CHRISTINA JONES-PAULY is an independent consultant on women and governance for various international agencies. She holds a Dr Phil in Comparative and Islamic Laws (London) and a Dr Jur in international law (Harvard). She was Human Rights Fellow at the Radcliffe Institute for Advanced Study, Harvard University, taught Islamic Law at Harvard Law School, and was Associated Researcher at the Socio-Legal Studies Centre, Oxford University. Before this she headed the Human Rights and Development Unit at the University of Bonn. She has worked on numerous human rights projects for the UN.

ABIR DAJANI TUQAN studied Islamic Law at SOAS, and is the first Arab woman to pass the Bar in Britain (Middle Temple), with First Class Honours in Islamic Law. She has spoken at various international conferences and in the media on Islamic family law.

Christina Jones-Pauly
with Abir Dajani Tuqan

WOMEN
UNDER ISLAM

Gender, Justice and the Politics of Islamic Law

Foreword by The Rt. Hon. Justice Thorpe

I.B. TAURIS
LONDON · NEW YORK

Published in 2011 by I.B.Tauris & Co Ltd
6 Salem Road, London W2 4BU
175 Fifth Avenue, New York NY 10010
www.ibtauris.com

Distributed in the United States and Canada Exclusively by Palgrave Macmillan
175 Fifth Avenue, New York NY 10010

Library of Islamic Law: 3

ISBN: 978 1 84511 386 5

A full CIP record for this book is available from the British Library
A full CIP record is available from the Library of Congress

Library of Congress Catalog Card Number: available

Typeset in Garamond by Artform, Oxfordshire
Printed and bound in Great Britain by CPI Antony Rowe, Chippenham
from camera-ready copy edited and supplied by the author

MIX
Paper from responsible sources
FSC www.fsc.org FSC® C013604

This book is dedicated to the memory of mentor,
friend and philanthropist Helen Maguire Muller
for her generous support and above all friendship.

CONTENTS

FOREWORD

Is Islam inherently anti-women? In this groundbreaking work Christina Jones-Pauly examines the history and practice of Islamic law as it affects women throughout the world. The book highlights the diversity of ways in which it has been interpreted, leading both to the progressive family-planning policies of Tunisia and the more conservative personal status laws of Egypt. Seeking to understand how a set of religious laws which initially empowered women subsequently became a tool for inequality, the book shifts the debate away from whether Islamic law itself is misogynistic or not, and looks instead at the contexts in which it has been applied, both in Arab and non-Arab cultures. The most important factor in determining whether court rulings are disadvantageous to women, is not, the book concludes, the conservativeness of the society, it is the institutions of that society, and in particular its pre-Islamic institutional history and the independence of its judiciary. In Pakistan, for example, the higher courts have been unable to resist popular and political pressure to criminalize extra-marital sexual relations, yet interpret the law themselves in a liberal way in keeping with the original spirit of the Quran and the hadiths. The book also provides innovative insight into a non-Muslim majority country, South Africa, with its powerful Muslim minority. Relying on extra-judicial forums to settle conflicts, the Muslim communities, now encouraged by an overarching state constitutionalism, are taking the Sharia towards new frontiers that would benefit Muslims world-wide. Interweaving legal scholarship and detailed on the ground case studies, *Women Under Islam* provides both a rich reference resource and new way of understanding gender politics in the Islamic world.

The Rt. Hon. Lord Justice Thorpe (Sir Mathew Thorpe), Court of Appeal
Head of International Family Justice for England and Wales

ACKNOWLEDGEMENTS

This book is the result of many years of teaching and researching on Islamic law. It is also just the beginning of the realization of a dream, a dream of an *ijtihad* of Islamic law. The root of the word is *jihad*, that is, exertion, this time with the intellect and heart. That means going back to the sources, the Quran and the practices of the Holy Prophet, exerting logic, reason, and fairness like the jurists of old did. This sets right the centuries of patriarchal interpretations and throwing light on the non-patriarchal views that can still shine through the century-old dust. It is also a book which aims to show how rational and just Islamic law was from its initial intentions. The history of Islamic law resembles the whispering game, a good pious compassionate Muslim friend of ours, a man, told me. The original spirit of the message gets changed and unrecognizable by the time it is whispered down to the present-day generations. This is not to say that there is no room for differing points of view. While Allah represents *al tawhid* (oneness and not division into a trinity), the law and its precise rules do not have to be one, for the Quran says that Allah has created from a single human seed many nations, tribes and religions, meaning symbolically, many points of view (49:13).[1] That is the essence of human reason and logic – but at one point, the spirit of the oneness of origin brings us all, from many tribes and religions and peoples, to agree on certain basics – treating all creatures of Allah equally, making Allah's justice available to all, not keeping certain privileges to oneself. This gives us the ability to acknowledge that we can learn from all cultures as well as come together to dignify our common human origins. This book is dedicated to that one spirit, as exemplified in the Universal Declaration of Human Rights because it celebrates humanity.

The book consists of case studies – two Arab and two non-Arab societies. The object is to show that Arab language and culture cannot and should not dominate the field. It is rather independence of thought and judicial integrity which has to dominate. I show that the judiciary at the higher levels is the main source of reform and sustenance of reform towards justice based on egalitarianism.

We would like to thank the many people who made this book possible: Amna Aouwidj, judge, member of parliament, Tunis; Lamia Ben Aba, advocate, Tunis; Naima Ben Aicha, director, Center for Arabic Women for Training and Research, Tunis; Sana Ben Achour, professor of law, University of Tunis; Samia Ben Khalifa, conservation of culture and crafts, Tunis; Soukayna Bouaroui, professor of law, University of Tunis; Zakia Bouaziz, director, Centre of Research, Studies, Documentation and Information on Women (CRÉDIF); Kacem Bousnina, head of association of parliamentarians and former governor of Sfax; Abdel Majeed Charfi, professor of history, University of Tunis; Abdulaziz Choulati, Institute for National Heritage, Tunis; Michael Philip Cracknell, Environnement et développement dans le monde arabe (Enda Inter-arabe); Samia Dahmani, English literature Ph.D. candidate, Tunis; Kais Darragi, Tunisian Embassy, London; Hassan Dhakouani, Palace of Justice, Tunis; Fathiya Baccouche El Bahri, advocate (Cour de Cassation), Tunis; Khédija El Madani, advocate (Cour de Cassation); Nabiha Gueddana, director, National Office of Family and Population; Naila Hachicha, business woman, Tunis; Alia Hamza, journalist, Tunis; Zahia Jouirou, social historian, Faculty of Letters, University of Tunis; Faiza Kafi, president, Union of Tunisian Women, Tunis; Lilia Labidi, professor of sociology, University of Tunis; Alia Mabrouk, novelist, Tunis; Nga Mahdaoui, artist, calligrapher, Tunis; Hamad Sahli, counsellor, Tunisian-Saudian investments, Professor of History Emeritus; Salwa Zangar, Institute of National Heritage, Tunis; Queen Dina HRH Princess Dina Adbul-Hamid of Jordan; Dr Essam Adel Allam, FGM Resource Center, National NGO Commission for Population and Development, Cairo; Karim A. Azmi, Nour Law Office, Cairo; Dr Ziad Bahaa-Eldin, Advisor to the Minister for Legal Affairs and Ministry of Economy; Prof. Dr Nagiba El-Ghamrawy, Cultural Attaché, Egyptian Embassy, Bonn; Prof. End Hill, Department of Political Science, The American University in Cairo; Fatma Khafagy, Women's Office, UNICEF, Cairo; Abdul Karim, Dar al Iftar, Said Mohammed, Al Azhar; Dr Fathi Naguib, Assistant Minister of Justice; Amina Shafeek, League of Egyptian Women Voters, trade unionist; Dr Hania Mohamed Sholkany, anthropologist, Cairo; Sheikh Muhammad Tantawi, Sheikh ul Islam, Al Azhar, Cairo; Mervat Talawi, former Minister for Social Affairs, Member of the National Council of Women; Ambassadress Nihad Zikry; Mona Zulficar, Senior Partner, Shalakany Law Office, Cairo; Justice Albie Sachs, Cape Town; Attorney M.S. Omar, Durban; Prof. Nadja Moosa, Cape Town; Justice J. Traverso, Cape Town; Justice Farlam, Cape Town; Hameed Haroon; Johari Abas; Muhammad Fizan; and Marlene Hickin, Oxford and Australia. We owe a huge debt to the late Prof. Sir J.N.D. Anderson, the late Prof. N. Coulson and Dr D. Hinchcliffe. Amedee Turner QC and Debby Turner like Aziz Dajani opened their hearts and home countless times in London for a weary traveller.

A word of special thanks I give to Denis Galligan, Director of the Centre for Socio-Legal Studies, University of Oxford, and his assistants, and to Frank Vogel, Director of the Islamic Legal Studies Program, Harvard Law School, his staff, and Peri Bearman. Stefanie Elbern and Karina Waedt of Bonn have been excellent assistants and very good friends. Peter Barnes' proofreading has been invaluable. The three who rescued the production of this book deserve special mention: Dorothy Stahl, Ekkehard Huebschmann and Alan Mauro.

A special word of gratitude I owe to the Radcliffe Institute of Advanced Studies, Harvard, which gave me a wonderful atmosphere under the auspices of the Rita E. Hauser Human Rights fellowship to complete the manuscript.

Finally I would to thank Abir Dajani for a long valuable friendship and for her contributions. She opened her house, made contacts and shared in various interviews and gave great moral support.

To simplify the formatting, words and names like Quran, Sharia, ulama, Ali, Umar, Abduh have been kept in an anglicized form.

All the faults are mine.

C. Jones-Pauly
London, Cambridge and Davos

INTRODUCTION

This book takes inspiration from the Quran, specifically the sura dedicated to women, An Nisa. One of its verses starts out warning men that they 'are never able to be fair and just (enough) as between women, even when you long to do so' (4:129). Yet in its formidable cleverness, the Quran does not leave men hanging with this thought. It gives them a solution to their problem of never being able to do enough justice to women. It says, 'but turn not away from them leaving them hanging, for if you reach understanding with them and practise self-restraint, then Allah is forgiving and merciful.'

The charge levelled against Islamic law as practised today is that it cannot do justice to women because it is stuck in a medieval frame of mind. The BBC once referred, for example, to Pakistan's 'medieval' laws that criminalize fornication and adultery. The object of this book is to look at whether Islamic law has such deep roots in the Dark Ages that it cannot extricate itself, or whether politics and die-hard cultural customs have overwhelmed Islam, or whether modern law courts are assuring the evolution of Islamic law. We undertake this task in the spirit of the great British jurist, Lord Denning, Master of the Rolls, whom I personally met. He was known for breaking precedent. Yet at the same time he reached back to even more ancient precedent in medieval common law to find justice for modern times.

We have gone back to ancient Islamic precedent to find justice. Islam was revolutionary in its gender relations for the time. The question is why did it stop? Why did it become mired in women-unfriendly fossilization? Can it get out of the mire? To answer these questions, examples of four societies which have taken Islamic law in entirely different directions with regard to women were chosen: Arab and non-Arab cultures; Muslim-majority societies; and one Muslim-minority society. All are governed by constitutions. All but one constitute ruler/states, that is, states where the ruler has remained in power for a long time or relied on martial law. The chapters are divided by country. The issues highlighted for gender justice differ from country to country because the respective historical and socio-political constellations have led each society to have different concerns. What may not be a problem for example in Tunisia is a problem in Pakistan and vice versa. In each chapter comparison is made, where appropriate, to similar dilemmas in Western laws and Mosaic, Christian or African legal systems.

The book starts off with the Muslim majority Arab society of Tunisia. It offers currently the best example of an egalitarian Islamic law for women. We search for its historical roots. We bring attention to the pre-Arab Berber politics and the role of women, then trace the history of the extra-judicial means that women used to maintain their economic and personal independence, mainly the marriage contract, in early Islam in Tunisia. The Quranic verses and the hadiths relating to women's economic independence are carefully analysed in conjunction with the evolution of the duty of the husband to maintain first his blood family and children and secondarily his spouse. We then move into the Ottoman period and emphasize the role that the emancipation of slaves in the mid-19th century played in the evolution of the law, since the Islamic legal justification on which the emancipation edict of the ruler at the time was based elaborated the principle of equality of all human beings. The establishment as well of the Sadiki College, which trained Ottoman Tunisian bureaucrats in all areas, including the judiciary, in how to harmonize modernization and Islamic law, was unique in the Arab world. Examined in detail are the trade union origins of the independence movement and its relation to the established ulama. This includes an in-depth analysis of the argumentation of two major intellectual figures who laid the groundwork for what is called the 'Tunisian way' in the modernization of Islamic law based on the concepts of equal dignity, conscience and liberty, which has led to abolishing polygamy as a right. We dispel the myth commonly heard in Arabic speaking countries and in the Western lands that the Tunisian law is secular and has no roots in Islamic law. This is simply not true. We identify the arguments put forth by Islamic scholars in Tunisia. To give even more texture to their arguments we compare their positions to Quranic texts and the hadiths. We perform *ijtihad* and challenge the conventional interpretations which limited the wife's possibilities to control her husband's polygamy. Another issue is veiling. It has been controversial through all time in Islamic law: interpretations of texts depended on the empirical assumptions made in any one age. We show how the logic of arguments that it be mandatory has long been challenged and how veiling was confused with the need to wear an outer cloak demonstrating how these controversies have been ignored or forgotten. The Quranic verses and hadiths on how far men may chastise their wives even to the point of physical constraint are presented in their historical contexts to show that women never accepted passively the pro-male interpretations. The textual basis of the abolishment of the husband's privilege to exercise extra-judicial divorce is examined.

The modern Tunisian issues that are discussed relate to the Islamic principles of birth control as a key to economic and social development and women as equal partners in the family in terms not only of rights but equal duties when the women have the means. The sustainability of the reforms despite efforts to undermine them from the conservative camps is discussed through the lens of the electoral politics of the women and the commitment of the judiciary to continuing the long tradition of harmonizing modernity and Islamic law.

In the chapter on Egypt the ancient pre-Islamic political culture is presented, then the politics of class stratification in the Arabo-Islamization process and its impact on the role of the religious legal ulama at the grassroots. The very diverse political role of women at various historical stages starting in the Mamluk and medieval period through the 1950s is emphasized. Examples of women from various classes who learned how to manipulate the legal system are cited. The differences in the intellectual debates in Egypt and Tunisia in the 19th and early 20th centuries are illustrated by the differences in the extent to which conservative institutions were preserved or transformed at the time. In terms of the modern period after the Second World War, the chapter reviews critically the monarch's control over the legislative process by which Islamic family law was reformed on a piecemeal basis. We then move into the era of militaristic socialist, as opposed to civilian socialist, revolutionary politics, which led to a focus for gender equality different from the one found in Tunisia, that is, gender equality was confined more to the political arena and less in the legal sphere. The impact of the post-socialist era on the speed of legal reform of Islamic law in family matters is analysed. The reluctance to reform Islamic law affecting women substantively and a preference for mainly procedural reforms are contrasted with the currently more substantive reforms.

We compare our interpretations of Quranic verses and hadiths with the compromised interpretations of the same Islamic texts. As the right of husbands to divorce is curtailed mainly by registration methods, we challenge the conservative construction of *talaq* as a fairly easy and quick method for husbands to terminate the marriage and destabilize the position of woman and child and take a closer look at the Quran and hadith provisions that contrast the easy pre-Islamic *talaq* practice with the more inhibitory Islamic prescriptions.

The issue of a woman initiating a divorce through the *khula* procedure by returning her marriage dower, has achieved great prominence in Egypt. We compare our *ijtihad* on the issue with that of the Egyptian legislator. A second major issue has been female circumcision. An added feature in the Egyptian chapter is the interaction between the laws of the Coptic community in Egypt and Islamic law institutions in terms of forum-shopping by Coptic women. The role of the higher judiciary in sustaining and even extending the reforms of Islamic law is discussed.

The chapter on Pakistan concentrates on the highly publicized issues connected with the Islamic model of criminalization of sexual relations (adultery and fornication between two unmarried persons) and honour killings. The prominent political and social role of Muslim women in the pre-Pakistan Indian Subcontinent is presented as background to the founding of the state of Pakistan. The diversity among the leading Muslim intellectuals in the face of the dismantling of large segments of Islamic law pertaining to slavery and to criminal law at a time of shifting power relations between the Muslim Ottoman Empire and the British Empire serves as background to an analysis of positions taken on women and principles of law reform. The chapter then traces the shifts in models of interpreting Islamic law, starting with *ijtihad* at the start of the creation of an independent Pakistani Muslim state, then moving into conservative interpretations of Islamic laws during the Cold War, ending in current reforms. Whether state enforcement of Islamic law is compatible with the Quranic prohibition of compulsion or force in religion (2:256) and with the contractual essence of Islamic law is discussed from a political and judicial point of view. The history of litigation by Pakistani citizens dissatisfied with the Islamization of the criminal law is traced as well as the confrontation between the political forces and the judiciary. As the political forces continued to press for restoring a pre-British Mughal empire type of penal Islamic law, we point out the transformation of Islamic penal law by the state's expansion of its discretionary *taazir* powers contrary to the hadiths and Quran. Sociological problems and increased violence against women have arisen because of the expansion of the state power that is used to circumvent the strict evidentiary requirements of Islamic penal law. Focus is then on the evolving case law revealing how the courts serve as mediators between international legal standards, political pressures and popularist interpretations of certain hadiths which men use to justify violence against women because of mere suspicion of extra-marital relations.

The final chapter concerns South Africa as a Muslim minority country. The early history of Islam there since the 1600s and the role of women as reflected in community rituals and in early court litigation are presented as background to the current problems. The contradictory legal status conferred on Muslims in terms of personal law in the pre-apartheid era is contrasted with the absolute refusal to recognize the Muslim marriage and any incidents thereto during apartheid. The impact of this historical legacy on the legislature and judiciary in post-apartheid liberated South Africa is analysed. Data is examined regarding the diversity of extra-judicial practices among the major Muslim communities in the different regions of South Africa, with some communities relying on contractual arrangements to guarantee women's rights, others relying on private arbitration bodies controlled by men to determine women's rights. The main issues to date relate to disputes among Muslims about women administrators of *waqf* properties and between Muslim organizations vying for control over certain mosques. Another issue is the extent to which the state will recognize Muslims' marriages by statute, which would expand the current judicial recognition. The draft law on Muslim personal status is critically commented upon in the light of South African Muslims' practices, the Quran and hadiths. We review the judgments of the post-apartheid Constitutional Court striking down certain African customary laws that discriminate against women and discuss their implications for Muslim personal law. A new interpretation of the Quranic inheritance verses is proposed in the light of recent constitutional case law, which holds the government to higher standards of equality than the legislator has applied up to now.

1

TUNISIA – THE IDEAL ISLAMIC REFORM

Introduction

Tunisia was chosen as the first country to deal with because it has a special place in the modern history of Islamic law. Tunisia reopened the door of *ijtihad*. *Ijtihad* means to make an effort to think about things and to think anew. It was commonly thought that Islamic law was fully developed and needed no new impulses. In the case of Tunisia *ijtihad* meant thinking about some fundamental issues in Islamic law. This entailed raising some basic questions about the essence of the spirit of Islam, how this essence has been interpreted through the ages by jurists and politicians, and for what purposes.

Many in Tunisia with whom we talked – men and women – attribute the opening of the door of *ijtihad* to one man – Habib Bourguiba, who led Tunisia to Independence from the colonial powers. As a Muslim, he saw that Islam had a strong message. This was one of social responsibility and quality. He was not alone in his view. Leading learned Muslim theologians and jurists preceding him and during his time of struggle had publicly written about this. At Independence, he consulted learned Muslim theologians and jurists. The result was a series of laws which give the fullest realization of equal social responsibility between men and women that presently exists in the Islamic world. These laws are all based on research of Islamic law sources. One of the most well-known of these laws is the code of family law (Code of Personal Status). It is applicable to all citizens, whether Muslims or Christians or Israelites or otherwise. It enacts an interpretation of the Islamic law sources which permit abolishing polygamy and personal divorce by the husband (only divorce before the court is permitted).

The 'Tunisian way' has raised many questions. One such question we raised everywhere we went in Tunisia: how is it possible? The answer most often given was that Tunisian men are generous. Tunisia has a long cultural tradition of taking women's interests seriously. A Tunisian father loves his daughter above all. The pre-Islamic legendary Kahina, Queen of the Berbers, offers a positive reinforcement of the faith in women's abilities to lead. She fought the initial Arab attempts to conquer northern Africa (Hannoum 109, 124, 125). From the Islamic era, the Prophet too had only a daughter and constantly admonished Muslims to love their daughters. We probed even more, asking under what circumstances this proverbial love can best flourish. The answers we got were varied – e.g., political and bureaucratic stability since modern bureaucracy was introduced into Tunisia a century ago and a dynamic alliance between intellectuals and policy makers. The class origins of women involved in the struggle were said to be middle class with more at stake in equality than was, for example, the case in Egypt where upper-class women dominated (Largueche). One obvious factor was hardly mentioned – that is, the civilian origins of Tunisia's founding generation, the generation that guided Tunisia to Independence and ruled in the first decades of Independence came from the trade union movement. This movement integrated Tunisians from other civilian sectors including young Muslim theologians and civil servants. The military never played a prominent political role. This factor is unique in the post-colonial Muslim world. If we accept the hypothesis that a military-influenced society by nature is hierarchical and accordingly patriarchal (see Huntington) then the 'Tunisian way' is a logical consequence of a non-military-influenced society.

The 'Tunisian way' has also attracted criticism in the Islamic world. It has been criticized as 'unIslamic', an unsound aberration. We wanted to examine whether this critique has any basis. On the basis of our examination, we can conclude that we do not believe that the criticism has any substantial basis. The critique is an indirect criticism of the sincerity of Tunisians. We found that Tunisians take the duties of Islam seriously. They do not fail in these duties any more than any other Muslim people. They do not just pay lip service. They determine what is the spirit and purpose of an injunction. This same approach can be found in their treatment of women's rights under Islamic law. The Tunisians have also offered a perfect answer to the criticisms from the secular West that the religious and the secular must be strictly separated.

To prove the point, this chapter on Tunisia goes into historical depth. It looks at the origins of Islam in Tunisia, the intellectual and political forces at work through the centuries, and the actual social practices. We look at how these factors impinged on women's rights and status. We compare these phenomena with what was said and done at the time of the Prophet. This comparison is crucial, for some of the issues raised at the time of the Prophet are the same as those of today. Others are obviously different from those of today. In any case, it is important to know what principles and basic attitudes were at stake at the time of the Prophet. Through these comparisons, we wish to show how Tunisians' interpretations of Islamic sources have remained true to the basic principles and attitudes which were propagated during the Prophet's lifetime.

Case law in Tunisia has been relatively faithful to the legislator's intentions and interpretations of Islamic sources. It is cited in this chapter occasionally to illustrate certain fine points of interpretation of Islamic law.

Historical roots

Islamic schools of thought – Maliki roots

The following sections identify some of the historical strands that have favoured the notion of equality before the law.

The dominant school of law in Tunisia has been Maliki. It has existed since the establishment of the first and oldest centre of Islamic legal learning at Qairawan (Ben Achour 82). The Hanafi school was introduced in Tunisia much later with the advent of Ottoman imperialism and colonialism in North Africa.

The premises of the Maliki school were formulated by Malik b. Anas (from Medina, d. 179 A.H./796 A.D.) in his treatise *Al Muwatta* ('that which is sure or paves the way'). It is the earliest collection of hadiths about what happened at the time of the Prophet. Legal conclusions were extracted from them. The collection was written in the spirit of the Arabic Medina tradition, i.e. 'This is the way we do it so in Medina.' This approach implied that this way was not the only way. Other opinions about what legalistic conclusions could be equally drawn from other hadith collections existed in other parts of the Islamic world owing to different cultural circumstances and needs. These opinions were equally legitimate. The Medina approach also stands for reliance on realistic juristic opinions, based on actual experience and circumstances, not on abstract hypothetical cases.

It was no accident that Malikism offered such an approach. Its founder resisted making his opinions the law of the land. He emphasized that he was only a human being. He refused to be seen as infallible, implying that anyone claiming to have the infallible truth (*al haqq*) is arrogant (Rahimuddin, v). In Tunisia this approach found fertile ground. It has allowed Tunisia, combined with its open geography and ancient history, to harmonize the Berber, Arab and Islamic cultures so that one can take the best of all worlds (Ben Achour 49).

The reason why Malik b. Anas rejected any claims to infallibility is obvious. Readers of the Quran find that God, the lawgiver, has imposed limits, but these are very general. Within these limits there is room to exert logic in order to interpret these limits when specific questions arise. Malik is said to have pointed out, as revealed in the Quran, one who listens to the Word follows the best meaning (sura Al Zumar 39:19) (Brunschvig 69–70). The fact that certain questions arise in certain parts of the globe will be cause for differences in the application and interpretation of the general Quranic limits. This process leads in turn to differences of opinion. Indeed questions that Medinans raised were different from those that Meccans raised because of the different social dynamics and different influential personalities. This phenomenon did not cease in the course of Islamic history. Coulson has attributed the Medinan denial of the right of a woman (at least a virgin) to make her own marriage contract without approval of her family to the Arabian tribal prerogatives of the males and the Kufan acceptance of the right of a woman to make her own contract to the ethnic diversity of that cosmopolitan centre (Coulson 1991, 30). Much later during the imperialistic Ottoman rule an exception was made to the general rule that the Empire followed the Hanafi school. A special provision was made for wives of migrant workers. It became possible for wives to seek divorce under Maliki law, which was easier than under Hanafi, especially under the following circumstances: a husband who had taken on another wife at his workplace failed to send maintenance to his wife in the country of origin (Alami and Hinchcliffe 29–30).

Ibadi roots

Another school of law that took root in North Africa was that of the Ibadiyya. They were an offshoot of the Kharijiten. The latter, at first partisans of Ali (son-in-law of the Prophet), 'left' the fold in the 1st century of Islam in Kufa. The Kharijite doctrine was characterized by three basic elements:

i) its emphasis on equality of the non-Arab Muslims with Arab Muslims (Coulson 1991, 103). They argued that capability and not descent from the Arab Quraishi tribe, should be the basis of leadership so that even an African slave could lead the Caliphate. This argument was based presumably on the hadith that the Prophet had warned against counting on kinship as the basis of authority (Cook 20);
ii) its rejection of the authority of most of the *sunna* of Caliphs Uthman and Ali;
iii) its insistence that opinions by jurisconsults which were not based strictly on the Quran were not valid.

After the Abbasids defeated the Kharijites in the eastern Islamic world in the 2nd and 3rd centuries of Islam, a more moderate sect of the Kharijites, the Ibadiyya, found resonance in North Africa. The Ibadi moderateness lay in its reluctance to approve readily of any rebellion entailing warfare among the believers based on self-righteous Quranic interpretations (Cook 59). Ibadi doctrine was also compatible with Malikism in terms of its preference for using *ray* (reasoning and adduction, akin to common sense) to interpret the Quran and hadiths over *ijma* (consensus).

The Fatimids (of Syrian Ismaili/Shiite origins, deriving their name from Fatima, the daughter of the Prophet) (Hodgson I, 492) colonized the Maghreb, dominating Tunisia. From there they launched an invasion of Egypt in the Middle Ages. It was an Ibadi who opposed them. He was born it is thought in 270 A.H./883 A.D. in Sudan as the son of a Berber and his slave wife: Abu Yazid al Nukkari (Sahib al Himar). He led the revolt in 332 A.H./943 A.D. Upon entry in Qairawan he had the qadi and governor executed. He then lost the support of the Berbers temporarily as he adopted a life of luxury (silks and Arabian horses) then regained it by returning to a simpler lifestyle. He led attacks on Tunis and Sousse. He was eventually defeated by the Fatimid invader/imperialist Al Mansur and died three years after the start of the revolt.

Although the Kharijite school of law is no longer existent, the Ibadiyya still exist in North Africa, Oman and East Africa. The Ibadi doctrine is no longer considered tainted with heresy. The mufti of Al Azhar University in Egypt has recognized the need to put all the other schools of thought and law on a par as legitimate sources of authority (Shaltut). The Ibadi doctrine was never officially a source of law in the history of Tunisian jurisprudence (only the Maliki and with the Turkish/Ottoman invasion, the Hanafi). Nonetheless its spirit of renewal based on rooting legal reasoning in the basic sources of the Sharia (Quran and *sunna*) and not simply relying on repetitive commentaries of jurists or hadiths when proof fails in the Quran to support one's point of view (Cook 19) has been consistently reflected in the development of Tunisian law.

The eventual fall of the Fatimids after a series of defeats in the Levant by the Frankish Crusaders in the 11th century did not make way for indigenous rule. The non-Arab Turks established themselves as the colonializing rulers in Tunisia from the 16th century into the 20th century. The Kharijite/Ibadi idea that non-Arab Muslims were to be treated as equal to Arab Muslims had long been realized, but did not result in indigenous Muslim rule. The non-Arab Turks conquering Tunis in 1574 A.D. were seen as oppressors by the established religious families as well as the rural Bedouins (Cherif I:53), but the Beys – recalling the repulsion by their forefathers of the eighth Crusade by St Louis against Tunis (Cherif I:42, 73) – had developed more national feelings than their Turkish counterparts in Algeria and spoke Tunisian Arabic rather than their Turkish mother tongue when born in Tunis (Cherif I:41). The society they conquered had already developed structures and attitudes that reflected the value of equality. It was possible for a woman to own valuable tracts of olive plantations, a major source of commercial income, by way of her husband repaying her a debt he owed her (Cherif I:55). The rural Bedouins had a political structure based on a council composed of delegates representing various clans and characterized by tendencies to equality as the authority of the chiefs could not be imposed, but rather had to be consented to by their tributaries. This potential was not fully utilized as the social distinctions based on age, sex and rank were not yet weakened by international commerce and a centralized state (Cherif I:58). Finally, the city of Tunis on the coast was not the only centre of culture. Qairawan lay in the interior and supplied Tunis with an important mufti (Cherif I:54, 78).

Historical practices: roots of equality in marriage contract traditions

The spirit of Malikism, that of taking into account differences of opinion logically based on regional cultural differences, flourished in Qairawan. As the most developed centre of learning in North Africa, it produced Maliki scholars who had lively debates on differences of interpretation. One of the main transmitters of the works of the Maliki jurist al Qarafi was a woman, Umm al Hasan Fatima bint Khalil al Kattani (Fadel 191, n. 24).

Differences did not remain on the interpretational level. In practice different traditions grew up and flourished in different regions of Tunisia. The differences in the traditions relating to the marriage contracts are illustrative. A common thread running through these practices was equal rights of the women in matters of divorce.

The Qairawan marriage contract tradition

The women of Qairawan and their fathers diligently developed their own marriage traditions that go back several hundred years. The women there were known for their wealth, earned from the profitable carpet making trade. This gave them confidence to assert themselves. The result was the well-known Qairawan marriage contract (Ben Achour 91). It was cited in the 9th century by jurists also in Cordova in Muslim Spain as well as in Muslim Egyptian sources (Goitein III:49).

The contract contained two kinds of stipulations: l) polygamy as a ground for divorce demanded by the wife; 2) revoking the right of the husband to polygamy (Institut National 114, 115). To illustrate: in the 4th A.H./10th century A.D. Caliph Mansur bi-llah (b. 301 A.H./914 A.D.) fell in love with Aroua, the daughter of Mansur b. Yazid al Himyari. The daughter agreed to marriage only on condition that the Caliph accept in the marriage contract that he not take another wife. These were no hollow words. There is evidence that some women took their husbands to court when they unilaterally took on a second wife. The wife of the governor Yazid ibn Hatim brought him before the qadi of Qairawan, Abu Kutaib, to enforce the marriage contract provision against polygamy.

The Qairawan practice reflects a liberal legal position. The right to divorce on grounds of polygamy conformed to the Maliki hadith in which it was reported that the first wife of Rafi bin Khadij[1] demanded divorce from him when he took on a second wife.

The right to stipulate that a husband could not take on a second wife unless the first wife had the right of divorce was not specifically addressed in the Maliki hadiths. Initially this left the way open to regard such a stipulation as not prohibited and therefore valid. Over time, however, this right was circumscribed. The schools of law (excepting the Hanbalis) took a more conservative direction. They began to opine that a wife could not stipulate in the marriage contract that the husband may not marry a second wife. This shift in opinion derived from analogous reasoning based on a non-Maliki hadith.[2] It was reported that there were marriage contracts in which wives were prohibited from demanding that a polygamous husband divorce the other wife. Which wife was not clear. At first, the jurists construed the reports to mean that the second would-be wife could not stipulate in her marriage contract that the husband divorce the first wife. This was fair, since a contract should not encourage a person to break a prior contract. By analogous reasoning, however, over time, this construct was extended to cover also the first wife. She was prohibited from stipulating that the husband not marry a second wife.[3]

Another kind of condition in Qairawan marriage contracts also raised some controversy. This was the condition that the wife not be removed from her hometown upon marriage. This issue was the subject of a Maliki hadith. In the Maliki report it was said that a woman negotiated as a condition in her marriage contract that she not be taken away from her hometown. How the husband should react is not clearly spelled out in the hadith. Should he refuse to sign the contract? May he choose on his own free will to accept it and thus bind himself?[4] Ibn Malik's comment on this report also does not address the facts explicitly. His comment implies that with regard to such a stipulation, it is clearly binding on the husband if it is intended to be a condition to which divorce is attached. Such ambiguities left the way open for practice to establish the norms. The Tunisian Qairawan women today insist that it is in their tradition that the woman not be obliged to follow her husband if he left Qairawan (Enda Inter-arabe: Mahbouba). In this regard they are supported by a non-Maliki hadith. The latter takes the position that once the husband agreed not to remove the wife from the place she wants to stay, then the stipulation is binding on him.[5]

The Tunis marriage contract tradition

Qairawan was not the only place in Tunisia that developed a regional tradition of marriage contracts. The so-called Tunis tradition had developed by the end of the 20th century. It was the result of practices of the Sheikh ul Islams, among the most learned in the land. They devised for their own families marriage contracts. These allowed their daughters to divorce without stipulating any ground. In this regard the Tunis tradition gave more options to a wife than the Qairawan marriage contract, which seems to have been limited to polygamous situations.

The Tunis tradition reflects a particular set of social circumstances. The practice of monogamy had become common among the elite. Hence limiting the right of the wife to divorce only in circumstances of polygamy had, from a practical point of view, become superfluous. So that when a husband remained monogamous, there were still causes other than concubinage that could make a marriage go sour or make a woman or man unhappy in a marriage. No contract could foresee all possible causes. As a result, the marriage contract that permitted a wife to divorce as she saw fit was more appropriate.[6]

Culturally, such contracts were possible only in a country where the fathers are known for their extraordinary love for their daughters. It is often said in Tunis that Tunisian fathers will do all they can to protect their daughters and help them further their careers and economic independence – even more so than in respect to their own wives. Daughters can never be divorced, spouses can.[7] Thus the Tunis contract is an example of how a rule that had origins in the culture of a closed patriarchal Arab society like the Medinan, as opposed to the cosmopolitan Kufan (Coulson 1991, 30), can work to the advantage of a woman as long as the culture promotes a close relation between father and daughter.

From a legal point of view the Tunis contract offered the advantage of being less vulnerable to attack than the Qairawan contract. The general rule in all schools of law excepting the Hanbali was that a stipulation restricting the right of a spouse was invalid in itself, e.g. a clause revoking or restricting the wife's right to maintenance or the husband's right to polygamy (Coulson 1991, 189). While the parties could agree to such stipulations and abide by them privately, they could not expect a court of law to enforce them. The genius of the Tunis contract lay in its generality. It did not remove any rights in particular. It thus fulfilled the spirit of understanding that the Quran enjoins. The Quran warns that the spouses should either hold together on equitable terms or separate in kindness (2:229). The Tunis marriage contract gave the wife the chance to have a divorce if she felt that there was no more fairness in her marriage. In this way she was given the same rights as her husband – who could exercise his right of *talaq* as he saw fit.

Sfaxian marriage contract tradition

In Sfax where the economy was based on commerce and agriculture (Sugier 141; Sethom 23), examples of marriage contracts made in the last hundred years by the more well-off bourgeoisie reveal more concern with the economic aspects of the marriage. The possessions that the bride brought into the marriage were specified. It seems that these exact specifications were an innovation that appeared in the 19th century, in contrast to the Middle Ages. The innovation may have been the result of the introduction under the French of the requirement that notarized documents were needed as evidence. The exact enumeration in favour of the bride of the trousseau and jewels and other valuable metals and pearls plus a slave-servant came to constitute the major part of the contract (Sethom 23). Sometimes it was specified which parts constituted an inheritance from a deceased member of the bride's family (Gargouri-Sethom 84). This assured the wife a document that saved her from disputes over what was hers and what was her husband's in case of divorce or death. It was stipulated that the father of the bride gave the valuables to the groom, who in turn was to give them to the bride on the marriage night. Other provisions in the contract listed the virtues of the marrying partners: the husband – just, generous and knowledgeable; the bride – virtuous and a virgin. The latter provision gave the husband an implicit right to annul the marriage contract if the bride were not a virgin. No mention was made of the sexual virility of the man. It would seem that the bride had an equal right to demand termination of the marriage tie if the husband turned out to be of a character contrary to what was expected, since the Maliki jurists were known to grant a petition from a woman for termination of marriage on grounds of a cruel husband (Coulson 1991, 185).

Comparing marriage contract practices with hadiths

The Tunisian practice of conferring on a wife the right of divorce equivalent to that of her husband conforms to the spirit of two hadiths – one non-Maliki and one Maliki. The lesson from both is that women are to be given the right to exercise options against polygamy.

The non-Maliki hadith is a report from Aisha. She is reported to have given an interpretation of the Quranic verse on husbands who were remonstrative towards their wives (4:128). The verse says that if the wife fears that the husband is being remonstrative (*nushuz*, usually interpreted to mean cruel or deserting, but really means disobedient) towards her, then she can arrange for ending the marriage. At issue was whether the term 'remonstrative' included a husband who wanted to take on a second wife. Aisha was of the opinion that it does. Hence if a wife feared that her husband wanted to take on another wife, then she was entitled to take action. She was to tell him that if he took a second wife, he need no longer feed her or sleep with her, in other words, they should part.[8]

The second hadith is a major Maliki report about an Ansari woman in the days of the Prophet. Malik b. Anas reported the reaction of the wife of Rafi bin Khadij, a Companion of the Prophet, to her husband taking a second wife. The first wife was the daughter of Muhammed bin Maslama Ansari. When she grew old her husband married a second younger wife, on whom he showered more affection. The first wife demanded divorce. Her husband complied. He set into motion the divorce procedure by pronouncing the first *talaq*. Just before expiry of the *idda* he reconciled and took his first wife back. Still he did not show equal affection to both wives. The first wife demanded divorce a second time. Again her husband complied. Still he could not show equal affection to both wives. The older wife demanded for a third time divorce. This time her husband reminded her that this time he would have to make the divorce final. The older wife then had a choice: between a final divorce or living with a co-wife and a husband who was not able to treat both wives equally. The older wife seems to have resigned herself and reconciled.[9]

The Maliki hadith has both a clear and an ambiguous message. The clear message is that a wife has an option to refuse or accept her husband's polygamy. She may demand divorce, regardless of whether she has so stipulated in her marriage contract or not. The ambiguity lies in the repeated demand of the ageing Ansari wife to her husband: she demanded divorce, twice. For whom is not so clear – for herself or for the second wife. From a hermeneutic point of view, it would seem that the wife is demanding that the husband divorce the second wife. She is prepared to bring her marriage twice to the brink. She is in effect demanding not a divorce for herself as her husband thinks. When she realizes on the third try that he is not prepared to divorce the second wife, she breaks down. The reader has much sympathy for her: she is older, her husband has not lived up to the Islamic injunction that he should love both wives equally. He is callous and selfish: it is said that he felt he had done no sin. The reader is left with a sense that an injustice has been done. What would have been just is not specified in the hadith. The reader is left to make up their own mind about what would have been just. One possibility would have been for the husband to divorce the second wife, then attempt to reconcile with the first wife, for as long as he had the second wife, he had no incentive to really understand and reconcile with his older wife.

Pre-Islamic marriage contract practice

It is interesting to observe that the Islamic law as developed by the *fuqaha* (jurists) – in this sense one should talk of *fuqaha* law and not Islamic law – relating to divorce clauses in marriage contracts was basically liberal compared to other religious laws at the time when the Quran was revealed. Termination of marriage by divorce, especially at the initiative of the wife, was not a self-assured right. Mosaic and Church cannon law did not allow for termination on the part of the woman except under very restricted circumstances. The Islamic approach resembled more that of the ancient Egyptian culture that occupies a central place in Semitic history. Ancient Egyptian law permitted termination of the marriage by divorce and allowed the parties to determine the terms of divorce. There is evidence of women securing for themselves in a marriage contract the same right as a man had to initiate divorce especially when the couple lived in a house owned by the wife (Lüddeckens 272). Otherwise, the wife had implicitly in some examples of marriage contracts the option to leave when the husband decided to take another wife. His taking another wife was seen as a sign that he hated the first wife (Lüddeckens 269, 273, 275), implying that the wife had the option under the contract to leave. Relatives of the couple could also be party to the marriage contract to serve as guarantors of enforcement of the contract (Lüddeckens 332). Thus use of the marriage contract as a means of equalizing rights between woman and man was not unique to Islamic law. This is not to say that the Islamic jurists consciously drew on parallels with ancient Egyptian culture or law (Lüddeckens 353). It is only to note that this is consistent with the Quranic spirit of universalism. The Quran intends that Islam see itself not just as unique but also as universalistic, identifying what was good in the past and allowing it to continue. The wife (Asiya) of the Pharaoh who rescued Moses, for example, is praised in the Quran for her sense of humanity and faith as one of the best women of the world (suras 28:9; 66:11).

Modernity

Ottoman rule

The Turkish conquest marked the start of the monopolization of power by the central state and the modern era with fixed territorial boundaries. Tunisia became distinct from Algeria. The 16th and 17th centuries – when the Europeans were exploring and trying to subdue the New World – brought about the integration of the tribes into the political system. This era also saw the creation of a cadre of civil servants for the emerging state. After the French-Ottoman Capitulations, the Tunisian Bay signed independently of the Constantinople Capitulations treaties with France in 1605 (Cherif I:80), a sign of the relative autonomy and peace that Tunis enjoyed as compared to Tripoli and Algiers (Cherif I:97).

Tunisian dynasty

One hundred years later in 1704 Husain b. Ali Turki founded the Husseinite dynasty that ruled Tunisia until Independence in 1957. Called upon or 'elected' (Cherif I:122) by the notables and religious authorities to fill in a political vacuum, he centralized power by combining in himself all the military and administrative titles that had been dispersed among various commanders: *bay*, *day*, *pasha*, *agha*. Born of a Turkish father with two wives and a Tunisian mother, he was born in Tunisia and spoke Tunisian Arabic (Cherif I:119).

The judicial system remained as before: a Hanafi mufti reflecting the Ottoman imperial preference for Hanafism and a Maliki mufti from the ranks of the old Tunisian families, but the Bay favoured the Maliki qadis over the Hanafi mufti, who bought his post in Istanbul (Cherif I:153, 296), and granted funds to restore and maintain the city of Qairawan (Cherif II:163), where the Bay also kept a residence (Cherif II:184). He did not disturb the power relation with Djerba, where the Ibadi were in the majority and to whose woman regent he paid a tributary. In the environs of Tunis he provided funds for the upkeep of a forest of olive trees as undivided estates that provided revenue in part for widows and orphans (Cherif II:339). Strengthening the Maliki jurists over the Hanafi had the effect of sustaining the more liberal approach of the Malikis to divorce, e.g. allowing a wife without a contract to petition for divorce before the qadi on grounds that the marriage had come to be a hardship for her (Coulson 1991, 185), a principle that has since then become the basis of the Shiite Iranian divorce reform in 1994 (Jones 1996b).

European pressures

Pressure from the Europeans on North Africa in the next century grew. The Europeans had grown accustomed to full-scale expansion in India and above all in the 'New World'. They met no opposition or competition from the Ottomans. The Ottoman Empire had no interest in this expansion (Lewis 58) and contented itself with relying on a slave economy, leaving the Europeans to compete only among themselves for world power (Sarsar). By 1815 when the Treaty of Vienna ended the Napoleonic wars, the Europeans began to divide the world into spheres of influence and set standards of morality. The Treaty obliged the European governments to abolish slavery as a crime against humanity. This was a direct challenge to the very basis not only of the southern United States economy but also that of the Ottoman Empire. The military strength of the Europeans that was needed to patrol the seas for abolishing the slave trade impressed the North Africans.

Establishing an educated bureaucracy

Upon the invasion of France into the neighbouring territory of Algeria, the Tunisian Bay reformed the military on European lines. Five years later, the Tunisian Bay Ahmad established the military and technical school at Bardo, the naval centre of the Bays. The language of instruction was French and Arabic. French military works were translated into Arabic. The concept of regimentation of learning, financed by the state, swept also through the halls of the religious school of the Zaytuna Mosque in Tunis. The religious establishment controlled the *bayt al mal,* the state treasury. Ahmad Bay systematized the nomination, retention and payment of the religious teachers at the Mosque. This spelled the end of an Islamic education based on the individual will and diligence of a particular learned sheikh.

Establishment of Sadiki College

It was not until 1875 that Sadiki College was established, founded by Khayr ad Din, and named after Sadok Bay. The aim was to combine for the first time technical studies with religious and legal studies, supported by state funds. A boarding school along with a day school enabled boys from the interior to attend. The school produced until Tunisia's Independence all the civil servants and political leaders of Tunisia, trained in the belief that it is possible to harmonize the secular and the religious.

Sadiki College represents the institutionalization of the concept of harmonizing the secular and the religious: the critical and questioning approach of secular learning, on the one hand, and, on the other, the emphasis in religious education on rote learning while leaving it only to the initiative of the brilliant individual to raise critical questions.

Roots of equality: emancipation of slaves in religious and secular law

The process of harmonizing the religious and the secular had already begun at the highest levels of policy making before being institutionalized at Sadiki. A prime legal example is the decree from Ahmad Bay of 23 January 1846 condemning slavery and favouring emancipation, an emancipation not only of the individuals enslaved, but also of the society. Tunisian Bays had long been under pressure from the European powers to free at least the slaves of European origin captured by the Ottoman military. As early as the middle of the 17th century Tunis had signed a treaty with Venice for the return of Venetians taken and enslaved in Tunis and in 1726 it was reported that there were four thousand Christian slaves in Tunis (Cherif I:80, 172). Women slaves especially gave cause for political dispute. For example, the British consul wrote a report in 1835 on a Greek woman slave who had escaped to a European consulate, which refused to return her to her North African enslaver. The European consulates sought to put pressure on the local government by threatening to expose the affair in the Western press. Ahmad Bay began corresponding with the British and French abolitionist anti-slavery groups from 1840 to 1842 (Société 78). Finally he issued a decree condemning slavery (slavery as an institution being outlawed only several decades later in the decree of 28 May 1890) (Sraïeb n.d., 16; Jones 1975, 28). The Bay gave two reasons for issuing the decree – one being humanitarian, i.e. aimed towards making emancipation easier for the enslaved; the second being political, i.e. aimed to stop the enslaved from rushing into foreign consulates for refuge.

Obviously the political aspects of the decree reflected immediate practical concerns of sovereignty. These political concerns did not remain paramount. They set into motion a reflective process about the essence of

Islamic law. This process was mirrored in the long explanation that the Bay issued to justify his decree. He started first with social facts. He found that most of the inhabitants of the land were in the habit of abusing the right of property over slaves and mistreating especially enslaved Africans. The Bay then examined the legal debate among the Islamic jurisconsults. He found that they were not in agreement on whether slavery, especially among Africans, was supported by a fundamental source of the Sharia. Even if there were a text supporting the legality of the institution of slavery, the Bay found that it could not be upheld, for the *consequences* of this legal institution are contrary to the basic tenets of Islam and the public interest. The result was that Sharia judges were no longer allowed to refuse the demand of slaves coming before them for emancipation. The Sharia Court was pronounced to be a place of inviolable refuge for petitioners. From this refuge all slavery cases had to be sent to the Bay. The Bay also established administrative centres – apart from the qadi courts – where notarized emancipation documents could be issued to any slave coming to demand their liberty.

The 1846 decree offers a good precedent on several levels. For one, it established the head of state as an arbitrator in fundamental Sharia rights when there is i) dispute among the jurists, ii) lack of a definite and clear text, and iii) abuse of the rights conferred on Muslims in the hadiths. Secondly, the decree upholds two basic principles of Islamic law: the tendency towards extension of liberty and liberating a person from a relationship that is socially abusive of another person.

Roots of equality: equality before the law independent of religion

As illustrated above, actual incidents like that of the Greek woman slave seeking refuge in European consulates precipitated fundamental changes in the Islamic law of slavery. Furthermore, the change was justified by the argument that the *fuqaha* had interpreted Islamic law without considering whether the consequences of a rule violated basic Sharia principles.

Yet another notorious incident spurred the Tunisian head of state to extend the principle of equality in Islamic law to free persons of all religions. In June of 1857 a drunken Tunisian Hebrew ran over a Muslim child with his cart. When seized by a crowd, he started shouting blasphemies against Islam and the Bay. He was immediately taken to a qadi court and condemned to death. The British and French consuls attempted in vain to intervene. The execution took place within 24 hours of the judgment. Riots based on anti-European feelings broke out. A French gunboat paid a 'courtesy call' off the coast of Tunisia. Negotiations began for issuing a basic constitutional document for regulating the relations between Muslims and non-Muslims, Europeans and Ottoman subjects.

The Bay was put under pressure to issue a decree allowing each group to have its own set of courts. The Bay resisted the notion of a pluralistic system. He wanted a code that would apply to all in Tunisia, regardless of religion or nationality. His legal argument was that Islamic law is based on truth. Truth is universalistic because it is based on justice and equity. In turn there is only one justice for all because justice assumes that all are equal before justice. Justice meant the guarantee of liberty of the enslaved, and it is equally through equal liberty for all that each can realize her/his own economic prosperity. He equated justice with piety. 'Whoever submits to justice approaches piety.' (Jones 1975, 34)[10]

Ten days after the gunboat visit the Bay Muhammad issued the *Ahd al-Aman* (Fundamental Pact) on 20 Moharrem 1274/10 September 1857. The Bay declared himself bound by the principle that Muslims and other inhabitants of the country were equal before the law and the principle that the weak are to be protected against the strong (Art. III). As a result of the principle that all inhabitants have the same rights, he refused to grant the Hebrew community separate courts (allowing only Hebrew assessors in cases of criminal trials). He agreed to an equal right to purchase and buy land in Tunisia for all, regardless of religion or nationality. Previously, Europeans had been forbidden to own land in the *dar al islam* and had circumvented the prohibition by entering into fictitious mortgages (Jones 1975, 40). The Bay also introduced the concept of equal duties based on ability. Each had an equal duty to pay a tax for the prosperity of the society, but the tax was to be set proportional so as to relieve the poorer (Art. II).

The Fundamental Pact was an important milestone in the history of Tunisia on the way to democratic consultation between rulers and the people while remaining within a totally Islamic context (Sraïeb 1995).

Constitutionality

Muhammad's successor, Muhammad Es Sadiq, continued the tradition of laying down basic principles relating to the exercise of power by the head of state. He promulgated a Constitution in January 1861. The Constitution specified the contours of a nationwide bureaucracy circumscribing the powers of the head of state. It gave a monopoly to the central government for collecting taxes, a right that hitherto had been sold out to private persons (Art. 103). Provision was made for administrative as well as civil court complaints against the agents of the government (Art. 71). Even the head of state could be called before a select subcommittee if he violated the Constitution (Art. 66).

Sadiq Bay remained firm on the principle that the Europeans would not be brought before special courts and therefore treated differently before the law. Before the law all were equal. He insisted on a court system in which well-educated judges were appointed and precise codes of law promulgated on which judges could base their arguments. It was only when the French entrenched themselves as a colonial power in Tunisia that the law and court system deviated from Sadiq Bay's ideals, for the French instituted courts for each religious group and nationality with corresponding laws. Equality before the law was not a colonial ideal.

A popular revolt broke out against the increase in the level of taxes paid to the central government and local leaders were removed from the rural bureaucracy. As a result, the Constitution was suspended for the next one hundred years. Nonetheless, the idea of a systematic bureaucracy at all levels supported by education at Sadiki College became firmly entrenched. The system developed steadily for the next one hundred years. The College opened branches in the interior as well, a brilliant move that tended to allow for some integration of all social and regional levels (Sraïeb n.d., 183).

The imposition of the French Protectorate in 1881 did not destroy this basis. This is important to note because Sadiki was the product of indigenous Tunisian reformers, not of the European colonizers (Sraïeb n.d., 256). Thus, the idea that critical and well-founded harmonization of the secular and the religious was possible, had indigenous roots. Without the stable development over one hundred years of an educated bureaucracy on which the central government and legislating authority could rely for enforcement of its laws, the legal reforms that Tunisia enacted in this century after Independence would not have been possible (Anderson, L).

Modern intellectual reformers of Islamic law – Taalbi

Sadiki College also became the centre of critical intellectuals. They began editing newspapers and pamphlets only three years after the formal imposition of the French Protectorate (Sraïeb n.d., 257). Their criticism of the foreign rule was balanced. It was directed not only against the wrongs of the French Protectorate but also the internal social inequalities.

One of the leaders of the Tunisian Constitutional Party who was popular among Sadikian students was Sheikh Abdelaziz Taalbi (Sraïeb n.d., 233). Sheikh Taalbi was a graduate of the Zaytuna Mosque, which had also benefited from the philosophy that motivated Sadiki College. This was largely due to the efforts of Sheikh Mahmud Qabadu, a professor of Arabic, who had translated the French military books into Arabic for the Bardo naval school. He wanted a curriculum of Islamic studies that combined science and religion (Sraïeb n.d., 27). Since the Bay's decree of 26 December 1875 graduates of Zaytuna had to learn in addition to religion and Sharia literature, history and mathematics. The sheikhs were subject to inspection from government administrators (Sraïeb n.d., 34).

Abdelaziz Taalbi, the son of a notary, was born in Tunis in 1874. He was inspired by the pre-Protectorate constitutional approach of Ahmad Bay, who had issued the *Ahd al-Aman* (Fundamental Pact) of 1857. He was born the same year that the liberal historian Ibn Abid-Diaf died. He was destined to carry on the open, democratic and critical intellectual tradition of Tunisia.

Upon the suppression of his newspaper in Tunis in 1897, Taalbi left for Turkey, Saudi Arabia and Egypt, from where he was expelled. Thereupon he moved to Algeria and Morocco. In 1901 Taalbi returned to Tunis. He launched an attack on the brotherhoods as pagan remnants. He was not the first to have been prosecuted for his attacks on the brotherhoods. Muhammad Shakir from Sfax was dismissed from his post as a young theological professor in 1902 for similar criticisms (Green 68, n. 64). The Sharia Court sitting with Maliki and Hanafi qadis wanted to try Taalbi. He went instead before a magistrate's court and was sentenced to two months' imprisonment in 1904.

In charge of editing *Le Tunisien* in 1909 (Green 99, 208), Taalbi became a member of the Young Tunisians, modelled on the Young Turks. The political programme of the Young Tunisians was directed towards arousing a national conscience. The aim was to convince Tunisians to take their social, economic and political fate in their own hands. The programme emphasized social equality. This won support from students at Zaytuna Mosque who came from outside the capital and found in the Young Tunisians allies for convincing established families to share power (Green 236). Emphasizing the fundamental right to liberty and driven by the dream of restoring the promises of the Fundamental Pact for a constitution, Taalbi supported the protest against the pluralization of the law. This was directed against a proposal in a Hebrew journal that Tunisian members of the Israelite religion should have access to the secular courts established by the French during the Protectorate, and which Ahmad Bay had refused to institute on the principle that all are equal before the law.

Taalbi also helped found the Liberal [Free] Constitutional Party of Tunisia (Destour) (*Al Hizb al dusturi al hurr al tunisi*) in 1920 (Sraïeb n.d., 286–89), preparing the way for Independence. He was not unique. This was also the time when the world press was reporting on the return of Mahatma Gandhi from South Africa to India to join the struggle of the Congress Party in India for Independence. Taalbi remained head of the party until 1923, when he left for a tour throughout the Middle East, thus giving credence to his pan-Islamism.[11]

Taalbi – The Liberal Spirit of the Quran

Taalbi took the principles of liberty and equality seriously on all levels, not just at the broad secular constitutional level. As a theologian, the Sheikh careful analysed whether these principles were positively encouraged by the basic sources of Islamic theology and law. He found that they were supported. As a good practising Muslim, he proposed how these principles should be realized in the daily lives of Muslims and their relations with one another. He thought of all Muslims, not just men who dominated the political scene, but also of women.

His seminal exposition was his book *The Liberal Spirit of the Quran*, published after his release from prison in Tunis in 1904, first in Paris in 1905 in French and Arabic as *L'esprit libéral du Coran/Ruh at taharrur fi'l-qur'an*.[12] His book has been described as a rapprochement between traditionists and modernists, using reasoning deduced from Islam (Green 188). The basic question he wished to answer was why the Europeans had been able to conquer the glorious Orient, from North Africa to China, and especially the Islamic countries. He sought the answer in religion, just as Max Weber, the Christian sociologist, sought many years later to explain why the German Protestant community was richer and more powerful than the almost equally large German Catholic community as a result of their differing theological doctrines (Weber). The Sheikh, like the secular sociologist, made two assumptions: i) that religious doctrines contain implicit promises of economic and political prowess on this earth and that such power is a reward for belief; and ii) that religious doctrinal interpretations like legal interpretations have practical economic or political consequences.

It is especially the second assumption that is central to understanding what Taalbi wanted to achieve.

As already mentioned, Taalbi admired the Fundamental Pact of Muhammad Bay, who had issued it in the spirit of the Emancipation Decree of Ahmad Bay. The latter spelled out the basic principle that law is not just a matter of applying principles. One must constantly re-examine the consequences of such principles to determine whether the consequences are in turn furthering the original principles, or whether they are undermining the original principles.

Taalbi on intolerance

Following the above line of thought, Taalbi took an historical approach. He started with the purist century of Islam, that is, the time when the Quran was revealed and the Prophet lived. He concluded that Islam at its birth was a liberal religion. Its basic principles at that time were respect for diverse opinions, freedom to intermarry, freedom of religion for non-Muslims, equity and justice. God promised respect from other nations not just because one is a Muslim or is rich and powerful, but because one is just and equitable (sura 60:8) (Taalbi Chap. III).

Taalbi found that over the centuries Islam lost much of this pure spirit. He attributed the loss to Islam having become ideologized. Ideologically, Muslims were to understand themselves to be the recipients of the last Revelation before the Final Judgment Day. Through the last Revelation God wanted to introduce Islam as a chastisement to the preceding monotheistic religions because they had become corrupt. It could never be admitted that Islam had fallen to internal corruption. To admit any corruption would be to admit implicitly that God might have grounds to punish Muslims too by revealing yet another religion. To avoid confronting this ideological taboo, the official doctrines agreed upon by the theological and juridical elite were to be regarded as impeachable as God's Word. The doctrines had to be followed, even blindly. Taalbi found that this ideology led to arrogance and intolerance.

Taalbi found that objectivity was needed as an antidote. He pointed out the mistakes that had crept into the other monotheistic religions and civilizations, Christianity and Judaism. For example, the Christians' celebration of Carnival derived from the pagan Bacchus festivals as demonstrated by

Frazer's Golden Bough (Frazer). Even the French had betrayed, he observed, the original principles of equality and liberty of their 'secular religion', whose constitution was the Declaration of Man (Chap. VIII). In Islam, learned imams and heads of religious brotherhoods had come to serve as intermediaries between the believers and the word of God. They presided over numerous religious ceremonies that were not foreseen in the Quran (Chap. XI). The Islamic *fuqaha* were also said to bear part of the responsibility for practice having fallen away from principle. Taalbi pointed out which cultural superstitions and malpractice of the societies that Islam had penetrated came to influence interpretations of the Quran and *sunna*. This was due in part to the importance attributed to *ijma* (consensus) in any one school of law or among the schools of law. Such adherence contradicts a fundamental function of the hadiths, namely, if there be a contradiction between the rule of a school of law and a hadith, then the hadith and not the rule is to be followed (Chap. X).

Taalbi ended his critique on a constructive note. He defined what it really means to be the bearers of the last Revelation of God. It means to be constantly on the alert against fossilization, to be always looking out for the renewal of the original spirit and principles. This is the basis of faith, not preservation of the consequences of century-long application of the principles, turning Islamic liberalism into fanaticism (Chap. XX). 'Count not your Islam as a favour upon me. ... Allah has conferred a favour upon you that He has guided you ... if you be true and sincere.' (49:17)

Taalbi on practices abusive of women's rights

One of the Islamic principles emphasized by Taalbi was that of equality. He relied on sura 49:13: All human beings are equal, all having been produced by a pair, a woman and a man. The only legitimate distinction that should be made is between those who can stand before God with dignity (and a conscience: *waqa*) and those who cannot (Chap. XVII). Neither the sexual classification of a person, nor belief, nor nationality is a criterion for making differences. To limit equality between men and women to issues of piety was to miss the spirit of this verse.

It was especially the corrupted influences that had assigned the women an unequal status in Islamic law. They were in need of emancipation like the African slaves at the time of Ahmad Bay. Taalbi analysed how the woman had come to be mistreated by the jurisconsults.

Veiling

The first violation against the woman was the veiling of her face. Taalbi traced this corruption of Islamic law to 'pagan' Persian culture that had crept into Islam (Chap. V). He cited Greek and Latin works that described the Persians as very courteous people, whose ways subtly influenced their Arab conquerors. Up to the end of the 2nd century of Islam, Muslim woman had not been subjected to the veil. It was due to the Persian influence that Muslim women started veiling their faces in order to fit into the Persian society.

Taalbi cites hadiths and Quran to prove his point. He quotes sura 24:31, which says that women are to lower their gaze and keep modest and not display their beauty or adorn themselves in order to flirt with strange men. Most of the jurisconsults had translated the phrase 'not display their ornaments (*zinat*)' as not display their 'face'. He found that the *ijma* of the jurisconsults had gone against common sense (Ghazali 63).

The other Quranic verses used to support veiling relate to the peculiar circumstances under which the Prophet and his household suffered (sura 33:53–54). He was receiving visitors who overstayed and were not polite enough to leave when the Prophet showed obvious signs of being overtired. The Prophet was also vulnerable through his wives. Imploring visitors could gain entry to his household by chatting up his wives. To avoid these problems, it was revealed that the Prophet's wives should guard their distance between themselves and visitors by speaking with imploring visitors through a screen or some barrier (*hijab*). In this way both the wives and the intruding visitors would not be tempted to be inconsiderate of the Prophet and not bother him unnecessarily. In this way they could assure 'purity for their ... hearts'. This interpretation is further supported by a hadith. It is reported that an imploring visitor did not take the hint to leave even when the Prophet excused himself three times, a sign that the audience had ended.[13] Given these circumstances under which the Quranic verse of the *hijab* was revealed, Taalbi opined that it was meant to be restrictive, not generalized. Using the *hijab* screen was intended to be necessary only for the wives and daughter of the Prophet. Taalbi supported his argument by drawing an analogy to the verse that prohibits the wives of the Prophet to remarry after his death (sura 33:53). This prescription was not meant to apply to all Muslim women.

Supplementing Taalbi on veiling: the verse of modesty

Taalbi's arguments about veiling were not intended to be all-comprehensive. They are succinct and persuasive. It should be observed at this point that he could have elaborated even more on the verses cited above. The purpose of the following paragraphs is to show how his arguments can be even further elaborated.

Sura 24, verse 30 lays down the principle of equality between men and women in respect to dress and behaviour: both are to lower their gaze and both are to be modest in dress. There is no mention of their faces. They are not asked to wear a dress that covers their eyes and their faces. Otherwise, if they had to cover their faces, one could never know whether they had actually lowered their gaze. With a covered face, they could gaze with great lust as much as they wanted without rebuke.[14] Without a face covering they would have had to exercise self-discipline, a virtue. It seems that the very illogic of covering the face was raised, but dismissed with two contradictory reports.[15] The closest headdress that one can imagine which would have fitted the verse of modesty is the type of scarf which stewardesses today on various Arab Gulf airlines wear – they are attached to a hat and swing gracefully down over their bosom then up over the shoulder. It provides sufficient modesty and freedom at the same time.

The very next verse 31, however, is clearly directed only to women. It relates to their ornaments. It addresses the almost universalistic practice of women adorning themselves, something not expected of men. The modesty of dress prescribed in the foregoing verse is extended to modesty of ornaments. The spirit of verses 30 and 31 is that both men and women have equal responsibilities. That is the mutual responsibility to keep their desires within limits. In this way the entire burden does not fall on a woman to hide her face. This conclusion is reinforced by a hadith. It is a report about a man who feels sexual lust towards a woman who is not his wife. He is told to go home to his wife and have intercourse with her, not to demand that the woman whom he lusted after cover herself so as to protect him from his own lust.[16]

As for the verses relating to placing a barrier (*hijab*) between the wives of the Prophet and imploring visitors, it is worth noting that again no distinction is made between the sex of the visitors. Not just a male visitor would be refused face-to-face contact with the Prophet's wives. A bothersome female visitor could be equally refused. The point was to distinguish between visitors who were badly motivated: coming out of turn or at improper times to get extra favours, visitors whose inconsiderateness was unfair to the Prophet and even other visitors. The screen was to serve as a reminder of fair play for all, regardless of sex.

Supplementing Taalbi on veiling: the verse of the outer garment

There is yet another Quranic verse used to justify veiling which Taalbi did not mention. This is sura 33:59. It says that the wives of the Prophet as well as all believing wives are to wear a covering (*jilbab*). The purpose was to prevent women from being molested when travelling about. What is not so clear is whether the covering is to be such that the women can be recognized as Muslim women and therefore would not be molested by men, or whether the covering was to prevent anyone from recognizing them as women.

The hadiths help somewhat in interpreting this verse. In one hadith one can deduce that veiling was not the practice in Arabia. In that hadith Aisha reported that Umar bin al Khattab pleaded with the Prophet that the latter should let his wives be veiled. It should be recalled that Umar was the one who had conquered Persia, where veiling was the practice. It is reported in the history of Tabari that the Arabian men had even adopted a Persian headdress (the *qalansuwah*) by 17 A.H. (Rosenthal, Yr. 17, 107).

The Prophet did not heed Umar's plea. Umar kept trying to convince the Prophet. He went again to the Prophet and reported that he had seen Sauda, the elderly wife of the Prophet – she had been a widow – at a gathering (Ahmed 49). In other reports of the same situation it is said that he recognized her during her toiletry at night in the open (Ahmed 54). Why he was able to recognize her is not clear – whether it was because of her height – she was known to be a tall woman – and therefore stood out, or whether she was in the habit of wearing ornaments and jewellery that made her easily recognizable. Umar said that because of this experience, he feared for the wives of the Prophet. It is again not clear whether Sauda was vulnerable to attack simply as a woman or especially as the wife of the Prophet.

Later on in connection with this encounter with Sauda, the Quranic verse was revealed that women should wear a coat (*jilbab*) in public gatherings.[17] The verse does not refer at all to covering the face. Reports from Safiyyah and Umm Salamah (who served as an imam for women) (Ahmed 61) reveal only that the women upon hearing the verses tore down their curtains to use as outer garments and placed them on their heads.[18]

The purpose of the *jilbab* was to avoid being molested (Razi XXV:230). It would seem that God basically favoured the Prophet's earlier approval of his wives being unveiled, but at the same time wanted to solve a problem of women being molested. A compromise was reached: a 'conditional' or 'circumstantial' verse was revealed. The verse refers only to wearing a covering under certain circumstances: when going to public gatherings and when there is danger of being molested. The conditional nature of the wearing of an outer garment is further confirmed in another verse. Sura 24:60 makes an exception to the wearing of an outer garment: women who are no longer of marriage age are exempted from wearing it, but are not to make wanton display of their ornaments.

Another report from Aisha gives even more insight into the problem. The hadith deals with women who had gone out to say the *fajr* prayer while it was still dark. Aisha mentioned that the women returned after saying their prayers so wrapped up that no one could recognize them as women.[19]

A similar hadith told of the Prophet taking care to wrap himself up when going to prayers. Aisha reported that he did not like to be wrapped up in a coat with designs on it because it distracted from praying. So he took to the habit of using a rough woollen wrap.[20] When this hadith is read in connection with the Quranic verses that enjoin both men and women alike to dress modestly and further address women in particular about their finery (24:30, 31), it becomes clear that men were probably accustomed to wrapping themselves when going out to prayers and gatherings, but women not. Women tend to want to display their finery. Hence they had to be spoken to directly so that they too would see the need to wrap themselves as the men did when going to prayers or gatherings.

The conclusion to draw is that wearing an outer garment in public is a matter of circumstances – that is, when Muslim women are vulnerable. They are especially vulnerable when going about in the dark – whether going to prayers or going to the toilet in open fields as is common in rural areas or having to go out at night to fetch water to cleanse themselves after intercourse with their husbands, as recommended by Aisha.[21] Under these circumstances, they should wear an outer cloak like that of a man so that they cannot be easily recognized. It would follow that a woman during the daytime would not necessarily have to be so wrapped up that no one can tell whether she is a woman or not. The same would hold true for women who live in areas where there is no danger of being molested. God would see no necessity for these women to adopt the Persian custom of veiling.

Taalbi's conclusions

With regard to veiling, Taalbi concluded that this was the instrument used by the patriarchs to keep the women secluded and restricted. They were denied any opportunity to contribute to Muslim life and civilization. Taalbi found that this violated the hadith proclaiming that believers are to get one half of their knowledge of religion from a woman and one half from men (Spellberg 27). It was no surprise that jurisconsults had supported the interests of patriarchs, for the same jurisconsults had tolerated the difference between the free and the non-free, the owner/enslaver and the enslaved.

Taalbi's juridical approach to interpreting the basic sources of Islamic law is clear. He relied on the plain meaning of the words of the Quran (Chap. XX). This assures believers of being able to use their healthy common sense in understanding what God expects of them rather than relying blindly on scholarly religious intermediaries. The consequence of such an approach is that the *ijma* of the scholarly elite is not binding if not compatible with the plain common-sense meaning of the text being interpreted. In other words, the *ijma* can become tyrannical, if the plain meaning is not allowed to serve as a corrective instrument of renewal.

The juridical maxim on which Taalbi relied is that of liberty: to reduce the freedom of a person, in particular that of a woman, is to reduce her opportunity to do God's justice and to serve the welfare of the community. Restriction of liberty may not be absolute for all time, only under circumstances that may temporarily require it, as a state of emergency. This principle in turn obliges the Muslim community, the Muslim state, to create the circumstances for liberty, not for restrictions. Concretely, this would mean, for example, when a woman is required to be veiled to prevent molestation, she is burdened constantly by fear of molestation – and fear restricts. The community should go to the root of the problem, which is the 'liberty' with which men molest women. The community should ensure a functioning court and policing system that gives the women confidence to sue and punish molesting men. The community also has a duty to develop its sanitation systems so that women and men do not have to go out when it is dark to perform their toiletries. The community also has to develop a safe transport system for believers on the way back and forth from prayers during darkness. Realization of such duties rather than placing the entire burden on women to veil themselves would be in the spirit of Taalbi. Not only is the Quran liberal, but also pragmatic.

Abusive practices against women: *dar jawad* (house of discipline)

Role of dar jawad

At the time Taalbi was arguing that the veil is not required, there existed an institution that literally restricted women physically. It was designed to break the will of high-spirited women. This was the *dar jawad* (National Union 18; Lakhdar-Ghoul). The exact origins of this institution in Tunisia are not clear. It seems to have existed since the 15th century. It was a house held by a person of repute to which husbands sent their wives to be corrected.

According to an account in the 1930s from a French visitor to one of the correctional houses for disobedient wives located in Tunis, there were forty women living there. The reasons were varied: a very young woman had refused to marry a man 30 years her senior. Another had been sent there by her husband because he wanted to avoid the daily quarrels between her and his mother. Yet another with a beautiful face had been sent there by her husband because he knew she wanted divorce. He thought if she were kept in the correctional house then she would have less chance to find another husband. A very young inmate had been sent by her stepmother for alleged insolence. A frequent ground for confinement was a quarrel between spouses that threatened to turn into a divorce dispute. The husbands did not want the women to stay in the matrimonial home.

The correctional houses were financed by the men who had had the women sent there. The period of confinement lasted on average a few weeks, at most a few months. Most of the inmates came from the lower classes. The women could be confined either by virtue of the private orders of their relatives or husbands or on order of the local qadi.

Confinement of the wife raised some legal questions for the Tunisian jurisconsults that undermined the practicality of making obedience a condition for receiving maintenance. It is reported that at the start of the 19th century the qadi of Qairawan and the qadi of Tunis entered into a discussion on whether a mother could still have custody of her children during her 'internment' (Lakhdar-Ghoul 51). It was held that she retained joint custody over the children for two reasons: first, her husband visited her regularly, and secondly, he was still responsible for paying her maintenance. This meant that while the husband had lost the services of his 'recalcitrant wife', he still had to pay for her maintenance and probably that of a relative or servant woman who had to take care of the household while the wife was in internment.

Living up to the reputation of Tunisian fathers, who, as mentioned before, are legendary in protecting their daughters, and supported by the Maliki teachings against husbands' brutality (Bellefonds II:294), some fathers went to great lengths to have their daughters released from confinement. One father exchanged his Tunisian nationality for the French nationality – which was regarded at the time as apostasy (Jones 1975, 264) – in order to have his daughter released (Lakhdar-Ghoul 64). Other fathers did not live up to expectations. In one case a young woman who did not get support from her father took the initiative to convert to the Hanafi school of thought (Lakhdar-Ghoul 64). The advantage was that she could marry without her father's consent and his assistance in negotiating a marriage contract, as prescribed by the Maliki school (especially for virgins (Sethom 22)). The disadvantage did not seem to impress her, for the Hanafi school offers a woman fewer grounds for divorce, e.g. she may not plead that the marriage has become a hardship for her as she could before a Maliki qadi. Perhaps she thought in case she needed a divorce she could reconvert to Malikism. When compared to the English common law at the time, the *dar jawad* represented a particularly pernicious violation of the Islamic spirit. Even 19th-century English common law permitted the wife to apply for a court writ against her husband who violated her right to peace in the marital home. This was especially important for women from weaker economic groups. The husband could also be ordered to give a security bond that he would do no harm (Siegel 21–23).

Evaluation of the legal basis of confining women

Arbitration

The legal basis on which the qadis were issuing orders to confine the women is doubtful. It is thought that the roots of such a house lay in the Quranic verse on a reconciliatory process between disputing spouses (4:35) and the verse of admonishment of wives (4:34). Sura 4:35 provides that if *shiqaq* is threatening, that is, the spouses are likely to split up after a bitter quarrel, then an arbitrator from the wife's family and one from the husband's family should try to mediate and reconcile. The bitterness with which the spouses quarrel with one another as a condition for the need for arbitration is mentioned in the hadith in which Yahya b. Said reports on the first *talaq* that the husband gave to the daughter of Abd al Rahman b. Hakam. The wife's father said that she should come to him although there were still two more *talaqs* to be pronounced before the divorce could be final. Aisha disputed the command of the father, saying that she should stay at her husband's place. Then Aisha was reminded that her own daughter Fatima had also left her husband's place for another place and this was allowed because of the nature of quarrelling involved.

Whether the main purpose of the arbitration is to save the marriage or assist in making the divorce process less acrimonious and more peaceful is not specified in the Quran or the above-mentioned hadith. Another hadith says that the arbitrators must be called and may decide what is needed: to reconcile or to have the partners separate.[22] During this period of arbitration – a time for 'cooling off' – it could hardly be expected that the spouses continued to live under the same roof. Thus the practice grew up in Tunisia of a good neighbour taking one of the spouses under his or her protection (*dar al iskan*) (Lakhdar-Ghoul 53). There was also the *dar sukna bi husna* to which a wife could go to talk over marital problems in peace (Largueche 266). Alternatively, a trustworthy woman (*amina*) was assigned by a qadi to live in the home of the quarrelling couple to observe their behaviour as a prelude to arbitration (Largueche 263, 267).

Women who left the marital home during the arbitration period because of acrimony between herself and her husband were the subject of controversy in the Maliki hadiths. The question was where the woman should go: whether to her father; whether she could live alone; whether she could stay in a house her husband had found for her to rent even though she could not afford the rent. Two fairly clear rules emerged, however. For one, all men in the community were to avoid passing by the house of a divorcee (or a woman in the process of divorce). Obviously they were not to tempt themselves into thinking that such a woman was ripe for plucking.[23] Secondly, the husband remained responsible for paying the rent until the divorce was final. This reduced the chances of an angry poor woman being tempted to find as quickly as possible another man or boarders to help her pay the rent before the marital dispute was settled.

Obedience

At some undetermined time the juridical emphasis shifted. Emphasis was no longer placed on the issue of where the woman could choose to go during the period of arbitration. The issue became one of chastising the woman. Attention was turned to sura 4:34 on chastisement of wives. What would have given rise to such a shift? The shift seems to have come about in response to quarrelling spouses reaching an impasse in the divorce negotiations and arbitration. In such a situation not even the arbitrators could help. Spouses could come to such an impasse if, for example, the wife was determined to get the husband to divorce her (so that she would not have to pay him), but the husband was determined to stay married. Under these circumstances neither would be prepared to reconcile. The arbitrators would be powerless.

The husband who lost patience with the Quranically prescribed arbitration would seek to take matters into his own hands. He would seek another verse to assert his power. Sura 4:35 would seem at first glance to provide for him a way out: the verse says that when a woman has been remonstrative, the husband may admonish her and abandon the marriage bed. The husband who does not want to divorce may declare the wife disobedient. The jurisconsults came to the aid of the husband. Declaring the wife disobedient became tantamount to outlawing her. Marital discord became associated with female insubordination. Disobedience became a ground for denying the wife maintenance (Engineer 117; Sonbol 1996, 280) if she did not remain in the marital home or did not go to live in a place her husband approved, e.g. the *dar jawad*. Out of the *dar al iskan* was made the *dar jawad*, a house for solitary confinement of the wife at the request of her husband or father.

At the heart of the *dar jawad* was the notion of marital obedience. From this notion derived the claim that the husband has the right to browbeat his wife. The *dar jawad* offers again a good example of how the Quran was interpreted to the disadvantage of women. The reason was that the plain meaning of the Quran and hadiths was ignored as well as the spirit of equality. In support of this point we need to re-examine sura 4:34ff and relevant hadiths on obedience and wife-beating.

Sura 4:34 starts out with a general statement: men stand by women in time of need as expected in a reciprocal relation. Men give support materially (food, money, which constitute *nafaqa*). The verse then goes on to talk of a specific class of men. There are men who are absent (e.g. for military reasons or for business). A Maliki hadith gives some insight into the problems of such businessmen.[24] The husband of Fatima bint Qais was away on business in Syria. He sent back home through his agent barley. Fatima wanted her usual portion of the grain for her support. The agent refused, saying that her husband had pronounced a *talaq*. Fatima, as reported, was livid. She would have been entitled to support at least for the next three months of her *idda* (waiting period after divorce before a woman may remarry). Thus one of the questions raised in this hadith and in sura 4:34 is whether the men are still responsible for supporting their womenfolk when absent. Do they have to leave behind enough support for them? Do they have to send them support from afar? Who is to have the power of attorney over the wealth left behind or sent to them for support? A general answer to these questions can be found in sura 4:34, which involves a play on words. The answer is that those womenfolk who are devout and pious and thus preserve the wealth as God would have them do are entitled to a power of attorney. The reverse is also true, namely, those womenfolk who are full of rancour and do not preserve as God would like them to do, do not deserve power of attorney. In the hadith literature dealing with questions of *nafaqa* (maintenance), the Prophet confirmed the right of pious womenfolk to give away part of their husband's wealth for charity.[25] The emphasis was not on general obedience of womenfolk to menfolk and in particular of wives to husbands. It is rather on obedience to God, to what God expects of women when the men are absent. If the women handle the wealth of the men properly, then they are obeying God. God is the only one to whom a Muslim, whether man or woman, owes obedience. The ultimate test of obedience is whether one is strong enough to refuse the commands of another, including those of a husband, if contrary to equity and justice. Otherwise, the concept of obedience becomes perverted.

Obedience and beating

If we proceed to the succeeding sentences in the same Quranic verse, we see that they are addressed to wives who have been in fact unfaithful in the absence of their husbands. Such a wife has caused discord (*nushuzahunna*). This is enough to make a husband brutal to his wife (implying that a brother who returns to find his wealth squandered by his sister would not be brutal to her). God understands that the anger of the husband is justified, but the question is whether he is justified in brutalizing the wife. Accordingly, the verse sets out how a husband is to express his anger. He is released from his marital duty to sleep with his wife, but he need not divorce her. The Quranic word used for 'abandoning' (*hajara*) raises two possibilities. The husband may 'emigrate' from the marital bed, or send the wife emigrating (Lakhdar-Ghoul 56). Furthermore, the Quran enjoins the husband who abandons the marital bed to be resolute. Finally, the concluding words of this verse warn the husband under these circumstances not to oppress the wife or treat her as a whore. This implies that he cannot abuse her as he likes and be fickle, for God is ever present, ever listening, even to our most intimate conversations. The husband is to give the wife a chance to repent, that is, she is to get a second chance to fulfil the trust placed in her.

The verb used in sura 4:34 for resolute withdrawal by the husband is *daraba*. It has been often interpreted to mean 'to beat'. It can also mean 'setting an example by shunning or absolute abstaining' (a kind of metaphorical self-beating). The hadith literature indicates that 'beating' is not what was intended. Rather abstinence was intended. The Maliki hadiths indicate that beating wives was a very controversial issue already at the time of the Prophet. The Prophet had advised Fatima bint Qais (mentioned above), who had complained very angrily about her husband who had not sent grain for her maintenance, about whom she should best remarry. She had several offers. One of them the Prophet asked her to refuse. It came from a man who never put his stick down (i.e., he beat his wives).[26] In other hadiths, it is said that a husband is not to slap his wife in the face.[27] A husband was also not free to wound his wife, for he is liable for paying compensation to her.[28] A series of non-Maliki hadiths reveal another side of the dispute about beating. Men had come to the Prophet to complain that their wives were getting too emboldened, whereupon it is reported that the Prophet then allowed them to beat their wives. The women, however, did not remain acquiescent. They in turn also went to the Prophet. How the Prophet responded is reported in two different accounts. One account has been construed to mean that the Prophet refused to lend an ear to the women.[29] Another more detailed, and therefore, more credible, report shows that the Prophet was very amused at the concerns of the men and indeed did take the concerns of the women seriously.[30] In the latter report Umar narrated his own concerns and those of the other Quraishi men – who were later to claim to be the sole successors to the Prophet's power – about their emboldened wives and their fears of the example set by the Ansari women, and especially the Prophet's wives Hafsa and Aisha, who had withdrawn themselves from the bed of the Prophet because they had disagreed with him. The Prophet listened patiently to Umar. Then the Prophet withdrew himself too from the bed of his wives for 29 days. Umar thought that this was a sign that he had divorced his wives for having talked back to him. But the Prophet surprised him. No, he had not divorced them. There is neither any mention that he had beaten them. What he did was to resolutely and stringently shun them. He set an example for 29 days.

Thus the meaning of the chastisement verse in the Quran (sura 4:34) is clearer when read in conjunction with hadiths reporting the behaviour of the Prophet and the discontent of the women about beating husbands. The clear intention is to require the dissatisfied husband who has decided to leave the marital bed to be stringent in his abstinence rather than to allow him to pick up his stick. This offers a much more civilized approach to marital discord. It also underscores the extraordinary sensitivity with which God perceives men and women. Men and women have different emotional ways of responding to conflict. Cultural conditioning arms each with different emotional weapons. A man will react with brute anger when he feels unjustly treated. A woman will react with unfathomable emotional hurt when she feels she has been unjustly treated. God warns each not to use these weapons to inflict hurt. In this way they will do justice to each other when exercising their equal rights to end the marriage because of serious discord. The jurisconsults did injustice to this scheme by associating discord with female insubordination. This was taken as a ground for denying maintenance and denying the wife the right to leave her home without the permission of her husband. It was also used to restrict the right of the wife to divorce to serious grounds, e.g. a cruel or deserting husband.

By interpreting sura 4:34 to permit beating, the jurisconsults did an astonishing thing. Such an interpretation gives a wife a status even lower than that of a slave. Several hadiths prohibit beating slaves. Ibn Malik reported that slaves were not to be overburdened beyond their capacity. Dawud reported explicit prohibitions against beating slaves.[31] If there were differences between a slave and his/her master or mistress, the slave was to be released (not beaten).[32] Alone on the basis of analogy with the hadiths prohibiting the beating of a slave, the beating of a wife should have been even more stringently forbidden. The fact that this was not the case is an indication of the extreme gender prejudices of the jurisconsults.

Disobedience by men

The *dar jawad* served to correct remonstrative disobedient wives, but there was no equivalent institution for remonstrative disobedient husbands. This fact reflects another construing of the Quranic verse on remonstrative husbands which did injustice to the spirit of equality in the Quran.

The word for disobedience appears twice in the Quran in the context of marriage. The word is *nushuzann*. It appears in suras 4:34 and 4:128. Verse 34 is written from the point of view of the husband: 'if you fear *nushuzahunnan* (on the part of the wife) ...'. Verse 128 is written from the point of view of the wife: 'if you fear *nushuzan* (on the part of the husband) ...'. In verse 34 the husband is given the right to emigrate from the marital bed. In verse 128 the wife is given an equal right to separate herself from him or send him away. She is asked to settle the discord by an amicable separation just as her husband is asked to settle the discord without outrage and enter into arbitration (verses 34 and 35).

Traditionally the jurisconsults construed the notion of *nashiz* in verse 34 relating to women differently from verse 128 relating to men. Women were placed under a duty to obey; remonstrative women were deemed disobedient. Men were not under a duty to obey. Remonstrative men were deemed cruel or deserting, not disobedient. Only recently have Muslim women begun to correct this misconstruction. In Malaysia a woman has recently sued her husband in court on the basis of his 'disobedience' towards her (Shah 5–6).

Tahar Haddad – successor to Taalbi

Although the institution of the *dar jawad* existed well into the 20th century, the writing pens of the Tunisian men did not cease to plead for justice and liberty for women. Another graduate of the Zaytuna Mosque, Sheikh Tahar Haddad, took up their cause. In 1929 he began publishing articles that reflected a new approach in the Liberal Constitutional Party (Destour), which Taalbi had helped found. The leaders of Destour became more conscious of the need to organize the working class into unions and cooperatives for political success. This was the start of laying a civilian power base, as opposed to a military power base, which has distinguished Tunisian politics and legal reform ever since the 1930s from its Algerian, Libyan and Egyptian neighbours. Tahar Haddad's writing also provided the theoretical underpinnings for the Neo-Destour Party, founded in 1934 and eventually led by Habib Bourguiba (Sraïeb n.d., 299).

In 1930 A.D./1348 A.H. Haddad published his treatise on *Our Women in the Sharia and Human Society/Imra'ana fi'l shar'ia wa'l mujtama'*. Similar to Taalbi, he intended to demonstrate Islam's understanding of the universalism of human nature and society. He met opposition from the ulama

(M'Halla 132). His book was banned and he left for Saudi Arabia, where he became a taxi driver and died in an accident in December 1935.[33]

What motivated Haddad was the debate on whether Islam was an obstacle to progress, one of the measures of progress being how the society deals with the question of equality of men and women workers. He answered that Islam *per se* was not anti-progressive or against equality. It was rather the decadent customs and myths of inequality that had crept into pronouncements made in the name of Islam. He equally stressed the greatness of Islam that had spread over a vast area from Morocco to Indonesia. He gave women credit for contributing to this greatness. He asserted that without the woman playing a role greater than the contemporary one of seclusion and subordination, Islam could not have been able to achieve its pre-colonial glory. What is unique in his discourse is that he conceives of the woman as an active historical agent in Islam.

The position that Haddad took in this debate about why Islam had lost its dynamism reflected not only an inner piety that sought to understand the fundamental principles and axioms of God's ambitions for Islam. It also reflected a political continuity. Already in the late 19th century the Tunisian Prime Minister at the time had analysed the political relationship between illegal colonial French rule and Islam. He was Khayr ad Din – a Mamluk slave trained as an administrator for Ottoman colonialism. He published in 1867, ten years after the Fundamental Pact issued by the Tunisian Bay and twenty years after the decree for the emancipation of slaves, a tract on the decadence of the Islamic civilization and the need for political reform. He blamed not only his fellow Muslims. He blamed also the colonials, who were so pernicious as to further their own interests by aborting the Islamic reform movement and favouring behind the scenes the retrenched Islamic conservatists while publicly denouncing the 'backwardness' of Islam (Khayr ad Din 117ff; Pensa 354). Tahar Haddad reasserted this two-pronged approach in his book on women: to regain for the woman in Islam her rightful place as an equal and free person, and to expose the conservatives as agents of the colonial powers who could continue their dominance as long as the conservatives rejected the liberalizing spirit of Islam. Haddad was brilliant and courageous enough to target the very heart of this resistance: the status of women. His tract was an embodiment of the best of the legendary dedication of Tunisian fathers to their daughters.

Like Taalbi, Tahar Haddad stressed from the start the theology of the historical intention of God's revelation of the Quran: it was to renew life and liberate women from the constraints of the Arabian society. Haddad added, however, to this approach pragmatic reasoning and sociological analysis. From this point of view Islam was not just for the glorification of God in order to guarantee a place in heaven. It was for improving the daily conditions of the lives of the people. Hence with regard to women's rights, Haddad was more interested in looking at the working lives of women and their needs. They were sociologically speaking one-half of society and a necessary source of labour for society, but in terms of the superficial and encrusted juridical interpretations of the Quran and hadiths, they were excluded from being recognized by the society. They had more duties than rights. It was time to follow the example of God and hear the pleas of the woman (sura 58:1).

Because the society thought more in terms of duties – men arguing that they had more duties than women and therefore deserved more rights – Haddad propounded the premise that women should be given equal duties and responsibilities like those of men. He supported his position with two suras: that of 4:32, which assigns a woman the earnings she has made and the man what he has made and holds each one responsible for administering their own goods and wealth; and that of sura 2:228, which gives a woman rights like those that a man has against her (Haddad 25, 29, 57). These injunctions, so argued Haddad, presume that women are actively in control of their lives, for these injunctions can be realized only if the woman is allowed to seize the initiative to control her own earnings rather than, as custom had it, handing over the responsibility to her relatives to do so. Haddad's positioning of equality in the context of social responsibility continues to bear a stamp on the modern Tunisian family law. Islamic history provided more than enough examples of active women, some famous like the businesswoman, Khadija, who employed her husband, the Prophet. In the time of Caliph Umar in the first two decades of Islam there was Hind bint Utbah. She petitioned Umar for a loan from the public treasury. He granted it to her on condition that she be responsible for paying it back, not her husband. She went off to engage in trading, buying and selling. By the time she had to repay it her husband had divorced her. She was kept to her word and she repaid the loan.[34]

Haddad on equality

Concerned with equalizing the duties and responsibilities of women with those of men, Haddad had to take on the difficult question of the entrenched attitude that women are subordinate to men.

The Quranic verse cited in support of the inferiority of women is sura 2:228: men have an advantage over women and therefore are in a class of their own (*daraja*) (or have rank over them). The second verse cited is sura 4:34: men stand by women in need (or men are protectors of women). These two verses were used by jurisconsults to justify giving women only one-half of the inheritance shares of men (with some few exceptions). The jurists then sought a premise to support their interpretations of these two verses. The premise was biological necessity. Men's advantage over women lies in their superior biological strength. This strength should be used to protect women. The premise was raised, however, to the level of dogma. Haddad challenged the logic. The dogma of inferiority of women rested not on Quranic logic, but on biological ideology clothed with Quranic interpretations. Haddad pointed out that there is no Quranic verse that prescribes the inferiority of women due to their biology (Haddad 41).

Traditional Tunisian practice and equality

It should be noted that Haddad's critical predisposition had roots in some Tunisian rural traditions. Haddad did not mention them as a source of authority, but they are worth mentioning as part of explaining acceptance in a large part of the population of the enshrinement of equality in the marriage laws after Independence. An example of such a tradition is found in Gabès – on the coast, next to the desert. As part of the marriage ceremonies lasting a week, games were played. They were partly intended to ease the tension under which both sexes stood at the time of marriage: the wife had to prove to be a virgin and the husband had to prove his virility. Some of the games simulated married life. In one in particular the newly-weds played the parts of a sultaness and sultan. They entered into an allegorical battle of authority and will. The lesson to be drawn was that there has to be a checks-and-balances relationship between the sexes, with no one dominating, and the one seizing domination having to compensate the other (Baklouti 92, 93).

Reevaluating the Quran and hadith on equality

Sura 2:228 starts out with prescriptions about divorce. It prescribes that women who have been divorced by their husbands (by *talaq*) have to wait three months to determine whether they are pregnant or not. If the woman is pregnant, the husband may decide to reinstate the wife – but only on condition that he wants to treat her equitably. This implies that he should not wish to take her back only to determine whether she bears him a male child, for example. On the other hand, there is nothing in the verse that prevents a pregnant woman from refusing the offer to return to her husband.

The verse then goes on to state that women have an equal right to men that balances out the right the husbands have against them. Then the verse takes a surprising turn. It ends with the words that the husband still has an extra right or advantage that the wife cannot match.

What can this extra right be? Is it that the husband has the advantage of being able to remarry without waiting, while the wife is restrained to waiting three months before she can remarry? The hadiths offer some insight. Whether the husband should have this advantage seems to have been a subject of debate, especially in regarding polygamous husbands. A Maliki hadith reports on a polygamous man who had already reached the limit of four wives. It seems that he wanted to marry a fifth wife, but obviously that would have been illegal. His only choice was to divorce one of the four then marry the fifth woman. The question then arose whether he had to wait for the fourth wife to end her *idda* before marrying the fifth woman. Qasim b. Muhammad and Urwah b. Zubair opined that he should not have to wait for the end of the *idda* of the divorced fourth wife. He could replace her immediately.[35] At the same time they said that the polygamous husband should have divorced the fourth wife over several sessions. This implies that he had tried to divorce her in one session in order to gain time, for several sessions would have meant a delay in marrying the fifth woman.

Legal restraints on divorced women forcing them to wait before remarrying were and still are not uncommon. The Mosaic law at the time of the Prophet was far less liberal than the Quran. Under Mosaic law a divorced woman who was nursing had to wait two years before remarrying (Cohn 98). Her husband did not have to wait at all. The Maliki jurists granted the same freedom to a Muslim husband, while reducing the waiting time for the Muslim woman. No effort was made to correct the imbalance.

A contemporary example of such restraints is the German family code. The code imposed up until recently in 1998 a waiting period on the divorced woman but not her former husband (Scholl).[36] Such a restriction had been imposed earlier on men for reasons of piety but was lifted. The restriction on women persisted because it represented the last vestiges of patriarchal interest in controlling the fruits of a woman's body. A man had to know who was his child, so it was thought. The restriction on women was lifted not because it was considered a violation of gender equality, but for other reasons. It was because it was found to be extraneous in the face of the family law provision that a former husband or the new husband has the right to contest the paternity of a child born after termination of the marriage as not being a child of the marriage bed. Additionally, any woman who applied to a marriage officer with a statement about who was the father of her unborn child was guaranteed a release from the prohibition, as the law had allowed a marriage officer discretion to grant such requests (Ss. 1592 and 1600 Buergerliches Gesetzbuch, Stratz).

Thus when sura 2:228 is construed in the context of divorce law, it loses some of its sting. It is more about discrimination on a specific point rather than a general endorsement of men's superiority over women. The hadith literature, by contrast, that is cited in favour of such an endorsement does not match the context of sura 2:228. The hadiths are more concerned with the future of women after death than their life on earth. They also reinforce the Judaic/Christian view of Eve as the cause of all evil, even though in the Quran it is the devil who is mentioned as the tempter, not Eve (suras 7:19–25 and 20:120–121). It was reported in the non-Maliki collections that Paradise has many persons who were poor on earth, but few women. Most of those in hell are women (whether most of them in turn are rich women is not specified). The reason given is that a woman, even if treated well by her husband in general, never forgets if he treated her wrongly just once.[37] If a man does not want to end up in hell too with such revengeful women, he is to avoid the allure of women, since it was a woman, Eve, who is to blame for the travails of the people of Israil.[38]

Indeed, when placed in an historical context, sura 2:228 contains a radical reform in favour of women's rights over pre-Islamic Arabic practice. The verse confers on the divorced wife an equal right. This is implicitly the right of the wife to refuse reinstatement. According to Maliki hadiths, *talaq* was a pre-Islamic Arabian and Mosaic institution. It was designed to give the husband the exclusive right to divorce the wife and even remarry her after divorce (as long as she had not remarried another in the meantime).

The hadiths speak of pre-Islamic husbands who divorced the same wife up to a thousand times. This implies that the wife could be reinstated a thousand times against her will.[39] In effect she was treated as a yo-yo. Sura 2:228 gives her the right to refuse to return once divorced on the third *talaq*. She has only to fulfil her *idda*.

To conclude, the Quranic phrase that men have an advantage or rank over women was taken out of its divorce context. In summary, Haddad was right to criticize the *fuqaha* for raising the 'men-have rank-over-women' phrase to a level of dogma. It is relevant only in the context of divorce. It does not contain doctrine about equality between the sexes. There is another verse that has a more general doctrinal character. That is sura Al Tawbah 9:71 which states that women and men are each other's guardians (*awliyya*) – seen by some to abrogate or restrict suras 2:228 and 4:35 (Shah 10–11). If the phrase in sura 2:228 that women have equal rights to match those of men had been read in conjunction with sura 9:71, then the Quranic spirit would not have been twisted to discriminate against women.

Haddad on polygamy

The second major issue that Haddad took on was the question of polygamy. Tunisian men had the right to have up to four wives plus slave concubines. Women had only the right to one husband, a clear major discrimination. At the time Haddad was writing his tract, polygamy was heatedly debated in North Africa. The Egyptian King Fuad had been presented in 1927 with a legislative bill that would have restricted polygamy based on the arguments of Muhammad Abduh, a prominent reformer. Abduh had argued that no man could hardly be expected to live up to the Quranic demands that the husband love his wives equally. The King refused to sign it into law (Ahmed 175). Haddad sided with Abduh. To support his arguments he analysed the two major contestations against polygamy, namely, that no man could ever do justice to two women (sura 4:129); and that if a man cannot do justice, then he should marry only one wife (4:3). This argument later became the basis of Tunisian legislation that invalidated polygamy. It is also the basis in part of the Pakistani law that requires the state to determine the capability of a man to marry a second wife.

Social effects of polygamy

Haddad did not stop at juridical arguments. He elaborated also the sociological consequences of polygamy (Haddad 65ff). He wanted to show how a legal institution like polygamy was having effects which were undermining the general welfare of the Tunisian Muslim society. He examined first polygamy in the rural areas at the time. He found that polygamy there was motivated by economic interests. It was the custom of men to marry several wives as plantation workers. Keeping them as wives was cheaper and easier in terms of controlling them than hiring paid labour.[40] Haddad then examined the psychological aspects of polygamy. He started from the premise of equality of feelings – husband and wife are motivated by the same feelings: each wants to be loved. When, however, polygamy is introduced, this balance is disturbed. It leads to men thinking in egoistic authoritarian terms. It fans flames of jealousy among women. Each seeks for herself and her children extra favours from the husband. Each seeks something extra from the resources available for maintenance or inheritance (e.g. more *inter vivos* or testamentary gifts).

Polygamy in the Quran and hadiths

Haddad's sociological and psychological approach to the reality of polygamy in Tunisia is particularly useful for evaluating the Quranic verses on polygamy, for the Quranic verse is set in a social context. It has much more contextual richness than most interpretations of that verse have done justice to.

Sunna: marry only a poor widow

The context of sura 4:3 is plain: it is conditional. It deals with a situational rule. That situation has to do with wars or other disasters. These can lead to a surplus of women with half-orphaned children. Someone or some institution has to take care of them. Otherwise, the fatherless children and their mothers, who have to work without help from their fallen husbands, brothers or fathers, will become even poorer. Surviving men will be tempted to exploit them sexually and the women and their children tempted to accept selling themselves. Or, as was common in the early centuries of Islam, enemy troops enslaved women as spoils of war. If, however, a Muslim man could show that he was married to them, then the women had better chances of being released from the enemy. Conversely, Muslim troops who captured from the enemy widows with children increased the surplus population of the female and fatherless children. The Quran insists on a solution to these problems. The community or state is the first addressee. It can intervene and help the widows with children. If the community fails – 'If you fear you shall not be able to deal justly with the orphans ...' (the introductory three lines of the sura) – then each man is allowed – not obliged – to assume individual social responsibility for helping these orphaned families. For this reason the Quran allows him to take the widows with children under his protection by marrying up to four. The *sunna* of the Prophet set an example that set a limit on polygamy. He set an example by marrying only widows (Aisha being an exception) (Spellberg 102). On the basis of this example those Islamic countries which insist on allowing polygamy should restrict the request of a man to take a second wife to only marriage with a poor widow with children.

It would seem after the Prophet's death that men became less concerned about the social function of polygamy. They were more concerned about the numerical restriction to only four. A quarrel arose about the number of wives permitted. Men who had been accustomed to having an unlimited number of wives were stunned to think that Islam drastically restricted them. The question was posed whether the imprecise phrase 'marry ... two, or three, or four' in sura 4:3 meant that a man was limited to a maximum of four, or to two plus three plus four, making a total of nine wives, the number the Prophet had. Ali bin Hussain answered firmly, only four. Aisha confirmed. It was not intended that all Muslim men have the same number of wives as the Prophet had had.[41] They were restricted to a smaller number of only four,[42] for to marry more than four widows with children would have placed a burden on any man that would be impossible to fulfil. The controversy about the numbers did not die down. Even centuries later in the Middle Ages the exegeses and the *ijma*, or consensus of scholars, which limited the maximum number to four, were challenged. It was argued, how can there be an *ijma* when there are even two jurists who disagree (Razi IX, 175).

After the Prophet's death, polygamy became a financial issue for the community. The Muslim community had expanded by conquest into many lands. Umar as military commander had to set up a fund for soldiers' pensions and their widows. At one point people came to Umar complaining. They wanted a raise in their stipends. He told them that it was their own fault that they did not have enough. Their lifestyle had changed. They had taken on more wives and hired servants. He was not about to support such a lifestyle.[43]

Polygamy as an issue of levirate marriage

When placed in an historical comparative context, the polygamy verse is best understood as an issue of levirate marriage. At the time Mosaic law forced the brother of a fallen soldier to marry the latter's widow. In effect this was a forced polygamous marriage. Not all Hebrew husbands or jurists approved of this rule of levirate marriage (Neusner 166). The Quran in sura 4:19 prohibits forced levirate marriages. Sura 4:3 reinforces this rule. In effect it releases both the brother of a fallen soldier and the latter's widow, even when she has children, from the obligation to marry. It goes on to say what should happen if the widow does agree to enter a marriage with her brother-in-law voluntarily. The Quran expressly requires a new marriage contract with the widow and a new dower. Her second husband (even if it happens to be her brother-in-law) cannot refuse her a second dower on the basis that she has already received one from her deceased husband in addition to a portion in the inheritance from the deceased. The succeeding verses relate to the administration of the properties of orphans (sura 4:6–10). They are filled with warnings against unjust administration of their wealth. As emphasized by Aisha in reports on how to interpret the polygamy verse, a man who decides to marry more than one widow with children takes on a heavy responsibility. He is responsible for securing their rights to their shares in the estates of their deceased father. This is a particularly heavy responsibility because it can lead to conflicts with the other relatives of the deceased who may accuse the new husband of diverting a share to himself.

Invalidating polygamy

The above arguments show how polygamy can be restricted according to the Quran and hadiths – so restricted that only the most pious of men would wish to practise it. Haddad, however, argued for the invalidation of polygamy. His argument is elegant in its simplicity: no husband can do justice to more than one wife; polygamy leads to social and psychological conflicts that sap social energy.

The purpose of this section is to present arguments which would support invalidation of polygamy even more strongly based on the Quran and hadiths.

There are several hadiths which further support Haddad's analysis of the social damage caused by polygamy. One manifestation of this damage is the pain felt by the woman. Aisha spoke of this pain. She spoke honestly about her jealousy of Khadija, even though she was already dead, for the Prophet often remembered her and praised her too much, saying that she lived in a palace in paradise.[44] At the same time, the Prophet too was aware of how painful polygamy can be. He realized that a husband could never do justice to a woman, as stated in sura 4:129, much less to two or three or four. Hence it is not surprising that the Prophet refused his son-in-law to marry polygamously. Ali had been requested by the Banu Hisham b. Mughirah to take on a second wife. Ali had nothing against this, but asked his father-in-law the Prophet for permission. The Prophet refused on the ground that it would hurt the feelings of his daughter Fatima (Spellberg 157). But if Ali was determined to marry another woman, he was advised to divorce Fatima, then marry the other woman.[45] Tunisian fathers would especially sympathize with this example set by the Prophet. Aisha and the Prophet prophesized paradise for the fathers and mothers who are benevolent to their daughters.[46] In other words a good Muslim is one who avoids a polygamous situation.

The broader social problems that the polygamy verse intended to solve, namely a surplus of women after war and to regulate levirate marriages, were not addressed by Haddad in detail. Perhaps this was because the social situation at the time in Tunisia did not at all correspond to the problem addressed in the verse, for the verse conditions polygamy on a surplus of women. Haddad stressed in the introduction to his treatise that Tunisian women constituted 50 per cent of the nation. In other words there was no serious surplus.

It is this very conditioning (Gätje 341) of polygamy on a surplus of widows with children, as after a war, which would justify invalidating polygamy. As long as there is no serious population imbalance, then polygamy may not be allowed. It would be suspended until such time as a population imbalance occurs. A similar situation arose in Europe at the end of the World Wars. There were arguments in favour of introducing polygamy as an especially '(pagan) Germanic' institution before and even after the Second World War. Some German Christian pastors argued that polygamy would solve the overwhelming number of widows with children (Schwab; Gätje 335, 341).

There is one problem, however, with the surplus-of-women argument. It can happen, at least theoretically, that a disaster could result in a surplus of men. Whether women would be given the same rights if such an imbalance should occur, i.e. an overwhelming surplus of men, is highly doubtful. So in the spirit of Quranic equality, polygamy should be allowed only if extremely drastic population imbalances occur, a rarity.

Even if the population imbalance were to be so drastic, there would still remain the problem of polygamy violating equality of rights and obligations between men and women. Among the early hadiths[47] the Prophet is reported to have warned that no Muslim man is to compete against his fellow Muslim and take away his fiancée from him. Equally so, no Muslim woman is to compete against another Muslim woman by being the cause of a divorce. Certainly a woman who agrees to be a second wife is provoking divorce.

When there is no drastic imbalance in the population, polygamy is not the final solution for taking care of widows with children. Sura 4:3 addresses first of all the state. It has to make an effort to support orphans and their mothers. This interpretation is supported by the Maliki hadith that says that the state shall take over paying for the rent of the house in which a divorced woman lives in case her husband is financially unable to pay.[48] The same would apply to orphans and widows. It was this social component of Islam which Haddad emphasized and which Bourguiba later realized. The welfare of a woman does not necessarily depend on individual men, but on the society as a whole that enables her in turn to contribute to the society.

Thus the key to women's rights was, in Haddad's opinion, education and learning. Education prepared one for participation and respect in the society. In this respect Haddad was underscoring not only the Islamic injunctions to learn as applying equally to all, but also the assumption of the Western society that a learned person has superior chances over an unlearned (Pensa 277).

Haddad on veiling

On the matter of women veiling themselves or keeping themselves in sequestration, Haddad again took a socially pragmatic approach. Veiling, he argued, had been so dogmatized that some local customs required a daughter to veil herself before her father. Haddad argued that veiling should not have been dogmatized since the jurists had disputed the meaning of the Quranic verses relating to modesty in dress. Some took the plain meaning of the verse, others interpreted it to mean veiling the face of the woman and keeping her sequestered. The debate had never ceased. As the issue was highly debatable, it could be judged only according to its social consequences.

Social disadvantages of veiling

Haddad thus enumerated the social disadvantages of veiling:

i) Veiling was not conducive to satisfactory marriages. Veiling prevented men and women from getting to know each other's character, tastes and interests before marriage. They had to contend with their parents whose tastes and interests were given more priority in the search for marriage partners. In Tunisia veiling had even led to mistakes in the identity of the bride or bridegroom. This was not frequent, but it made young people suspicious of Muslim marriages and induced them to dream of marriages with Europeans.

ii) Veiling and the consequent sequestration of women also had an effect on men. It had, complained Haddad, led men to adopt silly habits. They had become egoistical and thought they could do any kind of foolishness in cafés and restaurants without being under the watchful eye of their wives. This was a reference to the hypocrisy which the veil engendered. A man and a woman having an affair could go undetected because the woman was fully veiled.[49]

iii) For children, too, veiling had undesirable consequences. Veiled mothers preferred to let their children play in the streets without supervision.

iv) Veiling made the life of a woman complicated. For example, the rural women had never been able to afford to wear the veil because it would interfere with their labour and the economic sustenance of their families. By analogy Haddad argued that women working in the cities should be given the same right to labour without extra complications. Judging an opinion of law or injunction according to whether it makes life less complicated is nothing strange for Islam. It is emphasized in the hadiths that God takes care not to impose complications. Simplicity in dress as well as in rules is a virtue.[50]

Consequently, a good Muslim woman can avoid veiling in order to avoid the difficulties attached to that custom.

Legal arguments against veiling

Haddad also put forth legal arguments against veiling. He pointed out that veiling and accompanying sequestration undermined other rights given by the Sharia to women. One such right was that of a woman to administer her own property. Veiling restricted her movements and contacts with the outside world so that it handicapped her full enjoyment of her rights to her property.

Hadiths on sequestration of women

Haddad did not extensively quote Maliki hadiths to support his position, for the topic of sequestration of women and veiling does not occupy much space in Malik's collection of hadiths. This may be because the Ansari women of Medina, where Malik lived, were known to be of very independent spirit: Aisha praised them as 'the best of women [because] shyness would not prevent them from inquiring about religion and acquiring deep understanding of it.'[51] The few Maliki reports on veiling and sequestration indicate differences of opinion on the question of whether women in the state of *ihram* should cover their heads and hands. It was reported that women should not veil themselves, another reported simply about the practice. The practice of some women ran contrary to this prohibition.[52] The non-Maliki traditions, which Haddad referred to (Haddad 183), report positively on meetings between men and unsequestered women. Anas bin Malik is quoted in one such hadith about a meeting between the Prophet with an Ansari woman. The Prophet had her pulled aside to speak to while others were present. This has been taken to mean that men and women are permitted to meet privately as long as they are not secluded from other people.[53] Cases of women who proposed marriage face to face with a man were reported to indicate that a woman and a man may look at each other before marrying.[54] The Prophet indeed encouraged such meetings. He advised that when one wishes to marry an Ansari woman in particular, the man should look into her eyes, since apparently eye defects were common among the Ansaris.[55] There are also reports of contact between women and men in other areas, such as on the battlefields, where women treated wounded men and vice versa.[56] Once when a woman shepherdess had slaughtered one of her animals, some men were sceptical about eating the meat just because it had been slaughtered by a woman. The Prophet unequivocally ordered that it be eaten, thus sanctioning women being in the open and performing the same duties as men.[57] An account of a battle of the military commander Al Mughirah with the people of Maysan in Persia (*circa* 15 A.H.) illustrates the activism of the Muslim women. It was reported that Ardah bint al Harith b. Kaladah wanted to join the men in the battle. She took off her veil (*khimarah*, meaning a complete covering of her face), made a banner out of it and started waving it. The other women followed suit. This contributed to the victory of the men (Rosenthal, Yr 17, 170).

Haddad on marriage practice

On the institution of marriage, Haddad regretted that social customs had reduced it to a matter of costly festivities and vain expenses (Haddad 146). Especially for the urban middle and lower classes marriage had become a ruinous affair. The groom had heavy costs and the bride placed a burden on her family because of her trousseau costs. This had damaged women's own self-image. As daughters they saw themselves as sources of ill luck, at least in financial terms. Their lack of self-esteem affected eventually the exercise of their divorce rights. The right to divorce was often written into the marriage contracts, but the practical exercise of this right was problematical. Upon divorce, they had a Quranic right to damages if the husband were at fault (see below on *talaq*). But Haddad found that the women shied away from demanding damages upon divorce. They did not want to cause more financial burdens. They often agreed to give up their trousseau in exchange for a more expedient less costly divorce process.

As a result of financial burdens some families asked their children to postpone marrying until enough had been saved up for the festivities. This had the social consequence of a high rate of celibacy among women and men. Haddad regarded celibacy as morally debasing.

Decades after Haddad published his thoughts on this topic, some of the same basic problems remain. It simply has taken on other forms. Some couples who married under state law regard themselves not yet properly married until the festivities have taken place. These occur some years after the state marriage until enough has been saved to finance the social celebration. If a child is conceived before the public celebration, the woman sometimes aborts it because it is not seen as a proper child of the marriage (Labidi 1989, 91).

In certain rural areas, even to this day, such as in the Sahel, there are practices, however, which allow a bride to keep her own self-esteem. The young bride works to contribute to her trousseau. She embroiders and sews costly garments and linens.[58] So neither the father nor the groom has to bear the expenses of a trousseau.

Hadiths on marriage celebrations

Haddad did not expressly discuss the hadiths on wedding expenses. There are many references in the hadiths to the wedding festivities. It was taken for granted that while the marriage contract and ceremony as such were short and simple, the cultural habit of using the occasion to hold large festivities could not be stopped. The celebrants were admonished not to forget to invite the poor to the wedding festivities and invitees were warned never to turn down an invitation to a wedding.[59] This implies that generosity is expected at wedding celebrations, at least generosity by those who can afford it.

Haddad on* mahr *(dower)

One of the financial burdens that the Maliki law imposed for getting married was the dower, *mahr*. Haddad was not against the *mahr* in principle. He complained merely of it being too high. The social consequence was that women eloped with their lovers.

The level of the *mahr* differed in fact from region to region in Tunisia. A movement to keep the *mahr* low was started by an Algerian colony in Bizerte, where the marabout there imposed the minimum symbolic *mahr* as the standard tradition. The Tunisian Bay approved and had circulars issued from the 1920s to the 1940s to reduce the *mahr* in order to encourage young men to marry.[60] Some jurists recommended that the minimum *mahr* be only four Dinars (Gargouri-Sethom; Qairawani 65 *nikah*).

Since Tunisia's Independence the amount of the *mahr* has been reduced officially to one dinar. In some regions of Tunisia it takes the form of a wedding ring, or gifts to the bride from the groom's family, such as clothing or sacks of food or bottles of olive oil.

Haddad on the nature of marriage

Haddad lamented the poor attitudes of men towards their marriage partners. Husbands tended to see marriage either as a service to them or as a financial burden. Haddad observed that upon returning home from labouring, the husband was often impatient with his wife. She wanted to share her problems of the day, e.g. quarrels with the neighbours (Haddad 159). He had no time to listen. When a man had problems, he need not talk with his wife. He could distract himself outside the home. The woman, on the other hand, who was not allowed to gain any understanding of economic and social realities, found her salvation in making capricious demands for luxury items.

As a remedy against the socio-culturally misdirected Islam, Haddad argued for the return to the original simpler and purer conceptualization of marriage in Islam. Marriage is not just a social tie, but also a sentimental tie, the object of which is cooperation between husband and wife on an equal basis. The contemporary Muslim husband had forgotten the many exhortations in the hadiths to men to listen to their wives and enter into dialogue with them.

A man's task is not just to provide for the wife and buy a house without taking into account the feelings of the wife as some Tunisian men were wont to do. This was made clear in the famous hadith in which the Prophet speaks of the woman as a rib. The reference to the woman as a rib is surprising since there is no reference in the Quran to the rib (Ahmed 87). Even some traditionists opine that Eve was created before Adam (Cooper 145). The references to the rib indicate a certain influence from Judaic-Christian jurists who justified the subordinate position of women on the basis of the belief that Eve was fashioned from the rib of a man. In the hadith the Prophet warns men against trying to break the will of their women. Even threatening to divorce her if she does not bend to the man's will is not permitted: 'if you try to straighten her, you will break her, and breaking her is divorcing her.'[61] He enjoins men to really relish their wives, to make the concerns of their wives their own concerns. That would include taking seriously her conflicts with the neighbours. The Companions too told of their chatting leisurely and freely with their wives after the Prophet's death.

Haddad drew the conclusion that if husbands were not seeing their wives as equal partners then the woman became a mere symbol of sexual desire. This made the society no better than the Western societies which religious men in Tunisia were criticizing for treating the woman as a sexual object (Haddad 189).

A Quranic verse in support of Haddad's approach is sura 2:223. It analogizes a woman to a piece of land being prepared for tilling, not to a rib of a man. Land is precious, and if not treated properly, it will not be productive and it will resist. Land has its own laws of nature, which if not obeyed, lead to devastation.

Haddad on talaq

The arbitrariness to which a wife was subjected was, in Haddad's opinion, most obvious in the law of divorce, especially in regard to the husband's use of *talaq* (unilateral pronouncement by the husband of divorce). The law and practice, however, had come to diverge, to the detriment of the woman. Several of these practices even violated the Quran (Haddad 72). Nonetheless, they had established themselves in Tunisia with the approval – whether explicit or tacit – of even the most conservative jurists, the 'rigourists', the term used at the time to describe the traditional fundamentalists, or integrists.

The practices which Haddad especially criticized were:

the easily revocable initial *talaq* (first *talaq*)
the private divorce without court intervention
the drunken *talaq*
the 'husband of one night' after a final irrevocable *talaq* (third *talaq*).

Revocable talaq *and private divorce*

In general a husband had three chances to pronounce *talaq* before the divorce was valid. The first two *talaq*s were revocable, the third irrevocable. On the revocability of a first *talaq* Haddad took the view that revocation was not as easy as most husbands thought (Haddad 73). It was being used by a husband to punish or to harass a wife. The half-autobiographical stories of women of Haddad's generation confirm this abusive practice of the revocable *talaq*. They testify to the revocable *talaq* being used as an instrument of harassment on the first night of marriage or to goad the in-laws (Hejaiej 30, 72, 128, 130). Haddad pointed out that this ran contrary to the Quranic intentions that a *talaq* was revocable only if done in all sincerity and a desire to turn over a new leaf in the marriage. He cited sura 2:231: 'If you divorce women, and they fulfil the term of their *idda*, either take them back on equitable terms or set them free. But do not take them back to injure them, or to take undue advantage; if any one does that he wrongs his own soul.' The intention of this verse is reinforced by sura 2:225 in which God holds everyone accountable for the intentions in their hearts.

Thus in Haddad's reading of the Quran the first *talaq* was revocable only if the good intent of the husband could be objectively established. This meant that a husband could not be judge in his own cause and determine whether his *talaq* was revocable. Several hadiths deal with this question of how to assess the husband's intent. Certain phrases used by the husband were taken automatically as expressions of serious intention to divorce. Other phrases and gestures without words were regarded as ambiguous and in need of clarification.[62]

Haddad's emphasis on assessing intention served as the basis for the post-Independence Tunisian legislation. The family code (Code of Personal Status) requires all divorces to be brought before the court, which alone judges the intentions of the husband (or the wife for that matter, who may seek divorce). Haddad's approach also conforms to the hadith reported by Ibn Malik that arbitrators between the spouses are a must. The Quran commands them. The task of the arbitrators is to ascertain the intentions of both spouses and eventually separate or reconcile them.[63] The implication is that no husband may divorce without going to arbitrators. Neither the Quran nor the hadiths confer explicitly on the husband a doctrinal right to divorce without a final decision from the arbitrators. This leaves it to the discretion of a government to suspend the use of private divorce.

Drunken talaq

The Tunisian judicial practice at the time of Haddad recognized a drunken *talaq* as valid. This was a controversial issue in the hadith literature. Some said it was illegal, analogous to a *talaq* from an insane husband.[64] It is surprising that it was not declared illegal simply on the ground that a husband who has violated the prohibition against intoxicants should not profit from an illegal state. Malik was among those who reported that an intoxicated *talaq* would be valid. The argument was based on an analogy with murder: an intoxicated man who killed another still had to face the consequences, despite his state of intoxication.[65]

Haddad did not accept the argument. He showed how it violated the Quran. The Quran rejected an oath given out of inadvertence (sura 2:229).

Drunkenness is to be analogized to inadvertence. Haddad chastised the fundamentalist *fuqaha* of his day (the rigourists (*jamidin*, literally, those who are ossified or frozen in their thinking)) for obscuring the spirit of the Quran by allowing a drunken *talaq* (Haddad 78).

Revocable talaq *and one-night husbands*

The Quran, as Haddad cites (Haddad 74), permits spouses who have divorced after an irrevocable third *talaq* to remarry each other. But the remarriage is limited to only two times. The third remarriage could take place only after the wife had married another man and was divorced from him (sura 2:230). The Islamic rule represented a liberalization *vis-à-vis* Mosaic law. The Mosaic law prohibited a divorced woman from ever remarrying her first husband.[66] The Sharia, in contrast, did not put the woman under such an absolute restriction. It imposed only certain conditions for a remarriage between the same partners.

It was said that the Quranic verse on this subject was revealed to dissipate the anger of families who had no desire to go through rearranging marriage conditions for the same divorced couple.[67] The Prophet made the remarriage somewhat more difficult by adding the condition that the wife must also have consummated the marriage with the second husband before being divorced.[68]

The practice that developed in Tunisia was that the wife simply took one husband for one night. Whether the marriage was consummated in fact or not was not important. Haddad thought that this made a mockery of the Quranic version of the law. He rejected it even though the great jurist Abu Hanifa had justified it (Haddad 76). Haddad was thus implying that not even the great jurists of the past could be infallible.

Haddad on returning the* mahr *upon divorce

In the rural areas of Tunisia men were known to require the women to return the *mahr* (dower) upon a *talaq* divorce or to relinquish claim to an unpaid dower even if the divorce were initiated by the husband. This was a pre-Islamic practice – it still prevails under African customary laws – which had been abolished by the Quran (2:229: ‘it is not lawful for you to take back any of the gifts ...’) (Haddad 72). Even when the wife initiated divorce (*khula*) and offered to pay back the dower, she would be released from repayment if it were established that the husband had done injustice to her.[69]

This unQuranic practice, however, continued. It was facilitated by changes over the centuries in customs relating to payment of the dower. The Maliki rule was that because *mahr* is a necessary condition for a valid marriage, it should be paid upon marriage. If it were not paid at marriage, the wife had a right to claim the *mahr* any time she chose. This was in contrast to the Shafii school of thought (Brunschvig 73; Bellefonds II:218). In time the practice of paying the dower promptly at marriage became seldom. Since the 10th century in Tunisia it had become increasingly difficult for women to reclaim the full *mahr* from their husbands. The practice of deferred dower – due to Ottoman influence – took hold (Labidi 1989, 156). A small sum (like a down-payment) was delivered immediately at the marriage (*muqqadam*). A larger more valuable amount or gift (*muakhkhar*) became due upon divorce or death of the husband. Consequently, if at the time of divorce, the wife did not actually have the full dower in hand, she had to sue for it. If the husband proved recalcitrant, she often had to choose between a long-drawn-out process and acceptance of the husband's offer to facilitate and shorten the process in exchange for her relinquishing the dower. If the practice of paying the entire dower on marriage had continued, the tables would have been reversed. The husband would have had to try to sue the wife for return of the dower upon divorce at her initiative.

In some parts of Tunisia practices developed which tried to correct the Hanafi influence. Sfaxian marriage contracts, for example, show that the upper bourgeoisie, known for their agricultural and commercial wealth, developed a traditional practice that tried to protect the daughter. The written marriage contract specified the amount of the dower due before the marriage ceremony and fixed the date when the rest had to be paid. The rest (sometimes gold) was to be paid (usually) within two years after consummation of the marriage (Sethom 20, 24).

Haddad on post-divorce compensation: **mutaa**

As mentioned, the Quran prohibits husbands from demanding the dower back upon a *talaq* divorce. It goes even a step further, as Haddad reminded his readers. The Quran requires the husband to pay in addition to the *mahr*, a post-divorce gift, the *mutaa* (sura 2:241). This represented a certain liberalization *vis-à-vis* the Mosaic law. The Mosaic rule was that a divorcee was entitled to a post-divorce gift only if the amount had been specified in her marriage contract (Cohn 109, 110).

This Quran verse has been subject to many different interpretations at different times. In the 8th century it was interpreted as compulsory, but the amount was fixed at a low rate (Coulson 1991, 29–30). Later it was opined that the Quranic injunction was a matter for the husband's conscience. The husband who did not pay lost moral standing, however, in the community. He could no longer serve as an upright witness in court. The initial opinion that the compensation was a legal obligation was adopted by the Egyptian legislator (see chapter on Egypt).

In rural Tunisia, as mentioned, Haddad had observed that the husbands were demanding compensation from the wife upon divorce. She was to give back the dower. In other areas of Tunisia where the husbands permitted the wife to keep the dower,[70] the husbands were refusing to pay an additional post-divorce gift. The Tunisian judiciary supported the husbands. It was argued that the husbands had more than enough financial obligations upon divorce. They had to pay for the maintenance of the divorced wife during the *idda* (waiting period of at least three months) to establish whether the wife were pregnant. The judiciary did not emphasize the fact that the *idda* was not so much for the benefit of the wife as for the protection of the husband's interest in a potential child.

Haddad took another view: the *mutaa* is obligatory. He justified his view on the basis of the purpose of such an obligation. Marriage, he argued, is a contract which creates certain expectations of longevity of partnership and willingness to solve problems. If it is so easy to break without compensatory consequences, then the contract cannot be taken seriously.

Haddad's view is compatible with the two traditions which Malik reported on *mutaa*.[71] It is first reported that Abd ar Rahman bin Auf gave his divorced wife a slave, indicating the gift could consist of something of value, not just money. The second hadith confirms in its first part the rule that every divorced woman should get a gift. Then in the second part it goes on to say that there is an exception to this rule as uttered by Abd Allah b. Umar. That exception is in the case of divorce before the marriage was consummated. A woman divorced before consummation had an automatic right to one-half of her agreed upon *mahr* as specified in the Quran (sura 2:236–7). After specifying this amount the verse goes on to say that husbands still should be generous, meaning that the husbands would be expected to give more than the one-half of the *mahr*.

The question had obviously arisen whether the divorced woman could then claim also an extra gift like a woman whose marriage had not been consummated. In response to this question, Umar gave a restrictive interpretation – namely, that the divorced woman of an unconsummated marriage was strictly limited to one-half of the *mahr*. She was not to get an extra gift. Umar's interpretation implies a concern that the absence of consummation means lack of a deep emotional attachment or expectations on the part of either partner.

It is precisely this emotional link that characterizes a consummated marriage which Haddad emphasized by interpreting the Quran and hadiths in such a way that *mutaa* is obligatory and not voluntary.

Haddad on the wife's right to divorce

Haddad not only lamented the arbitrariness of the divorce rights of the husband. He also commented on the women's right to divorce. In contrast to the men, he noted, divorce by women was not arbitrary. When Tunisian women wanted divorce, they had to petition the qadi court. They had to have specific grounds, according to Maliki rules, e.g. divorce was allowed under the conditions in the marriage contract, or the husband had gone insane or had an infectious disease,[72] or he was not paying maintenance,[73] or he had not cohabited with her for over a year,[74] or he had taken an oath to refrain from sex for four months as allowed in the Quran[75] but had extended it beyond the four months,[76] or he had accused her of adultery and she had successfully rejected the accusation with an oath,[77] or she wanted to buy her freedom.[78] In practice Tunisian women's divorce petitions were for the most part granted. This implied that the courts found the women's arguments convincing and not frivolous.

Haddad then analysed this situation according to Quranic criteria. He found that women seeking divorce were acting more in accordance with Quranic requirements than their husbands. The Quran requires arbitration before a divorce can take place. The qadi courts existing at the time served as such arbitrators. Haddad presented arguments as to why men too had to be brought in line with Quranic injunctions and forego private *talaq*. They too had to subject their decision to divorce to arbitration, in effect they had to exchange arbitrariness for arbitration.

Haddad's point here was that the Quran requires in matters of divorce procedural equality for men and women. Both have to submit their desire to divorce to public arbitration by a court. Haddad did not debate the substantive grounds for divorce for husband or wife. He emphasized rather the need for a remedy against arbitrariness, for the husband who used *talaq* arbitrarily kept the wife in a state of uncertainty. She could not be sure when it was meant to be revocable or irrevocable which made it difficult for her to prepare herself for another future, either alone or with another man.

By not emphasizing the question of what are the substantive grounds for divorce, Haddad steered the debate in the direction of principles. The Sharia is there to remedy wrongs and to bring about equality so that one who has more power than another may not be tempted to be arbitrary. He saw the state as embodied in the courts as the best guarantor of these principles. Divorce cannot remain, according to the verse on arbitration, a matter of mere private differences between the spouses. Such an interpretation would be most incompatible with the famous hadith in which the Prophet called *talaq* legal but an abomination.[79]

Women's right to divorce in the Quran and hadiths: can the wife pronounce talaq*?*

As said, Haddad found that the Quran confers procedural equality on the husband and wife in the matter of divorce. This approach provokes less controversy. Nonetheless, the issue raises another interesting question of substance, indeed substantive equality. The question is whether the Sharia allows women to have an equal right to arbitrary divorce as men? To answer this question one has to begin with looking at whom the Quran and hadiths are addressing in divorce matters.

The Quran and hadiths presume that many believers were already practising divorce at the time. The men used their rights unashamedly to torture their wives, divorcing them up to 200 times.[80] This would seem obviously morally intolerable. Hence the Quran limits the number of divorces to three, just as it had limited the number of wives to four. It further imposes strict rules on when divorce should be spoken, i.e. when the woman does not have her menses (and the woman is not to hide when she has her menses or not).[81] It obliges each spouse to submit to arbitrators who pronounce divorce or reconciliation.

In the Quranic verses on divorce God addresses especially men because they were known to abuse divorce so much, holding their wives in suspense. It should not be overlooked, however, that God also addresses women. Women are said to have rights over men that men have over them, but men have one more over them (2:228). This raises the question: does the Quran give a woman a *talaq*-like right to divorce her husband?

When one examines the hadiths to find an answer to this question, one finds two different approaches. There are some hadiths in which some women take the approach that they may divorce their husbands in a *talaq*-like manner. There are also several reports of women who took another approach: they demanded that the husband pronounce a *talaq* and the husband is given no option other than to comply.

In the first category is a Bukhari report about those people who say that a woman may declare to her husband, 'I will not have sex with you' – meaning I will divorce you. The report says that such people are ignorant.[82] In contrast a Maliki report tells of an enslaved woman who pronounced *talaq*. According to the report, Zabra, a slave, was married to an enslaved man, but she got emancipated. Her husband remained enslaved. She went to one of the Prophet's wives, Hafsah, about divorcing her husband. Hafsah told her that she could decide to divorce her husband now, but she should think it over, not rush in thoughtlessly.[83] Zabra decided on divorce. She said the *talaq* three times and left her husband. In yet another report about one of the Prophet's wives, Aisha, it was said that she also took a generous approach. She was interpreting the verse (4:128) relating to recalcitrant husbands who disobey their wives. She said that the wife may take the initiative to tell the husband that he may no longer sleep with her or is no longer obligated to maintain her if he wants to marry another woman.[84] Finally, there is the Maliki report of Rubayyi, daughter of Muawwidh b. Afra. It is said that she divorced herself from her husband, left him, then told Abd Allah b. Umar what she had done. He accepted it and declared that she had to go through *idda*.[85]

In the second category of women seeking divorce are several Maliki hadiths describing women who demanded that their husbands divorce them, and the husbands did so accordingly. One hadith says that the daughter of Muhammed bin Maslama Ansari asked her husband to divorce her when he took a second wife. Just before the *idda* ended she asked for reconciliation and he granted it; then she again wanted divorce. He gave it. She demanded divorce a second time, and again she reconciled in the *idda*. Finally, when she demanded a third time a divorce, he reminded her that they had to really get divorced and no more reconciliation was possible.[86] The wife of Abd ar Rahman bin Auf also asked her husband to divorce her, and he did so, reminding her that she had to tell him when she no longer had her menses.[87] By that time her husband had become ill. He asked her whether she still wanted to divorce, implying she had a choice between becoming a widow with an inheritance or a divorcee without inheritance. She wanted divorce. It was further reported that an Ansari woman (no name given) had also asked for a divorce. The husband asked her to let him know when she was without menses so that he could then declare divorce.[88] He did and he gave her the divorce.

These hadiths are evidence of women who exercised a *talaq*-like divorce either directly or through their husbands and the husbands had no right to object. The *fuqaha* could have interpreted these hadiths in such a way that the right to divorce was equal for men and women. Instead, the *fuqaha* interpreted them in such a way that the rights of the spouses became imbalanced. This took the Sharia in the direction of the Judaic Talmudic rules, which gave the husband control over the divorce process.[89] The *fuqaha* devised a legal construct – the divorce 'option' – for this purpose. The construct conferred on wives a right to divorce but only if the husband had already conferred on them the option. This option was deemed revocable, as reported in a hadith. The divorced wife argued that it was not revocable. Zaid b. Thabi, however, decided against her without giving the reasons.[90] A similar construct was placed on the report of the wife Rubayyi cited above who walked away from her husband and got it approved by Umar. Her divorce initiative was construed to be a *khula* divorce, even though no mention is made in the hadith that she offered to pay her dower back to get the divorce.

Haddad on economic equality between spouses

Right of the wife to work outside the home

Haddad was concerned not only about protecting wives against the arbitrariness of men pronouncing *talaq*. He also dealt with the question of economic equality between spouses. At issue was whether women should be allowed to work outside the home. Restrictive interpretations of the Sharia had resulted in wives being subjected to the will of their husbands, who could refuse them the right to work.

Haddad began treating the issue by placing it in a social context. He found that the restrictions were the result of perversions that had crept into the Arab society. Over the centuries the male elite had accustomed itself to a lethal mixture of polygamy and slavery. Slave girls kept by men as marital partners or sexual objects had lulled men[91] into thinking that the essence of a woman consists in fulfilling the desires of a man and to devote her energies to him. Haddad took a survey among the Sharia judges at the time and found that this attitude affected the judicial practice in Tunisia relating to the poorer classes. It was common judicial practice to give a wife of a poor man who did not have enough to support her the right to borrow money for maintenance (Haddad 90) rather than to order the husband to allow her to work outside the home.

Haddad also examined the attitudes of women caught in such a male-centred society. He found that they accepted their lot for the most part. They competed for men's favours (Haddad 119ff). Encouraged not to work, they indulged in fantasies of luxury or actual luxury. Haddad was in good company on this point. The famous Egyptian Hanafi jurist and qadi, Ibn Abidin, who died in 1836, had held that under the Sharia a woman had the right to work even without the consent of her husband, as long as it was during the day. He profferred two reasons: one was spiritual. The woman needed work to keep her from devilish temptations (Meron 269–70). The other reason was a matter of social justice and equality. In the hadiths there are two categories of women who are allowed to work: divorced women who had to maintain themselves[92] and married slave women (Meron 269, 277–8). Ibn Abidin opined that a married free woman should also be added to these categories and treated equally. Otherwise, the married woman would be placed at a disadvantage compared to her sisters. Haddad added a novel argument for supporting the divorced woman. He argued that the amount of the *mutaa* due upon divorce had to cover the costs of a day-care for the children in her care while she worked (Haddad 60ff).

The Quranic verse which Haddad cited to support his position was sura 4:32, which confers on each spouse the right to keep their own earnings.

While Haddad's concern about idle women wasting their time in luxuries was appropriate for the more wealthy classes, and while the traditional jurists refined the details of their recommendations on the amount and kind of maintenance due, e.g. the husband had to give only a summer dress and a winter dress (Bellefonds I:259), and did not have to cover the short-term medical or religious expenses of the wife (Meron 221–6), the reality for the average Tunisian woman was otherwise. The reality corresponded to the Quranic verses and hadiths that foresee women having to work. The Tunisian women have a long tradition of working, both with and without the consent of her husband. The Qairawan women traditionally specified what kind of work they wanted to do and refused work they considered degrading. They had a monopoly in certain commercial work such as door-to-door sales or teaching carpet weaving (Enda 36, 37, 40). Other women who were married off to older men had to work when the husband retired and earned very little pension (Enda, 59). In Sfax the bourgeois husbands were freed of the duty to provide new clothes for several years for their wives because the wives' families provided her with a trousseau of clothes (Sethom 29). The middle-class families of Sfax sent their daughters as apprentices to women who were known for their mastery (*muaalim*) of embroidery for women's and men's clothing and their moral integrity, and who lived not far away from the home of their pupils (Zouari). The best in the trade had up to forty pupils. Entire families built their reputation on the skills of their women. A mistress of the trade worked with her own daughters, passing on the secrets of the trade to them. This had to mean for such families that male babies were not necessarily prized over female (Jouirou). Female progeny, who could help in expanding the trade and maintaining the family economic reputation, must have been equally regarded as indispensable. The women used the wealth earned through the trade not only to help family members in need, including husbands, but also to buy olive trees for themselves.[93]

Right of the wife to be compensated for work within the home

Haddad reinforced his view that a married woman has a right to work outside the home without her husband's permission by citing the Quranic right of a wife to be paid for performing work in the household of her husband (Haddad 59ff). It was specifically provided that if a woman nursed her child, her husband should pay her for this work.[94] He was arguing in effect that if a wife has to be paid for services in the household, then surely she had a choice – either to get paid for work at home or for work outside the home. The Quranic verses referred to are suras 65:6 and 2:333. They provide that a husband should pay a wife who nurses their child. The verse was issued in the context of divorce. If the divorced wife were pregnant, delivered at the end of her *idda*, and nursed the child, the husband still had to pay her for her expenses for nursing the child.

A general principle was distilled from this verse. It applied beyond the divorce context. That principle is that if the wife does something to the benefit of the husband, then he is to compensate her. Haddad recognized the power that this principle conferred on women. If she did work in the household, her husband had to compensate her. The inverse of the principle is that if he does not pay, then she may refuse to work in the household and work outside.

This principle represented liberation from the Mosaic rules, for under Mosaic law, a wife was under a duty to help her husband in his work or business. She was allowed to refuse only if she agreed to maintain herself (Cohn 104). Not even all European legal systems have acknowledged such freedom. Among the European legal systems, for example, the German civil code indeed went so far as to prevent this kind of situation by specifying that the wife was obliged to work in the household and the husband obliged to bring in money. During the late 1920s, at the time Haddad was writing, this provision of German law allowed a husband to threaten his wife with divorce if he felt that she was neglecting the household work by working to earn money, even if she needed the money to pay for the education of her children from an earlier marriage, who were not the responsibility of her second husband.[95] The latest reforms have not changed this pattern. It has simply been left to the discretion of the spouses to decide which one – the husband or the wife – shall take care of the household and which shall make a living.[96] The Sharia does not foresee such a division of labour in the marriage. The partners could agree to a division, but with the understanding that each has to compensate the other so that no one dominates the other on the basis of material earnings or neither is totally dependent materially on the other. The Sharia presented liberation to the wife from the Mosaic duty imposed on a wife to obey her husband by helping him in his work or business (as was also required under the original family law section of the German Civil Code of 1899). She was allowed to refuse only if she agreed to maintain herself.

Implications of the right to work and compensation for the rules of obedience

Haddad did not labour the implications of his position on the Quranic rights of the woman to earn her own living (4:32) and to be compensated for work at home (65:6). The implications, however, are far-reaching. Haddad was in effect saying that there was a conflict between a clear Quranic right of a woman to work and the jurists' interpretation that had subordinated that right to her husband's approval. The jurists had done this because they had subordinated the right to work to the law of maintenance. The jurists opined that the husband alone has the duty to maintain the wife (4:34) regardless of how much she earns or how wealthy she is (Bellefonds II:256). But this duty to maintain was interpreted to give him authority over the wife. She is to be obedient. Obedience means that she may not work outside the home if her husband refuses. The verse that a woman may keep her earnings has implications to the contrary: if she has a right to her own earnings, she may also decide when to earn. The latter verse has been subordinated to the principle of obedience, that is, she can obtain earnings by working as long as her husband approves of her working. Haddad's emphasis on the woman keeping her own earnings shows that no husband can be given the authority to nullify this Quranic right of the wife by refusing her permission to work outside the home.

This position is supported by the hadiths. Responsible working women are no strangers to the hadith literature. The hadiths contain stories of women who worked outside the home[97] and of women who expected slaves to do their housework.[98] Working women were not condemned. A woman too is not exempt from providing for her family. The hadiths speak of Asma bint Abu Bakr who was required to provide for her ailing mother, even though a non-Muslim.[99] Authority was given to a wife who wanted to make charitable contributions from the earnings of her husband even without his approval, an issue that raised controversy among the jurisconsults.[100] She could take from his properties without his permission only if she were in need and he were miserly.[101]

Obligation of the wife to work and the principle of obedience

Whether a wife has a duty to work if her husband orders her to do so was not an issue explicitly raised by Haddad. Certainly he would have been aware of it as discussed in the juridical literature. For this issue challenged the principle of obedience in the same way Haddad challenged the jurists' logic on whether the duty of maintenance should be so tied to obedience that it overrode the Quranic right of a woman to earn her own living.

The question of whether a husband could order his wife to work if he could not support the family was problematic for the jurists. It tested the limits of tying the principle of obedience to the rules of maintenance. Theoretically under the principle of obedience, the husband could have ordered her to work to provide for her own maintenance and she would have to obey. The result would have been counterproductive, for if she provided her own maintenance, she would no longer be dependent on him and therefore would not have to obey him in other matters. Furthermore, if she were charitable and shared her maintenance with him, he might have to obey her. In order to avoid these conclusions, the jurists found that the husband could not force the wife to work, but they differed on the consequences for the wife. Some held that she should accommodate him by accepting his decision not to pay for a servant or slave and do the housework herself; others held that her job is not to do the housework for the husband, only to share his bed (Bellefonds II:291) and to be pious.[102] Blinded by a one-sided emphasis on obedience of the woman, the jurists neglected the principles of mutual obedience and mutual material maintenance, which the Quran and the hadiths support. They failed to draw the lessons that the hadiths give us on women who were called to share the burdens of providing for their husbands and families.

There is much evidence in the hadith literature showing that maintenance (*nafaqa*) was a much-discussed issue, but not tied to obedience. In the Quran *nafaqa* has the meaning of being charitable with one's material means (4:38) when one has a surplus after meeting one's own needs (2:219). Likewise in the hadiths classified under the topic *nafaqa*, the primary emphasis is on *nafaqa* as a surplus, that is, that which remains over for one's family after one has met one's own needs.[103] Providing for other relatives and dependent persons is classified as charity (*sadaq*).[104] Who constitutes family, relatives, or dependents is not specified. Nor is it established whether family members have priority by virtue of their degree of relationship regardless of whether they are in fact capable of providing for themselves (i.e. not in a state of dependency). The essentially charitable nature of maintenance even for the family – i.e. charitable in the sense that it was not fixed in a contract – was not foreign to the social context into which Islam was introduced. The Mosaic law obliged a father to maintain his children only for the first six years of their life. Afterwards it was only a moral duty. If he did not continue to maintain them, he was constantly reminded by the court and the community to give charitable donations to his children (Cohn 94).

The hadith literature indicates that it was not very clear-cut who should be maintaining whom. Indeed there was a controversy about who should care for women who were in a state of dependency. For example, a woman of Mudar is reported to have said that the women were dependent on their parents and sons. It was disputed whether the report really should have said that the women were dependent on their husbands.[105] The fact that there was a dispute as to what the women actually said could imply that these women were not necessarily widows or divorcees or unmarried, they could have been married women. Maliki reports deal only with maintaining widows and divorcees. Zainab, daughter of Kab bin Ajrah, asked whether she could return to her relatives when her husband was killed. She was allowed after finishing her *idda* at her husband's home.[106] The widow of Saib b. Khabbab wanted to maintain herself after her husband's death. She had her own land to cultivate for that purpose. The question arose whether she should be allowed to do so. Her land was located some distance from her deceased husband's place. She sought permission to go there daily, which was granted.[107]

In other hadiths women raised similar questions as above, but in the specific context of how they could control the properties and assets of their husbands. Aisha favoured the right of the wife to give charity out of her husband's properties without getting his approval in advance, but her position was disputed.[108] Whether the charity is for use of the women themselves as maintenance because of dependency on absent husbands, absent for military or business purposes, or for use of others is not clearly specified in the hadith.

The Quranic answer to this situation of absent men is that men are protectors of women and are to be charitable towards them. Being charitable means to help them materially by sharing their wealth with them (4:34). While the menfolk are enjoined to be charitable to their womenfolk by leaving enough behind for their maintenance, the women are equally enjoined not to abuse the trust placed in them. What is curious is that the verse does not specify the nature of the relationship between men and women. This is left open. It could be between brothers and sisters, fathers and daughters, husbands and wives. Thus if a man absent on military duty or business left behind both blood relatives and a wife who was not a blood relative, certainly there could arise a conflict over whether the blood relatives had priority or the wife, or whether the wife was expected to rely on her own blood relatives (e.g. fathers and sons).

To solve this question, the verse was interpreted to refer specifically to the husband and wife relationship. The reasons were twofold: first, because the succeeding verses speak of reconciliation between spouses in case of a conflict and secondly, because the Prophet, as reported by Aisha, allowed Hind bint Utba, who did not have enough to live on because her husband Abu Sufayan was a miser, to take from his wealth without his permission to maintain herself and the children.[109] Hence not only were sons and fathers to be charitable to their needy mothers and daughters, but also husbands were to treat their wives like blood-family members. Practices in the Sfax region in Tunisia in the 19th century indicate the continued reality of this controversy. There a married woman and her family shared the expenses of her maintenance. She brought into the marriage her trousseau consisting of clothes and linens that she sewed herself and her father gave furnishings for the bridal household (Sethom 29). This was in line with earlier practices. *Fatwa*s from the 12th century A.D./6th century A.H. contain cases from Gafsa in which the fathers used the *mahr* paid by the groom to buy a house for their daughters in which the newly-weds lived, so that upon divorce, the wife had a house for her own maintenance (Shatzmiller 232–35). All of these practices were for the protection of the daughter. First of all, they prevented her from turning over her *mahr* to her husband for sentimental reasons. They also prevented the husband from badgering his wife with the argument that she should be grateful for all he was doing for her material welfare, since she and her father would have equally contributed. These practices represented a liberalization of the Mosaic rule that either the father kept the *mahr* for himself or the husband was to give the bride gifts that would belong to her, in which case he could always remind her that she would not have had them but for him (Cohn 100).

Other hadiths reveal that there can be women who are not dependent, women who had means of their own, like the Prophet's first wife Khadija. The Quran calls, too, upon them to be protectors of men and to be charitable to their own relatives and to their husbands ('The Believers, men and women, are protectors, one of another: they practise regular charity ...' (sura 9:71)). This is confirmed in the hadith literature. For example, Maimuna bin Harith had emancipated a slave, even though she knew that her poorer maternal relatives were in dire need of household help. The Prophet told her that she would have done better to have given the slave to her relatives.[110] Zainab, wife of Abdullah b. Masud, said to her husband that the Prophet had appealed to the women to be charitable. She said to her husband's face that she knew he had no means to provide for anyone. She had, however, some jewellery and asked her husband to go to the Prophet to ask whether she should keep it for herself or give it to another. Abdullah told her that she should go and ask herself. She returned to the house of the Prophet and met there another woman of the Ansari, who had the same question. The women told the Prophet's secretary that they wanted to know whether they could use their jewellery to provide for their husbands and the orphans in their care. The answer was that they could be charitable towards their relatives (Bellefonds II:262).[111] This implied that the term relatives also includes husbands. Umm Salama also asked whether she could provide maintenance for the sons of her husband Abu Salama who were dependent and helpless. She was told that would be charitable.[112]

Given the variety of situations and questions raised in the hadith literature, the jurists recognized that two principles could govern in the obligation of maintenance: either the principle of need and dependency regardless of family relationship, or the principle of a blood or marital obligation. No one principle was made the absolute determining principle. One sees from the different positions of the jurists on the details of maintenance that they vacillated between these two principles. On the one hand, between husband and wife, the principle was that the husband owed maintenance to his wife by virtue of their relationship and by virtue of the jurists' emphasis on the Quranic verse of obedience to the husband at the expense of the Quranic verse on obedience of the husband to the wife. On the other hand when it came to establishing how much the husband owed, the principle of need played more of a role. A less needy wife could spend her own earnings on herself. The principle of need contrasts with some European principles of maintenance from the 18th century, whereby the husband took over the entire property of the wife (Hattenhauer), but was then obliged to maintain her. He could determine what she needed. In contrast, some Sharia jurists (Shafii) could hold that the wife who is wealthy in her own right and keeps her wealth could get less (proportionately) than the wife who is poor (Bellefonds II:262). Need also played a role in the controversy that arose among Maliki jurists in Andalusia regarding the question of whether husbands had to pay rent to their wives if they lived in houses owned by their wives. It was held that if the wife were an orphan (i.e. without a father whom she could count on in case of divorce), then he should pay. Others were of the opinion that a wife otherwise could not charge her husband rent because this would undermine marriage as a partnership (Bencherifa).

In conclusion, when the Quran and the hadiths are read together in the light of practices in Tunisia on the issue of maintenance, one sees that the major issue was not one of obedience of the wife to an all-providing husband. In fact the practice tried to equalize the material contributions between the spouses so that the husband could not use his duty to maintain as a cudgel.

Summary: Haddadian principles of reform

The principles and ideals that Haddad propagated underlay the reforms Tunisia legislated after Independence. While Haddad has been seen as a pragmatist (Moncef 131), certain principles can be distilled from his work –

principles that could further serve to guide courts' interpretation of the Sharia as well as future legislative enactments.

His first principle is that of evolution, i.e. the Sharia can evolve. The principles in turn that govern this evolution protect against abuses. A prime example was the legitimacy accorded to *talaq* pronounced by a drunken husband.

His second principle is liberalism, or rather, the recapture of liberalism. The liberal spirit of the Quran and many hadiths aims at liberating people, not enslaving them, and especially women. This spirit was allowed to flourish for a short while, then was suppressed in the course of centuries, and finally had to be restored (Haddad 144). The major factor of oppression has been the jurists' favouritism shown to men. This bias was due to the economic and military power that men wielded. To curb this power, it is necessary not only to limit men's power over property and the means of production, it is equally necessary, if not more important, to free women from absolute control by men.

Haddad's third principle is justice. Islamic law has a moral object: namely to do justice between men and women, to show respect to women. This task cannot be left to individual men acting as husbands, sons, brothers, fathers, etc. They would be judges in their own cause. The most appropriate body is a court. The court is to mediate between men and women so as to cure the abuses.

The fourth principle is the necessity to assess interpretations of the Sharia according to the social consequences of any one interpretation. For example, if the Quranic verses and hadiths on veiling are so interpreted that a woman hardly has freedom of movement and cannot come to know her future husband in order to give an informed consent to the marriage, then such interpretations violate the rights of women guaranteed by the Quran such as the right to free consent to marriage. The solution is to reexamine the word and the texts in order to interpret them so that other basic legal principles are not violated.

Haddad's emphasis on principles is brilliant in its simplicity. This simplicity mirrors the very simplicity that Islam introduced as a reform movement. It confronted the abuses that had crept into Judaism and Christianity. It was intended to concentrate on essentials and not to get bogged down in details that lead to fossilization. The same fate that had befallen Judaic and Christian law also overtook Islamic law by the time of Haddad. The jurists had strayed too far from the spirit of the Scripture (Neusner V:

36). Haddad and Taalbi presented a challenge: they sought to recapture the original dynamics of Islam.

Haddad has not been idealized by all. He has been criticized by some post-Independence writers. He has been accused of advocating the evolution of Islamic law in the direction of French Western law (M'Halla 128). He has been contrasted with Khayr ad Din of the 19th century, who has been depicted as a 'true' Islamic reformer who did not want to emulate the West (Hamdi 205–6). This critique overlooks the fact that Khayr ad Din wanted Islamic law and administrative reforms because he felt that they were necessary to keep up with the Western powers. He accused the West of supporting and harbouring anti-reform sentiments in order to keep the Muslim world behind (Khayr ad Din 118–19, 132). What seems also forgotten is that Ahmad Bay, author of the anti-slavery decree, had also started a reform process based on the idea that a ruler can initiate reforms of Islamic law when the law itself produces social consequences that are contrary to basic principles of justice (Jones 1975, 30).[113] In short, Haddad and Taalbi fit into the mould already set in 19th century Tunisia. They were intellectuals, but in tune with political leaders. The fact that the gap between intellectual theorists and political leaders was never very large has sustained reforms of Islamic law in Tunisia.

Pre-Independence and reform of Sharia

The political leaders of the Tunisian independence movement incorporated the challenges of Haddad into their political programme, the likes of which has hardly been seen in the Arab world. This unique feature of the Tunisian political scene can be attributed to the civilian background of the major political actors of the pre- and post-Independence politics. The Tunisian leaders derived their political discipline from the socialist workers' movement and not the military. A civilian movement can accommodate women's interests more easily than a political movement controlled by the male-dominated military. A civilian-controlled body politic can also more easily recognize the continued need for a strong economic contribution by the woman and assess it as equal to that of the men, whereas a military-dominated economy tends to give more weight to men's productivity (Rejeb, R. 65).

Other factors also played a role in the efforts of the Tunisian pre-Independence politicians to rebreathe into Islam the reformative spirit that characterized and gave strength to Islam at its birth. These were international factors. International influence was nothing new in the history of legal reform in Tunisia (Ben Achour 220). Ahmad Bay's emancipation degree for slaves noted that Muslims had not only abused their own law, but that the Western powers were doing more justice than the Muslims to the Muslim slaves, thus allowing Muslim slaves to take advantage of the European court system (Jones 1975, 30). This kind of objectivity and ability to overcome false pride and admit one's own mistakes is another Tunisian virtue that has been a saving feature in Tunisian politics from time to time.

Hence one major international influence reflected in the Neo-Destourian agenda for pre-Independence discussions was the court system introduced by the French colonials. It was a triple court system based on international principles of citizenship. There was one set of courts applying French law, another Islamic law, and a third one Mosaic law, especially in personal status matters. Sadiq Bay had already foreseen in the 19th century the dangers of this pluralistic system: Tunisians were tempted to become French citizens in order to avoid the jurisdiction of the Islamic courts when to their advantage. They tended to be the more educated and wealthier who could afford lawyers to appear before the French courts. The Islamic courts were becoming the domain of only the poor and rural population.

Against this background, the Neo-Destour Party set great value on introducing a unified court system and a personal status code that would apply to all Tunisians regardless of religious or economic status. Yet the system was to be rooted in Islamic legal values, a point which has been totally missed by the international and Islamic community. To achieve this goal, the party needed a consensus on basic principles acceptable to all religions. Leaders of all religious communities (Islam, Christianity, Judaism) were informed and consulted (Yearbook 423).

The Neo-Destourians succeeded in realizing these aims. The French agreed to a unified court system valid for all Tunisians. A unified court system also required unified laws, equally applicable to all citizens. The result was the Personal Status Code applicable to all regardless of religion.[114] The Neo-Destourians also pushed through reforms in the area of *ahbas* (*habus*) (*waqf* – private and public religious land trusts which rendered much land inalienable *and* uneconomic). They abolished the *waqf*. [115] They realized the work started by Khayr ad Din,[116] who had sought to abolish the institution, but was blocked by the French, who were not much interested in curing the abuses of the private hubus (Jones 1975, 349).

The discipline and ease with which the Neo-Destourians achieved this led to Independence within one year of the Convention of 3 June 1955 between France and Tunisia (Jones 1975, 321), far ahead of the time schedule set by France (15 years).

Independence – equality before the law

Once Tunisia became independent, the Constitution of Tunisia was enacted.[117] Its provisions are true to the spirit of reform. Islam was declared the state religion (Art. 1). Islam is also deemed compatible with Article 6, which guarantees equal rights and duties for all citizens. The next major piece of legislation was the Code of Personal Status, which covers family and succession matters. Consistent with the principle of equal rights, the Code of Personal Status made man and woman equal in their rights and duties in so far as each has a right to marry[118] and be loyal to only one partner (i.e. to be monogamous)[119] and each has a right to divorce the other and an obligation to go before a court of justice to have such divorce pronounced.[120]

Problems of inequality in inheritance

There is one area in which the Code of Personal Status falls short of the spirit of equality. That is in inheritance law. The Code conserves the classical interpretation of the law of inheritance, under which a son takes twice as much as a daughter, the surviving widower twice as much as the surviving widow. One explanation for this approach may lie in the fact that drastic reforms were being made in land and property rights by way of the abolition of the *habus*. Many *habus* documents had denied women any share in the property. This device had been used to exclude married women and widows from their lawful shares under the Sharia (Ferchiou 1990, 42–4). It was a practice that abused the Sharia. Against this background the reinstatement of the classical law of inheritance in the Code of Personal Status can be regarded as a small measure that sought to emancipate at least married women and widows from abusive practices (Art. 93 CSP). One reform was introduced regarding daughters' inheritance. Tunisians borrowed a Shiite rule in favour of daughters. Under the Sunni rule that had dominated in Tunisia, a daughter had to share the inheritance with her paternal uncles, even when she was the sole descendant heir. The Shiite rule, on the other hand, excluded the paternal uncles. The Tunisians enacted the latter rule, whereby the daughter may take the entire estate if she were the only child even in the presence of a paternal uncle (Art. 143 CSP). In practice, however, in certain areas of Tunisia, the '*habus* state of mind' has not been completely overcome even up to this day. In one village the women still do not inherit their share because the land is a collective family resource essential for the survival of the family (Ferchiou 1985, 18–19; Jouirou). This motivates some women, however, to sell their jewellery that constituted part of their dower to buy lucrative olive tree lands.[121]

A second reason why the inheritance laws were not part of the discussion for reforms before Independence may lie in the frustration which men and women equally share in practice when it comes to obtaining their shares in an estate. The Islamic law of inheritance as practised over centuries has resulted in equal disadvantages for both sexes. This is because the law of inheritance has resulted in extreme fragmentation of properties. As a result one hectare has often had two hundred co-owners, women and men. The co-ownership can be dissolved only with the unanimous agreement of all (Jones 1975, 359). A strong personality in the family, whether an aunt or an uncle, who has taken over the administration of the property, often prevents all relatives from disposing of their shares, however miniscule. This continues to be a problem up to this day (Enda 59: Zaghouan). This practice has been strengthened by a reform in the Land Code. The Land Code allows one family heir to have the final say over an agricultural or commercial property that forms a productive unit.[122]

Assessing the Code of Personal Status

'Head of the family', cooperation, mutual obedience

As said, the Code of Personal Status is the only Islamic family law code in the Arabicized world which has realized the Quranic spirit of equality between spouses. The Code, however, is not perfect and the Tunisian legislators are constantly perfecting it with the help of women lawyers and judges. There remain provisions that are problematic. The following paragraphs deal with some of these problematic issues.

One such issue relates to the term 'head of the family'. Article 23 of the Code confers on the husband the position 'head of the family'. The term is not totally strange to Tunisian practice. Traditionally in certain parts of Tunisia, this term refers to the head of the extended family as opposed to the core family (Jongmans 110). Being 'chief of the family' does not always mean that the family felt obliged to accept decisions made by the family member carrying that office (Jonker 66). Being head of the family has significance rather for social rituals, i.e. the head of the family is responsible for receiving and distributing plates of food received from the neighbours who have sacrificed an animal as part of a family occasion. The head of the family need not be male. A female, especially the widow of the deceased head of the extended family, can also exercise such ritual function (Jonker 66). In certain regions the female head is responsible for placing a gift of food or money on the emptied plate that is returned to the family sharing sacrificial food (Jouirou 22, 25).

In the Code of Personal Status the term 'head of the family' has been restricted to the core conjugal family and been given a purely male character. The term is not used in the Code's provisions relating to maintenance obligations to members of the extended family (Art. 37ff). The restriction of the use of the term 'head of the family' to the conjugal sphere, contrary to some Tunisian traditions, raises a suspicion that it was simply taken over from the French civil code.

A closer examination of the provisions relating to the head of the family reveals that the term does not confer explicitly any rights. It imposes rather duties. The head of the family is obliged to take care of the necessities (*nafaqa*) of the wife and the children. He must be the breadwinner (*ail*).

This was a one-sided duty until 1993. Since 1993 the article has been amended. The wife has been given an equal duty to feed the family if she has the material means. She has not, however, been given the corresponding title of co-head of the family. How the two spouses are to arrange fulfilling their duties is further defined in Article 23 according to two criteria: firstly, according to practice, tradition and local custom, and secondly, by way of cooperation especially on meeting the financial, educational and travel needs of the children. Under the first set of criteria there are several traditions and customs that define the material contributions expected from the wife. Among the Qairawani, for example, the woman is expected to work. That allows her to have material means to put at the disposal of the family, but on condition that she finds the work is worthy of her dignity. This is opposed to the husband who is under a duty to work to maintain the family regardless of whether he finds it below his dignity or not. In the Sahel, a very conservative region, according to tradition, the wife brings into the family the furniture and house linens (Medimegh 110; CRÉDIF 1996b, 34). In Sousse the bride brings into the conjugal family more than

40 shirts for her husband, either sewn or purchased by herself (Medimegh 114, n. 5). In the course of the marriage her earnings are used for so-called luxury and comfort goods (Medimegh 110) as well as for buying a house if the husband does not insist on living in the house of his parents (Medimegh 111; Enda 22, 52; Jonker 62). In a survey of twenty women of low income, eight decided on their own to use their earnings to buy land and a house (Enda 115).

As for the cooperation expected of the spouses in maintaining the family according to Article 23, in practice the cooperation between spouses encompasses more than finances. It includes relieving each other of chores and sharing in child rearing. Working husbands of working wives tend to share the household tasks, especially in looking after the children: indeed 67 per cent of the working husbands of working wives engaged in more playing time with the children compared to 40 per cent of working husbands of non-working wives. Three times as many non-working wives struck their children physically than working wives, and the greater majority of the children of working wives had better school results (Rejeb, S.).

The amendments made in 1993 subjecting the wife to a similar duty as the husband to contribute to the family maintenance when she has the means had far-reaching consequences for the issue of wifely obedience. The link between a wife's obedience and her husband's duty to maintain was broken. The Code of Personal Status provided prior to the 1993 amendment that the wife was to be obedient. After the wife was given also the duty to maintain, the obedience provisions were revoked. The provisions requiring the spouses to cooperate in maintaining the children in effect require mutual obedience, as foreseen in the Quran (4:35; 4:128). The provisions are in keeping with the hadiths which show that women of means supported their families, including incapacitated men (see supra).

Despite all these reforms in the spirit of the Quran and hadiths, the retention of the title 'head of the family' exclusively for the husband is still a source of some tension. As said, Article 23 associates only duties with the term. The case law, however, has attached certain rights to the title of head of the family. For example, a husband who had decided that the marital home would be in a particular place because of his work against the will of the wife, who refused, apparently without reason, to live in the home, was allowed to deny maintenance to the wife (Sharif 61). His right to take the decision about where the matrimonial home would be located based on his work requirements was based on his capacity as head of the family, who has a duty to work in order to provide for the family. Denial to her of her right to maintenance was based on her being deemed *nushuz*, disobedient. Now that the law no longer allows a finding that a wife is disobedient, it would seem that the courts would be obliged to work out the concept of mutual disobedience based on the Quranic verses referring to *nushuz* on the part of the wife and *nushuz* on the part of the husband (suras 4:34 and 4:128). Cooperative consultation and mutual consideration are the result. In this respect the provision in the Code of Personal Status that the spouses are to cooperate in reaching family decisions is consistent with the Quran. If the spouses cannot reach an agreement, then the courts would have two choices: either to fall back on the provision that the husband as head of the family has to make the final decision that most enables him to provide for the family or to fall back on the traditions and customs as allowed under Article 23 of the CSP. Such a tradition would be that which allows a woman, especially from Qairawan, to make an agreement with her husband that he not remove her from the place where she wishes to live. In such a situation where there are two households to maintain, the courts would have an easier decision to make if the wife were also earning, for she could be made responsible under the 1993 reforms for making her contribution to the upkeep of the two households. If she is not earning, the courts may have to consider whether they impose on the wife who wishes to live elsewhere than the husband the duty to start earning. The latter would be more consistent with the equalizing intention of the legislator and the equalizing spirit of the Quran and *sunna*. This would tend to eventually make the provision that the husband is head of the family – a term that does not appear in the hadiths or the Quran – a dead letter. Otherwise, to continue to clothe it with a right to make a final decision would be an indirect way of reviving the notion of obedience that the legislator abrogated.

The position of head of the family has legal significance in revenue matters. If the minor children have income, then as head of the family, the father is responsible for their taxes. But since changes in the finance law in 1984, the head of the family no longer submits the tax declarations of his wife. Each may file a separate declaration (Aouij).

Hijab *(veiling)*

On even more contentious points, such as the *hijab* for women, Bourguiba had not been particularly concerned during the French colonialism in the

1920s. But at that time he did not see it as religiously relevant, having called it on occasion a matter of habit belonging to traditions of dress.

After Independence, Bourguiba strove for a pragmatic rather than legal approach. He did not attempt to enact a law, presumably because he saw the *hijab* as a piece of clothing, and to have police physically removing such would have been an insufferable intervention in personal freedom, although Bourguiba was accused by the Islamists later of having physically removed the veil of a woman (Hamdi 12).

Like Taalbi and Haddad, Bourguiba also knew that the *hijab* was a state of mind, a state of feeling secure or insecure. This mental state had to be undermined through indirect means. If the atmosphere were secure and if men knew that women had equal rights as marriage partners, then the '*hijab* state of mind' would dissipate.

The *hijab* became an issue of stormy public debate in the first 20 years after the enactment of the Code of Personal Status. In 1976 during Ramadan the theologian Professor Hend Chalbi gave an address on television on the liberation of the woman. He said that the Code of Personal Status was not the liberator of the Tunisian woman, but Islam, especially the *hijab*. He made no mention of what liberates men. The *hijab* became a symbol of the renewal of Islam. As the Islamists became more vocal, the government felt compelled to resort to quasi-legal measures. No law was enacted, only an administrative circular was issued. In 1981 Circular No. 108 prohibited wearing of the veil at public institutions, such as the university and schools, factories and in government offices (Medimegh 136).

While the Islamists stressed the *hijab* as a dress code for women, the government in the 1990s held steadfast in seeing what was really at stake. The *hijab* was – as Taalbi and Haddad had already discerned decades earlier – a symbol of excluding women from the public life of work (Cherif 60). It has more recently been regarded as a symbol of religious pressures on women to change their cultural freedoms or traditions, as had been argued in the hadith in which the Prophet answered Umar's call for veiling by pointing out it was only a Persian custom.[123] It has also been argued that the mandatory *hijab* has a chilling effect on the religious freedom of women to interpret the Islamic sources as not referring to a head veil, but rather to modest dress.[124]

Right to work

Constitutional guarantees protecting the right to work had long existed. The preamble of the Tunisian Constitution guarantees each citizen work, regardless of gender. Statistics on gender attitudes towards working women were gathered in 1991. They showed that the overwhelming majority (80 per cent) of women and two-thirds of the men (67 per cent) in Tunisia positively evaluated women's work as a contribution to development (Medimegh 103, 114, n. 1). This confirmed findings in the early 1980s that three-quarters of the population wanted their daughters to work and have their own earnings (Medimegh 113; Enda 63–4, 70). In the spirit of Haddad, the Tunisian legislator has acknowledged outright the right of the woman to work not within the family code directly but in the context of development and social support. In 1991 the special consultative committee for Women and Development was created. It is responsible for guaranteeing women's voice in the national development plans. In 1992 the former president of Tunisia, Ben Ali, publicly confirmed that work is women's key to progress, a gain for the woman, her family and the society.[125] A year later in 1993 the Tunisian legislator amended the Code of Personal Status to rescind the unilateral obligation of the wife to obey her husband's wishes.

Simply having a right is not enough. A woman's right to work is realizable only if she has the support of her family and the state for taking care of her children. Hence the Ministry of Youth and Children and local communal administrations subsidize up to 50 per cent of the costs of crèches. The Code of Investments accords advantages for enterprises that offer crèches for working mothers.[126] The law of July 26, 1994 on day nurseries was passed with an explicit view to realizing 'the right of the mother to work and the right of the child of a working mother to protection'.

*Dower (***mahr***)*

Haddad's critique of high dowries had struck a chord with the Tunisian authorities even before Independence. In the 1940s its minimum value was set at four Dinars (Qairawani 65 *nikah*). After Independence, Bourguiba again took a pragmatic approach. He strove not to have it legally abolished, but rather to have it reduced to a symbolic value. Bourguiba set an example by publicly marrying for only one Dinar (Medimegh 114). Indeed in practice the *mahr* is recorded as a symbolic amount that makes the marriage legal under Article 3 of the CSP. This is in accord with the classical Maliki rule – contrary to the conclusion of Imam Shafii who saw the *mahr* as only commendable, not an essential element of the marriage (Khadduri, Para. 166) – that an unconsummated marriage is voidable on the basis of the absence of a *mahr*. A marriage consummated without an agreement on *mahr* creates a *mahr mithl* (customary *mahr*), a debt on the husband (Toledano)[116] (Art. 13 CSP).

In various regions customary traditions have blurred the line between *mahr* and the gifts brought by each of the spouses or their families into the marriage. The Code of Personal Status attempts to make a distinction between gifts (*hadaya*) offered by the spouses after the conclusion of the marriage and the *mahr* (also called *sadaqa*) (Art. 28). All gifts are to be returned if the marriage is not consummated. The *mahr* is treated differently. Only one-half of the *mahr* must be returned if the marriage is not consummated. The case law reveals that it is difficult in practice to distinguish between *hadaya* and *mahr*. The Tunisian Court of Appeal has recognized that regional differences play a role. The differences blur the lines between *mahr* and gifts because of the principle of intention of the parties. This means that the court has to determine the intention with which the parties concluded the marriage and *mahr* contracts. And the intentions have to be interpreted in the light of the custom of the parties and of the place where the contracts were concluded (Sharif 70). What may appear as gifts in one region may be *mahr* in another and vice versa. So if what is alleged to be a gift is found actually to be part of the *mahr*, then only half of the alleged gift will be returned if the marriage was not consummated. If what may appear as *mahr* is fundamentally a gift, then the entire gift has to be returned. The courts are left with the task of classifying the valuables exchanged at the marriage as *mahr* or gift.

Against this background of blurred boundaries in marriages where the wife brings valuables into the marriage, the *mahr* can be reconsidered in a new light. The Quran speaks of the *mahr* in several verses. It treats the agreement to pay or the actual payment of the *mahr* as an act initiated by the husband. Sura 2:229 does not make it an obligation. Sura 4:4 reinforces the notion that the dower, the *mahr*, is a 'free' gift, voluntary. Sura 2:236 then regulates a situation in which the husband did not give or offer a dower, married but did not consummate the marriage, then wants to divorce. The Quran recommends a good heart in this situation. It says if he wishes to do justice, he should make a reasonable gift to the bride, presumably as compensation for pulling out of the marriage contract even before giving it a chance. But once a man has voluntarily entered into a dower agreement, he takes on certain obligations. Sura 2:229 orders a man not to take back what he voluntarily gave the wife. Sura 4:19–21 strengthens this point of view. Once a dower has been given, the husband may not take it back during the marriage out of anger or because he needs the money to marry another wife. Sura 2:237 regulates the case in which the husband has voluntarily fixed the amount of dower due, but still divorces the wife before giving the marriage a chance. He is to return one-half of the agreed amount.

The Quran also mentions how the woman may react to the offer of a gift of *mahr*. The voluntary nature of the dower is again stressed. Sura 4:4 gives the woman the freedom to return the *mahr* in part or totally, and the husband presumably is not to feel insulted. One of the Maliki hadiths partly reinforces the woman's freedom of remittance. While the hadith makes a demand for a *mahr* obligatory when the marriage is being arranged by the guardian, the final decision to accept or not accept the *mahr* is left to the wife.[127]

Sura 4:25 then regulates marriage with an enslaved Muslim woman. Here the husband is ordered to make a gift to the owners. It is mandatory. In order to avoid what looked like discrimination between free women and enslaved women, jurists tended to interpret the *mahr* for free women as equally obligatory. They differed, however, on whether the absence of an agreement on the *mahr* affected the validity of the marriage contract,[128] just as there was a discussion about whether sura 2:241 enjoining *mutaa* maintenance for a divorced woman beyond *idda* maintenance was a duty only on the pious man and not on the man who does not fear hell (Coulson 1991, 31). The *mahr* was treated by jurists as an obligatory sign of respect for the woman and not as consideration for the marriage contract.[129] Thus a *mahr mithl* (customary amount) was attached to a marriage contract as an implied clause when no *mahr* was agreed upon. As a side remark, it can be noted here that the impact of the institution of slavery on the evolution of Islamic law and rights of women cannot be underestimated.

While this argument for respect of the woman is laudable, it is incomplete, for the Quran requires not only respect for the wife, but also for the husband. Women and men are protectors of each other. Consequently the woman is also obliged to show an equal sign of respect to the husband at the marriage. So if the *mahr* is treated as a duty falling solely on the husband, then it becomes a legal device that introduces inequality of duties between women and men, and therefore a sign of one-sided non-reciprocal respect. To avoid this imbalance, the Quran gives the woman the power to mitigate the inequality imposed by the classical jurists as sura 4:24 permits the wife to exercise her right to remit the *mahr*. This is charity, which is praiseworthy. By exercising charity, the woman brings the couple back on an equal footing. The *mahr* is no longer then a source of financial security for the woman received at the expense of equality.

In practice, however, in certain regions in Tunisia this equality is restored not by remitting the *mahr* of the husband and his family, but by an equal exchange. Custom obligates the bride and her family to bring enough valuables into the marriage to relieve the husband of certain living expenses. The nature and significance of the marriage gifts and the *mahr* vary from woman to woman. Some who traditionally bring into the marriage animals given by their fathers (in Mornag, near Tunis) use the marriage gift as start capital for a small business (Enda 52). Others sell their wedding jewellery given by their husbands when the husband has no means to buy a house for the family that could be registered in his name (Enda 43, 59), so that in the end the husband is also benefiting from his *mahr*. If the husband's duty to pay the *mahr* is not to be abolished (Charfi), then at least the woman's customary duty to bring a gift into the marriage should also be recognized in the law. To achieve this end one could rewrite the provisions on *mahr* to redefine it. It would be an agreement between the spouses on something of value, however little, to be concluded at the time of the marriage as a sign of mutual respect. The agreement may be a mutual exchange of valuables, or a gift offered by the husband and accepted or refused by the wife, or a gift offered by the husband and remitted by the wife, or a mutual commitment by each to bring equivalent values into the marriage to finance the new household.

Properties accumulated in marriage

The Code of Personal Status, in accord with the Sharia, prohibits a husband from having control over the earnings of his wife and the properties she accumulates during the marriage (Art. 24). This is not an explicitly mutual provision. Nothing is said about the control of a wife over the properties of her husband. It seems to have been a self-evident assumption of the legislators that a wife has no control over the properties of her husband.

This means that if the spouses divorce, each is to take the properties they accumulated during the marriage. This is not easy to determine. Just as separating the *mahr* from the marriage gifts can be difficult for the courts in case of dispute, dividing the properties accumulated within a marriage upon divorce can also be difficult. This requires bookkeeping – oral or written – that gives proof of who has brought what in the family and who has provided which services for the family. Often the reality is different. Article 26 of the CSP foresees this common situation in which many spouses find themselves: there is no precise bookkeeping to prove which movables belong to whom. In that case the court decides on the basis of oath and on the basis of what goods would most likely belong to a woman and which to a man. And if one of the spouses runs a business, then goods in connection with this business shall be assigned to the merchant spouse, also under oath. With regard to goods that could just as well belong to a woman as to a man, the oath is again used.

Compensation for services of the wife during marriage

There is no codified provision, however, that matches the Sharia rule about how the husband is to compensate the wife for her services in the household, whether she is earning her own monies or not. Nor is there a provision that if a woman has contributed labour or her earnings to constructing a house, as happens frequently enough, even among poorer families (slightly less than half), then she is entitled to her equity share. Such a provision would be consonant with the Sharia principle that each spouse is entitled to what they contribute, whether in the form of actual movables or in the form of providing finance for immovables. Even in the absence of such a provision, the Sharia principle could still be applied. What hinders the realization of the Sharia principle is an administrative practice. That is the practice of registration of ownership. When a marital home, though built with the earnings of the wife, is registered in the name of the husband, and the parties separate, then the house belongs to the husband. A sample national survey in 1991 shows that 80 per cent of the houses were registered in the name of the husbands (Enda 123).

Community of property law

To deal with the unequal division of immovable resources between the spouses, the Tunisian legislators enacted the legal institute of community of property.[130] The law is not an amendment to the family law provisions of the Code of Personal Status or to the Code of Property. It is a law for itself. It permits the spouses to enter a contract at the time of marriage or during the marriage at any time. The contract may regulate only immovable properties used for the family (e.g. the conjugal or family house), not business premises, even those appended to the house. The law is intended to encourage women to take matters into their own hands. They are expected to insist on contractual arrangements under which they have a share in the house. The present practices vary. Some women buying a house with their own savings register it in their name and that of their husbands (Enda 32). The majority have it registered only in the name of the husband, regardless of who bought it. It is thus hoped that women would take advantage of the new law and not register the house they have built with their own income or savings simply in the name of the husband, but in both names, though women who buy the house themselves are known to register in the name of the husband in order to avoid affronting him (Enda 22).

The spouses may stipulate in the contract that the house shall be owned jointly, thus creating a community of property regime. This contract shall be registered at the office for immovable property (§14). Under the community of property regime, the inheritance rules are not affected (§3). This means that the heirs of each spouse shall inherit only that part owned by the deceased. All decisions relating to the improvement or the conservation of the house need not be taken jointly, except in regard to alienating the property or renting it out for more than three years (§17) or renewing a lien on the property for more than three years in total (§17). The contract has to be in force for at least two years in order to be valid.

The agreement shall come to an end upon divorce, or by judicial separation of goods or by mutual consent of the spouses (§18). The partition of the house is to be according to the provisions of Articles 116 to 130 of the Code of Immovable Property (§24). The partition articles are part of the chapter on partition (*qisma*) of property held in co-ownership. These provisions are intended for property held jointly, regardless of the proportions assigned to each co-owner. The community of property law does not specify whether joint ownership by spouses means in equal proportions (50–50). It seems that it is left to the spouses to decide whether the shares in the house are equal or apportioned according to financial contribution made or according to who has the most bargaining power. Apportioning can be difficult in the case where the house has rooms or space for the informal business of the wife or the formal business or profession of either spouse. In such a case the spouses could in principle, it seems, decide to base the joint ownership on a percentage that reflects how much of the house is used for business and how much for family life.

To keep a community of property agreement compatible with Islamic law, the Tunisian legislator seems to have treated the community of property contract as a partnership agreement that relates only to the family house.

Otherwise, there is some concern that the new community of property law may not be compatible with the Sharia injunction that spouses keep their earnings and properties separate and administer them themselves.[131] One has to look more closely at the Quranic injunction. An explicit reference to women and men keeping their gains and profits separately could be treated as a warning (not an obligation) to both spouses not to enter contracts with each other relating to their gains and profits. One reason could be that men tend to use such contracts to bypass the Quranic injunction that women have the right to retain power over their own earnings. Another reason could be that women have to be encouraged to act on their own will, not subordinate to that of their husbands, just as their husbands act on their own will, not subordinate to that of the wife, and just as God judges each separately for their deeds, not making one guilty for the deeds of the other. In this way the Quranic warning would represent an improvement over the Christian law at the time, which allowed the husband to be automatically the trustee of the wife's property on the assumption that a wife would not contradict her husband (Baker 99; Holdsworth 525).

What to do then when wives register the houses they buy with their own earnings and profits in the name of their husbands? Is not this practice contrary to the Quranic warnings to keep one's wealth separate? Under these circumstances a law that allows a wife to enter a contract with her husband regarding property serves two purposes. One is to cure the un-Quranic practice of wives who register the houses they bought with their own earnings in the names of the husband. They do themselves an injustice by not recognizing the Quranic injunction that they are to control the fruits of their work. The second purpose is to show social confidence in women to learn to act as adults, conscious of their own interests and responsibilities and the interests of their children. A wife, if she felt it in her best interests, can enter an agreement to be co-owner with her husband of a particular property by which each commits herself/himself to contribute a set amount to invest in or improve the property.

Freedom of contract between spouses has an analogy in Islamic law in agreements between heirs. Heirs may agree amicably among themselves that they shall divide their inherited property as prescribed by the *fiqh*, but then make gifts of their shares to top off the share of another heir. Spouses who inherit from their pre-deceased children can enter into such agreements so that they receive equal shares instead of the 2 to 1 ratio.[132]

If the spouses do not make a community of property agreement that regulates ownership of property upon divorce, other solutions have to be made available upon divorce for the wife who has used her earnings to buy the house which is registered in her husband's name. One such solution would be based on the Sharia injunction that the husband is to compensate the wife for her household work. That would mean that the wife is entitled upon divorce to an equity share in the family house though registered in the husband's name. That share would constitute the compensation due for her work. This solution has been accepted by the Muslim communities in Tanzania, where the case law allows the wife upon divorce to claim her equity share in the family house acquired during the marriage.

Otherwise, the marriage contract offers also possible solutions. Article 11 of the CSP allows the spouses to write into the marriage contract whatever they choose relating to their properties and earnings. They are allowed to regulate the ownership and partition of the family house as they stipulate. It has been reported that this possibility has hardly been used in practice (Aouij). If it were used, one Sharia limitation would most likely apply. That is, the husband may not be given the right to administer the properties of the wife. Rather the spouses have to jointly administer each other's properties, or make provision for alienation from one to the other.

One type of property that is excluded from the community of property law is the *mahr* (§4). This means that if the *mahr* consists of a house from the husband to the wife, then the parties may not agree that the house shall belong jointly to both. It is unclear whether this exclusion applies to a house bought by fathers for their daughters. It is a very old traditional practice (Shatzmiller 232–3) for fathers to use the *mahr*, when in the form of monies or valuables, to buy a house registered solely in the name of the married daughter as a protection in case of divorce.

Otherwise, bank accounts are also excluded from a community of property contract. Bank accounts may be maintained by spouses separately. This practice is not unknown, especially in families where the husband is a migrant worker, though upon return of the husband, the accounts can be switched to the name of the husband (Enda 27).

Population law

Independence brought with it many issues that were not pressing at the time of Taalbi and Haddad. One such issue was economic development. Most newly independent countries began seeking a way out of the non-diversified colonial economy in order to bring a higher standard of living for the population. Linked to this was the question of population control. Rapid population growth was an important factor that nullified all economic and social gains won with great effort.

Linking population control and economic development

In Tunisia monitoring of the implementation of national development plans took into account the impact of population growth. Documents in 1959 relating to the national economic plan showed that a growth rate of 2.6 per cent threatened to annihilate any economic gains foreseen for the ten-year plan 1956–1966 (L'Office National 1974, 321–7, 331–54). The evidence was compelling for Bourguiba. He was convinced that economic development could have success only if the population level remained stable or grew only in proportion to economic gains. For that reason he began within ten years of Independence to lay the basis of a demographic policy. He explained to Tunisians in various presidential speeches the interconnectedness between promoting the status of women, the evolution of society, population policy and development. In 1966 he frankly accused mothers who had dozens of pregnancies of wrecking the development plan, producing more workers than could be absorbed by the economy. He explained that if the population expected the government to provide education and social welfare services, the people also had to do their part by controlling the number of mouths to be fed, clothed and educated. The key actor in fulfilling this task was the woman, who had to have control over her body. Bourguiba gave a series of public talks warning against early marriages of minors, illiteracy among women owing to debasement of her status, reduction of a woman to simply being a sexual object with only instincts. The man was also assigned a new role. He had to change his attitudes. He had to see the woman as a partner capable of making a vital contribution to development. He had to stop being a social dictator.

Starting in 1961, a series of legislative enactments prepared the way for population control. Law 7 of 9 January 1961 abrogated several French laws: the law of 18 September 1920 which had prohibited the sale and importation of contraceptives, the decree of 22 June 1923 that prohibited the importation of contraceptive substances or instruments, and the decree of 1 January 1942 regulating advertising of birth control pharmaceuticals. Two years later the basic law was enacted to implement the equation between population control and development (Law 26 of 15 July 1963, modified by Law 46 of 1965). Family welfare payments from the state were limited to the first four children, then later to the first three. The age of marriage was raised to 17 years for women and 20 for men (Art. 5 CSP) and the marriage of underaged parties declared null (Art. 21 CSP).

The social readiness to cooperate was also measured. A questionnaire among rural and urban families showed a desire to reduce the number of children and that already 15 per cent of women were using contraceptives. On the basis of these results, twelve maternal and infant protection centres were opened in 1964. All consultations and distributions of contraceptives were free of charge. Men were also included in the programme. Midwives prized for their ability and wisdom in the community were given the responsibility to distribute condoms and sprays to men. The first two years saw success. The women coming for contraceptives were of child-bearing age, the average age being 31. More than half of the women who came were of the working class, many of whom were wives of day workers.

In 1968 population control was given ministerial status. The department for family planning was created in the Ministry of Public Health, which was made responsible for training of professional family planners and dispersing them among the population. The means of dispensing advice and knowledge were innovative. Rather than waiting for the population to come to the consultation centres, educational mobile vans were put into operation. This conformed to the unanimous proclamation of the UN Human Rights Conference in Teheran of 1968 that access to birth control information is a fundamental human right (L'Office National 1974, 13).

In 1969 Decree 364 of 6 October 1969 was issued to create the National Institute of Child Health. The tasks assigned to the Institute were to administer the maternal and infant protection centres in addition to elaborating programmes on conception and pregnancy. No specific mention was made of family planning as such. Implementation was through administrative directives (L'Office National 1974, 228).

In 1973 the Tunisian legislator decided no longer to shy away from the terminology family planning. It created the National Office of Family Planning and Population (Law 17 of 1973, 23 March 1973). The aim was to harmonize population issues with development through progammes supporting family health. This was accompanied by a programme for educating all families on family planning and population issues (L'Office National 1995, 271).

Tunisian officials were well aware of the religious risks that they might encounter in implementing a birth control programme. They were well informed of the unsuccessful introduction of the birth control programme in Egypt. The failure there was attributed to opposition from certain religious figures. A factor that may have played an equally strong role was the militarization of Egyptian society, for a militarized society, preparing for war and expecting many deaths can hardly be expected to be interested in birth control in the face of decimating warfare. Tunisia, on the other hand, had the fortune of having a thoroughly civilian political set-up. The base of its support consisted of workers, not soldiers.

Nonetheless, Bourguiba made conscious efforts to take the wind out of the sails of potential religious opposition. In his speeches conscientizing the public about the emancipation of the woman and the necessity of birth control for the human and economic development of the country, he cited solid religious support by saying that God only helps those people to transform their difficult situation to the extent that the people are prepared to transform themselves.[133] Social surveys were undertaken to test actual public opinion. It was found, for example, in 1973 that 94 per cent of midwives believed that Islam permitted contraception. One year after the creation of the National Office for Family Planning (ONPFP) and Population a conference was held in Tunis. As a result the ONPFP presented its research findings on the attitudes of Muslim classical law experts on family planning.[134] An opinion issued in 1937 by the Egyptian mufti Abdal Majid Salim was cited in which he had held that the wife or the husband might take measures to prevent the sperm from entering the uterus. Later in 1953 a commission of Al Azhar University in Cairo issued an opinion (*fatwa*) that the Shafii school of law did not prohibit using medicines (such as the pill) to prevent pregnancy. This was justified especially when frequent pregnancies would weaken the health of the woman and lead to higher medical costs, or when the couple feared that pregnancy would result in poverty for them and their family. As to be expected, there were jurists with opposing opinions, citing the need for fighters in the Arab-Israeli conflict.

The difference of opinions indicated that Islam basically treats sexual relations as matters of private discretion, including the number of children one wants to procreate. The Tunisian government thus decided that efforts to promote family planning had to stress family planning as a voluntary matter, a decision left to the couples. The government sought to educate couples on decision-making processes. This included counselling couples on what factors they should take into account. Two such factors were the capacity of the couple to feed and educate their offspring and the capacity of the government to provide enough infrastructure.

Few sexual injunctions in the Quran

In terms of Quranic teachings on sex, God hardly regulates the subject of sexual practices. The few injunctions are found in sura 2. Sura 2:222 enjoins coitus during the menses of a woman. It was reported that Imam Malik said that the verse was intended to be milder than the Mosaic rules that prevented women not only from having intimate relations in their menses, but also from eating, drinking or associating with anyone.[135] The penalty imposed by the Prophet for violating this Quranic injunction was reported to be a payment of one and a half dinars to the wife.[136] A limitation on sexual relations is found in sura 2:187. It is intended to prevent intimacy during the fasting period of Ramadan. Ramadan is a time during which Muslims are to strengthen their character by way of self-restraint (sura 2:183). Refraining from intimacy during the fasting period is deemed good for the character. This means that a man is to measure his virility by his ability to restrain himself. The virtue of restraint in general is implied in sura 2:223. This sura compares in general terms wives with fruitful land (*harth*). Land has to be treated well if it is to yield. The verse warns that when the husband desires intimacy, he is not simply to take the wife as he wishes. Before the intimacy he is to do a good deed. Presumably this would remind him to treat intimacy as a partnership and not just a matter of satisfying himself. The early Maliki hadiths contain rules to constrain a husband. He could not beat his wife as he liked if he were displeased for any reason including sexual. If he injured her, he was subject to paying compensation, the *diya*, as anyone else guilty of a tort.[137] It is reported that the Prophet forbade him to strike or slap his wife on the face.[138]

Such examples evidence the progressiveness of Islam at the time. It is only in the last century that law-makers in Western countries have permitted women to initiate tort and rape litigation against their husbands. Islamic progressiveness was not sustained. Medieval jurists had addressed the theme of marriage as an equal sexual partnership between man and woman, but eventually steered their analyses in a direction that placed a woman under the control of the husband. One reason for this deviation lay in the complicated issues that slavery increasingly posed for the jurists. Distinctions between how a free woman was to be treated sexually as opposed to an enslaved woman became a central concern. The distinctions had to be made in such a way, however, that the authority of a man towards both classes of women could be preserved (Johanson 77, 97).

Birth control in Sharia

The issue of preventing pregnancy is not treated in the Quran. It is not part of the verses specifying which actions are criminal subject to penal sanctions. Questions of how to deal with intimate relations were rather treated in the hadiths.

Preventing pregnancy by coitus interruptus

The early Maliki hadiths on *talaq*[139] speak of men who wanted to know whether they could prevent pregnancy by *azl* (*coitus interruptus*). The men were in a wartime situation. They wanted to satisfy their passion by seizing some of the women captives of the enemy. At the same time they did not want to risk impregnating the women because they wanted to sell them as slaves. So they thought they would use *azl*. Before implementing their plan, the men refrained and sought the opinion of the Prophet. It is reported that he said that preventing pregnancy is in principle allowed.

In another hadith a slave owner admitted that he had a better sexual life with his slaves than his wives, but did not want to have them all impregnated. So he sought advice about whether he could practice *azl*. It was said to him that he could do so, but a distinction was made between the enslaved women and his lawful wives. He could practice *azl* against the will of the enslaved woman, but if he were with his wife, he needed to have her consent.

The hadith above confirm Tahar Haddad's observation that men in his society had been spoiled by having enslaved women with whom they felt they could do as they liked. This infected their attitude towards all women.

Not all the hadiths approved of *azl*. Umar is reported to have said that he found *azl* personally repugnant. But he did not impose his personal attitude on others. He did not forbid it for others.

Preventing pregnancy by other methods

Other hadith on *radhaa* (fosterage/breastfeeding) report various opinions on how women could be protected from cohabitation in order to prevent pregnancy. It is reported that the Prophet had prohibited cohabitation as long as the mother was breastfeeding, whether enslaved or not, a wisdom that is recognized today in modern medicine which recommends a longer breastfeeding period for a healthier recovery of the uterus and stomach muscles.

The position of the Prophet seems to have produced a certain controversy about why this was recommendable. Some argued that the Romans and Persians were not in the habit of preventing cohabitation with a breastfeeding mother. Children conceived by breastfeeding mothers were born healthy. To prevent a woman from determining how long she should breastfeed and therefore refuse cohabitation with her husband, other hadith reporters tried to invent a Quranic verse that set a limit on how long a mother could breastfeed before consenting to resume cohabitation. Aisha, the Prophet's wife, entered the controversy. She came down on the side of the mother. The point of the Prophet's recommendation was to protect the health of the mother. She argued that since it is forbidden to cohabit at birth, then it should be forbidden during breastfeeding, for both are strenuous for the woman.

Traditional Tunisian practices

The traditional advice of midwives in Tunisia was less liberal than the position of Aisha. The woman could no longer determine whether she should refrain from intimacy as long as she breastfed. A set period of 40 days after the birth became customary. During this time the man had to restrain from sexual relations with his wife (Binous 47). In some regions he could distract himself with organizing a celebration with sweets on the seventh day after the birth, if the newborn were a boy (Jouirou 29). Otherwise, a midwife did not expect a man to complain during the 40 days. It was said that 40 days was short enough for a man not to fear that he would lose his virility (Labidi 1989, 290), for if a couple could be expected to withhold from intimacy for the same length of time during Ramadan, then why not when the health of the mother and child were at stake.

Medical treatment: non-punishable miscarriage and abortion

Medical practices that could result in miscarriage or abortion were the subject of debate in juridical works. A Hanafi medieval treatise, for example, opined that cupping or leeching could not be considered dangerous for a pregnant woman as long as the foetus had not moved and delivery was not approaching. Otherwise, such medical treatment was deemed too dangerous for the pregnant woman (Dien 66). The treatise did not make it clear who was to determine whether the pregnant woman felt movements or not. Implicitly it would have to be the pregnant woman herself who determined up to what time she would risk miscarriage or not.

As for aborting the foetus, the same Hanafi treatise recommended that midwives be prohibited from aborting once formation of the foetus was 'evident'. What constituted evident was not defined; this seems to have been left to the judgment of the mother and midwife. No specific punishment was recommended if the midwife violated this rule (Dien 104). In this regard, the treatise rejected the arguments of some jurists who advised setting a tangible time limit, namely 120 days – the minimum time that a foetus can be born alive. After 120 days of pregnancy, an abortion would not be recommendable. The treatise rejected this argument on the grounds that the 120 days was only for determining paternity in the case of a divorced wife or widow. The treatise preferred not to analogize abortion to paternity. It preferred an analogy with *azl*. This opinion is interesting from the point of view of balancing the sexual rights of men and women. If men were allowed to prevent pregnancy by practicing *azl*, then why should not a woman be equally allowed to stop the pregnancy by means of abortion. If one were to expand on the analogy, then the issue of consent would have to be dealt with. If *azl* were permissible only with the consent of the wife, then abortion would be possible only with the consent of the father of the foetus. This point was not specifically raised in the treatise. But one could also argue that if the society places on the woman the greater burden of child care, then the decision to abort or not should be left to the mother and the midwife because of their expertise in knowing best how to weigh the disadvantages of birth for the mother against miscarriage. Otherwise, if the society requires that father and mother share the burden equally, then the abortion should also be a joint decision.

Punishable abortion

Punishable miscarriage or abortion was treated in the hadiths relating to killings. The issue was raised whether a miscarriage or abortion was to be considered a killing and therefore subject to compensation, imprisonment or the death penalty. The Maliki hadiths established early that unwanted, that is involuntary, abortion was punishable by death. In one hadith as two women quarrelled, one threw a stone at the other. As a result the victim aborted. The Prophet is reported to have ordered the relatives to pay compensation in the form of a slave. The judgment stirred a controversy. The male relatives of the guilty woman objected because the foetus was not a human being. One could not see it, talk with it, or insult it. In other words, no one would have been concerned about its death in the womb before it saw the light of day. The Prophet argued back that their defence was like that of a soothsayer, that is, one has no real basis for predicting what can happen to a foetus. One cannot predict whether it will develop or not.[140] This implies that the issue was not whether a foetus is a human being or not. The point was rather that the foetus was an integral part of the body of the mother, so that an injury to any part of her body, causing her to lose a part of her body, was a tortious wrong to be compensated with damages paid to her. Hence abortion or miscarriage is not a theological issue of predicting when something will become a soul or a life, but rather a biological issue, closely tied up with the bodily integrity of the woman, not the foetus. From this point of view the woman and foetus are one, so that the woman is the determining factor. If, however, they are divided, the woman loses importance. She becomes minimalized and can be made an instrument of abstract predictions. The European and American jurisprudence has much to learn from the Islamic point of view and argumentation in this area.

In Tunisia long after the time of the Prophet, the issue of controlling birth by way of abortion remained a controversial subject of juristic opinion in the 11th century. Abortion was deemed in one *fatwa* to be allowed in the first 40 days of pregnancy. Some centuries later, it was disapproved of (Lohlker 18). A number of jurists from the various schools favoured the 40-day solution. Others among the Hanafis and Hanbalis argued for permitting abortions after 40 days (Lohlker 13, nn. 3 and 4). Some of the Hanafis – not all – took the approach that even after 140 days an abortion would be allowable in cases of hardship, such as the mother has not enough milk and the father cannot hire a nursemaid or the birth could not be natural and only, for example, by way of a Caesarean operation (Lohlker 17, Dien 101). In the case of married women, the consent of the husband was not required at any time (Lohlker 17). The classical jurists also held varying opinions on sterilization (Lohlker 26ff).

Modern abortion law

As part of the population policy, Tunisia enacted a law to regulate voluntary miscarriage (*isqat*). It was made punishable under the penal code in the chapter governing violence against the person. Both the Ministries of Health and Justice are jointly responsible for the enforcement of the legal provisions. The general rule (Laws 3 of 26 September 1973 and 57 of 19 November 1973) is that voluntary miscarriage is allowed up to the first three months (90 days) of the pregnancy, but it has to be performed by a medical doctor in a medical clinic or hospital. Beyond three months, separating the foetus from the mother may be medically performed if the physical health or mental equilibrium of the mother is at risk or the foetus is at risk of having a serious illness or infirmity. The medical doctor performing the operation must submit a justifying report prior to the operation. Otherwise, anyone inducing a miscarriage outside the safer conditions of a clinic is punishable with imprisonment of five years and/or a fine of 10,000 dinars. It is immaterial whether such a miscarriage is with the consent of the pregnant woman. If the pregnant woman herself induces the miscarriage outside the protection and advice of an established medical centre, she is subject to a lesser punishment of two years' imprisonment and/or 1,000 dinars. The medical regulation of miscarriage was urgent given the fact that 25 per cent of all beds in gynaecological clinics were filled with women, including married women, who had developed complications because of unprofessional abortions during the first years of Independence (Kilani).

Birth control methods: abortion versus contraceptives

In the early phases of the population control programme in Tunisia, the statistics showed that the number of abortions for married women compared to use of contraceptives was higher (Kilani). In the 1980s a study revealed that young married women sought abortions for special reasons. The marriage contract had been signed, but they did not feel themselves to be really married, as the public celebration was not to take place until some two to three years later (Labidi 1989, 91). As contraceptive methods became more publicized the number of interrupted pregnancies stabilized. Nearly three-quarters of the yearly 20,000 pregnancy interruptions are reported in the regions of Tunis and Béja, followed by Sahel. Only about 20 per cent of the women rely on involuntary interruption, about 12 per cent rely on the pill, 43 per cent on intrauterine devices, and 17 per cent on tying of the tubes (which is not sterilization).

Success of Tunisian family planning programme

The use of educational methods and mobile vans has led to good results. Infant mortality was 30.6 per cent in 1995, compared to 200 per 1,000 at the time of Independence in 1956 (Ministry of Public Health). The national average number of children is now 3.2 (CRÉDIF 1996). The fertility rate is lowest in the Tunis District with 2.46 and higher in more rural areas as in the Southeast with 3.41. The 1956 figure was 7.2 children per mother (Ministry of Public Health). Population growth has dropped from 3 per cent in 1966 to 1.84 per cent in 1995 (Office National 1995, 9). The crude birth rate in 1956 was 50 per cent, by 1994, 22.7 per cent (Ministry of Public Health), thus keeping the level of unemployment (15 per cent) the lowest in the Maghreb (Morrisson 28) and reducing the proportion of young people aged under 15 from 46 per cent in 1966 to 36.6 per cent in 1991 (Office National 1995, 10). The life expectancy of women is 73 years and for men almost 70. The average age of marriage for women is nearly 25 years, and for men even older, 30 years. Almost 35 per cent of women are single. Almost 44 per cent of all higher-educational students are women, 56 per cent of whom specialize in the arts and humanities and 44 per cent in medicine and biology. A little over 50 per cent of rural women are reported to use contraceptives, the national average being 60 per cent; prenatal consultation is high in rural areas at 69 per cent, but below the national average of 79 per cent; likewise birth delivery under the supervision of professional care (including qualified midwives) is high for rural women with 65 per cent, though below the national average of 75 per cent. Only 19 per cent of rural women have deliveries done by an unqualified midwife (CRÉDIF 1996). This is despite a relatively high illiteracy rate among rural women, combined with a literacy rate for rural men that has tended to be a little more than half that of all women. The rate of illiteracy among rural women was brought down from 84 per cent (55 per cent for men) in 1975 over almost 20 years to 60 per cent (32 per cent for men) in

1994 (CRÉDIF 1996), almost double the national average of *circa* 32 per cent (CRÉDIF 1994). While women have compensated for illiteracy (Hejaiej 8, 13) through personal authority, one can imagine how their already strong personalities could presumably be strengthened with literacy. The success of the birth-control programme among illiterate rural women also indicates that illiteracy need not be an obstacle *per se*. Mobile medical centres and winning over respected midwives play a far more important role.

Infanticide

The Tunisian law regulating voluntary termination of pregnancy did not have an exclusively medical purpose. It also had a social preventive goal. It is designed to offer an alternative to other social inhumanities such as infanticide or abandonment of a child (Kilani 14). Both practices are punished under the penal code.

Article 210 provides for life imprisonment if the father intentionally murders his own child. The mother is punished with two years' imprisonment if she murders the child at a particular time, that is, during or just after birth. Otherwise, the Tunisian courts mete out the same lifetime penalty to a mother who murders her child under the same circumstances as a father (Aouij).

When compared to the infanticide law in a European country like the Federal Republic of Germany, Tunisian law has long been more liberal. First, Tunisian law never distinguished between children born in or outside of marriage. The German law until relatively recently did make such a difference. It prescribed a milder sentence for the mother of a child to whose father she was not married (§217 of the Penal Code, a relict of the Prussian law of 1851) if the murder took place during or immediately after the birth. The sole reason for the milder penalty was that the mother was presumed to be in economic stress because the child was not of the marriage bed. This contrasted with the British infanticide law, which metes out a milder penalty only on the ground that the mother has been proven to be mentally imbalanced.[141] Only recently after severe criticism, has the German infanticide law been repealed (Hussels).

The Prophet was adamantly against killing children for the reason of economic stress, such as fear of lack of food for oneself. This was reported to be a sin, second only to having rivals to God and even worse than adultery.[142]

Abandonment of children

Article 212 of the Penal Code punishes anyone who exposes, including an attempt, a child to danger with the intent to abandon it with three years' imprisonment and 200 dinars. If a parent or grandparent abandons the child, then the penalty is increased to five years' imprisonment plus 200 dinars fine. The penalties are doubled in case the child is abandoned in a place where there are not many people. Since 1995 the penalties have been stiffened to 12 years' imprisonment if the abandonment resulted in handicapping (physically or mentally) the abandoned child (Art. 213).

Social responsibility

The abandonment of children as well as cases of infanticide are reported in the press, thus raising consciousness about social responsibility (Hejaiej 73). Figures on the actual number of abandoned children are not easy to find. A 1994 study quoted the official figure of 304 abandoned children (Taamallah 93). It is difficult to establish the actual unofficial figure. The solution to abandonment and infanticide that educated and professional women advocate is adoption as provided for in the Personal Status Code.[143] A Tunisian businesswoman, of a very prominent social and political family, and with two children of her own has typically taken action to set an example. She adopted an abandoned child, whom no one of her social class would have dared to adopt. The child's bright dark eyes and skin could not have contrasted more than with the blue eyes and blonde skin of the adopting mother. She plans to publish an article in a leading newspaper in Tunisia about her action. Her father was against the adoption. The reason he gave was typical. He argued that the child, coming probably from an adulterous relationship, had 'bad blood' and came from hell. He got a retort that silenced him: 'If I do not adopt this child, then her life will be hell. I am saving her from hell.'

The intention of the adoptive mother to publish an article is in the tradition of a Maliki hadith on the question of foundlings. In the report, Sunain found a child.[144] Whether the child had been abandoned by its parents because of an adulterous relationship or got separated from them because of war or a natural catastrophe, was not made clear. Sunain wanted to know whether he could keep the child. Apparently Umar had a suspicion that the man was lying. The child could have been his, but he could have been claiming that the child was a foundling, since it seems that the practice at the time was for the community to pay for the maintenance of foundlings. As soon as a trusted advisor vouched for the piety of Sunain, then Umar granted him permission to keep the child and to receive money from the state treasury. Some jurists treated this case as one raising questions about witnessing:[145] whether the standard number of witnesses were needed at all to prove the status of a child as abandoned and without parents, or whether it was a matter of vouching and giving a pledge for the good intentions of the person wishing to care for the child.

Since 1957 the Tunisian state has established a fund dedicated to financing abandoned children and families who take them in (Yearbook 1995, 271).

Infanticide, adultery, honour killings

A criminal case from the Court of Appeal confirms the negative attitude of the father of the mother mentioned above who adopted a child of a darker colour. At the same time, it illustrates the Islamic humaneness of the Tunisian legislature. In the case a 26-year-old married woman had given birth to a son.[146] Her 53-year-old mother came to know of the pregnancy only in the fifth month, too late for termination of the pregnancy. It seems that the daughter had been unable to solve her problem early enough. She had been traumatized by the poor health of her husband and a fear that he would react violently against her adultery (*sifah*). Both the daughter and mother were charged with infanticide after the child was born and disposed of in a field, where it was discovered by a woman who worked in the same field as the mother. A medical report confirmed that the child had been strangled on the day of birth. The daughter made a full confession, but then withdrew it in an attempt to save her mother from prosecution by saying that she was alone at the birth. The mother did not seem to attempt to deny her role. The two-year imprisonment sentence pronounced by the court was suspended under Article 53 of the Penal Code, which allows for leniency in case of mental distress.

No mention was made of the possibility that the daughter could have been charged also with adultery under Article 236 of the Penal Code. An accusation by the state authorities of adultery is possible only at the request of the spouse, whether husband or wife, who feels hurt by the adultery.

Both the man and the woman involved in the adultery have to be found guilty, implying that where one cannot be found or one is not found guilty, then no prosecution of the other party is allowed. If both parties are convicted, the penalty is five years' imprisonment and a fine of 500 dinars for each.

Before 1993 an honour killing by a husband of the adulterous wife and/or her lover was permitted by law according to Article 207 of the Penal Code. In 1993 the infamous Article 207 was abrogated. Since the abovementioned infanticide case occurred just one year after the abrogation of the husband's right to an honour killing, this may explain why the 26-year-old daughter was traumatized by fear of a violent reaction of her husband, which would have been legitimated under the law at the time.

The old law was clearly against Islamic *sunna* (the best, the just way). As cited above, the Prophet was said to have listed the killing of a child for reasons of hunger as even more sinful than adultery. By analogy, the killing of a child who is a product of adultery would be even more sinful than the actual adultery. The question of honour killings did not arise in the Maliki collection of hadiths. In the Bukhari collection it is treated as a matter of divorce. If the husband found his wife with another man, it was recommended that the husband not take justice into his own hands. The remedy open to him is divorce.[147] The story reported does not mention the case of a wife finding her husband with another woman with whom he is not married. By analogy, one would expect the same recommendation for the wife.

Protection of children

In addition to reforming the penal code, the Tunisian legislator has also taken measures especially focused on the child as Tunisia is party to the UN Children's Convention. It is hoped that this focus will convince women and men to see the child as a human being endowed with her/his own rights and dignity, not tainted by the relations between the parents, just as a woman is no longer seen as an appendage of her husband. The Child's Council was created in 1995 with the task to advise the Ministry of Youth and Children with the help of studies on the needs of the child and preparation of statistics.[148] The social aim is to sensitize the society to the needs of the child.

Fundamentalism

What has been called the 'almost mystical' (Hopwood 111) social pact that Bourguiba had with Tunisians as well as the strong pro-women's legislation came under open attack by the fundamentalists in the last days of Bourguiba's regime. The fundamentalists' movement was not entirely new in Tunisian history. They were once called the rigourists in the days of Haddad, whom they had also attacked, although he came from among their ranks.

Their vocalness in the 1980s coincided with economic problems that led to an enormous increase in the costs of living. By that time urban development had taken on a structure that introduced new social segregation. The upper classes were moving to the suburbs leaving the inner *medina* to the poorer, who then moved to housing projects for the low-income classes (Salem 24). Such a development facilitates a concentration of political fundamentalism in lower income groups. The response of Bourguiba was to increase the number of women candidates in municipal elections as a countermove, with the effect that 478 women assumed public office (Waltz 22). They had all been nominated by the National Union of Tunisian Women (founded in 1956, and winner of the 1978 United Nations Human Rights award).

The 20th century Islamic movement (Hamdi 1996, 1998) had been founded by Ghannouchi born into a poor family in Gabès. The leaders of the Islamic movement alleged that they had a monopoly on the truth and the way to individual salvation. The emphasis was on the individual's salvation, which in turn depended on the individual's morality, and morality was defined in terms of sexual behaviour. The same zeitgeist had gripped the North American society under the Christian Right. The individual corruption and hypocrisy of leaders were also attacked. This led to a debate on whether polygamy should be re-introduced partly on the basis of the behaviour of certain highly placed officials who were keeping a mistress alongside the wife.

The Islamic Movement (MIT) organized a demonstration in April 1987. The then Minister of Interior – ex-soldier trained at St Cyr – Zain al Abidin Ben Ali was ordered by Bourguiba to suppress it. The Islamists were accused of treason against the state. A court trial began in August 1987. In October 1987 Bourguiba signed over the prime ministership to Ben Ali. Ben Ali arrested more Islamists. Ben Ali had Bourguiba arrested on 7–8 November 1987. The senile President for Life and champion of women's rights at the age of 84 was declared incapacitated. Ben Ali became the constitutional head of state. Former Neo-Destour allies from the trade union movement who had been arrested were granted amnesty.

A year later on 7 November 1988 a solemn National Pact was announced. It had two purposes: to restore a consensus on the social vision of the country and to redefine that vision. All political parties and social and professional organizations signed the Pact. The Pact is to reaffirm the principles that each political party, including the Islamists, is to respect. These are commitment to gender equality, human rights, reaffirmation of the Code of Personal Status, commitment to civilian rule and tolerance (National Union 58). The Pact was essential for restoring the course set at Independence regarding women's rights. Two years later in 1990 the first multiparty elections, on the municipal level, took place. In 1994 Ben Ali was elected President. Opposition parties sit in the parliament.

The controversy sparked off by the fundamentalists on women's rights sent shock waves among the intelligentsia. All the questions relating to the wearing of the *hijab*, polygamy, equality between men and women in divorce broke open again and put into question the laws, which had been applied in thousands of cases for over twenty years. The assumption that there was a social consensus behind the better egalitarian interpretation of the Quran and hadiths began to be doubted.

The response was a series of social inquiry. Some studies concentrated on lower classes and rural women. It was found their understanding of Islam was not rational. Their understanding derived from an oral Islam mixed with magic that is supposed to help one out of a hopeless situation. This oral Islam was transmitted over encounters and social relationships. Knowledge of Islam was not based on the written Islam (the Quran and hadiths) (Jouirou).

The finding that the source of what one knows of Islam is linked to social encounters and relationships may prove to be a saving factor for the future of Tunisian Islamic legislation. The hierarchy of social relations in Tunisia is not rigid (Salem 21). There is social mobility. This allows for exchanges of knowledge across social classes. Nor is there dependency on a higher social class of ulama claiming a monopoly on interpreting written Islam (Salem). The exchange of information is being further promoted by the government's cultural campaigns. Prizes are awarded for the best essays about Islam.[149] The public spread of knowledge of Islam serves to counteract the literature exported from Saudi Arabia into Tunisia (Medimegh 14, n. 20). In addition, the state has established control over the qualifications of religious teachers in mosques and rooms of prayer.[150] This was facilitated by measures taken under the government of Bourguiba. The financial basis of the religious institutions had been undermined by abolishing the *waqf*, the religious trust (Jones 1975, 346, Cherif 1996, 66).[151]

One social relationship found to be very important in the promotion and preservation of the liberal spirit of Islam in Tunisia is that between father and daughter. It was found that the most efficient women on municipal councils (totalling 478) came from the lower classes and had fathers who had encouraged them to advance their careers (Waltz 28, 31). This encouragement of women's rights is a result of Tunisia's non-military tradition. Already in the last century a school certificate freed men from military service (Salem). This freed men of a largely patriarchal/hierarchical culture that militarization of a society breeds. Fathers did not need the military as a vehicle for social advancement. Daughters' education was an effective alternative vehicle.

The government has also concentrated on women's social networks as vehicles for spreading knowledge of Islam. Financial support for the National Union of Tunisian Women has enabled them to maintain a network of offices throughout Tunisia. They offer services for arbitrating problems of women, including family conflicts. Through this arbitration knowledge of the Islamic basis of Tunisian family law is being spread. To what extent the role of the Union is being supplemented or replaced by the bureaux for citizen's complaints for each ministry created in 1993 remains to be seen.[152]

The rural woman was projected onto the national scene during the national elections of 1999, which Ben Ali won. Campaign posters still displayed everywhere long after the election were strikingly pro-women rights. The candidate was seen shaking hands with a Tunisian woman, old enough to be his mother. She looks supremely self-confident and is in rural dress. This is the image that symbolizes the continued commitment of the government to strengthen and carry forward the long tradition of Tunisia to apply the interpretation of the *sunna* and the Quran that is best for women's rights so that men and women do not dominate or subordinate one another, but can treat each other as equals. In this way the egalitarian spirit of Islamic justice is achieved.

2

EGYPT – CONSERVATIVE INCREMENTAL REFORM

Introduction

Egypt has a long distinguished history, containing many firsts. While Tunisia is known for firsts in legal developments, Egypt is known for political and religious firsts from ancient times to modern times. In terms of politics, its state bureaucracy of 7,000 years is the oldest in the world. In terms of religion, it has numerous examples of ancient goddesses who were placed on an equal footing with male gods, just as god-like queens who were as astute as kings. Despite the multiplicity of gods and goddesses, Egypt was also the first to propagate monotheism in the ancient world. In terms of modern history, it was the first country in the Ottoman Empire targeted for European military invasion (by Napoleon). Most recently, it became the first Arab country to sign a peace treaty with the Israelis. Egypt is also the most populous Arab country.

Arabization and Islamization of Egypt and class stratification

The Arabization of Egypt started in the 1st century after the Prophet's death. Under the Arabian Umayyad rulers the language of the bureaucrats became Arabic, replacing Greek. The Arabs also introduced a new tax system, for Egypt was a rich country and thus an important source of taxation, just as it had also been since the ages of the Pharaohs. The Christian Copts in Egypt rebelled against the new tax system imposed by their new

Arab masters. The response of the new rulers was to resettle members of Arab tribes in Egypt. For a while the majority of the population remained Christian, while the elite became Arabic, belonging mainly to the military class. An Arabicized civil elite came into existence in the tenth century with the influx of Iraqis when Iraq experienced an economic crisis. The emigrating Iraqis consisted of both Muslims and Jews.

In the 10th century the Fatimids invaded Egypt. They came from Qairawan in Tunisia, the city most well known at the time for its mosque and university (Lev 5). The Fatimids assumed the reins over Egypt for two centuries. They brought with them the Qairawan tradition of learning. They founded the Al Azhar mosque and university to propagate their Ismaili (Shiite) ideas. The old mosque of Amr in Cairo they allowed to remain. There the Sunni ideas continued to be propagated. On the administrative religious level the Fatimids also made changes. They replaced the Sunni Maliki qadi in Cairo with an Ismaili qadi. While the Fatimids otherwise tolerated the Maliki and Shafii schools of law, they apparently did not take a kindly view towards the Hanafi school of law, as the latter was associated with their Abbasid rivals (Jackson 53ff).

Economically the Fatimid era was a time of prosperity. Trade flourished with Sicily, Venice and Genoa.

Women enjoyed prominence too. The tombs of two local Egyptian Shiite women were important places of worship (Lev 149). In the 11th century, the sister of the Fatimid ruler attained fame. She was Sitt al Mulk (Lev 34). She restored political, religious and fiscal order in the wake of a cruel intolerant ruler.

Prosperity did not last forever. The Nile no longer sufficiently flooded, leading to famine and illness. This did not stop the Fatimid administrators from continuing to demand taxes. As a result, instability broke out in Fatimid Egypt. A revolt ensued. A Christian Armenian military commander saved the Fatimid dynasty from toppling, but his successors – Arabs from Syria – imposed a military dictatorship, merging civilian and military functions. The Syrians relied militarily on indentured soldiers, called the Mamluks, who had been captured from the Black Sea area and enslaved. The Mamluks had won fame for having defeated the Crusaders in Palestine.

The Mamluks turned on their masters. They usurped military and political power in the 13th century and ruled until the 16th. On the eve of taking over full power, they selected a woman in 1250 to be sultaness. She was Shajarat al Durr, a widow. She then married her Mamluk military commander, whereupon she lost her position of power (Jackson 42–43).

The Mamluks were traditional Sunnis. They had no love for the tenets of the Ismailis propagated by the Fatimids. The Mamluks wiped out all traces of the Ismaili sect. The Mamluk era was the era of the famous jurist Ibn Taimiyya (of the Sunni Hanbali school of law). He attacked what he saw as the 'corrupted' religious class in Egypt and the popularity of the charismatic Sufi religion among the poorer classes (Berkey 164ff, 172).

The Mamluks also shifted the balance of the schools of law among the judgeships. Represented among the judges were the Maliki, Shafii and Hanafi schools, the Shafii, however, enjoying ascendance over the Maliki (Jackson 53ff).

The Mamluks were then defeated by the Ottomans in the 16th century. Under the Ottomans the social differences between the military elite and the civilian elite became even more pronounced. Under the Ottomans the rivalling political families among the elite were of Circassian and Bosnian origin. Followers of the Mamluks continued to regroup to seize power again, in the hope of re-establishing an independent Mamluk Egypt. The Ottomans continuously succeeded in crushing the Mamluk revolts.

With regard to women, the Ottomans also engaged in battle against certain classes of women. A chronicle on late 17th to middle 18th century Egypt mentions the immorality of a certain class of women. These were women singers, who were in great demand for the weddings of the wealthy (Crecilius 122). These women were organized into guilds. Mention is made of the police having been ordered to raid one of the houses of the head of the singers' guild, as part of an effort to stamp out so-called immoral acts.

As for the religious classes from the Mamluk era, local Egyptian ulama did not have a frictionless relationship with the new Ottoman rulers. The ulama appear to have enjoyed instead a rather good standing among the populace. They seemed to have been the only class which spoke out against abuses by the foreign Turkish rulers of the time in favour of the peasants and labourers (Crecilius 8) as well as free and enslaved women (Marsot 50ff). The ulama were thus assigned a mediation role among the various factions on the political and social scene. They mediated between the Ottoman officials and Mamluk military factions attempting to reinstate Mamluk rule (Eccel 23–4; Delanoue 21) as well as between the ruler and the people (Marsot 75). Their role was more distinct and pronounced than that of their counterparts, for example, in Saudi Arabia (Kechichian 55). There is evidence that even in the first century of Islam during the period of revolt of the Abbasids (members of the Prophet's family) against the Umayyads (members of the Prophet's in-laws related to his wife Aisha), learned scholars from Egypt were subject to inquisitorial vetting on their views about the creation of the Quran, had refused to accept the doctrine of the Abbasid Caliph Al Mamun (813) and were said to have died in prison (Lapidus 380) during the Islamic Inquisition (Makdisi 12).

The basis of power of the Ottoman rulers, like that of their predecessors, remained the collection of taxes from the rich harvests of the Nile delta. But the periodic non-flooding cycles of the Nile brought famine in the wake of insufficient flooding. These developments did not topple Ottoman rule. Instead, the hardships led to the development of popularist religious movements connected with local saints. These movements attracted especially devout women (Crecilius 116) as well as political devotees.

The modern state – arrival of the Europeans

The first major dent in the Ottoman rule came with the French military occupation of Egypt under the command of Napoleon (1798–1801). The occupation was short-lived, but it was a sign of a weakening in the power of Constantinople. The ruler appointed by the Ottomans to control Egypt saw new opportunities. He was Muhammad Ali, an Ottoman ruler of Albanian origin. After the Napoleonic invasion he sought to attain more autonomy for Egypt from Constantinople. Inspired with the vision of re-establishing an independent Mamluk-ruled country, he revolted against Constantinople but was defeated.

Nonetheless Muhammad Ali was able to establish the first family dynasty in Egypt, along the lines of those found in Europe at the time. The founding of the dynasty meant that the Ottoman sultan had no more control over the appointment of successors. Muhammad Ali's successor was Ismail. Ismail achieved another first in the Ottoman history. He wrestled from the Ottoman Empire the title of Khedive (1867) to distinguish Egyptian rulers from the Bays in other parts of the Ottoman Empire. The Muhammad Ali dynasty lasted until Egypt became a republic in the 20th century.

Under the Ottomans the weight of importance among the various schools of law shifted. The Hanafi school of law enjoyed official status in Egypt as part of the Ottoman Imperium. Still the head of Al Azhar University was allowed at first to remain Shafii (the Shafiis having taken over from the Malikis since the start of the 18th century (Eccel 133)). Shafii influence at high levels, however, declined. In the second half of the 19th century, the Ottomans replaced the Shafii head of Al Azhar with a Hanafi.

The Ottoman Empire finally came to its own demise. After the First World War the Empire dissolved. Its various parts were parcelled out among the European imperial powers. The British assigned themselves to Egypt. Twelve years after the First World War Egypt finally became independent in 1936. Official British colonial presence was limited to British troops, who were stationed in the Suez Canal zone. The monarchal dynastic form of government instituted under the Ottomans in Egypt continued in the new independent state in the form of a royal kingdom.[1]

Reform movements in the 19th century on women's rights

Culturally, Cairo was a magnet, not only for educated men, but also for women intellectuals. The Egyptian state under the Ottomans had not neglected the education for females. A state girls' school was established in the early 1870s.

Women littérateurs and essayists were not uncommon in Cairo. Among them (Kader 65ff; Wiebke 606–7) were Aisha Ismat Taimur (b. 1840), a poet who published in Egyptian newspapers tracts on the need for education of women. Another personality was Zainab Fawwaz (b. 1845 or 1860), who had emigrated from Lebanon to Cairo. She published in connection with the World Exhibition of 1893 in Chicago a lexicon of the biographies of over 400 women from the Arab world and Europe to prove that Arab women had important social positions and influence. She also published novels evolving around family sagas. Marie Elias Ziyada, who had studied Islamic philosophy under the tutelage of sheikhs at Al Azhar University just before the First World War, held literary salons for over 20 years in Cairo (Kazem).

Men and women intellectuals did not shy away from the subject of emancipation of women. Zainab Fawwaz wrote many letters and articles on the subject. Her writings are thought to be more precise and specific than even those of one of the leading male writers on emancipation.

Issues of veiling and equality

Among the men, Qasim Amin (1865–1908, a member of an aristocratic Turkish family and a lawyer and judge of the Court of Appeal) was acclaimed as a great male intellectual publicist arguing for a renewal of social interpretations of Islam and for the emancipation of women (Walther 607, Kader 58). He published a book, *Tahrir al mar'a* (The Liberation of Women), in 1899 as a series of articles in a newspaper. A contemporary of Taalbi in Tunisia, Qasim Amin argued against the practice of veiling women as an example of how customs had corrupted the original intentions of Islam. Islam had originally intended to liberate the woman from denigrating Arabian social customs. Qasim Amin argued that in practice Islam had not achieved the goal of influencing the social customs. The reverse had occurred. The social customs influenced Islam too much. The customs went beyond even the limits set by the Sharia. If Islam had achieved the upper hand over social custom, instead of vice versa, then, so Qasim Amin argued, the Muslim woman would have been in the forefront of emancipated women in the world (Ragaï 99). Instead, because of the veil, the Muslim women had become subservient. Veiling he regarded simply as a custom, a custom that was not the fault of Islamic tenets or Islamic law (Ragaï 111). He argued that in fact the social consequences of veiling were against tenets of Islam. He analysed the social consequences of veiling to support his point: the veil was a symbol of servitude because it prevented women from completing their education and earning their own living. Because he analysed the phenomenon of veiling as a social practice, not a religious one affecting a woman's or a man's faith in God, he concluded his analysis with advocating the prohibition of the social practice of veiling (Ragaï 105).

As to be expected, the publications of Qasim Amin provoked a heated intellectual discussion. His most ardent opponent was Muhammad Talat Pasha Harb (Hassan, Harb 1914), equally a lawyer, an advocate of national economic self-help and the founder of the Bank Misr. Pasha Harb argued that the heart of the issue was whether there could be equality between men and women, since Qasim Amin had argued in relation to the veiling that God had established equal obligations and privileges for women and men. Equality in the opinion of Pasha Harb could never be sanctioned. He relied on a Quranic verse to support his argument that women, like orphans, are weaker in all aspects, physically and mentally, than men, and therefore cannot be treated as equal.[2] He interpreted the verse to mean that women need protection and therefore can never be given rights equal to those of men because their responsibilities were different. He certainly was in good company with some contemporary European scholars who were also arguing at the time for excluding women from certain professions in the name of 'protecting' them. This made the veil, according to Pasha Harb, a 'social necessity' (Ragaï 122). He feared that the cessation of the custom of veiling would lead to women exposing themselves indecently as European women. He ignored the capacity of the Egyptian Coptic women to remain modest in their dress despite not wearing the veil. He ignored too the Quranic verse that would have undermined his 'protectionist' arguments. That verse speaks not only of the weakness of women and children, but also the weakness of men. It further says that the cause of the weakness of women and children, as well as of men is oppression by others. The verse concludes with a statement that it is a duty in the name of Allah to make them all – women included – strong by removing the oppression and the oppressors.[3]

The intellectual strivings of Qasim Amin against veiling were not sustained with the same intensity as he started out with. Qasim Amin had a protégée, Malak Hifni Nasif (1886–1918), who later published tracts on the veiling of women (Walther 609, Kader 59), which were more conservative (Kader 66ff) than the positions taken by Qasim or his Tunisian counterpart Taalbi at the turn of the century and later Tahar Haddad in Tunisia.

Issue of polygamy

Another woman who entered the debate on women's rights was Bahissant El Badiah (Ragaï 124ff). She centred her concern on polygamy. She argued vehemently against this legally approved privilege for men. Like Qasim Amin she argued from the social point of view, that is, one analyses the social consequences that a law or practice has in order to determine whether the consequences in themselves lead to violations of legal principles. She took in account not only the disadvantages of polygamy for the woman, but as well as for the man. Polygamy, she argued, led men to immorality, because men had to lie to their wives; and it sapped their health and their wealth. Usually a husband took on a second wife because he was unhappy with the first. By taking on a second wife, he was in effect insulting and making the first wife unhappy. El Badiah argued that the husband did not need polygamy to solve his problems with a first wife. He already had a remedy if he were dissatisfied. That was *talaq*. He could divorce his wife, releasing himself and herself from an unhappy situation. He could find satisfaction by remarrying, and the first wife, too, by being released from a polygamous marriage.

Religious reformers: Muhammad Abduh

It was men, however, who dominated the intellectual discourse on jurisprudence and Islamic law and had an impact on policy. These men were mainly theologians. One of the most well known was Muhammad Abduh (1849–1905), born of a peasant family in Lower Egypt. He became grand mufti of Egypt (Saeed 128ff). In his early years he was a mystic. He was later sent into exile (including a stay in Tunisia) for a while because of membership in a politically revolutionary group which fought against foreign and despotic domination of Egypt. Upon return he was named a judge, a member of the legislative council and finally mufti.

Training of Sharia judges

Abduh undertook a study of the Sharia Court system in 1899 (Eccel 87). He identified problems in the application of the law. Transparency of the rules of the Sharia and training of the qadis were two practical concerns for Abduh. Many judges were apparently applying the law poorly as the sources of the law were highly dispersed among volumes of commentaries (Eccel 90–1). As for training, Abduh proposed a school for qadis (*Madrasat al qada' al shar'i*) to train them not only in Islamic law, but also to give them a general liberal education. The school was opened in 1907, just after Abduh's death (Shaham 15). It presented competition to Al Azhar and was closed in 1929. It did not survive, unlike Sadiki College in Tunisia which flourished

Defining **ijtihad** *and* **ijma**

Abduh had clear ideas about how the sources of Islamic law were to be used. He advocated the Quran as the primary source of the Sharia. He favoured reopening the door of *ijtihad* in interpreting the Quran. He specified the criteria that the exercise of *ijtihad* had to meet: *ijtihad* was to conform to the spirit of Islam and the common good most appropriate for the social circumstances of the time. He tackled also the attributes of *ijma* as a further source of law. *Ijma*, he argued, has to be rooted in universal reason, not parochial religious self-interests.

Compilations and codifications of Islamic law

Abduh was equally clear about a pragmatic approach to solving the practical problems of interpreting and applying the sources of Islamic law. For this purpose he advocated compiling the positions of all four Sunni schools of law in a kind of compendium, since that would be easier to consult than the many academic juristic treatises from which the qadis could choose.

Apart from pragmatic concerns, Abduh had also a modernist agenda. He pointed out the modernistic jurisprudential advantages of a uniform compendium of Islamic law tenets. A compendium would, he hoped, lay the foundation for achieving a certain consistency in the jurisprudence. This was especially important for Egypt, where three schools of law (*madhab*) were applied in different regions in Egypt: the Malikis dominating in Upper Egypt, the Shafiis in the Delta (the tomb of Imam Shafii being in Egypt) and the Hanafis, the official school of law of the Ottoman Empire, used mainly in Cairo (Abdal-Rehim 97).

Thus it was not surprising when Abduh recommended codifying the Sharia. For this task Qadri Pasha was entrusted by the ruler Ismail to write a code. The draft code, however, was not to be as broad in scope as the intended compendium of all four *madhab*. The code was to be modelled on Hanafi law, in keeping with the official declaration in 1856 that the Hanafi *madhab* alone had the status of being the official school of law for Egypt (Eccel 79). The code was completed, but was never officially adopted. This was due again to opposition from the ulama, who were said to fear that codification meant losing control over the interpretation of the law (Eccel 90–1; Hill 1987, 4, 132, n. 2).

Reform movements: Salafiyya, Rashid Rida

Muhammad Abduh founded the Salafiyya reform movement during his tenure as mufti. The influence of this movement was felt also in Tunisia, where Taalbi was one of its members. As a result of this influence, he helped form the Young Tunisians Party composed of nationalist lay persons and theologians.

After Abduh's death in 1905 the mantle of leadership fell on Rashid Rida (1865–1935). Rida gave voice to the Salafiyya movement in his journal *Al Manar*. Rida, born in Tripoli in Lebanon, travelled widely in the Ottoman Empire and finally settled in Egypt. He acted not only as a publicist, but also devoted attention to institution building. He founded in 1911 a university (*Dar al da'awa wa'l irshad*) with the aim of teaching Islam according to modern standards, similar to the long-established state-supported Sadiki College in Tunis. The university met the same fate as Abduh's school for training Sharia judges. The university had to close within a year of opening for lack of funds.

Rida differed somewhat from Abduh in his approach to applying Islamic law. As a scholar he turned to classical Islamic law scholars who had advocated reform. He particularly favoured classical Islamic scholars such as Ibn Taimiyya. Rida also differed from Abduh regarding the weight to be accorded to the basic authoritative sources of Islamic law. Rida did not emphasize the Quran as the primary source of Islamic law. He emphasized giving equal weight to the hadiths. Because of his emphasis on giving equal weight to the hadiths as to the Quran, Rida has been considered more conservative than Muhammad Abduh. He also advocated retaining a scholarly class like the ulama, of which he was a member, with their monopoly over the interpretation of Islamic law, even a reformed version (Saeed 130 *et seq.*).

Ideological underpinnings of reform

It can be only surmised that the more classical approach of Rida to reform had ideological underpinnings. By referring back to classical scholars, Rida was in effect finding roots for reform in an era when Islamic rulers were the colonizers and imperalists and not the colonized. Abduh, on the other hand, can be said to have been open to a more syncretic approach under prevailing circumstances.

Secular reform movements: Haykal

Among the secularists advocating change was Muhammad Husain Haykal (1888–1956). He was a lawyer, novelist, founder of the Egyptian Democratic Party and one-time minister of education in the 1930s. He contributed frequently to the journal *Al Jarida*, which also advocated change. As minister of education in the 1930s he blocked attempts of the Al Azhar ulama to have their graduates appointed to government schools without state certification. In 1908 he wrote that he was against the veiling of women and for education of women beyond primary school (Smith 39).

Ideology of class

Even though a secularist, Haykal mirrored the distrust of his class, the religious intellectual class, towards the peasants' popular culture. He emphasized, for example, in 1911 the need to invest in higher education, while keeping the pace of primary school education slower, so that an intellectual aristocracy could maintain social order. He differed from his class only to the extent that he advocated a secular rather than a religious aristocracy (Smith 45, 56). In fact he argued explicitly against a religious aristocracy. He reasoned that Islam is anti-clerical and permits each individual Muslim person to exercise *ijtihad* (Smith 144, 150). As a practising Muslim, he believed in equality before God for all believers. As a landowner, however, he believed in a strict hierarchy in economic and political matters. He believed that it was part of divine order that each accept her/his own economic lot and recognize the authority of village patriarchs. The patriarchs, however, he admitted, were to be controlled by moral sanctions, for they were obliged to help those born into an inferior lot and therefore in need (Smith 121).

Islam and the state

The elite-controlled structure which Rashid Rida advocated essentially holds sway today in Egypt. This system maintains a religious class of ulama, which requires a clear division of labour in regard to the interpretation of Islamic law. The state government is dependent on opinions issued by the ulama classes relating to Islamic law interpretations on any one topic. It does not matter whether the opinion has been orchestrated by the government or is totally independent of government predilections.

This structural relationship between government and religious elite is what distinguishes Egypt from Tunisia. Tunisia has a more integrated system in which knowledge of Islam is not confined to one class. The head of state of Tunisia and the country's civil servants see themselves as good Muslims capable of understanding Islam and choosing wisely among interpretations of the basic principles of Islamic law. A monopoly of specialists is not taken for granted as a matter of principle. Historical legacies, too, play an important role in explaining the differences of approach in Egypt and Tunisia. The Egyptian ulama class has a historical reputation of serving as mediators between the powerful and the less powerful, speaking out on behalf of the lower classes against abuses, especially in rural areas (Shoshan 94–5). In Tunisia, in contrast, the reformist government of Khayr ad Din in the 19th century left a legacy of integrating the ulama into government policy and institutions, thereby neutralizing the more conservative ulama (Green 117, 232). In the first half of the 20th century in Tunisia the trade union movement, from which Bourguiba sprang, also provided a forum for voicing the concerns of lower-income labourers independent of the religious class.

Thus when the clerics have a good popular reputation and have built up an infrastructure for spreading their version of Islam, as in Egypt, then the government is in a more difficult situation. In addition in Egypt the government has faced not only a clerical class with a monopoly on classical learning, but also Islamist groups which try to compete against the clerical class. Up until recently the government under the guidance of Mubarak and the ulama joined forces in fighting the challenge that young radical Islamists mounted against the traditional ulama, whom they accused of being too pro-state (Skovgaard-Petersen 220, 225).

Under such circumstances the state is faced with several choices. One choice is to enter the fray and compete with religious groups in respect to the interpretation of Islamic law. In this scenario the government would have to assign all competing parties set roles. Another choice is for the state to devise the rules by which the religious groups shall compete and arbitrate, but the government stays out of the competition (Skogaard-Petersen 380). A third possible choice is for the government to devise its own infrastructure for disseminating information on interpreting Islamic law that is equal in effectiveness to that of the clerics who hold a monopoly. The intention of the government may be either to break the clerical monopoly or to create an effective system of checks and balances on that monopoly (Hijab 50; Saeed 125).[4]

The difference of approach of the government in Egypt and Tunisia raises some questions about the debate on secularism and Islamic law. The debate has been phrased in terms of whether Islamic states should make a clear division between religion and state, that is, whether the state should refuse to enforce the tenets of any religion. The implied purpose of such division is to allow equality of all citizens before the state law and to allow an equal chance for all to switch their religious loyalty. In the light of Islam the terms of the debate may have to be rephrased.

The emphasis in the debate perhaps should not be so much on a clear division between church and state as emerged from European Christian history (though in practice the division is not as clear-cut as the theory). Rather the emphasis perhaps should be more on the purpose of secularism, that is, to allow equality before the law. The question then becomes whether this equality can be achieved without dividing religious authority from state authority. Tunisia has managed to achieve this. It is a secular state that is based precisely on not dividing religious authority from the state. The state embodies both the religious and the state power. Tunisia has a legal system that derives from Islamic law but applies equally to all citizens regardless of religious affiliation. How has this been possible? It has been made possible because the state has retained the monopoly on interpretation of Islamic law. This monopoly is achieved only when the state is seen as consisting of a head of state or organs of governance on the one hand and citizens on the other. Both sides have to be perceived as being in consultation about the best interests of the society at large. If the state authority perceives itself as a democratic reflection of the citizens, that authority has to retain the right to *ijtihad* (Cherif 1994, 66), the right to interpret the Sharia for the good of the society. By retaining the right to *ijtihad*, it can choose an interpretation of the Sharia which best serves the Quranic spirit of justice and equality. This power can extend even to deciding even how far Sharia should be applied as a state law in contradiction to the injunction that there is no compulsion in religion (sura 2:256).

Otherwise, a division between 'church' and state, which removes the state power over the interpretation of Islamic law and allows a small group of scholars and clerics to interpret Sharia leads to the very opposite of what secularists want to achieve. The division of power allows the interpretation of the Islamic law to remain in the hands of a small group of scholars and clerics, who are not part of the democratic process. Their reflections on the law mirror the interests of that narrow class of clerics and not the wider society. Equality is not guaranteed. The state denies itself the power to exercise *ijtihad* in the interests of equality of all citizens regardless of religion. The non-assumption by the government over the power of *ijtihad* is in itself a denial not only of the democratic principle, but also of the basic spirit of Islam, whereby a variety of consultations is better than a monopoly held by clerics holding limited dogmatic opinions.

Court systems

This section deals in detail with the court system as it has evolved in Egypt. The aim of this presentation is to show how the system had become so complex that it made adjudication difficult, discouraging women from using the courts. This section also shows that the basic strategy of judicial reform in Egypt is incremental, rather than revolutionary.

Courts before the Nasir era

By the time Muhammad Ali's dynasty was established in the 18th century, Egypt already had a complex court system (Brown 23). There were Sharia courts, Coptic courts (today 6 per cent of the population) and Catholic courts (called Milli courts). The Sharia courts were located in the mosques, according to a chronicle of Egypt (Crecilius 207–208).

Muhammad Ali retained these courts and added new civil and commercial courts. The civil courts had not only judicial, but also administrative and legislative functions, rendering them more like councils than courts. A network of these council/courts covered village and provincial levels and Cairo. They heard minor cases and prepared cases for higher courts (Brown 24). These council/courts fed into the Council of the Assembly of Justice, the *Majlis Jamaiyyat al Haqqaniyya.* Muhammad Ali also established a council with representatives from the ulama for matters of inheritance, guardianship and serious crimes (*Diwan al Wali*) (Eccel 96ff). This became in 1829 the *As Shura,* consultative council, consulted in some cases about the compatibility of legislation with the Sharia (Skovgaard-Petersen 100ff).

Subsequent rulers were bold enough to tackle the Sharia courts, but only in relation to procedural and organizational aspects. The proceedings had to be written and only written documents could be accepted as evidence in certain transfers relating to gifts and land. These reforms in 1856 and 1876 were justified by the argument that it was necessary to preserve the force of the Sharia and to restore its original principles of justice and equality (Eccel 79–80). By the end of the 19th century the Sharia courts were organized into a hierarchical appellate system. At the bottom were the district courts: then came the provincial; the system culminated in a High Court (*Nizarat al hakkaniya*) where the mufti and the chief qadi presided (Eccel 85ff). Corresponding to the court structure, a divided bar was established. There was a Sharia bar and a non-Sharia bar established by Law No. 15 of 1916 (*al Muhamun as shariyyun*) (Shaham 68). The position of the mufti was also reorganized. The mufti was given two hats to wear. Not only was the mufti a member of the highest Sharia court, but was also assigned an executive position within the Ministry of Justice in 1880. The mufti's task was to define the law in cases of doubt, similar to the position of the Sheikh ul Islam in the Ottoman Empire (Skovgaard-Petersen 101ff, 241).

As the European imperialist powers won more economic influence in the Ottoman Empire, they pressured the Egyptian government to add to the complexity of the court system. As a result, the Mixed Court was added in 1876. It was a sign of non-confidence of Europeans in the local judicial system. The Mixed Court had jurisdiction in civil and commercial cases involving Egyptian and European parties. The Mixed Court quickly became an irritant in the eyes of the government when in debt claims it ruled against the Khedive of Egypt at a time of declining finances (Brown 28).

Alongside the Mixed Court there existed the consular courts. They had jurisdiction in personal status cases of non-Egyptians, regardless of their religious affiliation.

In the 1880s the Egyptian government sought to rival the powers of the Mixed Courts. The government created the Native Courts, later known in the 1930s as National Courts, with civil and administrative jurisdiction (*al Mahakim al ahliyya*), as an alternative to the Mixed Court (Brown 230, Eccel 96ff). A break was made with tradition: administrative competence was separated from judicial duties. The judges were chosen on the basis of their legal training and not administrative experience (Brown 31).

When the British occupied Egypt at the start of the 1880s, they introduced cantonal courts with simplified procedures and lay judges (local leaders) in 1912. They were relatively short-lived, being abolished in 1932 (Brown 39, 56; Hill 1979, 52).

After the Second World War the court system was streamlined, but only somewhat. The Mixed Court was abolished. Its commercial and economic jurisdiction fell to the National Courts. The National Courts adopted the continental European law principle that the law of nationality applied to foreigners so that foreign law continued to be applied to non-Egyptians, much to the relief of Europeans.

The post-war period saw also the adoption of a French-influenced system. In 1946 the *Majlis al Dawla*, Council of State, was installed. In terms of its review powers, all draft legislation of the government had to be submitted first to the *Majlis*. In terms of judicial powers, it adjudicated in administrative and ultra vires actions (Brown 71). The *Majlis* started the tradition in

Egypt of judicial review of the constitutionality of legislation. Its most well-known chairperson was Al Sanhuri. He belonged to the political opposition of the Wafd Party, which had held power up to the Nasir revolution in 1952. Al Sanhuri had no fear of issuing stays of execution of government measures. He ruled against the government on a law which it had not submitted to the *Majlis* as required under law. As shown below, this set a powerful precedent for present-day judicial practices (see below on Sadat's personal status decree).

Courts after the Nasir revolution

The monarchy was overthrown in a military coup in 1952. The revolutionary socialist government of President Nasir (Nasser) was established. The new government tackled the court system. It consolidated the courts. The religious courts, the Sharia and the Milli (for Christians), were abolished under Law No. 462 of 1955, in force since 1 January 1956. (Najjar 320). The Copts it is said did not protest as the ex-Minister of Justice, a Copt, had been in favour of such a move. Only the Catholics protested momentarily (Brown 66, 92). The National Courts assumed their jurisdictions. While this was a bold move in terms of form, in terms of substance, it was not innovative. The religious law continued to be applicable. The new courts were to apply the religious law according to the confession of the parties. In the case of the Christians, the churches still to this day have to give an opinion before a court judgment is issued (Hill 1979, 92).

The National Courts have jurisdiction in civil matters (Hill 1979, 17). At the first level are the summary or petty sessions courts (*mahakim juzaiya* (*guzai*)). They have jurisdiction over marriage dowers or change of domicile, for example. At the next level are the first instance courts (*mahakim ibtidaaiya*), which hear appeals from the summary courts and where divorce petitions are heard as well as inheritance cases involving large amounts. Both courts are divided up into specialized chambers: for personal status matters, commerce, housing, revenue, guardianship, labour and injunctions.

Cases from the first instance courts go on appeal to the *mahkama al istianafi*. At the next level is the Court of Cassation (*mahkamat al naqd*). It can interpret the law and hear retrials as well as break with precedent, that is, it can find that an earlier interpretation of the law is no longer appropriate. It has civil and criminal chambers (Hill 1979, 21).

In the course of the years following the coup, however, the Nasir administration deviated from its original streamlining policy. It re-introduced complexity into the system of courts. It created special courts alongside the National Courts. First was the Court of Revolution (*mahkamat al thawra*) (Brown 80). It was used occasionally against sedition (1953–1954, 1967, 1971). Then came the People's Courts *mahkamat as shab*, similar to those established after the revolution in Mozambique) with lay judges (Brown 80, Hill 1979, 52). These did not last very long, only from 1954–1955. They were used mainly for prosecuting members of the Muslim Brotherhood.

In support of Nasir's nationalization policy a special Court of Sequestration was established (*mahkamat al hirsa*) (Brown 110). The State Security Courts were established in 1958 to deal with offences against price control laws (Brown 112). Extra-military courts came into existence in 1966. Civilians were subject to their jurisdiction in regard to crimes involving the armed forces (Brown 114). In 1969 a new Supreme Court was established. It stood over the Court of Cassation (*mahkamat al naqd*). Its function was to assure that the National Courts and Court of Cassation issued judgments that were consistent with the tenets of the socialist revolution (Brown 91).

To strengthen the enforcement of the laws enacted in the spirit of socialism the office of the Socialist Public Prosecutor was created. Its function was to secure the rights of the people, the security of the political system and commitment to socialist behaviour (Brown 95).

Courts under Sadat and Mubarak

Sadat took over the reins of government after Nasir's death in 1970. Sadat continued the policy of creating special courts. In 1980 the Court of Ethics was created to protect values from dishonour. It replaced the Court of Sequestration, which had been created to uphold the nationalization policies of the revolutionary government. The new Court of Ethics handled cases brought by the Socialist Public Prosecutor involving offences against the political and economic order. Persons who had amassed large wealth were investigated and funds sequestered to prevent such persons from leaving the country (*mahkamat al qiyam*) (Brown 110). The Court of Ethics also heard disputes over disqualification of candidates running in labour union elections, but its decisions upholding qualification were often overturned by the administrative chamber of the State Council (Rosberg 201).

One significant development was the renaming of the Supreme Court, which had been placed over the Court of Cassation in 1969. In 1971 it was renamed the Supreme Constitutional Court (Brown 94). It has taken on in the course of the years a pronounced profile, making itself independent of the executive in the tradition of the former *Majlis al Dawla*, which had laid down the principle of judicial review of the constitutionality of legislation under Al Sanhuri. It has developed a bold jurisprudence with a liberal socialist orientation, even in disputes involving competing interpretations of Islamic law. At the same time it serves as a guardian of democratic procedures. For example, it declared the 1983 election law unconstitutional because of restrictions placed on voters' rights. It also declared Sadat's presidential decree on divorce unconstitutional because the executive had bypassed parliament on a matter which could only be the subject of a parliamentary enactment and not of a presidential decree, which was reserved for urgent state matters (Brown 105).

Upon the assassination of Sadat in 1981 Mubarak succeeded. Under his government the jurisdiction of the military courts was strengthened in so far as the President of the Republic may transfer cases to the military court. The military courts were seized with jurisdiction over the trials of the violent fundamentalist Islamists in 1992 (Brown 114).

Summary of the court system

In summary, the judiciary consists of the following courts, as established under the Constitution of 1971 (amended in 1980):

National Courts (Summary, First Instance, Appellate, Cassation) – with general jurisdiction, including Sharia personal status law (Arts. 165–7 of the Constitution: *Mahakama*, as elaborated in the Law of Judicial Authority No. 46 of 1972). Since 2004 family law chambers have been introduced in the Summary and First Instance Court levels (starting in Cairo, Giza and Sharkiya with their own family-disputes-settlement offices separate from the other court chambers – to protect children asked to give evidence) (Law 10 of 2004, 18 March 2004). Family law appeals go to a specialized circuit of appeal.

State Council – for administrative disputes and disciplinary cases (Art. 172 of the Constitution: *Majlis al Dawla*).

State security courts – functions prescribed by law (Art. 171 of the Constitution: *mahakam amn al dawla*).

Supreme Council – headed by the state president, to be consulted on draft laws relating to judicial organization (Art. 173: *Majlis ala*).

Supreme Constitutional Court – jurisdiction over the constitutionality of laws (Arts. 174–8 of the Constitution: *mahkama dusturiya al aliya*).

Military courts – functions prescribed by law (Art. 183 of the Constitution: *askari*).

Consultative or Advisory Assembly – to be consulted on draft laws as to their compatibility with Islamic law (Art. 195 of the Constitution: *Majlis as shuri*).

Political background since 1952

The complexity of the Egyptian court system reflects the complicated political situation – internationally and nationally – in which Egypt found itself just before the monarchy fell and for almost 20 years afterwards. Already in 1948 as the Palestinian war erupted, martial law was declared in Egypt (Shepard xvi). Four years later the Egyptian military staged a coup. Nationalization of the Suez Canal followed. As a result, Egypt became embroiled in a war with the British and French. Then followed the crisis with the Palestinians and the Israelis. The Egyptians had financed the Palestinian liberation movement, in the hope that it would suffice to simply aid the Palestinian cause. War, however, broke out. The Egyptian government stood behind the Palestinians and directed resources towards a war costly in funds and human capital.

On the national front politics moved from a strategy of alliance to polarization. The Nasir government had come to power in an alliance with the Muslim Brotherhood (*jamiyat al ikhwan al muslimun*). The Brotherhood had been founded after the First World War shortly before Egypt's Independence. Thus it had already existed 24 years before the military coup under Nasir's leadership and had its own autonomous base of power. It had been founded by Hasan al Banna as a society for moral guidance, an alternative to two other similar organizations (Eccel 513ff; Abdelnasser 25).

The alliance between Nasir and the Brotherhood showed cracks shortly after the military coup. Differences arose over the plans of the Nasir government to introduce a programme of Arab socialism. A tract in support of the government was distributed. It was written by a member of the classical ulama class. It supported moderate socialism as a legitimate tool to fight class exploitation (Eccel 402, 411). A response quickly appeared presenting counter arguments. It was published by the Muslim Brotherhood in the form of a pamphlet written by Sayyid Qutb, a member of the propertied and pious class (Shepard). He criticized the socialist tract for undermining the right to private property (including private *waqf* for religious and charitable support). In his tract, *Social Justice in Islam* (1949), reissued under the auspices of the Muslim Brotherhood in 1954 (*Al aadalah al ijtimaaiyya fi al islam*), Qutb, of a propertied family, defended private property as the basis of Islamic life (Eccel 412; Akhavi). He was hanged for treason in 1966.

The mufti at the time, Hasanayn Makhluf, expressed sympathy for the position of Qutb. The mufti opposed nationalization and sought to strengthen ties with the King of Saudi Arabia (Skovgaard-Petersen 173), who was within the ideological and financial ambit of the United States, which opposed Nasir's ideological and financial alliance with the Soviet Union.

In terms of women's rights at the time, the Muslim Brotherhood had no problems accepting a woman in their ranks of leadership. She was Zeinab al Ghazali. She championed women's rights, specifically, the right to active participation in public life, the right to work outside the home and the right to have the husband pay for household help. She herself set an example for others. In order to have a free hand to leave the marital domicile to participate in political activities, even late at night, she wrote into her marriage contract the right to divorce in case her husband decided to restrain her from engaging in various activities. When her husband no longer wanted to abide by the agreement, she promptly divorced him (Hijab 56–7).

In the course of the ensuing decades the Egyptian governments banned, unbanned, and rebanned the Brotherhood, depending on the extent of political unrest in the country. Between the government and the Brotherhood began a struggle over control over the popular mystic orders, which have long roots in Egyptian history (Saeed 123). The struggle culminated in an attempt to overthrow Nasir. Nasir won the upper hand and had many Muslim Brotherhood members imprisoned. Nasir went so far as to nationalize Al Azhar University. The result was that many Egyptian intellectuals went into exile. The Saudi Arabians gave refuge to those Egyptian intellectuals who propagated conservative reformism (Skovgaard-Petersen 189).

After the death of Nasir, Sadat came under pressure from the market-oriented international lenders of capital for development. He modified the previous socialist course of Egypt. This change of course evoked intellectual opposition, such as by Hasan Hanafi, a philosopher of the Islamic left. He accused Sadat of abandoning Nasserite social policy (Akhavi 378). Sadat also started a new religious policy. He began to have the state sponsor religious programmes in the hope that these would prove to be viable alternatives to those of the Muslim Brotherhood (Hijab 5). By this time the Brotherhood had splintered into various groups. Some used terrorist tactics to destabilize the regime. These culminated in the assassination of Sadat after he signed the 1979 peace treaty with Israel.

Against this political turbulence on the national and international scene, what place did family law and women's rights have? It is not surprising that these concerns too were overlaid with the social consequences of war and insurrection. The internal political turbulence had brought with it intellectual polarization. The wars with Israel sustained the dominance of the military (Nowaihi 110; Najjar 321). A militarization of a society necessitates in turn hierarchization at all levels of society, including within the homes of soldiers, mobilized for long stays away from home. Thus it is no surprise that the issue of reforming the family laws affecting women's rights stirred heated debates in Egypt. Militarization of the society – however good the cause may be – not only exhausts its resources for social needs; it also affects the relations between men and women. Mobilization of men in a *jihad* requires strict hierarchical obedience from men. Men need to be assured that the women left behind know their place in the home, under the leadership of an absent husband, and are as obedient as a soldier to his commander. Even in the classical writings of the jurists some of the Hanafi authors explicitly linked obedience of men to the ruler to women's obedience to their husbands and loyalty to him as lord of the house (Meron 221). They were interpreting the Quranic warnings to men not to be disobedient towards their wives and their wives not to be disobedient to their husbands in a context of militarization and not in the context of equality between spouses.

Another factor that has militated against reforms in family law and women's rights was the antipathy of the upper classes towards the poorer classes. The socialist revolution had not completely overcome the long tradition of social cleavages and hierarchy (Saeed 131; Najjar 322). The upper classes had little interest in relying on laws and courts to settle personal family disputes. This has long historical roots. Throughout the centuries in Egypt it has been observed that each social and economic class has different attitudes towards the use of courts to claim rights, the poorer having frequent recourse to courts, and the elite generally finding it vulgar to mix with the masses in such public fora like courts (Crecilius 234; Hill 1979, 9, 59, 90; Eccel 8). Naguib Mahfouz's novel, *Miramar*, is a brilliant portrayal of the entrenched attitudes of the ruling elites in general and of men in particular towards the servant class and women. A central character, a peasant girl, who is a servant in the boarding house, has to fight for her personal and sexual dignity against men boarders, regardless of whether the men are loyalists of the old regime or supporters of the revolutionary regime (Mahfouz 1998).

Efforts to codify and reform the law of personal status

As already mentioned, Qadri Pasha wrote and published a Code of Personal Status (Bellefonds I:37)[5] at the end of the 19th century. It was never enacted. As a result, there is no one code regulating family matters. Instead there is a myriad of statutes regulating different aspects of family matters. The Qadri Pasha code merely serves as a reference point for the law-makers.

The basic piece of legislation that governs personal status is a law enacted in 1920.[6] It regulates basically maintenance. This law was amended in 1929[7] and 1985.[8] This law is evidence of the reluctance of the early Egyptian state to interfere in family religious law. It preferred to limit interference to the materialistic aspects of marriage and divorce because these involved civil processes of execution of orders before the National Courts rather than the Sharia courts.

Law of 1920

After consultation with the Sheikh al Azhar, the Maliki Sheikh, the Mufti, other ulamas and the council of ministers, the Sultan of Egypt promulgated Law No. 25 of 1920 on maintenance and certain aspects of personal status.[9] The law was intended to deal with husbands who were not paying their wives maintenance. Maintenance was pragmatically defined as a civil debt on the husband.

Nature of maintenance – a debt

Classical debate

The legal nature of maintenance was the subject of dispute among and within the schools of law. Within the Hanafi schools there was a division of opinion on the nature of maintenance: was maintenance an element of the marriage contract? Or did it have the nature of a contract separate from the marriage? Or could it be classified as an exchange of mutual gifts, the wife giving her husband obedience in exchange for his giving up his freedom to spend his income as he liked, though his wife retained the freedom to spend her income as she liked (Meron 26–39).

The Hanafis did not all agree with the Maliki and Shafii opinions. The Maliki and Shafiis opined that maintenance was a contractual matter. Some of the Hanafis disputed this approach because it was feared that this would give the wife the chance to contract out of maintenance for herself (though not her children).[10] This would have released the husband of the duty to maintain and rendered maintenance a matter of mutual charity. It would also have deprived the husband of his claim to his wife's submission to his will (Meron 22, 212, 241).

1920 legal approach – debt

The final version of the 1920 law treated maintenance arrears as having the nature of a debt, which was closer to a contractual approach.

The debt could be created in three ways: l) by way of a legal presumption, that is, the married status creates automatically on the husband the obligation to pay maintenance to the wife; 2) by way of a court order; and 3) by way of a contractual agreement between the spouses.[11] The law's recognition of the varying ways in which the maintenance debt could be created was an acknowledgment of the legal differences of opinion among the classical jurists. There is no overriding principle of Islamic law on this matter which could be taken for granted.

The debt on the husband could be extinguished in two ways: 1) the husband fulfilled it by paying the arrears; or 2) the wife waived the debt. This meant that the husband could not automatically extinguish the duty to pay arrears by simply divorcing his wife.

Restrictions on duration of the idda *for purposes of maintenance*

The 1920 law also specified the times during which the husband had to pay maintenance. He had to pay as long as the marriage existed and for a limited time after divorce. The post-divorce maintenance payments were due only during the *idda*. The length of the *idda* depended on whether the divorced wife was pregnant or not.[12] When she was not pregnant, it lasted three months, assuming that she had her menstrual cycle once a month. If she were pregnant, the *idda* could last for at least nine months and beyond. There were women who were claiming that they were pregnant for years far beyond nine months because the foetus had decided to go to sleep. Under Maliki law a foetus could sleep for up to seven years, under Hanafi law two years, and Shafii four (Coulson 1991, 174). The law in 1920 put an end to this by limiting the *idda* to an absolute maximum of three years.

The law prohibited the courts from hearing evidence that a woman in *idda* had intervals between her menstruation periods lasting longer than a year. That meant that women could still bring evidence that the intervals were from one to eleven months, up to a maximum of three years.

The position of the woman who was breastfeeding was not as precisely regulated under the 1920 law. It was provided that if she had no menstruation while breastfeeding, then the three years would start to run only after the breastfeeding. By implication, if she had menstruation during the breastfeeding, then she would get maintenance for a maximum of three years. But if she had no menstruation, she could prolong the maintenance payments for as long as she breastfed. There was no time limit set on the duration of her breastfeeding. Such provisions left room for judiciary discretion. The civil courts would have had to consult with the qadis in the religious courts about what was a reasonable time limit on breastfeeding. Or else the question would have to be referred to the qadis for resolution. This would prolong the duration of the original maintenance litigation brought in the state civil courts.

Buying on the credit of the husband or divorcing the husband for failure to pay maintenance?

Classical legal approach

The classical Hanafi law did not permit a wife to divorce her husband on grounds of his failure to pay maintenance. The wife had two possible legal remedies open to her. For one, she could buy on credit in his name. Then the debt was owed to a third party. Or the wife could put out her own money, then claim it as a personal debt against her husband (Quadri 109, n.9). In contrast to the Hanafis, the Malikis and Shafiis permitted the wife to seek divorce on the ground that the husband was not paying maintenance.

1920 legal approach

In the Egypt of the 1920s the statutes regulating debts had become so complicated, that the Hanafi solutions were rendered impractical. By the 1920s written evidence was required to prove a debt. A wife had to present written evidence of credit from third parties. Or she had to present written documentation of what she had spent from her own income for her own maintenance. Furthermore, a poor absent husband would most likely be so credit-unworthy that his poor wife could not even take advantage of the Hanafi rule allowing her to buy on credit. Even if she did not buy on credit and used her own meagre income, it would not have been enough to maintain both herself and her children.

Thus it is understandable why the law of 1920 did not regulate the wife's right under Hanafi rules to buy on credit. Instead, the lawmaker sought another solution. It turned to the Maliki and Shafii rules. The Egyptian qadis of the latter schools were accustomed to giving the wife two options. She could either sue for maintenance arrears or the qadi gave her a divorce for lack of maintenance.

*Forced divorce (*tatliq*) for lack of maintenance*

Under the 1920 amendments, once the evidence established that the husband had no means to pay, or if he had means, but ignored an order to pay arrears within a time limit set by the court, the qadi could order a forced divorce (*tatliq*).[13]

The 1920 law set limits, however, on this form of 'forced' divorce for failure to pay maintenance. The divorce order was equivalent to only a revocable *talaq*. This meant that the wife had to enter *idda* upon receiving the court order. The husband could revoke the court-ordered divorce only if he declared that he would start paying the arrears. The law left open the question of when the revocable divorce could become irrevocable. Was the divorce irrevocable as soon as the *idda* expired? Or did the qadi have to reissue the divorce order two more times, giving the husband two more times to reconsider and pay the arrears?

Absent husbands

Classical legal approach

If a husband were absent for four years and left no means of maintenance, the Hanafis insisted on, first, a declaration of presumption of death of the husband, which was possible only after expiry of his presumed life expectancy (90 years), then, secondly after that period, a declaration of widowhood (Coulson 1971, 196). The Maliki and Shafii, in contrast, recognized such a declaration of widowhood after four years of absence of the husband. There had arisen in the Islamic literature a controversy about whether a Hanafi court could apply the Maliki *ijtihad* so that the wife need only wait four years before seeking a divorce. The Ottoman jurist Abu Suud of the 15th century was against applying the Maliki rules outside Maliki territory. Four centuries later in the 19th century Ibn Abidin of Egypt disagreed on the basis that social necessity required choosing the best rule from among the various *ijtihad* (Karaman 689).

The Egyptian law-maker adopted the tolerant approach of Ibn Abidin. The 1920 decree combined the Maliki, Shafii and Hanafi rules for an absent husband who sent no news to his wife. In such circumstances the Egyptian court was not allowed to issue an order of divorce for lack of maintenance. The court had to demand that the Ministry of Justice start a search for the husband. The search could last up to four years. If after four years, the husband was still not found, the court was to notify the wife of the futility of the search.[14] She was then to enter *idda*, equivalent to that for a 'putative widowhood' (Coulson 1971, 198). After the expiry of the *idda*, there was no order of divorce. There was instead a declaration that the woman was now eligible for remarriage. That meant that the absent husband retained a limited marital right. The law permitted the husband, if he reappeared, to reclaim his wife, despite remarriage, on one condition. That was, that she had not consummated her new marriage.[15]

Out of the combination of opinions of the two schools came in effect a compromise. The missing husband who returned retained his status under Hanafi law to a limited extent and the wife could have limited relief more quickly under the Shafii rules. She had to wait only four years instead of 90 years. This approach mirrored the strategy of the brilliant jurist Sanhuri, who sought to make out of the old something new (Hill 1987, 93).

Divorce owing to defects in the husband

Classical legal approaches

Again the Maliki qadis were accustomed to allowing women to divorce on the ground of defects in the husband, e.g. illnesses like insanity, sexual diseases, leprosy. The Hanafi were stricter. They had recognized only the incapacity of the husband to consummate as a defect and ground for divorce by a woman. The Hanafis had obviously considered consummation to be a marital obligation that was fundamental to the essence of the marriage.

The 1920 law adopted the Maliki position. It conferred on the wife the right to petition for divorce for reasons of illness of the husband. The law-maker, however, wanted also to give due credit to the Hanafi conservatism and not make it too easy for the wife to divorce. Hence the law-maker invoked a general principle that was to govern the petition for divorce because of defects in the husband. The principle was harm. This meant that the wife no longer established her case by merely presenting certificates proving the ill-health of her husband. She had to bring evidence of medical experts showing that she was harmed by continued cohabitation.[16] There was no automatic presumption that the condition of her husband was harmful to the wife. Woe, however, to the wife, who had known before the marriage of these illnesses. Even if she had thought at the start of her marriage that she was capable of dealing with such defects in her husband or had banked on his being cured, the law did not take into account the fact that her capacity to handle the situation could change in the course of the years, thus rendering the marriage a hardship. Divorce on grounds of such defects was possible only if the wife did not know of the defects at the time of the marriage.[17]

The nature of the divorce order in these cases of dire illnesses of the husband differed from that in maintenance cases. The divorce order for reasons of defects and illnesses was immediately irrevocable.[18]

Forced talaq *(*tatliq*)*

The 1920 law reflects the extreme caution of the law-maker in interfering with the husband's prerogative to initiate divorce. In cases of default in maintenance payments, the wife did not enter a petition for divorce, i.e. she could not initiate divorce. Thus she could not replace her husband's will with her own will. Only the court could initiate the divorce and thus replace her husband, and not even entirely. The qadi could issue only a revocable *talaq*. This left the husband room to react and exercise his will. A court-ordered divorce, a forced *talaq* (*tatliq*), was of only temporary effect.

The aversion to forced irrevocable *talaq* has long roots in Egyptian history. In past centuries the political powers had been known to interfere in marital relations and force the husband to utter a *talaq*. This was an abuse which may have led to an overreaction, that is, an extreme protection of the husband's *talaq* prerogative. A following report in the Egyptian Chronicle can be used to illustrate this point (Crecilius 208):

> During the time of Ali Pasha al Izmirli (1717–1719) (1129–1132) a woman married to a money-changer fell in love with one of the soldiers. She went to the commander demanding that he divorce her from her husband and marry her to the soldier. She promised to give him the share of the divorce settlement as 'the price of your coffee'. By settlement she meant the rest of the delayed *mahr* which her husband owed her upon divorce. He told the money-changer to divorce. He refused as she was the mother of his children and he had lived with her eleven long years. The commander ordered him to be beaten. He relented, divorced the wife and was released. The commander then demanded that the money-changer pay the divorced woman the delayed *mahr*, but the husband said that he had divorced under duress and so did not have to give it. He was locked up. The commander said he should stay locked up until he agreed to pay the delayed dower, the *mutaa* and the *nafaqa* for the *idda*. Friends of the money-changer came and paid the money. He was released. Then the commander told the professional witness (notaries, *shahid*) to draw up a marriage contract between the newly divorced woman and the soldier. He said he was acting as her agent (as a father would do). The commander then used the money he got as the *mahr* for the marriage of his soldier. The notary refused, saying that he could not marry them until the *idda* was over. But the commander was impatient, saying that

marriage was better than adultery and the contract was drawn up. She left with the soldier. The notary then moved away to another town and did not return until the commander left Cairo.

This report can be interpreted in several ways. One way is to interpret it in favour of the husband's right to retain control over divorce. On the one hand, it shows that a wife who did not love her husband any more had no chance to divorce. Lack of love was not a ground for petitioning for divorce. Her only way out was to collude with political authority. Her husband, however, was doing his best, providing for her and the children. He had no reason to divorce her. He seemed to still love his wife and not to be the sort of person who would have arbitrarily divorced his wife. He appears to be the innocent party in this story. So the moral of the story would be that good husbands should be left alone to exercise the *talaq* when good reason is there. The state should not interfere.

Another way to interpret the story is that husbands' control over divorce can be arbitrary. In this case one has to pay close attention to the behaviour of the commander. The commander forced the *talaq* because he was motivated by professional interest as well as his own greed. He had a professional interest in keeping his soldiers happy and in making some financial gain. He was judge in his own cause. He was thus acting no better or no worse than a husband. A husband is equally judge in his own cause when he exercises *talaq* unilaterally. He is judge of his own conduct towards his wife, of whether he is sensitive or insensitive to her needs and vice versa. *Talaq* is only a privilege, a right, not even a duty. Thus exercise of such a privilege conflicts with a fundamental principle of justice that one may not be judge in one's own cause,[19] which is the case in *talaq* when the sole judge is the husband.[20] If the wife had a corresponding privilege, whereby she is also judge in her own cause, i.e. both become judges in their own cause, then the violation of that fundamental principle of justice might be tolerable. If the state is not going to tolerate an outside authority abusing the husband's *talaq* and forcing him to exercise *talaq*, then why should the state tolerate a husband abusing his own *talaq* privilege and not take steps to prevent abuse.

Nonetheless in 1920 the state was more interested in protecting the husband's right to *talaq* from abuse by the state than protecting the wife against abuse of *talaq* by the husband.

Law of 1929

Nine years after the 1920 law on divorce King Fuad of Egypt issued another decree-law to modify the law of divorce. He consulted with the Ministry of Justice and Council of Ministers before issuing the decree.[21] The decree changed the law on maintenance claims during the *idda* and conferred on the wife the right to initiate divorce petitions on grounds of harm and/or absence of the husband. The law added provisions relating to the husband's right to exercise *talaq*.

Measuring post-divorce maintenance in the idda

The new provisions relating to post-divorce maintenance during the *idda* expressly laid down the financial capability of the husband as the sole criterion for measuring the amount of maintenance due. The amount of maintenance due was to be measured according to the means of the husband and not according to the needs of the wife. His status was decisive, not hers.[22] This meant that in regard to the legal nature of maintenance, the decree-law emphasized maintenance more as an integral element of the marriage. Maintenance was thus treated as inherent to the husband's marital obligations, and less as a function of the contractual rights/duties of the wife. This was a partial return to the approach of many Hanafi jurists, which de-emphasized the wife as a creditor of her husband and more as an entitled donee (Meron 226). Her right to maintenance was treated as a debt on the husband only for the one month preceding her petition to the court (Bellefonds II:27), given that she was entitled to receive her maintenance at the start of the month in general (Meron 292, 143). This approach was also more aligned with the Shafii rule that the husband's wealth was the sole measure of maintenance (Bellefonds II:262).

Not all of the Hanafi jurists accepted the point of view that only the means of the husband was the measure. Many were willing to take into account the status of both spouses when setting the amount of the maintenance. If one were rich and the other poor, then the average of their fortunes was taken as the measure of maintenance (Meron 227; Alami 117). One sees in the diversity of approach to this question a jurisprudential struggle. The Islamic jurists of old had adopted different points of view and rules because they classified the legal nature and principles of various duties and rights differently. Even the hadith collections had dealt with and classified *nafaqa* differently. Malik had not even listed *nafaqa* as part of the chapter on marriage, only mentioning it as a matter of paying for the upkeep and lodging of a divorced wife as long as she had to stay in *idda* to determine for the sake of the husband whether she were pregnant or not. In later glosses it was taken for granted that the husband was to maintain and lodge the wife (Qairawani 47). While Bukhari included a chapter devoted to *nafaqa*, Muslim placed *nafaqa* in the book on charity (*zakat*, with a sub-chapter on gift, *sadaq*). The Egyptian law-makers did not have an easy task in trying to determine which of the basic approaches they should adopt.

Length of the *idda*

The decree-law of 1929 introduced a new time limit on the duration of the *idda* for purposes of maintenance. The decree in effect abrogated Article 3 of the law of 1920 on the length of the *idda*.[23] The earlier maximum of three years was reduced to one year from the date of the divorce.[24] This clearly meant that even breastfeeding women were limited to three years.

Divorce by the wife for reasons of absence of the husband from the marital home

Another change made in 1929 added to the list of reasons for which a wife could initiate a divorce petition.[25] The 1920 law permitted the qadi to take the initiative to impose divorce if the husband failed to maintain her. Previously a husband could stay away from home as long as he wanted as long as he left behind enough property to maintain his wife. The 1929 decree-law removed this absolute prerogative. Now the husband was allowed to be absent – even if he were not in default of maintenance – up to one year. Beyond that he had to show that he had a legitimate reason for his absence. This meant practically, however, that he was not fulfilling his wife's sexual needs. It also meant, practically speaking, that a woman did not have to worry about whether she was obedient to her husband or not. The wife's petition on grounds of absence for a year or more was not automatically to be granted. The qadi had to give the absent husband a chance to correct the situation by asking him to return within a certain time or to make arrangements for the wife to move to him. Failure of the husband to comply with the request resulted in a divorce. The divorce pronounced by the court was deemed irrevocable.[26] If the husband of course had good reasons to be absent, the wife had to put up with non-fulfilment of sexual relations.

What constituted legitimate reasons for the absence of the husband was an issue left to the discretion of the court.

These provisions indicate that the Egyptian law-maker was adopting the view that sexual relations do not belong to the essence of marriage. The only sexual act that is an essential element for the marriage is consummation at the start of marriage, a duty on both spouses, breach of which has legal consequences. When one of them does not agree to consummate, then it is ground for ending the marriage contract. In popular belief the woman can be forced to consummate, but in law, the situation is more complex. Hanafi jurists wrote much about whether the husband had a duty to perform sexually in the marriage once it was consummated. Much of the debate was based on one premise, namely, the hierarchical nature of the relationship between husband and wife. The issue could never be resolved, however, because the premise of hierarchy contradicted the premise on which the rules relating to sexual consummation at the start of the marriage were based: that premise was the equality of the spouses. The consummation of the marriage was allowed only if the wife had given her consent to the marriage contract, just as the husband had given his. If once having consented, she still did not wish to consummate the marriage, the husband had only one remedy at law. Nowhere in the Quran or the hadiths is it mentioned that the remedy is the right of the husband to force consummation of the marriage. The sole remedy mentioned is that he may recover half of the marriage dower, the *mahr*.

Despite differences of opinion on whether the husband had a unilateral, or mutually agreed upon, duty to satisfy his wife sexually, Hanafi and Shafii jurists agreed that it was not morally correct for a husband to ignore his wife sexually (Bellefonds II:298), Ibn Hazm of the Zahiris (Bellefonds II:299) even classified such abstinence as *haram* (forbidden). This led to conferring on a qadi discretion to decide what penalties he could impose on such a husband if the wife complained. The Malikis and Hanbalis left the matter to the spouses to decide what they wanted to do to cure the situation. The husband obviously could divorce his wife if he no longer wanted to satisfy her sexually or she no longer wanted to satisfy him. The wife could also ask a Maliki qadi for divorce, pleading that the lack of sexual relations would prejudice her. The Hanbalis demanded that she tolerate such a situation up to four months of abstinence (Bellefonds I:298–9).

Again the Egyptian legislator took a mixed approach. It relied on the Maliki interpretation of the principle of mutuality in conjugal relations, but used the Hanafi strictness to temper its liberality. This approach mirrors the legal philosophy of the jurist Sanhuri of the time. In 1920 he was still a young lecturer-at-law. In his later writings he stressed the need to introduce changes in the laws only gradually and with temperance. This guarded the principle of respecting established legal relations and expectations (Hill 1987, 36). People had to be given time to rearrange their relations. This meant a compromise in the legislation, liberalizing, but with temperance (for Hanafi spouses), and restricting rather than forbidding former liberalizations (for Maliki spouses).

The 1929 decree-law had certain ambiguities. When read in conjunction with the 1920 law, the new law meant that a husband who was both absent and in default of maintenance payments was subject not only to a revocable divorce for default in maintenance, but now also to an irrevocable divorce on grounds of absence. The difference between the two laws was procedural. Under the first law the wife could file a petition relating to maintenance and the qadi could decide whether to issue a revocable divorce. Under the second law the wife could file for divorce on grounds of absence and the court could issue an irrevocable divorce. In this way, from the point of view of the wife, she did not have to place all her eggs in one basket. If one petition failed, then the she had a chance to submit the other petition. If she succeeded in both petitions, then it was simply a matter for a higher court to disentangle whatever contradictions might have arisen.

Divorce by the wife for reasons of harm

The second ground that the 1929 decree-law specified for a divorce petition by the wife was injurious acts by the husband. She has to prove that he had made the marriage impossible for her, a hardship in effect. The concepts of 'impossible' or 'hardship' are not defined in the law. It could cover a multitude of tortious acts such as mental and physical cruelty. Injury has also been defined so as to include situations in which the husband tried to take control of the wife's own property, thus threatening her financial and physical security in the marriage (Shaham 123, 132).

Even if the wife succeeded in proving her case for harm, a divorce order was not automatic. The court had first to order both spouses to appear before the court for an attempt to reconcile them. The duration of such a reconciliation process is not specified. If reconciliation proved to be impossible, then the court could order divorce on grounds of hardship and harm. The decree is irrevocable.[27]

Arbitration process

If the evidence presented by the wife seeking divorce failed to convince the court of the existence of hardship, she did not necessarily lose her case. Arbitrators had to be appointed. This solution shows the sensitivity of the law-maker towards the situation of women who feel driven to seek divorce. It is presumed that a woman who seeks divorce must have serious reasons to go so far. For that reason alone her petition cannot simply be rejected for lack of sufficient evidence of harm. Her seeking divorce is evidence alone that something is seriously wrong between the two spouses.

The 1929 decree-law provides in detail for the arbitration process. As for who could be appointed as arbitrators, only men were eligible: two from the families of each of the spouses. The families were to propose the arbitrators. They could qualify for this task if they were propertied. Presumably the idea behind this provision was that a well-off person would have more objectivity and be less subject to manipulation. Such a provision also reflected the social deference in a conservative patriarchy to the propertied classes as sources of authority and respect. Even provision was made in case there were no family members meeting these qualifications or the families were not interested in getting involved in the marital quarrel. In the latter case, other persons could be appointed. To qualify they had to know of the personal problems of the spouses and be knowledgeable of reconciliation techniques.[28] This readiness of the law-maker to allow reconciliation by friends reflected also a recognition of social changes in Egypt. The former grand mufti Muhammad Abduh had already complained at the turn of the century before last that many poor and even well-off persons were breaking their ties to their families and extended kin (Eccel 87).

The tasks of the arbitrators were clearly specified. They were to determine the causes of the conflict between the spouses and to reconcile them. They were to specify the terms of conditions each had to meet for continuing the marriage.[29]

If the arbitrators failed to reconcile the spouses, then they were to determine who was at fault, the injuries for which the husband was responsible and the injuries for which the wife was responsible. Then they could decide on irrevocable divorce.[30] It was thus possible to order a no-fault, equal-fault, proportional fault or one-sided fault divorce. Presumably their findings were the basis for negotiating the terms of a divorce settlement, whereby either had to compensate or return properties, or the financial status quo at the time of the divorce was to be maintained.

In case, however, the arbitrators could not agree among themselves about proportioning fault or about the outcome, the court was to be notified. The court then was to order them to try again. If they failed once more, two more arbitrators were to be appointed, a total of four.[31] Whether any time limits were to be set is not specified in the law. That lay within the discretion of the court. Given the even numbers appointed, a tie vote was always possible, thus extending the time needed to reach a consensus or majority vote.

The final decision as to whether a divorce should take place and the terms of the divorce settlement lay actually in the hands of the arbitrators. The court was not to interfere. The court was to order what the arbitrators had decided.[32]

Subjecting the court to the decision of the arbitrators was not novel in Egypt. It is still practised by the large Coptic Orthodox minority (6 per cent today). Grounds for divorce by either spouse is even stricter under Coptic personal status rules, divorce being allowed only for reasons of adultery or apostasy. A reconciliation process is necessary. The decision reached by the arbitrators is sent to the court, which is to follow that decision (Rugh, Bergmann and Ferid).

Problems of maintaining the wife during arbitration and litigation

What is not specifically regulated in the 1929 decree-law is the financial and living position of the woman while she is in litigation and arbitration. During this phase she would not qualify for *idda* maintenance as she was not yet divorced. At the same time, if she refused to stay in the marital home as long as the quarrel between the spouses was not settled by arbitration, her husband could argue that he was obliged to maintain her only if she returned to the marital home. However, the very process of arbitration implied that rules did not have to be applied strictly. It could be inferred from the law that the arbitrators had the authority to convince the spouses to accept either that the husband continue to maintain the wife, whether she agreed to stay in the marital home or wanted to stay in another lodging, or that the wife agree to pay for her expenses during this time of limbo. At the same time if the wife were dissatisfied with the arbitrators on the decision of maintenance, feeling that she had been compelled because the cards were stacked her, or because it was taking too long before an agreement on maintenance could be reached, the decree-law did not prevent her from complicating the process. There was nothing in the law to stop her from petitioning the court for maintenance during the arbitration process. The result would have been that she was involved in three proceedings: the one for divorce on grounds of harm, the arbitration process and the petition for maintenance.

1929 restrictions on talaq

While the 1929 decree-law extended the grounds for divorce by the wife, it restricts the husband's *talaq* prerogative. He may no longer give a *talaq* while in a state of drunkenness or under force.[33] He may not give a conditional *talaq* (e.g. if you or I do x tomorrow, then you are divorced),[34] since this is regarded as a way of intimidating the wife (Fahmi 39). He may no longer issue a single *talaq* as an irrevocable *talaq*.[35] That means if he did not revoke the first *talaq* at the end of the *idda*, it did not become automatically irrevocable. He has to repeat it two more times, and the wife has to undergo *idda* two more times before it could become irrevocable. That naturally extends the time period of the divorce process. If the wife were pregnant or breastfeeding when the *idda* started, then the husband would have to wait longer than three months before the divorce could take effect.

By regulating the *talaq* process, the law-maker was attempting to purge the society of some of the practices which had corrupted the divorce process as originally foreseen in the Quran and hadiths.

Talaq *in exchange for compensation*

One area of *talaq* is not regulated in detail in the decree-law of 1929. That is utterance of *talaq* in exchange for a compensation payable by the wife. The law-maker obviously recognized the practice as valid, as it is provided that a *talaq* is 'revocable, *except* [emphasis added] when pronounced for the third time, when pronounced before consummation of the marriage, *when pronounced in exchange for a compensation* (*talaq ala mal*) [emphasis added] ...' The purpose of this short provision was simple. The law-maker wanted merely to distinguish a *talaq* in exchange for compensation from the wife from the normal *talaq* process. Thus only one *talaq* is specified as necessary for such a divorce to take effect.[36] This meant that the divorce was quicker. The husband could not delay the wife from separating herself from him since he did not have to issue three times *talaq*. The wife had to undergo only one *idda*.

By defining a *talaq* in exchange for compensation as irrevocable, the law-maker was in effect uniformizing the judicial practice. Not all schools of law agreed on the irrevocable nature of the *talaq ala mal* (Bellefonds II:442). As a result, the qadis, depending on the school of law, had been able to give divorce in exchange for compensation with differing effects as to revocability and irrevocability.

A *talaq* in exchange for financial compensation paid by the wife has long been practised in Egypt (Shaham 149). The extent of the financial advantages conferred on the husband has varied considerably from case to case, the most extensive losses being reported to have been among poor women especially, even to the extent of their agreeing to waive the *idda* maintenance and child support (Shaham 108).

The concept of *talaq ala mal*, as used in the 1929 decree-law, reflects the acceptance of the law-maker of the peculiarly Hanafi differentiation between *khula* and *talaq* by way of a compensation agreement. Abu Hanifa defined *khula* as an agreement without compensation. It is merely an agreement to end the marriage and all outstanding credit claims that spouses may have against each other. There need not be any specific agreement on compensation. This was different from *talaq ala mal*. The latter constituted a divorce with a specific agreement of the wife to pay a specified compensation. Without this specification, compensation was not due (Bellefonds II:443).

The notion of compensating a spouse upon divorce is not exclusively Islamic. The Coptic Orthodox Church also recognizes compensation as part of divorce. The terms and conditions differ from those in the Islamic schools of law. The Coptic rules indeed require compensation. As divorce is a matter of fault, the spouse found to be responsible for the termination of the marriage is required to compensate the other spouse for all disadvantages which the divorce entails (Bergmann and Ferid).[37] As a consequence, if for example, the wife has committed adultery, she is to compensate her husband for the ensuing divorce.

*Marriage dower (*mahr*)*

Apart from divorce, the 1929 decree-law regulates litigation about the amount of the *mahr*. Establishing the amount of the *mahr* was necessary, for example, in cases of return of half of it if the marriage were not consummated; in cases where the husband sought conjugal rights over the bride, alleging that he had paid the entire dower despite allegations by the wife that it had not reached her hands; in cases of a *talaq* in exchange for return of the *mahr*; or in inheritance cases if the husband had not finished paying the *mahr* by the time the wife died. In any disputes relating to the *mahr* the burden of proof is to lie on the wife.[38] If she could not bring enough evidence, then the court would base its decision on the statement of the husband supported by an oath from him. The court, however, has to determine whether his statement under oath is credible. To do this the court has to establish what is the customary *mahr* of a woman of the social and economic status concerned. If the statement of the husband under oath does not deviate from the custom, then the court would be entitled to rely on it.

This provision laying the burden of proof on the wife was based on a presumption that the wife or her family had more say in setting and receiving the *mahr* than the husband or his family. She would have more interest in preserving the documents or properties or gifts received as the *mahr* than the husband. So the burden was placed on her to keep track of the *mahr*. This provision was an exception to the usual procedural rule that the burden of proof usually lies with the person initiating court proceedings. The position taken was based on an opinion of the Hanafi jurist Abu Yusuf (Fahmi 44).

The solution thus chosen for regulating disputes over the *mahr* reflected the practice in Egypt of secret and public dowries. For the sake of prestige a marriage contract contains a high sum, but in secret the families have agreed to a lesser sum. Or the husband has signed a promissory note that contains a sum different from that in the marriage contract. Tradition also entitles the father or agent/guardian of a bride to receive the dower directly for purposes of buying the bride's trousseau so that the husband has no chance to convince her to use the dower for his benefit. The law-maker was prepared to take into account such traditions (Shaham 29) and not upset popular expectations of financial arrangements. Otherwise, the law could have simply provided for enforcing two presumptions in the light of the usual traditional practices: one, that the agreed upon dower in the public marriage contract was the dower to be enforced; second, that the dower had been paid to the guardian and not directly to the wife. The burden to refute these presumptions would have then fallen on the husband.

Whether the law-maker had any knowledge that the social practices of those who preferred to go to Maliki qadis regarding the *mahr* differed from those going to Hanafi qadis is not clear in the explanatory notes attached to the 1929 decree-law. This would have been interesting to establish, as the legal position of some Maliki jurists differed from that of Abu Yusuf. According to Malik, a dower claim needed to be proven only in connection with proof of consummation. The full amount of the dower would be due to the woman or her agent/guardian only if consummation had been established. Without consummation only one-half could be claimed by the woman if not paid, and if the groom had paid in full, he could claim back only one-half of that amount. Given that consummation or non-consummation was the determining factor, disputes over the *mahr* were regulated according to the rules of burden of proof for consummation. So if a woman were living in her own house with her husband who contended that he had not consummated the marriage (and therefore would not have to pay the full *mahr*), then his word would be taken as true. If she lived in the house of her husband and he denied that they had consummated the marriage, then her word would be taken as true (Mokhtar 56).[39] Maliki jurists admitted that in judicial practice the application of the principle that a dower dispute is in effect a consummation dispute led to divergences from Malik's opinion. If the dispute arose before consummation, the wife and the husband were given equal chances to testify on oath. If both took the oath, or both declined, then the marriage was annulled. If the dispute arose after consummation and related only to prompt dower, not the delayed amount due on divorce or death, then the presumption of credibility was in favour of the wife, if her claim were brought shortly after the consummation. If brought long after the consummation, then the presumption was in favour of the husband (Toledano 156, 67).

Changes in personal status laws from 1929 to 1979

The next period of fifty years saw procedural changes in the personal status law (without major substantive changes), proposals for reform, rejection of proposals and political declarations on the status of the woman after the revolution under Nasir.

Statute of limitatis on maintenance claims

A 1931 law on personal status related largely to procedural matters. Basically the substance of the rights conferred on women in 1920 and 1929 was not altered, only the procedural realization of these rights. For example, a statute of limitations of three years was imposed on maintenance suits initiated by women (changed in 1985 to one year).[40]

Scope of maintenance claims for unregistered marriages

In case, however, the marriage was not officially registered, a woman could bring a maintenance suit only if the husband did not deny the marriage.[41] In cases of contention the only factor that saved women were their children. Courts did not award maintenance, but rather wages and lodging for taking care of the children or breastfeeding them (Shaham 173). No mention is made of the right of the wife to claim repayment of costs she might have borne for a servant during the marriage or repayment of her household services in case her husband had not provided her with a servant. Nor is mention made of whether the wife's claim for contributions in terms of work hours in the business of the husband were to be treated as part of maintenance claims (as occurs under the Iranian family law statute (Jones-Pauly 1996, 323)) or separately as a contractual claim.

Imprisonment of non-paying husbands

Finally, for a recalcitrant husband, a proceeding could be started in criminal court for his imprisonment up to 30 days.[42]

Criminal proceedings against disobedient wives

The 1931 law provided for the court chamber for personal status to handle cases in which the husband alleges disobedience as a defence in a claim for maintenance from the wife and has already initiated proceedings in the criminal court for an order of forced return of the wife. In the personal status litigation he may present the evidence from the criminal proceedings. The police had the power to physically force the wife to return to the conjugal home. This was unlike Tunis, where the wife was sent not to her husband's house, but to a shelter, where she could stay until a resolution of the dispute.[43] Since 1967 use of the police to enforce conjugal rights has been prohibited by administrative order, though still occasionally used (Hill 1979, 82; Shahan 73).

1945 rejection of proposals regarding polygamy

A law was proposed in 1945 by the Ministry of Social Affairs for restricting polygamy along the lines of the law later adopted in Pakistan. It was proposed that the husband not be able to marry a second wife without the approval of a court. This represented a compromise with the position of the grand mufti Muhammad Abduh, who had argued for the abolition of polygamy with allowance for exceptions in extreme circumstances. The proposal was dropped in the face of conservative opposition (Najjar 320, 322).

1962 social role of women in the Charter of National Action

The revolutionary socialist government of Nasir concentrated on the social and work situation of women, avoiding trying to co-ordinate political policy with legal changes because of the confrontation it would cause with conservative religious elements. The Charter of National Action of 1962 proclaimed gender equality, and like the Neo-Destourians in Tunisia, emphasized the role women have to play in shaping development in the country. This required free movement of women. The hope was that men would exercise self-restraint, that is, they would not exercise their rights to curtail the movement of women and thus these privileges would fall into disuse without the law having to interfere.

1979 reforms

No changes in the substantive divorce rights of women occurred until Sadat came to power. It is not surprising, since during the Nasir era Egyptians were preoccupied with surviving the war against Israel. Under Sadat peace was made with Israel.

Fifty years after the King of Egypt had introduced reforms in 1929, Sadat after consultation with the Council of Ministers and the Council of State issued in 1979 a presidential decree containing major changes.[44] He bypassed parliament because the new draft law evoked heated and long debates, bringing parliament to a deadlock. He justified the decree as an emergency enactment. He argued that the Egyptian society had changed drastically since the last substantive reforms in 1929 and was in desperate need of having an updated law. It was known colloquially as 'Jihan's law'. This was in reference to the efforts and influence of Jihan Sadat, the wife of the president, to reform the personal status laws.

The presidential decree had a short life. It remained in force four years after Sadat's death in 1981 until May of 1985. The Constitutional Court declared it unconstitutional in a case of maintenance brought by a wife, whose husband raised constitutional arguments against the validity of the 1979 law (Najjar 337, 342). The Constitutional Court struck down the law basically on procedural grounds. It ruled that a presidential decree was not appropriate for matters of personal status. A presidential decree is generally restricted to extreme emergency situations. Matters of personal status are not matters of urgency (Botiveau 1985). Thereupon the Egyptian parliament passed in July of 1985 a modified form of the decree of 1979 as submitted by the government of Mubarak.

The 1979 presidential decree continued the process started in 1920 for expanding the grounds of divorce for women and for setting formal limits on the use of *talaq*. It struck new ground, however, in two areas. It regulated polygamy, but remained cautious by dealing only with the procedural aspects of polygamy. It regulated obedience, and with regard to maintenance it entrenched the concept of imbalance between duties and rights of men and women.

Polygamous marriage as ground for divorce owing to harm

Regarding divorce by women the 1979 decree expanded the provision in the 1929 decree-law that a woman could get a divorce by bringing evidence of injurious acts by her husband that made the marriage impossible or harmful for her. The 1979 provisions specified that the notion of harm would include the act of polygamous marriage by the husband. Her petition for divorce on this ground was subject to three conditions:

i) the husband had not obtained her consent to a new co-wife;
ii) the husband was already married to another woman and had kept this secret;
iii) the wife brought her petition for divorce within one year (statute of limitations rule) of being informed of the polygamous activity of her husband.

These same provisions dealing with the right to divorce mentioned marriage contracts containing clauses – similar to those in Qairawan in Tunisia – that conferred on the wife the right to divorce in case the husband engaged in polygamy either in secret before the marriage or after the marriage. The 1979 law read into the marriage contracts an implicit clause that polygamy gave ground for divorce, even if not explicitly mentioned in the marriage contract. The burden of proof, however, became crucial. It was provided that if the wife did not have a divorce clause in her marriage contract specifying polygamy as a ground automatically for divorce, this was no reason for her to be denied a court order of irrevocable divorce. Hence if she and her husband had agreed explicitly to such a clause, then breach of the clause would serve as the basis for an automatic court order for divorce. The wife had only to bring proof of the polygamous marriage. Proof of injury was not necessary. In the absence of such an explicit clause, the burden of proof that lay on the wife was more complicated. She had to show not only that there was a polygamous marriage in fact, but also that the polygamous situation injured her, e.g. the husband was not treating the wives equally.

The opposite situation, of course, could equally occur. The wife could agree to a marriage contract clause that deprived her explicitly of the right to divorce in case of polygamy. For such situations the 1979 decree was somewhat ambiguous. It referred to a wife having one year to bring her petition from the date the harm occurred, 'regardless of her manifest consent'.[45] The implication is that even if a wife had agreed to a co-wife and believed that she could live with the situation, it could occur that she finds she can no longer tolerate it. Or it could occur that the husband ceased to treat the wives equally. In such a case the burden of proof for establishing harm would be heavier than otherwise.

Registration of *talaq*

The 1979 decree continued in the vein of the 1929 law, which set limits on the exercise of *talaq*. The 1979 decree required the husband to register the *talaq* with a notary, just as the marriage had to be registered. The *talaq* could not take effect from the date of registration, but from the date of personal notification to the wife of the registration.[46] The husband was subject to imprisonment if he gave false information about his domicile, that of the divorced wife and his social situation.[47]

Registration of polygamous marriages

The 1979 provisions regulating polygamy were also more procedural than substantive. As marriage must be registered for purposes of family law litigation, the 1979 decree extended the registration requirements to cover polygamous marriages. The husband had to specify each time he married the names and domiciles of all his wives. Certainly this was absolutely necessary in order to fulfil the Quranic limits on polygamy. A man is limited to four wives. He must also maintain all four equally. If the strict limitation to only four wives is to be protected from abuse as well as the right of all wives to equal maintenance, then registration would be needed.

Linking maintenance to obedience

The maintenance provisions of the 1979 decree were even more explicitly restrictive of the wife's rights to maintenance, in contrast to the 1920 and 1929 provisions. The latter two laws conferred on the wife the right to divorce if the husband is not providing maintenance or is absent without legitimate reason. Under the 1979 provisions the wife could not claim maintenance if she were 'disobedient' without legitimate reason. The term 'disobedience' was restricted to meaning that she had left the marital home. As a result, if she left home and the husband stopped providing maintenance, then she could no longer sue under the 1920 and 1929 laws for a maintenance order and eventually divorce for lack of maintenance. The 1979 decree permitted the husband to get a police order requiring her to return to the marital home. The wife was given the right to respond within ten days explaining why she left home and refused to obey the order. Once she responded she regained her right to maintenance. If the husband then chose not to comply, and the wife insisted on not being reconciled, the court was then obliged to start the procedures for arbitration and eventually divorce under the 1929 decree-law.

What is not clear is the role of private maintenance agreements between spouses. A marriage contract, for example, could contain a clause that the husband will provide maintenance even in the event that the wife leaves the marital home because she is suing in court for a divorce on grounds of his polygamous or harmful acts. In this event the law did not specify where the burden of proof lies. That is, if the husband were alleging disobedience, yet has a marriage contract regulating the right of the wife to be absent in case of litigation, it is not clear whether as part of his petition he was to give evidence that no such contract clause existed. If the burden of proof lay on him, then the wife would have to be exempted from having to respond within the ten day limit to a police order to return to the conjugal home in order to preserve her rights to maintenance under the marriage contract.

From one point of view the 1979 restrictions on the wife's right to maintenance paralleled earlier provisions on husbands who refuse to provide maintenance. Under the 1920 and 1929 laws the absent husband is the target of the law. He has to answer for his default, subject eventually to penal action. In the 1979 law it was the absent wife who was made accountable, subject to forfeiture of the right to maintenance and penal action.

From another point of view the 1979 decree entrenched an imbalance between the rights and obligations of the spouses. It presumed inequality of the spouses' obligations. The 1979 decree spoke of the 'absent' wife as someone who does not submit herself to her husband. The 1929 decree law speaks simply of the husband who does not fulfil his debt of maintenance. Another choice of terminology could have been made. Using the Quranic terminology, that applies the term *nashiẓ* to both men[48] and women,[49] the law could term an absent or non-paying husband as well as an absent wife as disobedient. Each would be subject first to an order to return to the conjugal home. If either failed to return within the time limit specified, and the husband additionally failed to provide maintenance, then the court could start a process of reconciliation, arbitration and eventually divorce. In addition, the spouse bringing the allegation of disobedience would have to bear the burden of showing whether the issue of disobedience is regulated in a contract between the spouses.

Further restrictions on the right to maintenance

Two other restrictions in the 1979 decree were also imposed on the wife's claim to maintenance: her apostasy (an issue discussed in more detail below)[50] and her leaving the marital home for work. Even where the wife's right to work was guaranteed by law or by custom, the husband still could contend that her working harmed the family life or that she was using her work as an excuse for something else.[51] The antidote to the law's restrictions, of course, would be a private marriage contract that bars the husband from intimidating the wife with a refusal to maintain her on grounds of her work situation. This was the solution, as mentioned above, adopted by a well-known Muslim Brotherhood woman fundamentalist.

Post-divorce maintenance: *mutaa*

While restricting the women's right to maintenance, the 1979 decree also expanded the right to post-divorce maintenance under certain circumstances: where the wife had consummated the marriage, had sexual relations with her husband, the marriage was valid, the husband used *talaq* to divorce her without her consent, and she was not at fault. She was to enter *idda* as usual. She would be entitled as usual to maintenance during the *idda* up to a maximum of one year, depending on the menstrual intervals, pregnancy or breastfeeding. The 1979 law added in addition to the *nafaqa* for *idda* the *mutaa*. The *mutaa* is a gift upon divorce which is obligatory in the Quran. It is to be of a reasonable amount. The verse has been interpreted at times in Egyptian jurisprudence as non-obligatory and other times as obligatory (Coulson 1991, 31–2).[52] The 1979 decree defined 'reasonable amount' as a minimum of two years of maintenance. Beyond that the length of the marriage, the husband's financial capacity and the circumstances of the divorce would be taken into consideration for higher amounts. This provision was Maliki-influenced. The condition that the wife be practically innocent again reflects, however, efforts to temper Maliki liberality. No mention is made, in cases of women who worked for the family businesses of their husbands, of including in *mutaa* compensation to the divorced wife for her contributions as permitted in Iran (Jones-Pauly 1996, 324).

Arbitration process

As for the divorce procedure the 1979 decree sought to regulate in even more detail the arbitration process.[53] It set a limit of six months on the deliberation by the arbitrators. Previously the arbitrators could have taken as much time as they wished. The decree also changed the relationship between the arbitrators and the court. It removed the obligation on the court to accept the decision of the arbitrators. The final decision lay with the court, to accept, reject or modify.

Co-maintenance

The 1979 decree explicitly exempted women from the duty to co-maintain their children.[54] That was imposed explicitly on the father. The law-maker did not seem to take into account the debate in the hadiths and *sunna* about the various meanings attached to the word for maintenance, about the relative financial independence of spouses *vis-à-vis* one another and their financial interdependence within the extended family (See Tunisia above). In this way the law-maker's approach resembled more that of many European legislators. The latter have emphasized the core family over the extended family and through the centuries eroded the wife's financial independence (Jones 1995; Jones-Pauly 1998). The 1979 decree, however, had a saving feature. It did not explicitly forbid spouses from regulating maintenance matters in their marriage contracts. Thus it would still have been possible for those parents who stress equality and reciprocity of duties and rights to reach their own private contractual agreements about sharing maintenance costs of children as well as regulating payments of the father to the mother of wages for breastfeeding.

As regards the maintenance obligations and polygamy as a ground for divorce the 1979 decree raised an important aspect of Islamic law, namely, the role of contract in family matters. The contract can be used to limit or extend the rights of either spouse, just as it can in matters of inheritance when women confer their shares on other relatives in exchange for support in a contractual agreement (Moors 53–5). Such a contract can be independent of the jurists' legal interpretations, especially as allowed by the Hanbali school of law, which may have been more influenced by the nomadic lifestyle in Arabia than the other schools of law which have roots in urban centres (Coulson 1991, 48–9). Certainly the advantage of allowing contractual arrangements is that it can supplement family law. For no family law, as legislated, or as advocated by any one of the thousands of Islamic jurists, can ever cover or do total justice to each individual marriage. A marriage is as different as the individuals in it. But a contractual approach also presumes a parity between the spouses and their families negotiating the contract and thus would have to allow for continual renegotiation as circumstances change. Literacy of both parties is also demanded. The contract thus serves in a way the function that equity has served in the European systems, especially in the English common law system, which had its own set of equity courts. The contract can mitigate and correct the ulama's or jurists' interpretations of the law, which are not to be taken as infallible. On the other hand, it can also introduce more injustices that again have to be corrected by the law itself as litigated before the courts. It is small wonder that there was a campaign to have more women make use of the marriage contract to assure their equality rather than their renunciation of rights (Zulficar).[55] The contract as a source of law introduces a higher degree of plurality in the law, which can be justified by the assumption (which is rebuttable) that each knows what is in her/his own best interest at any one time. The contract also reinforces private family traditions which over time form the basis of 'house law', as was prevalent among the leading ulama families in Tunis in the last century (see above) as well as in contemporary Germany.[56] Such a plural approach would also continue the 'situational' approach that has long characterized the jurists' development of the Sharia (Coulson 1991, 47). Such a 'situational' view can be said to rest on the principle (in the Sanhuri tradition) that the jurists' interpretation of the law is there to give guidance, but in the end it is the individual people themselves who have to decide what law is most just for their situation. They can decide either by making agreements or by litigating before a third party who will decide for them.

1985 law

Once the 1979 decree was declared unconstitutional for procedural reasons, the Egyptian government under Mubarak continued to press for reforms in the personal status law. Parliament finally enacted in 1985 a modified version of the 1979 decree. Law No. 100 of 1985 was introduced as an amendment to Decree-Law 25 of 1929 and Law No. 25 of 1920.

General conditions for maintenance for the wife

The 1985 law amends the maintenance provisions of Law 25 of 1920. The 1920 law had basically defined the legal nature of maintenance as a debt on the husband. The 1985 law is more concerned with the conditions that determine the husband's duty to pay and the wife's corresponding right to be paid. This new emphasis on conditions implies another view on the legal nature of maintenance. The nature of maintenance consists of a marital obligation arising from the marriage contract.[57] The Quranic basis cited is the general verse in Sura Al Nahl, which contains general moral principles for respect for God's creation, for authority, for female babies, for those who command justice and for support of family.[58] This favours a Maliki approach to maintenance in general as a contractual matter, as opposed to the Hanafi view of it as debt. Remnants, however, of the debt nature of maintenance remain, e.g. in the specification that once the husband defaults on maintenance payments, this is to be treated as a debt towards the wife.

The maintenance obligation, as was also defined in the 1979 decree, is placed in the 1985 law squarely on the shoulders of the husband, as it is specified that the obligation exists even when the wife has her own means. This reflects a more Shafii view.

As for the amount of maintenance due the 1985 law does not modify the express specification laid down in the 1929 law that the level of the maintenance is based solely on the financial capability of the husband.[59] Such a rule gives preference to the Shafii view that only the capacity of the husband counts (Bellefonds II:262), and thus makes it more difficult for courts to opt for those opinions of jurists who favoured a level of maintenance that is an average of the social levels of the spouses if they belong to different economic classes.

The nature of the maintenance is specified. It includes not only food, clothing and lodging, but also medical costs. Medical costs were controversial among the classical jurists. The modern Egyptian legislator settled for the opinion of Shaybani that an ill wife is entitled to maintenance (Meron 222).

Another element of maintenance that is not excluded, but also not expressly mentioned, concerns domestic servants for the wife. Egyptian practice long provided that a husband had to provide a servant for the wife, especially if she had children. Otherwise, in the absence of children, a servant was required only if the husband could afford this.[60] This was partly in accord with the opinions of classical Hanafi jurists, for the jurists permitted wives to claim from their husbands the costs of a household servant (or the costs of a wife's own slave, when slavery was allowed) (Meron 217–18).

The rule whereby wives could claim costs of household help has implications for other rights. The right to claim household help reinforces the wife's right to work. The right to household help provides the basis for arguments for contemporary women against husbands who dispute the wife's right to work on the ground that it interferes with her home duties. A defence would be that the jurists have obliged husbands to provide their wives with a servant – even part-time if that is all that he can afford – so that they can exercise their constitutionally and Quranically guaranteed right to work and thus earn their own living without prejudice to the welfare of the family.

Household furnishings do not belong to the classical list of things the husband must provide for maintenance. These things are governed by custom. Customarily they are brought by the wife as part of her marriage trousseau (*jihaz*). They go with her when she leaves the marriage. This custom is very old and well established, taken for granted, for example, in Mafouz's *Palace of Desire*, when the husband who has divorced his wife while in a state of anger regrets the loss of the furniture as a result of his abuse of his *talaq* power (Mafouz 1997, 281). Coptic spouses too are known to follow this custom (Fahmi 99; Rapoport). Because of the increasing value of the household furnishings, it is important that the wife keep in a safe place the list with the signature of both spouses and/or their families in case the husband divorces or evicts her or drives her away through abusive behaviour (Shaham 3; Hoodfar 66, 160). When husbands have divorced their wives and evicted them, it has been common for the wives to have the former husband jailed for illegal possession of the furnishings (Fahmi 80).[61] As the practice of an expensive trousseau was and still is prevalent in North Africa, the Maliki jurists were particularly preoccupied with contests over the furnishings. While in some instances the amount of the trousseau was larger than the amount of the *mahr*, in Egypt it was common that the amount of the two were equivalent as the bride and her family used the dower to purchase the furnishings. Some Maliki jurists had nothing against this practice. On the other hand, some Hanafi jurists wanted to keep the two matters separate as the trousseau was ascribed the nature of a gift transaction between relatives unrelated to the marriage (Bellefonds II:237, 247). Egyptian court practice has recognized claims for recovery only of the *jihaz* when it has been paid for with the dower monies (Shaham 37).

Obedience as a condition for maintenance during the marriage

While the 1920 law never explicitly made the wife's right to maintenance during the marriage dependent on obedience to the husband, the 1985 law explicitly does so. It essentially reaffirms the case law that has developed in Egypt. The courts have long held that the wife's right to maintenance is contingent on her being obedient, but have set limits on the extent of obedience required of wives (Shaham 96–7).

For purposes of a case where the husband disputes the wife's claim to maintenance on grounds of disobedience, the 1985 law defines disobedience on the part of the wife as adamantly withdrawing herself (*mumtania)* from obeying (*ata*) the husband, then further interprets 'withdrawal' to mean leaving the conjugal household without reason and refusing to obey a court order to return. The wife has thirty days to justify her actions.[62] During that time she may claim maintenance. If she refuses to give a justification, then she has to forego maintenance. She may either wait for her husband to divorce her, or she may petition for divorce on grounds of breakdown of the marriage (impossible to live together). If she decides to petition, then the court is to set in motion the procedure for arbitration and thus eventually for divorce.

In the provisions regulating the right of the wife to maintenance in general,[63] disobedience is painted with a broader brush. The wife's right to maintenance is conditioned on

i) her not adamantly withdrawing (*mumtania)* herself of her own accord without reasons;
ii) her not engaging in something over which her husband has a say;
iii) her not going out of the marital home without the permission of or without informing (*idhn*) her husband;
iv) her not leaving the house for work if the husband complains that her leaving the house is prejudicial to the welfare of the family and asks her to desist.

The wife's defence to a charge of disobedience is that custom or necessity allows her to leave without permission. Or she may rely on a provision in her marriage contract (Botiveau 1993, 222–3) or on the initial acceptance by her husband, i.e. consent by habitual silence, of her commitment to working (Shaham 82). Presumably women could also argue in their defence before the courts that it would be illegal to render the Quranic right of each spouse to their own earnings[64] ineffective if the wife were denied the right to work. Some working women, however, already consider this provision of law that deems them disobedient if the husband wants them to stop working to be highly theoretical, since they believe that no husband would stop his wife from working as life is too expensive to live on one income (Hoodfar 153). In their eyes the law merely preserves the myth of a gender construct without serving any practical purpose.

The definitions of obedience in relation to maintenance claims reflect the willingness of the legislator to be circumscribed by the terms of the debate laid down in the classical Hanafi literature. The very term used in the law of 1985 to denote disobedience derives from the Hanafi jurists. The term used is not *nushuz*, but rather *mumtania.* The term *nushuz* was used in Hanafi literature to refer to a wife who was married, but who because of illness did not move into the home of the husband. Abu Yusuf argued that only the wife who became ill after having moved into the home of her husband would have a claim to maintenance even though she is too ill to fulfil wifely duties, including intercourse (Meron 63). Shaybani in contrast was of the view that maintenance is still due to any wife who has fallen ill (Meron 257). The Egyptian legislator favoured the latter opinion by providing in the 1985 law explicitly that an ill wife does not lose her maintenance. The law leaves open to judicial interpretation whether an ill wife who stays at her parents' home, for example, is still to be considered disobedient or not.

As for the term *mumtania,* meaning a woman who makes herself inaccessible (to her husband), it was used in the classical Hanafi literature in different contexts. In strict terms it referred to the lack of obligation of maintenance by a man towards a woman to whom he should have no sexual access, that is, both parties had to restrain from intercourse, e.g. when it was discovered that the marriage was actually void (Meron 100). The Hanafi jurist, Kasani, however, used the term to cover valid marriages. The house of the husband was referred to as the place where the wife was 'tied to' certain duties, just as the husband was tied to the duty to maintain (*mahbus*, derived from the word for 'tying up' of property in a religious endowment, a *hubus*, so that it could not be freely inherited). In the case of the wife, this meant that she would not be free to do as she wished. Her situation was analogized to that of a qadi, who cannot earn a living in addition to fulfilling judicial duties (Meron 40), not even enter a sale directly without an agent mainly in order to avoid bribery (Dien 67). Hence a wife could not make herself inaccessible to the husband, no more than a qadi could become inaccessible to the people without suffering the consequences.

In contrast to the classical literature, the hadiths use the root of the term *mumtania* (*manaa*, restraining, making something impossible) in a variety of contexts. In the Bukahri hadiths when the Prophet was asked whether a wife should ask for permission to go to the mosque, he answered categorically that the husband is not to restrain her at all.[65] In effect, the husband is not to deny her access. The implication is that if the husband demanded that she ask, or if she simply informed him of her going to the mosque without asking for permission, and he restrained her, then he would be in the wrong. This enlightened attitude towards women leaving the home was reinforced in another hadith. One of the wives of the Prophet, Sauda, was out at night. Umar was also going about and saw her. He spoke to her in a seemingly chastising tone. She went to the Prophet and mentioned the incident to him. In response to her situation, the Prophet received a divine inspiration and asserted that women are allowed by God to go out for their own needs.[66] This was a way of telling Umar, who was also out at night, probably fulfilling some need too, that a man is equally 'tied' to his home and family and cannot do as he pleases. He is to go out, too, only for his needs or to fulfil his duties. Later in the Middle Ages disputes developed among the jurists over details such as to whether a woman could go to the public baths without her husband's permission (Dien 39). Those in favour of permission reflected an exaggerated reliance on what was believed to be Umar's demands for obedience over reason (Dien 105, 117) rather than on the Prophet's enlightening efforts to avoid gender differentiations. Another version of the same story contains an added comment that the woman could only go out fully covered.[67] Whether this version led elite women in certain areas to resort to the veil as a way of moving about incognito in order to circumvent men's increasing efforts to control and demand permission is still to be established by social historians.

In Muslim's *Sahih* collection of hadiths the term of *imtinaa* ('inaccessible wife') is used in a purely conjugal situation. It refers to a woman who refuses her husband sexual access or abstains from intercourse.[68] This kind of behaviour attracts the angels' attention, it is said. She is said to be cursed by the angels. While the angels may be displeased, there is no implication that her act has any influence on her maintenance rights. It is not just the wife who can decide to abstain. Muslim reported an incidence when the Prophet abstained temporarily from fulfilling his sexual duties as a husband.[69]

If we turn from the hadith literature to examine the Quran, we see a certain compatibility between the two sources. Neither ties obedience to maintenance. The root of the Quranic term used to refer to disobedience is *nashaẓa.* The term is used in relation to both women and men. When used in relation to women, it does not overtly condition maintenance on obedience (Sistes 5).[70] The obedience of women in sura 4:34 refers to obedience towards God and towards equity, not towards the husband. The women are enjoined to be fair in guarding the wealth entrusted to them by their husbands, who may be absent on business or at war, just as a man would be expected to protect the property of another who is away. The disobedience of women is referred to as a reason for a marital dispute, which the husbands can try to settle by refraining from sexual relations, but which may eventually require arbitration that could lead to reconciliation or to divorce. The disobedience of men is referred to also as a reason for marital dispute. The two spouses are enjoined to try to settle the dispute and husbands are to exercise self-restraint, but if this is not possible, then they may divorce. In effect, disobedience on the part of either spouse is ground for divorce after arbitration is attempted. In this sense both spouses have equal claims.

Thus a statutory provision that is directed only against the wife who is declared disobedient because she leaves the marital home upsets the equality of claims conferred in the Quran on both spouses. A further provision in the 1985 personal status law is needed. Provision also should be made for the husband to be declared disobedient when he leaves the home or when the nature of his work is prejudicial to the interests of the family. If the intent of the legislator is to encourage spouses to stay together, to prevent any spouse from leaving the marital home and to ensure mutual respect by each informing the other, all that would be needed would be a provision whereby either wife or husband could seek a court order of return to the marital home or an order to desist from prejudicial work. If either refused to comply, then a Quranically justified right of divorce on the basis of disobedience and disrespect would ensue. Such a solution would serve to strengthen what has been observed about the social ethic of men in Egypt. It has been observed that they give priority to family matters over work when there are problems at home (Sabbagh 133).

In this way maintenance claims or disputes over whether the wife is misusing the support she gets would be decoupled from the issue of *her* obedience alone. Maintenance as an issue can stand on its own. When kept separate from the issue of obedience, the parity between spouses as laid out in the Quran would be preserved. The Constitutional guarantee of the woman's right to work and of the state's obligation to assure that she can reconcile work and family duties (Art. 11) would also be preserved. Thus if it happens that the husband becomes disobedient because he leaves the marital home and has no reason or no wish to exercise his power of *talaq*, then he should be held liable for continuing to maintain the wife. Likewise if the wife has been disobedient by leaving the marital home and she has no reason or wish for petitioning for divorce, the husband still could not refuse to pay maintenance. He is, according to the Quran,[71] to seek arbitration. During the arbitration time he would pay her maintenance. He may practically at any time exercise his power of *talaq*. The use of *talaq* would end his obligation to make maintenance payments. Why he does not exercise *talaq* is his problem and not that of the wife. Obedience is irrelevant. Legislation which would decouple maintenance from obedience/disobedience would also conform to the judicial practice of some courts.

A report on actual divorce cases shows that some judges have little sympathy for a husband who does not exercise the power he has when the wife has left. He is not acting 'like a man' when he refuses to use such power and end his ongoing maintenance obligations. He is only humiliating the wife (Hill 1979, 74–5).

When placed in the general Egyptian culture, again one sees that obedience is not exclusively a Muslim concern. It is a general Egyptian cultural factor that is also upheld in the Egyptian Coptic law. The Coptic wife is required to obey her husband (Bergmann and Ferid).[72] The wife has a right to leave the house without her husband's permission if the reason is to further her studies. This right can be withdrawn if the parties so agree in the marriage contract (Bergmann and Ferid).[73] Like the Muslim husband, however, the Coptic husband may bar the wife from working or studying if he can prove that this interferes with the welfare of the family and he earns enough to maintain the family.

Egyptian women are known for being employed in large numbers by the government, which has made a conscious effort to give them opportunities. The proportion of Egyptian women diplomats is famously high.[74] The 1991 statistics showed that women made up at least 20 per cent of the labour force owing to a redefinition of agricultural work. This figure would probably be even higher if the informal sector were included, for the figure estimated alone for female-headed households lies between 15 and 22 per cent. In the rural areas almost 70 per cent of the families depend on the work of the women (45 per cent in the urban areas) (Nassar). There is evidence too of women controlling and putting to work the money earned by their husbands (Atiya 19). One study has nonetheless revealed that working and earning one's own money may not necessarily change the psychological attitudes of women and men towards one another. The study revealed that earning did not confer any authority on the woman. She still felt that her husband had the authority to withdraw his consent to her working (Nassar 194, 196). The results of this study, however, are contrary to those from another finding in Cairo (Hoodfar 271). Such attitudes might change if there were a campaign to educate women about the Quranic verses on the right to one's own earnings and the mutual obedience owed between spouses. But such a campaign would require a commitment by the state elite to pull back from what has been called the 'rhetoric of schizophrenia', which aims at limiting women's authority in the family on the one hand, but increasing on the other hand their visible presence at the level of public representation (Cheriet 96–7).

Apostasy and maintenance

A husband is generally obliged to pay maintenance even if his wife is of another religion.[75] This principle does not hold true in cases of apostasy. The 1985 law adds the apostasy of a wife as a ground for denying her maintenance.[76] Apostasy is not defined. It has been left to the courts to determine whether this provision is in accord with the Quranic injunction that there is to be no force in religion.[77] Equally it is left to the judges to decide how to define apostasy: whether it is limited only to denunciations of Islam or includes reconversion of a woman to a religion of the Book (Christianity or Judaism) from which she had previously converted to Islam, as happens in some cases of Coptic Christian women married to Muslim men. As, however, the 1985 law treats maintenance as an element of the marriage contract, the odd situation could arise whereby the husband refuses to pay the maintenance, but insists on staying married without all duties attached. If the wife brings a suit for maintenance, the courts may have to insist that the husband choose to divorce the wife.

The question of apostasy is not only an Islamic one in Egypt. The Coptic rules even forbid marriage between a Christian and a non-Christian (Bergmann and Ferid).[78] The very nullity of the marriage bars a claim to maintenance. If the marriage is originally between two Christians, but in the course of the marriage, one becomes an apostate, this is ground for divorce. Apostasy means converting to another religion, leaving Christianity to become an atheist, converting to a specified sect such as Jehovah's Witnesses, or being banned by the Church (Bergmann and Ferid).[79] That means that if a Coptic wife who converted to Islam sought to sue for maintenance, her husband could institute a divorce proceeding to end the marriage and thus his maintenance duty. Equally he could decide to pay the maintenance and remain married to her.

Full obligation of the husband and partial obligation on the wife for maintenance of children

The husband is explicitly made the sole person responsible for the maintenance of the minor children.[80] The wife is not obliged by law to maintain them. The criteria for the maintenance of minor children is the financial capacity of the father *and* the needs of the children. This rule holds during the marriage as well as in a post-divorce situation. The measure of the amount of maintenance owed for children is thus different than that for post-divorce maintenance of the wife consisting of the sums due during *idda* and the parting sum called the *mutaa*. For the divorced wife the sole criterion is the financial capacity of the husband.[81]

There is a time limit on the maintenance duty of the father. He is responsible until the daughter is married or has her own means and the son has reached 15 years of age or can earn independently. Age 15 is the age of majority in Islam (*bulugh*). Once the husband contests that the children can be independent, the wife may be held responsible for their further maintenance. This has happened in Pakistan, where a wife spent her own resources on the education of her sons who had attained puberty (age 15). She was denied a claim against her husband for her contribution towards the maintenance and boarding school costs of their children from the time of their puberty.[82] She received reimbursement only for the time she supported the sons before they reached 15 years of age.

Otherwise, spouses may deviate from the rules of the law by resorting to contractual agreements, as has long been the practice in Egypt (Shaham 166). They may regulate maintenance matters so that both spouses share equally in the maintenance regardless of the children's age, or apportion the maintenance according to financial capacity and/or needs.

The wife's right to divorce on grounds of polygamy

Polygamy is an issue that the Egyptian legislator has addressed at various times since the mid-1940s. Various laws regulating polygamy have been drafted but not enacted (Najjar 320). While official statistics do not show widespread polygamy (*circa* 8 per cent), it is a class-related phenomenon. Most polygamous marriages take place apparently among the lower income groups (Azer 71–3).

In addition to the right to ask the court for a divorce on grounds that the husband does not fulfil his maintenance obligation or that the marriage is a hardship, the wife may under the 1985 law petition for a divorce on the ground of the husband's polygamy. This is in effect an extension of the hardship rule. The burden of proof lies on her. She has to prove that the polygamous situation makes married life impossible. Her petition for divorce on this ground, however, is time-barred. Her petition has to be submitted within a year of her knowing of the polygamous marriage.

The 1985 law is more restrictive on the wife than the 1979 presidential decree. The 1979 decree presumed that polygamy was a hardship on the wife who petitioned on that ground for divorce. Otherwise, she would not have bothered to petition. The 1985 law removes that presumption and lays the burden on the wife to prove that polygamy is a hardship for her, even though the Arabic word for harm (*dirr*) means in itself second wife. The law does not go beyond the court practice. The courts have been reported to ask women who have left the marital home because of a second wife whether they felt harmed by the polygamous situation. If the wife answered positively, arbitration was ordered as a prelude to a possible divorce or reconciliation (Hill 1979, 75).

The law thus protects to some extent women who have not written or did not wish to write into the marriage contract a right to divorce on grounds of polygamy. Up until 1985 the right to divorce because of polygamy was enforceable only through a marriage contract. Those who did not have such a clause were at a disadvantage. What remains somewhat ambiguous is the case of a woman whose marriage contract expressly bars her from petitioning for divorce on the basis of polygamy. The law provides in general that the initial consent of the wife to a co-wife does not bar her from showing that polygamy has in fact made her marriage impossible. It is not specified, however, whether this consent may take the form of an informal oral consent, or shall be expressed as a formal term of the marriage contract.

Apart from anti-polygamous clauses in the marriage contract, it has also been a practice in Egypt for husbands to confer on wives a right to divorce on grounds of polygamy. The husband takes an oath that he will use *talaq* in case he takes a second wife. The same held true it is said in Medina, where polygamy was not customary, rather frequent divorce and remarriage (Shaham 105; Stern 32; Stowasser; Yamani).

Why the law has limited the wife's petition for divorce on grounds of polygamy within one year of knowledge of the situation is not clear. Injury can arise at any time and knows no time limits, as the husband can begin treating a co-wife unequally at any time during the polygamous marriage, not just within the first year of her knowledge of the polygamy. The time limit in effect gives the husband a licence to violate the Quranic prescription of equal treatment and love of wives[83] once the year is over. The experience of a young maid in Cairo illustrates this point. A married man asked her to marry her. He told her that he would not divorce the first wife, with whom he had children, but he did not love the first wife and never would.[84] A man's fickle love is not limited to one year. The young maid finally decided after visiting the first wife and three children that the man could not possibly support a second family.

Placing the burden of proof on the wife to show that the polygamous situation is harmful to her and makes marital life impossible reflects an overemphasis on polygamy as a *right* of the husband. When examined closely, the Quranic conditions, in contrast, present polygamy strictly as an obligation – at least as a way to score moral points under certain circumstances, especially after a wartime situation, and not as a right.[85] These circumstances are that the co-wife has to be a war captive or an orphaned widow in need or an orphan in need and not qualifying for social support from the state. It would follow that a wife would have the right to ask for divorce by proving simply that her polygamous husband had married a woman who did not meet these conditions. Proof of her state of mind and health would thus become irrelevant. The hadiths concerning polygamous marriage are silent on this. They reflect discussions only about the issue of whether a second wife-to-be could insist in her marriage contract that the husband divorce the first wife in order to avoid a polygamous situation. It was held that she could not do so.[86] The hadiths also show how Aisha classified polygamy as an example of the husband's disobedience (*nushuzann*) to illustrate the Quranic verse on the recalcitrant or *nushuzann* husband (4:128), thus supporting the Maliki hadith on the older woman who was unhappy with her husband marrying a younger wife as analysed in the next paragraph.[87] The only other *sunna* on *nikah* (marriage) that would relate to polygamy contains a prediction of a time when there will be an extreme surplus of women.[88] This implies strongly that polygamy is to be treated more as a 'situational' obligation, to be fulfilled under certain specific social circumstances, and not as a right. Otherwise, it can be prohibited for as long as those conditions do not exist in great mass. The Egyptian Constitutional Court has held that as the opinions of the *fuqaha* (classical jurists) are not imbibed with irrefutable 'holiness', consistent with the opinion of the classical jurists Ibn Hazm and Abu Yusuf (Chejne 71), so *ijtihad* on this issue of polygamy is justified.[89] Given the social nature of the obligation of polygamy under strict social and economic circumstances, any good Muslim interested in an equitable society could question whether a polygamous marriage for reasons of pure desire is tantamount to being asocial. Thus it should suffice for a wife who seeks divorce because of polygamy to show two elements: 1) that the polygamous marriage was not exercised as a social necessity; and 2) that there can be no social necessity if the state treasury is responsible for caring for orphaned widows.

But what of women, as shown in the Mailiki hadith about the marriage of the daughter of Muhammed bin Maslama Ansari, who did not want a divorce, but wanted their husbands to be considerate of them? One hadith in particular illustrates the dilemma poignantly. The older wife asked for a divorce when her husband took on a younger wife. The older woman demanded divorce twice but each time she reconciled with the husband before the *idda* ended. She had hoped in vain he would reflect on why she was asking for divorce. By the third time she asked for divorce, he warned her that it would be final. When analysed in some depth, however, the hadith raises some very difficult questions about the rights of a woman who does not really want divorce. What are the options for this unhappy couple? The husband, it is reported, felt that he had committed no sin. This raises a subtle challenge to the reader. The sensitive reader asks whether the husband can objectively judge his own conduct and the real wishes of his older wife, for the question that the husband put to his older wife is a rhetorical one: 'What do you wish?' Then he answers his own question with a threat: if you wish divorce then I shall leave you. He has not understood what the older wife really wants. She wants a divorce, but it is ambiguous for whom. For herself or for the second wife? By initiating the divorce process, she is telling him indirectly that she is unhappy with polygamy. Her request for a divorce is also a veiled threat to her husband: it is either me or her. She brings the marriage to the brink, hoping that he will choose to divorce the second wife. The husband is heedless of what she really wants. He hardens in what he wants: he wants to keep the second wife and get rid of the first. Both are terribly unhappy in the marriage. If the couple had gone to a qadi, there would have been two legal questions at issue: does the wife have an automatic right to divorce herself if her husband takes a second wife? Does the husband have the moral and therefore legal obligation to divorce not the first but the second wife if his first wife does not agree to polygamy and if he has proven himself incapable of treating the two wives equally? Answering the first question is the simpler. If the first wife is unhappy then she should be free to leave the marriage that has become polygamous. An answer to the second question is more complex. To do justice to the wishes of his older wife, the husband has to divorce the second wife. This is a limit on his freedom of feelings. Still it gives him the chance to try again to reconcile and love his first wife. If after divorcing the second wife and staying married to the first, he still cannot love the first wife, he has not lost his freedom entirely. He still has the option to divorce the first wife and only after that divorce may he take on a second wife. Jurists, however, tended to prefer simpler solutions. Hence the easier solution of giving the wife a right to divorce in her marriage contract was adopted over the more complex solution. Justice, however, would have demanded a more differentiated complex solution so that the husband does not selfishly give in to his own feelings without taking into account those of the wife. Selfishness is not a virtue in Islam.

Aisha offered in one hadith a more differentiated solution for women who did not wish to divorce, but who disliked polygamy. First of all, she classified polygamy as cruelty or desertion by the husband (i.e. *nushuz* on the part of the husband – see below regarding *nushuz* as meaning causing grave marital discord). Then she advised the woman who is in such a situation to enter into an agreement whereby the man does not divorce the woman, but they remain married; he is not obligated to maintain her and neither is she under a mutual duty to have sexual relations. The husband, if he is a good Muslim, would accept such an arrangement. If he does not, he exposes himself to being called a poor Muslim, for Aisha points out that the Quranic verse in 4:128 explicitly says that such a settlement brings about justice and peace (*sulh*).[90] The legal consequences of such a settlement for the wife who does not wish to divorce and is prepared to live practically 'celibate' are to her advantage: she has no problems relating to the custody of her children. She has her own separate accommodation. She is responsible for earning her own living. She may inherit in case her husband predeceases her. These advantages have to be relativized since they represent only a maximization of advantages in a system in which the male jurists interpreted the Sharia in their own interests in order to give a man more privileges.

Registration of a polygamous status

The husband is required, as under the 1979 decree, to specify his status when he registers each marriage.[91] He has to give the names of all women to whom he is married and their address. The 1985 law improves on the 1979 decree by requiring the official registering the marriage to notify the current wives of the new co-wife. This attempts to solve the problem of secret polygamous marriages that has long plagued Egypt (Kader 65).

Registration of *talaq*

The 1985 law adds a new paragraph to the section in the 1929 law dealing with *talaq*. Article 5 of the 1929 law makes every *talaq* revocable up to the third *talaq*. The 1985 law keeps the husband's exclusive right to *talaq* intact.

It introduces Article 5A as a procedural matter. The husband is to register the *talaq* within thirty days of the date of pronunciation. Presumably this is the third irrevocable *talaq* that has to be registered, although nothing would stop a husband from registering each of the two revocable *talaqs*. The *talaq* (presumably the third and final) takes effect only when the divorced wife is made aware of it. She may be present at the time of registration, or if she is not present, then she has to be given certified notice of the registration. Only at that point are her inheritance and financial claims on the husband affected. This means that the husband may still divorce a wife when he is absent from her or she from him.

The 1985 law does not take a stance on the debate in the hadiths about whether a husband had to pronounce *talaq* only when the wife is not in her menses, an issue which determines whether the husband may pronounce *talaq* in the wife's absence. The Quran prescribes that the husband is to use *talaq* only in conjunction with a proper calculation of the *idda*. The men are warned that the calculation of the *idda* has to be precise. This verse meant that husbands who had been pronouncing the first *talaq* while the wife was in her menses, were not giving the women the benefit of a full *idda*. With the *talaq* begins the *idda*,[92] which was the length of three periods of cleanliness. So if a husband pronounced a *talaq* in the middle of the menses, then the *idda* would have to be less than a full menstrual cycle. Thus the *idda* could not be properly calculated and the maintenance of the women during *idda* would be cut short. Consequently the *talaq* had to take place while she was not in menses. As soon as the menses began after the *talaq*, then the *idda* could be properly calculated on the basis of a full menstrual cycle. It is no wonder then that the Prophet is reported to have clearly said that a *talaq* pronounced while the wife has her menses is not valid because of the Quranic injunction that the divorce be pronounced in such a way that the *idda* can be properly calculated according to the woman's menstrual state.[93] It was Ibn Umar who was of another opinion, who felt that his divorce of his wife during her menses was valid.[94] He was obviously worried about a woman whose menses might be delayed or whose menses lasts for longer than a month after the *talaq* had been pronounced. But in such a case, the solution would have been to set a time period for such exceptional cases rather than making his solution a general rule for most women, for the Maliki hadiths say explicitly that the rule is to be followed even if a long time is required.[95] Furthermore, the Quran specifies the simple solution of setting the *idda* at three calendar months only in the case of older women and younger women who for some reason do not have monthly periods.[96]

Thus the rule that the husband may pronounce the divorce only when the wife is not in her menses discouraged divorce *in absentia.* This was another safeguard against the arbitrary use of *talaq*. In a case where the spouses were absent from one another, for whatever reason, then divorce *in absentia* could take place only if the wife informed the husband whether she was in her menses or not, as happened in the case of an Ansari woman, reported by Imam Malik to have informed her husband when she was not in her menses because she wanted a divorce from him. Her husband obliged her.[97] Likewise in the case of Abd ar Rahman bin Auf, he asked his wife to inform him when she had ended her menstruation so that he could give her the final divorce. By the time she had completed her cycle, he was ill. She informed him and he divorced her.[98] The present-day legislated solution to the problem of divorce *in absentia* is not by reference to the menstrual state of the woman, but by reference to the state's ability to inform her of the husband's actions and thereby reinforcing the husband's powers. The legislated requirement of notification of the husband's wishes removes the rule of mutuality of notification provided for under the Sharia. Under such a rule of mutuality the wife has to inform the husband when she does not have her menses, and the husband has to inform her of his use of *talaq*. The principle behind this mutuality is equality. Both spouses have the equal duty to inform.

Registration of the *talaq* has raised several problems since 1929, when the decree-law required that husbands issue three *talaqs* and not three-in-one. Notaries have been known to register a *talaq* as final without necessarily requiring evidence of whether it was pronounced under the proper circumstances (Shaham 147). The new requirement that the wife be given notice of the registration of divorce provides some check on collusion between a notary and a divorcing husband. The registration allows the wife to challenge the irrevocability of the *talaq* on grounds that it was not pronounced at the proper time during her menstrual cycle. Yet such a challenge places the burden of proof on her, whereas, it should be on the husband to prove that he had divorced properly acting on information from the wife about her cycle.

The requirement to register a *talaq* is not designed to be comprehensive. The law leaves open certain questions about delegation of the power of *talaq* from the husband to the wife. The law is formulated in such a way that it is the husband who has to register the divorce. Yet the provision that she is deemed to be notified if she be present at the registration could be read to imply that she could register the divorce on behalf of her husband because she divorced herself on his behalf, in which case he would not need any formal notification. This could be the case as long as the spouses are not members of those Shii who believe that the husband alone may pronounce *talaq* and may not delegate it (Bakhtiar 502). Otherwise, the hadiths report several instances of controversies between spouses about the delegation of the power of *talaq* to the wife. The Quranic basis of the power of delegation derives from the Prophet speaking to his own wives. If they found that they could not accept the hardships of being married to a famous man, then he allowed them to leave whenever they wished.[99] On this subject Aisha's interpretations are key. Apparently there were questions during her lifetime about whether the delegation of *talaq* was in itself a *talaq*. She denied this. The delegation of *talaq* was to be treated as an option exercisable by the wife.[100] Once this point was settled, further controversies – at least as presented in the Maliki hadiths – turned on whether the option once exercised was revocable or irrevocable. It was not clear whether the option meant that the wife had only one revocable *talaq* or whether it entailed the full power of *talaq* over three periods of cleanliness. If the latter, then she would have had to exercise the option three times as her husband would have done; if the former, then only once as the equivalent of three times. Ibn Umar is reported to have given two different opinions on this matter.[101] In one instance he decided that the extent of the power of option depended on evidence about the intention of the husband (Shaham 107, n. 31). If the husband swore that he gave only a revocable power, then the option was only for one *talaq*. Another time Umar is said to have told a husband who complained that he had given his wife the power to divorce that he had to abide by the wife's divorce, meaning that the divorce was final. When read together, these two decisions imply that the presumption is that the husband when delegating the power to divorce has delegated his full power. The burden of proof to the contrary should rest on him, namely to establish that he delegated only one revocable *talaq*.

Post-divorce maintenance: *idda* and *mutaa*

The 1985 law retains the provisions in the 1979 decree which extended the terms of maintenance during the *idda*. The 1985 law amends the provisions of Decree-Law 25 of 1929 relating to maintenance during *idda*. As mentioned, the 1929 decree-law used as the sole measure of the *idda* maintenance the financial capacity of the husband. It also limited the duration of the maintenance to a maximum of one year from the date of the *talaq*. The

Quranic and *sunna* criteria – length of the menstrual cycle or of the breast-feeding or of the pregnancy – were no longer applicable.

The 1985 law adds that the husband is also obligated to pay the Quranic *mutaa*, the price for using *talaq*, as specified in the Quran.[102] The Quran specifies that this is a 'duty on the righteous' men who use their power of *talaq* and that the amount is to be reasonable. No other conditions are specified. The 1985 law, however, specifies another condition, namely, that the wife cannot have consented to the divorce or have been at fault in the breakdown of the marriage. This provision complicates and lengthens divorce procedures in so far as the husband can contest paying the *mutaa* on the ground that his wife's behaviour was reprehensible and that was why he used *talaq*.

This linking of the *mutaa* to the innocence of the wife being divorced reflects the Egyptian culture. The Coptic rules also require a post-divorce payment (a compensation) to the partner who is not guilty of breaking up the marriage.[103]

Post-divorce lodging

The 1985 law adds to the 1929 provisions on maintenance during the *idda* a new provision relating to lodging – distinct from furnishings, which belong to the wife's trousseau – as part of maintenance after divorce. The husband who exercises the power of *talaq* is obliged to provide separate living quarters for the minor children of the marriage and for the woman who has custody of the children (often the mother and former wife or a female relative of the mother). They may not stay in the conjugal home. That is reserved for him. He is to have found lodging for them during the *idda*. If, however, he has not provided lodging by that time then the children and their custodian may continue to live in the conjugal home until the custody ends, not just until the *idda* ends. He thus has to move out of the conjugal home. If the custodian of the children does not wish to live in the conjugal home, the husband may not insist that she stay there. She may petition the court for money to rent another place for herself and the children. Because of the housing shortage and high cost of urban housing, the term separate living quarters is not so easily defined. There are incredible stories of husbands who have allowed the children and divorced wife to stay in the conjugal home. To meet the requirement of separate quarters for themselves and the divorced families, they simply build a cement wall in the middle of the flat.[104] As soon as the custody ends when the children become of age, the divorced custodian must leave the conjugal home.

This provision of the law was contested as un-Islamic and therefore unconstitutional before the Constitutional Court.[105] The constitutional provisions at issue were Articles 2 and 34. Article 2 provides that the main starting point (*masdar*) of or source of legislation (*tashri*) is the Islamic Sharia. Article 34 guarantees safeguarding of private ownership against expropriation without justification or compensation.

The plaintiff in the case had divorced his wife. They had minor children. She had the custody of them. He refused to give up the conjugal home exclusively to them to reside in. He sought to be able to stay in the marital home with them. He refused to be set under the time limit to find alternative accommodation for the children and the mother. Under the practice preceding the 1985 law, a husband had only to provide money for separate accommodation of the divorced wife during her *idda* and during the time she had custody of the minor children, not to find a flat for them.

First of all, the husband argued before the court that providing for a double household would render him destitute. This financial burden would interfere in his right to exercise *talaq*. Only wealthy men could afford then to use the *talaq*. In addition, he argued that it would be inequitable to provide the divorced wife cum guardian with lodging if she herself had a home of her own (either her own property or that of a relative). Finally, he argued that the requirement in the 1985 law that the husband give up the conjugal home had the effect of expropriating his property without compensation.

The court reviewed the considerations that had moved the legislator to allow minor children and their divorced mother as their custodian to continue to live in the marital home if the husband had not provided alternative lodging. It found that the prior practice of giving the divorcee cum guardian only monies for maintenance and lodging had led to the mothers using the money to take the children often to their own relatives. This practice had resulted in the children suffering from the resentment relatives showed towards them. To avoid this situation, the legislator conferred on the judge the authority to decide whether monies were more appropriate for renting separate lodging or entitlement to the conjugal home for the period specified. The divorced wife cum guardian was also given the option to stay in the conjugal home or to be given money to find an alternative home on the ground that it would be harmful to her state of mind if she were obliged to stay in the conjugal home on the ground that this was cheaper for the former husband. If she were on particularly hostile relations with her former in-laws, and was breastfeeding, this would not be conducive to her nursing and caring for her children in peace.[106]

The court also dealt with the equity issue raised by the plaintiff. If the guardian of the children were not the divorced mother, but rather a relative, such as a maternal aunt or grandmother, then the situation was different from that imagined by the legislator concerning accommodation of a guardian who is the divorced wife. The custodian who is a relative would more often than not already have a home of her own or a home provided for by her husband. It would not have been the intention of the legislator to require her to move out into the former conjugal home or alternative lodging with the minor children.

As for the infringement on the right to *talaq*, especially of economically weaker husbands, the court answered that such a right has to be weighed against the right of the minor children to be maintained as well as the right of the divorced wife to maintenance during the *idda*.

The expropriation argument is given short shrift. The law allows property to be burdened as required by a social function and social welfare. No Muslim is to use property in such a way as to go against the social welfare, and men especially not to retaliate against their wives. In the case of minors, they need continuation of lodging and should not have to suffer as victims of the recklessness of their *talaq*-wielding fathers.[107]

The final ruling was that the new Article 18A had to be interpreted in such a way that it was not unconstitutional. This means that if the divorcing husband is economically weak and the divorced wife cum guardian or other female guardian of the minor children has a lodging of her own, or has the resources for a lodging on her own with the children, then the husband is not obliged to find suitable lodging for them. If these circumstances are not present, then the husband has to find suitable lodging.

The court also clarified a certain ambiguity in the law. The law requires the husband to find separate lodging during the *idda* before it ends. If he finds it, the family has to move out of the conjugal home. If he has not found any suitable lodging by the time the *idda* has expired, then the children and their guardian may stay in the conjugal home as long as the guardianship lasts. In effect, he has to move out. At the same time, the law says that if the conjugal home were not rented out, and he found suitable lodging for the family after the *idda*, then he could live in the conjugal home alone. In that case the family would have to move out as soon as he found lodging for them. The law did not specify what would happen if the conjugal home were rented out. The court ruled that if the conjugal home is rented out, then the husband (presumably by analogy) is not to be pressured to find suitable lodging within the *idda* period.

The court did not go into the detail of debates in the hadith literature on where the divorced wife must spend her *idda*. The court was concerned rather with general rules. It found that the divorced woman may continue to stay in the conjugal home as long as the divorce is revocable, that is after the pronouncement of two *talaqs* and during the first two *idda*. The reason is, as the court wrote, that this offers a chance for resuming married life in so far as the husband may revoke the *talaq*. The wife may choose to leave the conjugal home if she fears that she will be abused by the husband's family[108] or she and her husband quarrel incessantly.[109] Once the third *talaq* is pronounced, there is no chance of resuming marriage life. The court did not rule that the divorced wife has to spend her third *idda* outside the conjugal home, for the Quran prescribes that she not be turned out or leave on her own accord,[110] though it was a practice according to the Maliki hadiths that she spend her last *idda* elsewhere[111] while claiming the costs presumably of staying elsewhere than in the home of the divorcing husband since the *idda* is for the benefit of the husband to determine whether she is pregnant from him. The court simply appealed to the pious value of providing maintenance.[112] It seems that the court was upholding in effect the Maliki practice, whereby the divorced wife cum guardian moves out during the last *idda* to suitable lodging, indeed can be forced to move out.

The court did not challenge the assertion of the plaintiff that *talaq* is a right since this was not the core issue. Nonetheless the decision gives occasion to reconsider the nature of the *talaq* power. It is not a right in the sense that it is inherent to human nature, or rather to a pious human nature. It is also not a right in the sense that it can be curtailed only by what is absolutely necessary for preserving the rights of others, for the exercise of *talaq* is heavily circumscribed in the Quran and *sunna*. It had its origins in an Arab tribal custom of men playing with and manipulating their wives. They could threaten them with divorce and revoke the threats a thousand times or more.[113] Islam set a heavy limit on this practice. It limited the threat of *talaq* to two times. On the third round it was irrevocable. The Quran also prescribes when it could be pronounced: only when the wife did not have her menses,[114] and the husband had to ask her to inform him about her state. And if there is a genuine danger of a final break between the spouses, then they are to go into arbitration with third parties.[115] This implies that the husband is to refrain from pronouncing the final *talaq* until the arbitration is ended. The Quran also restricts the use of the threat of *talaq* to situations of aggravation or disobedience on the part of the wife,[116] e.g. as in the case of a woman who thrashed her husband almost to death with her slipper upon learning that she had been deceived about his polygamy (Atiya 118). The one instance in which the non-orthodox *talaq* allowed by the Shafii jurists, that is, three *talaq*s in one sitting irrespective of the menstrual cycle of the woman, was only in the case of a non-consummated marriage (no *idda* required). If the woman, though married, had fallen in love with someone else before the consummation and was pregnant, then a quick *talaq* by the first husband would have solved the problem with mercy and discretion. Otherwise, the unabbreviated orthodox *talaq* can be described at most as a right of social necessity. It is to be exercised only under prescribed conditions. To avoid a husband becoming judge in his own cause (Ragaï 100) as to whether the marital situation is so aggravating as to require a threat of *talaq*, arbitration is required. Eventually the Egyptian legislator may have to consider enacting a law which requires at the time of registration of the two revocable *talaq*s the registration of evidence of arbitration. As long as this evidence fails, the final *talaq* would not be valid and the husband still liable for maintenance payments.

Reforming the wife's right to divorce – Law No. 1 of 2000

The Egyptian legislator enacted as its very first law of this millennium several amendments to the personal status laws.[117]

The principal aim of the new law was to allow the wife to petition for divorce more expeditiously. She would not have to find experts and witnesses to support reasons for divorce as required under the Decree-Law 25 of 1929 and Law 100 of 1985. She could save time also by having all matters relating to divorce settled by one court. If she does not have her marriage contract registered (*urfi* marriage), she can now get a court declaration of divorce that would allow her to remarry.

General background

This new law had a long history. In 1974 there was a powerful film *Oureed Halam* (I Need a Solution) by Hosn Shah.[118] It portrayed the weary path of Faten Hamama to prove her grounds for divorce. It took her years. At the same time a lower family court judge in Cairo observed year after year the judicial hardships suffered by many poorer women who came to his court. Out of a sense of compassion he was resolved to help them and to do justice for them. He retained this dream all during his judicial career and never forgot it even as his esteem in the world of law rose to the highest levels. He finally was able to realize this dream when he was asked by Mubarak's government to draft what has become Law 1 of 2000.[119] He observed that the Egyptian culture is one of discretion and privacy. Women have great difficulties airing in a public forum like a court all the problems that have driven them to seek divorce. In this respect the law which requires her to explain her reasons for wanting a divorce places a heavy burden on her. In situations of polygamy women have a particularly difficult time expressing why polygamy presents a hardship. Very strong emotions and fears are involved. Articulating them can be difficult. Articulating them can evoke feelings of self-shame. It has been reported that men's favouritism leads women in polygamous situations to become murderously jealous of one another, fearful of the father favouring the step-children, and forces them to resort to witchcraft. To pour out these feelings is painfully embarrassing (Atiya 129–134 on a fisherwoman). For rural women, complaints are not even expressed necessarily in words. Rather symbols are used. Siwan women, for instance, express their marital discontent by the way they arrange their jewellery (Vivien). Judges used to grant divorce according to symbolic custom. Women who wanted a divorce on the ground that their husbands were not fulfilling their conjugal sexual duties simply laid a slipper before the judge upside down (Hill 1979, 85). The new law, which regulates the use of a *khula* divorce petition by the woman, relieves her of having to go into detail about her private married life. As the new law also reduces the time required for getting a divorce degree, it saves the poorer women lawyers' fees.

Hanafi madhab

For the first time the personal status law states that the source of the law for questions not covered in the statute shall be the opinions of the Hanafi classical jurist Abu Hanifa and only those opinions that are most acceptable and most likely (*arjah*) to have stemmed from him.[120] This is a deviation from the long-standing practice of the legislator, the judges, and the Sheikh ul Islam at Al Azhar[121] to draw on all schools of law. Such a provision also circumscribes the courts' use of *ijtihad* (Vogel; Akhavi 398, n. 42). The new provision reflects partly the position of the Egyptian thinker Sayyid Qutb (d. 1966), who was hanged for his Muslim Brotherhood activities.

Procedural matters

Under the 2000 law jurisdiction is conferred on the court within the area of domicile of the plaintiff or the defendant to hear personal status matters relating to maintenance, wages to women for breastfeeding and child care (Shaham 108), custody, the *mahr*, the trousseau bought by the wife or her family (*jihaz*), marriage gifts (*dota*), furnishings, divorce by court order (*tamlik*, not *talaq*), *khula* divorce, and release of debt (e.g. of dower debt or past maintenance).[122] If the matter is one of custody, then the competent court is that in the district of domicile of the guardian or the minor. If the matter relates to an absent person, e.g. a husband not paying maintenance, then the competent court is that of the last domicile of the absent person.

All personal status suits relating to maintenance and wages (e.g. suckling wages) are exempted from judicial fees.[123] As for the fees of the lawyer in any personal status suit, these shall be determined by the court. If counsel has been named as legal aid counsel, the fees set by the court shall be paid by the public treasury. This is not to detract from the legal aid which the bar association has agreed to extend.[124] The court may also use its discretion to appoint a social worker to report on a case within two weeks.[125]

Maintenance fund

The law of 2000 establishes, similar to that in Tunisia, a family fund for implementing maintenance orders of the courts in favour of wives, divorcees, children and relatives entitled to maintenance. The details of the use of the fund and recovery by the state from recalcitrant husbands (or presumably women made responsible for maintaining their parents or younger siblings, for example) are to be issued by the Ministry of Justice.[126]

Divorce by court (**tamlik**)

The latest personal status law contains a surprising provision (Art. 172) relating to divorce litigation. If the confession or faith to which both spouses belong does not allow divorce, then their courts are barred from hearing a divorce petition.[127] It would seem that this applies to religious groups such as Roman Catholics or non-Muslim sects (referred to as *taifa* and *milla*). Explicit reference is not made to a Muslim *madhab*, such as the Hanafi, which does not permit a woman to get a divorce except when her husband is missing. The new law did not abrogate Decree-Law 25 of 1929 or Law 100 of 1985, both of which confer on all Muslim women, regardless of the *madhab* of the spouses, the more liberal Maliki provisions for divorce.

Limited divorce relief for unregistered marriage contracts (**urfi** *marriage)*

The law of 2000 also provides for limited relief for unregistered marriages, the *urfi* or customary marriages. The *urfi* marriage is not infrequent in Egypt. It is a valid Muslim marriage, in the presence of two witnesses and provable by a paper pledging commitment to God and signed by the witnesses. It is not a formal marriage contract. No dower is involved, no other conditions attached. It is a way to avoid the high costs connected with marriage and wedding celebrations as well as to circumvent pressures of parents against marriage with socially less prestigious partners. Because the *urfi* marriage paper is not registered, it is not recognized by the government for official purposes. This has prevented women from suing on the contract in court (Karam 146; Shaham 65). For the spouses of an *urfi* marriage, it is perfectly acceptable as a religiously valid union. This form of marriage is a practical solution for widows of soldiers who would have lost their pensions if they were to formally register their remarriages.[128] As an unregistered marriage, the *urfi* marriage often remains a social secret. The *urfi* marriage, however, entailed problems for women who sought to leave it. If the husband refused to divorce the wife, she was barred from seeking divorce from a court because an unregistered marriage was not justiciable. Even if the couple separated on their own accord, the unregistered *urfi* marriage paper still prevented the wife from remarrying.

The 2000 law allows women to terminate the marriage by bringing before the courts either a petition for divorce (*tamlik*) or for annulment (*faskh*).[129] The only condition is that they must bring written evidence of the marriage. This can include an unregistered paper. In this case the only type of divorce permitted is a court-ordered divorce (*tamlik*), meaning that the wife of an *urfi* marriage still does not qualify for the *mutaa* payment due under the 1985 law in cases when the husband pronounces *talaq* and the wife is not at fault. It is not expected that more educated women with higher social status will make use of the new law because going to court is not socially acceptable, but it may serve the interests to some extent of the poorer women.

Arbitration procedures for divorce

Law 1 of 2000 differentiates between reconciliation and arbitration procedures depending on the type of divorce: *talaq* divorce, mutual-consent divorce, divorce as exercised by the wife under her marriage contract and court-ordered divorce. For *talaq* divorces, mutual-consent divorces and divorce under the terms of the marriage contract the law requires only that at the time of the registration of the divorce, the registrar is to notify the spouses of the risks of divorce and to urge them to undergo arbitration with relatives from both sides. Arbitration is not required as a condition for registration.

For court-ordered divorces, the law is stricter. A reconciliation and arbitration process is required (like in Tanzania) as a condition before a court-ordered divorce may be issued. At the same time, the new law aims to shorten the arbitration procedure for court-ordered divorces. It confirms the provisions in the 1985 law that the two arbitrators should come from the families of the spouses if possible. While the 1985 law required those nominated to give the dates of commencing the arbitration and a proposed termination date, the new law sets definitive deadlines on the nomination of the arbitrators. The nomination is to take place no later than the second court session on the divorce action. If one of the spouses has failed to make a nomination, then the court is empowered to appoint an arbitrator.[130] By the third court sitting the arbitrators have to present their conclusions to the court. Whether the maximum of six months deliberation period accorded to the arbitrators in Law 100 of 1985 still applies is not clear. It seems that the time accorded lies solely within the discretion of the court and according to the court calendar. If by the third court session, the arbitrators have not reached a unanimous decision, the court will hear their differences of opinion. The authority of the court to make the final decision is made even clearer in the new law. It is for the court to decide whether to accept the arbitrators' conclusions or one of the proposals of any one arbitrator or to judge as it sees fit in accordance with the evidence presented.

Time limits are specified only in the case of quarrelling spouses who have children. The reconciliation process may not be under one month (30 days) and has to take place at least twice. The maximum time allowed is two months (60 days).[131]

The use of family arbitrators is not only prescribed in the Quran when it is feared that a couple shall break the marriage tie. According to custom in certain parts of rural Egypt relatives are assigned a central role in mediating between spouses long before a divorce so that marital disputes are nipped in the bud. For example, if a woman of the Siwan oasis in the western desert of Egypt wears one of her elaborate silver chains behind her head instead of both on her chest, this is her way of complaining that the husband was being unfair to her. His relatives are to intervene to correct the situation (Wickering 50).

Family Courts Establishment Law of 2004 – procedural advantages for women and the new role of women experts

Under the 2004 Family Courts Establishment Law (10 of 2004, 18 March 2004), the parties are obliged to submit to a pre-hearing meeting with the staff of the newly established dispute settlement offices attached to the courts. The office is headed either by a jurist or by social and psychological specialists in family matters. The officers enlighten the parties about the consequences of persisting in court litigation, then advise them on an alternative settlement, a settlement aimed at maintaining family stability (Art. 6). Unlike litigation, counselling costs nothing: no fees are charged. If the parties decide on counselling, a time limit is set: the efforts to settle may not exceed two weeks (Art. 8). If a settlement is reached, then it becomes self-executing without further court action. If the parties decide on litigation, then the minutes of the counselling sessions are sent to the court, though they may not be sent without the signature of the parties. If the parties fail to reach a settlement, then the family court takes on the dispute. The court bundles together all personal status litigations affecting the particular family in dispute and settles all matters ancillary to the disputes. For example, if a divorce is ordered, then issues of maintenance and custody are settled by the same court. The court establishes a special unit for execution of its judgments (Art. 15), including imprisonment. The parties no longer have to go from court to court. In inheritance matters the Family Courts Establishment Law confers jurisdiction on the president of the family court to issue certificates of death. He may refer the matter to court in case of difficult disputes (Art. 4).

Besides consolidating procedures and saving many women and men from wasting time going to various courts, the new family court law introduces a particularly interesting innovation, requiring that a woman expert be part of the judicial proceedings. When hearing a dispute the three justices constituting the court may not sit alone. They must be joined by two assessors. These are modern experts with a social science background: social workers and psychologists. Experts may be drawn only from a list controlled or constituted by the Minister of Justice in agreement with the Minister of Social Affairs or Minister of Health depending on the nature of the case. In keeping with gender progressiveness, at least one of the expert assessors sitting with the judges must be a woman (Art. 2). If the matter goes to appeal, the requirement of expert advice is dropped. The court is free to forego or seek expert assistance as it deems suitable.

Because every family dispute will invariably involve a woman, the Ministry of Justice is interested in assuring the presence of women social experts, but it is also starting to train young women law graduates for service in the new family courts. While this is laudable, confining women to that area of law perpetuates the stereotype of women as best suited only for family-related areas. It will be up to the new women judges, with the support of the first woman Supreme Constitutional Court judge (Tahany Al-Gebaly), to devise strategies once in the judicial service to sensitize their male colleagues to women-friendly justice as well as to take the opportunity of expanding the number of women in other types of courts.[132]

Khula – *extending the grounds for divorce by women*

The crown jewel in Law 1 of 2000 is Article 20 regulating *khula*. In practice *khula* has always been possible and indeed been long used in Egypt (Abdal-Rehim 105; Shaham 107; Tucker 54).

An elderly man in the village where the first woman to bring a suit under the new law lives, said in an interview that it was common that a woman got her divorce papers from the public notary upon returning her dower.[133] The long-standing popularity of *khula* rested on the advantages it had over *talaq*. The exercise of *talaq* entails maintenance to the wife during the *idda*, accounting for property the wife brought into the marriage and paying the remainder of the *mahr*. *Khula* entails no financial burdens on the husband (Tucker 54).

The new law defines the parameters of *khula* and prohibits certain types of *khula* agreements. Essentially *khula* is defined as an agreement between the spouses to divorce on terms they specify. The registration of the *khula* agreement is not specifically required by the new law. In practice it has been often but not always registered, much to the annoyance of some judges (Shaham 108). The new law requires it to be registered if a court is to hear any litigation involving the terms of the *khula* agreement.[134] If it is not registered it is not justiciable.

An arbitration and reconciliation process is not required in the case of a *khula* divorce agreed upon by the spouses. If they register it, the registrar is required only to urge them to undergo an arbitration process with their relatives.[135]

When the spouses have not been able to reach an agreement, it is the wife who may petition for a court order of divorce. She must meet the following conditions:

i) she relinquishes financial claims against the husband (e.g. foregoing the deferred dower and maintenance debts, and renouncing the right to maintenance during the *idda*; *mutaa* would be irrelevant, as explained below);
ii) she returns the *sadaqa* (wedding gift) the husband had bestowed on her (not necessarily on her parents);
iii) she states that she hates life with her husband, that they cannot possibly continue marital life and that she fears violating God's commands because of such hatred.

The new law contains one important element that aims at reforming current practices. One of the practices that the law has outlawed is that of the divorcing wife agreeing to renounce maintenance for the children and to restrict her custody rights (or, presumably extend her custody rights in exchange for financial advantages favouring the husband) (Shaham 108). This was a practice found to exist especially among women from the poorer classes. Women also agreed to renounce suckling wages, that is, payments when still breastfeeding at the time of divorce. The origins of these practices have not been investigated. But they resonated with the interpretation of one of the best-known Shafii Quranic exegeses from the Middle Ages. Such practices were recommended for women who did not want to be divorced. A woman was advised to make peace with her angry husband by offering to give up the dower and child support, and by reducing the number of times he had to have sex with her. She would be in effect appealing to his greedy instincts.[136]

In some instances, when the women discovered after the divorce that they in fact could not survive without financial help from the former husband and father of their children, they returned to court to contest the validity of the *khula* agreement (Shaham 109). Whether they were successful in their petition depended on whether the judge found the agreement had met all formal contractual requirements (Shaham 111–12).

Law 1 of 2000 seeks to remedy the situation by expressly forbidding compromising the rights *vis-à-vis* the children as the price for a *khula* divorce. The explicit exclusion of custody matters from *khula* contracts is a rejection of the opinion of some classical Maliki jurists that women could agree as part of *khula* to extend their custody of the children as long as this did not harm them (Bellefonds II:440–1; Toledano 79).

Because the text of the law in general refers to the maintenance (*nafaqa*) of the minor children, the question of whether maintenance includes suckling wages is not explicitly regulated. This could leave room for judicial discretion to decide whether suckling wages are an integral part of maintenance of minor children. It is also open to the judiciary to decide whether it will construe the law in such a way as to do justice to the classical opinion that a clause requiring a wife to renounce suckling wages is valid only if the offer for *khula* came from the wife (Bellefonds II:439, 441), not the husband; or whether it will consider such payments as an obligatory right conferred by the Quran[137] which would be hardly negotiable. Choosing the latter approach would entail a detailed discussion on the central role of contractual agreement in Islamic law, as a means of deviating from state law or the opinions of the schools of law, such deviation being based on the assumption that no legal rule can be comprehensively equitable. No legal rule can ever foresee those myriad individual situations that will always deviate from the norm and yet require that justice be done to them too. This approach presumes that while uniformity is the goal of state law, it is not necessarily the goal of justice, which is to reach an equitable remedy for individuals. Such a divergent approach is especially attractive for rulers in a society where the differing social and economic strata play a prominent role in the different attitudes towards the use of the court system.

It is clear from these express prohibitions in Law 1 of 2000 that no court ordering a divorce on the basis of *khula* may permit a woman to forego support for minor children. The text of the law does not regulate private *khula* contracts so explicitly. It is not prohibited to write such provisions to the disadvantage of the wife or children in even private contracts; nor is it explicitly provided that such contracts are not justiciable because they contain inequitable clauses. In the event of litigation one would certainly expect the judiciary to rule in favour of nullity of such clauses, given the legislators' awareness of the problems that had plagued *khula* divorces in the past and their intention to cure the situation.

Where there is no litigation, however, a problem arises. The law provides for the parties to make their own *khula* agreement without going to court for approval of its provisions. Presumably even an agreement under which the wife renounces custody or maintenance for the children would, in practice, stand. Given this practical possibility, the legislators may have to consider again whether there is a need to amend the rules for notarial registration of divorce agreements, in such a way as to prevent clauses which affect minor children's maintenance rights and the right of the mother to suckling wages. Thus the legislators will have to decide whether they wish to take more responsibility for closing the gap between judicial practice, which would prohibit such clauses, and social practice, which would tolerate and enforce such clauses, or whether they wish not to interfere in basic contractual freedom, in the hope that people will eventually internalize the law and voluntarily accept it as equitable for themselves, as apparently has happened with regard to the adoption in private agreements of the state law's limitation on the duration of the *idda* (Shaham 152).

Arbitration in **khula** *divorce*

If *khula* is classified logically as a divorce pronounced by the court (*tamlik*), parties to a *khula* suit may have to undergo a reconciliation and arbitration process. If they have children, the arbitration would last at least 30 days, if no children, less than a month. At least two sessions have to take place. The process is not to exceed 60 days. A Constitutional Court decision has interpreted the statute to this effect even though *khula* is not explicitly classified as *tamlik*.[138]

Irrevocability of a **khula** *order*

The *khula* divorce, whether agreed upon by the parties without litigation or ordered by the court, is irrevocable.

A court decision in favour of *khula* cannot be contested or challenged in any way.[139] An appeal is thus in practice denied.

Consent of the husband?

The new law did not specify that the court decree granting a *khula* divorce may be issued without the consent of the husband. Absence of the need for consent is implied by the fact that the court is responsible for issuing a divorce decree in its own right and not on behalf of the husband. This again implies that the *khula* divorce does not require the consent of the husband, since a distinction is made between private *khula* divorce agreements and *khula* divorce pronounced by the court. Such a distinction reflects a combination of Hanbali and Hanafi thought. The Hanafis treated *khula* as a contract, consisting of an offer from the wife and acceptance by the husband, or vice versa (Coulson 1991, 138; Bellefonds II:440). Hanbali jurists tended to treat *khula* as an annulment of the marriage, probably because it involved the return of the dower, the consideration in the marriage contract (Spectorsky 1993, 427). Accordingly, when the husband offered divorce by *khula*, the offer was considered unretractable. It was for the wife to decide when to accept it. Acceptance was deemed to have occurred when the dower was actually repaid, not when she agreed, as in a normal contractual situation (Bellefonds II:427–8). If she made the offer, she could leave the marital home as of right. When the marriage was deemed terminated was not clear. It was said the marriage ended only once the husband took the dower back (Spectorsky 1993, 251–2); it was also said that it terminated once it was established that the amount of compensation she offered or the amount of the debt which she was to forgive her husband was fair (Spectorsky 1993, 231).

Khula *in Islamic law*

Customary basis of khula *in the Quran, Africa and ancient Egypt*

Khula has a long history in Islamic law and mirrors a custom among some African peoples that requires the dower be paid by the husband's family to the family of the bride. If the marriage breaks down, then the wife's family is to return the dower. A reduced amount may be returned only if the husband is largely responsible for the breakdown (Coulson 1991, 138). The return of the dower has an economic advantage for the husband's family since with the returned amount they can afford to find another wife.

An exception to the general rule of return of the dower in African societies by the bride's family can be found among the Thonga ('Ronga') of south-eastern Africa (South Africa, Mozambique, Zambia). The women are known for their independence, reflected in the saying, 'You marry the body, not the head; the head is ours.' Their laws and customs permit a woman to get a divorce on grounds of ill-treatment by her husband or on grounds of mutual consent. The latter is conditional on the woman being able to pay back the *lobola*, the marriage gift, herself without the help of her family (Webster 256, 259).

Similarities can be found also in ancient Egyptian marriage contracts, which allowed both spouses the right to divorce. Husbands could release (meaning of the root of the word *talaq* in Arabic) their wives from the marriage. Wives could choose to leave the marriage. If the spouses lived in the house of the wife's family, then she was allowed to release her husband (Lüddeckens 272). The wife who left took only half of the marriage gift she had received from the husband and left all the wealth accumulated by both spouses during the marriage to her husband (Lüddeckens 258, 271, 274). Today *khula* is seen by some Muslim women as a very simple transaction. A contemporary popular conception of *khula* is expressed by a young Muslim Zanzibari woman who is adamant about appearing fully veiled in public but equally adamant about her right to divorce: 'The Word of God is just. God gave us women who are unhappy with our husbands *khula*. It means we just have to pay him and the divorce takes place whether the husband wants it or not. No questions asked, no quarrels. It is very simple.'[140]

The word *khula* does not appear in the Quran. Its basis is deemed to be the Quranic verse on the return of the dower upon divorce. In general the Quran prohibits the husband from taking back the marriage gift conferred on the wife.[141] If he wanted another wife, he had to pay a fresh dower. This is a clear difference from the African tradition which gives the husband the dower back upon divorce. An exception is made, however. The husband may accept from the wife something in exchange for the benefit that she will get from terminating the marriage contract. Because of the exceptional nature of *khula*, it is not surprising, as mentioned above, that the Hanafi classical jurist Abu Hanifa limited the concept merely to an agreement to forgive any outstanding debts which either spouse had towards the other; compensation as such was not to be part of the arrangement (Bellefonds II:443). The distinction between a *khula* divorce and a *talaq* divorce in exchange for compensation seems to rest on an oblique reference in the hadiths to interpreting the Quranic verse on fear of a breach between spouses because of irreconcilable quarrelling between them (*shiqaq*) (sura 4:35) to mean that if the efforts to reconcile go on indefinitely and the quarrelling never ceases, then the simplest way out would be to have the husband end the impasse by merely pronouncing a *talaq* in exchange for compensation.[142]

Khula *in the hadith literature*

The early Maliki hadiths report how women used the *khula* verse in the Medina community. The most dramatic story is that of Habiba, a daughter of Sahl Ansari.[143] She was terribly unhappy with her husband, so miserable that she visits the Prophet in the middle of the night as he goes out to say his morning prayers. She tells him that either it is her life or her husband's. She threatens suicide or murder if she has to continue to be married to him. When her husband appears on the scene the Prophet tells him of Habiba's decision. She promptly offers to give him back all that he has given her. She has it with her. Her husband is apparently dumbfounded, though nothing is reported of his response or defence. The Prophet orders him to take what she offers, and Habiba returns to her parents. As portrayed by the young Muslim woman above from Zanzibar, the *khula* procedure as performed in the days of the Prophet was quick and without much ado. No witnesses were called. It was enough that the wife had threatened suicide or murder. She had become a danger to herself and to her husband, ready to commit a criminal act forbidden by God.

Later, women made the procedure even simpler. Rubayyi, daughter of Muawwidh, left her husband. She then went with her paternal aunt to Abd Allah b. Umar to inform him of the separation. There was no objection. Apparently Rubayyi had paid back what her husband had given her. The only question to be solved was the duration of the *idda*. The *idda* of Rubayyi was ordered to be that of any other divorced woman. In another report it was said that Umar confirmed that a woman could leave on the basis of *khula* without even getting permission from the courts, that is, the courts did not have to verify the desperation of the wife.[144] This is an important report. It implies approval of gender equality in divorce. In effect, the *khula* divorce is for women the equivalent of the *talaq* divorce by men. A woman may leave the husband, the only condition being a financial compensation or reckoning of outstanding debts with the husband, just as *talaq* allows a man to leave the wife, the only condition being payment of *mutaa* compensation and any remaining *mahr* to the wife. No court is needed to pronounce the divorce in either *khula* or *talaq*. This is an argument which had already been used in the debates on *mutaa* in relation to the draft of the 1979 'Jihan's law' (Najjar 333).

The 2000 Egyptian law is stricter than the hadiths. It allows *khula* without any interference from the courts or arbitrators only if the spouses negotiate between them how much the wife is to return to the husband. Otherwise, if the wife acts unilaterally, as in the case of Habiba or Rubayyi, the courts impose the arbitration process.

Another version of the story of Habiba as reported by Aisha puts another slant on the discourse. It was said that the husband of Habiba used to beat her so severely that he had broken one of her bones.[145] When the husband was called before the Prophet, he specified what he had given her as dower, namely two gardens. The Prophet promptly ordered him to take them back and leave her alone. The only controversial point was the length of the *idda*. Ibn Umar was reported to have said that a woman who left her husband in return for compensation needed only to wait for one menstrual cycle.[146]

Thus over time *khula* became controversial. On the one hand, it enabled desperate women to leave a marriage, a revolutionary concept, for at the time the Hebrew and Christian communities denied women any chance to leave of their own accord. On the other hand, it opened women up to being blackmailed by greedy husbands who wanted to have the dower back in order to marry another wife. A husband who wanted to get back the dower he had given for one wife could refuse to use *talaq* to divorce her, but make her life so hellish that she would decide to leave the marital house on the basis of *khula*. Aisha's portrayal of what happened in the case of Habiba illustrates this problem. Her husband had beaten her into using *khula* so that he could get his property back. Ibn Malik was well aware of this blackmailing of women into resorting to *khula*. As a consequence, he was of the opinion that if a woman had exercised *khula* by agreeing to give back her dower because her husband had pressured her by beating her, holding her prisoner or ransoming her, then she had a case in equity before the courts. She could prove that he had forced her. In that case the court would uphold the divorce, but allow her to keep the dower. Later Maliki jurists expanded on this protection for the wife. If she paid for her divorce, then learned that she could have sued for divorce on grounds allowed without having to suffer financial losses, she was allowed to claim back the monies paid to the husband (Bellefonds II:434–5).

In contrast to Malik's opinion, Egyptian law bars any further action on *khula* once pronounced by the court. It remains to be seen whether the courts will satisfy themselves that the wife is not acting under pressure or being blackmailed. If it is found that she is under pressure, it would be possible to recommend that the court still pronounce divorce, and for reasons of equity order that the dower be returned to the wife.

Monetary limits on **khula** *compensations*

As for the amount that was to be paid, Malik was of the opinion that it not exceed what the husband had given to the wife. Even this opinion is broader than what the Quran seems to have intended. The basic rule is that the husband should not claim back the marriage dower upon a divorce. However, in the case of a divorce by the wife, the Quran speaks of an exception to this rule. The exception does not speak of return of anything but the dower amount. Therefore, the exceptional recompense that the husband receives in a *khula* divorce cannot exceed the value of the dower.

The Egyptian law of 2000 by contrast is even broader than the Quran or Malik's opinion. The court order specifying the nature of the *khula* payment may cover not only the wedding gift (*sadaqa*) from the husband, but also may specify that the wife renounce all future financial claims. The renunciation should not cover the claim to *mutaa* because the 1985 law prescribes *mutaa* in circumstances where the wife is not at fault (though in the context of *talaq* by the husband).[147] The only relevant financial claim for purposes of *khula* would relate to the issue of maintenance during the *idda* following an order for a *khula* divorce. This *idda* would be equivalent to the third *idda* of an irrevocable *talaq*, i.e. a period of three menstrual cycles. Certainly it was a controversial point in the hadith literature whether the non-pregnant wife during the third *idda* had a claim to lodging costs and maintenance during that period, regardless of where she chose to live, or whether she was limited to lodging in the matrimonial house without the husband incurring extra costs, or whether she had a right both to lodging in the matrimonial home and to maintenance.[148] There was no possibility of saving the marriage by the time of the third *idda*, yet her undergoing the *idda* was required for the benefit of the husband. On this point the Egyptian courts may have to adapt and extend the opinion of Abu Hanifa, who opined in the case of a husband who divorced his wife by *talaq* that he pay maintenance plus lodging during the final *idda*. By analogy, the Egyptian courts could exercise their discretion and ask whether it is fair to accept renunciation by the wife of maintenance apart from lodging during the *idda* as a valid condition in a *khula* agreement.

The *khula* provisions of the 2000 law could make inroads into the old rule that the furnishings (as part of the *jihaz*) belong to the wife. If the wife's family has used the *mahr* given by the husband to buy the furnishings, then return of the *mahr* upon a *khula* divorce could technically include turning the furniture over to the husband. To avoid such a result, one could resort to the approach of some Hanafi jurists to categorize the furnishings as a gift transaction between the bride and her family, rather than as dower. The resolution of this issue may depend on the equity of the situation, a principle applied by the Egyptian Constitutional Court in its interpretation of the lodging provisions of the 1985 law (see above). The court found it equitable to ease the financial burdens of the husband when the wife, as guardian of the minor children, is not financially weak. By analogy, it could be equally found that where the wife is financially weak, she would not have to return the furnishings as part of her returning the *mahr*. In such a case the *mahr* returned could be limited as well to the lesser sum of a customary *mahr* (*mithl*).

Evidentiary requirements under the Egyptian **khula** *law*

The requirements in the 2000 Egyptian law mirror an attempt to combine various classical opinions (Bellefonds II:424–5). The result places more of a burden of proof on the wife than any one of these opinions originally intended. First, the new statutory law requires the wife to present various statements to the court to prove she has grounds for a *khula* divorce. She is to state her hatred of her husband and reasons why it is impossible to continue the marriage. Under classical rules the statement would have been simpler and focused on her own fears. She would have had to state merely that she is a danger to herself or to her husband if she continues in the marriage. As for the wife's statement about how much compensation she is prepared to give to the husband, the statutory law reflects a combination of the Shafii, Hanafi and Maliki opinions. The Shafii made *khula* conditional on the wife offering evidence of the dower she had received. The Shafii opinion was reflected in the Egyptian draft Code of Personal Status written by Qadri Pasha, which prescribed restricting the wife's offer of compensation to what could constitute a dower (*mahr*) (Bergmann and Ferid).[149] In contrast, the Hanafi and Maliki opined that return of the dower was not an essential condition of *khula*. Return was discretionary, for it was reasoned that a husband gained certain advantages from a *khula* divorce. If he had divorced by *talaq* in the proper way, he would have had to wait for the divorce to become irrevocable over three *idda*. He would have been responsible for maintenance of the wife for such a long period of time. Further, he would have had to wait for this long period of time before being able to marry another wife, if he had already reached his limit of four wives. With the *khula* divorce that the wife gave him, the divorce was immediately irrevocable, meaning that the *idda* was much shortened, to his benefit. Accordingly, from an equitable perspective repayment of the dower to him was discretionary. Otherwise, she was to forgive any outstanding debts her husband owed her, but such debts were not to exceed the value of the dower. Such debts did not include her claim for maintenance during the shortened *idda*. By combining these opinions rather than choosing one over the other or adapting one or the other, the statutory law requires the wife seeking *khula* to offer evidence not only of what constituted the dower she received but also of what constituted any outstanding debts her husband owed her.

In fairness, on the other hand, the above evidentiary requirements of the 2000 Egyptian law have to be evaluated against the customs and practices that have taken root in Egyptian society. It became common for a husband to offer a *talaq* divorce in exchange for compensation by the wife. When one considers that this form of *talaq* was placing extreme financial burdens on women who sought to leave the marriage, the 2000 law can be regarded as an improvement, for the law limits the nature of the financial compensation that the wife may offer in exchange for divorce to two categories: namely, the marriage *sadaqa* and financial claims she otherwise might have against her husband. The court is to establish on the basis of the evidence produced the amount of the marriage *sadaqa*. Then it is to establish whether the wife would qualify for post-divorce maintenance and whether she has any financial claims other than maintenance-related against the husband and which she would renounce. Once the divorce is granted, the wife need not negotiate any further with the husband about what more compensation he wants before divorce can take place. If the Egyptian courts interpret narrowly the scope of the *sadaqa* and financial claims to be renounced, then the effect of the new law may well be to eliminate over time the customary agreements on *talaq* in exchange for extortionary compensation. Poorer women and their families might then come to prefer petitioning for *khula* in court over concluding private divorce contracts. On the other hand, broad interpretations that would extend *sadaqa* beyond wedding gifts to encompass all kinds of gifts during the marriage, and that would restrict the concept of maintenance-related debts to exclude her contributions to the wealth of the husband, would provide no incentive to go to court.

Comparison with Pakistani jurisprudence on **khula**

The Pakistani courts have established clear-cut principles for *khula* divorces which could be of persuasive value for Egyptian courts. The Pakistani High Court has declared *khula* is a right conferred on the wife. For this reason it does not need the consent of the husband.[150] *Khula* is prescribed on only two conditions: that the wife is desperate and that the wife return the dower, which ordinarily the husband would not be entitled to. Hence return of the dower is a favour to him and he should be happy simply with that. The Pakistani courts rely on some of the non-Maliki hadiths that report on women who elaborated a little more than the famous Habiba did in their pleas for divorce the reasons why they wanted to leave the marriage. They had no complaints about the husband's character or piety. Married life with him just could not be endured. As to the amount the wife was to pay back, there is only reference in the *sunna* to the property that Habiba was given as a dower (a garden) without any reference to renouncing debts or financial claims.[151]

The Pakistani courts have reaffirmed the right of the wife to get a *khula* divorce merely on the basis of her statement of being fed up with the marriage. She is not required to bring any evidentiary support of her statement.[152] The justices have reasoned that just as the husband need not present evidence of his reasons for exercising his right to *talaq*, *khula* is the wife's equivalent of this male privilege.[153] The jurisprudential basis of this interpretation lies in those hadiths where there is no indication that the Prophet required women seeking *khula* to present evidence beyond their statement that they wished to leave the marriage and were prepared to return the dower.

Controversies in Egypt over the **khula** *law*

The 2000 law was hotly debated in Egypt. The first litigation began as soon as the law was published.

The debate turned largely on what consequences it would have for the different economic classes. Many felt that the *khula* law only benefited the wealthier classes. A wealthier woman can afford to renounce financial claims and repay the *sadaqa* more easily than a poorer woman. It is for this reason that the Iraqi Code of Personal Status of 1953 did not allow poor women to renounce their maintenance claims in *khula* proceedings (Bellefonds II:447). Others in Egypt argue that poorer women are not at a disadvantage if they only have to return the *mahr*, since it tends to be low. However, the situation is problematical for rural women who have received gold as their *mahr* and have already used it for the benefit of the husband: to buy a piece of land for him or to pay for the costs of his migration to the Gulf to find work (Sholkamy 121). If this woman ever sought a *khula* divorce, the courts would be confronted with a question of equity: if the husband has already benefited from the dower paid, then all that could be demanded of the wife would be to renounce any financial claims she might have against him. It would be recommendable that the courts issue an order of *khula* without repayment of the dower on the equitable grounds that the husband had already received his compensation.

One advantage that the *khula* law is said to have for the poorer woman relates to costs. The fees that a poorer woman would have to pay an advocate to get a non-*khula* divorce might be higher than the cost of the recompense she has to pay to her husband, as the *khula* divorce is supposedly quicker.

As for the wealthier classes, *khula* has consequences for them too. It is known that many men in Egypt convey properties to their wives or register wealth and real estate in their names in order to avoid taxes. Their wives are in effect tax havens. The *khula* divorce law would have the effect of forcing husbands to seek tax havens other than their wives, especially if the courts limit the recompense to only the marriage dower, exclusive of any other gifts or conveyances made in the course of the marriage.[154] It has been said that the *khula* law offers wealthier women who have a lot of their husbands' wealth registered in their names the possibility of absconding with the wealth after obtaining a *khula* divorce. This was apparently the reason why a provision in the draft new law that would have given women the right to leave the country without permission of their husbands was defeated in parliament.

The concerns about the *khula* law being less advantageous for the lower-income classes have been belied by the fact that the first litigation under the new law was brought by a woman of little income, who had taught herself how to read and write. This was Wafaa, a 32-year-old peasant woman from Sigin Al-Kom in Al Gharbiya.[155] Her husband was a health assistant with his own small business, which had prospered over the years. Wafaa felt that he was ashamed of her not being as educated as he was. He allegedly beat her up violently on several occasions. According to a newspaper interview, Wafaa admitted that she had tried to commit suicide, although they had children. Her husband apparently had offered to divorce her if she wanted and told her she could go to court. Why she did not seek a divorce on grounds of harm is not clear. Her husband married a second wife, a woman who had helped in the house when Wafaa fell ill after her son's death and could not fulfil her wifely duties. Wafaa felt that she was not being treated the same as the second wife, and again threatened suicide. Finally Wafaa decided to attempt to divorce and found a lawyer. The lawyer apparently started a reconciliation and arbitration process in order to get the husband to fulfil his duty under Islamic law to treat the two wives equally. Actually Wafaa had several options under Egyptian law: she could have sued on the grounds of physical abuse, but she had no police records. In her public interview, however, she asserted that she did not believe that beating was a proper ground for divorce. She was happy that her husband had not taken out his frustrations on someone else. She could have sued as well on the grounds of the hardship that polygamy brought her, but apparently she was time-barred (up to one year from the date of knowledge of the polygamous marriage). Her conception of *khula* is that a woman has to take much abuse until she can bear it no more – in contrast to the opinion of the young Zanzibari woman cited above – then she qualifies for *khula*. Her husband in his interview believed too that a wife is prepared to tolerate extreme situations if only for her children's sake. Certainly, suicide attempts by the wife are a sign of desperation, which forms the basis for a *khula* divorce. What Waafa and her husband seemed not to have known is that accepting abuse by either spouse is not sanctioned by Islam and requires compensation from the abuser.

Constitutional challenge to the **khula** *law*

About a year and a half after the enactment of the new *khula* law, a husband sued for a declaration that the law was unconstitutional.[156] He challenged only parts of the law. In the same year as the enactment of the new law, his wife had been awarded by the Alexandria Court of First Instance for Personal Status Matters in 2000 divorce by *khula*. The couple had been married for only three years. She had returned the dower and the wedding jewellery and relinquished the deferred dower. She stated that she could not bear to live with her husband, that she feared she would anger God by continuing to live with a man whom she loathed[157] and that she wished to leave him. In accordance with the procedural requirements, the Alexandria court appointed arbitrators, who found that reconciliation was impossible and recommended a *khula* divorce.

The statutory provisions made the decision incontestable. The husband wanted the incontestability of the order to be declared unconstitutional on the grounds that the basic right to litigation was violated. State Counsel opposed the petition. The husband also maintained that Islamic law required his consent to the *khula* divorce, even though consent was not specifically addressed in Law No. 1 of 2000.

The Constitutional Court declared *khula* divorce to be an irrevocable type of divorce, similar to that of an irrevocable *talaq*. The jurisprudential basis lies in the hadiths, where the Prophet pronounced the *khula* divorce to be final and incontestable. The term 'incontestable' was thus being interpreted as meaning irrevocable. It would seem that while a court decision pronouncing a *khula* divorce is not appealable, the only issue that can be contested is whether all the conditions of a valid *khula* were met.

The court went beyond the issue of whether a *khula* is an irrevocable divorce. It ruled that any matters connected with *khula* litigation are equally incontestable, even the amount of the dower to be restituted. The trial court's decision is final in all respects. The reason is that husbands would pursue further litigation in order to irritate the wife and not with honest intentions.

Another element of incontestability that the court tackled related to evidence. Does the wife have to present her reasons for her statement that she abhors her husband and can no longer stay in the marriage? The court answered in the negative, but indirectly. It ruled that it has only to verify that she has made such a statement, that she has restituted the dower and that the arbitrators have not been able to reconcile the parties. Neither the court nor any one else is to bring witnesses as to her reasons. God is the only witness to her detestation of her marital life. An appeal is possible only when the purpose is to establish whether the lower court fulfilled the formal requirements of the law. Nothing subjective will be part of the review process.

As for the issue of whether the husband has to consent to the *khula* offer, the Constitutional Court noted that Islamic schools of law differ on this point, but persons in authority have a right to choose from among the schools. One criterion for choosing one view over another is whether one position eases the burden on the judges and the judicial system. In this case, the Maliki position was preferred as it did not require the court to obtain the consent of the husband. Such a position offered persons in authority, namely the judges of the Constitutional Court, the chance to avoid aggravated quarrels between spouses that would prolong litigation, perhaps endlessly. The court further interpreted the spirit of God's revelations to mean that accord is better than strife. Where there is a chance to end the strife, then that is the better way out. Strife overburdens not only the spouses but also the legal system and God does not wish to overburden humans. Another aspect of the Maliki position which the court adopted is the argument that requiring a husband's consent opens the door to malice on his part. The object of law is to erect barriers to such evil.

The court appears to have thought that *khula* is not a mechanism for making women equal to men in terms of the right to divorce. The husband still retains the right of a private *talaq*. Instead of taking the equality approach as the Pakistani courts have done, the Constitutional Court sought to argue that the law is intended to take mercy on women and rescue them from abusive situations. It argued that the law aims to rescue wives from oppressive husbands who are obdurate and rigid, and who are not ready to accept the fact that their wives are alienated from them for good. If the wife abhors her husband, then to make her stay with him because he does not consent to a divorce is to deny her God's mercy. The husband who refuses to consent to accepting the wife's offer to relieve him of financial burdens is violating a cardinal principle of the Islamic faith, which is to avoid forcing someone to stay in a relationship that is not peaceful, especially when the arbitrators find that there is no chance of reconciliation.

The court's use of the general principle of mercy and of avoiding long-drawn-out strife is a powerful argument for future cases, where the facts could be different. While in the case in question it happened that the arbitrators sided with the wife, the court laid the foundation for any future cases in which arbitrators might disagree with the wife. The statute confers on the judiciary the right to reject or accept the decision of the arbitrators. The court protects itself against future contentions that the husband's consent is needed when arbitrators agree with the husband. When the court finds that a wife abhors her husband, regardless of what the husband or arbitrators say, the court will apply the general principle that strife is not to be prolonged in the private or the public sphere. So the court may in future justify granting *khula* even when the husband and arbitrators do not.

From a procedural perspective the case raises an interpretation issue that the Constitutional Court did not discuss. The first-instance court in Alexandria by appointing arbitrators seems to have interpreted Law No. 1 of

2000 in such a way that *khula* is classified as a court-ordered divorce, and therefore the spouses must first enter arbitration. The wording of the statute does not say clearly whether *khula* is a court-ordered divorce or whether it stands in a category of its own, as it is not contestable like other court-ordered divorces. It could be argued that the spouses in *khula* proceedings need not be subject to arbitration. Certainly from the perspective of the Pakistani case law, *khula* is the wife's equivalent of *talaq* so that the court would simply urge arbitration rather than order it. The Alexandria court interpretation reflects more the public policy point of view that *khula* is not to become a means by which women destabilize marriage as an institution. The argument is flawed in so far as it presumes that *talaq* is not a destabilizing factor as well.

In summary, the Constitutional Court decision is a victory for women's rights in so far as it upheld Law 1 of 2000. The decision also reduces the number of potential obstacles to exercising the right to divorce for women. They do not have to offer evidence of reasons for abhorring the husband any more than the husband has to give a reason for using *talaq*. The husband's consent is not required. Nonetheless the decision has not cleared the obstacle course completely. It interpreted the law in such a way that women have to go through arbitration in order to divorce. The arbitration requirement has been extended and is not restricted to non-*khula* types of divorce, namely divorce that has to be proven on specific grounds such as cruelty, desertion or failure to pay maintenance.

Women's Council

At the same time as the new divorce law came into force at the start of March 2000, a new women's organization came into being. This is the National Women's Council, replacing the former Women's National Commission.[158] Suzanne Mubarak, the wife of Hosni Mubarak was named head of the Council. Thirty other members sit on the Council. They have included the former Minister for Social Affairs, Mervat Talawi, the left-wing trade unionist Amina Shafeek, the advocate Mona Zulficar, the Director of the Social Research Center of the American University in Cairo, Hoda Rashad, and the Sheikh ul Islam of Al Azhar, Sheikh Muhammad Tantawi. One of the functions of the Council is to propose draft legislation and advise on how government's draft legislation affects women. Government appropriations and private donations finance the Council. It has developed its own research on the most effective way to analyse women's problems in social and family contexts and conducts public awareness campaigns. The council would also be in a good position to monitor the implementation of the divorce law. Whether it will establish a network of local branches throughout the country remains to be seen. It could take as a model for such branches the National Union of Tunisian Women, or the 25 *fatwa* councils that Sheikh Al Haqq, former mufti and Sheikh ul Islam of Al Azhar, ordered to be set up in 1990 and 1991 in each of the governorates (Skovgaard-Petersen 289).

Female circumcision

Public debate and litigation

Apart from personal status and divorce issues, the circumcision of women in Egypt became a source of great tension. The practice is widespread in Egypt. It became a public controversy when the television company CNN aired a documentary on circumcision at the time of the international Cairo conference on population control in 1994. In an interview the day before the documentary, the Egyptian Minister of Health stated that the practice of genital circumcision of females was rare in Egypt. On the very next day the documentary aired contrary evidence and depicted live the circumcision of a young Egyptian girl (Issa 351).[159] The minister then denounced the practice and action was taken. In 1994 an NGO Task Force to combat female genital mutilation was established as part of the National NGO Commission for Population and Development. Its main aim is to eradicate the practice, not through legislation, rather through resource centres for women and public awareness campaigns that undermine the popular moral justification for circumcision. A public debate began immediately on the question of whether circumcision should be prohibited by law and whether such a law would violate or conform to Islamic law. The then mufti of Egypt, Muhammad Tantawi, later the Sheikh ul Islam of Al Azhar, took the position that female circumcision is not mandatory under Islamic law and therefore could be restricted for medical reasons. The then Sheikh ul Islam of Al Azhar, Jadd al Haqq, gave an opposite opinion, namely that circumcision is a practice permitted by Islamic law for reasons of public morality and welfare and therefore cannot be prohibited.

Two years after the International Conference on Population and Development the Minister of Health, Professor Dr Ismail Sallam, issued Decree No. 261 on 8 July 1996.[160] In the light of the Islamic law controversy on female circumcision, the decree did not forbid circumcision of females *per se*, but classified it as a medical matter. This enabled the ministry to limit the performance of female circumcision only to medical personnel. Accordingly, it became illegal for non-physicians to perform circumcision, a widespread practice. Even medical personnel, whether in public or private medical centres, were restricted. They could perform the operation only under the following circumstances: it had been proposed by the treating physician; the female concerned had a disease; and the chief gynaecologist at the hospital in question had approved. The intention of the ministry in taking this approach was to carve out a less emotionally-charged administrative or procedural path through a political minefield. It is reminiscent of the approach often taken by the Egyptian law-maker throughout Egyptian modern history, e.g. in respect of religiously valid *urfi* marriages. Such marriages are not prohibited as such, but administratively are not justiciable before the courts for all purposes like registered marriage contracts. Certainly in Europe this approach is also resorted to in emotionally-charged questions such as abortion; for example, in Germany a certificate of counselling about the risks of abortion is required before an abortion may be performed within the first three months of the pregnancy.

The Egyptian courts eventually became the battlefield where the debate was to be decided. A group of Muslim men brought an action before the Administrative Court in Cairo for annulment of the decree from the Ministry of Health. The court restricted its ruling to the procedural parameters set by the ministry. In the light of the fact that some medical professionals were in fact performing and being paid for circumcising females,[161] the court found that the ministerial decree was an ultra vires intervention in the exercise of professional freedom and discretion. The ministry appealed. The appellate court decided to deal head-on with the issue of the Islamic legal aspects of female circumcision, in addition to the rights of the medical profession. It favoured the opinion of Sheikh Tantawi endorsing restrictions, and upheld the ministry's decree.

Circumcision in Islamic law

The controversy over the legal status of circumcision has produced a number of opinions from scholars and ulama. In 1994 a book appeared on the subject by a law professor, Dr Abdel Aziz Al-Sukkari,[162] who argued that there is no clear command in the *sunna* regarding circumcision. This was followed in the same year by the publication of the opinions of the two highest ulama in Egypt, Sheikh Tantawi, then mufti, later Sheikh ul Islam of Al Azhar, and Jadd al Haqq, then Sheikh ul Islam since 1982. In 1996 the World Health Organization, which opposes female circumcision, published a pamphlet-treatise explaining that female circumcision is merely custom and not *sunna*. The author was an Islamic scholar from Riyadh (Sabbagh).

The two opinions of Sheikh Al Haqq and Sheikh Tantawi are of particular interest because they come to different conclusions, the former in favour of female circumcision, and the latter against. This difference of opinion reflected what has long been allowed in Islamic law, namely the freedom of diversity of opinion, especially when there is no Quranic or *sunna* text on a matter, or the hadiths are weak. The media in part, however, treated the difference in opinion as a sensation and reduced the debate to a matter of 'belief' – which Sheikh was to be believed – rather than emphasizing the long-honoured tradition among the classical scholars of disagreeing on the basis of rational argumentation, just as justices of a supreme constitutional court come to different conclusions when applying the same sources of law.[163] The classical Islamic law scholars differed in the past on circumcision for males and females (Sabbagh 11–17; Rispler-Chaim 85–6). The Egyptian ulama equally have had differing opinions since the 1950s. For Sheikh Al Haqq this was not a new topic. He had already issued in the 1980s an opinion in favour of female circumcision against doctors' disapproval of the practice (Krawietz 224, 231). He supported the popular belief that female circumcision is needed to maintain a woman's chastity and modesty. In 1994 he repeated his opinion. Sheikh Tantawi, on the other hand, took the side of Mahmud Shaltut, Sheikh ul Islam of Al Azhar until 1962. Sheikh Shaltut had written that there was no legal basis for female circumcision, thus rendering it a subject that medical personnel should handle, and that chastity and modesty are matters of attitude, which could be achieved by education (Rispler-Chaim 86, 90; Krawietz 224, n. 18, 234). At the core of Sheikh Al Haqq's argument was an evaluation and acceptance of the popular understanding of why female circumcision is thought to be a necessary Islamic ritual. At the core of Sheikh Tantawi's argument is an evaluation of how popular custom can deviate from the wording and spirit of the sources of Islamic law.

To appreciate the differences of opinion between the two jurists, the social backdrop and the classical attitudes towards circumcision as well as the philosophy of diversity of opinion in the Sharia should first be understood. We will start with a discourse on diversity then turn to the social backdrop and classical attitudes.

Diversity of legal opinion

Very early in Islam, private jurists took the initiative to establish their central role in the formation of the Sharia. They studied the Quran and hadiths in depth. They wrote treatises of law, expressing their opinions about how to interpret the Quran and the hadiths. The result was a large body of literature laying down various interpretations of the Sharia. As several schools of law developed over time, diversity of opinion also grew, between and within the schools. Reports in the hadith literature vary on whether diversity was a disputed topic and how it was to be evaluated. Ibn Malik's collection of hadiths did not contain any debates on the subject. The non-Maliki collections contain more references to diversity. The concerns reported during the lifetime of the Prophet related not to juridical opinions so much as to disputes about what the Quran contained. The Prophet warned that if while the Quran was being recited orally, before it was written down, and a dispute arose about correctness or the content, then the recitation of that verse should cease.[164]

Among the jurists, diversity did become a topic of discussion. Diversity was not condemned *per se*. Law by its very nature is a matter of argumentation. Argumentation can thrive only on the freedom to express honest opinions and the freedom to engage in avoiding injustice. Thus, it was impossible for the jurists to condemn diversity of opinion *per se*. It was rather the method of argumentation that was of concern. Among the classical jurists, Shafii is credited with the most thorough systematization of methods of argumentation (Coulson 1991, 55ff). He formulated the ground rules of jurisprudence in the Sharia relating to the number of sources of Islamic law and the methods for interpreting them. The classical rule is that the two major sources of law are the Quran and the hadiths. The two major methods for interpretation are *qiyas* (analogy) and *ijma* (consensus).

Shafii, however, did not have the last word. He had a formidable opponent in Ibn Hazm (d. 1064 Cordova),[165] an Andalusian jurist who died about two hundred years after Gaza-born Shafii died (d. 820 Cairo). Ibn Hazm did not challenge the basic scheme propagated by Shafii, but made major revisions. He accepted that the two major sources of law were the Quran and the hadiths. Regarding *sunna* as reported in the hadiths he was very cautious. He ranked the most reliable reporters in order of their closeness to the Prophet. Women who were the favourite wives of the Prophet he deemed especially reliable. Then came Abu Bakr, the first caliph. Umar ranked after Abu Bakr (Chejne, 114, 144).

It was mostly on the methods of interpretation that Ibn Hazm challenged the Shafiite jurisprudence. *Qiyas* he rejected. He argued that it had become a source of disputes and heated controversies (Chejne 171). Not that he was against controversy – even the Companions of the Prophet had exercised the freedom to have well-founded differences (*ikhtilaf*) (Chejne 114). The problem was that the disputed differences had become totally unrelated to reality, causing unsound and unfounded argumentation. The result was manifested in extremely pedantic legal treatises that did not do justice to the sources of law, the Quran and the hadiths. *Qiyas* he characterized as mere belief that drawing analogies established proof, where there was actually none. Thus *qiyas* had led to widespread sophistry (Chejne 173) and wide support of *taqlid*, that is, jurists were simply repeating what earlier jurists had argued and extending the latter's arguments by way of analogy, without any evaluation of the source on which the original argument was grounded (Abu Zahrah 285). This was illogical and dangerous because one cannot pass judgment on matters the reality of which one has not determined for oneself (Chejne 144). Ibn Hazm replaced *qiyas* as a method of interpretation with logic (*burhan*). Logic is more rigorous than *qiyas*. It requires basing conclusions on the evidence in the Quran and the hadiths. He had good support for this position in Abu Yusuf, who had criticized indiscriminate use of the hadiths without applying logic to interpreting them (Wheeler 71).

As for *ijma* – reaching a consensus among the jurists – Ibn Hazm did not reject it as a concept. He presented, however, a more rigorous definition of *ijma* than Shafii. *Ijma* had to mean full agreement, not just a majority opinion. *Ijma* when applied to the opinions of the Companions of the Prophet meant establishing the points on which they had reached total agreement (Abu Zahrah 356). If one Companion was of a different opinion, it could not be said that *ijma* existed among the Companions on the point at issue. Among the jurists, *ijma* had to be based on sound logic applied to the two basic sources of law, Quran and *sunna*. There had to be total agreement among the jurists in order for a rule to be binding. An alleged *ijma* that is based on illogic and wrongful interpretation is invalid *ijma* (Chejne 114).

Circumcision as social and medical practice

Keeping in mind the plea of Ibn Hazm to look at the reality of matters before passing judgment, let us now turn to the social reality of female circumcision. Female circumcision is known to be a largely African practice, with its roots in ancient Pharaonic Egypt. There is evidence in paintings from ancient Egypt of circumcision of females and males, but the female mummies do not show evidence of circumcision (Berkey 21). Later Byzantinian and Andalusian medical literature contain references to an unseemly growth of the clitoris in some women. It was said that in some it excited the women sexually because of contact with their garments. It was also said that it grew to such an extent that it looked like a penis and was uncomfortable for sexual intercourse. The medical remedy was to have it cut (Berkey 22, 24). A medieval treatise on local government rules and public order (*muhtasib*, vice squad or *Ordnungsamt*) regarded issues of body organs like private parts to be essentially a medical matter. Only physicians were permitted even to look at private parts, thus implying an interest of public authorities in restricting interference in the personal and private sphere, including prohibition of partial emasculation of any man, even a slave (Dien 60, 87, 103). It was recommended that the public authorities control who performed the operations, as many were done by women tattooists and manicurists. Questions also arose as to distinctions between the liability of a surgeon and that of an imam performing the operation (Berkey 27). In the preceding century there were reports from the USA that clitoridectomy was regarded too as a matter of purely medical treatment in extreme pathological cases (Berkey 31).

In present-day Egypt, girls are circumcised either individually or in groups in a kind of initiation ritual, as in many African cultures (Atiya 137). The depth of the cut into the female genitals, and therefore the extent of the medical harm done, varies very much depending on the person, usually a woman, performing the circumcision.[166] From interviews with women of the poorer classes, it is clear that circumcision is popular for various reasons. Some have said that it distinguishes Muslim from Coptic Christian women (Atiya 79; Krawietz 234) just as it has been considered a way of distinguishing Muslim men from 'infidels' (Sabbagh 13). Despite popular belief to the contrary, there is evidence of circumcision practised by some

Coptic women, historically and in the present day (Berkey 20, 23; Early 105). For some it is needed as a cosmetic measure to prevent the labia minora from growing long and ugly (Early 102). For others it is to protect family honour (Sabbagh 206) and to control the sexual appetite of women, though women have made empirical observations that the circumcision resulting in clitoral exposure (Early 103) can have the contrary effect, that is, it whets the sexual appetite (Atiya 113).[167] The Freudian notion of a frigid woman, as popularized in the West, is obviously foreign to populist Islamic cultural expectations. Another function of circumcision is said to confirm that a young woman has a uterus (Spenlen 39).[168]

Khitan ***in the Quran and sunna***

Why the practice of female circumcision is widespread in certain geographical areas of the Muslim world and not in others, and whether there is a correlation with how the classical jurists treated circumcision in a particular area is unknown. The word used by classical jurists for circumcision was *khitan*, or *khafd* (less often). *Khitan* referred to both male and female circumcision. The word does not appear in the Quran. A Quranic reference to Abraham's obedience to all of God's commands has been stretched to being deemed a very obscure command to perform male circumcision, a Talmudic Old Testament requirement from God (Sabbagh 13ff, ftn 167 above: Abu-Sahlieh 5–6).[169] In the hadith literature there are some but not numerous references to *khitan*. This would mean that circumcision was to a certain extent well known. The most detailed hadith most often cited in regard to female circumcision is from Abu Dawud, who warned that it was weak (ftn. 167 above: Abu-Sahlieh 17). According to the hadith, a woman in Medina performed circumcision operations on women. The Prophet is reported not to have prohibited it, but to have cautioned against it. He told the woman not to cut too severely so as to interfere in the sexual enjoyment between spouses. Two prohibitions that can be inferred from the account relate to the method of incision and to the purpose. It is not allowed to make deep cuts (Sabbagh 19) and the purpose is not to reduce the sexual appetite or satisfaction of women. It is interesting to note that the hadith, though weak, is reported by an Ansari woman. Ansari women were known for their independent attitudes, regarded by Umar as arrogance (see Tunisia chapter on obedience and beating). Whether Ansari and Qureshi women differed in their attitudes towards circumcision is not clear. This, however, is implied in certain juridical works citing other equally weak hadiths alleged to have been addressed specifically to Ansari women urging them to be circumcised (Sabbagh 19, n. 28). These hadiths propagandized circumcision as a matter of health and cosmetics. Circumcision would give a woman a glowing face (ftn. 167 above: Abu-Sahlieh 17). When seen in the context of the rivalry between the more independent Ansari women and the supposedly more 'compliant' Qureshi women, it is no wonder that circumcision for women became controversial in the juridical literature.

Classical juridical opinions on **khitan**

One of the proponents of female circumcision was Ibn Taimiyya (Berkey 21, 31, Ibn Taimiya 18). When asked whether there should be *khitan* for women, he answered definitively in the affirmative. He classified it as a matter of ritual purity, just as *khitan* for men was for reasons of health and purification. He defined, however, *khitan* for women as a question of *khafd.* This means 'diminishing', implying a diminishing that could go either way – diminishing their sexual appetites or diminishing hindrances to sexual enjoyment (ftn. 167 above: Abu-Sahlieh 17). Whether he was referring to the problem of women who had unusual and unseemly growths in the clitoris, thus restricting *khitan* to these medical cases, is not clear, but unlikely. For he further generalized that Tatar and European women (Rispler-Chaim 88–9) suffered from strong sexual appetites because of a defect in their private parts, in contrast to Muslim women regardless of their nationality. No medical authority was cited to support this seemingly ethnic prejudice. He cited in support of female *khitan* in general a weak hadith. He did not, however, support the undiminished practice of *khitan. Khitan* had legal consequences. If it resulted in injuring a woman, compensation was due. In this opinion, this was the kind of enlightened regulation that the Sharia introduced to control the practice.

It is this injury aspect which was emphasized, especially in the Maliki juridical literature. First of all, the Maliki hadiths do not contain references to the purposes of circumcision as do the other hadiths. The non-Maliki sources of reports from Abu Huraira on what constitutes cleanliness include cutting nails, plucking hair under the armpits, clipping the moustache, shaving the pubes *and* circumcision. The reports from Anas and Aisha on the same subject leave out circumcision in the list of what constitutes cleanliness.[170] While it is not immediately clear in some reports referring to *khitan* whether they had both men and women in mind, other reports from Abu Huraira clearly indicate that the *khitan* being recommended was only for men.[171] The Maliki jurists gave a husband the right to cancel a marriage contract if he found that the wife had a defect in her private parts, especially if it obstructed sexual intercourse. He did not even have to pay the dower, according to some jurists. A controversy arose about whether, upon a complaint by her husband, the wife could be examined without her consent, or whether her word was to be believed (Toledano 43, 122). Hanafi jurists, on the other hand, tended to deny the husband a right to void the marriage in case of a defect in the wife, thereby denying him the financial advantage of not having to pay the dower. It was argued that he had the power of *talaq* if he were dissatisfied with his wife. This difference in approach could explain why it was observed already in the Middle Ages that female circumcision, which obstructed penetration, was more prevalent in the east than in the west of the Islamic empire (Berkey 35, n. 14), where the Maliki opinions dominated (assuming that sexual enjoyment without obstructions created by *khitan* was the rule, and a few exceptional cases of *khitan* resulted in voiding the marriage).

Out of the variety of attitudes towards circumcision for females and the variety of interpretations from jurists, two main threads of argument emerge. One is that circumcision is not prohibited in the Sharia, but where it is practised, it may not have the purpose of diminishing the sexuality of a woman. The second is that *khitan* is a medical matter. The medical aspect involved treatment of purely bodily growths in women (somatic concerns) as well as psychological and sociological effects of such growths (enhancing or diminishing sexuality or modesty). Juridically, the opinion of Sheikh Tantawi, in favour of treating female circumcision as a matter of health (including psychosomatic cases) thus requiring reliance on medical judgment, is a logical outcome of clear interpretations of the Quran and the hadith literature. Amid the great diversity of classical juridical opinion on female circumcision, the one common thread running through them was the need for a medical assessment. To mix social demands for modesty in both women and men (as required by the Quran)[172] with the practice of female circumcision was to confuse issues just as large parts of the general lay population had been doing for decades. The opinion held by Sheikh Tantawi was consistent with his tireless efforts to present a *tafsir* (exegesis) of the Quran in language understandable by the layperson. It is also in keeping with his family situation. He had a daughter who is a medical doctor (Skovgaard-Petersen 251–2) and he was open to seeking the expertise of non-clerical professionals in order to ground Sharia interpretations in a firm factual foundation, e.g. through talks with astronomists for calculating the new moon; or with the doctors' union on questions of liability insurance for protecting poor patients (Skovgaard-Petersen 172, 198, 263, 280–1, 379).

Conclusions

In the 1980s members of the intellectual class in Egypt regretted that women had not been able to benefit from the liberationist spirit of Islam. Women were subject to an interpretation of Islamic law that was unjust and distorted. As a result, the personal status law was defective. Reforms of polygamy and unilateral *talaq* championed towards the end of the 20th century have not been implemented (Nowaihi 101).

Two decades later the intellectuals continue to plead for a reformed personal status law which conforms to the Quran's liberal spirit of equality between men and women. The intellectual capacity to conceptualize and articulate the reforms is impressive. The implementation fails. The cause of non-implementation is said to lie in the very conservative nature of Egyptian society and in deep class divisions. Once the financial and intellectual energy of Egypt was no longer tied up in the Palestinian wars, a chance arose again to re-examine the personal status law. By that time, however, society had become even more conservative, owing to migrant workers from Egypt flocking to the more traditional Arab Gulf states.

One significant factor contributing to the conservatism is said to be labour migration, despite the improved material development that accompanied returning migrants (Nada 65, 70–1).[173] Egypt had once exported its ideas and its well-trained professionals to the Arab Gulf states, but as the economic situation reversed, Egypt became dependent on its labour force migrating to the Gulf and Saudi Arabia to find work and send back their earnings to their families in Egypt. In these areas the men, and their wives when they accompanied them, grew accustomed to a very restricted version of Islam in non-democratic patriarchal societies. As a young woman who worked for voter registration in Cairo noted, she had spent several years in Libya with her husband and had become so accustomed to covering her head that she found it difficult to remove the covering once she returned to Egypt, although her Egyptian colleagues were not covering on the grounds that the Quran only requires modest clothing and a covering of the breast.

As a result of many Egyptian workers migrating, some have been attracted to attend courses abroad to qualify as religious teachers. Upon returning home they infiltrate the homes of upper-middle-class women to teach them at home about Islam. They are taught that obedience is unilateral – the wife to the husband – and that they should not go outside the home to work. These teachings are reinforced by a new phenomenon that more wealth from the Gulf States and Saudi Arabia has brought. The new upwardly mobile middle-class women can afford not to work and to stay at home as housewives. This reality is being ideologized: it is being justified by distorted interpretations of the Quran rather than being analysed as a result of the effect of wealth.

Possible solutions to the problem of social conservatism make for a lively debate among women intellectuals in Egypt. Some wish to see a massive information campaign by the government to counter the conservative teachings of migrant workers trained in the Gulf. This would be supported by submitting to the private press articles focusing not only on foreign and political affairs, but also on social issues. For example, the story of a chauffeur for a well-off businessman, who admits to beating his working-class wife because she wanted a bank account in her own name, is illustrative. Upon learning from his employer, a man, that Islam allows a woman to control her own earnings, he stopped beating his wife and allowed her to keep her own bank account. It is thought that a public campaign would benefit many more men like the chauffeur, with an emphasis on the Quranic injunction to make those whom society treats as weak, e.g. women, strong by ceasing to oppress them (sura 4:75).

Other intellectuals wish to see a massive industrialization programme. It is hoped that the creation of a strong economy itself would create new material conditions that would force people to interpret Islam in its proper liberationist spirit.

All seem to agree on the positive contribution of one person to carrying Islam's liberationist spirit forward. That person is the late Sheikh Tantawi (d. 2010). His relation to the government was institutionalized but without compromise to his integrity as a thinker. It is said that President Mubarak and Sheikh Tantawi reached an agreement whereby the government will continue to support the Dar al Ifta, which is housed in a modern building with the latest electronic equipment for educating schoolchildren and the public about Islam, and where Sheikh Tantawi held audience. In turn, the Sheikh did not shy away from pronouncing his views of the Sharia on politically and socially controversial issues, something which could not be taken for granted in the past (Skovgaard-Petersen 257). This did not mean that he had to agree with the government. Sheikh Tantawi was known to maintain his freedom of thought. He was a *mujtahid* of integrity, basing opinions on facts and logic. His capacity to grasp the essential spirit of the basic sources of the Sharia (Quran and the hadiths) was phenomenal. He was known for emphasizing the basic orientation of the Sharia towards sharing wealth and protecting the poor (Skovgaard-Petersen 266, 280). For this reason, for example, he issued an opinion against the government's land-reform scheme on the grounds that it would have deprived the poorer tenant farmers of legal protection.

His charisma was thoroughly Islamic. He embodied the best of the tradition of the Egyptian ulama. He was available for anyone who has a problem or wishes to discuss a question. He was flexible enough to accept callers without standing on the ceremony of Western-style appointments and without regard to the social status or religious affinity or gender of the seeker of advice.[174] This ensured public confidence in his integrity and openness. At the same time, he maintained the strict division of responsibilities between his office and other state authorities. He was known for rigidly maintaining the division of authority between the Sheikh ul Islam and the Egyptian courts when he received petitions from persons dissatisfied with a court judgment.[175]

The obvious strength of his character and Islamic-law scholarship, however, should not blind one to the complexity of the institutional system in Egypt today. The position of Sheikh Tantawi and his relationship to the government indicates a system of checks and balances in public life which is much more complex than has been captured up to now in the political science theories of democratic checks and balances, above all the independence of the judiciary.

Besides agreeing on their admiration of the Sheikh ul Islam, several women intellectuals seem to agree, too, that the religious and political structures along with the class divisions in Egypt are too complex to permit any but painstakingly gradual reforms in laws affecting the personal status rights of women. What reforms have been achieved through the legislature have been sustained by the highest court and even extended. This reflects the realization on the part of the court that its independence is not only from political influence but also from partisan religious influence. It walks a tightrope. The next step in Egypt after the Supreme Court set a precedent of appointing a woman judge to its bench is to appoint a woman mufti, even if it has taken eight centuries since that same idea was already proposed in the 13th century just before the Egyptian Mamluks took over in the name of slave power (Fadel 190; Mian Hammad Murtaza v Federation of Pakistan, Petition 1/L 2010, fed. Sh. Crt., 29 Sep 2010).[176]

3

PAKISTAN – ORTHODOX MODERNITY

Historical background

Muslim ruler/states in the Indian Subcontinent

This chapter covers a non-Arab Muslim society, Pakistan. It has a long history as part of the Indian Subcontinent. It was subject through the centuries to waves of varying rulers: Muslim conquerors fought as early as the 10th century with the Hindu rajas who controlled the area from Kabul to the Punjab, and Genghis Khan invaded in 1221. The Indian Subcontinent's borders were determined under the colonial British. Its population included a majority of Hindus, not Muslims; the latter were scattered throughout India, with pockets of concentration. Bengal had fallen under Muslim rule in 1204 when conquered by the Delhi Sultanate (1206–1526), whose rulers originated from the Persian Tajiks (a silver coin was struck in the first decade of the 1200s in Calcutta to commemorate the victory.) The Mughal empire succeeding the Delhi Sultanate produced some of the greatest examples of Islamic architecture, the Taj Mahal and the Lahore Fort gardens (now in Pakistan). Strong Muslim rulers had either collaborated with or fought against the British. For example, the Begums of Bhopal in central India ruled a principality which had been founded by an Afghan commander in the early 1700s. The women rulers who succeeded saw fit to ally with the British during the Mutiny of 1857,[1] while the Nawab of Oudh (with his capital at Lucknow), Wajid Ali Shah, was said to support the rebellion, along with his wife the Begum Hazarat Mahal. The Bhopali

Begums in the end proved to be the more foresighted. The largest Muslim principality in the Subcontinent was in Hyderabad, ruled by the Nizam.

Introduction of British legal thought in the Subcontinent

India had a long tradition of Islamic scholars before the arrival of the British. General Cornwallis, whose army had retreated when the American colonies won Independence in 1781, presided over the introduction of new laws into a legal system which had been founded on Islamic law, with recognition of Hindu, Buddhist and customary rules in civil matters. The major concern of Cornwallis was to change the penal law, the basis of which was Islamic, applicable to all persons regardless of religion. Cornwallis undertook the task in a piecemeal way rather than with a revolutionary overhaul of the entire set of laws. He began by removing the power of heirs of a murder victim to exercise discretion to waive the death penalty and ask for compensation instead. This power was transferred to the ruler/state, which replaced compensation with imprisonment. Later he asked Muslim scholars to write a *fatwa* on whether murder required *qisas*, a life for a life, i.e. the death penalty. Then he prohibited mutilation of a thief's hand (Yousaf; Jones-Pauly 1999).

In the following century the Mutiny roused the British from their complacency and gave both Muslim scholars and rulers as well as the British occasion for rethinking the direction of legal reform (Klein; Jones-Pauly 1999). A commission was established for determining the shape of the Indian legal system. A compromise was reached – mostly on pragmatic grounds – between universal laws for all in the Indian Subcontinent and pluralistic sets of laws governing personal status and was justified by British notions of equity. The key universal laws were the penal code, the evidence code and civil and criminal procedure codes. The notion of repugnancy was introduced as the bridge between the statutory universalistic laws and the pluralistic personal status and inheritance laws or customs. Repugnancy introduced the yardstick against which all local customs and rules were measured. If found to be repugnant to written statutory law or equitable justice, the rule in question was declared inapplicable. The concept was not foreign to Islamic juristic thinking. During the same period the Ottoman Empire too was redesigning its legal system and laws. The Ottoman Land Code of 1858 revised the traditional Islamic inheritance rules. The justification was equitable development, for the object was to curtail the extreme land fragmentation which was economically detrimental to agricultural development.

Legal scholarly dialogue – Syed Ahmed Khan and Badrudin Tyabji

It was a time of juxtaposed legal systems, each one vibrant in its own right, each one having a different power base. Such juxtaposition was not new in Indian history – it had been the case under Mughal rule too. What was new was the effort to harmonize and systematize, which included the concept of freedom of choice – to what extent members of a given community could choose to move in and out of their own community-law systems and the universal system. Comparison became the order of the day. In these circumstances it is not surprising that one of the foremost Muslim legal thinkers at the time began writing about Islamic law as a system. He did not take it for granted, nor confine himself to analysing individual rules and their derivation from sources. He began to examine it from a philosophical point of view – its purposes, its vision of human nature, its vision of the origins of laws. He was Sir Syed Ahmed Khan (1817–98). He is claimed as one of the intellectual fathers of Pakistani Muslim identity. He served as a judge in the British service and on the Legislative Council of the British Viceroy. To the chagrin of some Muslim leaders who resented the fall of the Mughal Empire, he propagated mutual respect between Muslims and the British by writing a book on the causes of the Indian Mutiny, in an attempt to counter arguments that blamed Muslims, and wrote a commentary on the Bible in response to British works on Islam (Muir). He was keen for Muslims to recognize that education was the path to take in order to realize their rights under British rule. His approach can be contrasted with that of British legal scholars who tended to see Islamic law through other lens. First of all, they wished to master its intricate rules and crystallize them in the same way as their own laws. What was missing was a true dialogue of legal systems. Such a dialogue would mean knowing each system so well that one could participate in internal critique. That is to say, an Islamic scholar would know British law well enough to be familiar with the internal critical debates surrounding British law reform, and a British scholar in turn would be familiar with the critical debates among Islamic scholars. The aim of such an exchange is to discover how each legal system can benefit from the other and admit its own failings. It was the uneven power relationship between colonized and colonizer which prevented such a dialogue.

One of the crucial results of the debate was the realization among Muslim thinkers that education was essential for the community. Aligarh University, originally the Muhammedan Anglo-Oriental School begun by Syed Ahmed Khan, was founded as the main centre of Muslim learning, near Agra. Among its later sponsors of women's education was the Begum of Bhopal, Jehan (Sultan; Lambert-Hurley).

Starting a social reform movement for Muslims and a magazine in 1870, called *Tahdhib al Akhlaq*, Syed Ahmed Khan's works also became known in Arab Islamic centres through the Arab periodical *Al Manar*, started in 1898 by Syrian-Egyptian Rashid Rida. Regarding communal strife, Ahmed Khan had apparently less faith in cooperation between Muslims and Hindus: he was against the participation of Muslims in the Indian National Congress, a political party, founded in 1885. He also initiated the All India Muhammedan Educational Conference in 1886 to project Muslims' views. He was opposed by Badruddin Tyabji (1844–1906), Chief Justice of the Bombay High Court and the foremost Muslim scholar on the application of Muslim personal status law in secular state courts.[2] A president of the Indian National Congress, he argued against the creation of separate Muslim and Hindu states. He opposed the veiling and sequestration of Muslim women; the women in his own household removed the veil. He argued that making it mandatory would be against the Quran. He was in good company: the Begums of Bhopal had not worn veils. Only the last Begum Jehan donned it, and only for political purposes whenever she held an audience with a British colonial official. In 1876 Tyabji founded his own organization for the advancement and betterment of Muslims, called *Anjuman-i-Islam*.

Later in opposition to both Syed Ahmed Khan and Tyabji, Viqar-ul-Mulk called for the establishment in 1906 of the Muslim equivalent of the Indian National Congress. This was the All India Muslim League. Its later leader, Muhammed Ali Jinnah, joined forces with the Indian National Congress in the fight for Independence, then supported the founding of Pakistan. Jinnah himself had married into a wealthy Bombay Parsi family. His only daughter, Dina, later married a Parsi, thus exercising her right (probably not consciously but out of love) as a Muslim woman to have the same right as a Muslim man to marry someone of a monotheistic religion.[3]

More traditional movements were also afoot. The Deoband *madrassa* or seminary (influential today in Durban, South Africa) had been founded in 1866 by Haji Muhammad Abid, continuing the tradition started in the

10th/4th centuries of schools of law attached to a mosque and financed by a *waqf* (Makdisi 21). It emphasized traditional hadith learning, while Syed Khan focused on Quranic *ijtihad.* Associated with the Deoband was Maulana Muhammad Qasim Nanotvi, whose spiritual mentor Haji Imdad Ullah had been so closely involved in the Indian Mutiny of 1857 that he sought refuge in Mecca. A later associate was Maulana Ubaid Ullah Sindhi, who went to Afghanistan in the First World War to set up a provisional Indian government to fight the British. After the Allied victory he left for Moscow, Istanbul and Mecca.

Another group which came into existence at the time of Syed Ahmed in 1894 was the Nadva Tul Ulema in Lucknow (long regarded as the hotbed of the Mutiny). The group was intended to bring together ulama scholars at the Dar ul Uloom. The founding of this group was more in line with the position of another contemporary of Syed Ahmed Khan, Jamal ad Din al Afghani (1838–97), an Iranian Shiite scholar and government advisor who spent time in India (just before the Mutiny), Iraq, Afghanistan, Mecca and Istanbul, and was well known for his impassioned dislike of the British defeats of Muslim military powers in the region (Indian princely states during the Mutiny and Afghanistan in the second Anglo-Afghan War). He advocated calling the ulama together for a consensus on *ijtihad* rulings,[4] while Syed Ahmed Khan opined that the ulama as a group were not inclined to perform the necessary *ijtihad.* Nor did he think that such a consensus was conducive to freedom of speech. He preferred to exercise his own intellect and win influence over minds in this way (Ahmad 59–60).

Though opposed politically, both Syed Khan and Tyabji agreed on the same guiding principle of Islamic law – rationalism (Makdisi 12, 16, 18) – to counter blind adherence and duplication, that is *taqlid* as opposed to *ijtihad* based on argument and investigation of facts as well as texts, *ijtihad* being used in the sense that it is needed, in the same way that prophetic inspiration was needed in its day, so that the Revelation could be clarified under changing circumstances (Makdisi 36). Part of the object of this chapter is to demonstrate how to this day this rationalism can be traced in contemporary Pakistani judges' analysis of sources of Islamic law. A parallel movement in Tunisia at the time was the founding of Sadiki College by Khayr ad Din, aimed at training bureaucrats in harmonizing scientific epistemology and Islamic religious knowledge. Among Muslims in the Subcontinent this was left to the private efforts of a scholar like Sir Ahmed Khan, who acknowledged the influence of the reformer Khayr ad Din on his thinking (Ahmad 59).

This was an era of shifts in world power relations. On the eve of the Mutiny of 1857, the British had fought the costly Crimean War, suffered disaster a decade before in the first Anglo-Afghan War of 1842, and had taken up a crusade to abolish slavery worldwide, the economic basis of both the southern United States and the Muslim Ottoman Empire. Great Britain had entered into several treaties which were to impact on the power of the Ottoman Empire and Muslim states, e.g. engagement with Persia over Herat in 1853,[5] a treaty with the Sultan of Sokoto (Emir of Believers) in 1853 for protection of British merchants,[6] a treaty of Peace in Perpetuity between the Chiefs of the Arabian Coast (Trucial Sheikhdoms of Oman) in 1853,[7] a treaty between Austria, France and Great Britain guaranteeing the independence and integrity of the Ottoman Empire in 1856,[8] an agreement between Great Britain and Aulaki (South-Western Arabia) for the suppression of the slave trade in 1858,[9] a treaty between Great Britain and Zanzibar for the suppression of the slave trade in 1873, Zanzibar being one of the largest suppliers of slaves for the Persian Gulf and India.[10] Muslim intellectuals were grappling with the significance of all these events for Islamic law – the abolition of slavery as an Islamic legal institution alone meant a revolutionary change in legal thinking, for treatment of slaves, no matter how much better than in some Christian domains, had consumed much juristic energy, and its rules were often referred to in order to draw analogies with other domains of law, including penal law. The peace treaties between the British and Arabian Muslim princes turned the concept of *dar al harb* (non-Muslim lands as enemies of Muslims) and *dar es salaam* (Muslim lands as friendly) upside down. Afghans had declared *jihad* on Persia during its siege of Herat in 1837 and in 1841 against the British (Nawid).[11] All these events sent shock waves through the Muslim intelligentsia who had to synthesize their significance and decide whether to reform or to retrench. The positions that various intellectuals took on the political and military imbalance which accompanied the outburst of intellectual energy in the 19th century must have coloured their attitudes towards the direction Islamic juridical thought should take, for national, religious and ethnic pride were at stake. It was not solely about correcting injustices. Today we observe a similar shift. It is human rights and the women's movement that both incinerate and stimulate debate.

The start of Independence

The Muslim question and the Indian independence movement – the birth of Pakistan

By the time the Indian Subcontinent, under the leadership of Gandhi, a lawyer, began its struggle for Independence, the world had shifted again – the Boer War, the Suffragette Movement, the First World War and the dissolution of the Ottoman Empire had pushed intellectual thinking in the direction of framing the world in terms of rights, in particular the right to self-determination, whether as a state, a minority group or an individual. In India the Muslim question had long been debated. Rulers of Muslim states became concerned about their status in a future independent Hindu majority state. The son of the last Begum of Bhopal began to negotiate for the right of rulers to opt out of an independent India and found their own states. If this had been realized it would have meant that Hindu majority India would become fragmented territorially between a Hindu state and some smaller states dominated by Muslim rulers: even where there were already Muslim rulers, such as in Bhopal and Hyderabad, the Hindus were still in the majority among their subjects.

The attempts of the Muslim rulers to gain independence failed (Zaidi). Instead, it was agreed that the once-independent Indian government would become sovereign and compensate the rulers for loss of position and of quasi-autonomy which they had enjoyed under British rule. Muslims, however, pushed for a separate state in the far west of the Subcontinent, bordering on other Muslim states like Afghanistan. This was the ground for the birth of the state of Pakistan. Much to the chagrin of Gandhi, the Muslims obtained a separate state in 1947, in exchange for the non-fragmentation of most of the territory of India. Pakistan comprised the former Indian provinces of East Bengal, West Punjab, Sindh, North-West Frontier, Baluchistan and a portion of Assam ('Sylhet'). The leader of the Muslim League, Muhammad Ali Jinnah, like Gandhi a lawyer and known as the Quaid-i-Azam (Grand Leader), became the country's first governor general.

The result was one of the most tragic examples of large-scale ethnic cleansing that has ever taken place – seven million dead. The Hindus and Sikhs moved into Punjab in northern India and the Muslims crossed over into Pakistan. Today Muslim families are assigned the task of protecting important Sikh shrines which remain in Pakistani Punjab, where Sikhs once protected Muslim shrines before Partition. Pakistan inherited the legendary Pathan-dominated North-West Frontier, which includes the Swat Valley, supposedly the scene of Alexander the Great's campaigns and controlled under the British by the Yusufzai-Pathans. Pakistan became territorially fragmented into western and eastern Pakistan, eastern Pakistan consisting of Bengalis, with a long intellectual history (their most famous son being Rabindrath Tagore, Nobel Prize Laureate) and affiliation at least among the elite with Persian culture. Marriage contracts among Bengali Muslims were, and are to this day, written in Persian, as Persians had played a prominent role in recording early Indian history.

Pakistan, like modern Punjab, was born out of blood and bitterness. Its first President, Jinnah, was a moderate Muslim (married to a Bombay Parsi, as mentioned above), who sought to create a legal system in the spirit of Syed Khan and the reforms undertaken in various other Muslim majority countries. The rationalist tradition of *ijtihad* was reclaimed as the basis of Islamic law.

Pakistan was the first country to have a constitution which declared its *raison d'être* to be upholding Islamic culture and becoming a counterweight to Hindu culture and power. It redefined the nation state. Nationalism was not to be based on blood, ethnicity or language, but on religious affiliation. What is often forgotten, however, is that it was closely related to the desire of certain Muslim rulers to maintain their positions of power. Indeed, Abida Sultan, granddaughter of the last Begum of Bhopal and daughter of the Nawab, who had tried to negotiate the Independence of Bhopal state, fled to Pakistan upon its birth. Because she became a Pakistani citizen the Indian government deprived her of the right to succeed to the title of Begum upon the death of her father the Nawab. Her flight to Pakistan made a dramatic story. She escaped with only her jewels and without informing her family. Once in Pakistan she married well and became Ambassador to Brazil. She was a close associate of Fatima, Jinnah's sister. Abida's sister, who remained Indian, succeeded to the titular leadership of Bhopal and the princely lands. She was Sikander Saulat, and became a member of the Bhopal assembly in 1957 under the name of Sajida Maimoona Sultan. When the Indian government under Indira Gandhi relieved the strain on the national budget of payments to the princes by ordering all payments to be ceased,[12] the nephew (Hamidullah Khan) of the Pakistani daughter of the Nawab negotiated with the Indian government regarding the retention of certain family land holdings. The nephew eventually succeeded his mother, Sikander Saulat, who had married the Nawab of Pataudi in Punjab. The current Nawab of Bhopal and Pataudi then set an example of how Muslims and Hindus can coexist, at least at the elite level. He married a Hindu, Shamila Tagore, of the famous Tagore family and a famous movie actress. She converted to Islam, which facilitates custody of children, in case of divorce or separation, and inheritance. While Bhopal acceded to India, the rich Nizam of Hyderabad sought independence from both Pakistan and India. He was forced to decide for India when his Hyderabad troops were defeated by the Indian army.

Muslim exceptionalism in Indian law versus law reform in Pakistan

Muslims remaining in India are exempt from the universal laws governing certain personal status matters for all citizens. For example, the law abolishing polygamy for Hindus and all other groups does not apply to Muslims. The same is true for other laws granting women rights to post-divorce alimony and equality of inheritance rights. In effect, while Hindus were prepared to accept legal reforms of their own traditions, Muslims felt compelled to remain more nationalistic about their own rules. The All India Muslim Personal Law Board was formed for the express purpose of exempting Muslims from legal reforms. The Indian politicians have pandered to the Board for political votes, and the Indian courts are left with the task of reforming Islamic law and conferring on all women, Muslim or not, entitlement to post-divorce maintenance.[13]

The All India Muslim Personal Law Board did not keep pace with the initial reforms which Pakistan introduced in personal status matters.[14] The Pakistani legislature introduced, by using *ijtihad*, a new Muslim family law.[15] It did not abolish polygamy but did place limitations on it. No man may marry a second wife without his first wife's consent and the approval of the Arbitration Council. He must prove to the Council the necessity of a second wife, e.g. the first wife is too ill to take care of the household, or has not produced children. Violation of this provision entails imprisonment. If he takes on a second wife without permission, he must pay a prompt dower, or else it can be taken in the form of arrears in land revenue. In terms of inheritance the grandchildren have the right to step into the shoes of their predeceased parents and not be disinherited by collateral relatives when the deceased has left only daughters and no sons, or no first-degree children at all. The husband's *talaq* is not effective until he gives notice to the local council (under the Basic Democracies Order 1959) and submits to an Arbitration Council (Lyon 182; Ali, S.S.) for an attempt at reconciliation, under pain of imprisonment.

At times the Hindu–Muslim, India–Pakistan animosity seeps into the law. For example, a Pakistani challenged the constitutionality[16] of a law designed to stop elaborate and expensive weddings, because even if the wealthy could afford them, they set a poor example for the poor burdened with wedding-cost debts. The petition pleaded violation of the right to trade and business (Art. 18 of the Constitution) and protection against discrimination (Art. 25). The Supreme Court upheld the law as in accord with the Islamic Sunnah of the Prophet, who expected the family to invite not just relatives but also the community and to keep the event simple. It attributed the social evil of ostentatious expensive weddings and high dowers to Hindu customs, without any reference to expensive weddings in non-Hindu contexts, e.g. in the Arab world.

A Muslim ruler/state – in need of an Islamic law?

As said above, Pakistan was the first modern constitutional state to be founded explicitly as a Muslim state. Often the Islamic Republic of Iran is accorded this distinction, but the difference is that Pakistan never became ruled by clerics as did Iran. The Pakistani constitution established a governance structure in which the clerics or ulama are assigned a particular role and not given political power. Their role will be discussed in more detail at a later point.

Constitutional 'Objectives Resolution' and Islam

In 1949 two years after Independence, the Pakistani Constituent Assembly adopted the principles which were to guide the drafting of the first Constitution. These were incorporated in the Objectives Resolution which named eight essential principles:

1. sovereignty in God Allah alone but delegated as a sacred trust through the Pakistani people to the State of Pakistan with the object of sovereignty being exercised within Allah's limits;
2. exercise of the State power and authority through popularly elected representatives;

3. principles of democracy, freedom, equality, tolerance and social justice, as enunciated by Islam;
4. a federated form of government;
5. enabling Muslim citizens to order their individual and collective lives in accordance with the teachings of Islam as set out in the Holy Quran and Sunnah;[17]
6. adequate provision for minorities to freely profess and practise their religions and develop their cultures;
7. guarantee of fundamental rights;
8. an independent judiciary.

1962 Constitution – from Mirza to Ayub Khan

Pakistan relinquished its dominion status and became the Islamic Republic of Pakistan under the Constitution of 1956. The president of the country had to be a Muslim, whether a woman or a man. Five seats were reserved in the parliament for women. The Constitution was suspended and abrogated in 1958 upon the imposition of martial law under President Iskander Mirza and General Ayub Khan, who later ousted Mirza. Ayub Khan belonged to the old British Punjab Regiment.

In 1962 Ayub Khan had a new constitution passed, which created a strong presidential form of government with control over the parliament. The right to vote was not universal. Parliament had six women members. The Islamic principles named in the Constitution were not to be subject to any judicial review. To reinforce the curb on the judiciary, he introduced the Advisory Council of Islamic Ideology, whose members were made responsible only to the government for recommending how it could best ensure Muslims would live their lives according to Islamic teachings. In effect the people were not entrusted with any authority in interpreting Islamic law or seen as trustees of Allah's delegation of democratic authority to them. The tone went from enabling to ensuring.

In 1965 elections were held and a woman stood for the presidency. Fatima Jinnah, the sister of Jinnah, the founding father of Pakistan, stood for election, and lost.

Ayub Khan laid plans for moving the capital city from Karachi in Sindh to Islamabad in Punjab.

End of the 1962 Constitution, and the rise of Zulficar Ali Bhutto, the 1973 Constitution, and Islamist challenges

The Constitution of 1962 had a short life. Martial law was again established in 1969 under Yahya Khan. In 1971 Bengali nationalism triumphed and East Pakistan seceded to become Bangladesh. India had attacked Pakistan and supported Bangladesh militarily. Pakistan had lost over 50 per cent of its population. The defeat spelt the end of Yahya's regime and Z.A. Bhutto became Prime Minister. He was a landowner from Sindh (Karachi). He had been Foreign Minister in Ayub Khan's government; he had resigned over disagreement with the Tashkent Agreement between India and Pakistan on a ceasefire in Kashmir. Bhutto nationalized major industries and banks and in 1973 the National Assembly promulgated a new constitution.

In 1977 his Pakistan People's Party was challenged by the Pakistan National Alliance, whose manifesto was the Quran. When the votes showed a majority win for the People's Party, the National Alliance claimed election rigging, not without cause, but its demands for a fresh election were refused. The National Alliance then agitated, urging people to defy the police and security forces. They convinced mosque leaders to declare a *jihad* against Bhutto on the grounds that he was a left-wing socialist.

General Ul Haq – Islamic democracy?

Again the military intervened and General Zia Ul Haq imposed martial law. Ul Haq reflected the interests of the Punjab military class. In early 1978 the political parties met to discuss new elections, but in 1979 Ul Haq declared all political parties moribund. A month later with the Soviet invasion of Afghanistan, Pakistan became a close ally of the United States and gave refuge to the Afghani mujahedin fighters, who were pitting Islam against communism. Not ready to concede power to a democracy based on political parties, General Ul Haq established an Islamic body, the Majlis ul Shoora, as a substitute for the National Assembly. The Majlis was not to have parliamentary powers. It was more of an advisory body. In 1979 he decreed the application of Islamic penal law, the same year Z.A. Bhutto was hanged for the murder of a fellow party member. Ul Haq used the democratic instrument of a referendum in 1984 to endorse the non-legislative Majlis body. In effect a pseudo-Islamic institution was utilized to avoid introducing a democracy based on authentic Islamic principles and the original founding principles of Pakistan. General Ul Haq knew that whoever consolidated control over Islam controlled the people, which is nothing new in terms of early Islamic political history (Lapidus 377; Agha).[18] He also did not wish to encourage any socialist or left-wing politics because of the Soviet influence on his doorstep in Afghanistan and for fear of alienating Afghani refugees fleeing into Pakistan. He died in a plane crash along with the US ambassador in 1988. Ul Haq was succeeded by a civilian government and parliament was restored. It adopted the name Majlis e Shoora (National Assembly).[19]

Making history – the first woman Muslim prime minister

In 1988 the Pakistan People's Party again contested the elections, this time under the leadership of a woman, Benazir Bhutto, the daughter of Z.A. Bhutto. Pakistan made history as the first modern Islamic state to elect a woman leader. It was the second modern state at the time applying religious law to achieve this distinction (Israel under Golda Meir). President Ghulam Ishaq Khan dismissed Ms Bhutto's government in 1990 for reasons of corruption. When the President dismissed the next duly-elected Prime Minister, Mian Nawaz Sharif, and appointed a caretaker premier, the Supreme Court quashed the appointment and the ousted premier was reinstated. The President and premier then both resigned. Despite the political turmoil, the penal code was amended in 1990 to add aspects of Quranic law on murder and compensation as an alternative to the death penalty.[20]

In the ensuing elections of 1993 Ms Bhutto was re-elected, along with a new President, Farooq Ahmad Khan Leghar, also of the Pakistan People's Party. During her tenure she made some alterations to the Islamic *hudud* laws. Her government largely abolished whipping as a sentence but kept it intact where prescribed in the Quran.[21] In November 1996 she was again ousted by the President on charges of corruption and the National Assembly was dissolved. Mian Nawaz Sharif was again elected premier in 1997. During his tenure he attacked the judiciary when the Chief Justice released certain civil servants who had been arrested by Sharif's government. The Chief Justice opposed extending the jurisdiction of special courts for speedy trials, which Sharif had instituted to bypass the judiciary. During Sharif's tenure Islamic penal injunctions were expanded to cover murder. The Penal Code was amended to introduce the notion of *diya*, compensation to the victim's family if they did not insist on the death of the perpetrator. The courts could normally order the death sentence as part of the *qisas* principle, a life for a life and it could be commuted only with the consent of the heirs of the victim.[22]

Nawaz Sharif's government ended with General Parvez Musharraf (of Sindh origins) taking power in 1999. The Constitution of 1973 was revived through the Legal Framework Order, 2002, by executive order.[23] The Order permitted the Chief Executive of Pakistan to amend the Constitution in any way thought fit and such would not be challenged in a court of law (Art. 3).[24] The Chief Executive became the President with a term of office for the next five years (until 2007). Non-Muslims and women received reserved seats in each provincial parliament. In the fifth year of his rule the legislators passed a law which punished honour killings.[25]

After general elections in 2002 the National Assembly affirmed the executive order by enacting the Constitution (Seventeenth Amendment) Act of 2003. In 2005 local government elections were held. Musharraf has since resigned.

The 1973 Constitution – basis of applying Islamic law

In summary, throughout all these political changes the 1973 Constitution was suspended in 1977, then restored in 1985 then suspended in 1999, restored in 2002 and amended in 2003.

The Islamic law legacy of General Ul Haq remains to this day. One of the major laws which he introduced, without the benefit of parliament, is known as the Offence of Zina[26] (Enforcement of Hudood) Ordinance VII of 1979 (Zina Ordinance), one in a series of *hudud* ordinances. He reintroduced the Islamic penal law based on *taqlid*, that is, blind adherence to interpretations from past eras, the very kind of interpretation of sources which Syed Ahmed Khan had critiqued a century previously. This chapter is devoted mainly to the many issues which have arisen from this ordinance.

Later in 1991 after Ms Bhutto was dismissed, the Majlis e Shoora constituted as parliament passed the Enforcement of Shariat Act during the premiership of Mian Muhammad Nawaz Sharif. The following discussion provides the constitutional background to the application of the Zina Ordinance and the Shariat Act.

The Pakistani Constitution of 1973, from the Bhutto era, reflected the fears that had been expressed among Muslim leaders before the partition from India that Muslims might not be able to live their laws as freely in a Hindu majority society under the more socialist and secular-oriented leadership of the first generation of Indian leaders like Nehru and his daughter. The preamble of the Pakistani Constitution guarantees that Muslims shall be enabled to order the individual and collective spheres of their lives in accordance with the teachings and requirements of Islam as set out in the Holy Quran and Sunnah.[27] Non-Muslims, consisting of Hindus and Christian minorities, would be by implication exempt. This implication has proved not to be necessarily the case – some of the Islamic penal provisions introduced and analysed below do indeed apply to non-Muslims.

First challenge – may the ruler/state enable Muslims to live by Islamic law by enforcing Islamic law?

This enabling provision in the Preamble may seem on the surface self-explanatory and non-controversial. In fact it became the subject of dispute one year after the promulgation of the Offence of Zina (Enforcement of Hudood) Ordinance VII of 1979. The challenge came in a 1980 case before the Supreme Court. The litigants disputed the right of the state to enact Islamic rules carrying penal sanctions, specifically the *hudud* criminal rules. The litigants contended that how Muslims lead their lives under Islam is a matter of free choice and conscience, not to be defined by a state constitution.[28] The way to leading a life according to God's prescriptions was by enabling a person to search her/his own conscience and to make a free choice to lead one's life under Islam, as there is no force in religion.[29] The petitioners also used the language of the 1949 Objectives Resolution, which provided that Allah is the sovereign, but delegates his sovereignty to the people. They argued that since God is the chief legislator for Islam the parliament could enact no Islamic laws. Muslims had to find the law for themselves in the Quran and hadiths and regulate their lives accordingly.[30]

The Supreme Court rejected these arguments. It concluded that the state has the authority to enact penal laws in order to enable Muslims to lead an Islamic life, even though such laws might violate their consciences. The court rather supported its position on the basis of secular law, 'secular' meaning here simply the law as legislated by the state rather than by a religious body. The court quoted the 1973 Constitution as amended by Ul Haq's executive order in 1980. Article 227 provided: 'All existing laws shall be brought in conformity with the injunctions of Islam as laid down in the Holy Quran and Sunnah, in this Part referred to as the Injunctions of Islam, and no law shall be enacted which is repugnant to such injunctions.'[31]

Therefore, so argued the court, it is the Constitution which guarantees the state's right and duty to enact Islamic laws.

The court made clear that the Constitution itself is not subject to the Injunctions of Islam, since Article 203B (c) (Definitions) exempts the Constitution from such norms: '... law includes any custom or usage having the force of law but does not include the Constitution, Muslim Personal Law, any law relating to the procedure of any court or tribunal or, until the expiration of [ten] years from the commencement of this Chapter, any fiscal law or any law relating to the levy and collection of taxes and fees or banking or insurance practice and procedure ...' This meant that no one could challenge the Constitution as being against the Injunctions of Islam nor challenge the Injunctions as unconstitutional (Redding). Ergo, this exemption kept the Constitution as the fundamental law of the land.[32] Thus any law enacted under the constitutional powers of the state has the nature of law and the law in question was to punish violations of its prescriptions which happened to derive from Islamic prescriptions. To the layperson this sounds like legal sophistry. The judgment nonetheless can be acclaimed as politically clever. It leaves open the way to future constitutional changes that may enable Muslims to take another path towards leading an Islamic way of life other than by threat of punishment by the state under Islamic penal law.

The reasoning in the judgment had an impact much later, as evidenced when the Enforcement of Shariat Act was duly promulgated by the Majlis (parliament) under Prime Minister Nawaz Sharif in 1991. The Enforcement of Shariat Act X of 1991 proclaims the Injunctions of Islamic law as laid down in the Holy Quran and the Sunnah shall be the supreme law of Pakistan (Art. 3 (1)) (Kennedy). At the same time the Act protects judicial independence. No court judgment shall be challenged. The Act states that the courts are to interpret statutory laws in conformity with Islamic principles, yet it acknowledges that there are multiple pluralistic Islamic law interpretations, two or more, in which case courts are to choose the one most compatible with the Constitution (Art. 4). Nor shall the constitutional guarantees of the rights of women be affected (Art. 20). In the light of the Supreme Court's ruling that the Constitution is the fundamental law of the land, the Enforcement of Shariat Act represents a compromise. The Constitution remains unamended and so by implication is supreme or at least equally supreme. Such a compromise is typical of the *modus vivendi* which the British scholar Sir Norman Anderson perceived to be necessary if statute and Sharia were to coexist (Anderson 1957).

The court did not respond in detail to the plaintiff's argument that when the state purports to enforce the religious text it violates the verse against compulsion in religion (2:256). This goes to the very core of the nature of Islamic law (Rosen). It is a legal system which functions with parties' consent and agreement. Several areas of law reflect this. Marriage in itself is a contract which regulates the rights and duties of the parties and can go as far as negating the husband's privilege of polygamy as well as allow the wife to deviate from the usual conjugal duties. In Western law, by contrast, marriage is by origin a sacrament and except in property matters is less negotiable. Even with regard to the marriage dower in Islam, the wife is given expressly the Quranic option to agree to waive it.

Another issue which the Supreme Court did not respond to was the petitioners' argument that if Allah is the supreme legislator for Islamic laws, then the state may not legislate in this area. General Ul Haq instead answered them. He decreed a constitutional amendment by inserting in Article 2A[33] the original aims set out in 1949 for a constitution:

> The principles and provisions set out in the Objectives Resolution reproduced in the Annex are hereby made a substantive part of the Constitution and shall have effect accordingly.

The Annex reiterates God as sovereign who entrusts the people who in turn entrust the state to exercise the limits of Allah:

> Whereas sovereignty over the entire universe belongs to Allah Almighty alone and the authority which He has delegated to the State of Pakistan, through its people for being exercised within the limits prescribed by Him is a sacred trust…

What is curious is that not even this amendment fully answers the contentions of the petitioners, for it does not specify the relationship between sovereignty and the power to legislate. If it is intended that God legislates and delegates this power to the people who delegate it in turn to the state of Pakistan, but as a trusted agent of God's legislative power, then people and the state must exercise this legislative power only as God would want them to. If this is so, then the unity of God's power and authority is split into three units (God/Allah, i.e. the principal, and the agents, i.e. the people and the state), contrary to the doctrine of *tawhid*, the indivisibility of God. The petitioners' arguments imply another theory that retains the *tawhid* of Allah/God. According to that theory Allah/God can never entrust power to another entity, because Allah/God retains that power to preserve *tawhid.* The Prophet never entrusted or delegated power either. He appointed no agents nor left any legacy as to who should succeed to his power and authority. So neither the people nor the state are under a mandate to exercise powers like Allah/God would as Allah/God's agent. If that were so, then they would closely resemble the Catholic doctrine which asserts that the Pope, head of the state of the Vatican, is God's direct emissary and delegate and every priest is a representative of that divinity – a doctrine which vehemently goes against that of *tawhid.* What the people and the state can do instead is to take responsibility for legislating. The term 'legislating' must be carefully defined. Legislating is not an act that God/Allah has delegated. Legislating is merely a human act of constituting a body, consulting and debating according to certain pre-determined rules of order, with the object of issuing rules that meet certain formal requirements. Muslims who wish to legislate as agents of Allah or trustees would have to duplicate and enact the entire Quran. This would not make sense. So one is left with preserving Allah/God as One, who does not by nature share or delegate authority, but as One who inspires the conscience of each individual to enact laws that are not hypocritical, that do not impose injustice or perpetuate inequalities. Otherwise, to equate what Allah/God mandates and what a jurist from the first century of Islam opined could amount to an act of blasphemy.[34]

The Ordinance as a form of enacting Islamic penal law

The 1979 Zina Ordinance has remained an ordinance and not made into a law even when parliament was reinstated since Zia Ul Haq. Thus the validity of the Ordinance has been called into question by activists. President Musharaff assured the life of the Ordinance under the Legal Framework Ordinance of 2002, confirmed by the parliament in the 18th Amendment Act of 2003. During his regime the legislature decided to maintain the Ordinance though amended it with an Act, namely the Protection of Women (Criminal Laws Amendment) Act, 2006 (Act VI of 2006, assented to on 1 December 2006).

How is Islamic law determined?

Once the Supreme Court in 1980 ensured the Pakistani state's right to apply Islamic penal law by enacting a statute or an executive ordinance, the next issue at stake is how the court is to decide which of the many Islamic legal interpretations of the Injunctions in the Holy Quran and the Sunnah will be selected and applied.

The Constitution of 1973 specifies the procedural parameters. First of all, the legislative organ of the government may enact laws that incorporate the Injunctions. Secondly, the courts may control such enactments by judicial review. Any citizens may petition the courts to exercise judicial review; such petition is to be brought before the Federal Shariat Court.

Legislating Islamic Injunctions into law – all schools of law represented

Article 227 (of Part IX of the Constitution) requires that all laws conform to the Holy Quran and the Sunnah (Injunctions of Islam). The President of Pakistan is to appoint a Council for Islamic Ideology. Ayub Khan's Advisory Council for Islamic Ideology of the 1960s thus became mandatory. It may have from eight to 20 members, who must represent as many schools of Islamic legal thought as possible. At least one member must be a woman, two must be Supreme Court or High Court judges or former judges, and at least eight must have been conducting Islamic research and teaching for 15 years. In a strict sense ulama may not be members, as is required for the Federal Shariat Court. Judges who can show a long career in Islamic studies can also qualify.

No member of the executive, neither the President nor a Provincial Governor, nor the legislature at a national nor provincial level is required to consult the Islamic Council about the Islamicity of a proposed law. The legislature consults it only if two-fifths of its members agree to do so.

Otherwise, the Islamic Council has a duty to advise and recommend how the Majlis e Shoora or the executive can give effect to Islamic Injunctions. It is to compile those Injunctions which can be given legislative effect. Neither the executive nor the legislature is required even to seek the advice of the Islamic Council. They may choose to ask advice, enact without asking advice, or seek advice retroactively. They are only under a duty to consider, not necessarily to follow, the advice of the Council. Hence the legislative branch remains independent, as representatives of the electorate. Such independence allows the legislators and executives who are

Muslim to be ultimately accountable to their own consciences and not become blind followers of a clerical class, true to the spirit of Islam.

A second bite of the cherry – judicial review of Islamic laws

The Constitution guarantees the right of every citizen to petition the Federal Shariat Court to review a law for its conformity to the Holy Quran and the Sunnah of the Prophet (Art. 203D (1)).

Article 203C of the 1973 Constitution creates a Federal Shariat Court.[35] Its members must be Muslims (not gender-specific), and not more than eight in number. This number includes the Chief Justice of the Court. The Chief Justice should be a justice of the Supreme Court or a High Court, or at least be qualified to be a Supreme Court justice. A maximum of three Shariat Court judges should be ulama versed in Islamic law.[36] Thus the majority on the court are not ulama.

To serve as a check on the power of the executive or the legislature to enact a law without consulting first about its conformity with Islamic Injunctions, the Federal Shariat Court is given jurisdiction to initiate its own review of a law (Constitution, Art. 203D (1): of its own motion). Or it may order that a *hudud* case being heard in a subordinate criminal sessions court be transferred to the Shariat Court (Constitution, Art. 203DD (1); the proviso to Art. 20 (1) of the Offence of Zina Ordinance gives the sessions court summary jurisdiction).

The court is under an obligation not simply to give an order. It must give a reasoned judgment with grounds and specify why the law or part of it is repugnant.

Under either procedure any law declared repugnant to Islamic Injunctions shall become ineffective on the day specified by the court, after giving the executive or legislature reasonable time to consider how to change the law, that is if the decision does not go on appeal to the Supreme Court.

Defining Islamic Injunctions – how wide is the sunna*?*

The Constitution defines Injunctions of Islam in two different ways. In the section relating to the enactment of a law it provides that the law is to conform to the Holy Quran and the Sunnah (Art. 227, Part IX, Islamic Provisions). The preamble uses the same definition of the Injunctions ('Wherein the Muslims shall be enabled to order their lives in the individual and collective spheres in accordance with the teachings and requirements of Islam as set out in the Holy Quran and Sunnah'). In the section on reviewing the law for their Islamic content the Constitution requires that the court use the criteria of the Holy Quran and the Sunnah of the Holy Prophet (Art. 203D of Part VII, the Judicature). This difference in terminology – Sunnah versus Sunnah of the Prophet – can have serious consequences. The difference is important because the successors and Companions of the Holy Prophet established their own *sunna*, the *sunna* of the *sahaba*, which can be distinguished from the *sunna* of the Holy Prophet in so far as they do not always quote the words of the Holy Prophet. Since the Federal Shariat Court is to represent as many schools of law as possible, the issue of differences in how Sunnis and Shiites treat *sunna* should be reflected. Sunnis wanted to give equal weight to all Companions in opposition to the selective condemnation or acceptance by Shiites (Tayob 205; Hamdani 8). As will be shown below in the discussion of the Zina Ordinance, the penalty of death by stoning derives from a *sunna* of the Companions and not directly from the words of the Holy Prophet.

Judicial review of Islamic laws

The bulk of this chapter is devoted to the judicial review of the *zina* law in Pakistan – its substantive provisions, its application and judicial review.

Constitutional scheme of the judicature

As described above, the Federal Shariat Court is a superior court of special jurisdiction for the purpose of attending to questions of repugnance to Islamic Injunctions. Otherwise, the judicial system in Pakistan is universal. It consists of the High Courts of each Province and subordinate District Courts, Magistrates' Courts and Criminal Sessions Courts. At the apex sits the Supreme Court. The Supreme Court hears appeals from a High Court if the monetary value of the case is a minimum of 50,000 rupees (Art. 185 (1)) and from the Shariat Court (Arts. 203D (2), and 203F). In actuality the Supreme Court frequently exercises appellate Shariat jurisdiction, as it is called. The Supreme Court also has transferral jurisdiction. It may transfer a case from one High Court to another High Court if in the interests of justice (Art. 186A). The Supreme Court has exclusive extraordinary jurisdiction, without litigants seeking a remedy. This is when the President of the country seeks from the Supreme Court an opinion on a question of law of considerable public import (Art. 186). The force of decisions of the Supreme Court lies in their binding nature. Its enunciations on questions or principles of law bind all other courts, including the Shariat Court (Art. 189).

It is not clear from the Constitution (Art. 203F (2A))[37] whether the Federal Shariat Court has exclusive appellate jurisdiction over Islamic criminal law cases (*hudud*), or shares it with other High Courts. The Federal Shariat Court is concerned that litigants rush preferably to the High Courts under the latter's writ jurisdiction to hear the *hudud* cases, and the High Courts have interfered under powers granted in the Criminal Procedure Code in courts handling *hudud* cases.[38] The Federal Shariat Court conferred on itself exclusive jurisdiction over appeals in *hudud* cases.[39]

Social backdrop of the Offence of Zina Ordinance

Six years after the 1973 Constitution came into force, the Offence of Zina (Enforcement of Hudood) Ordinance VII came into operation under the martial rule of General Zia Ul Haq. It reintroduced Islamic penal law, sparking a lively public debate which spilled over into the courts. This is not surprising. The criminalization of sex goes to the heart of any society's basic behaviour, whether open or behind closed doors. It opened a floodgate of litigation which had not existed before.

A brief digression into Western laws illustrates the point. It was only in 1997 that the German parliament abrogated the criminal statute penalizing infanticide.[40] The law, enacted in 1871, had discriminated against women on the basis of whether they were married or not to the father of their child. If the mother were not married and she killed her baby while giving birth or immediately afterwards, she was not guilty of murder. Instead she was subject to a milder punishment. If she were married and killed the child, then she was subject to the penalty for murder. This amounted on the one hand to discrimination against the married woman. On the other hand, the law reflected discrimination against the unmarried woman (or a married woman who had a child from an affair). The softer penalty was justified not on the ground that the unmarried woman suffered temporary insanity, but because society would have condemned her for having a child out of wedlock. By committing infanticide she justifiably avoided such social shame. The law in effect also discriminated against children. Those born of a marriage were socially more worthy than those not born of a marriage.[41] The real motive for infanticide, according to a study by a superior court judge, was economic.[42] This position contrasted with the English Infanticide Act of 1939, which makes no distinction between married or unmarried women, adulterous or non-adulterous. Like the German law it apportioned milder penalties for women who caused the death of their child but within 12 months of birth. The grounds, however, were different, being based on medical empirical evidence – a woman was known medically to suffer mental stress after childbirth. So it was the state of mind of the woman, not her marital status, which determined whether she would be charged with murder or manslaughter. It had to be proven that her balance of mind 'was disturbed by reason of her not having fully recovered from the effect of giving birth … or the effect of lactation…' (Craig).[43] Motivation because of economic straits was no excuse. In terms of criminalizing sexual affairs of married persons outside marriage, it is the US army that presents the most prominent example of continued criminalization of adultery. The grounds seem not to be because it is a mortal sin[44] as defined by classical Christian exegetes, but because it is bad for discipline.

Solving social conflicts by punishing sexual crimes

The debate sparked in Pakistan over the law that punishes adultery, abduction and sexual relations between unmarried persons reflected social problems. Abduction, elopement and rape have been and still are serious problems. The roots lie partly in unjust family relations, e.g. women are pressured to marry elderly men, then elope with younger men for love or to escape beatings. Or close male relatives sexually harass their sisters-in-laws who are forced on economic grounds to live and work in the household of a better-off sister (Raban 9, 12).[45] Conflicts among family clans contribute to sexual conflicts, e.g. when women are caught between political and personal vendettas.[46] Or if a man is having an illicit relationship with a woman, the latter's relatives can seek revenge by abducting a woman relative of the man they feel has wronged their own woman relative. Or friends can arrange such vendettas.[47] Or parties who are about to be sued try to intimidate the plaintiff by trumping up allegations of rape against the male relatives of the plaintiff.[48] Polygamy, even when the husband has to seek permission, has heightened the conflicts. It has led to strained relations and pushed the wife to ask for *talaq* (divorce). If the woman thereafter remarries, vengeful husbands allege that the *talaq* was invalid, then accuse the remarried wife and her new husband of *ẓina*.[49]

The upshot of prosecutions under the Offence of Zina Ordinance was that men if convicted of rape suffered much heavier punishments than in Western jurisdictions. In this sense rape was taken as a serious offence, analogous to the murder of a woman's soul.

On the other hand, many of the victims of the Zina Ordinance were women. When the woman alleged rape against a man, she was often booked in turn on a charge of consensual sex. Such actions reflected the attitude that has plagued Western jurisprudence, where men are given the benefit of the doubt because of the prejudiced stereotyped thinking that women basically do not say no to men, but rather put themselves into situations where they know men will have sex with them. In terms of results, early statistics were showing that of all women in prison, the overwhelming majority (eight out of ten) were charged with *zina*.[50] Other statistics on the overall prison population were showing more men in prison than women convicted of *zina* (Kennedy 1987, 318).[51]

Police corruption in charging zina

The large number of women in prison on charges of *zina* was not just a reflection of sexual patterns of fornication or adultery. The number also reflected a police practice related to charging men for rape, i.e. forced *zina* (*zina bil jabr*). When a man was charged with rape, the police simultaneously charged the woman accuser of consensual sex with the alleged rapist. Women's groups actively protested against this practice. It discouraged women from bringing charges of rape because they knew by doing so they would be subject to being charged in turn. There were some examples of a different practice – the accused rapist got the charge reduced from forced sex to consensual sex, but the woman was not charged.[52]

In February 2005 these practices were seriously exposed as a product of corruption. The Supreme Court upheld a conviction against three men who had raped a young schoolgirl in the sixth class, about 12 or 13 years old. She was snapped up when going out to buy a notebook and even abducted from her home town of Faisalabad to Karachi. Her mother, with her blind husband, went searching for her and finally found her in jail. The mother had her released on bail. The accused were found guilty on the basis of the evidence and sentenced variously to 25 years' imprisonment, life imprisonment, 30 lashes and fines of 20,000–30,000 rupees. On appeal they argued that the girl had wanted to marry one of the abductors and that she had confessed to consensual sex. It was true that she had submitted to the police a confessional statement, then afterwards testified that she was forced. The Supreme Court found that her confession was flawed because she feared her family would be killed by the more influential perpetrators and because the police had pressured her. The court further found that the mother in pursuing the case had no motives of rancour, as is common in such cases – 'a poor lady with a blind husband can by no stretch of imagination implicate falsely such influential persons due to whose influence she failed to lodge even a proper F.I.R. [First Information Report] and filed a complaint under the compelling circumstances'.[53] The court upheld the convictions.

A year later the Federal Shariat Court followed suit, deciding to terminate current police practices. It ruled that when charging a man with rape, the police are no longer simultaneously to charge the woman prosecutrix with illicit consensual sex.[54] It was hoped that this judgment meant, too, that the Shariat Court itself was terminating its practice of converting on its own initiative charges of rape into charges of consensual *zina*.[55] The Federal Shariat Court and the Supreme Court, however, did not discuss the causes of these practices. At the root of the practice of preceiving consensual *zina* as the flip side of forced *zina* (rape) was a total misunderstanding of the standards of proof. It was thought that absence of forced intercourse established in and of itself consensual intercourse by default. The standard of proof for rape cases was and still is is beyond reasonable doubt.[56] It had not been made clear to the public prosecutor or some of the judges that the same standard had to apply in order to establish consensual *zina*, for *zina* is a crime. Solid proof, proof beyond doubt, is at the core of the Quranic verses on consensual *zina*. Hence just as it was incumbent on the courts to establish in rape (*zina bil jabr*) cases the element of coercion beyond reasonable doubt, it was obligatory to establish the element of consent beyond reasonable doubt in consensual *zina* (*zina bil raza*) if no four witnesses were present. This misunderstanding or prejudice is not limited to Pakistan. In the West this principle is also just being learnt: men having intercourse with a woman who is in a drunken state are now liable to be charged with rape. Rape is defined as not having obtained the woman's free consent. Signs of violence or assault need not be proven.[57] In an Islamic context the slightest intimidation of a woman would thus amount to lack of consent and hence rape.

While the two recent decisions on police practice were most just and contributed to the reforms of the Zina Ordinance in 2006, the problem was more complicated and ran deeper in terms of practices and attitudes of prosecutors and lower criminal court judges. As will be shown in the cases below, the practice, for example, of charging a woman with aiding and abettting in her own abduction was a contradiction in terms, for enticement or abduction means being taken against one's will. Her aiding and abetting would indeed be cause for acquitting the alleged abductor or enticer of the charge.[58]

Nonetheless, acquittals of men were problematic. The total number of appeals (518) against acquittals out of the total number of criminal cases handled by the Federal Shariat Court was a little more than half of the appeals against convictions (849).[59] Acquittals in *zina* cases meant usually that the woman victim was appealing. More detailed statistics are needed on just how many of the appeals against acquittal as well as conviction are by women.

Judicial review of the Offence of Zina Ordinance

It did not take long before the Ordinance was challenged as unIslamic under the constitutional provisions allowing anyone to petition for review of a law that the law-maker (in this case Zia Ul Haq) alleges to be Islamic. One of the first cases challenged the penalty of death by stoning.

Terms of the Offence of Zina Ordinance

As background to the analysis of the judicial review, a brief description of the main features of the Ordinance is needed. The Ordinance introduces classical Islamic law, which punished adultery and relations between unmarried persons, carefully differentiating penalties for slaves from those for free persons.

Under the Ordinance, if convicted of adultery, then both parties are subject to death by stoning, the *hadd* penalty, and the stoning is to be carried out by those witnesses who deposed against the accused, if available (Art. 17), but conviction is difficult because one needs either four upright male witnesses (eight female witnesses as permitted in classical law are not specified) who see a man actually penetrate a woman in the act of sexual intercourse, or a confession[60] from both the man and the woman charged.

The second major *zina* offence consists of illicit intercourse (fornication) between two unmarried persons hence no adultery is involved. The penalty is 100 lashes. Again, conviction is possible only if four upright male witnesses have seen the actual sexual penetration of the woman or both have confessed.

Because of these difficult evidentiary requirements, the Offence of Zina Ordinance introduced some innovative elements. If neither four upright witnesses nor sufficient confessions were available, then the courts relied on circumstantial evidence. Prosecution was by the state and not left to private complainants. Proof was to be beyond a shadow of a doubt. If the court convicted, then the penalty was not death. Instead it was up to ten years' imprisonment and whipping for consensual *zina.* For rape it was from 4 to 25 years, whipping and rigorous imprisonment. Gang rape was exceptional. It had to be punishable with death (Art. 10 (4) prior to the 2006 reforms). Consensual intercourse between unmarried persons, while punishable by whipping, was also punishable by death (Art. 6 (3) (b)). These were called the *tazir* (*taazir*) punishments, that is, enacted at the discretion of the ruler of the state, not prescribed explicitly in the Holy Quran as the limits (*hudud*) of Allah/God. (See below the section on 'Postscript' on amendments to the Ordinance which removed rape from the Zina Ordinance.)

The Offence of Zina Ordinance, prior to the reforms in 2006, also criminalized abduction, kidnapping, selling/buying for prostitution, compelling women (not men) into marriage and enticing or detaining women (not men) for purposes of illicit intercourse. Interestingly it is only in the last two of these offences that the Ordinance was gender specific, otherwise gender neutral. Rape (*zina bil jabr*) too was not gender specific.

There are safeguards against the application of the death penalty for *zina* proven by the strict standards of four witnesses or confession. The punishment of death by stoning is not automatically applicable upon conviction on the evidence of four witnesses or confessions. First of all, if the conviction is based only on a confession, the accused is allowed to retract and thus be freed (Art. 9 (1)). If conviction is on the basis of four eye-witnesses, any one of them may retract (Art. 9 (2)). Secondly, the death penalty must be subject to review by the appellate court (if from the Shariat Court, this is the Supreme Court – Art. 5 (3) of the Ordinance). This procedural safeguard has meant that no one has been executed by stoning to date.[61] Finally, if the Federal Shariat Court decided to order the transfer of a *hudud* case from a lower Sessions Court to the Shariat Court, the latter may not reverse an acquittal by the lower court (Art. 203D of the Constitution). If the latter has ordered execution, then the Shariat Court may order suspension of execution (Art. 203DD (1), and proviso to (2) of the Constitution).

The Ordinance also applies, curiously, to non-Muslims, even though classical legal interpretations presumed each community would handle its own affairs.[62] The Ordinance, however, makes some exceptions for non-Muslims. If charged they may have their cases heard by a non-Muslim judge (Art. 21). Their witnesses may also be non-Muslims (proviso to Art. 8). If convicted, they are subject only to 100 lashes as they are not *muhsan* (sane, adult and Muslim – Art. 2, Definitions, Arts. 5 (2) for *zina* and formerly 6 (3) for rape). For that reason the law-makers reserved the right to impose the death sentence against non-Muslims only in cases of rape if circumstances warranted (former Art. 6 (3)).

Also exempted from stoning or whipping is a perpetrator who is a minor. A minor is someone who is under the age of 18 (for boys) or under the age of 16 (for females) or someone who has not reached puberty (Art. 1). He or she is punishable only by whipping (Art. 5 (2) (b)). This represents an adjustment of the classical interpreters of Islamic law, as 15 was considered to be the age of puberty and therefore the age of adulthood (*bulugh*).

The Ordinance does not explicitly provide that pregnancy of an unmarried woman constitutes rebuttable evidence of *zina*.[63]

Problematic logic of the Offence of Zina Ordinance

One of the major objections to the Offence of Zina Ordinance related to its provisions on forced *zina*, namely rape (*zina bil jabr*). The classical interpretations of Quranic verses on adultery presumed consensuality, not force. The term *zina* was associated only with consent. The Ordinance oddly used the term to refer to both forced and consensual intercourse; it made no distinction between forced and consensual sexual intercourse. All that had to be proven was actual sexual penetration, whether the parties were consenting or not.

Without such a distinction, a major problem lay in applying the standards of proof. Because the term *zina* meant a *hadd* offence and a *hadd* offence required proof by four witnesses, a person who alleged rape had to get four upright witnesses who saw her being forcibly penetrated. This means that just as a conviction for consensual adultery or illicit sex was nearly impossible, rape went unpunished as well for lack of proof.

The use of the term *zina* to refer to rape also raised confusion in cases where a woman could not prove forced *zina* beyond a reasonable doubt. An accused rapist would argue in his defence either that there was no sexual intercourse at all or that intercourse did take place but the woman had consented. If the woman complainant alleged intercourse, supported by medical evidence of intercourse, and she failed to prove that it was forced, then the assertion of the accused that it was consensual was interpreted as a complaint from his side against the woman of consensual *zina*. This led in turn to police investigating whether the parties were guilty of consent. This in turn led to the rather tangled situation of an accused rapist implicating himself as guilty of consensual *zina* or demanding that the woman be charged with consensual *zina* with another man. Further complicated legal questions abounded: how to protect the man acquitted of rape against double jeopardy (i.e. being prosecuted on another charge on the same facts) and how to protect women against being penalized for bringing rape charges?

This is why it became important for the police to rely on confessions. Such a situation opened the door to police misusing confessions to discourage rape charges. The accused rapist (male or female) could offer a confession, but the victim also was asked to confess to being forced into 'consenting' to intercourse. This was a contradiction in terms. A victim cannot confess.

The classical jurists handled this issue more logically than the Ordinance did, as will be illustrated with court cases analysed later in this chapter. From the perspective of the classical jurists, if a woman (now also a man in modern Pakistan) alleged that she was forced into being sexually penetrated against her will, the issue for the classical jurists was one of her credibility and the surrounding circumstances, not her confession to being forced.

Under the classical interpretations if a woman brought a charge of rape, this was treated generally as a matter of her own self-defence. For example, an unmarried woman found pregnant had to give some explanation of her condition, at least according to some jurists (not all). An allegation of rape by a man or a *jinn* (a spirit) was an acceptable defence. At issue was her credibility, whether her description of the surrounding circumstances were credible or not, e.g. she had shouted for help but being in an isolated area no one heard her pleas for help; or she had been drugged into sleep while the intercourse took place. Her allegation of rape gave her a merciful chance to escape being charged with consensual *zina*. For the jurists her allegation of force was sufficient to exonerate the unmarried pregnant woman from suspicion of consensual *zina* for lack of *mens rea* (Quraishi; Sonbol 2000, 311)[64] and thus obviated the need even to further charge her with consensual *zina* and search for four upright witnesses.

What the classical jurists had not dealt with in great depth was a charge of rape brought by a non-pregnant woman – what standard of proof did she need to produce, four or only the usual two witnesses?[65] What was the penalty? This seems not to have been a major issue with the jurists. The issue was treated under different headings. Malik's *Muwatta* treated a case of forced intercourse under the chapter on *hudud* (prescribed punishments) as did Dawud's *Sunan*. The penalty was whipping for a slave and stoning for a free man (marital status not clear). Bukhari's *Sahih* classified it as *ikrah* (coerced, hateful), meaning it had no prescribed penalty like a *hadd*.[66] The *Muwatta* treated it again under the chapter on mortgaging of property and pledges (for enforcement of judgments) (*rahm*), proposing that the rapist be penalized with paying the dower (*mahr*) to the victimized woman. A Maliki gloss treated it under the chapter on judgments relating to coercion.[67] The reason for lack of systematic treatment may be that cases of rape were associated with elopement or abduction. If it were established that a man had eloped thinking he could change a woman's mind, then took her against her will, he had to pay her the dower and thereby redeem her honour. If the woman were married and raped, the husband could save his honour too by simply divorcing the victimized woman. The Companion and Commander of the Faithful Umar was said usually to release a man accused of rape if he agreed to marry the woman (Sonbol; Fahmy 366).[68]

Modern vocabulary translates the term rape into *ightisab*, meaning to coerce, as distinguished from *zina*. The Pakistani Ordinance used the term *zina bil jabr*, which means forced intercourse, which is the essence of rape. Nonetheless, it raised the ire of women activists because it applied the protective evidence requirements of consensual *zina* to rape. What was overlooked in the heated debate was that the *taazir* provisions of the Ordinance were more than adequate for prosecuting and punishing rape on the basis of forensic evidence, witnesses, statements, circumstantial evidence and cross-examination. Four upright witnesses were not needed. There were thus two ways to prosecute rape – one, through four witnesses or confession, with certain death for the rapist, the second by *taazir*. If anything, the penalty for *taazir* rape should have been raised from the minimum of four years to a minimum of ten years, ten years being the maximum for consensual intercourse. Death would be imposed only in highly exceptional circumstances.

To give the ruler/state the benefit of the doubt on not lessening the penalty for rape issues, it should be noted that a discretionary death penalty for an offence not explicitly named in the Quran like rape (assuming Quranic *zina* is strictly consensual), raises some issues. May the ruler/state extend capital punishment beyond what the Quran prescribes as the limits (*hadd*) of Allah/God? (Coulson 1957, 53–4) For the Quran is very careful not to make capital punishment a general remedy in criminal law. Hanafi jurists were known for arguing against allowing the ruler/state to impose the death penalty as a discretionary *taazir* punishment.[69] The Quran names only one crime where it is allowed without question – in rebellion against Allah, the Prophet, the social order (*hiraba*) and spreading evil destruction in the society (*saa*). The jurists have taken this to cover highway robbery and general terrorist activities. The penalty can be one of several: outright execution, crucifixion, mutilation of hands or feet, or exile, yet the Quran also provides one exception for those who repent.[70] The only other possibility for capital punishment is in the case of murder – but that is subject to a number of constraints, e.g. all family members of the victim must agree to capital punishment and if one dissents, then the family is entitled only to compensation.[71] Hence it would seem that the maximum *taazir* punishment would have to be limited to life imprisonment, even for rape. This might explain why the Pakistani Offence of Zina Ordinance took the route of classifying rape as *zina*, for it was reported in the *sunna* (hadiths, not the Quran) that the only other crime that can be punished by death is *zina*. So by classifying rape as *zina* this might allow the ruler/state to apply the death penalty to rape. Gang rape was made (and still is) punishable by death. The flaw in this argument is that gang rape could fall under the Quranic classification of terrorizing society. Re-classifying rape as *hiraba*, a terror to society, would conform more to a woman's perspective: any rape, single or gang, is terror. Given the human rights campaign against the death penalty, life imprisonment would more than suffice for rape.

The following sections will analyse the case law to show the issues that arose in relation to applying the death penalty in cases of criminalized sex, such as adultery, non- or pre-marital sex and rape.

Case law under the Offence of Zina Ordinance

1981 challenge to hadd *– is death by stoning unIslamic?*
Case 1 – yes, it is unIslamic

Besides the issue of whether the state violates the Quranic injunction that there is no force in religion[72] when it forces Muslims to accept Islamic law as state law, the Federal Shariat Court was faced very soon after the promulgation of the Offence of Zina Ordinance with the question of whether the penalty of death by stoning prescribed in the Ordinance conformed to Islamic Injunctions as laid down in the Holy Quran and the Sunnah of the Prophet. As noted above, Article 227 of the Constitution enjoins that laws conform to the Holy Quran and Sunnah, while Article 203D enjoins judicial review according to the Holy Quran and the Sunnah of the Holy Prophet.

Differences in what is in the Quran and what is in the Sunnah of the Prophet or the Companions was at the heart of the litigation which arose in 1981, two years after the promulgation of the Ordinance.[73] The litigants sought a declaration that the so-called Islamic death penalty of stoning to death for *zina* was unIslamic in so far as it did not accord with the Holy Quran. Their argument was based on the text of the Constitution, which required that the law accord with the Holy Quran, not just the *sunna* (Quran *and* Sunnah, not Holy Quran *or* Sunnah). The Federal Shariat Court adjudged the petitioners' arguments to be legitimate, declaring the death penalty by stoning contrary both to the Holy Quran and to the Sunnah of the Holy Prophet. The justices ordered the ruler/state to change the law so that the only penalty for *zina* would be 100 lashes in public for the offender, without any distinctions of marital status or gender.

The well-reasoned arguments of the court are well worth analysing. The majority of the justices, with one judge dissenting, argued that stoning was not ordained in the Holy Quran or in the Sunnah of the Holy Prophet and therefore could not be applied as a prescribed *hadd*. The verses the justices relied upon were:

> Sura An Nisa (Women) (4:15) (4:16)
> (15) 'As for those of your women who are guilty of lewdness, call to witness four of you against them. And if they testify (to the truth of the allegation), then confine [banish] them to the houses until death

shall take them or (until) Allah appoint for them a way (through new legislation).'
(16) 'And for the two men of you who are guilty thereof, punish them both. And if they repent and improve, then let them be. Lo! Allah is relenting, Merciful.'

Sura Bani Israil (17:32)
(32) 'And come not near adultery. Lo! It is an abomination and evil way.'

Sura Al Nur (24:2)
(2) 'The woman and the man guilty of fornication, flog each of them, with a hundred stripes; let not compassion move you, in this case, in a matter, prescribed by Allah, if ye believe in Allah and the Last Day: And let a party of the Believers witness their punishment.'

After examining these verses, it was clear to the justices that the Holy Quran does not name stoning (*rajm*) as a *hadd* punishment. So where did *rajm* originate? The justices found that stoning was first introduced by the Sunnah of some of the Companions, who had succeeded the Prophet. But on which *sunna* (i.e. practices, dictates and advice) should the justices rely? They opted for giving the Quran precedence over the Sunnah of the Companions, reasoning on the basis of the Constitution. Justice (rtd.) Salahuddin Ahmed, then chairing the court, found that the Constitution in Article 203D referred to the Holy Quran and the Sunnah of the Prophet as the only tests for what is Islamic. The Offence of Zina Ordinance was a law subordinate to the Constitution. While the preamble of the Ordinance referred to the Holy Quran *and* the Sunnah, section 2 of the Ordinance defining *hadd* referred to its being ordained in the Holy Quran *or* Sunnah. In order to make this subordinate legislation consistent with the Constitution, Justice Ahmed decided to deem Sunnah as used in the Ordinance to mean exclusively Sunnah of the Holy Prophet.[74]

The Sunnah of the Companions on stoning (*rajm*)

Having established the constitutional supremacy of the Holy Quran as a source of law over the Sunnah of some of the Companions, the court proceeded in good Islamic style of argumentation to analyse why it was not prudent to accept the hadiths from which the law-makers derived the application of the penalty of *rajm* (stoning). The Sunnah prescribing *rajm* was said to derive from the hadith of Caliph Umar, the Commander of the Faithful, who took the young Muslim Arab community to venture outside Arabia. He led armies in major conquests of Persia/Iraq and other non-Arabian lands. In that hadith Umar is reported to have said that there had been a verse in the Holy Quran prescribing *rajm* for *zina*, but by oversight it had been left out in the written versions of the Holy Quran.[75] The court deemed this hadith to be too weak and illogical. The Holy Quran cannot be supplemented by a verse that should have been inserted but in fact does not appear in the written Revelation.[76] Furthermore, another Sunnah from Caliph Ali, also the son-in-law of the Holy Prophet, and father-in-law to Umar (who had married Fatima's and Ali's daughter Um Kulthum), disagreed with Caliph Umar. Ali reasoned that stoning was only the Sunnah of the Holy Prophet and not of the Quran. It could not have been from the Revelation because the Prophet had ordered stoning even *before* sura 4:15 requiring four witnesses for *zina* had been revealed. The implication was that stoning was more a matter of custom or discretion, not Quranic, for the Holy Prophet would have cited exactly what verse had been revealed as the basis of his decision to stone.

The Sunnah of the Holy Prophet on stoning

The court then proceeded as required by Article 203D (1) of the Constitution[77] to determine whether the *rajm* (stoning) penalty was to be found in the Sunnah of the Holy Prophet. The court found that the Holy Prophet had imposed varying punishments in cases of *zina*. He had indeed ordered, on occasion, stoning. But it was not clear whether the sentence was issued before the Revelation in the Holy Quran that imposed only stripes.[78] Even when the Holy Prophet ordered in some cases stoning, knowing that whipping had already been revealed, there was still a problem of interpreting the intentions of the Holy Prophet and reconciling the apparent conflict between the Quranic silence on *rajm*/stoning and the varying sentences he had meted out.[79] To resolve the issue, the court reasoned that the Holy Prophet knew that whipping was prescribed in the Holy Quran, and therefore was *hadd*, but he had ordered stoning only as a discretionary (*taazir*) punishment if aggravating circumstances so merited.[80]

Why stoning is discretionary, not *hadd*

The court used *qiyas* (reasoning by analogy) to support its argument that *rajm* must have been discretionary. It drew analogies with and compared other *hadd* punishments for crimes just as heinous as *zina* in order to show how such punishments had a discretionary element. In cases of murder or feuds (*qatl/hurub*) or *hiraba* (treason, war on Allah/God and the Holy Prophet), the Quranic verses allow a choice of penalties, requiring the exercise of discretion. They are not fixed. There can be death for retaliation (*qisas*) (here the court cited sura 2:178) or death by crucifixion (*salb*) (sura 5:33). Alternative penalties are possible, such as in the case of murder, namely remission and compensation, or in the case of treason, cutting off the hand or exile.[81] It followed, so argued the court, that if in such serious crimes as these there is an alternative penalty to death, then the choice of penalty involves a certain degree of discretion, or *taazir* (Allah/God does leave room for reasoning according to different circumstances.). Then surely the same principle would apply in the case of *zina.*

Which of the two penalties for *zina* – whipping or stoning – would be the more appropriate *hadd*, asked the court. For an answer the court relied on the basic criminal law principle that the nature of the penalty must fit the nature of the crime, that is, the harsher the crime, the stiffer the penalty.[82] Accordingly, compared to murder and grievous robbery, *zina* merited whipping as a unique *hadd* penalty. It would not fit the nature of the crime to impose death by stoning. Thus the court reconciled with the help of *qiyas* the Quranic whipping prescriptions for *zina* (which have been interpreted in classical legal texts as relating only to unmarried consenting adults) with the varying punishments found in the *sunna.* At this point the court did not consider whether it would distinguish consensual from forced *zina* (rape) in terms of a suitable penalty; for rape in the eyes of a woman is worse than murder or treason.

Differences of opinion among jurists on *hadd* for *zina*

The court then turned to the differences of opinion among the classical medieval jurisconsults. The court noted that Hanafi jurists had also exercised discretion about what was the most appropriate penalty depending on the status of the accused, not just the nature of the crime.[83] In the case of slave adulterers, whipping was preferred over banishing them to their houses or sending them into exile, as the Quran enjoins, for banishment would have disadvantaged the enslaving owner.[84] But for married free women stoning was preferred. Thus the court found that this classical explanation was unjustly motivated by economic considerations for slave owners.

Given the variety of opinions having roots in the then social and economic considerations of the day, the court expounded its final argument. This was as follows: in the light of so many opinions there arises the issue of the benefit of doubt. It is a basic principle of criminal law to give the accused, who is possibly subject to losing her/his life, the benefit of the doubt, and apply the lesser penalty of whipping.[85]

Classical reasoning on whipping and stoning – roots in slave law, economic and military needs

Here it is worthwhile to digress briefly into the reference the court made to the socio-economic origins of different punishments for *zina*. The arguments of the founder of the Shafii school and the much-acclaimed architect of systematizing traditionalism in Islamic law (Makdisi) are revealing and confirm the court's views. In his masterpiece, the *Risala*,[86] Shafii attempted to justify why there are two punishments for *zina*. Crucial to his argument is the fact that enslavement in his day was perfectly legal and very much part of the juristic discourse. He did not start his argument with the original *zina* verse (4:15, 16), which punished women by confining them to their houses and men too, but allowed for repentance. Shafii started instead with the verse on marrying enslaved women (4:25), which allowed them the same privilege as freed women to be married and to receive their dower. The man who married an enslaved woman was warned not to do so out of lustful motivations. But the verse went on to provide that if a married enslaved woman fell into shame (*fahasha*, the same word that was taken to mean adultery or fornication in sura 4:15, 16), her penalty was nonetheless half that of the freed married woman who fell into shame too.[87] As Shafii rightly argued, an enslaved woman convicted of *zina* could ask why her penalty was less than that for a freed woman. But half of what? Half of banishment or stoning or lashes? Some jurists opined that banishment and repentance had been replaced by the verse on whipping, others were for banishment and whipping,[88] others were for the hadith-based stoning even though it did not appear in the Quran. Shafii then argued that if there had been no Sunnah of the Prophet meting out occasionally the sentence of stoning or no hadith from Umar supporting *rajm*, then one could have concluded that the enslaved woman would get 50 lashes and the freed woman the full Quranically prescribed 100 (sura 24:2). That would make perfect sense in terms of sheer mathematics. This would not work, for obvious reasons, with stoning. But the references in the Sunnah to stoning involved only freed women: there is no reference to enslaved women. Logically then – if the goal was (and is) to minimize the conflict between the Holy Quran and the Sunnah – one could deem the whipping a lesser penalty to be claimed by enslaved women and men, while stoning could be reserved for freed women and men. This would solve the mathematical dilemma that the Quran had presented. Shafii did not cite which hadiths he was relying on. Perhaps he felt the reader might be aware that the hadiths from chapters on *hudud* in Malik's *Muwatta*, Bukhari's *Sahih*, and Dawud's *Sunan* all made references to the whipping punishment only in regard to adulterous slaves, while all other references to stoning did not specify whether the persons involved were enslaved – thus implicitly they related to free persons. In Dawud's *Sunan*, however, the references are to the freed and the enslaved. A man who committed adultery with a woman who was enslaved by his wife was subject to stoning if his wife had not made the slave lawful for him.[89] Otherwise he was subject to flogging and to compensating his wife with another slave. The Quranic verse which further punishes adulterers and adulteresses after their whipping with a prohibition to marry except with another of their ilk, or a non-believer (i.e. not a Muslim, Christian or Jew) is ignored, for such a verse would presume logically that the crime is not punished by death, only whipping or banishment,[90] for if the person were dead there would be no need to speak of marrying after the conviction.

Even if one accepts Shafii as a man of his time, who accepted differences between the enslaved and the free, and between men and women, there is still a flaw in his logic. *Hadd* can be prescribed only by the Quran, not by the *sunna*. The whipping verses do not distinguish between married or unmarried, free or enslaved, any more than do the original Quranic verses on banishment and exile or repentance. There are two possibilities, using analogous reasoning. Just as the verse on *hiraba* allows the community to choose among the penalties listed, why should it not be equally logical that it be intended that the community combine the Quranic penalties on *zina*? As mentioned earlier, a hadith from Malik's *Muwatta* shows that whipping and banishment were combined for a free man, even if he did commit adultery with an enslaved woman. Her lashes and her time of banishment could have been half that of his. Stoning, which is not

Quranic, could have been treated as a backstop to the truly Quranic *hadd*, whipping and banishment, but not elevated to *hadd*. When circumstances were heinous, then a slave adulterer could be equally stoned like a free person, for the half punishment would apply only to the punishments named in the Quran, whipping and banishment. Besides, Shafii admitted an exception to the verse enjoining in general half the punishment for slaves when murder was involved. The slave murderer would not get the benefit of the verse.[91] The difference made in punishments for the enslaved and the free adulterer – whipping for one and stoning for the other – was not really inevitable from the logic of the Quran or the *sunna*. The rules were, as the Pakistani court pointed out, and as Hanafi jurists admitted, derived from the logic of the economic interests of slave owners. Once modern law no longer permits analogy to slave law, the distinction gets translated into one between the married and the unmarried adulterer. There is no inexorable logic in this distinction either.

Why the stoning verse became such an issue in the first place was not discussed in the court decision. What is interesting is that the argument for stoning is attributed to Umar. This is not surprising. The great historian of Islamic history, At Tabari, recorded that Unar as a military commander was very conscious of the need to keep discipline in the frontier towns outside Arabia among his troops and prevent temptation. Nor did he want his Arab troops flogged in order to avoid humiliation.[92] He needed commanders who kept their reputations clean. It was recorded that Umar once recalled a commander of the frontier town of Basra in Iraq who was allegedly seeing a lady who conferred her favours only on military commanders and noblemen.[93] The witnesses had not seen the actual intercourse though they had found the commander between the lady's legs. Hence there was not sufficient evidence to convict him. After the hearing Umar warned him that if the testimony had been true (which it probably was), he would have had him stoned. This was a warning, and the governor was never caught again in outrageous situations. Thus a potential penalty of death by stoning would have served as a psychological deterrent against breaking discipline. Furthermore, public order in a religiously pluralistic ruler/state was an especially sensitive matter, as illustrated in the second major hadith cited in favour of stoning. In that hadith the Prophet had the Torah law applied to a Jewish adulteress and adulterer, namely death. If members of the Jewish and Christian communities had been allowed to continue to impose the death penalty on their own adulterers and the Muslim rulers had no control over that, while the Muslims would not have been subject to death for adultery, only whipping, this could lead to tense situations. An expedient political solution had to be found. The most expedient would be to argue that the pre-Islamic Revelation for the *kitabi* imposing death for adultery would have been be renewed for the Muslim community.

Lessons from the Pakistani 1981 judgment declaring stoning to be *taazir* not *hadd*

The Pakistani decision of 1981 provides an excellent lesson. It teaches us to scrutinize much more carefully the roots of arguments which produced the classical Islamic rules. The object of such a scrutiny is twofold – to discover the socio-economic and political biases of jurists at a particular point in time, and secondly to avoid those rules which are rooted in a set of values to which we no longer subscribe, namely, enslavement, inequality, economic discrimination.

In summary, the court held that *rajm*, stoning, is discretionary and must not be applied to *zina*. Only whipping constitutes *hadd*. The reasons are: i) where the verses of the Holy Quran are clear on a point of law, they suffice, and it is not required to turn to anything else for their interpretation;[94] ii) the benefit of doubt due to lack of *ijma* among jurists and of reasonable doubt about the logic of hadiths (or jurists, one could add) should go to the accused not the prosecuting state.[95]

Fate of the 1981 Pakistani judgment

The decision of the Federal Shariat Court to strike down *rajm* (stoning) as not *hadd* spelled a political disaster for General Zia Ul Haq, the architect of the Offence of Zina Ordinance. He reacted immediately, amending the Constitution so that the court could review its own judgment, a violation of the balance of powers.[96] The court forcibly changed its judgment in 1983, which will be analysed next.

The 1983 Challenge to hadd – is death by stoning unIslamic? Case 2 – no, it is Islamic

Summary of the 1983 court's judgment

Faced with an order to review, the Federal Shariat Court reconstituted itself in 1983 to review its prior decision of 1981 against stoning. The government formally brought the petition and the original petitioners in the 1981 case became the defendants.[97]

As was to be expected, the defence attorney for the original petitioners argued that the 1981 Presidential Order from Ul Haq could not apply retrospectively without violating a fundamental principle of the rule of law. The court, not surprisingly, dismissed the argument, and overturned its 1981 decision. There was one dissenting judge – the only member who had sat on the 1981 bench.

All the other five justices declared the Offence of Zina Ordinance to be in accordance with Islamic Injunctions in the Sunnah. They analysed the wording of the Ordinance: section 2 said simply that the mandatory *hadd* punishment of stoning was based on the Holy Quran *or* Sunnah, thus not exclusively on the former. However, it was pointed out that the preamble to the Ordinance proclaimed that it was in accord with the Holy Quran *and* the Sunnah. In response, the justices held that where the Ordinance refers to the Holy Quran and the Sunnah, the word 'and' should be read to mean 'or'. Thus the mandatory 100 stripes was according to the Holy Quran and the mandatory stoning in accord with the Sunnah.

The court, however, did not limit its arguments to semantics. It articulated what lay behind them – that was the vexatious question of *ijtihad* – namely how far can modern judges re-examine the sources of law and their relation to one another. The court's answer was: not at all – the courts need not question anew the relation between Sunnah and the Holy Quran. Justice Zahrool Haq in his own separate concurring opinion wrote the most detailed justification of this position. He laid the reason for rejecting *ijtihad* at the door of the political rulers. The Pakistani rulers could be deemed to have closed the door of *ijtihad*, at least in the matter of the age-old controversy of whether the Quran is supreme over and thus trumps contradictory Sunnah.[98] Furthermore, even to opine that the Holy Quran is supreme over Sunnah in case of conflict would mean adopting the ancient *khawarij* position – that the Holy Quran alone is sufficient for judging whether a rule conforms to the Injunctions of Islam or not.[99] By even citing the Kharijites, the Justice was displaying the most liberal feature of the application of Islamic law in Pakistan, namely its openness to the plurality of opinion in an effort to seek justice. He judged the Kharijites on this point to be 'misguided, even though all schools of Islamic legal thought are deemed applicable in Pakistan'.[100]

The court did not address the issue of whether stoning is disproportionate to the crime of consensual intercourse, that is, whether the punishment fits the crime. One can only presume that the principle still holds, but with a caveat. The principle might be subject to another criterion, namely where the Sunnah prescribes a particular punishment it will be presumed without critical analysis that the circumstances match the penalty. So perhaps it is just as well that the court did not expound on this point since it would have further undermined the rule of law.

Dissenting opinion from the 1983 judgment

The dissenting opinion of Justice Aftab Hussain agreed with the grounds of the majority opinion of the 1981 court, but refined some of the arguments. He maintained that at most the ruler/state has the right to give itself the power to impose the stoning penalty under its discretionary powers of *taazir*, but it could not maintain that it was imposing the penalty as *hadd* in the name of the Holy Quran. The ruler/state had imposed *rajm* (stoning) in excess of the Book of Allah.[101]

Impact of the 1981 and 1983 decisions

The controversy in the judiciary and the political pressure placed on the judicial process resulted in the ruler/state amending the Constitution in an effort to clarify its position. It sought the support of historical figures in the independence movement by incorporating the statement of principles from 1949 into the Constitution and by adding Article 2A.[102] The ruler/state, however, did not attempt to resolve the question of how many and which of the opinions of past jurists, including those of the *khawarij*, remain valid. This would have undercut the very nature of Islamic law and its wealth of juridical knowledge. Islamic law is by nature a lawyer's law, a lawyer's paradise (Anderson 1957, 21; Arabi 13[103]). It consists of such a palette of opinions on such a wide variety of subjects from so many corners of the world that one is challenged to argue back even more meticulously.

At the heart of the controversy between the 1981 and the 1983 judgments, aside from the blatant political pressures involved, lay the juridical question of how to reconcile the Holy Quran and the Sunnah of the Prophet and Companions in cases of inconsistency. The approach was to see this as a challenge. Was it merely a seeming inconsistency which required simply finding a way, in principle or in empirical analysis, to distinguish them (as is done in common law jurisdictions when court decisions conflict), or to reconcile them, or simply to abrogate and overturn precedent? On the issue of whether stoning was mandatory for *zina*, the 1981 court distinguished between mandatory and discretionary punishments for *zina*. It found to be mandatory only what the Quran prescribes, in this case whipping. When the Sunnah prescribe other punishments for the same crime, then these reflect the discretionary exercise of judgment by the Holy Prophet or the Companions.

The 1983 judgment, on the other hand, found that there can be two different mandatory *hadd* punishments for the same crime – one prescribed by the Holy Quran and one by the Sunnah. With regard to the right of the courts to exercise *ijtihad*, the 1983 court limited its pronouncement to one point – it adjudged that *ijtihad* is no longer exercisable on the question of the relation between the Holy Quran and the Sunnah. In fact, however, subsequent case law applying the Offence of Zina Ordinance reveals that *ijtihad* is still alive and well.

Despite the revision of the 1981 judgment – due more to political circumstances than juridical argument – there are aspects of the 1981 judgment which remain unchanged. They have not been subsequently refuted. These are: i) The Constitution and statutes are the basic sources of law, enabling the application of Islamic law; ii) The courts may directly compare the Holy Quran and the Sunnah to evaluate for themselves the strength of a Sunnah, while there is no question about the strength of authority of the Holy Quran; iii) The courts may re-examine the arguments of the traditional ancient jurisconsults in the light of the social assumptions and concerns of their day, for which the rule was made, e.g. the distinction which the great jurist al Shafii made between punishments for adulterous enslaved Muslims and freed Muslims, thus preserving the economic interests of the enslavers. Once the courts have understood these underpinnings, they are allowed to take into account the fact that these social concerns and aims are either no longer relevant or contradict our conscience, then formulate alternatives more appropriate rules in the name of combating the sin and evil of hypocrisy.

Abolition of the Punishment of Whipping Act

One statutory change that resulted from the distinction the 1981 judgment made between mandatory *hadd* and discretionary *taazir* punishment was the repeal of the old British Whipping Act of 1909 and the abolition of whipping for *zina* under the regime of Benazir Bhutto. Whipping for all offences except where it is prescribed as *hadd* was abolished.[104] In practical terms this meant that where the Offence of Zina Ordinance ordered the *hadd* penalty of 100 lashes for consensual *zina* then whipping is permitted. In the light of the issue in the 1981 judgment – whether the *hadd* is not prescribed in the Holy Quran or the Sunnah of the Prophet or Sunnah of the Companions – the Abolition of the Punishment of Whipping Act defines *hadd* as the punishment found in the 'Holy Quran *and* the Sunnah'.[105] Given that the Sunnah, as Shafii had pointed out, referred to whipping only in relation to slaves, and enslavement is now unethical and illegal, it would have been more accurate and appropriate to limit the definition to the *hadd* in the Holy Quran, but politics is in practice the art of compromising legal principles.

*Challenge to the discretionary (*taazir*) punishment for* zina

Also in 1981 litigants challenged the discretionary punishments for consensual and forced *zina*, prescribed in section 10 of the Offence of Zina Ordinance.[106] Section 10 provided that if there were neither four upright witnesses to testify to seeing actual penetration, whether consensual or forced, nor confessions from the parties charged with *zina*, the case was not lost, but needed to be proved by other means, namely by circumstantial evidence, direct statements, forensic evidence, etc. Proof had to be beyond reasonable doubt as in any other criminal case. If a conviction was won on the basis of such proof, then the punishment was not death by stoning but rather imprisonment, whipping and/or fines. For this reason the offence was named *tazeer* [sic] *zina* (*zina bil raza*) or *tazeer* [sic] *zina bil jabr* as opposed to *hadd zina* (*zina bil raza*) and *hadd zina bil jabr.* [See Postscript on changes relating to *zina bil jabr.*]

In the litigation challenging even discretionary punishments, counsel for the defendants asked the Federal Shariat Court to strike down Section 10 of the Ordinance as inconsistent with Islamic justice. The idea was that if there was not sufficient evidence to convict someone on a charge of *zina*, subject to the *hadd* of stoning or whipping, then why should the ruler/state charge them again for the same offence but liable to a lesser *taazir* punishment (fewer lashes and fewer years in prison in lieu of death). Since the court was already under pressure because it had struck down stoning as *hadd*, the case was dissolved because of a procedural issue. If it had continued, it might have led to reconfiguring the Ordinance in such a way that consensual *zina* would be nearly impossible to prove for lack of four witnesses and rape would have been proven by another way.

Later in 1986 the court dealt *obiter* with Section 10's discretionary punishments in a case involving false accusations against a wife for adultery under the Offence of Qazf Ordinance, also introduced by General Ul Haq.[107] Section 3 of that Ordinance defined *qazf* (*qadhf*) as imputation of *zina* with intent to harm a person's reputation, whether that of a woman or a man (Jones-Pauly 2000).[108] A husband had accused his wife of *zina* on an oath pronounced four times. She responded with a counter-oath, also pronounced four times, denying the charge. The oaths were enunciated in accord with the procedure known among classical jurists as *liaan*, which is also used in paternity cases: when a spouse, like the wife in this case, responded with a denial, then she was not liable to any further prosecution. The husband in question then divorced the wife. She, however, had been charged with *zina* subject to *hadd* under the police practice of charging *zina* when there was prima facie evidence on the basis of the husband's accusation. The State Counsel, however, felt that the wife was liable to further prosecution. He argued that he could not pursue a charge of *zina* subject to *hadd* (consensual adultery liable to a death sentence), since her denial on oath settled that point, but he would pursue prosecution for consensual adultery liable to discretionary punishment.

The case was not easy. Two Federal Shariat Court judges favoured the State Counsel, one dissented and one reserved his opinion. In the absence of a majority opinion, the matter was referred on a point of law. The Chief Justice, Aftab Hussaini, consulted the work of Shafii. A similar case or question had apparently come to the fore centuries ago. Shafii had been of the opinion that the counter-oath of a woman averts the *hadd* penalty – thereafter she may not be further subjected to any penalty, even a discretionary one.[109] The Chief Justice, however, consulted further. He cited opinions of later jurists who had commented on and glossed Shafii. They said that while the woman's oath averted the *hadd* penalty, one still had to evaluate the evidence brought forth by the accusing husband when he gave his oath. If the oath did not provide sufficient evidence to support a *taazir* penalty, then the wife was fully acquitted of the entire matter. If the evidence was substantial, then she would be liable to being recharged with a *taazir* offence.

Justice Ali Hussain Qazilbash dissented. He relied first on sura 24:8 ('But it would avert the punishment from the wife, if she bears witness four times (with an oath)...'). He then referred to the Sunnah of the Holy Prophet, who had acquitted an accused wife of any punishment upon her taking the oath of denial. When she gave birth afterwards to a child who resembled a man other than her husband, the Holy Prophet still refused to reopen the case. He did not impute *zina* to her. He said he would have punished her only if the *liaan* procedure had not taken place. Thus he did not subject her to double jeopardy. On the basis of his gloss of these sources, Justice Qazilbash concluded the following: if the husband had circumstantial evidence in support of *zina* liable to discretionary punishment, but not to a death sentence, then the husband should not even be allowed to take the *liaan* oath of accusation. The very purpose of the oath was to allow a husband (or wife, as the Quran is gender-neutral on this point) a chance to challenge his wife when he is only suspicions of her and lacks the evidence of four witnesses. Thus *liaan* meant suspicions cannot amount to evidence, and hence the ruler/state may not proceed to try to get a conviction under *taazir* provisions for the same offence.

Thus by analogy to the Offence of Zina Ordinance, it can be said that the majority opinion in the *liaan* judgment answered *per obiter* the question of whether a person acquitted of a charge of *zina* subject to *hadd* was in turn chargeable for *zina* subject to discretionary punishment. The answer would have been in the affirmative. Whether this conformed to Islamic legal principles, the answer probably would be, no. The original opinion of Shafii without a gloss from later commentators recognized the double-jeopardy principle – why subject a person to the same charge twice, especially when the Quran provides for settling disputes in a relatively peaceful and merciful manner? To do otherwise would be to fall into the sin and evil of vengeance, which is not justice.

Proving adultery or consensual zina

Quranic protections

Proving *zina* was never easy under Islamic law because the Quran prescribes four upright witnesses (sura 4:15, 16). According to dissenting Justice Qazilbash in the *liaan* case of a husband mentioned above who accused his wife of adultery, the strict Quranic evidentiary requirement upset husbands in particular (why not wives, is not made clear). Even if he caught his wife in the act of adultery, he still could not have her convicted because his testimony alone was not enough. He needed upright witnesses, who were not tainted with self-interest as a husband would be, and no less than four. To ease the husband's ire, while preventing him from acting rashly, Allah/God revealed to the Prophet a special mechanism. This was the procedure of oaths. If either the husband or the wife accused the other of adultery, for whatever reason – including, it would seem, finding the spouse in flagrante delicto – the requirement of four witnesses was dropped. The accusing spouse had to give an oath four times as to the truth of his allegation, then give a fifth oath invoking a curse upon himself if he were lying.[110] The wife had a chance of a rebuttal. She could take an oath, also four times, that he was lying, and a fifth one invoking Allah's wrath if her husband were right. If she rebutted the charge with these oaths, then the charges had to be dropped.

Otherwise, the Quran went so far as to use the requirement of four witnesses to protect the reputation (in effect to avoid the slandering) of a woman accused of having an affair. If someone voiced suspicions that a woman of good repute (*muhsina*) had had an affair or led a questionable sex life, four witnesses were still required. The verses are a warning to men not to be quick to attack women as sexually loose. Chaste men are not explicitly protected. If the slanderer cannot find four witnesses, then he is to be punished with 80 lashes and never qualify as a witness for anything again, unless he repents.[111] This procedure represented a triumph of rationality over the ordeal method which had been sanctioned by some Mosaic jurists earlier, whereby a wife accused of adultery had to survive a barley drink ordeal to prove her innocence (Jones-Pauly 2000).

This system of criminalizing sex outside the marriage bed while requiring almost impossible evidence for a conviction was a stroke of brilliance and of wisdom. It satisfied two demands of the day – to criminalize adultery and pre-marital sex, as long practised in communities prior to the Islamic Revelations, on the one hand, and on the other to prevent men from using their sexual privileges to kill or stigmatize women. The Quran equalized women with men in the arena of sex. This is the significance of the revolutionary requirement of four upright witnesses. It is a pragmatic approach as well to humans whom God/Allah knowingly created as sexual beings. People will have affairs and will have pre-marital sex to the end of time, but society does not have to be obsessed with their sex. There are far more important matters that need to occupy our attention, such as charity, justice, mercy, honesty, equality, protecting the weak, saying prayers, fasting, avoiding hypocrisy. Leaders who prefer to legislate on sexual matters could take an example from the historical reports about some of the virtues that Caliph Umar championed. He dismissed any leader who did not visit the sick, including sick slaves, who did not sit in front of his house for all to consult and who treated the weak unfairly.[112] When he sent Abu Bakr to replace the disgraced Al Mughirah in Basra as governor, Umar commended him to the people for his social and political vision. He promised them that his governor would take from the wealthy and more affluent and give to the poor and rid their roads of undesirable elements.[113]

Theoretically if two unmarried persons were living together and it were publicly known, no one could charge them with violating the law unless they brought forth four upright witnesses to the act of intercourse. Upright people are hardly concerned with peering into others' bedrooms to catch them in the act of intercourse. It is very poor manners. When one does, however, find four upright witnesses to the sexual act – the Quran and some of the *sunna* provide for that too – there is the punishment of whipping and banishment. The couple practically would have to invite four witnesses into their bedroom during the intercourse, in which case both punishments of banishment and whipping preserved the right of the community to uphold its sense of decorum and its feeling that the two sex offenders have humiliated or harmed their partners or their families and in turn should feel the pain also of humiliation by being publicly whipped. At the time of Allah's/God's Revelations the Roman and Christian laws permitted a husband to kill a woman caught in the act of adultery; the woman, however, was not accorded the same privilege. So a woman had to think twice before killing her errant husband and to keep her anger under control; otherwise she would be charged with outright murder. A husband, on the other hand, could kill on the spot and plead outrageous provocation because of an affront to his authority over a woman. It is curious that the *sunna* on *zina* dealt with convictions on the basis of confessions to adultery or pre-marital sex, not on the basis of four upright witnesses.[114] This is revealing on two counts. First, sexual behaviour is to be interpreted as a matter of private freedom and conscience, not for prying neighbours much less the ruler/state trying to satisfy their sexual fantasies. Hence convictions are valid only if the persons involved have a bad conscience and wish for punishment by confessing. Secondly, persons who confess are asked to make sure they are not abusing their own conscience, for they were asked in the *sunna* whether they had actual intercourse or had just engaged in physical affection and fondling, private or public.[115] Affection and fondling were not punishable offences and if they raised suspicions, then the suspicions had to be proven, and with four witnesses.

Even Caliph Umar, the great military commander, was reported to have been chastened when he spied on his community. He was in the habit of taking nightly inspection walks. One night he found some Muslims drinking. The next morning, when he confronted one of them, the accused asked him how he knew. Umar told him that he had seen him 'with his own eyes'. The accused reminded him of the Quranic Injunction against spying and retorted: 'Did not Allah forbid you to spy on people?'[116] So Umar forgave the man his indiscretion of drinking in public.[117]

It has been observed that rulers were frustrated with the extremely high standards of the Quran because their job was (and is) seen as to get convictions, yet the Quran does not so easily allow convictions. Hence jurists found ways for rulers to circumvent the high standards with such notions as *taazir*, a ruler's discretion, and the creation of special courts paralleling and competing with the qadi courts. In this way the jurists and the ruler totally missed the social and spiritual point of the *zina* and sexual slandering verses (*qadf*), which was to leave people alone in their sexual lives and to teach them not to justify aberrant behaviour, like killing in a passion, or ranting and raging against loose sexual *mores*, and to dispense with the notion that a man has total control over a woman and her feelings.

Confessions as proof of zina *– a verdict of stoning*

It is the way convictions were arrived at and the evidence used which occupied most of the case law dealing with the Offence of Zina Ordinance. The following sections analyse problems connected with the proof of *zina*.

About seven years after the introduction of the Offence of Zina Ordinance a husband accused his wife and his friend of adultery.[118] He alleged that the two had run away together and engaged in 'illicit' intercourse. In fact the police found the two living together in the same house and arrested them. They pleaded that the complainant husband had in fact divorced the woman and that they were now lawfully married to each other. The man was initially charged nonetheless with rape, *zina bil jabr*, subject to *taazir* (why not with consensual *zina* was not clear). The case was first prosecuted at the district sessions court.[119] The trial judge changed the charge to *zina bil jabr* subject to *hadd*, namely death, on the grounds that the evidence was confessional on the part of both defendants. The judge awarded accordingly stoning to death in a public place. The case went on appeal to the Federal Shariat Court. Even if the parties had not appealed, the death sentence could not have been executed without a review from the Supreme Court (Art. 5 (3) of the Offence of Zina Ordinance).

The Federal Shariat Court set the death sentence aside for various reasons. First, on procedural grounds:[120] a person charged with a lesser offence, like rape subject to a discretionary penalty (*taazir*), may not have the charge changed to a more serious offence carrying the death penalty, though the reverse was possible. Secondly, on evidentiary grounds, pleading marriage as a defence did not amount to a confession to *zina*. Failing a valid confession, the prosecutor had not brought four upright witnesses who had actually seen the accused in the act of penetration. The court remanded the case to the trial level to determine whether there were facts other than the defence of marriage which could constitute a confession.

In this case the court was following precedent from other similar cases in which the police and the state prosecutor were treating a defence of marriage as a confession. As stated by Chief Justice Muhammad Siddiq three years earlier in 1985: '… [the State Counsel] … strongly relies upon the defence pleas … that they married each other and were leading life as husband and wife … It is significant to note that even sexual intercourse is not admitted by the … appellants with each other in their statements … They have only alleged marriage with each…. [T]o establish the charge of Zina, it is necessary to show that a man and a woman … have … committed sexual intercourse' (at 403–4).[121] In other words, marriage does not mean it was consummated and living together does not in itself alone establish *zina*. No one witnessed them in intercourse, presumption is not enough under Islamic law, and so the court acquitted the accused.

The judgment confirmed a view that the Quranic law of *zina* is to protect people's private sex lives from prying public eyes. Living together is not an offence in itself. One should not even have to plead a defence of marriage or prove one is married. Four eyewitnesses to intercourse are needed – nothing more, nothing less.

In another case the Federal Shariat Court held that a simple assertion by the two accused of *zina* that they are of the age of majority and live together as man and wife suffices as a defence.[122] When a man and woman living together are charged with *zina* and assert that they were married after the divorce of the woman, the state prosecutor was to prove beyond reasonable doubt that the *talaq* of the first husband was invalid.[123] The court acquitted the appellants.

Through the years, the police also became too enthusiastic in some instances to act immediately and rashly on informers' wagging tongues. In one case the Federal Shariat Court had to chastise the police.[124] In Lahore an informant had asked the police to come quickly to a place where it was suspected that the accused and a woman named Mst Goshi were preparing to commit *zina* together on a cot as they had entered a room together. The man was found and convicted at the Sessions Court and an arrest warrant was issued for the lady. On appeal to the Federal Shariat Court, Justice Manan criticized the police. They had misused their power by trespassing in the house of the accused without a warrant, violating the constitutional guarantee of the fundamental right to privacy (Art. 14). The appellant was acquitted and the arrest warrant discharged. It was a key decision, for it cited the Constitution as the fundamental law of the land.

Retracting confessions – police coercion

The Offence of Zina Ordinance allowed the accused to escape the *hadd* punishment of stoning or whipping if she or he retracted a confession before the punishment was executed. In Umer Farin and 2 ors v The State[125] a husband complained that in his absence abroad his wife had an affair with the accused and ran away with him. The husband had been married to her 15–16 years and their children were still minors. The wife was found with her lover and both were arrested. The police took confessional statements from both.[126] At the trial the woman and the man retracted their confessional statements because they said they were extracted through third-degree police methods, whereupon the judge changed the terms of the charge. He charged and convicted them of enticing a woman away with criminal intent to have illicit intercourse (then Art. 16 of the Ordinance). The woman defendant was declared not only the victim but also the abettor of the crime. A more logical approach would have been to drop the charge of enticement and find another more appropriate charge, as enticement involves exercising undue influence and defrauding the victim. A woman deemed to abet cannot by definition defraud herself.

The case went on appeal to the Federal Shariat Court. The appellate court found the opposite of the trial judge with regard to the confessions. It opined that the confessions were voluntary. The crux of the case was, however, weighing the significance of retracting confessions, whatever the grounds. The court found in favour of the State Counsel's arguments, namely that retraction of a confession means one is no longer liable to the *hadd* punishment – stoning in this case – but it can become the basis for a lesser discretionary charge. A higher charge may be reduced to a lower one. Retracting a confession can serve as evidence in an ordinary non-*hudud* criminal case if found to be voluntary and true. The truth of the confession has to be established with the help of collaborative evidence. The woman had stated that she was pregnant. The court held that her statement of pregnancy plus the fact that her husband had not had access to her for some time and statements from her parents as well as her minor daughter provided such collaborative evidence. The couple were sentenced to five years' imprisonment and twenty lashes.[127]

The judgment was problematic. Confessions extracted by police brutality are nothing new in the history of Islamic law. In a Sunnah of the Companions it was reported in a case of alleged theft that the people of Kila had taken into custody the alleged thieves.[128] The case came before the Companion Nuaman bin Bashir and he released the accused. The community was upset and asked him why he had done this before beating them or investigating the matter. He chastised them for wanting him to beat them. He answered that the people had found their stolen goods on the accused. Was that not enough that they had recovered their property? In the Sunnah of the Prophet there was no instance of a confession extracted by a third person. All instances of confessions were voluntarily made at the time of the public hearing, or the accused had to be asked whether he wanted to confess before being taken into custody, not afterwards. On the basis of both Sunnah, using a retracted confession even for an offence subject only to a *taazir* punishment could be violating the Injunctions of Islam, for it is the retraction which suffices. Once retracted it should be declared inadmissible evidence and could not be further collaborated.

Another problem in the judgment about the retracted confession lay in allowing the husband to initiate accusing his wife of *zina* upon his return. The procedure for such a husband is, as noted above, that of oath-taking (*liaan*). It gives the wife a chance to deny the accusation. If she does so then afterwards it is discovered that she gave birth to a child not her husband's, then she is still not to be charged with *zina*. In such a case, the woman cannot be charged even if one wanted to because the *liaan* procedure precludes opening up a case for *zina* (for fear of violating the principle of double jeopardy).[129] The option is then divorce, not a further charge. This follows in the footsteps of the Prophet, who ordered divorce between the parties under such circumstances. There was no charge of *zina*.[130]

Confession by the woman, denial by the man

Another case[131] raised the issue of whether only one party can be convicted of *zina* on the basis of a confession when the other party does not confess. A brother accused his sister aged 17–18 years and a man of *zina*. Both were recovered from the same house and charged with consensual *zina* liable to *taazir*. The man pleaded innocence, while the young woman confessed. The trial court acquitted the man but convicted the woman. The Federal Shariat Court ordered the case to be transferred to its jurisdiction for reasons of justice. It could not under the law reverse the acquittal (Art. 203DD (1), and proviso to (2) of the Constitution). The court's opinion was that: '… to maintain conviction of the present appellant … where the co-accused had been acquitted, will whittle away the confidence of the people in our judicial system, particularly when the offence in question could be committed by the two jointly and not alone by any of the accused.'[132] At stake was some confusion about whether pleadings are the same as confessions. Justice Gul Muhammed Khan pointed out that a 'yes' to the question, 'Do you plead guilty' is not the same as a confession. Then he examined the law of confession from the perspective of some classical Islamic jurists. Abu Hanifa, he held, insisted on a confession repeated in four different sessions for a conviction of *zina*. Shafii and Malik, however, subscribed to the view that one confession suffices. Justice Khan cited several jurists who preferred the four-times confession as mandatory. In the end nonetheless the Justice did not declare which opinion he would favour. He left a strong hint of an *obiter dictum* that a four-times confession was necessary, whether for *zina* liable to *hadd* or to *taazir*. Otherwise, he disposed of the case on the grounds of the absence of a full confession. He then examined the nature of confession. Aside from whether one or four confessions are required, a confession must first meet certain standards. In order to be accepted a confession must not only be voluntary, but also true. He found that the so-called confession of the accused woman could not have been true.[133] The forensic evidence disproved it. The medical report showed there had been no sexual intercourse during the time the two accused had been staying together in a hired house and posing as husband and wife for some seven days. The Justice then went a step further. He deemed an untrue confession to be a retracted confession. While Islamic jurists allowed a person to retract a confession, the Justice asked, but what is to be done when a person had given a false confession and its falsity is proven? The court reasoned that the person would want to tell the truth and therefore by not telling the truth she was presumed to have retracted the statement. The accused young woman was acquitted as the man had been.

This judgment is an excellent example of how procedural and evidentiary rules can protect persons from violation of some basic principles that undermines the morality of the law. *Zina* relates to intercourse and penetration. It cannot be performed alone, rather it takes two persons. To punish one of the intercoursees and acquit the other raises too many doubts that should go to the benefit of the one party left to bear the brunt of the charge by herself and not by that of her mysterious male partner. The questions that raised doubts were many. Did the woman confessing *zina* have sex with someone else other than the one who denied having it with her? Was the woman's confession motivated purely by bad conscience or by a desire to appeal to the conscience of the man so that he would marry her and save her from her brother's fury, wishing that if Caliph Umar had heard the case he would have ordered him to give her at least her dower? Under Islamic rules if someone has made a charge of *zina* then fails to prove it, that someone is subject to 80 lashes. Does this mean that the ruler/state or prosecutor will be subject to lashing if it agrees to prosecute a case based on a complaint brought by the husband, brother or neighbour but loses? It is these kinds of absurdities which arise from underestimating the dangers of prosecuting intercourse and which undermine the inner morality of the law.

A look at the *sunna* confirms the importance of keeping basic principles of morality and human decency intact in a society bent on suppression and coercion. In certain, not all, Sunnah of the Prophet, women stood up for their rights. If a man confessed to intercourse and named the woman involved and she denied it, then only he was stoned or whipped, and she released, or he was simply charged with false accusation. One could say, at first blush, that convicting only one of the sexual partners, while acquitting the other, might have been legitimate. At a second look, however, it is clear that the person confessing, as reported in the Sunnah, was pleading in public to be punished and doing so completely voluntarily. Nowadays it is different. What Muslim man would go around confessing in public to his sexual sins and asking the ruler/state to punish him? He waits instead for someone to discover his sins and to be charged by the police. This is a far cry from the Sunnah. It is nowadays other people who are complaining and causing the police to bring charges. This constitutes interference in a person's conscience about their sex life. It is no longer about the sinner taking the initiative and expiating himself publicly. In the Sunnah the believer had the choice – to go public or to stay silent. It was not a choice the public could make for believers, nor could the public serve as the keeper of consciences. Hence a confession should not even be accepted if there had been a charge brought by the ruler/state on behalf of complainants. A confession could be accepted only if a person turns her/himself in. Besides, with regard to women who confess today, it is known that they live in a society which intimidates them. Their confessions in particular, even when seemingly free or seemingly self-motivated, have to be carefully scrutinized.[134]

Unmarried pregnancy – does it prove zina?

In this section, three different judgments are discussed. They are arranged according to the name of the woman affected.

Taslim Bibi – a disgrace

One of the first cases involving unmarried women just seven months after the Offence of Zina Ordinance became law did not bode well for the woman named Taslim Bibi.[135] She claimed that while she was working in the fields loosening dirt the accused found her there and raped her. He threatened to kill her if she told anyone about it and at the same time promised to marry her. Out of fear and humiliation she did not reveal this to anyone. When she discovered she was pregnant two months later, she reminded the young man of his promise. He refused to honour it. Taslim Bibi informed her parents of the encounter in the field, and two days after the birth of her baby daughter her father took her to the police to lodge a complaint against the accused, the putative father. Taslim Bibi was detained. The baby died two months later while the mother was in detention. The accused man belonged to a notable village family and witnesses on his behalf testified to his good reputation. He denied that he had raped the woman. He said that her charge against him was an attempt to blackmail him into marrying her. He then counter-claimed against Taslim Bibi, alleging that the intercourse has been consensual. In other words, he did not deny having had intercourse, he denied rape. Taslim Bibi pointed out to the court that the accused was in effect accusing himself as well by confessing to having committed the crime of voluntary *zina*. She maintained nonetheless that he had forced her into having intercourse, but if the court did not accept this, then at least it should recognize that she had intercourse for fear of being hurt. The trial judge did not believe her and convicted both of consensual *zina*, though the young man was acquitted of rape. He went on appeal, Taslim did not; why is not made clear.

The Federal Shariat Court reversed the lower court's decision and acquitted the man of consensual *zina* on grounds of lack of evidence beyond a reasonable doubt that he had consented. Technically the acquittal of the man would have meant that as the man had neither consented to nor been forced into intercourse, Taslim Bibi also could not have consented. Instead the pregnancy was the indirect proof against Taslim. Even though she had not gone on to appeal, the court took it upon itself to chastise her and her parents. The court did not refer to the general Islamic principles of *zina*, namely that no one may accuse another of *zina* without bringing four witnesses and that a reasonable denial by a woman, even a pregnant woman, constitutes self-defence to protect her from being killed. The court instead called her unmarried pregnancy 'disgraceful for the entire family'. Obviously the pre-Islamic cultural normativeness had more impact than the more protective Islamic Injunctions.

Jehan Mina – the triumph of social Islam and of stoning

Some three years from the date of the Offence of Zina Ordinance the unmarried 15-year-old Jehan Mina was living with her father. She worked temporarily as a domestic servant for her ailing aunt. Her father died and her mother remarried. Jehan then went to live with her grandfather. After her aunt no longer needed her, she went to live with her uncle. She began showing signs of pregnancy. On being questioned by her uncle, she said that her aunt's husband and his son had been forcing her to have intercourse with them. The accused denied this, alleging that Jehan's uncle was angry with them over a land dispute. Jehan's aunt confirmed the dispute, but alleged that Jehan had been raped while grazing cattle in the mountains. The grandfather ordered Jehan to come back to him so that he could kill her to salvage the family honour. Her uncle, however, refused to give her up. At the trial the two accused men were acquitted of rape, *zina bil jabr*, but Jehan was convicted of consensual *zina* and sentenced to death by stoning under section 5 of the Offence of Zina Ordinance. The reasons were twofold: the pregnancy in itself was proof of intercourse; and she had stayed silent for six months before admitting to what had happened. The appeal court upheld the acquittal of the men on the grounds that the only evidence against them was the statement by Jehan, which did not establish a case beyond reasonable doubt. The court refused, however, to acquit Jehan. Because she could not prove rape, the pregnancy served indirectly to prove consensual *zina*. Her death sentence was commuted. The reason was grounded more in mercy than legal analysis. Because of her tender age, so reasoned the court, and the loss of the companionship of her parents, she was sentenced to (only) three years' imprisonment and ten lashes. The punishment was to commence once her baby reached two years of age, when she would cease breastfeeding, according to Islamic Injunctions.[136] Again the Islamic Injunction that four upright witnesses are needed for a conviction of *zina*, pregnancy not being sufficient proof, was overridden by cultural norms. The culture had to punish her. She had been saved from an honour-crime death at the hands of her grandfather and from death by court order, but society still demanded its price – at the very least she had to suffer imprisonment. The society demanded no price from the man who had not had the courage to speak up,[137] who did not follow the pious example of a Muslim man in a Sunnah of the Holy Prophet who spoke up to protect a woman found giving birth to a child in the marketplace (see Safia Bibi below).[138]

Safia Bibi – the triumph of Islamic legal norms

The third case about whether pregnancy in itself constitutes sufficient evidence for a conviction of *zina* turned out better than Taslim Bibi's. It represented a triumph for cross-border female solidarity. This was the infamous case of Safia Bibi,[139] a case which like that of Amina Lawal and Zafran Bibi raised an outcry around the world (Lee). The accused woman, 20 years of age and almost blind, worked as a domestic. Her father alleged that the grandson in the house where she worked had raped Safia. She testified she had been raped on two occasions – once by the grandson and again by the son of her employers. Safia gave birth to a child, who died in hospital. Her pregnancy was forensically established, as was the potency of the alleged rapists. The trial criminal court judge acquitted the accused grandson of *zina bil jabr* for lack of evidence beyond the statement of Safia. The court then turned on Safia. The judge found her guilty of consensual *zina* subject to a *taazir* penalty in the absence of four witnesses or a confession. She was sentenced to three years' imprisonment and 15 lashes plus a fine. The grounds were manifold: she had been pregnant, had not complained of the offence while pregnant and had kept quiet for ten months. The court rejected testimony from a witness that Safia Bibi had complained to her mother about rape.

By the time the case went to the Federal Shariat Court, public opinion was highly sympathetic to Safia and against the lower court. On appeal to the Federal Shariat Court two issues were to be decided – i) whether one sexual partner can be acquitted while the other is convicted; ii) whether pregnancy of an unmarried woman is sufficient evidence to convict her of *zina*.

On the issue of whether *zina* requires the conviction of both parties or the acquittal of both, the court, under Chief Justice Aftab Hussain, had to review its doctrine pronounced in Mst Bakhan v The State, *PLD* 1986 Fed. Sh. Crt. (FSC) 274, as discussed above, which held that no one party can be acquitted or convicted without the other, even though one party has confessed. The court consulted the classical literature. It examined the position that the medieval jurist Abu Hanifa would have taken. It found that he would have acquitted both parties for the simple reason that the denial of one disproved the confession of the other. On the other hand, the court found that Shafii would have allowed conviction of only the confessing party, but the confession of one party would never suffice to convict the other, unless other independent evidence were available, similar to English common law.[140]

In the case at hand Safia had not confessed, but was her pregnancy similar to a silent confession as it were? Would pregnancy suffice to convict her alone of consensual *zina*, or to convict her alleged rapist of *zina bil jabr*? On the question of whether pregnancy would suffice to convict Safia the court could have efficiently disposed of the matter by ruling that consensual *zina* subject to *taazir* had not been proven beyond reasonable doubt because there was no evidence of the woman servant being sentimentally attached to the man she accused of rape.[141] The court failed to cite this fundamental principle of criminal law.

Instead, the court chose to review Islamic literature on pregnant women and *zina*. The court found that the Hanafi and Shafii jurists tended not to disagree on this matter. They would have found that pregnancy is not sufficient evidence of a woman's consent to intercourse, which forms the crux of *zina*, not the pregnancy *per se*. An exculpatory statement on her part that she was raped would have sufficed for her defence.[142] What evidence she would have had to bring nonetheless to pursue charges against the man was not discussed by the jurists. Their main concern was providing a defence for her, without elaborating on what evidence she needed to prosecute her rapist. The court interpreted the Hanafi and Shafii positions to mean that a pregnant woman needed only to defend herself against charges of consensual *zina* and need not be concerned, as her father was, with naming and accusing the rapist. The court then turned to Malik Ibn Anas's position, which placed the burden of proof on the unmarried pregnant woman. She had not only to assert that she was raped in order to exculpate herself, but also to prove the credibility of her story, perhaps not to the degree of beyond a doubt, but at least plausibly. She had to prove that she had raised an alarm, complained about the coerced intercourse, or show she was bleeding from the rape.[143]

The court then decided that the requirements of the three schools of law were in fact fulfilled in this case. The evidence that Safia had complained to her mother satisfied the Maliki requirement. But the Hanafi and Shafii positions (that pregnancy is not equivalent to a confession) were in any case to be preferred as they were more consistent with present-day ethical consciences.[144] Safia was acquitted.

This judgment should be read in conjunction with another case in the same year (1985), but in the Supreme Court. In Muhammad Sharif v The State[145] the Supreme Court reviewed the Maliki position on pregnancy. It found that the burden of proof of self-defence on the unmarried pregnant woman was lessened to the extent that Maliki commentaries gave more benefit of the doubt to a woman in an isolated rural area than in a crowded urban area. A woman alleging rape in the lonely countryside could shout as much as she wanted but no one would hear her. At the same time the court noted that the special social condition of women in any one society or era differs and has to be taken into account. Where women are known not to speak out for reasons of shame or decorum, no matter where they are located, in the country or a city, then the Maliki position is unfair, for it presumes that women are outspoken and cannot be intimidated.

The Supreme Court did not cite some of the Sunnah of Umar. In addition to having advocated elevating stoning to a Quranic penalty because it had been left out of the Quran through oversight, he was also reported to have expanded the evidentiary requirements for *zina* in order to widen the net of convictions: through witnesses *or* confessions *or* pregnancy.[146] Perhaps the Supreme Court did not cite these hadiths because it could not have answered satisfactorily the question of whether pregnancy suffices for a conviction in the light of other *sunna*. Dawud's hadith[147] narrates the story of a woman bearing a child in the marketplace. She was naturally asked, who the father of the child was; the woman did not answer. The question was put again in front of the Prophet and the woman was again silent. A young man came to her rescue saying he was the father. The people said he had a good reputation and so was credible. In a hearing before the Prophet it came out, however, that he was married – presumably not to the woman bearing the child. He was stoned because it was said he had confessed. He had not exercised his option to remain silent as the woman had done. In another Sunnah of the Prophet a woman from Ghamid did *not* remain silent.[148] She told the Prophet she had committed fornication. We are not told whether she was married or not. He sent her away. She kept returning to him. She told him she was now pregnant and later she informed him she had given birth. Finally he had her executed by stoning. As Shafii pointed out in his *Risala*, the *sunna* prescribing stoning related to married free persons while the *sunna* prescribing whipping related to slaves, married or unmarried. If so, then we can presume that the pregnant woman of Ghamid (in another version, she was of the tribe of Juhainah) who was stoned was not single, but rather *married*. We have no evidence otherwise that the Sunnah of the Prophet ever condemned an *unmarried* pregnant woman to stoning. Not even Malik's *Muwatta* reported such an event occurring before the Prophet or the Companions. Malik only wrote his own opinion about what should happen in the case of an unmarried pregnant woman. He prescribed how an unmarried woman may protect herself from public sanction by asserting rape and how to make herself credible before a judge, who might feel obliged to question her, as happened in the case of the woman having borne a child in the marketplace. Malik did not specify what was to happen to her if the judge or the public did not believe her. Malik only then advised the putative father and rapist to take care before marrying the woman or at least offer a dower (perhaps as compensation as was usual in the Mosaic Old Testament law in case of rape)[149] and to wait for the end of the three months *idda* before marrying.[150] This original prescription took on another dynamic as time progressed. The late medieval and modern-day Maliki jurists interpreted Malik's counselling to mean that the *sunna* required an unmarried pregnant woman to be stoned. This is a huge presumption based on a leap of faith, not reasoned argumentation, for Malik did not say, 'Find the rapist and have him along with the woman stoned.' A presumption is not enough to make a case for justifying the jeopardizing of a woman's life. Malik was well aware that the *sunna* contained no case of an unmarried woman being stoned solely on the basis of pregnancy. The *sunna* referred to pregnant women who were married and free (not enslaved). But again, we have to keep in mind that the free married pregnant woman who was stoned took the initiative to proclaim and confess her sins, even when the Prophet sent her away to contemplate the consequences. Otherwise, a pregnant woman as found in the *sunna* exercised the right to remain silent, even in the face of an inquisitive or upset public when delivering a baby in the marketplace. Thus the rule that would emerge from the *sunna* would have to be as follows: a *married* woman who freely confesses – without being charged or goaded – to having become pregnant by someone other than her husband would be liable to be stoned. An unmarried woman who freely confesses without being charged or complained against would be whipped. In both instances though the key condition for a conviction is that she takes the initiative to confess openly and ask explicitly for punishment. Under today's conditions of social suppression of women, such a confession would have to be extremely closely scrutinized together with the woman's psychic stability. In the light of the *sunna* reporting a woman giving birth in the marketplace, Malik's self-defence rules for unmarried pregnant women can be interpreted as pragmatic advice on how to handle a situation that excites the public. The woman would have the right to remain silent. As for how to handle an inquisitive crowd, if a brave man does not step forward to protect her, the woman can protect herself with an allegation of rape or unconsciousness. Her statement should suffice. It would fall then to the judge either to present this as a fait accompli terminating the case or to request the crowd to bring evidence of four upright witnesses.

One has to be perfectly clear, however, that the *sunna* of self-defence of a woman in a case of *hadd* for consensual *zina* was not addressing the issue of punishment for rape. The advice is unclear as to what to do when an unmarried pregnant woman charges rape, but wants her rapist to be punished and not simply plead that her allegation of rape means that she is not guilty of consensual *zina*.

Comparison with Zanzibari law on unmarried pregnancies

At this point a digression into Zanzibari law (Spinsters Act) on the same issues is useful. The Zanzibari decree regulating pregnancies of unmarried women, called spinsters, makes an interesting comparison with the Pakistani approach.[151] It was first enacted nine years before General Ul Haq issued the Offence of Zina Ordinance. The Zanzibari law went to the heart of the problem of unmarried pregnant women – not a moral problem, but a financial and social problem: who is going to bear the burden of the costs of the pregnancy and maintaining the child? This question is especially crucial in a subsistence economy, where the family is the main source of support. Quranically, Zanzibar rests its approach on the verse which enjoins kindness to a pregnant woman as a parent.[152]

Zanzibar penalized relations between unmarried men and women only if pregnancy resulted. The law was enacted in response to parents who were reluctant to send their pubescent daughters to school for fear of premarital pregnancies, but it was extended to cover all unmarried women, including widows and divorcees. Most pregnant girls are at least 16 years of age, but if the girl is under 14 years of age, then her sexual partner would be subject to punishment for defilement under the penal laws (Khamis).

The law at first imprisoned both parties. The idea was to secure the name of the man who had impregnated the woman and have the case investigated initially by the Regional Commissioner and a Special Committee established for such purposes. Now parties are sentenced to what is called an offences centre or to community service. The main purpose of securing the name of the man was to make him pay for maintaining the child. The family of the impregnated woman use the time spent in submitting criminal charges and pleadings to negotiate with the man's family about marriage. If marriage turns out to be out of the question, then at least maintenance is secured. The law closely followed the Sunnah of Umar who tended towards marriage and/or compensation in the form of a dower as a solution to unmarried pregnancies. At the same time, like the Pakistani ordinances, the Zanzibar law did not respect the *sunna* where the unmarried pregnant woman and her partner decided for themselves how much they wish to expose their consciences to public scrutiny or to Allah/God alone. The ruler/state is not to pressure them into exposure.

Married pregnancy – does it prove zina?

If an unmarried woman is accused of having an affair with a married man, then she would be liable to the *hadd* of stoning to death under the Offence of Zina Ordinance. If she had an affair with an unmarried man, then she would be liable to the *hadd* of whipping. If a married woman, however, has an affair, then she would be liable always to stoning. If there are no upright four witnesses or she does not voluntarily confess, then she was liable to the *taazir* penalty of at least four years of imprisonment. She ran a particular risk, more so than her unmarried sister. The married woman's husband nowadays could call for a DNA test to determine whether he is the father of the child if he suspects that his wife had an affair.

The High Court in Lahore decided to protect 'family cohesion' and therefore shielded the married woman from the modern-day scientific DNA proofs.[153] The High Court held that DNA evidence did not fit into the evidentiary scheme of *zina*, which is particular to Islamic legal interpretations. The complainant, the husband, Syed Imtaz Ali, sued and had Muhammad Azhar arrested on suspicion of *zina* with his wife. The husband had his daughter submit to a DNA test, since he thought she was not his child. The lab reports confirmed his suspicions. They concluded that Syed Ali was excluded from paternity of the child and could not be the biological father.

The High Court called an Islamic law scholar and advocate, Muhammad Ismail Qureshi, and consulted the work, *Tafheen ul Quran*, by Syed Abu-ul Aaala Maudoodi. The High Court read for itself, however, the Quranic verses on the evidentiary requirements for *zina* and the oaths a suspicious husband must take. The High Court found that the only proof admissible was by four witnesses, voluntary confession (though the Quran has nothing to say about confessions in relation to *zina*, it is obviously inferred here or assumed it is from the Sunnah) or by oath. DNA results did not fit into this scheme.

The High Court explained what it believed to be the social values which the Quranic evidentiary requirements were protecting. These were to avoid stigmatizing children. Other legal systems have similar aims, having presumptions in favour of a child being deemed to be of the marriage bed unless the husband brings absolute proof of impotency or lengthy separation from the wife.[154] To use DNA for establishing *zina* in a private matter would not serve the larger purpose of why *zina* is punishable. The law should be aimed at punishing only lewdness in public, where four or more persons could witness this vulgarity. The High Court noted that DNA could be useful evidence in other types of cases, e.g. establishing paternity for purposes of maintenance. The High Court could have added that husbands' use of secret DNA tests is a modern-day form of spying, which even Caliph Umar had had to be reminded to avoid.[155]

With these social aims in mind the High Court held that the Quran requires first the suspicious husband to give an oath. Then the wife has to give an oath. If she refutes his oath then that is the end of the matter. If she does not, then she can be charged with *zina* liable to *taazir*, not *hadd*, for DNA is not equivalent to nor does it replace four witnesses to the act of intercourse. The oath is precisely for the purpose of giving the wife a chance to defend herself against suspicion. Even when the allegation is true it is up to her conscience to decide whether she wishes to keep the matter private between herself and Allah/God. Her reasons can be as valid as those of her husband, who chooses another route, that of publicizing his suspicions. The same applies to the wife who suspects her husband has sired a child outside the marriage bed. Her husband has the same option of privacy when taking the oath demanded by the wife.

The High Court held that the accused should be released but on bail until the *liaan* oath procedure had taken place, if it ever did.

The decision upheld the spirit of the Holy Quran and the Sunnah. The difficulty of proving *zina* is a sign that the ruler/state is not to interfere in the privacy of consensual sex unless the parties so wish, when their conscience cannot bear the burden of sin. It was a warning to the police and the public to exercise great restraint.

There are certain elements in the DNA decision which raise some questions. The judgment refers to legitimizing or stigmatizing a child. A child is a child and no distinction should be made in terms of legitimizing or stigmatizing, for to label a child is to blame a child for the actions of its parents and amounts to guilt by association. The High Court referred as well to the need not to destroy the stability of the family. The notion of protection of the family is a difficult concept from a juridical perspective. Is the protection for the individual members of the family or for the family as a conceptual entity? For a family is no juridical person as such and has no legal standing, not even in the Injunctions of Islam. When two spouses have taken an oath or a court orders an oath, because one is suspicious of the other, the oath-taking means in practical terms that the marriage is over and the family split. So it is more the cultural sentiments about family than legal principles which influenced the High Court's decision not to use DNA as proof.

Nonetheless the law of *zina* as promulgated in the Offence of Zina Ordinance will catch up with the pregnant married woman plagued with a suspicious husband. Whether he divorces her of his own will without the *liaan* oaths or because of them, he can still use DNA to contest paying maintenance for the child. At that point *zina* liable to *taazir* (fornication under the Penal Code) will raise its head. Already the state prosecutor in the case noted that DNA would be useful for a later prosecution he planned for *zina* liable to *taazir*. The prosecution would not need four witnesses, or even circumstantial evidence, only DNA. How the prosecution would fare depended on whether the future court would follow the precedent of the Federal Shariat Court, which ruled out pursuing prosecution of a woman who had given an oath of denial in a *liaan* procedure.[156] If it would not accept this precedent, then the future court would have to decide whether it will instead follow the established principle that one cannot convict the married woman without her sexual partner (unless she was impregnated artificially without intercourse) or not.[157] If a court nonetheless would still decide to convict her of consensual *zina* (now called fornication under the Penal Code), then she should plead violation of the constitutional principle of privacy and dignity (Art. 14)[158] and argue that the Quran and the *sunna* also are aimed at protecting sexual privacy and dignity.

Proof of zina *by witnesses*

While the vast majority of cases before the Federal Shariat Court relied on circumstantial evidence and statements of various witnesses, the Quranic four witnesses have never appeared. It has been rumoured, though, that where the prosecution actually found four upright witnesses to an act of intercourse, the judge asked how it was possible that they had achieved this – it is so rare. The witnesses answered that each peeped through the keyhole one after another. The judge then promptly dismissed their evidence – witnessing had to be simultaneous by all four. One can also question whether witnesses who stoop to peeping through a keyhole are truly upright.

Proving rape* (zina bil jabr *subject to* taazir*)

Zina bil jabr under the Offence of Zina Ordinance (prior to the 2006 reforms), was defined basically as intercourse without the consent of the victim. The case law has been mixed, as anywhere in the world. There is evidence of judges trying to protect the honour of women. There is evidence to the contrary, showing that judges are worried that men are being overly prosecuted. One consistency emerged – a young woman who alleges rape more than likely wins her case. (See Postscript on rape under the Women Protection Act.)

Protecting women

In Ghulam Sarwar v The State,[159] the judges took care to put rape in a sociological context. The plaintiff, a Christian, aged 15–16 years, had been working in the fields, threshing. The accused appeared with a companion, caught her, dragged her away and raped her. She raised the alarm, others came and the accused with his companion ran away. They were later caught and arrested. The medical report confirmed sexual intercourse, but found no marks of violence. In his defence, the accused, a young boy, pleaded that the girl had consented. He labelled the plaintiff a woman of 'easy virtue' and accused her of trumping up charges due to political enmity between their families. The trial court nonetheless convicted him of rape. He was sentenced to ten years' imprisonment and 30 lashes, plus a fine. The Federal Shariat Court on appeal found that the lack of violence supported the plea that the victim had consented. The court them changed the charge to consensual *zina*. On further appeal the Supreme Court restored the original conviction. Justice Muhammad Afzal Zullah held that the absence of scratches on the plaintiff's body was not indicative of her consent. Justice Zullah opined that the function of the *zina* law was to protect women against being molested, and not men against so-called loose women: '... ordinarily in respectable village communities, of Pakistani Muslim society, the protection of the females of ... agricultural labourers against all molestation, is that of the landed gentry. Here in this case, the petitioner has broken these well-established norms and is a slur on the good name of Muslims in his village. He violated a young lady of Christian faith and taking undue advantage of the victim participated in what it appears was, an action of gangsterism. He deserved no leniency in the matter of sentence.'[160]

Another social element taken into account was the age of the plaintiff.[161] A girl in her teens would be more submissive than a more mature woman, it was observed. The implication is of course that more mature women would have a more difficult time proving that they did not consent, as it seems to be assumed in the judicial male mind that she is more capable of warding off an attacker than her younger sister, thus constituting more a manifestation of prejudice than of a desire to teach men to restrain themselves.[162]

While Justice Zullah chastised the accused for violating the village social code, he did not comment on the slur which the accused made against the reputation of the girl, namely that she was of 'easy virtue'. There was a case to which all judges should refer in rape cases in order to put a stop to such deprecatory language: that is a Federal Shariat Court case.[163] In that case Chief Justice Aftab Hussain advised the young accused to be careful in his defence plea about how he characterized the plaintiff. She was a mature woman, married with children and was appealing against an acquittal. She lost the case on appeal because the attack occurred in the dark and the identity of the attacker was not established beyond reasonable doubt. The accused had called the plaintiff a 'loose woman'. The Justice stated that such sullying of a woman's reputation would make the accused open to a charge of *qadhf* (*qazf*), slandering someone's sexual reputation. In the light of this case any accused man in future should plead in his defence only consent, without adding what he thinks about the reputation of the woman. Unfortunately the court did not change the charge into *qadhf* (*qazf*). The courts have not all consistently followed the line of Justice Hussain against slurring. It was declared in another rape case that if the victim added a charge of *qadhf* (*qazf*) this would amount to unnecessary harassment of the accused.[164] The Protection of Women Act of 2006 now supports the judiciary's observations that false charges merit punishment of the accused who slanders the plaintiff.

Whether women alleging rape and abduction are overprotected – damages for the victim

The issue was raised of whether women victims of rape were being overprotected, to the detriment of doing justice to male perpetrators.[165] In the case, the plaintiff, aged 20, had returned to live with her mother due to strained relations with her husband. One Muhammad Sharif proposed to procure a divorce for her then to marry her. The plaintiff's mother refused the offer. The plaintiff was induced to visit the family of the accused, Muhammad Sharif, whereupon she was abducted to Sindh, where she was kept for seven months. Upon their return to their home area, the plaintiff went to her mother's house and Sharif to his own house. The young woman brought charges of rape. At the hearings it was revealed that the she had a child by a man other than her husband. It was established who the father was. The Federal Shariat Court found Sharif guilty of rape and sentenced him to five years' imprisonment, ten lashes and a fine, which was to be paid as compensation to the plaintiff. On appeal the Supreme Court changed the charge to consensual *zina* liable to *taazir* (Art. 10 (2)), convicted the man of consensual *zina* but confirmed payment of the fine to the plaintiff. The Supreme Court did not charge the woman with *zina*. The case was complicated because the original charges were not only *zina bil jabr* but also abduction for purposes of rape under Article 11 of the Offence of Zina Ordinance. Abduction carried a sentence of life imprisonment. The Supreme Court observed that life imprisonment did not fit the crime, which was not serious enough to warrant life imprisonment. The Supreme Court suggested the legislature change the law so that judges could exercise as much discretion in meting out punishment for abduction as for rape. From a women's perspective the reverse should have been asserted – life imprisonment for rape and a discretionary penalty for abduction. The amendments in the 2006 Act for the Protection of Women have not heeded the judge's advice. The sentence of abduction remains life imprisonment. In the case of rape the courts have discretion to sentence to death or imprisonment between ten and 25 years. (See Postscript.)

Another judgment illustrates similar problems when the woman alleged both abduction and rape.[166] The medical report in the case showed that she had been habituated to intercourse, the vagina easily admitting two fingers. Nor did she show marks of violence. The police evidence showed that the plaintiff had moved about with the defendant freely and without resistance. The Federal Shariat Court held that the charges had not been proved beyond doubt and acquitted the accused. The key to the court's decision lay in its not separating the crime of abduction from that of *zina bil jabr*. Just because someone abducts another for the purpose of having sex, and the person being abducted agrees to being abducted, does not mean that in the course of the abduction she agrees to forced intercourse. So while abduction charges may be dropped because the victim is found to consent to being abducted, rape charges can still be upheld.

In a 2004 case[167] the Shariat Court did not follow the Supreme Court's opinion that lack of marks on the body of the victim is not a sign of consent, and therefore should not be put forth as evidence.[168] The Federal Shariat Court found that the plaintiff had been subjected to sexual intercourse on the basis of medical evidence, but she showed no bodily marks of violence. She alleged she had been forced at the point of a gun, but the weapon was never found. Police officers' investigations showed the woman had consented. On the balance of the evidence the court found that the man should be charged instead with consensual *zina* (fornication) and reduced his sentence to two years. While the 2006 Protection of Women Act prevents the courts from transforming charges from rape to consensual *zina* or vice versa, the 2004 case is still troubling because it regards the absence of bodily marks as indicating a woman's consent.

Protecting men – use of repentance to mitigate punishment

The Quranic verses on *hudud* stress punishment as well as mercy if the sinner repents. Following the two verses on requiring four upright witnesses to testify to lewdness among women and among men, and prescribing banishment as the appropriate punishment, is a verse which speaks of Allah's mercy: 4:17: 'Allah accepts the repentance of those who do evil who know no better and repent soon afterwards…' 4:18: 'Of no value is the repentance for those who continue to do evil…'

Again in regard to *qadhf* (*qazf*) – that is, a slanderous charge of *zina* against a chaste woman – the Quran prescribes the 80 lashes against the slanderer 'unless they repent thereafter and mend their ways …' (sura 24:45). Further, in the case of the heinous act of fighting Allah or the Prophet or spreading evil in society (*hiraba*), repentance is also recommended: '[Punish them] except for those who repent before they fall into your power …' (sura 5:34). Thieves, whose hands can be cut off so all know (in the hereafter) their evil as a warning (sura 5:38), may too be forgiven ('But if the thief repents after the crime and amends his (her) ways, Allah turns to them in forgiveness …', from sura 5:39). The only offence for which there is no compassion or mercy is *zina* punishable with 100 lashes (sura 24:2).

While the Federal Shariat Court found in 1981 that stoning does not constitute *hadd* and therefore is not mandatory for *zina* because stoning is not prescribed by the Quran, it did not discuss whether the law-makers should have amended the Offence of Zina Ordinance in order to conform to the Quranic spirit of mercy when a crime carries a drastic punishment.

Since 1981 litigants have now and again brought up the issue of Quranic mercy when there is repentance. In Parvez Iqbal v The State[169] the appellant had been charged with abducting and kidnapping a woman with intent to compel her into marriage. The facts showed that the woman had resisted and in the scuffle the appellant had pulled a knife. This resulted in another charge under the Arms Act. The relatives of the victim offered a compromise and agreed to drop charges under the Arms Act. Thereupon the appellant asked the court whether the compromise could be extended to dropping the charges of abducting and kidnapping, since they carried a penalty of life imprisonment. Upon review of the Sunnah in various hadiths and classical legal commentaries, the court found that *only* in cases of *hiraba* (fighting Allah/God and the Prophet, spreading evil or highway robbery) could the offender repent and restore the damaged or stolen property. The decisive factor in the judgment was a Sunnah from the Holy Prophet: 'Forgive Hudud among yourselves but when a matter of *hadd* comes before me, it becomes compulsory.'[170] The court interpreted this to mean forgiveness is strictly a private matter. So if an accused repented and the accuser forgave her/him before entering a charge with the ruler/state authorities, then there would be no prosecution. Once the accuser brought charges, however, and a prosecutor was involved, forgiveness even in the case of repentance was not possible. Nor can the ruler/state or prosecutor apparently ask the complainant to forgive and have charges dropped if the accused repents.

More than a decade later, however, the Federal Shariat Court to some extent changed its opinion.[171] In a rape case the Chief Justice Ijaz Youssef allowed a compromise. The plaintiff and her brother had alleged rape. The accused was convicted and sentenced to five years' imprisonment. On appeal, counsel for the plaintiff and her brother sought to forgive the appellant and to nullify his conviction. It seems that they were motivated by a desire to reduce the bad blood that the case had caused between the families. The court responded that forgiveness could not transform conviction into acquittal, but held that forgiveness would serve as a mitigating factor in sentencing. As a result, the sentence for rape was reduced from five to two years' imprisonment.

Whether by reducing repentance to a private matter or by permitting repentance to mitigate official sentences, the courts are revealing the difficulties that arise when a ruler/state applies a religious law. 'Allah gives and takes away. Allah/God punisheth and forgiveth whom Allah pleaseth and hath power over all things.' (sura 5:40). Alone is the power of the Divinity to impose rules then demand repentance and show mercy.

In the face of such divine power the courts ought to reconsider how they deal with repentance in order to ensure that they are not misusing a religious concept to cheat women out of their right to be given their just due for the harm sexual violence inflicts on them and to exemplary punishment or damages. Under the Quranic verses women have a right to demand whipping or banishment. Imprisonment as under the Pakistani laws was reported in some hadiths only in connection with apostasy and divorce.[172]

If the courts grant the rapist the right to repent and be forgiven for his sexual violence against a woman,[173] what are the criteria and conditions for allowing this? The hadiths give the most concrete guidance on this point. Repentance is reported only in cases of capital punishment for *zina*, and as far as can be seen for consensual *zina* (fornication) not rape. In the reports the culprit repented before the stoning. What is striking is that it was the perpetrator alone who decided to have his/her own life taken. Such a person made an open confession in public.[174] No one charged him, no one had to prove a case against them. This kind of repentance in the face of such a drastic punishment represents the culmination of a deeply religious internal struggle. Persons who were so remorseful as to ask the judge to take their life represent a desire to expiate one's sins. Regret, combined with a desire for expiation, necessitates mercy and can lead to forgiveness, whether in this life or the afterlife, but tends to exceed the boundaries and capacities of law made for this life. Hence in the hadiths on death for *zina* there was only one circumstance under which mercy and forgiveness come into play – when the perpetrator could not bear the sin/offence he had committed. So he regretted it, voluntarily demanding punishment. Such conditions no longer exist. No anti-adultery law today dares to provide for acquittal when the perpetrator cannot bear his offence any more and begs for punishment by an open confession.

When the punishment, however, was not as drastic as death, a deep religious experience of repentance was not expected or required, as reported in the hadiths. Such less drastic punishments consisted of compensation, whipping or imprisonment. For that reason repentance and forgiveness could not appropriately be entertained by the judge. It is only after a conviction that forgiveness comes into play. For example, the plaintiff might wish to make a gesture of reconciliation towards the family of the accused in order to keep peace in the community. She may decide to return the compensation or to offer to meet the medical expenses the accused might have incurred while in prison or for the psychic trauma resulting from a public whipping. It is not for the courts to mitigate a sentence of compensation, whipping or imprisonment – they should think equally about the trauma a woman has suffered from sexual violence – who is going to pay for her medical expenses for physical or mental illness? Will the accused be so repentant that the court orders him to pay for these?

If the courts otherwise decide that they can indeed intervene to apply the principles of forgiveness in cases where only imprisonment is ordered, they might first have to consider the question of whether imprisonment can count as a punishment as drastic as death. Certainly the Quranic list of punishments reveals that the right to life and the right to socialize with one's friends and family are at the core of Allah's message. Death is a highly exceptional punishment. Imprisonment is not even prescribed, being described only in the case of the Prophet Joseph, whose length of imprisonment evoked great sympathy in the hadiths. Even though thieves might have a mutilated hand that hinders them from earning a livelihood, they are not imprisoned away from their family. The option to demand compensation to pay the family for murder itself underscores the futility of imprisonment, for in prison how can a person earn enough to pay?[175] Communal service is more in keeping with the Islamic spirit than prison, as exemplified in Zanzibar, where a couple convicted of *zina* are punished not with imprisonment but with communal service. It is these background considerations that the courts should analyse before permitting forgiveness of imprisonment sentences for rapists (see start of chapter on Cornwallis).

May a husband kill a wife or her partner for adultery?

The Quran does not speak to this issue specifically. The Sunnah of the Holy Prophet on the other hand did so very clearly. There are two categories of reports on the subject – one, on how to deal with a husband killing a wife and/or her partner, in the light of the Quranic requirement of four witnesses, and second, in the light of the oath procedure, *liaan*, prescribed for an accusing husband (or an accusing wife).

Sunnah on killing a wife or her lover in the light of the mandatory four eyewitnesses

From the perspective of witnessing, some of the Sunnah of the Holy Prophet stated clearly, no killing. A husband was not allowed to kill when he caught his wife in adultery or had reason to believe she was having an affair. His lone witnessing of an event could not replace that of four upright disinterested witnesses. This was made clear in a hadith in which Saad ibn Ubaida asked the Prophet, ' "What do you think: when I find a man with my wife? Shall I grant him a respite until I bring him four witnesses?" The Messenger of Allah, May Allah bless Him and grant Him Peace, replied (emphatically): "Yes".'[176]

Nonetheless husbands did kill their wife and her lover when found in adultery; and they went to the authorities, not to confess because they had a poor conscience, but to ask whether they were liable. In the Sunnah of the Companions, when confronted once with an inquiry into liability, the governor of Syria, Al Muawiya bin Abi Sufyan (son of the business woman Hind Bint Utbah, and later the first Umayyad caliph), did not know how to respond. He found the case difficult and consulted Caliph Ali, the son-in-law of the Prophet. Ali advised him simply to follow the Sunnah of the Holy Prophet. Four witnesses were required; without them the husband was liable for punishment. One version says that the punishment for a wife-murderer was beheading.[177] Beheading implied that allowing husbands to kill on the basis of suspicion of unproven *zina* would lead to a plague of evil and terrorism in the land, amounting to *hiraba*, necessitating a drastic punishment.

The other versions of hadiths were more circumspect and less clear, probably reflecting the anger of men who wanted to give in to their passions and assert their hold over women. In Bukhari's *Sahih* Saad b. Ubaida was quoted as saying: ' "If I found a man with my wife, I would kill him with the sharp side of my sword." When the Prophet heard that, he said: "Are you surprised at Saad's sense of jealousy (*ghira*, often translated as honour, self-respect, solicitude or zeal)? I have more sense of solicitude (zeal) than Saad and Allah has more sense of solicitude (zeal) than I." '[178]

Dawud reported more ambiguous versions, reflecting perhaps local pre-Islamic sentiments. On the conversation between Ubaida and the Prophet reported in the *Sunan* collection of hadiths, the tension was evident. Dawud categorized the issue as a matter of compensation for murder (kitab *diya*). The Prophet said: 'No, do not kill your wife.' But Ubaida retorted: 'Why not?' Then the Prophet spoke of his sense of *ghira* (solicitude) and that of Allah. The Prophet ended with a word of authority: 'Listen to your chief.' Then Abd al-Wahhab added: 'Listen to Saad's side of the story.'

Another version of Ubaida's persistence was categorized by Dawud as a matter of *hudud* because the Quran's mandatory rule of four witnesses to obtain a conviction for *zina* was being discussed. It was reported that the people asked Ubaida, the husband: 'The prescribed punishments have been revealed. So if you find a man with your wife, what will you do?' Ubaida (and Abu Thabit) said, 'I shall strike them with a sword so much that they become silent (dead). Should I go and gather four witnesses?' Until that time the need would be fulfilled. So the people went to the Prophet, who said: 'The sword is a sufficient witness.' Then he added: 'No, no, a furious and a jealous man may follow this course.'[179]

In these examples it is clear that Ubaida was mocking the verse on witnesses – how could anyone expect a man seeing his wife with another man to go and find four witnesses? The Prophet acknowledged his fury, but told him Allah is even more zealous about protecting us from ourselves.

Sunnah on killing a wife or her lover from the perspective of the liaan *oath*

The hadiths prohibiting killing on grounds of unproven *zina* are clearer in relation to the *liaan* oath. This is the only way for a husband to deal with finding his wife with another man.

Dawud's *Sunan* told the story of Hilal bin Umayya.[180] He was already known to the Prophet, who had heard him repent of some transgression. Upon returning home after a trip he found a man with his wife. It was night, but he saw them and heard them. He wanted to kill his wife, but the next day he went straight to the Prophet for judgment. Agitated, he told the Prophet that he had found a man with his wife and that he had seen and heard them himself. The Prophet also seemed upset. Then the verse from Allah was revealed: 'For those who make charges against their spouses and have no witnesses other than themselves …' The Prophet then told Hilal that Allah made life easier for him, meaning he did not need four witnesses. So Hilal's wife was summoned and the Prophet explained to her that the punishment was more severe in the afterlife than here. They took four oaths to be followed by a fifth. Hilal swore four times by Allah that he spoke the truth. She swore four times by Allah that he lied. Before Hilal took the fifth oath invoking God's wrath if he had lied, again the Prophet warned him that the punishment in the afterlife was more severe. Hilal took the oath. When his wife's turn came, she hesitated, then said: 'No, I shall not bring disgrace on me and my family.' She took the fifth oath calling on Allah to curse her if Hilal had spoken the truth. The Prophet then separated them. He released the wife of all liability and forbade anyone to charge her with adultery. Anyone accusing her or her child would be liable for punishment. For Hilal the Prophet ordered that the child would be his if it were born with reddish hair, light buttocks, wide belly and light skin. If it were born with curly hair, fat limbs, fat shins and fat buttocks and darkish skin, then it would be the child of the adulterous man. The child when born was darkish. The Prophet said the punishment for her would have been drastic had Allah not revealed the verse for the oaths. The story ended well for the child – he supposedly later became the chief of the Mudar tribe.

Husbands still did not seem convinced they should give up prior pre-Islamic rules. Bukhari's *Sahih* related how after the verse had been revealed, Uwamir asked Asim bin Ali: 'Suppose a man saw one with his wife and kills him? Or what should he do? Please ask the Prophet on my behalf.' Asim accommodated him and asked the Prophet, who found the question disgraceful, even impudent. Asim went back to Uwamir, upset that the Prophet was annoyed. So Uwamir, just as persistent as Ubaida above, decided to visit the Prophet and asked the same question in a public audience: 'If a man sees a man with his wife, would he kill him? Would *you* kill him? What should he do?' The Prophet told him that Allah had already revealed a solution for him and his wife. He asked him to fetch his wife. When she came they underwent the procedure of oath-taking. Uwamir lost the case, since his wife swore she had not committed adultery. He asked the Prophet: 'If I should keep her as a wife, I have lied.' So he divorced her even before the Prophet separated them.[181]

Present-day court decisions on killing a wife or her lover

It is against this background of the Sunnah of the Holy Prophet that the Pakistani courts were to judge a man who killed on grounds of unproven adultery or fornication. The following is a discussion of some of the cases.

Allowing acquittal for the murder of a wife's lover

A sessions court judge had convicted a husband who had killed his wife's lover on grounds of suspicion of unproven adultery and sentenced him to seven years of rigorous imprisonment and a fine of 20,000 rupees, or three more years of imprisonment in default of paying.[182] The appellant, Ali Muhammad, had left his house with his brother around 1:30 in the morning, supposedly to prepare for redirecting the water to irrigate their fields when their turn came at 4 a.m. At some point between 1:30 and 4 a.m. Ali Muhammad strangled his brother to death and was helped by some others to drag the body away. Ali Muhamad had suspected his brother of a liaison with his wife. He pleaded guilty, asserting provocation because he had found his wife and brother in a compromising position in the room next to his. The medical autopsy confirmed death by strangulation and chest and head-wounds caused by a blunt instrument. The eyewitnesses, the two helpers, testified that the murder was premeditated. It had been rumoured that his wife Maqsoodan was having an affair. The trial court rejected a plea for acquittal. The convicted husband went on appeal to the Lahore High Court.

The High Court cited the then new Penal Code amendments which admitted of Islamic versions of the law of murder. A husband who had killed someone who had committed *zina* with his wife was potentially punishable but not liable for the death penalty. The Code did not make explicit whether *zina*, that is, actual penetration, had to be proven before the murder or whether the husband could alone decide whether actual penetration had taken place. Also the law had not provided that self-defence could extend to causing the death of another. So the High Court held it would have to rely on Islamic Injunctions.

The High Court decided that under Islamic Injunctions this was a matter of self-defence and protection of privacy in the home, not premeditated murder. The High Court relied on quotations from the Sunnah of the Holy Prophet on when a person had been found peering into someone's house. If the house owner poked a stick in the eye of the peeping Tom, the house owner would not be liable for damages, since the house owner was protecting privacy. The High Court also cited a work written about the times of Caliph Umar, who had decided that when a girl whose honour was at stake threw a stone to defend herself and killed the aggressor, she did not have to pay the family of the dead man compensation (*diya*). As a result, the High Court found: 'What is commendable is to stop the evil by force … Defence of person/property and honour is commendable … I do not visualize Islam would turn table on the person who instead of losing life takes life of another while defending his person, property, etc. In fact Islam does extend the right to the aggressed to take the life of the aggressor in such a situation.'[183]

The High Court then drew an analogy between the right to self-defence when defending property and the right of the husband to defend himself against a man having an affair with his wife. The High Court relied on a Quranic verse, which it interpreted to mean that men have rights over women. The husband in this case was defending his rights over his wife. That verse read in its opening sentence, according to the judge's interpretation: 'Men are in charge (*qawwamun*) of women …' (sura 4:34 for women, An Nisa). The judge did not consider a more woman-friendly interpretation: 'Men are upright (the root of *qawwamun*: *qama*) towards women …'

Because the High Court found that men were in charge of women – that is, they have entitlement over them – and because the Quran further urges a man to take life only when forced to, it concluded that when one's rights (*haq*) are being threatened, one may take life without liability. In support of its conclusion the High Court cited Bani Israil, sura 17:33:

> Nor take life which Allah has made sacred – except for just cause. And if anyone is slain wrongfully we have given the heir authority (to demand *qisas*, or forgive), but let one not exceed the bounds in taking life for one is helped in the law.

In the case in question the lover had trespassed into the accused's house at night and the husband had heard him with his wife. One could not expect him 'to watch the sex act in peace', watch the honour of his wife being violated. So he surprised them and strangled the intruder. He had no other choice, opined the High Court, for the Quran also instructs: 'Help not one another into sin and transgression' (sura 5:2). This is at the very end of the verse. It actually starts:

> Believers, violate not the sanctity of the symbols of Allah, nor of the sacred month … And let not the hatred of some people in (once) shutting you out of the Sacred Mosque lead you to transgression (and hostility on your part). Help one another in righteousness and piety, but help not one another in sin and rancour. Fear Allah, for Allah is strict in punishment.

The case was not only one of self-defence but also of necessity the High Court decided. It cited sura 2:173 (Al Baqarah): 'But if one is forced by necessity without wilful disobedience nor transgressing due limits, then one has no sin.' Again only the end of the verse was cited. In fact it starts out with necessity with regard to diet restrictions:

> He forbade you dead meat and blood and the flesh of swine, and that on which another name has been invoked besides that of Allah. But if one is forced by necessity without wilful disobedience, nor transgressing due limits, then is one guiltless. Allah is Oft-forgiving and Most Merciful.

The High Court then equated necessity with provocation, so what is done in provocation is as though it were done out of necessity. Hence what would be otherwise forbidden, i.e. to kill, is allowed. If the murdered brother had run away and the husband given chase, then the rule of necessity would not have applied, opined the High Court *obiter dictum*.

Not surprisingly, the High Court acquitted Ali Muhammad. As 'custodian of the honour of his wife (he) had the right to kill the deceased while he was having sex with his wife'. Therefore he incurred no liability under *qisas* (life for life, i.e. the death sentence for the death of a victim), or *diya* (compensation to the victim's family).

At the core of the decision is the notion of the wife's honour and of who owns it. The wife herself does not own that honour, but rather her husband is its guardian and so may decide by whom and when it is violated and how to punish that violation. This amounts to a Roman-like *pater potestas*, respecting local custom and local gender power relations, but not the Sunnah of the Prophet. In the case of Hilal above, his wife, before taking the oath of denial, was reported to have said: 'I will not disgrace myself and my family' – she was in effect the custodian of her own honour.

The High Court did not analyse the issue of how much evidence in a case of unproven *zina* a husband needs to prove he was sufficiently provoked into murder. Hilal in the hadith, like Ali Muhamad, had been severely provoked. Hilal said he saw and heard his wife with another man like Ali Muhammad. But Hilal restrained himself, sought a remedy in the correct way and underwent the oath procedure. This oath procedure, which Allah revealed as the solution for provoked husbands, has many implications. Even if the husband had actually seen the intercourse, as a lone witness, or even if he had had four witnesses, this would still not have given him the right to kill the alleged adulterer with impunity. Because husbands are too quick to get upset about control over their wives, Allah introduced safeguards – first the four witnesses, so that the husbands do not serve as self-interested witnesses, then the *liaan* oath. If a husband were allowed to murder with impunity, on the basis of provocation due to unproven adultery, then the Revelations prescribing the oath procedure and the need for four witnesses to convict the wife would have been for naught. Provocation due to reasons other than unproven adultery might be another matter.

The High Court opined that the doctrine of necessity gave the husband the licence to ignore these prescriptions on an exceptional basis, which latter was the need to protect the husband's right to control his wife's honour. The High Court did not put the case in an historical context at all. It did not see that the Sunnah acknowledged as a fact of life that every husband wanted to use this excuse. That is precisely why Allah revealed the verses to protect a wife from such possessiveness and lack of evidence. In this regard the Quran was exceptionally forward-looking compared to other religions. In the medieval era Christians, for example, treated wife-murdering leniently on the grounds of provocation. It was common thinking that since the wife had sinned, then her husband was aiding God by eliminating her and thus the sin.[184] The Quran offered a far more humane and much more intelligent method of dealing with the issue.

One Quranic verse which the court might have cited to aid the murdering husband to deal with his anger is sura 42:37 Al Shura:

> Those who avoid the greater crimes and shameful deeds and when they are angry even then forgive.

In other words, one ought to forgive even at the moment of anger, then consult the adjudicators in the community in order to restrain oneself from undertaking drastic deeds like murdering a wife and/or her partner on the basis of unproven allegations. The High Court would have done well to have recalled from the 1983 judgment in the case of Jehan Mina the story of an exemplary man who controlled his anger.[185] Jehan was unmarried and pregnant and her grandfather wanted her killed. Following the court judgment, however, her uncle saved her from the custom.

Honour killing as provocation

In a case of a brother who killed his sister the Sunnah of the Holy Prophet on husbands who kill their wife or her lover was cited; the brother in effect likened himself to a husband.[186]

The brother along with two companions had beaten his sister and the man with whom they found her. His sister escaped, but her alleged lover was beaten to death. The trial sessions judge convicted the three men and sentenced them to 25 years of imprisonment. On appeal the men argued that they had been provoked, on the basis of the custom of *ghairat*, i.e. honour killing. They had seen the sister enter the house of the deceased in the dead of night. At first the brother pleaded that he and his companions had seen the deceased raping the sister and they came to aid her. The medical report, however, confirmed that the marks of violence on the sister were from their beatings and not from the alleged rape. Testimony established that the killers had no ill-will or grudge against the deceased.

The men cited in their defence the Sunnah of the Prophet as found in the narration of Ubaida, discussed above. The very word for honour killing, *ghairat*, is derived from the word *ghaira* which the Prophet used in responding to Ubaida's pleas to be allowed to kill his wife found in a compromising position. Ubaida had seen no sense in asking a husband seeing his wife committing *zina* to wait to get four witnesses to prove her crime. It was not the answers of the Prophet that counted, the accused contended – it was what the Prophet had done or not done. The brother and his companions who had beaten the sister and her lover interpreted the hadith to mean that the Prophet had taken no action against Ubaida; the Prophet had not objected.[187] The High Court did not cite other hadiths to contradict their interpretation.

In terms of case law the High Court did not cite the judgment in which it was held that just because a man and woman are in the same room does not mean they have had sexual intercourse.[188] They may have only embraced.[189]

With regard to honour killing, *ghairat*, the High Court held that a killing on the basis of custom deserved consideration. It amounted to grave and sudden provocation, transforming the homicide into culpable homicide carrying a sentence of less than 25 years. The High Court reduced the sentence to five years.

Enhancing a sentence for murdering a wife

Four years after the acquittal of Ali Muhammad for the early-morning murder of his brother whom he suspected of a liaison with his wife, another case arose in which the wife was shot dead and her lover wounded.[190] The event occurred in the daytime and both the wife and the other man were fully clothed. Abdul Razzaq pleaded guilty to killing his wife. He had returned from offering the Zohar prayer when he saw his wife Nek Bibi in an 'objectionable position' with Ahmed Jan. He shot his wife on the spot, killing her. Ahmed Jan ran away. Razzaq followed him, and shot and wounded him. The lower court found the husband guilty of intentional murder, and sentenced him to three years of rigorous imprisonment and a fine of 2,000 rupees (in default whereof, one month more in prison).

The advocate defending the husband cited the case of the acquittal of Ali Muhammad. The defence rested on the Quranic verse cited earlier that was interpreted to give a husband control over his wife. The defendant added that the Quran gives a husband two options – either to divorce the woman or kill her, and the husband alone can decide which option to take. He was allowed to transgress Allah's law out of necessity, and was not to help any one in sin. He had taken life for a just cause. He did not cite the Quranic verse that requires the husband and wife to take the option of an oath to deny or confirm the suspicion, nor did he cite the hadiths that gave as options an oath, divorce or both.

The court did not endorse the husband's arguments. It pointed out their illogical consequence. First of all, if the law allowed all men to rely on unproven suspicions, then every woman might be killed. Avoiding frequent murders by husbands was the cornerstone of the Quranic verses requiring four witnesses for adultery and oath-taking for suspicious husbands. If husbands did not respect these injunctions then they would undermine the Quran, which places a premium on objective eyewitnessing. Here, in this case in particular, the parties were fully clothed, in broad daylight, and in the presence of other people. *Zina*, the court reminded the husband, is not to be presumed even if a man and a woman lived in the same room. *Zina* is not living together: rather, actual carnal knowledge has to be proven. The court was implying that the necessity argument expounded by husbands to justify killing a wife or her lover would actually turn the rule of necessity into a farce – it would become a licence to kill.

The court, however, did not dispel the idea of a wife being likened to the property of her husband. It cited a part of the Hanafi commentary *Hidaya*, in which the definition of *zina* was carnal knowledge with a woman who 'is not his property'. While such a definition would have befitted the era of enslaved persons, when a man was guilty of *zina* if he had intercourse with his wife's slave without her permission, it is inappropriate to carry the language of the past over into modern discourse, which condemns enslavement. As the Tunisian theologian Haddad had observed in the 1930s (see chapter on Tunisia), the presence of enslaved women in society had long spoiled the men even after the rejection and repeal of all Islamic Injunctions regulating slavery.

The court then explained the larger social Islamic context of *zina*. The option was not as Razzaq had argued, to divorce or to kill. 'Islam does not save Muslim society from *zina* by solely depending on punishment with *hadd* or *taazir*, but introduced preventive and reformative methods. Penal punishment is a last resort.' The court went on to state that *zina* is a grave sin too, not just a legal offence. To prevent sin, Allah/God had provided and even ordained marriage. There was to be no celibacy. Allah/God had also allowed polygamy to contain people's sexual desires. The idea was not to bind people to a scaffold for flogging on a daily basis and punish those who did not take advantage of preventive methods.

The court found that the husband could not be deemed to have suffered sudden and grave provocation upon seeing his wife in flagrante delicto, even less so with regard to wounding the other man. The latter was seen fleeing with the accused in pursuit. The court refused acquittal and raised the sentence from three to five years.

The court nonetheless left the door open for future acquittals of angry husbands who feel they can exercise what they think are their customary rights, even though contrary to the basic Quranic principles. Because so many men are motivated by the notion of honour, the court opined that each case would have to be settled on its own merits and much would depend on the strength of the evidence a husband brought forward.

What is clear from the above cases is that the Quran and Sunnah have been used as tools to justify a popularist interpretation of a religious text or a pre-Islamic custom to the effect that murder for reasons of unproven adultery or fornication is allowed. There is no popular understanding or internalization at all of the basic principles of the Quran's humaneness and of its protection against such customary beliefs. Such recalls the days of racial segregation in the southern United States and of apartheid in South Africa, where the Christian scriptures were used to justify grave discrimination against Blacks. Whites took justice into their own hands and expected the law to give them licence to kill. The internalization of an alternative scriptural message of justice and equality took a long time. It is perhaps from this process that men can learn how to free themselves from the idea that they 'own' their women and their honour. Husbands in the cases above relied heavily on the Quranic verse of 4:34 to give them dominion over their wives, even to the point of killing them. When a sura is so interpreted as to have life and death consequences for women, it is a sign of an urgent need to dispossess men of a pro-male and highly materialistic interpretation of the famous sura 4:34, for such an interpretation is based on the notion that merely because men provide maintenance for their wives, they can control them (see chapter on Tunisia).

What is also striking about the two judgments on killing out of provocation is that they did not cite and compare the various hadiths, along with Quranic verses, since the Constitution requires examining the Quran and Sunnah. They tended to rely on textbooks rather than exercising *ijtihad* themselves in the same meticulous way that the Federal Shariat Court had in 1981 when a petitioner challenged the notion that death by stoning is mandatory. It may have become a matter of economy of effort, since mining through the Sunnah absorbs enormous time. Taking the time and effort, however, would have been most important, as men rely on a popularist pre-Islamic understanding of the hadith of Ubaida, which contradicts the legal logic of the Quran and other hadiths reporting on the Holy Prophet.

Is an honour murder because of *zina* permissible under any circumstances?

The next two cases illustrate a pernicious use of unproven *zina* to justify an honour crime against one's sister or daughter.

Whose honour is protected? – the husband's or the daughter's?

Nasiruddin married Kher Bibi, but just after the wedding and their first night together, he returned her to her father, alleging that she was not a virgin and thus implying that she had committed *zina* at some point before the marriage. He argued he had been deceived and given damaged goods, so to speak. Nasiruddin even added he thought he knew who the man in question was, namely his own brother. They all confronted Kher Bibi, who denied having committed *zina*. Nasiruddin well knew the consequences of his narrative. He had with cool calculation provoked his bride's family, instigating the father and his brother, Kher Bibi's uncle, to have her killed. She was brutally killed with a Kalashnikov. The evidence at the hearing revealed the tragic truth behind her murder: the husband of the young bride, it was revealed, was actually impotent, had constructed a lie in order to hide his own defect. He was the damaged goods, so to speak, not Kher Bibi, but he laid the blame on her.

The father and uncle along with Nasiruddin were sentenced at the trial level,[191] the father to death, the uncle to life imprisonment and Nasiruddin also to life. The family of Kher Bibi then petitioned the higher court for leniency and forgiveness in the name of Almighty Allah, and to forego the *diya* (compensation to the family for death of a family member). Her family said that it would not even object to an acquittal. State Counsel vehemently opposed (to use the words of the court) the petition to apply the Islamic Injunction for forgiveness, yet reminded the court it could issue a punishment under its discretionary *taazir* powers. The court decided not to acquit, but rather to reduce the sentences to 14 years for the father and uncle. It then categorized Nasiruddin as having abetted the crime and reduced his sentence, too, to 14 years' imprisonment.

May a brother suspecting unproven zina *kill for the sake of honour?*

The Supreme Court then became involved in reviewing the practice of *ghairat*, killing for honour.[192] The case gave the Supreme Court the opportunity to revive the issues of constitutionality in the discourse on Islamic Injunctions. The Supreme Court reviewed the constitutionality of the customary belief in *ghairat*, which renders many women vulnerable to, or even fair game for, any impulsive killing by a male relative at any time on suspicion of unproven *zina*.

In 1998 the accused appellant, M. Akram Khan, fired three shots into the chest and abdomen of Niaz Muhammad, who died on the spot.[193] The motive for the killing was *ghairat*. The killer pleaded he was suddenly provoked when he saw the deceased talking with his sister, Mst Hamidan, in the fields owned by Mst Khatan. This was not the first time that the two men had quarrelled. On another occasion (for reasons unknown) Hamidan's brother had attempted to harm Niaz, but at the time was released on bail after a compromise had been reached. The Supreme Court in reaching its decision relied on the sound reasoning of the lower High Court which had heard the case. The upshot was that no one may take the law into their own hands by killing to save a woman's honour in order to avoid the possibility of suffering the shame of having someone charge a female relative with *zina*. The High Court had sentenced the accused to death.

The Supreme Court further issued a clear opinion aimed at ending killing for honour. It held that honour killing violates Articles 9 and 8 (1) of the Constitution which protect life and set limits on custom. Article 9 guarantees the fundamental right to the protection of life and prohibits deprivation of life 'save in accordance with law'.[194] Article 8 (1) prohibits any custom contradicting the Constitution.[195] The Supreme Court found that provocation based on the custom of *ghairat* violates the right to life. It may not serve as a mitigating plea in sentencing. The death sentence was confirmed.

The Supreme Court judgment would technically have a great impact on lower courts, which have reduced sentences on the grounds that provocation involving honour is a mitigating factor. In other words, the Supreme Court decision would have invalidated the 1994 order of the Lahore court, mentioned above, which reduced the charge against a brother who had beaten his sister and killed her lover, from intentional murder to culpable homicide, because of grave and sudden provocation owing to belief in the custom of honour killing.[196]

The judgment declaring the honour killing unconstitutional was a necessary step towards reforming the law. It is hoped that the Supreme Court will take the opportunity to review how in the popular mind the *ghairat* custom is embedded in a misunderstanding of the Sunnah. The word *ghaira*, which appeared in a Sunnah of the Holy Prophet when Ubaida was pleading the right to kill his wife for adultery, reflects a pre-Islamic notion, which when translated to mean only honour of the husband, is without awareness of its many-sided meanings. The story of Ubaida reflects a faction in society which would have agreed with the social order prevailing in Christian lands at the time that allowed a man to kill his wife as long as he proved he had been provoked by her adultery.[197] Men today who identify with Ubaida are disinclined to reflect on how to place this hadith in the context of the Quran and the Sunnah of the Holy Prophet.

The Supreme Court has the added task of also reinterpreting the Quranic verse which men believe is the basis of the *ghairat* practice, namely that which they believe gives them control over women as their 'protectors' (sura 4:34).[198] The object of such a judicial exercise is to expound on the Islamic Injunctions in such a way that people can learn to accept over time that their popularist understanding of Sunnah and Quran is unjust. This involves a meticulous review of the sources, similar to what the Federal Shariat Court had accomplished in 1981 relating to the challenge to the mandatory nature of stoning.[199] Again, the economics of mining sources may be a hindering factor.[200]

It should be made plain to the public that the learned justices are better equipped for the task of interpreting the Injunctions. If there is the political will to support the Supreme Court over the popularist groups, this would strengthen the judicial resolve at all levels, not just the Supreme Court.

Reforming Pakistani Islamic criminalization of laws: honour killings and *zina*

Recommendations from the National Commission on the Status of Women

A year after taking power, Musharraf created the National Commission on the Status of Women in 2000,[201] which derives secretarial support from the Ministry of Women Development. Three years after the Supreme Court's decision of 2001 holding honour killings unconstitutional and thus no longer to be considered a mitigating factor in sentencing for murder, the Women's Commission held a workshop in the spirit of the court decision. It wanted to see action that would root the court's decision in statutory law. A study by the commission showed statistically that the rate of acquittal in the regional courts was high, ranging from 42 to 92 per cent depending on the area. Acquittals of course result from poor investigation into facts and lack of sufficient evidence to convict beyond a reasonable doubt. Whether the reasons lie in police corruption or in police sympathy for honour killing was not made clear. Even where there was a conviction, the punishments were too light to fit the crime.

The commission, chaired by retired Justice Ajida Razvi (first woman ever appointed to the High Court), had conducted research into the sections of the Penal Code dealing with murder from the perspective of Islamic Injunctions (*qisas* and *diya*, compensation). The workshop concluded that honour killing amounted to a victimization of women and was against Islamic justice.[202] The workshop participants sought exemplary punishments for men murdering women so that a man would not be exempted from the death penalty for honour killing, especially when the woman who is killed is a mother leaving minor children behind. Even if the members of the family agreed to compensation in lieu of death, the ruler/state, it was argued, should reserve its discretionary right to impose a harsher penalty. The argument was not asking for an innovative move from the part of the ruler/state, as it had already reserved in the Offence of Zina Ordinance its discretionary (*taazir*) right to punish when the prosecutor could not produce the Quranically mandated four upright witnesses to convict for consensual *zina.*

Seven months after the workshop, at the end of October 2004, parliament passed a law amending the Penal Code so as to raise the penalty for honour killing. The President assented to it in January 2005 (Welchman).[203]

The law expressly prescribes a minimum of ten years' and a maximum of 25 years' imprisonment for a killing motivated by a man's sentiments or honour (or jealousy). The statutory changes support the Supreme Court's decision declaring that an honour killing is not to be regarded as caused by a provocation entitling the accused to a mitigation of sentence. As for allowing families to forgive the sentence, and therefore reduce it, thus undermining the purpose of the Penal Code amendments, much will depend on whether the Supreme Court can ensure that its 2001 opinion on the unconstitutionality of honour killing is understood and strictly followed by all lower courts in such a way that such unconstitutionality bars courts from granting an acquittal demanded by a family as part of forgiveness and from reducing a sentence to under ten years in prison.

The keystone of course in the matter of honour killings is the offence of *zina*. The allegation that a woman relative or wife committed *zina*, which is a crime, is the basis of the motivation or pretext for the killing. As the Women's Commission has observed, the legal order of the ruler/state is at stake. The ruler/state has to assert its right to defend lives and property,[204] in other words, not leave such tasks to a kind of 'honour protection militia'. To achieve this, the ruler/state had to recognize the need for a total revision of the Offence of Zina Ordinance. A special committee was set up in 2000 under the direction of the Women's Commission to address the question of whether to repeal or amend the Ordinance. The committee was divided, despite clear positions taken by women leaders.[205] Enacting the law against honour crimes may have been putting the horse before the cart. While men are subject to heavier penalties now for honour killing if the killer is convicted on evidence beyond reasonable doubt, men may well resort even more to bribing police (Mehdi)[206] or prosecutors to ensure acquittals, or have a case come before the local panchayat council to defeat the legal process.[207] The impact of raising the penalty for imprisonment for an honour murder will reveal itself in time. If the penalties introduced to stop fornication and adultery in the Offence of Zina Ordinance are any guide, the prognosis is not particularly optimistic.

Role of the courts

The higher courts still have an important role to play. They can breathe life into the verdict in Taslim Bibi's case – that resulted in the acquittal of her lover/alleged rapist – so that women can benefit as well.[208] When he appealed against conviction for consensual *zina* (while Taslim did not), the

Federal Shariat Court found that he had to be released for lack of sufficient evidence to prove beyond reasonable doubt his consent to having sex with Taslim Bibi. On this principle many a woman would also be released if the same standard applied to her. As the police can charge the woman with consensual fornication or adultery on circumstantial evidence (formerly under *taazir* in the Zina Ordinance, now under the Penal Code), the courts can as a countermeasure insist on proof of her consent beyond reasonable doubt. In this way, the discretionary prosecution powers of the ruler/state would reflect more closely the aim of the Quran's requirement for four witnesses to the intercourse, namely to protect privacy.

Unholy alliance between zina *and honour killings*

As long as the Offence of Zina Ordinance makes *zina* a crime and the Penal Code fornication a crime, men will feel justified in using it as a pretext and work harder at not being convicted. Beyond the question of honour killings, the Women's Commission no doubt will emphasize the ruler/state's responsibility to the women traumatized by *zina* or fornication proceedings, whether they were convicted or acquitted and who are traumatized by living under the threat of an accusation of *zina* or fornication. The law was having a negative impact even on girls' education, as illustrated in one case report.[209] Razia, 13 years of age and pubescent, used to study in the 7th class. She told her parents that a certain Naseem Shah had been teasing her on the way to and from school. The elder brother of Naseem was put on notice but in vain. So the girl's father abandoned her education. The parents asserted that their daughter was kidnapped and held for sex by Naseem with the help of others. The testimony of witnesses, including the younger sister was that the house had been broken into and her sister knocked down. Razia was unconscious for a while but no sexual attack could be established medically. The case could not be proven beyond reasonable doubt, and Naseem was released. Either her parents were trying to cover something up, or the young girl was actually briefly kidnapped. In any case the whiff of a possible case of *zina* or fornication because a girl is teased by a man endangers her education.

The two cases cited earlier of the impotent husband who set his wife up for an honour killing[210] and of the brother who shot a man because he saw him walking in the fields with his sister[211] are dire but prime examples of how legislating for an Islamic concept has propagated a general mistrust of women. From a jurisprudential perspective it has strengthened misunderstanding of the principles of Islam and of their historical significance in relation to other women-unfriendly religio-legal practices existing at the time of the Revelation.[212] The decision of the ruler/state to introduce consensual *zina* (*zina bil raza*) subject to discretionary *taazir* punishments and circumstantial evidence seems to have confirmed men's belief in their right to cast out the evil of *zina* with a selfish self-righteousness that in the end abuses women. Fear reached a level that could be said to warrant a true state of *hiraba* – where women are terrorized. The arguments of necessity and the rights of a man over a woman, which men who murder their wives and women relatives put forward to justify ignoring Allah's injunctions, can be answered with accusing these men of committing *hiraba*, spreading another kind of evil throughout the land, worse than *zina*. There are different ways of handling this problem. In the name of compromise one way forward might have been to revamp the provisions on *zina bil jabr* (rape). Rape subject to *hadd* would be eliminated, as it is not within the ambit of offences subject to *hadd*. *Zina bil jabr* subject to *taazir* would stay. Or *zina bil jabr* would be treated simply as *hiraba* (terrorizing women) subject to the maximum *hadd*. The Protection of Women Act 2006 adopted this approach in part, but placed the provisions on rape in the Penal Code, removing them from the Zina Ordinance (see Postscript). Another approach would have been more straightforward: the *ijtihad* approach. Let the Quranic verses on *zina* rest in peace just as the verses on slavery, for the hadiths and the jurists' expositions of Islamic Injunctions show how the institutions of enslavement and of the criminalization of sex were closely linked. It is time to give full reign to the Quranic spirit of privacy and of non-puritanical respect for people's sexual lives (as reflected in the impossibly high standards set to convict). It should be left to the religious conscience of the individual to feel the burden of sin to the extent that he or she wishes to expiate the sexual sin, not to the people or the ruler/state. It is time more men came forward to show courage in taking responsibility rather than watching from the sidelines in silence as their female partner, pregnant or not, is prosecuted and traumatized.

Conclusions

The women of Pakistan can certainly be grateful that no stoning has ever taken place in Pakistan. The safeguards in the Offence of Zina Ordinance – confirmation by an appellate court – have proved effective. In the very few death sentences which lower courts have imposed on a pregnant woman and two consenting adults, the higher court has consistently reversed the death penalty. Nonetheless, while escaping stoning, a woman's life is still threatened. Many women accused of *zina* extra-judicially by their husbands or male relatives are 'executed' in honour killings. In such cases the law has not instituted judicial safeguards against acquittals or reduced sentences for wife- or sister-murderers. The highest court in the land, the Supreme Court, has had to carve out a judicial safeguard by holding honour killings unconstitutional.

The higher court, from the start of politicians' Islamization by criminalizing sexual acts, has played a crucial role in dampening extremism. It started as early as 1981 to declare the so-called mandatory *hadd* punishment of stoning unIslamic. It exercised *ijtihad*, reviewing the sources of and exposing the historical disagreements about stoning. This was in the spirit of the initial Pakistani Islamic legislation which circumscribed male privilege in polygamy and in arbitrary divorce. The higher courts have been faced with two contrary pressures in the last three decades. One was the political insistence on installing a particular type of Islamic law; the Offence of Zina Ordinance, for example, introduced under the military regime of Ul Haq, adopted a conservative view of adultery and fornication. At the same time, the classical view was supplemented by provisions which gave the ruler/state wide discretionary powers to prosecute consensual *zina* (fornication) when the state prosecutor was frustrated by the extremely high Quranic standards requiring four upright witnesses. So on the one hand the classical Injunction was adopted while on the other hand it was undermined. When the Federal Shariat Court saw fit to strike down the classical view, it was confronted with a political fiat – it had to review its own *ijtihad* and reverse it. The court did so under duress, thus rendering its second contradictory decision illegitimate. The second contrary pressure, which the higher courts have faced more recently, comes from conservative elements within society who are opposed to an interpretation of Islam that upholds gender egalitarianism. These elements have propagated an interpretation of Islamic sources that places men above women and allows them to stand in judgment on their women's sexual lives. Whether this represents a deep-seated resentment on the part of men, educated or not, against the family law that attempts to control their sexual appetites for polygamy is not clear, but plausible. The instrument used to enforce these views has been honour killings, based on a popularist lay interpretation that reads the legitimization of pre-Islamic custom into Islamic sources. This mirrors the ruler/state's misuse of Islamic sources for its own political agenda when the Offence of Zina Ordinance was introduced. The higher courts sit between Scylla and Charybis – the popularist notion of what Islamic law is about on the one hand and the politicians' early interference in the judicial exercise of *ijtihad* on the other. The higher courts have not lost their bearings totally. They remain in general truer to the spirit of Syed Ahmed Khan, the intellectual father of Pakistan, who defied the conservative ulama and exercised his right to independent rationalism in arriving at an Islamic law that evolves and is humane and egalitarian. If anything, the higher judiciary may have to find a way to become more assertive and exercise more control over its subordinate courts in order to bring more clarity into the discourse on Islamic law. At the moment, judicial authority is too much in competition with popularist lay groups and politicians. While the judiciary has established itself as an arbiter in the debate, its next task would be to establish itself as the final arbiter to be respected by both laypersons and politicians.

Postscript on the Protection of Women Act 2006

As this book was being prepared for publication, the adultery law in Pakistan was amended. The following is a short comment on the changes, showing that most of the jurisprudential concerns raised in past years remain with us. It is important to keep a historical record and analysis of the Pakistani experience with *zina* over the decades for the benefit of what happens in other countries where the classical Islamic views prevail. Nonetheless while the Pakistani amendments are welcomed, the conceptual underpinnings are still problematic.

Like Haiti in the years of 2005–2006 Pakistan was under great pressure from the international powers and their own women's movements to introduce laws to punish trafficking in women. On the coat-tails of these changes came amendments to the adultery laws. The result in Pakistan was the Protection of Women (Criminal Law Amendment) Act of 2006.

The Protection of Women Act rests on four pillars: first, it transfers all of the *taazir* offences and punishments of the Zina Ordinance on *zina bil jabr* (rape) and consensual *zina* (fornication) to the Penal Code. It leaves intact the ordinance *hadd* offences and punishments that criminalize consensual *zina* (fornication and adultery). Hence there are two kinds of fornication, each subject to different evidentiary requirements. A conviction under the ordinance for fornication or adultery requires four witnesses while a conviction under the Penal Code for fornication can rest on circumstantial evidence. Secondly, the provisions in the Zina Ordinance requiring four upright witnesses are strengthened in so far as no charge of *zina* can go forward for litigation without vetting the uprightness of the witnesses. Thirdly, and most importantly, it stops the practice of prosecutors and courts from changing charges in the middle of court hearings depending on the kind of evidence available. Fourthly, a false accusation of *zina* is punishable.

The Act allows the Offence of Zina Ordinance to continue to punish consensual adulterers with stoning and consensual intercourse between unmarried persons with whipping. The evidentiary requirements of four upright male witnesses remain the same, even though classic Islamic Injunctions allow eight upright women.

One would expect convictions under the Ordinance to fall drastically. Certainly in the past extremely few *hadd* convictions were possible and those in lower courts were consistently overturned for lack of four eyewitnesses to the act of penetration. The legislature made a special attempt in the Act to better Islamicize the vetting of witnesses, for in the past overzealous and jealous members of the family and of the public brought forward dozens of witnesses who proved to be less than upright, and police evidence had been tainted by bribes. Trials may become shorter as a result. There may be more of an effort to find pious men who can witness. Eyewitnesses are not to be accepted if they have committed major sins. Or the courts could decide slightly to relax the standards of uprightness. The vetting of witnesses and the complainant is to take place at the time the court accepts jurisdiction over the case, not during the trial itself.

Certainly the past practice of changing the charges in the middle of a trial produced confusion in case law, as the courts were well aware. The switching of charges back and forth confused the judges on the standards of proof for criminal cases. If rape could not be proven beyond reasonable doubt, then the case was transformed into one of consensual intercourse, but without maintaining the same standards of proving consent beyond reasonable doubt. The amendments prohibit transforming a case of *zina* under the Ordinance or a rape case under the Penal Code into a case of fornication under the latter. No fornication case under the Penal Code may be converted into a *zina* case under the Ordinance or into any other offence. It is unclear whether a rape case can be transformed into a *zina* case if there are four witnesses. Yet whether the courts will understand any better than under the Ordinance that consent is subject to the standard of proof beyond reasonable doubt cannot be assured through the 2006 amendments.

The past practice of shifting charges manifests a deeper issue. This is the issue of the difficulty of combining concepts from two types of prosecutorial systems. In the hadith reports on cases of *zina*, what is striking is that it was the offender who was responsible for going public and asking for punishment. Otherwise, outsiders who sought to bring charges would have been accused of violating the law against spying. The prosecutorial ruler/state system rests on the principle of intrusion, even if under the guise of protection. The interface between these two approaches still requires further study.

Even though the offences of rape and consensual sex appear now to have been neatly divided between the Ordinance and the Penal Code, there remain some conceptual problems. The offence of consensual intercourse between unmarried persons consists of two terms under two different statutes – one is *zina*, under the Ordinance, and one is fornication, under the Penal Code. *Zina* is to be proven Quranically with four witnesses but Islamic law also requires proof beyond reasonable doubt even when there are four truthful and upright witnesses, for witnesses can in fact, no matter how upright, get confused in their observation and recollection of the facts. Fornication is to be proven by truthful and credible witnesses, for even the non-Islamic systems dismiss charges if the witnesses prove not to be truthful and 'upright' in the sense that their reputations are scrutinized and may be attacked in the course of a trial. Substantively there seems to be no difference in the definitions of *zina* and fornication – both relate to consensual intercourse between unmarried persons. So one can ask what is the substantive difference between the old law and the new, or whether there has been only a cosmetic change. Under the old law of *zina* subject to discretion (*taazir*), *zina* amounted to no more than what is now called fornication. What is unclear is whether the concept of *zina* as adultery under the Ordinance can be covered as well under the definition of fornication in the Penal Code as intercourse between persons who are not married to each other, not just between unmarried persons.

These ambiguities reflect issues stemming from differences in the basic principles that underlie two different systems, and from trying through the law to reach political compromises between polarized positions – those disliking Islamization *per se* and those championing a classical, uncritical Islamization. The situation might not become too grave as long as one can eventually rely on the courts to introduce some sense into the process by carrying out careful research on the Sunnah and Quran and applying *ijtihad*.

The amendment rendering cohabitation an offence under the Penal Code is surprising. The Code punishes a man who induces a woman to believe that they are lawfully married, and so may cohabit. Whether in the course of cohabitation they actually have intercourse seems irrelevant. The maximum penalty is 25 years' imprisonment. This provision runs counter to the Islamic spirit that lies behind why the Quran and Sunnah required four witnesses to an act of intercourse in order to convict on a charge of illegal sex. As pointed out in this chapter, these prerequisites reveal the extraordinary merciful spirit behind the Quranic revelation. It protected men and woman living together or being together in the same room from spying and harassment by inquisitive and suspicious neighbours who did not know at all whether the two had intercourse. It is in this spirit that Pakistani courts convicted men who have killed sisters or wives or daughters only on the basis of suspicion, because they found a woman and a man together in the same field or room.

Certainly removing the rape provisions from the Ordinance has much improved its overall conceptualization. Rape subject to the *hadd* evidentiary requirements that there be four male upright witnesses to the act of forced penetration was not supportable by the Sunnah or Quran. The minimum imprisonment for rape under the Penal Code has been raised from four to ten years; the maximum penalty of death remains, and the maximum imprisonment of 25 years. However, if some thought that by transferring the rape provisions and adding fornication to the Penal Code would escape Islamic law, one has some doubts. Since all the laws including the Penal Code are subject to the constitutional provisions that they are to conform to the Islamic Injunctions, there is no guarantee that the transfer of old Ordinance provisions to the Penal Code will remove them from the ambit of Islamic Injunctions, for instance, in the case of rape, for the fine which courts may impose could amount to the value of a marriage dower.

The Protection of Women Act is welcome. It rests, however, on the shoulders of the jurisprudence of the Pakistani courts whose justices cut a path for such legislation. Many judgments (not all) as cited in this chapter reveal the astuteness of some of the justices and courts who have worked towards countering the tendency, in some quarters of Islamic scholarship or Islamic popularism, to undermine those Islamic Injunctions found in the Sunnah and Quran which uphold a spirit of equality and respect between the sexes and of social mercifulness.

4

SOUTH AFRICA – CONSTITUTIONAL CHALLENGES FOR ISLAMIC LAW

Introduction

South Africa represents the second non-Arab cultural context in this study. The country represents the one example in this book of a highly multicultural and legally pluralistic society. The South African Muslim groups mirror within themselves the country's cultural diversity. When aggregated as a totality, these groups and their communities[1] form a small minority, but are economically strong compared to their percentage of the population (Van Wyck). The Muslim groups have their origins in immigrant minorities who first came to South Africa from what is now called Indonesia and Malaysia, because of the Dutch military takeover of the Western Cape and the East Indies. Later waves of Muslims came from then British-occupied India, because British industrialists controlling the sugar plantations and railway construction imported labour.

Post-colonial apartheid South Africa was a regime of discrimination and terror. Muslims were divided into so-called non-white population groups, distributed across the range of colours, being classified as black, coloured or Asiatic. Thus Muslims were as subject to the discriminatory system as the majority of the African population. This discrimination along with the cultural diversity within the Muslim communities have both left their imprint on the historical development of Islamic law in South Africa.

While this chapter divides the South African legal developments along the lines of the two basic communities (Melayu and Indian), which brought Islam into South Africa, it is not intended to imply a favouring of communalist or unitarianist politics (Jeppie 87–8).[2] The intention is to understand the proliferation of diversity within a country that is unifying itself under an inclusive Constitution that also allows for cultural breathing-room.

The major issue affecting Islamic law in apartheid South Africa was the question of its recognition. Was it to be recognized on a par with all other legal systems deriving from the African laws, or from the European-based Christian law or the state statutory laws?

After the liberation from apartheid, the place of Islamic law is again being debated. The basic source of law in South Africa for all of its inhabitants is not Islamic law, but rather a Constitution legitimately adopted by a legislative assembly representing all citizens of several religious and non-religious persuasions. The Constitution guarantees at the same time the right to freedom of religious belief and of culture, subject to the principles of the Constitution. The right to one's own culture was a concession to Afrikaaners' political pressure to gain protection for linguistic (not economic) minorities. Against this background, contemporary South Africa represents an example of how within a pluralistic country Islamic law can accommodate differences as well as be integrated into an universal system of law.

The following sections will deal with a history of the Muslim groups in the Western Cape and the issues arising from recognition or non-recognition of Islamic law.

A brief history of the Muslim Malay community

Political origins of the Muslims in the Western Cape

The Muslim community in the Western Cape is the oldest in South Africa, and it can call upon a tradition of resisting injustice – one of its earliest members led a rebellion in the 17th century. He was the leader of a counter-assault against the Dutch seizures in Bantam (now part of Indonesia), Sheikh Yusuf at Taj al Khalwati al Maqassari. He was defeated, and the Dutch punished him by exiling him to the Cape of Good Hope, in 1694 (Esack 21). There he was confronted with another challenge – a ban which the Dutch immigrants had imposed on the exercise of the Muslim religion. This was a prime example of colonial rule as a gross violation of the rule of law, and the result was the secret practice of the Muslim religion. It was not until a century later that another Muslim leader in the

Cape rebelled. This was Imam Abdallah Qadi Abd As Salam (who wrote *Maarifat al Imam wal Islam*). He led a protest against the ban on freedom of worship by celebrating Friday prayers in the open in 1793. He, like Sheikh Yusuf, had been banished to the Cape because of political conspiracy against the Dutch in the Straits of Malacca (Esack 23). Because of his protest activities in the Cape, he was again banished to Robben Island. It took 31 years for the ban to be lifted, following the British occupation in 1804.

Apart from using the Cape as a place of exile for anti-European/anti-Dutch political leaders, the Europeans imported Muslim workers from the East Indies into the Cape. These workers (who are now from Malaysia and Indonesia) were effectively enslaved. In the 1700s the number of Muslims surged. The increase has been attributed in part to a law existing at the time called the Statutes of India Regulations (also known as the Statutes of Batavia) of 1715, which prohibited enslavement of any Christianized convert. Because this was not in their interests, which were to hire the cheapest labour, European immigrants sought to get around the statute by encouraging their slaves to convert to Islam (Davids 59). When the British took over they made English law applicable alongside the Roman-Dutch law in 1806. In the ensuing century this practice of converting slaves to Islam became superfluous. The British enacted a new law in 1838 which emancipated all slaves and prohibited slavery and slave apprenticeships regardless of religion. By 1842 Muslims constituted one-third of the then Cape Town population and slightly less than half of the total registered voters (Davids 62, Esack 24). They also formed the larger part of the poorer labouring classes (Davids 65).

Early Muslim institutions in the Cape

After a century of living in the Eastern Cape, the early Muslims began to establish their own institutions. Despite the ban on worship, a religious school was founded in 1793, catering to both enslaved and free students. The language of instruction was Melayu (Davids 62–3, 69). The first unofficial mosque was built in 1798. It became the official Dorp Street Mosque in 1804 (Esack 23). A religious festival in connection with the Prophet's birthday, but which is peculiar to South East Asian Islam, was imported. It was a colourful women's festival involving the cutting of orange-tree leaves. For purposes of this festival women were allowed access to the entire mosque, even the section reserved for men (Davids 63). The festival proved popular and so was held more often even on occasions other than the Prophet's birthday. In the 1850s South African European authorities sought to curb the festival's frequency because of certain complaints of nuisance. The religious leaders (maybe all male as we have no evidence yet of women leaders) were asked to voice their opinion about the religious necessity of the festival. They held that it was not doctrinally essential to hold the festival so often. The leaders agreed that it would be limited to once a year. This decision brought in its wake a severe restriction of women's participation and presence in the mosque. Whether at the time this restriction was met with dissent from the women is not apparently known.

Schools of Islamic law in the Cape

The initial Muslim religious leaders of the Cape community belonged to the Shafii school of law and theology. This is not surprising, since the Shafii *madhab* (school) prevailed in Indonesia and Malaysia. In the middle of the 19th century this began to change. The Ottoman caliphate in Istanbul took an interest in extending the influence of the Hanafi school, which dominated imperial Ottoman officialdom. In 1862 the Sultan sent Abu Bakr Effendi to the Cape. He was a Kurd from Iran, married to an English Muslim woman, and author of *Al Bahr al Din* (printed in Istanbul, 1871). The Hanafi Mosque in Long Street was established in 1870.[3] Controversial questions arising in the community were sent to Istanbul for official answers (*fatwa*s).

By the end of the 19th century, missionaries from Mecca had penetrated the Cape. They convinced several young men to study Islam in Mecca (da Costa 8). Around the same time, the fame of the reform-minded Egyptian mufti, Muhammad Abduh, had reached South Africa in the wake of his tours in the North African Maghreb region. At the start of the 20th century, Abduh received a request from a Muslim living in the Transvaal in South Africa to issue a *fatwa* (1903) on two problems. The question related to the relations between the Shafii and Hanafi schools of thought and between Muslims and Christians in South Africa. In his answer Muhammad Abduh took into account the particular characteristics of the situation of Muslim groups in South Africa, while at the same time giving them the benefit of the wider perspective of Muslim groups around the world. With regard to relations with Christians, he saw no problems in Muslims eating meat slaughtered by Christians, especially because of their tiny minority situation. As for diversity of praying practices according to established schools of thought, he also found it perfectly normal, as elsewhere in communities around the world, that one group could pray according to one school of law under the leadership of one imam and another group according to another imam of another school (Green 184, 194, n. 30; Skovgaard-Petersen 123–33).

In summary, the Cape Malay (Malay/Indonesian to be more accurate (Jeppie)) community groups were able to hold their own as representatives of a major religion. This was not only because of the strength of their numbers, but also because of the strong personalities of the Muslim leaders exiled and banished from South East Asia to the Cape. Over time the variety of cultural influences on the Cape Malay Muslims grew. The Melayu language gave way to Afrikaans and English. The international ties with learned Islamic law scholars and theologians outside South Africa and the East Indies became equally diverse.

Islamic law in South African jurisprudence – the 'Malay' Cape community

After having won recognition of their religion for purposes of religious worship, at the start of the 19th century, on a par with all other religions, the Cape Muslim community still faced considerable obstacles to the recognition of Islamic law in various civil and matrimonial disputes.

Is a Muslim wife a wife? – evidentiary problems – 1836

One of the first reported cases relating to Islamic law was in 1836. At issue was the recognition or non-recognition of a Muslim marital bond on a procedural point, in particular a rule of evidence. The rule was that the wife of a plaintiff husband could not give evidence in his favour, for fear that it would be biased. In the case at hand the plaintiff was a Muslim, who wanted to call his wife as a witness. The defendant objected. The plaintiff's lawyer counter-argued that a Muslim wife was not a wife for purposes of the rules on witnessing since a Muslim marriage was not recognized by South African law as valid. The reason was that it was a potentially polygamous marriage, which had no legal standing. According to case law no form of marriage would be tolerated that competed with Christian monogamous marriage. The court then called for the wife to give evidence about her marital status. She testified that she had been married to the plaintiff in a religious ceremony. The court further heard a Muslim 'priest' who testified in support of the wife. In the end the court struck a surprising compromise. It recognized the fact that in the eyes of the Muslim community the plaintiff was married to his witness. This was sufficient to bar the wife from being a credible witness in the case. This procedural part of the court ruling upheld in effect the principle that a Muslim religious marriage recognized as such by the community of the parties would undermine the need for unbiased evidence. At the same time, the court nodded in the direction of the case law which did not recognize Muslim marriages for any purpose. The court gave the plaintiff an option: if the judgment went against him on the substance of the matter, then he could move to have the court annul the judgment on the grounds that he had not been able to submit his evidence.[4]

May a Muslim woman mortgage her property without her husband's consent? – 1887

About 30 years later, in 1887, a Muslim woman who owned land attempted to mortgage it. The registry of lands had documented that she in fact owned the land and that she was married under Muslim rites. The Registrar of Deeds, however, refused to register the bond. He wanted the husband's consent to the mortgage. Such consent was considered standard, since non-Muslim European women still stood under the coverture of their husbands in property matters. The woman objected and hired a lawyer to contest the matter. He did not argue any Islamic law provisions that would have permitted the wife to dispose of her property as she liked. Instead, he argued that South African state law did not recognize Muslim marriages. They were polygamous, which was repugnant to the South African *ordre public*, meaning, it offended a basic sense of justice of the ruling powers. The lawyer concluded, therefore, that as the marriage of his client could not be recognized, obtaining her husband's permission was superfluous. The court[5] ruled against the woman's advocate, and required the husband's consent. The court put forth an argument of presumption, finding that for purposes of a deed transaction by a woman, the Registrar of Deeds was to presume that the deed book had correctly registered the true marital status of the transferor as married and was not obliged to verify the nature of that marriage. The court further argued that such a presumption was valid because the state had appointed Muslim marriage officers who were to solemnize marriages for Muslims and have them registered. The licensing of

Muslim marriage officers was an indirect recognition of the validity of a Muslim marriage. The court in effect imposed on Muslim women the same standard restrictions as would have applied to a non-Muslim European South African woman who needed the consent of her husband to make property transactions. With regard to the recognition of Muslim marriages, this judgment continued the policy set in the previous judgment, which showed a readiness to recognize Muslim marriages for certain well-defined purposes and not categorically to refuse recognition. What is even more curious about the judgment is the presumption that there was not only an *ordre public* that rejected non-Christian polygamy but also an *ordre public* that sought to keep women under the control of husbands. It was presumed offensive to have any woman who sought to disengage from such control, regardless of her religion. Here gender counted more than her faith.

Are Muslim marriages equal to African customary law marriages? Is dower justiciable? – 1893

Not too long afterwards, in 1893, the Supreme Court of South Africa had to deal with the question of whether Islamic marriages and African customary marriages were to be treated alike.[6] The case arose out of a dower claim under African laws. The groom sought return of the dower from the father of the bride as the wife had deserted him without cause. A year before this case, a lower court had held that dower, known under African customary laws as *lobola*, was illegal because it was construed as consideration for 'immoral cohabitation'.[7] Hence it could not be recovered in a court in the Colony (as South Africa was then known); there was a similar problem with Turkish marriages (Jones-Pauly 2008, 315–16). Children were nonetheless recognized as offspring of a *lobola* marriage. The Supreme Court reviewed the case law, undertaking a historical discourse on what makes a marriage valid. The discourse was culturally limited, as the court started with ancient Roman law, a source of authority for Roman-Dutch law, applicable in South Africa alongside English common law. Roman law allowed explicit or non-explicit marriage contracts. As a result even when the wife was simply taken to the home of her husband with her consent, they were deemed married. Even the absence of the husband upon her arrival was irrelevant. Later, the Roman canonical (religious Catholic Christian) law required the presence of a priest for the validity of a marriage, in addition to consent from both parties. The Dutch South African law, in contrast, did not require the presence of a religious officer.

Marriage could take place before a secular or a religious marriage officer appointed under Act 16 of 1860. That same Act provided for the appointment of not only Christian marriage officers, but also Muslim officers. Thus a Muslim marriage before a Muslim state-appointed officer was procedurally valid and therefore recognizable. The same could not be said for a marriage under African customs and laws, for the statute creating marriage officers made no explicit provision for the appointment of a Tembu law or 'native' African customary marriage officer. In practice, this meant that if Africans wished to marry before state-appointed officers, they had to go to Christian or Muslim or secular officers. Furthermore, transfer of dower was not a prerequisite condition (as under African customary laws and some Islamic schools of law) for solemnizing marriages in South Africa. Yet the court found that the absence of a provision for African customary marriages was no reason for a refusal to recognize African marriages. The rescuing principle was found buried in the standard rules of conflict of laws. That is, as long as a marriage is valid according to the customs or laws of the place where it is contracted or celebrated, it is valid everywhere, including South Africa. As the *lobola* marriage was valid under custom, then it had to be recognized. The court found that no state is to refuse to recognize a marriage contracted in another place just because other customs dominate. The court then went one step further: it qualified its own general rule. A marriage celebrated under other customs, had to meet two criteria. One was that the marriage had to be between two unrelated persons (not incestuous). The second element was that it could not be polygamous. Thus transfer of a dower could be a legitimate part of the solemnization ceremony without detracting from the essential character of the marriage. In its conclusion, however, the court quashed an important part of the ruling from the court below. The higher court held that the Tembu marriage in its essence was not tantamount to an immoral cohabitation.

The Supreme Court's judgment was pivotal. It placed all marriages on the same level of recognition as long as they met three minimum conditions: 1) solemnization either before a state-appointed marriage officer, who could be religious or secular, or 2) a valid celebration under the customs or religious law of the parties; or 3) in essence non-incestuous and non-polygamous. Dower, which is important in an Islamic marriage and in African customary law marriages, was also elevated to the status of recognition. It was construed as an ancillary element of marriage. This opened the way to rendering a dower claim justiciable. Thus the Supreme Court overturned the precedent case law which had deemed dower an immoral consideration rendering the marriage invalid. At the same time, the Supreme Court judgment emphasized monogamy. In this respect it confirmed an earlier judgment in which it was explained that all persons in the Colony, regardless of religion or origin, should be encouraged to enter into monogamous marriages.[8]

Does a Muslim woman's right to sue without consent of her husband depend on her being married monogamously? – 1905

The issue of when a Muslim marriage can be deemed polygamous or monogamous arose in 1905. Again, a Muslim Malay woman, acting independently of her husband, met with opposition. She sought to recover rent and damages plus an order of eviction with regard to certain property that she owned. The defendant objected to her *locus standi*. She was married and under the Roman-Dutch law at the time, a woman could not sue in court unassisted by her husband. The plaintiff testified that she was a washerwoman by trade and was the wife of a Malay Muslim priest [sic] in Cape Town. The evidence showed that the marriage had indeed been solemnized in a mosque, though without a written contract. The court then sought to determine whether the Muslim marriage met the test set out in precedent case law. One key test was whether the marriage was polygamous or monogamous. The court at first presumed that a Malay Muslim marriage would be polygamous. The wife testified to the contrary. She brought forward evidence that under Malay Muslim custom, the husband could not marry polygamously. Hence it was a monogamous marriage. In the light of these circumstances, the court reversed the initial presumption, and formulated a new rule of presumption in favour of recognizing marriages regardless of religious or customary law, namely that all marriages are deemed prima facie valid unless proved otherwise. The impact of the new rule was devastating for the wife's initial claim for eviction and recovery of rent. Because the marriage was recognized, the woman was not allowed to sue without her husband's assistance.[9] No heed was paid to Islamic law permitting women to sue in their own right. Again, the underlying *ordre public* which held non-Muslim women under the control of their husbands, in effect prevailed for all women regardless of religion.

Is a Muslim Marriage monogamous for purposes of inheritance? – 1908

Only three years later, in 1908, a complicated inheritance case arose – the Estate Oeslodien case. Before the estate could be divided it had to be decided whether the Muslim marriage of the deceased was recognizable. The deceased, a Malay cleric, had died in 1853. He bequeathed the *usufruct* of his landed property to his wife and to his brother's children and the latter's descendants. He had created in effect a personal *waqf*, a family trust. The descendants contested the division of the sale proceeds of the property almost half a century later. The court had to decide which of the descendants were children of 'legitimate' Muslim marriages. It began with the marriage of the deceased cleric, the testator. He had married according to Muslim rites, as had his brothers also. None of them had married before a state-registered Muslim marriage officer under South African law. Hence none of the marriages had been registered. First of all, the court regretted that the couples had not chosen to fulfil the formal procedures necessary for recognition of any marriage in South Africa at the time. Nonetheless the court recognized that it was possible for these couples to conclude valid marriages without such formalities within their own legal systems. The court thought of a European analogy, that is, Scottish law, which recognized a marriage as long as the parties proved their consent in the presence of witnesses. No marriage officer was required to be present. The court did not mention that certain Islamic schools of law took the same position as Scottish jurists, but then explained why the procedural requirements in South Africa for the presence of a marriage officer, regardless of religion, was deemed important. This was to give anyone the opportunity to object to the marriage and to have the marriage registered. If Malay Muslims did not wish to accept this system, then the court could not recognize the marriage, though it was valid under Islamic law. The court then dealt with the substance of a valid Malay Muslim marriage, taking cognizance of the fact that the Malays were in practice monogamous. It took note of writings on Islamic law which cited the Prophet being in favour of monogamous marriages. On the basis of this information, the court should not have had any problems recognizing Malay Muslim marriages. Practice had made them monogamous and Islamic legal arguments could be made in support of this practice. The court turned a blind eye to these facts, finding it more important to encourage Muslim Malays not only to practise monogamy, but also to conform to the state's efforts to encourage registration of marriages with state-approved Muslim marriage officers. As a result, the court concluded that all the marriages were 'illegitimate', and hence it declared all the descendants of unregistered Muslim marriages to be children of 'illegitimate marriages'. They were denied inheritance. The court then carried out an about turn. It created a way out of the quandary it had just constructed. This was a case of testate inheritance not intestate, and in testate cases, the uppermost principle is the intention of the testator. As the latter was a Muslim religious leader, the court presumed that he was satisfied that the children named in the will were children of a valid Muslim marriage. His intention to benefit such children and their descendants was unambiguous.[10] The case is important for its two *obiter dicta*. First, it based the validity of marriage on universal procedural registration requirements, irrespective of religion. Secondly, it recognized a Muslim marriage as long as it was de facto monogamous.

Reversing the recognition of Muslim Malay marriages – 1910

The ruling recognizing the de facto monogamous Muslim Malay marriage in the Estate Oeslodien case lost some of its force in a criminal case ruling two years later, in 1910. Again Muslim marriages and African customary marriages were compared. In a criminal jury trial for murder, the Crown had called to the witness stand the wife of the accused. She stated that she and the accused had been married according to their African law and custom (which of the many customs and laws was not specified). She added, however, that she was the first and only wife of the accused. In effect their marriage was de facto monogamous. The defence objected to her testifying because of the rule that a wife may not testify against her husband in criminal proceedings. The court eventually found the accused guilty.

On appeal one of the issues to be decided was the admissibility of the wife's evidence. The admissibility question was tied to the issue of the nature of the accused's marriage. In its own words, the appellate court felt called upon to pronounce on the principles of recognition of unregistered marriages and monogamous marriages celebrated under non-Christian rites. The court did not dwell on the precedent case law preaching non-recognition of a marriage purely on the procedural ground that it had not been registered, in an effort to encourage this one unifying element in a sea of diverse types of marriages. Instead, the court framed the issues in terms of the substantive nature of a marriage and sought to find common ground from another angle. It referred to the case of the Malay washerwoman, Mashia Ebrahim in 1905 (see above), in which it had been decided that the marriage of a Muslim Malay woman could be presumed to be monogamous for the purposes of preventing her from suing in her own name without her husband's assistance. The court also referred to an earlier criminal case involving witnessing in a de facto polygamous African marriage. In that case the testimony of the second wife[11] of the accused was admitted. The reason given was that only the first wife would be recognized as a wife for purposes of non-admissibility of a spouse's testimony. In effect, persons were free to enter into polygamous marriages under their own rites, but only the first marriage would be recognized for purposes of criminal litigation. The court found support even in English ecclesiastical law for such a position.[12] The second wife, not the first, could thus be admitted as a witness. The court then consolidated its arguments by citing precedent that clearly distinguished the legal consequences of de facto monogamous marriages from de facto polygamous marriages. The court rounded off its arguments by concluding that the marriage at hand, though celebrated under African law and custom, which made it potentially polygamous, was in fact monogamous. Therefore the wife's testimony against her husband was not admissible. This conclusion sustained the legitimacy of the preceding case law relating to Muslim Malay marriages. De facto monogamy opened the door to legal recognition. By upholding such a precedent, the court was taking the jurisprudence in the direction of finding not only procedural but also substantive commonalities. A de facto monogamous marriage now served as a limited common basis for all religious and cultural groups in terms of legal recognition.

Reversing trends (Transvaal influences) – 1910

In 1910 the courts began to take a turn in the opposite direction. This coincided with a change in statute law in the Transvaal. Law 3 of 1876 had explicitly provided that polygamous marriages were invalid. This was repealed in 1885 (Law 4). The new law provided that the diverse laws and customs (of 'natives') would be recognized as long as consistent with 'principles of natural justice'. The new law was consistent with case law at the time, which held by and large that the state logically had to recognize the validity of marriages which had met the state procedures of registration and solemnization before a state-appointed marriage officer, and that the onus of proof lay on anyone, including the state, attempting to declare the marriage invalid.

The new statute and the case law received a setback in a court ruling on just what was a principle of natural justice. In 1910 the Transvaal Supreme Court ruled that it was not intended in the new law that any polygamous marriage be deemed consistent with justice.[13] In essence, the court was reviving the impact of the repealed statute.

In another ruling the Transvaal Supreme Court criticized precedent case law. It assailed the principle that the first wife is the lawful wife for purposes of litigation, even when her husband has the possibility under his own law to marry a second wife.[14] The court held: '[I]t appears to me the *better principle* [emphasis added] that when a man marries under a system which allows polygamy, his marriage is polygamous, and therefore not recognised by this court, whether he marries one wife or two'.[15] Thus according to the new principle, a de jure polygamous marriage should take precedence over a de facto monogamous marriage.

The 'better principle' had a profound effect on the recognition of Muslim marriages. De facto monogamy could no longer be the criterion for recognition. Marriages under Islamic and African laws and customs were presumed automatically to be de jure polygamous. There was not even an inquiry into whether such a presumption was correct – whether a de jure monogamous marriage could be allowed under Islamic law depending on the intention of the spouses when concluding a marriage contract, oral or written. The 'better principle' ruling also undermined the judiciary's efforts to introduce procedural uniformity by way of registration of all marriages. For even if the marriage had been registered before a state-certified marriage officer, and the parties had remained monogamous, procedural compliance would have no legal advantages at all.

The Transvaal Court and other courts following it did not question their own presumptions about the de jure nature of Islamic or African laws. They neglected to inquire into the details of Islamic or African laws in order to determine whether the so-called 'right' of men to polygamy was restricted, even prohibited under certain circumstances. Instead, a cultural blindness set in. The courts became preoccupied with distinguishing between 'civilized' laws, meaning 'us' European immigrants presiding over the courts, and 'uncivilized' laws – meaning 'them', without access to judgeships in higher courts.[16] This disparaging approach resulted not in judicial intelligence, but ignorance. It also provoked in the Muslim and African groups a self-defensive posture with respect to law, tradition and custom. Self-defence does not always create the best environment for nurturing critical self-examination, especially of legal premises.

The judiciary's position on polygamous marriages began to harden. It no longer looked at the facts of an individual marriage to determine whether it were monogamous de facto. It looked only at the de jure situation.[17] De jure polygamous marriages, including Muslim marriages, came to be called in legal parlance 'unions'.

Despite this hardening of positions, the peculiarities of individual cases still forced the courts to refine their positions on de facto vs. de jure polygamy. In 1951 – three years after the Nationalists' takeover of government, bent on apartheid – a dispute arose about the return of the marriage dower, *lobola*, under African laws and customs. The husband had married his first wife under African law. Later he married a second wife, but under Christian rites. The first wife left the matrimonial home because she was opposed to having her marriage rendered de facto polygamous. Her family did not wish to return the dower paid by her husband, arguing that under their law and custom the husband was not entitled to it if he were at fault in driving away the wife. The trial court regarded the first non-Christian marriage as an immoral union because it was de jure polygamous. Nonetheless it ordered the first wife either to return to her husband and live in such an 'immoral' state, or to live apart and return the dower to her husband. The case went to appeal. The appellate court felt the need to clarify the relation between recognized marriages and non-recognized non-Christian marriages. First of all, the appellate court chastised the lower court for ordering the first wife to return to cohabit with her husband or have the dower refunded. Such cohabitation, the appellate court opined, would undermine the de jure monogamous nature of the second Christian marriage and thereby endanger its recognition by the courts because it would become de facto polygamous by order of the court. The appellate court then turned to comparing marriages and unions in terms of the incidents connected to each category. A 'marriage' and a 'union' differed in terms of one of the incidents. A union was characterized by the polygamous incident in so far as the husband could take a second wife. Otherwise, the material incidents were the same for both.[18] As a result, a wife in a de jure polygamous union could still claim maintenance, for instance, like a wife in a de jure monogamous marriage. The appellate court then examined the early precedents on whether dower would be considered a justiciable material incident of a marriage or a union. Some of the case law had held that dower was 'inconsistent with civilised principles' and therefore not enforceable (despite the 1893 ruling mentioned above). The appellate court concluded that the husband could not claim his dower from a deserting wife. Curiously the court then went on to give another reason why the claim for dower was not enforceable, applying a combination of moral arguments. The court found that the husband had created a situation which made it impossible for the first wife to continue in the first marriage. She obviously wanted a de facto monogamous marriage, a morally laudable desire. By denying her this, he was at fault under African law and custom. He had rendered himself ineligible for a claim to dower even under the African custom and law.[19] Even though it was African law and custom, which were at stake, the same principles enunciated in the case had huge implications for Islamic law. The Muslim marriage had been long deemed non-recognizable because, like African marriage, it was de jure polygamous. Now the dower as an incident of a Muslim marriage under Islamic law would also have become equally 'uncivilized' like an African law dower.

Competing case law in the Cape, 1910–1937 – What is justice?

Despite the turnabout in the jurisprudence in 1910 that undermined the importance of de facto monogamous marriages (and reflecting probably the political differences between the Afrikaans influence in Transvaal and British influence in the Cape), another court, the Supreme Court of the Cape of Good Hope – in the same year, 1910 – took pains to preserve recognition of Malay Muslim marriages. The petitioner had divorced her husband (details of which were not specified in the judgment). She testified that she had married and divorced according to Malay rites. After the divorce the children were at first in the custody of their grandmother. Then the ex-husband took the children. The mother was now seeking return of the children. She argued that the law entitled her to sole and exclusive custody. Her reason was that her Muslim marriage could not be recognized; hence her children were not children of a 'legitimate' marriage and belonged only to her.[20] The court gave various hints that implied that it was ill-disposed to grant her custody. It dwelt on the fact that the mother had married a second man who was known not to be kind to children. It noted in passing that the first husband was entitled to custody. While this implied that his entitlement derived from Islamic law, the court did not delve into the legal details of custody under Malay Muslim law. In the end, not surprisingly, the court followed earlier rulings on Malay Muslim marriages. It concluded that such marriages were presumed to be valid unless otherwise proved. The court placed the onus on the mother to prove that her marriage had not met the requirements of South African rules relating to registration or de facto monogamy, was therefore invalid and any offspring should be in her sole custody.[21]

In the Cape the presumption in favour of recognition of Malay Muslim marriages continued well into the 1930s. In a case in 1937 a widow sought a declaration that she was the lawful widow for purposes of claiming workman's compensation.[22] She alleged marriage in a Malay mosque in 1903 at Uitenhage. The officiating religious leader had since died. Two other religious leaders swore to his having officiated and to the fact that the deceased husband and the applicant had lived together as man and wife. Procedural problems, however, arose. There was no record of registration of the marriage. It was not necessarily the fault of the parties; it was well-known that all records at the District Registry in Uitenhage were missing, lost or destroyed. Still the applicant could not produce an original certificate of marriage. Nor had the late officiating religious leader registered himself as a marriage officer under South African law. The court overlooked these difficulties. It argued that ever since 1860, the fact that the state had appointed marriage officers for non-Christian faiths, that is, for Muslims and Jews, made it incumbent on the courts to presume that the marriage had taken place according to the relevant rites. The benefit of any doubt was in favour of the asserted validity of the marriage. In the case at hand, the burden then lay on the company, which was refusing to pay the compensation, to prove the contrary to the presumption of legitimacy. The court found that the company had not put forward such evidence.

The status of women

The image of the status of women in the South African Malay Muslim community that emerges from the court cases is relatively positive. Women in fact wanted marriages to stay monogamous. They were economically active, earning their own income. They sought to keep custody of their children. The South African non-Muslim courts passing judgments in family disputes were inconsistent in their attitudes towards the Muslim women seeking justice. At times they supported their independence, at times worked against it. They did not have an overall social image or vision of the role of women in the Muslim Malay community. It seems they were more concerned about whether to impose a Christian vision of monogamy, and about preventing integration of Muslims into the European community, in order to uphold racist divisions.

The Muslim Asian Indian community

The second wave of Muslims arriving in South Africa came in 1860 from the Indian Subcontinent. They brought with them a different cultural approach to Islam, and also came to South Africa under different political and legal circumstances than the Malay Muslims. This affected their relationships among themselves in South Africa and with members of their communities back home. They were not as autonomous as the Western Cape Muslim communities.

While Sheikh Yusuf of the Western Cape is celebrated as the first Muslim leader in South Africa, Sheikh Soofie Saheb (known in full as Hadrat Hajee Shah Goolam Mohamed Soofie Saheb Siddiqui Chistiya al Qadri Habibia), who landed in 1895 from India on the eastern coast of South Africa, in Natal, has not enjoyed the same fame (Jeppie 71). Hailing from near Mumbai in India, he succeeded his father as imam of his town. He studied in Baghdad at the end of the 19th century. He left for South Africa at the instruction of his Sufi master in Hyderabad to spread the Chistiya order, settling in Riverside near Durban, where he had a a mosque, madrassa and an orphanage. His legal counsel was Mahatma Gandhi. He spread his work to Pietermaritzburg. After 15 years in South Africa, Soofie Saheb died in 1911. His son continued his work until 1940, when he too died. The daughter-in-law of Soofie Saheb then took over. This was Khatoon Bibi Soofie, who died in 1991. The Chistiya order has emphasized reverence for the Prophet and the importance of the hadith literature on the actions and sayings of the Prophet for the formulation of Islamic legal rules.

Short history of the immigration regulations for the Muslim Asian community

Members of the Soofie Saheb congregation included Muslim families who had emigrated from British India across the Indian Ocean to Natal on the east coast of South Africa. Many had been induced to come to work on the sugar plantations. This demographic shift impacted on the type of Islamic law practised in South Africa. It was no longer purely the 'Malay' Muslim law and custom that courts had to determine, but now the Islamic law of the Indian Subcontinent. The British colonial courts in the Sub-continent had a long history of developing what were known as 'Anglo-Muhammedan' interpretations of Islamic law. The question of citizenship had to be considered as a determinant of what law applied in each case. The Malays on the south-western coast of South Africa were South African citizens. The Indian immigrants on the east coast represented a mixture. Some were South African citizens, some were still citizens/subjects of British India. As long as litigants were not citizens of South Africa, but still subjects of British India, conflict of law rules complicated the issues. The South African courts had now to make reference to the vast Islamic law jurisprudence from Indian courts and to textbooks of Islamic law written by Indian jurists.

The immigrants were further subject to special South African laws enacted to apply particularly to them. An Indian Immigration Trust Board was created at the end of the 19th century,[23] and was entrusted with the 'government' of these immigrants. It was made responsible for enforcing all engagements of labour, recovery of passage money (e.g. return passage in case a labourer became unfit to work), interest, fines and penalties (e.g. when a labourer neglected to perform work) sued for and recoverable under the law. It also maintained a registry of the immigrants.

The Board appointed a so-called Protector of Indian Immigrants. Immigrants coming into Natal were bound to enter a service contract of five years with an employer allocated to them by the Protector. It was not just the employment conditions of single men and women that were regulated: the employment conditions of family members also came under scrutiny. Women and younger persons could be assigned only to 'lighter varieties of labour'. Spouses could not be assigned to separate employees. Marital partners and their children too had to be assigned to the same employee. Unification of families was to be guaranteed.

The Protector of Indian Immigration was also given power to intervene in the personal family affairs of the labourers. The Protector was automatically named as administrator of their estates. In the event an immigrant died intestate, without a will, the Protector had the power to possess the property and to establish who had rights to it, then expeditiously deliver it to such persons.

The Protector also took charge of the administration of family life, being appointed as registrar of marriages, births and deaths for the immigrants. Failure to give notice of births or deaths was punishable with a fine. Upon the arrival of immigrants, the Protector was to demand from each immigrant a certified copy of their marriage registration from India. If the certificate were lost during the course of the journey, the Protector was to register the particulars stated by the parties concerned.

The provisions relating to the registration of marriages did not solve the basic problem of whether Indians' marriages could be recognized under South African law. British Indian law recognized the validity of all marriages, regardless of religious belief; it did not limit such recognition to monogamous marriages, whether de facto or de jure, or only to the first wife of a polygamous marriage. South African law-makers, however, were not prepared to be as generous as British Indian law. Immigrants were allowed to import their laws and customs only to a limited extent. The South African immigration law, called Introduction of Indian Immigrants into the Colony of Natal (No. 25, 1891), provided that polygamous marriages would be recognized subject to two conditions. These were largely procedural. First, the marriage had to be registered with the Protector. Secondly, it had to be registered by 1872. Thereafter, no polygamous marriage could be registered, even with the Protector. If parties nonetheless entered polygamous marriages within the colony of Natal, the marriage would not be recognized.

This was not the first time that the South African law-makers were confronted with partial retroactive recognition of immigrant marriages. Already after the Crimean War, members of the British–German Legion accepted an offer of the British government to settle with their families in the area of East London. They landed in February of 1857. Four months later a law was enacted for recognizing a marriage and its offspring if it had been solemnized or entered into without such formalities as would have been required under South African law.[24] The only limitation on recognition was that an incestuous marriage or a prior existing marriage could not be so recognized. In effect a bigamous or polygamous relationship was still not recognizable.

On the other hand, celebration of a polygamous marriage was not prohibited or penalized. Its recognition in court was prohibited and therefore not justiciable. This approach reflected traditional South African jurisprudence, which sought to encourage monogamy in every cultural and religious group.[25] It was not, however, consistent with the treatment of African marriages in Natal. Ironically, the Zulu Code[26] recognized polygamous marriages among the Zulus in the same year as the Indian Immigration

Law was passed in 1891, which removed recognition of polygamous marriages among Indian immigrants.

The one area in which the Protector did not have authority was that of divorce. If married Indian immigrants wished to divorce, then they had to go before the South African court in their district. The law specified only two grounds for their divorce: adultery, and continuous desertion for one year. The parties had to be non-Christian and the marriage monogamous. Once the divorce was granted, the courts were to register the decree in a special Register of Indian Immigrant Divorces. A certified copy of the decree was to be sent to the Protector.

Another area where the courts had equally exclusive authority related to nullification of marriages. The religious law of the parties was immaterial: the marriage to be nullified had to be monogamous. Grounds for nullity were strictly limited: impotence at the time of marriage, not at the time of the petition; an incestuous relationship; lunacy at the time of the marriage; bigamy; and marriage under coercion or fraud.

South African jurisprudence on Islamic law for Muslim Asian Indians

Despite the efforts of the European immigrant law-makers in South Africa to regulate polygamous marriages of Indian immigrant labourers, the South African courts were still confronted with complications. One reason was that the Indian immigration law had prohibited the recognition of a polygamous marriage that an Indian had contracted in Natal. This left open the question of recognition of a polygamous marriage legally contracted in India.

Partial recognition of Muslim marriages for intestate inheritance by children (1917 Seedat case)

It was this problem which a South African court had to solve in 1917.[27] An Indian immigrant had married under Islamic law in India. He had four children from the marriage. Afterwards he emigrated to Natal. Later, on a visit to India, he married a second wife and had six children with her, some of whom were born in Natal. It is unclear from the court record whether any of the wives had also emigrated to Natal. When the husband died, he left a will to be executed in Natal. He specified that his estate was to be divided among his spouses and children as required by Islamic intestate inheritance law. At issue was the amount of the South African succession tax to be paid by the heirs. A surviving spouse was exempt, but the children were not. The question before the court was whether the two surviving widows qualified as 'spouses' for purposes of the succession tax law, and whether the 'children' were legitimate heirs under South African/Natal law. Counsel for the family members argued for recognition of the polygamous marriage. He presented multiple arguments: first, Natal law prohibited recognition of only those polygamous marriages celebrated in Natal. Secondly, as the marriage had been contracted outside Natal in a place where polygamous marriages were recognized, conflict of law rules applied. Accordingly, a marriage would be valid according to the law of the place of celebration, that is, British India at the time. Thirdly, it could no longer be argued that a polygamous marriage was abominable to public order since Natal had recognized Zulu polygamous marriages.

In response to counsel, the court split hairs. It held that Roman-Dutch law was the law of the land. Under that law a polygamous marriage was an *abominandum*, incapable of recognition. The court then tried to reconcile this principle with the statutory recognition of polygamous Zulu marriages. The court made life easy for itself by simply saying that any exception to the principles of *abominandum* had to be made by the legislature. The court awaited from the legislators a decision on whether to enact a law similar to that of the Zulu code for the express recognition of polygamous marriages of Indian immigrants. Hence the marriage of the deceased Indian immigrant, Seedat, would not be recognized judicially as valid. That meant that the spouses were not recognized as wives and surviving spouses.

As for inheritance by the children, however, the court turned to another standard. It used conflict of law rules for purposes of inheritance. Inheritance by children from parents whose marriage was valid under the law of domicile was not an abomination under Roman-Dutch law. The South Africa court then had to satisfy its conscience. By allowing inheritance by offspring of a polygamous marriage, it might look as though the court were indirectly recognizing polygamy. In support of its position that this was not necessarily so, it turned to an old English case, in which the marriage of the parents of the potential heir had been illegal under Scottish law, but not voidable under English law. Because the child was thus an offspring of a non-voidable marriage under English law, it could inherit in Scotland. The law of the domicile of the child was paramount.

The Seedat judgment set a precedent for driving a wedge between the treatment of African law marriages and Islamic marriages. The legislature widened the gap by creating special courts to hear cases under African laws and customs.[28] No special Sharia courts were set up for applying Islamic laws.

The Seedat judgment also continued an unsatisfactory state of confusion. The responsibility for regulating polygamous marriages remained unclear. The court had insisted that the legislature regulate the question of recognition of Muslim marriage laws. The legislature, on the other hand, had already regulated the marriages of Indian immigrants by a special ordinance, tailored to fit the judiciary precedents, which had refused to recognize polygamous marriages.

Reversals: no recognition of Muslim marriages for purposes of child custody (1932 Docrat case)

By the 1930s, the approach to Muslim polygamous marriages of Indian immigrants had changed. All avenues of accommodation were closed. The 'indirect' recognition of polygamous marriages for purposes of inheritance by children or of custody of children disappeared for Muslims. The occasion was litigation involving a father who sought custody of his child.[29] He had married in 1908 in Stellenbosch, in the Western Cape, according to Islamic rites, and had a child with his wife. She died in 1926, and an uncle on the mother's side took custody of the child. The father then sought recovery of the child. The court recognized that the applicant was indeed the father of the child and the husband under Islamic law of the child's mother. The marriage had not been contracted in the presence of a Muslim marriage officer, and therefore was not registered. The court declared the marriage as non-existent. It then declared the effects or incidents of such a marriage also as non-existent. Accordingly, the child was not the child of a 'legitimate' marriage and the natural guardian of such a child was the mother. The court took pains to point out that this did not entail a 'moral stigma on the parties', but was merely a legal obstacle. The court even rejected, without giving reasons, the father's argument that as the natural father he should succeed to the custody of the child when the natural mother died. The court allowed the mother's family to retain custody. The custody rules of Islamic law were thus not broached.

Recognizing Muslim Indian marriages for purposes of testate inheritance by children (1946 Fatha Mahmomed case) – the role of customary practices

Over the course of time the non-recognition of Muslim marriages became fixed in cement in the jurisprudence. There remained only one tiny opening in the testate inheritance law. In a case in 1946 the Supreme Court in Natal established that a deceased Indian testator who had married under Islamic law had not registered the marriage.[30] His children were declared not to be the children of a 'legitimate marriage'. The testator's will and intention, however, rescued them. The father had written in his will that his 'heirs' included the children of a marriage which he regarded as legitimate under Islamic law. The court felt compelled to follow the clearly stated wishes of the testator. It permitted the children of an 'illegitimate' marriage to inherit under the will. The court drew its principle from a precedent from 1908 involving Malay Muslims in the Western Cape. The Malay Muslim marriage in question had also not been registered.

This appears to be the first time that a South African court linked the Malay Muslims to the Indian immigrant Muslims. There was an attempt to generalize about Muslim customs regardless of their cultural backgrounds. Two customary practices were involved in the suit. One related to a 'levirate' marriage. In this regard, the court noted that the widow of the deceased son of the testator had married her brother-in-law 'according to the custom of the Mahomedan rites'. There was no evidence taken of the fact that this kind of 'levirate' marriage is nowhere encouraged in the Quran.[31]

The second customary practice related to the division of property under the will. The testator had bequeathed his immovable property to his son and grandson in equal shares. He prohibited alienation of the property (sale or mortgage). The property was to remain with his descendants in perpetuity. Under Islamic law this constituted in effect a personal *waqf* (religious trust). Neither the court nor the litigants raised this point. The court treated the intentions of the testator as a matter of *fidei-commissum.* It was unclear, the court opined, whether the testator wished to have a *fidei-commissum unicum* or *multiplex*. *Unicum* meant that the property remained inalienable only for the son and grandson and their descendants. *Multiplex* meant that it endured longer. The court solved the ambiguity on the basis of public policy. Doubts about what the testator meant were weighed against extending the *fidei-commissum* more than necessary, for it tied up the property. Free marketing of property was more important for the public welfare. A prohibition to sell or mortgage did not speak for extending the *fidei-commissum.*

The apartheid era and Islamic marriages

Discrimination in recognition of polygamy (Hindus, Muslims, Africans) – (1958, Mehta case)

The racist apartheid era came into full swing in 1948 with the electoral victory of the Nationalists. During this time, however, the judiciary attempted to modernize its position on polygamous marriages. A case arose in 1958,[32] the circumstances of which were virtually the same as those that had arisen in a case 50 years earlier.[33] This time it concerned a Hindu rather than a Muslim marriage, but the same principles were at stake. The deceased had married in Bombay in 1913 or 1914 according to Hindu rites. Hindu law permitted him to marry a second wife, but during his lifetime the marriage was de facto monogamous. He emigrated to what was then Rhodesia and died there in 1950. He left property to his surviving spouse. As in the case 50 years before, the surviving widow sought an exemption from payment of estate tax as a 'surviving spouse'. Only lineal descendants were to pay the tax. The Master of the High Court in charge of administering estates objected on the grounds that the marriage was de jure polygamous, hence not recognizable, and the wife should not qualify as a surviving spouse, as decided in Seedat's case 50 years ago. The court held otherwise, overturning the Seedat precedent. It argued that in Seedat the court had refused to recognize polygamous marriages because they were deemed 'uncivilized' and therefore contrary to public policy of civilizing the 'natives'. Since that time, polygamy had come to be recognized in a number of 'civilized' countries. Besides, the majority of the inhabitants of South Africa were living in polygamous marriages, at least de jure. Reasons for not recognizing de jure polygamous marriages had to be restricted. The only reason for non-recognition would be a situation in which the marriage actually detracted from the incidents of a monogamous marriage. This seldom occurred, so the court pronounced intuitively.

The judges, however, had different opinions on the issue of whether the public policy of South Africa had changed its attitude towards polygamy. One judge opined that it had so changed, since many other countries had no problems in recognizing polygamous marriages. Another felt that South

Africa had not changed its policy. The latter judge wanted to limit the recognition of polygamous marriages to certain purposes strictly as a matter of necessity, that is, anyone desiring recognition of a polygamous marriage would need to show strong reasons to overcome the basic presumption of public policy against polygamy.

In the end, all the judges agreed that the surviving spouse of a de jure polygamous marriage, but de facto monogamous marriage, could be recognized as a 'spouse' in a legitimate marriage for purposes of exempting her from estate tax.

The court left open the issue of public policy. It was aware that there was a difference of opinion on this issue. In the past, de facto monogamous Malay Muslim marriages had been recognized by some courts, but rejected by others. The court did not wish to issue a final statement on this issue, such as whether de facto monogamous marriages also presented an exception to the public policy of non-recognition of de jure polygamous marriages or were in themselves recognizable in all cases as conforming to the public policy of encouraging monogamy.

Disallowing insurance claims by members of polygamous families (Hindus) – 1960

Whether the public policy of South Africa had changed remained the subject of controversy. Two years after the Hindu-marriage inheritance case (Mehta), the Supreme Court of South had to deal with the same issues with respect to a marriage celebrated under African law and custom.[34] It was a case of the dependents of a married man who were seeking compensation from an insurance company for the death of their provider. The insurance company argued that they did not qualify as 'legitimate' offspring or dependents because the marriage of the deceased was polygamous, and therefore not recognizable for any legal purposes. The question was whether this marriage was contrary to public policy. The lower court found that even though the marriage was not recognizable, the incidence of the duty of a husband to maintain the wife could be recognized as a material interest to be preserved under the law. On appeal, the judgment was quashed. No exception was to be allowed. Accordingly, the claim was denied.

Disallowing insurance claims for African polygamous families – is marriage a contract? – 1961

A few months after the denial of an insurance claim for a Hindu family, a similar case arose under African law.[35] A widow claimed damages for loss of support due to the negligent killing of her husband. She too had been married de jure polygamously (under African law and custom). Her counsel was well aware that it would be almost impossible for her to win because of the earlier judgment. As a result, the claim was presented not as a claim deriving from matrimonial status, but rather from a contractual agreement. The widow averred that she had entered into an oral agreement with her husband that he would maintain her and the children in exchange for her not leaving the house to work. The court rejected her argument on the basis of the history of the law of claims for loss of a breadwinner. Such a claim had not existed in Roman law, nor in English common law.[36] The English Parliament had to enact the Fatal Accidents Act (originally in 1846) to allow such claims. The Roman-Dutch law as applied in South Africa had admitted such claims on the basis of equity, but was limited originally to members having the status of belonging to the family as recognized by the law. Hence the claim derived from the marriage as status, not from contract. Certainly a factor which influenced the court not to alter the jurisprudence on this point was its racial prejudices. The woman making the claim was African, the defendant was a European company. The rule had been in South Africa that in claims between persons of different 'cultures', African laws and customs had no place in the judicial arena.[37]

The contractual argument would have been especially useful in claims by Muslim dependants. Contractual agreements between family members and spouses are especially given credence as contractual claims are not derivative from family status.

Allowing maintenance claims for polygamous families if de facto monogamous – Muslims

The jurisprudence relating to claims for loss of a family breadwinner changed 12 years later. A Muslim wife claimed maintenance from her deserting husband.[38] She had married him in Malawi, then they had emigrated to Rhodesia. The husband argued before the court of first instance in Rhodesia that the marriage, though de facto monogamous, was de jure polygamous, and therefore was not recognizable in the courts. No incidents of marriage, such as maintenance, were justiciable. The case went to appeal to South Africa, as was possible at the time. The court held that precedent decisions had been issued in a time of religious intolerance of polygamous marriages, but times were changing. A more recent decision on a change in public policy regarding recognition of a Hindu marriage for purposes of inheritance by the surviving widow had set a signal for tolerance. Accordingly, it was held that since polygamous marriages had been recognized, even if exceptionally for some judges, for purposes of inheritance (with respect to a Hindu marriage in the Mehta case), then they would be recognized for purposes of maintenance. In further support of its ruling the court cited more recent jurisprudence from English courts allowing deserted wives of de jure polygamous marriages celebrated outside Great Britain to sue for maintenance under the Matrimonial Causes (Polygamous Marriages) Act of 1972.

Upholding polygamy for Indian Durban Muslims against the wishes of the wife (1983, Osman case)

In the 1980s the issue of de facto monogamous Muslim marriages versus de jure polygamous marriages raised its head again. A couple in Durban had undergone an arranged marriage celebrated under Muslim rites.[39] The antenuptial contract rejected Roman-Dutch rules of community of property and kept the properties of the spouses separate, as allowed under Islamic law. The marriage lasted only seven months. The husband issued what was regarded as a *talaq*, a unilateral divorce of his wife. In the meantime he sought to marry a second wife, again under Muslim rites. The first wife applied in a South African civil court for a restraining order. The court dealing with the case noted at the start that the Muslim marriage was not recognizable because it did not fulfil the procedural requirements of a valid marriage in South Africa. The first religious ceremony and the future religious ceremony were of no legal import. The first wife argued that the anticipated second marriage amounted to adultery and a humiliation for her. The court answered that it 'had the impression that Islamic law allowed a man more than one wife at a time'. It did not call for evidence of the status of monogamy in Islamic law. It did not refer to a precedent case in the 19th century, in which the South African court noted that the Prophet was against polygamy.[40] The court rejected the wife's plea for an interdiction of her husband's impending second marriage.

Reviewing South African jurisprudence on maintenance and dower for Muslim polygamous marriages – Is Islamic family law valid custom? (1983, Ismail case)

In 1983 the appellate court was faced with a case which brought together all the issues raised in the preceding last 100 years – the validity of Muslim marriages in relation to claims for dower and for maintenance.[41] Most of the South African jurisprudence on dower and maintenance derived from claims under African laws and customs for *lobola* (dower). The 1983 judgment brought the entire South African jurisprudence in these areas under review. The parties had married in the Muslim community in Pretoria in 1976. They did not, however, take advantage of the South African statutes which permitted marriages to be performed before Muslim marriage officers appointed by the state. This was because the marriage had been concluded without the simultaneous presence of both bride and groom. The court noted that it was customary among Muslims for the bride not to participate in the marriage ceremony. The source of this information was not cited. Nor was the marriage, once concluded, registered as provided for under South African statutes. Nor did the couple exercise their option to have the marriage converted into a de jure monogamous marriage, and so registered as provided for under the Indians Relief Act 22 of 1914 (see General Law Amendment Act 57 of 1975).[42] The parties had reached a tacit agreement that the marriage would remain de facto monogamous.

The parties also agreed to a dower. The husband gave and delivered to the wife gold jewellery. He agreed to pay the remaining dower of 7.5 ounces of pure gold upon termination of the marriage by reason of divorce, annulment or death. After the ceremony, the wife gave the husband the jewellery for safe keeping.

After about two years of marriage the husband stopped maintaining the wife. After another two years, the husband terminated the marriage by issuing three *talaq*s. He then also refused to pay the wife maintenance for the *idda*, three menstrual cycles for a non-pregnant wife, which is used to determine whether the wife is pregnant or not. The wife sued for maintenance in arrears, plus interest at 11 per cent per annum, maintenance for the *idda*, return of the gold jewellery she had given the husband for safe keeping, or alternatively payment of its cash value, and finally, payment of the deferred dower of 7.5 ounces of pure gold.

The wife at first took her dispute before the Muslim leader of the Pretoria community, the 'Moulana' (defined by the court as a high-ranking ecclesiastical officer-bearer of the Muslim creed, who had to pass an examination at a recognized Muslim religious institution in order to qualify for this position). He heard both parties in the dispute, and granted all the wife's claims. The husband refused to abide by the Moulana's decision. The wife then sought relief in the state courts of Transvaal to enforce her claims. The Moulana's decision was taken by the court as evidence of applicable Islamic rules.

Given the tendency of South African courts to deny recognition of a Muslim marriage, even when de facto monogamous or monogamous by contractual agreement between the spouses, counsel for the wife argued that she was not basing her claims on her marital status. This approach was similar to that taken by counsel in the case of wives married under African law, who sought compensation from insurance companies for the negligent death of their husbands. Counsel argued that the dower payment and maintenance were a result of a contract, and even that the marriage was not de jure polygamous, because the parties had entered into a contractual agreement that it be monogamous.

Counsel also added a new argument. The wife's claims were based not only on contract but also on custom. Even the monogamous contract was a custom. This was a clever strategy since the South African courts had long been accustomed to considering custom in family matters. Custom was specially applied in disputes involving African marriages. In regard to Muslims, there was the precedent case in 1946 of Fatha Mahommed (see above), a testate case in which customs of the Muslim community of the deceased were taken into account.

In the Ismail case in question, the wife's counsel convinced the court that it had to consider whether the Islamic marriage and family practices constituted legitimate custom. This meant that the custom had to meet the criteria which the South African courts had developed over time for what constituted a custom enforceable by the courts and what constituted proof of that custom. At the start of the judgment, the court laid down what were asserted to be the relevant Islamic customs and their sources. It believed that the sources of custom were the Quran and the hadiths as well as what was accepted by the couple's community as binding. The elements of binding Islamic custom for the purposes of this case, so the court opined, were: marriage before an imam; agreement to have a monogamous marriage; payment of a dower, whether immediate or deferred; payment of maintenance during the marriage and during *idda* upon termination of the marriage; and adjudication of disputes and claims before the Moulana.

As for the nature of the marriage, the court noted that the Quran allows the husband to enter a polygamous marriage, with a maximum of four wives, but under certain conditions. He must be capable of and willing to treat the wives with 'absolute equality' in all material and non-material aspects of a marriage. As a result, the court noted, in fact, 98 per cent of South African Muslims had de facto monogamous marriages. The information formed part of the pleadings, but no statistical source was cited, or information given as to whether the statistics differed from community to community.

Regarding termination of the marriage by the husband pronouncing three *talaq*s, the court noted that the custom permitted the husband to communicate, in one sitting and directly to the wife, an irrevocable *talaq*. Another way to terminate the marriage was by annulment, but this required a judgment by the Moulana and had to be based on a finding that the husband had misbehaved or had refused to give the wife a *talaq* when she wished to leave the marriage.

Having deemed the applicable Islamic rules as 'custom', the court then proceeded to measure such custom against South African case law regarding when a custom may be recognized. Recognition of custom rested on certain set criteria. First, the custom must have existed for a long time. The court found that the Quran and hadiths as sources of custom have a long history. Secondly, the custom must have been uniformly observed by the community concerned. The court found that the Quran and hadiths have long been observed by the South African Muslim community to which the parties belonged. Thirdly, the custom must be reasonable. The court found that adjudication before the Moulana was fair and reasonable since he respected the principle of *audi alteram partem* (the parties having a chance to be heard). Fourthly, the custom must be certain, and the custom may not contravene statutory law. The court decided that none of the Muslim customs involved in the case at hand were prohibited by law. Finally, the custom may not be *contra bonos mores*, that is, against public morality or policy. As the South African legislature had appointed Muslim marriage officers to celebrate and register Muslim marriages, such a marriage, even marriages that were not registered, were not by nature contrary to the moral fabric of the society. But the court defined the notion of 'moral fabric' narrowly. The object of recognizing the celebration of Muslim marriages was to have the effect that the man and woman entering into a union were not committing a crime by agreeing to live together.

The court then distinguished between two definitions of *contra bonos mores* – one narrow and one broad. In the narrower meaning a practice or custom is *contra bonos mores* when it is morally reprehensible or sexually immoral. In its wider meaning, it refers to the principles and institutions of a society as a whole. In this instance that larger society as a whole was South African society. The court found that in terms of the narrow definition of *contra bonos mores*, there was nothing reprehensible *per se* about the Muslim marriage customs or 'tenets of faith'. In the wider sense, however, it was the very nature of the Muslim marriage itself which undermined South African principles and institutions. Muslim marriage was by nature and de jure polygamous. To recognize it as legitimate would be a slap in the face for the basic South African principle that marriage is (or should be) by nature monogamous. Anything deriving from a polygamous marriage thus had to be rejected, since recognition of incidents would only encourage couples to continue to accept de jure polygamy.

The court also added two more arguments, based on the 'nature of the conjugal relationship'. The growing modern trend was towards absolute conjugal equality between spouses. The court felt that polygamy would undermine equality, which would also be compromised in terms of the different divorce rights of the spouses. The Muslim husband could unilaterally divorce without going to the Moulana, while the wife who sought divorce had to appear before him. The court's second argument was linked to public policy. The state had an interest in imposing a hard-to-break notion of the conjugal tie. Muslim customs, the court opined, had a different notion of that tie. It could be easily broken without any reason on the part of the husband or by the wife on the sole ground of 'general dissatisfaction'.[43]

In effect, the court was rejecting the early South African case law, which recognized de facto monogamous Muslim marriages in the Malay Muslim community in South Africa. The court did not countenance the earlier arguments that recognizing all incidents deriving from de facto monogamous marriages would encourage, rather than discourage, couples to remain monogamous. Why the Ismail court did not bother to look at the earlier jurisprudence is not clear. One can only surmise that it wanted to force Indian couples to 'take advantage' of the law which allowed them to transform their de facto monogamous marriages into de jure monogamy.[44] Recognition of de facto monogamy would have rendered the conversion law practically useless.

The court did consider, however, the arguments of the wife's counsel that the state's policy of encouraging monogamy was inconsistent, the state having legislated recognition of African polygamous marriages for certain purposes. The court responded again with distinctions. The state's action did not represent a change in basic policy, since it was acting out of expediency. For the Muslim communities in South Africa, expediency was not required, since the proportion of all Muslims in South Africa, who practised de facto polygamy amounted to only two per cent. In plain English, the court was saying in effect that there were so many polygamous Africans that their customs could not be ignored except at the peril of the very existence of the state. The court held that this tiny portion of Muslims would not suffer any 'real hardship' for lack of recognition of their de facto and de jure polygamous marriages. This response can be criticized as illogical, since the court was in effect denying the majority of Muslims with de facto monogamous marriages the chance to enforce the incidents of their marriages.

The court did not confront head-on the argument of counsel that the Muslim marriage is not by nature polygamous. He said that it is what the parties take it to be according to their contractual understanding. In the case at hand the parties understood the nature of their marriage to be monogamous. This was allowed by Muslim customs of the community. Probably the court did not know how to deal with the argument or else could not understand it because it regarded marriage from a South African statutory point of view. Marriage was a status, an institution that was governable only by law, unalterable by contract. The court simply concluded: 'Their tacit understanding cannot affect the inherent nature of their relationship.'[45]

Once it had refused to recognize Islamic marriages, the court then turned its attention to the claims of maintenance and dower as material incidents deriving from the marriage.

The wife's counsel argued that a maintenance claim was a proprietary claim, separate from the nature of the marriage. The court rejected this approach. It held that maintenance was not a contractual matter but an incident of a marriage. The court found that Islamic maintenance 'customs' flowed from the marital status and not from mere contract. If the basic polygamous Muslim marriage could not be recognized then maintenance claims in relation to it could not be recognized. The court did not care to determine whether it could draw an analogy with the situation affecting maintenance claims by wives of de jure polygamous marriages under African law and custom. A maintenance claim had been regarded as a proprietary claim, recognizable as separate from the question of the nature of the marriage.[46] Again, this was probably due to the court's view that these were only expeditious political exceptions for Africans which were not to be extended to other communities unless the legislature so decided.

The Muslim custom of dower, however, posed another dilemma for the court. Dower was not a strange concept for the court – South African case law had long dealt with it in the African communities, where it was known as *lobola*. In general, South African courts regarded *lobola* as 'uncivilized' – reprehensible – and therefore not enforceable in the courts. The legislature had overruled case law with a statute which prohibited the courts from refusing to enforce *lobola* claims. The South African courts regarded this as an exceptional rule, not to be extended to other communities in South Africa by the courts. Only the legislature could provide for a widening of the exceptions. This can be interpreted as meaning that the courts still regarded the dower as uncivilized and the legislative exception as again only an expedient measure. To counter these attitudes, counsel for the wife introduced a tactical argument that would distinguish the Muslim dower from the African. He argued that dower in Islamic custom was not quite the same as *lobola*. The Islamic dower was to be treated as a marriage gift, rather than obligatory like the *lobola*. The custom among Indian Muslims was to have an immediate dower and a deferred dower. The immediate dower vests in the wife as her property as soon as the husband delivers it to her. The deferred dower becomes a debt due when the marriage ends by death or divorce. In the case at hand, the immediate dower consisted of six ounces of gold, and the deferred dower 7.5 ounces of gold. The court accepted the argument. The wife had given the six ounces of gold to her husband for safe keeping and sought the return of it. Her counsel said that she was the owner and the husband was keeping her property illegally.

The court was convinced of the distinction. In its eyes, she as owner of the jewellery chose to hand it back to her husband. This was an act of free will on her part and was not required by Muslim customs as part of the conjugal relationship. In other words, the deposit of the jewellery for safe keeping with the husband was not an incident of the marriage. Therefore her claim for return constituted a claim on a 'contract of deposit'. Without being aware of the implications, the court, in effect, had converted what was set out as a claim under Muslim custom for redelivery of the paid portion of the dower into a claim under Roman-Dutch law on contract. Again the court placed a barrier between the African and Muslim communities.

As for the deferred dower, the court equated this to *lobola*. *Lobola* flowed from the marriage as the deferred dower did. The Muslim dower was thus as 'uncivilized' as the *lobola*. Because the legislature had not seen fit to make an exception for Muslims, the courts were not going to do so in order to preserve the public policy against recognizing any incident of a polygamous marriage. Curiously, the court did not add to its public-policy argument against polygamy the inequality argument that *lobola* and dower raise, for it is only the duty of the husband to pay. The question of whether there is a reciprocal or equivalent duty on the part of the wife was not raised.

Neither counsel nor the court offered any arguments for how they distinguished a marriage dower-gift that arises only because of the marriage from a deferred dower-debt that also arises only because of marriage.

With Ismail v Ismail the court anchored South African case law against any further recognition of Muslim de facto monogamous marriages on the grounds of their de jure polygamous nature, even if the spouses agreed to the contrary. The decision remains a major source of law, and is still cited by courts. It is also important as a benchmark for another reason: for the first time, a South African court had to recite in detail aspects of Islamic marriage law, though it was treated as custom.

Post-Ismail contradictions in South African case law – does de facto lifestyle or de jure lifestyle determine the applicable law?

A year after Mrs Ismail lost her case, another judgment raised the question of whether the de facto family lifestyle should be material or not in determining the application of custom.[47] The case dealt with child custody. The parties had married under Christian rites instead of African law and custom. They worked as teachers and had one child. Evidence was brought to show that their de facto lifestyle was Western. They lived with their child in the home of the paternal grandfather. Frictions developed and the wife left with her son, taking him to her mother and leaving him there. The father then sought the return of the child, which the mother and maternal grandmother resisted. They sought the application of the African custom of giving custody to the maternal grandmother. The court refused to apply the custom because the parents had lived de facto not under African custom, but under 'the law of the land'. The decision in effect exemplified the inconsistency in South African case law with regard to the significance of de facto or de jure marital and family lifestyles. Under the criteria of this decision, the Ismails' Muslim marriage would have qualified as Western and therefore recognizable under the law of the land.

Post-Ismail: Problems of **contra bonos mores** *in de jure monogamous marriages (1984, Cumming case)*

The issue of what is or is not *contra bonos mores* was not confined to Muslim de jure polygamous or de facto monogamous marriages. It arose also in connection with de jure monogamous marriages a year after the Ismail judgment. Specifically the question related to an antenuptial property contract for a marriage celebrated under Christian rites.[48] In that case, the court defined the criteria for determining which provisions of a marital contract would be contrary to good policy or public morality. The spouses entered into an antenuptial agreement about division of property in a written contract. Accordingly, the law deemed them to be married out of community of property. In the antenuptial agreement the husband conferred on the wife a car and a house, but subject to certain conditions, the major one being that should she predecease the husband or should the marriage end, the property would revert to the husband as sole owner. The house which was conferred on the wife became the conjugal domicile; it was also registered in her name. The marriage ended in divorce, whereupon, the wife sought an ejectment order against her ex-husband. He counter-claimed for a declaration that ownership of the house should revert to him under the marital contract. He also sued too for an order that the house be re-registered in his name. The court had to determine whether the reversionary clause was valid, or void for reasons of *contra bonos mores*. The first question the court raised was: what is the function of the marriage law? It found that the law aimed to favour sustaining the conjugal tie and to make it difficult to break. As a consequence, the law disfavoured anything which prejudices continuing the marriage tie. This included anything which undermined the bond of loyalty that spouses owed to each other and encouraged one to engage in conduct intended to end the marriage without being penalized. In this case Mrs Cumming argued that the reversionary clause was prejudicial. It undermined the husband's commitment to sustaining the marriage because divorce would bring him no financial disadvantages. He would revert to his pre-nuptial status and the wife would stand to lose more than he. The unsaid corollary of this argument was that community-of-property marriages had higher chances of not breaking up because the husband would stand to lose too much financially.

The court held that Mrs Cumming would have to establish for purposes of *contra bonos mores* that the reversionary clause was incontestably harmful to the public interest. This involved presenting convincing evidence that the reversionary clause would inevitably lead to the husband not taking the marriage tie seriously. Otherwise, it was pure speculation (or 'fanciful' to use the court's exact words) that such a clause would easily cause breakdown of the marriage and therefore be *contra bonos mores*. A mere chance that the clause might induce the husband to take his duties lightly was not enough to declare it *contra bonos mores*.

The court found that there was not only the principle of the stability of marriage at stake, but also the principle of contract agreement. The contract was between two competent adults, and the husband had not exercised any duress on the wife to sign. The purpose of the law was also to uphold agreements.

The third principle at stake was the freedom of the donor. The husband in this case as a donor had the right to determine the conditions of giving, and the law also had to protect this freedom.

All in all, the court held in favour of the reversionary clause. The freedom to contract and determine the conditions of a donation prevail also in the marital context as long as there is no compelling evidence that such freedom undermines the stability of the marriage.

The antenuptial contract in this case arose during the apartheid era. Such a contract was recognizable for the Christian community, but the deferred Muslim dower could not be recognized as an antenuptial contract. Such was *contra bonos mores*. The issue of *contra bonos mores* was decided in a political context in which each culture in South Africa was to be treated as autonomous. At the same time, the legal culture against which all laws and customs of each autonomous group were measured was the Roman-Dutch and English common law. In post-apartheid South Africa, another question arises. That is, whose *boni mores* serves as the basis of comparison? Is there a dominant *boni mores* common to all cultures in South Africa which exists alongside a subordinate version within each of the cultures? Or are all of equal value and weight depending on the circumstances of each individual case?

Specifically, as in the case of Mrs Cumming, who had to give up her car and her house to her ex-husband, would a marriage contract with a reversionary clause be contrary, for example, to Islamic law and custom? – for Islamic law does not permit revocable gifts. A gratuitous transfer must be absolute, without conditions (Coulson 1991, 168).[49] Such a reversionary clause would be regarded as 'uncivilized', and thus *contra bonos mores*. One could speculate that a revocable gift between spouses might impede honest and open relations. Islamic judges in the Middle Ages in Andalusian Spain were well aware of problems connected with settlement of properties between spouses. For example, there were disputes over monetary obligations when the conjugal home was the property of the wife. The question arose as to whether a wife could charge her husband rent for living in her house. Some jurists held that the wife could indeed do so, as she might have done in regard to any other person. Other jurists opined to the contrary, believing (or fancying, to use the South African court's language in Cumming) that if the wife were allowed to charge her husband, this would undermine the stability of marriage and the nature of marriage as a partnership. A third opinion took the middle ground. It was held that the wife could charge rent to her husband as a precautionary measure to secure her own future. She could do so, however, only if she were an orphan without any relatives she could rely on in the event her husband divorced her or left her a widow (Bencherifa 225).

Summary of South African jurisprudence on the application of Islamic law

Before moving to the next section, which analyses the fate of Islamic law in post-apartheid South Africa, a summary overview of the situation under apartheid would be useful.

During the apartheid era, a body of South African court decisions accumulated which represented a variety of positions, not necessarily consistent with one another. These positions can be summarized as follows:

– Claims relating directly to the marriage were not recognized as justiciable, that is, no divorce or nullity actions could be brought. The reason was that public morality could not tolerate or encourage polygamy. In effect disputes had to be settled by dispute-settlement mechanisms of the parties' communities, or by the parties themselves.

– Claims relating indirectly to the marriage were recognizable as justiciable, if (i) the matter flowed from the marital status, such as for witnessing purposes, inheritance or custody, and if (ii) the marriage were de facto monogamous. Two reasons were developed in support of these positions, at different points in time. The earlier one was that the claim was not directly concerned with the marriage. The later reason was that public morality had shifted against polygamy and so permitted exceptional justiciability only of proprietary interests.

– Claims relating indirectly to the marriage, such as for custody and inheritance, were not recognizable because the basic underlying marriage was not recognizable, as long as the marriage was de jure polygamous. De facto monogamy was immaterial.

– Claims relating to dower were not justiciable, unless regulated explicitly by statute, as in relation to marriage dower (*lobola*) under African law applicable as 'custom', but not in relation to the deferred dower (*mahr*) in a Muslim marriage. But if the dower had been delivered, but deposited with the husband for safe keeping, then the wife could recover it under a deposit contract.

– Claims relating to incidents of a marriage based on the application of Islamic law as 'custom' were not justiciable even though the individual customs were not *per se* against *boni mores*. They were non-justiciable because the underlying marriage was de jure polygamous.

– Claims based on a contract between the spouses, regulating maintenance, dower or custody, or even the de facto monogamous nature of the marriage, were not justiciable because the contract flowed from the de jure polygamous marriage of the contracting parties, who had not taken advantage of the statutory provisions for converting the marriage into a de jure monogamous marriage.

South African case law had dire consequences for Muslim families. The non-recognition of Muslim marriages rendered the children simply offspring of a 'non-marital union'. This deprived them and their parents of certain rights: the children could inherit only from the mother; the child upon becoming an adult was responsible for maintaining only the mother; and the father had no custodial rights over the child (Omar 1982).[50] In matters of intestate inheritance the problems were acute. Non-recognition of Muslim marriages left the South African courts no choice but to impose the general law on the distribution of the estate. As a result, when a Muslim husband died intestate, his estate did not go to his wife or children because they could not qualify as heirs in a 'legitimate' marriage. It went either to distant relatives, or failing them, to the state. Only if the Muslim marriage were celebrated abroad and the spouses were domiciled abroad at the time of the celebration, could the children be recognized as children of the marriage and thus 'legitimate' heirs, as long as the law of the place of marriage recognized them as children of the marriage (1917 Seedat judgment).

Another frequent problem confronting Asian Muslim lawyers during the apartheid era (Omar 1982, 486) concerned inheritance rights of divorced wives. Muslim Indian spouses would marry under South African civil law and also according to Muslim rites, to cover all their bases. In case of divorce, however, the husband would commonly divorce the wife according only to Muslim law, not South African state law, then remarry only under Islamic rites. If he died intestate, only his first wife inherited. The second wife was excluded because of the non-recognition of her Muslim marriage.

Judicial recognition of Muslim marriages in post-apartheid South Africa

Introduction: constitutional background – cultural rights

As the apartheid regime came to its negotiated end, one of the major questions to be solved was the recognition of Muslim marriages. A major change in the direction of the courts' case law on this issue occurred because of the new principles enacted in the Constitution of 1996. In the following sections, three post-apartheid judgments will be discussed – one which revolutionized the courts' approach, bringing case law back to the earlier courts' original tolerance towards Muslim marriages; one which attempted to restrict the changes; and one which reaffirmed the constitutional changes. As background to these decisions, certain provisions of the new constitution should be understood.

The new South African Constitution forms the basis of the current legal culture in South Africa.[51] Three provisions of the new constitution are of particular relevance to Islamic law. Section 15 (3) – relating to freedom of religion – permits parliament to enact laws which would recognize personal and family law based on the parties' religion and marriages celebrated according to religious law.[52] Parliament is not required to do so, but may. The only limitation is that the terms of recognition must comply with the

Bill of Rights (Chapter 2, Art. 7–39) and other provisions of the Constitution. One such provision is Article 9, which guarantees equality before the law. It is prohibited for the state or anyone else to discriminate on the basis of gender or marital status (Art. 9 (3) and (4)).[53] Article 30 confers the right to participate in the cultural life of one's choice.[54] Again the limitation on the exercise of this right is consistency with the Bill of Rights. Article 31 prohibits preventing anyone from enjoying her/his culture and practising her/his religion, as long as this is consistent with the other basic rights listed in the Bill of Rights.[55]

The so-called 'right to culture' was debated and contested during the constitutional conference. It constituted a kind of compromise in face of the demands from some of the conservative Afrikaaner immigrant community (Volkstaatraad) for a constitutional right to self-determination on the basis of a cultural nation (Volkstaat, or nation state).[56] A constitutional commission was formed to hammer out the issue of cultural rights (Commission for the Promotion and Protection of the Rights of Cultural, Religious and Linguistic Communities in South Africa). In a memorandum from this office, the then President of South Africa, Nelson Mandela, had the accent set on the linguistic aspects of culture. A multilinguistic plan was to be worked out.[57] When the commission sponsored a conference in September 1998, delegates were invited from smaller groups like the Amandele, the Phuti, the San, Tamils, the Griqua, and even proponents of a 'white' Afrikaaner Volkstaat.[58] The Nationalist Party, which had been the ruling party under the apartheid era, issued a statement that protection of cultural, language and religious communities was needed and was a matter of human rights. The statement emphasized protecting the 'mother tongue' in schools. Everyone knew that this was a veiled reference to the historical struggle of the Dutch-language settlers to place Afrikaans on a par with English as the second official language of South Africa. The debate became polarized. The Deputy President at the time, Thabo Mbeki (later President of South Africa), openly addressed the polarized positions on the dilemmas. On the one hand the 'white' minority wanted its cultural and language groups protected against the 'black hordes'. On the other hand 'black' cultural and language groups, suppressed during apartheid, wanted a new lease of life and to be promoted.[59] The challenge as seen by Mbeki was more than linguistic: it was to unite the population of South Africa around common aspirations and a common identity, which could also respect diversity. Mbeki was against the institutionalization of 'autonomous mechanisms' for each cultural group.

The issue of culture was clearly an explosive one. For decades the South African courts had deprecated the marriage culture of Africans, Muslims and Hindus as 'uncivilized' and regarded their own Roman-Dutch culture as superior. When a non-Christian marriage was recognized in law, it was only for certain exceptional purposes. This 'moralization' of the clash of culture was essentially subjective. Neither the apartheid law-makers nor the courts had adopted Alfred Whitehead's more objective philosophical definition of culture, namely: 'Culture is activity of thought.'[60]

Ryland v Edros – Muslim marriages are recognizable

It was not long after the new constitution came into force that the courts had to hear a case involving the application of the constitutional right to culture, in an Islamic divorce proceeding in the Western Cape. The couple came from the Malay Muslim community. The occasion was historic – the Malays formed the oldest Muslim community in South Africa. Their customs and practices had been the subject of the initial South African case law on Islamic law. It was only fitting that Malay practices were once again the subject of the first South African case law on Islamic law in post-apartheid South Africa.[61]

The parties in the case had celebrated their marriage according to Islamic rites in 1976. They had three minor children of their own, and two whom the wife had brought into the marriage. In 1991 the husband divorced his wife. He pronounced *talaq* three times, rendering his decision irrevocable. The local religious council, the Muslim Judicial Council, notified the wife of the divorce. The wife brought a criminal action against her ex-husband, accusing him of marital violence, but he was acquitted. The husband then brought a civil action in the courts against his wife, seeking to evict her from the matrimonial home.

The wife pleaded in her defence that her ex-husband had failed to give her reasonable notice. She also filed a counter-claim for maintenance and her share of the marital assets, basing her claim on the contractual nature of the terms of their marriage. She alleged that she and her husband had agreed that all contractual terms were to be governed by Islamic law: all her claims were based on these terms. She claimed maintenance for the *idda* period (the three-month waiting period after the divorce to determine whether she was with child); a *mutaa* gift, a kind of consolation or compensation for termination of the marriage without just cause; and an equitable share in the husband's assets as compensation for her contribution thereto.

She justified this claim by pointing out that throughout the marriage she had worked as a cashier and assistant in various jobs. She bought food and clothing for the family members and performed all the household chores. Her husband operated a small-scale firm manufacturing clothing. She conceded that he had also contributed to the household expenses.[62]

The husband admitted that he had married under Islamic religious rites, and he also agreed with his wife that the incidents of an Islamic marriage flow from the terms of the contract into which the parties enter. The contract may be oral or written; in this case it was oral. He differed, however, on whether all the terms of the contract were necessarily or exclusively governed by Islamic law – certain terms were to be governed by the territorial law (in this case Roman-Dutch), even though oral. The one term he pleaded that was not subject to Islamic law was the wife's claim to maintenance during the *idda* period after the divorce. The husband argued that the claim was proscribed by the statute of limitations under Roman-Dutch law because the claim was made more than three years after the event.

The other two of the wife's claims, he admitted, were to be interpreted according to Islamic law – namely the *mutaa* or compensation payment and the repayment of the wife's contribution to the husband's wealth. The husband did not dispute that Islamic law requires a *mutaa* payment to the wife upon divorce. He disputed the facts, however, alleging that the wife was to be blamed for the break-up of the marriage (he alleged adultery), not he alone. Also, in regard to repaying the wife for her contributions to the husband's wealth, the husband did not dispute the principle of the matter. In effect he recognized that she had a potentially equitable share in his assets, but he disputed the conditions under which a wife could claim her contributions to the husband's wealth. He alleged, first, that the contribution could not be indirect, such as through her labour, but had to be direct. Secondly, remuneration for indirect contribution through labour had to be an explicit part of the contractual agreement between the spouses. In this case this was not an explicit term of the contract.

As for the issue of eviction from the marital home, the court was spared examining the Islamic rules on the matter, since the parties reached an agreement at the pre-trial conference that the wife would move out by a certain date. The wife had only complained that she had not received reasonable notice of eviction. She did not appear to have contested whether she could be evicted at all. The experience of divorced women in Egypt with eviction would have been of use in the case. The Egyptian Constitutional Court had ruled that a basic principle of Islamic property law is that property may be burdened with a social function if the welfare of vulnerable parties so requires. Hence if the divorced parties have minor children, the wife's right to continued lodging in the marital home may take precedence over the right of the husband to evict her by issuing a *talaq*.[63]

Ryland issues – which Islamic school of law applies?

The first legal question raised by the court was which school of law was applicable to the interpretation of the marriage contract. This was unusual in a Muslim marriage case in South Africa. It is attributable to the fact that the judge (Farlam, J) hearing the case had already amassed considerable experience in questions of Islamic law, as he had served as an attorney in disputes over who held religious authority in Muslim organizations. In that earlier position he had become familiar with the various schools of law and their definitions of who is a Muslim.[64] The judge noted that each of the spouses had obtained expert opinions, which agreed that there were four schools of law. It was further agreed that the Shafii school would apply to South African Muslims in the Western Cape because many were descendants of immigrants from Malaysia, where the Shafii doctrine dominated. There appears to have been no dispute between the experts about whether the court should be bound by any one school of law, depending on the distant origins of the parties. There was no discussion of the fact that the Al Azhar Islamic University in Cairo, along with the Pakistani courts, has long recognized that not only one school of law is binding. Applying a combination of schools that best suits the circumstances is the better approach.

Ryland issues – does the application of Islamic law entangle the secular state in religious doctrinal disputes?

The second major legal issue raised by the court related to whether the state courts should apply any Islamic school of law, because differences in rules could reflect differing theological positions. At stake was whether the application of religious law would violate the principle that the state avoid entanglement in religious doctrinal disputes. Justice Farlam raised the issue on his own initiative, not at the request of the parties. He had found it imperative to do so since he had read an article on the 'revelational nature' of Islamic law (Cachalia). The court made it clear that it did not wish to decide on matters of religious doctrine, even in relation to proprietary or contractual issues, since that would endanger the constitutional guarantee of equality of religion and freedom to exercise one's religion. Counsel for each spouse then submitted, at the request of the court, their views on the subject. They both agreed that there was 'no clear barrier between the religious and secular spheres' in Islam. Yet the post-divorce dispute, in their view, did not involve deciding any points of religious doctrine and so would not 'entangle' the court. The court was satisfied with this explanation, and so found that it did not risk entangling the state in religious disputes.[65]

The avoidance of doctrinal entanglement contains the seeds for a novel application of Islamic law, which can involve examining not only jurists' texts, but also the revelational source – that is, the Quran, clearly a religious document, as illustrated in many an Egyptian and Pakistani court judgment. In South Africa the anti-entanglement doctrine may prevent the courts from relying on basic Quranic scripture for understanding the terms of Islamic law. Instead, the courts may apply Islamic law only in the context of a contract concluded with the intention that Islamic law should apply. What constitutes Islamic law would depend on proof brought by the parties as to what they understood to be the rules of Islamic law, including their interpretation of Islamic law according to their community customs when concluding the contract. In this case the court would not be so much concerned with determining what Muslim jurists have to say about the rules of Islamic law, but rather how a community interprets Islamic law according to their own customs. The second duty of the court would be to assess whether their understanding of Islamic law was consistent with the South African Constitution and public morality as determined by the constitutional Bill of Rights.

In terms of the principles of Islamic law, contract is a basic freedom and necessity – a necessity because the positive, or legislated, law cannot be expected to cover all the interests and needs of each and every person, even in family matters. Hence marital partners and family members are permitted to take responsibility for deciding the terms of their relationship, including succession matters. The contract may regulate how the parties themselves interpret the Quran and hadiths, even adding to the differences of opinion among the four schools. For example, a contract between spouses could theoretically prohibit polygamy or even confer on the wife the right to a second husband, depending on whether men outnumber women in the community. The validity of the contract would be determined on the basis of the constitution or public policy, not on any judicial interpretation of Islamic law *per se*.

The non-entanglement approach has implications for the other communities in South Africa. It would enable every cultural and religious community in South Africa to be placed on the same basis. A Christian or Hindu or an African traditionalist could be called upon to show how each party had regulated the incidents of the marriage, through contractual agreements based on their understanding of their customs and laws, subject to public-order criteria as determined by the constitution.

Ryland issues – is Ismail good law?
Are incidents of Muslim marriages justiciable in the courts?

The third major legal question which the court had to resolve was whether it could recognize the dispute as justiciable, since case law inherited from the apartheid era had ruled out the jusiticiability of Islamic marriage disputes on the grounds that Islamic marriage was de jure polygamous. In other words, the court had to decide whether the 1983 decision in Ismail v Ismail was still good law. The court found that the *ratio deciendi* of Ismail was that the terms of Muslims' marital contracts derived from the underlying Islamic marriage. Since the marriage was de jure polygamous, it was contrary to South African public order and morality to enforce polygamous arrangements. Public morality tolerated and encouraged only de jure monogamous marriages. The court then had to decide whether the standards of public morality had since changed. It did not make an assessment of whether the Ismail judgment had overlooked some key early case law before the apartheid regime came to power, and therefore should be distinguished as an anomaly. Instead, the judge used the opportunity to look to the new South African Constitution for guidance on public policy and morality. The court cited Article 39 of the Constitution requiring that the courts, when developing South African common law, promote the objects of the Bill of Rights.[66] The previous common law was based on a notion of intolerance of non-Christian matrimonial culture. The new Constitution introduced the notion of tolerance of religious beliefs and equality. These new values had what the court called a 'radiating effect'. That is, while the specific recognition of Islamic marriage was not guaranteed by the Constitution, the notion of tolerance was to radiate outward so as to influence how the judiciary was to treat a spousal contract in the context of an Islamic marriage.

Justice Farlam carefully pointed out that in Ismail, the judges had refused to separate the contractual proprietary issues from the issue of recognition of the de jure polygamous Muslim marriage, although such a separation had been allowed for de jure polygamous African-law marriages.[67] The refusal was based on the argument that *boni mores* did not allow recognition of any incident of Muslim marriage. Justice Farlam then decided that he would do what the Ismail court had not done, namely treat the contractual incidents of the marriage separately and render them justiciable, because the Constitution represented a new public policy. Without citing the pre-apartheid case law on Malay Muslim marriages, the court in Ryland in effect was reverting to the former tolerance that South African courts had shown in separating contractual proprietary incidents, inheritance questions and questions of coverture (rights of a husband over his wife and her property) from the issue of the nature of the marriage.

Ryland issues – recognition limited to de facto monogamous Muslim marriages

The Ryland court also raised the question of the relevance of de facto monogamous marriages that has plagued the South African courts for centuries. Justice Farlam noted that the marriage between Ryland and Edros was de facto monogamous. This was a material fact that would limit the application of the final judgment, as the court concluded that its *ratio deciendi* would not 'necessarily be applicable in such a case [of actual polygamy]'.[68] The implication here is that in the case of a de facto polygamous Muslim marriage, the contractual incidents may not be justiciable. The court did not specify the reasons for this delimitation, but one may surmise that the reason is that the Constitution stresses equality as the basis of public policy. Polygamy would not meet that test, since polygamy is not an equal right for men and women.

Ryland – which terms of a Muslim marriage contract are recognizable?

After overturning Ismail and recognizing the wife's claims as justiciable on the basis of a proprietary contract, the court then continued to examine whether the terms of the contract were justiciable. The court defined its task narrowly. It was 'not asked to recognize the marriage but merely to enforce certain terms of a contract made between the parties which are in a sense collateral thereto'.[69] The criterion which Justice Farlam used to determine whether the contract was enforceable or not was whether its terms were contrary to public policy or *contra bonos mores*. The test for public policy is whether the enforcement of the contract would be offensive to the morals of the entire South African community, including all religious groups, or be opposed to fundamental principles.

The court held that none of the terms of the contract was offensive. Such an agreement relating to i) post-divorce support, ii) division of property, and iii) compensation for divorce without just cause would be equally imaginable for the Christian religious community in South Africa.

Ryland – prescription of claim for idda *maintenance*

The parties, however, disagreed on the conditions attached to the above three terms of the contract. The husband's counsel maintained that the claim for *idda* was subject to the rules of prescription. He argued that the wife had sought to realize her claim out of time, beyond the statute of limitations, set at three years in South Africa.[70] The wife's counsel claimed that prescription is not even an implied term of a Muslim's marriage contract. The claim is valid for all time, thus placing a debt on the husband without term.

The Islamic law experts hired by the respective spouses agreed that the opinions of Islamic jurists on prescription (*mudiy*) varied considerably. The wife's expert pointed out that the Shafii jurists generally opined that a maintenance debt could not be prescribed. This position was common to both Malikis and Hanbalis (Bellefonds II:276). The husband's expert witness did not cite such authority. Rather, he added another dimension to the debate, by emphasizing that since unpaid maintenance was classified as a debt, it had to be proved. The rules of proof of a debt would apply.

In the end the court relied on South African statutory law and case law. At issue was whether a party to the contract could implicitly renounce his benefits under the statute of limitations. The court cited but disagreed with precedent case law that favoured renunciation of such a benefit. The reason was that prescription serves a public good and renunciation undermines this public good. Hence an implied term of a Muslim marriage contract renouncing prescription is unenforceable, as contrary to the public good in South Africa.

As to when the prescription time began to run, it was agreed among counsel for the parties that it should run from the date of the pronouncement of the *talaq*. *Idda* was defined simply as a period of three months after repudiation (*talaq*).[71] Whether the timing of the calculation of the *idda* depends on the timing of the *talaq* was not discussed, because according to the jurists' interpretation of the Quran, each of the three *talaq*s is to be pronounced when the wife is not having her menses (see chapter on Egypt above).[72] This means that the *idda* begins after each of the three *talaqs*, so the total minimum length of *idda* would be nine months, instead of three as calculated by the parties in Ryland.

Neither the expert witnesses nor the court referred to the Quran on the issue of maintenance debt for the *idda* period. Nor did they compare the Shafii position to that of the Hanafi jurists, which is closer to South African statutory law. Such comparative information might have been useful for the education of the court. The Quran contains no fixed rules about prescription. Prescription could be implied in the injunctions relating to divorce. The Quran says that when there is a danger of a married couple breaking up, such as when an initial *talaq* is pronounced, the danger is not to continue indefinitely. A set of steps to deal with the danger are prescribed. There is to be arbitration, presumably immediate, to stop the break-up from progressing further.[73] Family members are to be appointed to reach a solution. The object of the arbitration is to try to reconcile the parties, but if all effort fails, then negotiations are started for settling the financial consequences of a divorce. However, no time limit on the duration of the arbitration or negotiations was set. Only recently has the Egyptian legislature imposed such a time limit.

On the issue of prescription of a maintenance debt, several Hanafi jurists differed from the Shafii. These Hanafi jurists did not classify maintenance as a normal debt. As a result, several jurists concluded that if the husband had not been paying maintenance, the wife's claim for arrears was subject to a prescription of one month. An exception was made, however, if the amount of the maintenance had been fixed by a court or by an agreement between the spouses, then the claim was not subject to prescription of any duration (Shaham 69, 70, 80). In the 1920s the Egyptian law-maker introduced a blanket prescription of three years for maintenance claims. This was done as an exercise of the state's discretionary power to set limits as a matter of equity (*istihsan*) as to when a claim could be brought, in order to reduce legal uncertainty by simplifying the rules (Shaham 80; Meron 144).

Is the post-divorce gift of mutaa *obligatory?*

On the issue of the payment of the *mutaa* as a consolatory gift, both experts in Islamic law agreed that the *mutaa* is prescribed in the Quran.[74] No conditions are attached to it. Both conceded that the jurists in the four schools of law had different opinions about whether the *mutaa* is obligatory. Some argued that it is only morally recommendable to pay *mutaa*. The Hanafi jurists held diametrically opposed views about the obligatory nature of the *mutaa* (Coulson 1991, 31–2). Both expert witnesses testified that the Shafii argued that the *mutaa* is obligatory, but conditional on the fact that the husband initiated the divorce and the wife was not at fault in the break-up of the marriage. In effect, the husband would have the burden of proving that she had provoked the *talaq*. The husband in Ryland had asserted that he had been driven to pronounce *talaq* because his wife had sought the company of other men. The court held that there was not enough evidence at the time of the hearing to establish whether the wife was at fault, and postponed a decision on the *mutaa* until such time as the issue of the fault of the wife could be resolved.

The court accepted without debate the suggestion from the experts that the Shafii opinion on *mutaa* was determinative for the case. Later the wife's counsel submitted an alternative expert opinion, pointing out that there had been an evolution in Islamic legal thinking. A 'rigid observation of a single school of thought' is by and large no longer acceptable in many Islamic countries. All opinions of the various schools of thought are examined and the logic and appropriateness of any one opinion or a combination of opinions is applied.[75] For some unknown reason, the court did not refer to this supplementary expert evidence in its final judgment. If the court had taken cognizance of the alternative opinion, then it would have adopted another approach to the question of the payment of *mutaa*. It would have found that the Quran and several hadiths enjoin the payment of the *mutaa* to the wife upon divorce. No specific conditions are attached. The Hanafi opinions, which supported the obligatory nature of the *mutaa* without reference to whether the wife's behaviour had provoked the breakdown of the marriage, are consistent with the Quranic provisions. In the light of the variety of opinions, the court might have defined its task differently. It could have first attempted to determine the intention of the parties to the contract. But if the parties had not deemed the *mutaa* to be an implied term, then the court would have to decide which of the possible opinions on the obligatory or non-obligatory nature of *mutaa* would meet the test of public policy or public morality.

Ryland – may the wife be compensated by an equitable share in the husband's wealth?

On the last issue, relating to compensation to the wife for her tangible and intangible contribution to the husband's accumulation of wealth, the court was confronted with disagreement between the two expert opinions. The expert for the wife testified that the Shafii position was unclear. Therefore the court would have to look to other schools of law or to the legislation in Malaysia, which is traditionally a Shafii jurisdiction. The Malaysian Islamic Family Law Act provides for a division of assets acquired during the marriage upon divorce, consideration being given to the extent of the contributions each spouse made to the welfare of the family, including caring for the children and the family home. The wife's expert witness emphasized that the Malaysians would not enact a law unless they were sure that it conformed to Islamic law.[76]

The second expert opinion, written for the benefit of the husband, merely stated that remuneration after the divorce for labour during the marriage was not entertained in Islamic law without an explicit prior agreement. No sources from the Shafii school were cited.[77]

The court concentrated its analysis on the Malaysian statutory law and literature cited by the wife's expert witness. Among the literature, the court seized upon an article which stated that the basis of the laws was a synthesis of custom (*adat*) and Islamic juristic texts (Ibrahim 185).[78] The custom recognizes jointly-held property between the spouses, including not only property jointly acquired by the spouses, but also property originally acquired by one spouse, but improved by the sole efforts of the other. Islamic law was said to lack a basis for jointly-owned property. Nonetheless there was nothing in Islamic law that prohibited recognizing such a custom.

The court concluded that the core of the Malaysian recognition of joint property was custom. So the wife in the case at hand had to establish a similar custom in the South African Malay Muslim community, but she had no evidence to that effect. Her expert witness had indeed undermined her position by citing evidence of uncertainty in the Muslim community. He opined that 40 per cent would say that Islamic law allows joint property, 40 per cent would disagree and the remaining 20 per cent would not know. Custom has to be proved in South African law, and counsel for the wife could not provide such proof. The court finally ruled that in the absence of firm evidence of custom, there was no Islamic injunction that would compel recognition of a wife's equitable share in the creation of joint property or assets.[79]

In a last attempt to salvage the wife's claim to joint property, the court cited a code of Muslim law in the Cape that might provide some guidelines for the courts. There appears to be a codification of Islamic law in South Africa that was applied in the early years of the colony (Chijs; Visagie), and which has not been repealed. The court felt that it should not delve further into the issue of its applicability as counsel had not relied on this source of law. Additionally, there is some evidence that the code might have been abrogated implicitly by the Dutch ban on the exercise of the Muslim religion. When the British removed the ban, it was not clear whether they intended to lift only the ban on the exercise of religion or also wanted to reinstate the code of Islamic law.[80]

Evaluation of the Ryland court's decision on refusal to recognize joint property

The wife's counsel noted to the court that Islamic law is unclear about joint property, then challenged the court to undertake its own investigation in order to find the best view. The court did not take up the gauntlet. If it had, it would have had to assess in detail the many positions on joint property under Islamic law. The first place to start with would be the Quranic verse that entitles each spouse to separation of property.[81] The European notion of coverture was not part of the Islamic tradition. The fact that a married woman could own property without the control or consent of her husband has been the pride of Islamic law, especially since this right existed long before the British introduced the Married Women's Property Act, liberating women's property from their husbands' control (Coulson 1991, 14; Shaham 27, 73; Doi 158; National Council 30; Shatzmiller). Muslim women can acquire property by their own efforts. Or they can invest the marriage dower for their own benefit, or they can rely on their share of inheritance from family members. These are all rights that the women may claim, though customary practices can prevent them from realizing these rights in fact (Moors). Separation of properties was an important issue in the Middle Ages for Andalusian Muslim judges, for example, who were faced with questions about whether the husband living in the house of the wife was liable to pay rent to the wife. There were various opposing opinions on the issue. It was the general opinion, however, that he should pay rent when the wife was an orphan, and thus would have no source of family support should he divorce her (Ibn Iyad 225).

Given the general principle that marriage did not automatically mean community of property, the verse on spouses each keeping their own earnings can be interpreted in a variety of ways. First, it is clear that the husband does not take the property of the wife and she does not take his. The spouses are not prohibited, however, from entering into an agreement about other arrangements, e.g. sharing equally in the profits accruing to the properties during the marriage, or sharing proportionally as agreed upon. If the spouses have not explicitly agreed on how to split the profits after divorce, the verse can be interpreted to mean that each spouse gets back the share they have earned from the investment they made in the property of the other spouse. In other words, the wife's share in the wealth of her husband or vice versa could be based on an explicit term of the marriage contract or an implicit term whereby each gets back what they contributed. Thus in the absence of an explicit agreement, a share in the accretion of wealth of the other spouse is implied, based on the concept of active material contribution to that accretion, as in a business partnership.

An implied share can also be based on indirect contributions. This entails remuneration for services that benefit the other spouse, who otherwise would have had to pay someone else for services. In modern times Iranian women relied on the notion of remuneration in order to convince the revolutionary legislature to enact a law which requires husbands to remunerate their wives for services contributed. Divorcing husbands are to repay their wives on the basis of the Quranic verse that allocates a woman the right to what she earns (Jones 1996). The wife bears the burden of proving the nature and extent of her contributions to her husband's wealth.

In Egypt divorced wives may claim remuneration for specific services, e.g. breastfeeding their child. This derives from the Quranic verse which requires the husband to pay the wife for suckling their infant child. He is not allowed to determine unilaterally what to pay her, but is to consult with her about a fair recompense.[82] In Egypt the law allows a divorced wife to claim remuneration for her breastfeeding services, but the Egyptian legislature has not treated this right as an implied term of the marriage contract. An explicit prior agreement is required.

In sub-Saharan Africa, Tanzanian and Zanzibari courts have developed an extensive case law on what constitutes an equitable share in the property of the other spouse. The principle used is that each spouse is to show how she or he contributed directly or indirectly to the wealth of the other. Each spouse is awarded upon divorce the contributions made during the marriage. The rule is derived from the Marriage Act, which is a universal law, applicable to all marriages in Tanzania – African customary, Christian, civil or Muslim (Jones-Pauly 1998).

The court or counsel in the Ryland case could have also changed the nature of the wife's claim for an equitable share by adopting another interpretation of the Quranic verse allowing women to keep their earnings. The verse may also be interpreted to mean that the wife is under no duty to help maintain the family. Maintenance is the sole duty of the husband. In the Ryland case there was evidence that the wife had contributed her earnings to family support. This did not constitute a gift to the husband to aid him in fulfilling his duty to maintain the family. Her claim for an equitable share in the assets could have been transformed into a claim to be reimbursed for all her contributions to the maintenance of the family. On the other hand the court might have found this unilateral duty of maintenance resting solely on the man, contrary to public policy, public morality and the constitutional emphasis on equality. In this case it would have found support in the example of the Tunisian legislature, which amended the family code (*Majallat al ahwal as shakhsiyya*) to hold wives responsible for contributing to the maintenance of the family when they are financially capable of doing so. The justification was that equality requires equality not only in rights but also in duties.

Ryland – implications for the future application of Islamic law

Justice Farlam raised on his own motion the question of future treatment of cases of Muslim matrimonial disputes in South African courts. He made clear the *ratio deciendi* of his judgment, which is that the courts will examine the implied (presumably also the explicit) terms of Muslim marriage contracts and measure them against the principles of public policy as defined in and informed by the new constitution. To help it determine the Islamic law governing implied terms of contract, the court will rely on expert opinion and evidence of custom. The final yardstick of whether an Islamic rule is applicable or not will be public policy. On a comparative note, this is consistent with a decision by a French court, which declared that the absence in Muslim family law codes of a provision for compensatory payments to a spouse who would suffer a decline in her/his economic status due to divorce is against French public policy. The French courts would require the divorcing spouse to pay such compensation when living in France.[83]

The Ryland judgment is the first time in South African reported case law where the courts have applied Islamic law as law and not as custom. Without explicitly articulating the nature of Islamic injunctions, the Ryland court in effect overturned the Ismail court's approach. In Ismail, Islamic Injunctions were regarded as customs, subject to certain standards of proof. In Ryland, Islamic injunctions were treated as a corpus of law, which is proved by legal experts, separable from religious doctrine *per se.* At the same time, the Ryland court understood the relationship between custom and Islamic law. Islamic law applicable in any one community or geographical area can be interpreted so as to fit local custom and local custom interpreted so as not to contradict a fundamental principle of Islamic law. The Ryland approach can be seen as judicial activism, regulating and ruling on any traditional or religious family law. This is in keeping with the spirit of section 15 (3) of the Constitution, which confers on parliament discretion to legislate on traditional or religious, personal or family law for purposes of recognition of marriages (Rautenbach).[84]

Determining what a fundamental principle is in Islamic law may prove, as the Ryland court itself experienced, not so easy, given the huge juridical literature that has been passed down through the centuries. In an interview Justice Farlam admitted that he might have decided differently if he had been given more information about the wide variety of interpretations that Muslim countries have adopted.[85] He did not realize that a Muslim marriage can be regarded, as in Tunisia, as de jure monogamous. Up to now the South African judges had only assumed that a Muslim marriage was automatically de jure polygamous, being totally unknowledgeable about other points of view. For example, in Tunisia, the concept of a de jure monogamous Muslim marriage is based on the interpretations of the Quran and hadiths which indicate that polygamy is unjustifiable, for two reasons. First, most societies do not have a large imbalance between men and women. Secondly, a woman does not feel loved at all when competing for affection with a second wife. Love is the first commandment in a marriage. Besides, the Prophet did not allow his son-in-law Ali to take on a second wife because it would have hurt his daughter. As for the notion of joint property, Justice Farlam was also keen to learn that the Quranic injunction providing for separation of the earnings of each spouse can be legally interpreted so as to allow common property (not community of property), which would be divided between the spouses upon divorce according to what each had contributed and earned during the marriage. This did not necessarily have to be a question of customary practice. Again,

Tunisia was taking a lead on this issue (see the chapter on Tunisia above). In the end, however, the Justice was pleased that public policy can be used as a yardstick for interpreting and applying Muslim personal law, as legislators in other Muslim countries also apply Islamic injunctions within the parameters of public policy.

Not only would Islamic law be subject to the limits of South African public policy, but also to the limits of the doctrine of non-entanglement in doctrinal issues. In other words, the South African courts would decline to apply Islamic law in family or personal status matters if such matters involved the court in deciding doctrinal questions. What remains open, however, is whether the courts would feel free to use the Quran and interpret it or apply only the opinions of jurists as interpreted by the expert witnesses. It may depend on whether the South African courts would concentrate on the legal texts of the Quran rather than the religious.

Nonetheless one outstanding issue remained unresolved: the issue of how to treat the different categories of Muslim marriage. For South African jurisprudence there are three categories of Muslim marriage, namely the de facto monogamous, the de facto polygamous, and the de jure polygamous Muslim marriage. At least in the Ryland case the de facto status counted more than the de jure. Justice Farlam wrote an *obiter dictum* that a de facto polygamous Muslim marriage would not be treated the same as a de facto monogamous marriage for purposes of public policy.[86] Here again, the Tunisian interpretations may prove useful to the South African courts. While the de facto polygamous Muslim marriage in Tunisia is regarded as void and even incurs penal confinement or fines, certain incidents of the marriage are still justiciable. The children are of the marriage and the wife must be maintained during the three-month post-divorce *idda* period after the nullification of the marriage.[87] Taking this example, the South African courts could decide which incidents of even a de facto polygamous Muslim marriage are recognizable and which are not.

Amod v Multilateral Motor – trial court

The next case to arise after the Malay Cape Town Ryland judgment was in the Asian community in Durban.[88] The plaintiff had married her husband in 1987 according to Islamic rites, but the marriage was not registered. They had two minor children. In 1993 the husband died in a motor accident caused by the negligence of the other driver. The surviving spouse lodged a claim for herself and the minor children for compensation for loss of support. The insurance company agreed to pay compensation for the children, but not the surviving spouse, on the grounds that the marriage was de jure polygamous.

The Durban court had to deal with an old problem that has plagued South African courts since long before the new Constitution. The courts regarded any claims related to the incidents of a potentially polygamous marriage as non-justiciable, on public policy grounds. The only way to remedy the situation was by legislative decree. Indeed the legislature had passed laws that restricted claims only to certain incidents of such a marriage and to only certain marriages. The legislature had recognized, by statute, certain claims arising out of African marriages that were potentially polygamous. These were claims to the marriage dower, the *lobola*, and claims by the first wife, but not the subsequent wives, to maintenance. The South African courts were reluctant to extend by analogy this limited recognition to non-African potentially polygamous marriages. In their view, the legislature had explicitly to permit such extensions.

The courts had also consistently refused to extend the limited recognition of proprietary rights to insurance claims by surviving spouses. Such claims included compensation for loss of a breadwinner.

The Durban trial court followed previous South African case law and denied the widow her claim. The court argued that her de jure polygamous Muslim marriage blocked her claim. If courts were to admit such claims, then in the case of de facto polygamous marriages, the insurance companies would be inundated with multiple claims from several wives of the deceased.[89] While this appeared on the surface as a practical reason, it had very racist consequences. The court was upholding in effect a long tradition of denying black women the right to lay claim to the compensation due under the insurance contracts their husbands had signed and paid for. In the 1940s and 1950s one of the reasons given for refusing claims from widows of marriages under African law for loss of support was racist: no woman of a de jure polygamous marriage could sue a European for damages.[90] In the 1960s the courts changed their arguments to emphasize impracticability. They held that even if it could be proved that the deceased or injured husband was obliged under any one communal law to maintain a wife and children, the insurance companies would be faced with multiple claims from several wives who would allege they had been polygamously married to the deceased.[91] This would prolong litigation and burden the insurance companies. No thought was given to the real possibility that even Christian marriages could give rise to multiple claims, for the current wife and the ex-wife, who is dependent on alimony payments, could equally bring claims as dependants for loss of support.

In reality the court's deference to the argument that the insurance company might suffer a flood of claims from polygamously married wives was an indirect attempt to save the defendant company. It was well known that the Multilateral Motor Vehicle Accidents Fund was in a poor financial state. To save it, claims on the Fund would have to be capped.[92]

The Durban trial court also entirely overlooked the precedents of Mehta[93] and Kader,[94] in which the South African courts held that the common law as developed in Seedat, which prohibited enforcement of succession rights in de jure polygamous marriages of non-Christians (in that case Hindus), was based on public policy at that time, which had since changed. In effect, there were South African precedents for using public policy as the basis for a progressive development of the common law.

Faced with the then recent judgment in Ryland, that allowed claims to be justiciable even when the marriage is Muslim and potentially polygamous, the Durban court tried to distinguish the Amod case from the Ryland. The court interpreted the Ryland judgment to mean that only claims arising from the terms of the marriage contract *per se* were justiciable. Insurance claims were outside the terms of a marriage contract. Furthermore, and most importantly, Ryland had not declared the Muslim marriage fully legal *per se*, equal to a marriage under the civil law.

Amod v Multilateral Motor – on appeal

The defendant widow, Hafiz Amod, appealed to the Constitutional Court. That court sent it to the Supreme Court of Appeal on technical grounds,[95] also perhaps because of a congested docket. The reason was that the Constitutional Court hears matters that involve direct application of the Constitution. The Amod case involved rather the application of the common law. The Supreme Court, being more experienced than the Constitutional Court in common law, would be the more appropriate court for deciding how the common law should or should not be developed in a constitutional matter. If the Supreme Court of Appeal failed to develop the common law within a constitutional framework, then the widow could lodge an appeal by direct application of the Constitution.

The case went before the Supreme Court of Appeal.[96] Not surprisingly, the Supreme Court decided to further develop the common law so that the Muslim widow could win her claim. The then Chief Justice Mahomed (presumably of Muslim heritage) had the honour of writing the opinion of the court. He emphasized certain aspects of the Muslim marriage. It was based on a marriage contract, one of the terms of which obliged the husband to support the wife. Secondly, he noted that the marriage was de facto monogamous.

The insurance company argued that South African common law did not allow compensatory claims for loss of support unless the marriage were on a par with a civil de jure monogamous marriage. Only common law marriages, which had to be monogamous, could qualify dependants for an action in loss of support.

In answer to the insurance company, the court looked to the constitutional provision relating to the development of common law. The courts are commanded when developing the common law in South Africa to promote the objects of the Bill of Rights.[97] The court felt compelled to delve into the history of the common law on compensation for loss of support, and to understand its evolution before deciding whether it was necessary to develop it further. The common law limited an action brought for loss of support to those whom the deceased was accustomed to aliment *ex officio*, for example his parents, his widow, his children, all of whom are close family. The word 'accustomed' did not necessarily mean that the supporter was obliged, only that he did in fact support.

Historically South African common law had shown itself capable of developing this principle of a close familiar relationship by extending the action to a husband for the loss of support from the wife, who normally does not support her husband nor is obliged to support him. Up until then, it was thought that only the wife could take advantage of this remedy. The South African courts justified the extension on the grounds that the principle should be adapted to the conditions of modern life, without doing violence to the principle of dependency itself. Later the action was extended to cover the claim of a divorcee, no longer married to the deceased at the time of the accident, but dependent on the alimony payments he had been making to her. In Zimbabwe the action was extended to cover a widow married under African law and custom.[98]

The court then crystallized the principles for determining whether someone qualified for compensation for loss of support: a legally enforceable duty of the deceased to support; a right of the claimant to support that is worthy of legal protection; and finally applying the criterion of *boni mores* to determine what is worthy of legal protection.

The court then asked itself whether the factual evidence satisfied the above principles. It found that the deceased had a legally enforceable duty to support, such duty arising from a marriage contract which was legally enforceable, thanks to the Ryland judgment. Secondly, the court found that the wife's claim for support was worthy of legal protection, as the marriage was public and de facto monogamous. Finally, the court held that *boni mores* makes such a marriage worthy of protection in the same way as it protects a monogamous Christian or civil marriage. The basis of *boni mores* is the post-apartheid Constitution. To hold otherwise would mean that the *boni mores* were based on limiting protection to only one religious kind of marriage, namely Christian. Such a restriction would be discriminatory. Even prior to the Constitution under the apartheid era, the *boni mores* had already changed by virtue of recognition of claims from widows of African customary marriages. It was true that the South African courts had refused the claims of African widows, as in Nasionale v Fondo.[99] But the legislature found the ruling so unfair that it overturned it by enacting §31 of the Black Laws Amendment Act 76 of 1963, so that widows of African marriages could sue for loss of support if the competent government official certified that the claimant widow had actually been married.[100] This modernized legislation, plus the Ryland judgment, provided proof enough of the contemporary *boni mores* for purposes of applying common law.

The court concluded that the common law is to be developed so as to extend to de facto monogamous Muslim marriages the same protection it gives to monogamous Christian marriages. The legislature is free to make a law extending compensation actions to Muslim marriages, just as it did for marriages under African law and custom, but this does not exonerate the courts from developing the existing common law principles and applying them in conformity with the Bill of Rights.

The appellate court did admit that it limited the application of common law to de facto Muslim marriages, and left unresolved whether de facto polygamous Muslim marriages would qualify for the same treatment. The court noted in an *obiter dictum* that the values of equality and religious freedom could be used eventually to resolve the open questions. The resolution may be more problematic than the court foresees. The principle of equality is a double-edged sword: on the one hand, the unequal treatment of African and Muslim de facto polygamous marriages and Muslim de facto monogamous marriages is discriminatory. On the other hand, the inequality between spouses in a de facto polygamous marriage does injustice to the woman, who does not have an equal right to enter polygamous marriages.

Islamic law on support in case of accidental death

The Amod case did not involve interpreting and applying Islamic law *per se*, as the Ryland case had. Nonetheless the case does raise some issues that some Muslims may want to consider from a so-called 'Islamic' point of view when taking out insurance policies or applying for benefits under insurance. This is certainly true for those who consult learned Muslims on how to lead a 'Muslim' life.[101] Under Islamic public law the negligent death of any person, whether responsible for supporting others or not, has been treated as a penal matter as well as a matter of compensation. The relevant Quranic verse is quite clear.[102] If the deceased was a believer (narrowly interpreted as only a Muslim, broadly interpreted as any believer in a monotheistic God), then the penalty was emancipation of a slave and compensation to the survivors. It was not just any slave who should be emancipated – it had to be a believing slave (Muslim or believer in a monotheistic God). If the deceased were a Christian or Hebrew or a person with whom the Muslim community lived peacefully, the same rules applied. If the deceased belonged to a community at war with the community of the negligent perpetrator, then no compensation was due, only the freeing of a believing slave. If the culprit was too poor to afford to free a slave or had no slaves or had insufficient means to pay compensation, then fasting or repentance before God sufficed as the penalty. The rule is not foreign to common law approaches. If the culprit is bankrupt or has no means, then the dependants claiming compensation are left with empty hands. The nature of the compensation in Islamic law was left open – leaving it to the parties to agree on a monetary amount, material support or work time. The category of persons entitled to the compensation was restricted to the 'family' of the deceased. Family was interpreted by jurists as the lawful heirs, not so much dependants as persons who were expected to inherit (Shaheed 66, 182). In the opinion of many jurists, but not all, the amount of the compensation due varied according to whether the deceased person were female or male. It can only be inferred that this was based on the assumption that a woman would not, like a man, have full responsibilities for supporting her family members, only partial responsibility. As for who is responsible for paying the compensation, the Islamic jurists reasoned that the person responsible for the negligent death was directly responsible for paying the compensation, unless waived by the victim's family. If the responsible person were dead, then her/his heirs became responsible. If the victim's family waived compensation, then a court could impose a penal measure. By contrast, under South African law it is the insurance company which is responsible for paying the claim for compensation. If the dependants of the victim do not submit a claim to the insurance company and thereby waive their rights, the government steps in only if the death contravened criminal law and merits a penalty.

The very question of whether such insurance payments conform to Islamic law has been controversial. In general, insurance as practised by many businesses in non-Muslim countries has been held to contravene the Islamic rules against interest (*riba*) (Vogel 1998, 153). On the other hand, *riba* aside, the fund can be regarded for Islamic law purposes as a social necessity. It protects families of accident victims if the perpetrator is indigent and has no means to compensate the surviving families or dependants. This conforms to the *Muwatta*'s hadith that enjoined the creation of a social fund for needy cases. According to the hadith, when a divorcing or deceased husband did not have or did not leave behind sufficient funds to maintain the wife during the *idda*, then the community or state would be responsible for financing her.[103] Alternatives for funds that do not formally charge *riba* are being discussed for Muslims. This issue will be covered in more detail below.

The Amod decision has a certain irony about it. It reaffirmed non-discrimination against Muslim marriages, but raised for Muslims other controversial questions about benefiting from a certain type of insurance. It would be interesting for the Gender Equality Commission to monitor empirically whether the decision in favour of the Muslim widow for loss of support has led to a change in private insurance companies' practices, to the detriment of widows submitting claims, or whether the companies see an opportunity to expand the range of their clientele.

The holdings of the Supreme Court of Appeal in Amod have long-term implications for the future development of Islamic law. The court eliminated discrimination against Muslim de facto monogamous marriages, and treated Muslim marriages on the same footing as any other marriage for purposes of developing the South African common law on compensatory benefits for dependants of road accident victims. These two holdings of the court point in the direction of a universal common law for all family laws and customs in South Africa, similar to the Tunisian and Tanzanian vision. The basic law is the same for all, but the particular customs of any community will be taken into consideration in the application of the universal law. The Amod decision represents from this point of view a difference between the judiciary and the legislature. The latter, by enacting the Recognition of Customary Marriage Act only for African marriages,[104] has set a trend of keeping the marriage laws of cultural communities separate from another. This has permitted discrimination against women because the right to polygamy is granted unilaterally to men.

Recognizing Muslim marriages for inheritance purposes – Daniels v Campbell et al

The Constitutional Court of South Africa has added intestate succession to the areas where the Muslim marriage is recognized, so that a surviving spouse may inherit.[105] Juleiga Daniels had married under Muslim rites in the Cape Town Malay Muslim community under the apartheid regime in 1977. Her husband, Mogamat Amien Daniels, died in 1994. He left four children of another marriage and four grandchildren. Juleiga and her husband lived for their entire marriage in a municipal council house in a low-income suburb. At first Juleiga rented the house in her name. Later, when she married Mogamat, the council transferred the tenancy to his name as the husband, as was customary at the time. Later again in 1990 the couple were given the opportunity by the council to buy the house at a discount. The deed of sale was signed by both spouses, and noted that the couple lived in community of property. Throughout the marriage Juleiga worked as a domestic and sold goods in front of her house to supplement her income. She contributed her earnings to the rent and later the purchase price of the house. When Mogamat died intestate, without leaving a will, his children sought to evict Juleiga and claim the house for themselves as descendants. They argued that she was not a legally married spouse for the purposes of the Intestate Succession Act,[106] which provides that the spouse (gender neutral) will inherit, along with descendants, if any. The term 'spouse' is not defined. Nor was Juleiga, the children alleged, entitled to the benefits of the Maintenance of Surviving Spouse Act,[107] which allows the spouse of a 'marriage dissolved by death' to claim from the estate of the deceased a reasonable amount of maintenance until remarriage or death. The Master of the High Court, which is responsible for administering intestate estates, refused to recognize Juleiga as a spouse of a marriage, because her marriage, as a Muslim marriage, was de jure polygamous, though de facto monogamous. The case had been first decided in the High Court of South Africa (Cape of Good Hope Provincial Division), where Lady Justice Van Heerden had decided that the statutes were unconstitutional in not specifying that a 'spouse' meant a spouse of a civil, customary or religious marriage. On appeal the Constitutional Court decided that in the light of the equality spirit of the Constitution it would be discriminatory not to allow a Muslim widow to be treated the same as any other widow in a monogamous marriage concluded under civil law or customary law. The terms 'spouse' and 'marriage' were not defined in either of the applicable statutes. The courts could define the terms. So Justice Sachs ordered that a phrase should be read into the statutes as though they had included the words: 'and spouse shall include a husband or wife married in accordance with Muslim rites in a de facto monogamous union'.

Daniels – community of property

The Constitutional Court made short shrift of the matter, by simply following the equality and public policy doctrine established in Ryland and carried on in Amod. The High Court, on the other hand, had gone into more detail about the Islamic law aspects of the marriage. It is worth looking more closely at its understanding of Islamic rules, even though the statements made about them were *obiter dicta.* First, the court noted that the tenancy deed specified that the couple lived in community of property, but stated that this could not have been true, as Islamic laws do not recognize community of property. The court relied on the report from the South African Law Commission on Muslim Personal Law. Establishing whether spouses were in community of property is important for the distribution of the estate. It means that only the half of the estate attributed to the deceased spouse would be inherited. That is, the children would share in only one half of the estate, as the other half belonged to the surviving spouse. However, any assets or property which the surviving spouse had brought into the marriage or had received as gifts or inheritance from another relative would be deducted from the estate prior to distribution. Spouses of African customary marriages are now automatically regarded as being in community of property and of profit and loss, as long as they are de facto monogamous. As long as the couple have not reached an antenuptial settlement to the contrary, the courts assume that Muslims automatically have no community of property. If they reach an agreement to have community of property it should be registered.[108]

Interestingly it seems that neither the parties nor the court asked about what was the custom of the Malay community, as Justice Farlam had done in the Ryland case. There was no indication that there might have been custom by which spouses pooled their earnings for the specific purpose of buying a house. The absence of an inquiry about custom might indicate a trend towards universalizing Islamic rules rather than tailoring their interpretation to community customs.

The view of the court that Islamic marriages do not automatically entail community of property should be reviewed more critically. The Quran provides only that each man and each woman is to have a right to his or her own earnings. This means literally that a man and a woman have to keep track of their own earnings. Islamic laws do not automatically impose community of property on spouses. It is left to agreement between the parties. In other words, no community of property is presumed unless shown to the contrary. The agreement is not limited to a particular point in the relationship between the spouses. It does not have to be antenuptial. It can take place at any time during the marriage, or there can be a property settlement agreement after divorce. Tunisia enacted a law that regulates community of property agreements (see chapter on Tunisia above). The legislature found that such agreements are not contrary to Islamic law, as the spirit of Islamic law in general stresses freedom of contract over status. However, it could be argued that a contract cannot be made to cover something that is already explicit in the Quran. The Quranic verse provides that the woman keeps what she earns and the man keeps what he earns. This can be read in two ways. One is that neither the woman nor the man can agree to give the other blanket permission to own 50 per cent of the other's earnings. A second way is that each is to keep his or her earnings unless they decide otherwise.

As for each woman and each man being responsible for their own debts, there is no explicit verse governing this point, but the verse on earnings implies that each remains responsible for their own debts unless otherwise agreed.

Daniels – gift or bequest?

Apart from the community of property issue there are two other issues that arose, but were not dealt with by the courts. One relates to the possibility of a gift, and the other to the possibility of a bequest.

Mrs Daniels had asserted that her husband had *given* her the house. It is not clear from the judgment whether she was claiming a gift. A gift in Islamic laws takes effect only if there is delivery. It appears that there was no delivery of the deed to Juleiga. On the contrary, it stayed in the name of her husband. The High Court noted that statutory law does not recognize oral deeding of property. The transfer has to be in writing.

Alternatively the High Court could have also interpreted Mr Daniel's words as constituting an oral testament to the effect that his wife should inherit the house. In this instance, the wife could attempt to claim up to one-third of the children's half of the estate, as a Muslim testator may not bequeath more than one-third (leaving aside disagreement among the jurists about whether a bequest to a relative had to be approved by the other heirs).

Daniels – maintenance of a widow

As for Mrs Daniels claiming maintenance from the estate, this could have been cause for future litigation. The Islamic law expert (Shouket Allie) had testified that an Islamic marriage contract did not allow a widow to claim maintenance support until remarriage or death. She was entitled only to her inheritance share of one-eighth of the estate. From the two court judgments, it is not clear whether the expert spoke to the point that the surviving spouse can claim maintenance during the three-month waiting period. Unlike a divorced woman, who might claim a post-divorce gift, as according to some jurists in Egypt, this would meet her needs to survive, Juleiga would not have claim on any such gift upon termination of her marriage by death. A widow is allowed to claim only debts that her husband may have owed her, her unpaid marriage dower, if there were any, and her contributions to the wealth of her husband. In case of the latter, then her contributions to the rental and later purchase of the house would be claimable.

In support of her claim for maintenance from the estate of the deceased spouse, Mrs Daniels could have cited a hadith in which the Prophet's wife Aisha refused to allow any relatives of the Prophet to share his personal estate because she said he wanted his wives to be maintained from what he left.[109]

Daniels – estate distribution

As for the ultimate distribution of the estate, the trial and constitutional courts gave the impression that the Islamic rules would not be applied. The statutory provisions would instead govern the estate. If it were found as a matter of fact that Mr and Mrs Daniels were living out of community of property, then Juleiga would be entitled to a child's share in the entire estate. If it were found for a fact that Mr and Mrs Daniels had agreed on community of property, then Juleiga would be entitled to one half of the house. The other half she would have to share with her step-children and grandchildren: her share would amount to a child's share. In other words, nine persons would have an equal share in one half of the house. This one half could be reduced, however, by the contributions that Mrs Daniels had made to help her husband finance the house. From a practical point of view, the trial court believed that it was impossible on the facts to determine exactly how much the wife had contributed and how much the husband had contributed. The Tanzanian courts have had great experience in trying to disentangle spousal contributions, even though they complain in some cases of the great difficulties and sometimes clamour for an automatic presumption of 50-50 ownership. The South African courts may well wish to examine the case law from Tanzania, even for Muslim couples.

Extra-judicial practices in South African Muslim communities

The Ryland, Amod and Daniels judgments all set precedents for the judicial recognition at least of de facto monogamous Muslim marriages for purposes of resolving matrimonial disputes and for compensation for the death of a Muslim spouse. The issue of the recognition of de facto polygamous Muslim marriages remains unresolved and is still being debated. The debate can be seen as part of the larger question of whether Islamic laws have a place in the South African legal system comparable to that of any other religious law, such as Judaic law or any other cultural and community law, for instance African laws and customs. The merits of the various positions taken on this issue I believe can be best analysed contextually, that is, within the framework of the extra-judicial practices of the Muslim communities. Hence this section is devoted to examples of practical problems that face some of the leading authorities of the Muslim communities when applying their understanding of the principles of Islamic laws. First, family practices affecting marriage and divorce will be discussed in respect of the Cape then the Durban areas. The succession and inheritance practices in both shall be analysed.

Family law: marriage contracts

The lack of full judicial recognition of Muslim marriages in South Africa has meant that the Islamic rules as practised are the result of Muslim communities' own interpretation and application of the Sharia under the social and political circumstances peculiar to South Africa.

The Ryland judgment brought the importance of marriage contracts to the attention of the entire Muslim community in South Africa. The contract which was the subject of the litigation was not an explicit one. The court dealt with the implied terms. The immediate impact of the Ryland judgment was to encourage some couples to reflect consciously on the terms of their marriage contract.

The issue was raised in the Muslim newspaper *Al Qalam* (Durban), which is published by the Muslim Youth Movement of South Africa.[110] The movement is known for its open-mindedness. Five months after the Ryland judgment, *Al Qalam* interviewed (in January 1997) three recently married couples.[111] One couple had decided to marry under the civil law. The two others took pains to negotiate a contract containing terms other than those recommended by the religious leaders present at their religious marriage ceremony. The conscious conclusion of a marriage contract has certain advantages for the courts. Such a contract would allow South African courts in the future to raise questions of intention of the parties in case of ambiguity rather than relying strictly on implied terms of Islamic rules in a marriage contract.

Standard marriage contracts in the Cape Muslim communities

The Cape Muslim community is the largest in South Africa (Mahida 59). Hence it is appropriate to start with this community. In the Cape the standard marriage contract originally drawn up by the local imam is the norm. A typical example is one drafted by the imam of the Islamia College in Cape Town, who ironically enough served as the expert witness for the husband in the Ryland case, where there was no explicit contract.[112] He is a celebrant of Muslim marriages as well as an arbitrator in matrimonial disputes, and also issues *fatwas*.

The standard contract he offers contains a one-page explanation of the general features of a Muslim marriage.[113] The explanation emphasizes that a written contract drawn up prior to the marriage is an antenuptial contract and is to be seen as an 'essential act of prudence'. Explicit reference is made to the right of the bride to demand such a contract.

The negotiable nature of the contract is also stressed. Each party is to stipulate her and his wishes and needs. The minimum issues to be negotiated are four:

financial security;
dispute resolution;
acceptable and unacceptable behaviour during the marriage;
acquisition by the wife of the right to dissolve the marriage.

Guardianship of children has obviously been left out because the South African statute law on custody and guardianship of minor children is universal to all cultural and religious groups. The main determining principle is the interests of the child.

Who negotiates marriage contracts?

It is the experience of the imam[114] that nearly all women in his community want written contracts. In practice, however, the women do not always get their way – it is not just the bride and groom who negotiate. The parents too are given copies of the standard contract to study and negotiate its terms. While the spouses themselves must sign the contract once negotiated, parents are encouraged to sign as witnesses. In the event that there is a breakdown of the marriage, the parents serve as witnesses if there is a dispute about the terms of the contract.

If parents object to a marriage, their protest is overcome by elopement. If the prospective bride is or becomes pregnant, and the prospective husband is keen to continue the relationship, then the family of the bride tries to re-enter the picture to negotiate the terms of the marriage contract. The pregnancy gives them more leverage.

Marriage dower

As for the marriage dower (*mahr*), the standard contract suggests a gift of a copy of the Quran and one Krugerrand. This represents about 1,800 rands (*circa* USD 300). It is to be paid at the time of the solemnization of the marriage.

The standard contract also includes a section on a deferred dower. This is to consist of 'a suitable house in a suitable area'. This means that on divorce, the wife would have a claim against the husband for a suitable house. This provision has several implications. If the husband has registered the marital home in his name and not the wife's, then the wife could try to enforce a lien on the home in the form of her dower debt. If this were refused by the South African courts, then the implied term of the marriage contract is that the husband would provide funds to the divorced wife to buy a suitable house.

This provision is similar to that favoured by the classical Hanbali school of Islamic laws. It takes the position that the wife may stipulate in her marriage contract that the husband never expel her from her house (Spectorsky 1993, 67, s. 51), assuming that the house belongs to her in full or even in part. This contractual term is quite practical when compared with customary practices in southern Tunisia and the present law on lodging in Egypt. In southern Tunisia the father of the bride tends to negotiate a high enough dower to invest in a house in the name of his daughter. In Egypt, provision of lodging after divorce has not been treated in constitutional court case law as an implied customary term of the marriage contract. It is treated as a matter of compromise between two rights. On the one hand it is treated as a matter of maintenance during the *idda* waiting period after divorce for three menstrual cycles, or the length of a pregnancy. On the other hand it is treated as a matter of equity towards the husband, in whose name the marital home is often registered. A third consideration is social welfare. Consequently, if the ex-wife as mother of the children of the marriage has no means to move out of the conjugal home with the children, then the ex-husband as father of the children is to provide suitable alternative accommodation.

For South African jurisprudence, in the light of the Ryland judgment, the issue of a suitable house as part of the deferred dower owed to the wife upon divorce is of great import for future jurisprudence. As the Ryland judgment is based on the implied terms of a marriage contract, it could be argued that one of the implied terms of a Muslim marriage contract in the Cape is granting the deferred dower in the form of a suitable house.

Marital behaviour

The standard contract lays down two terms relating to 'matrimonial bliss'.

Matrimonial bliss is not elaborately defined. It refers to a commitment to 'higher values' of marriage. This is understood in practice as loyalty and no adulterous affairs. Marital bliss also includes spiritual, emotional and sexual fulfilment. This confers on the wife a right to sexual fulfilment in a marriage; otherwise she is entitled, according to the standard contract, to a divorce.

In practice if the wife is unhappy in the marriage, a divorce does not necessarily take place. First, an effort is made to renegotiate the antenuptial contract or negotiate a new post-nuptial contract. This happens especially when the husband has committed adultery. The wife is deemed to have a claim to divorce. The adulterous husband in the Cape is said to be open to negotiating a post-nuptial marriage contract as the price for holding the marriage together. There is a difference, however, as the imam has observed, between the wealthier Indian Muslim community and the lower-income Malay Muslim community. Women with wealthier husbands are prepared to tolerate their husbands' escapades in exchange for more financial security set out in a post-nuptial contract, while women with husbands having less well-lined pockets tend to seek divorce rather than renegotiate the contract.

As pointed out by the imam, under certain versions of orthodox Islamic laws, if the adultery of the husband had been proved, he would have been subject to the death penalty. Most likely it would not have been proved because of the impossibly high witnessing standards of four witnesses to the intercourse. In that case the wife would have the chance to take an oath of accusation.[115] In a divorce proceeding, she could use the oath as evidence of the hardship she would suffer if she were to stay in the marriage.

Polygamy

While adultery may be tolerated in some circles in the Cape, polygamy is hardly tolerated in practice. It is grounds for divorce. Despite the general intolerance of polygamy, the standard Cape contract confers on the husband a formal right to polygamy, conditional on the harmonious coexistence of the wives. The first wife receives the option to divorce in case of polygamy, but the exercise of this right is hedged by the condition that the wives are completely incompatible. Who has to bear the burden of proof of incompatibility in the divorce proceedings is not specified.

Thus the Quranic condition that the polygamous husband acts justly by loving all his wives equally is reflected in the standard contract because he has to assure harmony among his wives. At the same time it adopts the minimalist view of the Hanbali school of law, which allows a wife to divorce her husband if he marries polygamously. The contract does not adopt the prohibitive Tunisian view, which stresses the Quranic pronouncement that a man can never do justice to a woman and so for that reason the marriage will not be polygamous.[116]

It will be left to the negotiating parties themselves to decide whether they wish to modify the polygamous clause in the standard contract. This may depend on whether they make themselves familiar with the various classical jurists' arguments about polygamy clauses in marriage contracts. They could start with the Hanbali view that a polygamy clause does not affect the essence of a marriage (Coulson 1991, 190; Bellefonds II:90–1). A non-polygamous marriage is no less a marriage than a polygamous one. The classical arguments have not been so much about whether polygamy is an absolute right of every man or an obligation on every man to marry widows with children after a war that has decimated the male population. The arguments have rather assumed that each man will decide for himself whether polygamy is a right or an obligation. Instead, the jurists seemed more preoccupied with finding answers to specific situations rather than with principle, since several hadiths show that polygamy was hotly debated (Ahmed 66, 99; Goeje). There seems to have developed a practice of second wives insisting in the marriage contract that the husband divorce the first wife in order to assure monogamy. This clause was deemed inequitable and unenforceable. The most the second wife could demand was that she have the option to divorce. What is not mentioned is the case of the husband who keeps his various marriages secret from the wives. If a husband who is already married enters into a second marriage contract without telling the second wife, who has insisted on a monogamous clause, problems relating to a secret marriage (*nikah al-sirr*) arise (Rapoport 2002, 185–8). If the husband were to fulfil his second marriage contract, he would have to divorce the first wife, which would be unfair to her. The only way out of this dilemma was to allow each wife the right to exercise an option to divorce in the event that she discovered she was a co-wife. In effect, using the divorce clause as the way to handle polygamy represented a compromise. It triumphed over the principle of contractual freedom whereby the parties would have organized their sexual life as they liked, including banning polygamy.

If today's jurists were to treat polygamy as a right, then the husband could explicitly agree not to exercise this right, just as an heir can voluntarily forego her/his prescribed share of inheritance. If polygamy were treated as an obligation, then a contract could still specify the conditions under which that obligation would be exercised, such as in the aftermath of war, during drastic shortages of men in the local population, limiting marriage to widows with children.

Financial security

The standard marriage contract offered in the Western Cape regulates the material contributions which each spouse brings into a marriage. Gifts to any one of the spouses remain the property of that individual spouse. The contract is silent on gifts made to both spouses. Presumably, the gift would belong to each on a 50-50 basis.

As for contributions – whether monetary or in kind – made by each spouse that increase or save the assets, possessions or properties of the other, the value of that contribution is assigned and attributed to the contributing spouse. In cases of uncertainty, equity (fairness) shall be the determining factor.

The imam has observed a difference between the Indian and Malay communities on the point of finances. The Indian families tend to insist on more financial security for the bride in case of divorce. The Malay couples tend to emphasize the right of the wife to maintain control over the assets which she brings into and acquires during the marriage.

Community of property

Accompanying the standard marriage contract is a separate agreement on community of property. It specifically provides for no community of property. Each spouse is to retain and possess all assets as though the marriage had not taken place. Each is accordingly not responsible for the debts of the other contracted before or after the marriage. All inheritance portions, legacies, gifts or bequests also remain the exclusive property of the receiving spouse. There is to be no community of profit or loss between the spouses. Each retains all profits accruing to herself or himself during the marriage.

This agreement to exclude community of property conforms to the basic Islamic principle – to each spouse her or his own earnings[117] and debts. It has been the pride of Islamic jurists that Islamic law had from the start recognized the married woman's right to own property in her own name at a time when the Christianized European laws made the husband automatically trustee of the wife's property. The general aversion to community of property can be attributed also to problems of debt, especially in tenant-farm communities or trading and commercial communities. Under the community of property scheme, the debts incurred by a husband would consume the contributions which the wife had also made to his finances and she would have nothing from her earnings. Likewise, a businesswoman who had incurred debts could have consumed the earnings of her husband.

Nonetheless there is no rule which prevents spouses from entering a contract governing their property relations during the marriage. Whether the contract is valid or not depends on the legal nature of the transfer of properties and assets. If the transfer takes the form of a gift, then the disposition is valid only upon actual delivery. A future right that has not yet accrued cannot be given away (Coulson 1971, 222). If the transfer is of a contractual nature, then the object of the consideration has to be specified. This may constitute specific services that a spouse is to render to the other. Or if a spouse receives a benefit from the property belonging to the other spouse, then the benefiting spouse has to pay the other spouse or confer an equivalent benefit.

An alternative arrangement would be an agreement between the spouses amounting to a partnership agreement, in which one spouse agrees to contribute a certain sum specifically destined to pay for the debts of the other.

One kind of debt that would not be subject to a partnership agreement would be the *mahr*, the marriage gift. That is the sole obligation of the husband: the wife has no equivalent obligation. The *mahr* is not just a prenuptial engagement gift, but an essential element of the marriage, in so far as, even when the amount has not been specified, a wife may always claim the amount that is customary for her status and region (*mahr al mithl*). The dower belongs in law to the wife. She may claim it at any time though in practice, she receives a part at the marriage ceremony and may claim the remainder upon termination of the marriage by divorce or death of the husband. This means that if the spouses wanted to enter into an agreement in favour of community of property, the dower would have to be expressly exempted, or the wife may specify that she has consciously renounced her right to it.[118] This is not a problem in urbanized Tunisia, where the law expressly permits spouses to opt for community of property. Urbanized Tunisians pay a symbolic one dinar for the dower. In the Cape community by contrast, the customary dower of *circa* 1,800 rands, paid at the marriage ceremony, represents a sizable sum for the working classes, and even more so if a deferred dower consists of a suitable house.

Right of the wife to education and to leave the marital home

The exemplary Cape marriage contract provides for rights relating to the development of a spouse's own personality. For example, each spouse grants to the other the right to pursue higher education, whether in the home country or abroad. In one instance known to the imam, a bride added the specific condition that her husband take her within a year of the marriage to Malaysia to study.

The decision on the location of the marital home is not left to the husband, but is to be taken mutually.

The wife's right to work – whether voluntarily or for a salary – is conditional on her work promoting the welfare of the community. If that provision is construed widely, then normal contractual employment or self-employment would be included, because employment contributes to the economic welfare of the community in general.

Right of the wife to travel

The exemplary Cape contract confers this right unconditionally on the wife, yet limits it to the criterion of reasonableness. She may travel when and where she wishes as long as her reason for travelling is acceptable and occasional. No stipulation is made in regard to travel necessitated by her profession, which could be frequent. She is not to travel, however, alone, but is to be accompanied by a male relative. This relationship must be such as would render him ineligible for marriage with her. The husband's right to travel is not restricted, not even in terms of whether its frequency would be detrimental to the welfare of the family. No rule in the Islamic laws would make such a provision illegal, though the spirit of inequality would disqualify the differentiation made in the exemplary marriage contract.

Maintenance during the marriage

There is no provision in the Cape marriage contract relating to the wife contributing to the maintenance of the family, even if she has the means. Such a provision would, however, be permitted. On the issue of maintenance duties, there does not appear to be much flexibility among the learned ulama in the Cape. The husband is regarded as the sole provider, and he alone is obliged to pay maintenance. The wife is totally exempt from contributing to maintenance of the family.

This restrictive approach is contrary to the interpretation that the Tunisian legislature has adopted. The Tunisian position is based on various hadiths on maintenance and charity, whereby a wife who has means is to contribute to the maintenance of the family. These hadiths reinforce the Quranic verses conferring on spouses reciprocal duties. In one sura, revealed to a community weakened after a near defeat in the defence of Medina (Uhud), men were reminded that they were to stand by women in time of need, morally and materially.[119] The suffering of both women and men in supporting the Prophet's cause was acknowledged without gender differentiation.[120] In another sura, revealed later when the Muslim community was strong, men and women were enjoined to engage in reciprocal protection (*awliyya*).[121] Whoever does good works, whether woman or man, is rewarded.[122]

The Tunisian interpretation has important implications for succession law and for patriarchal attitudes in families. The general rule that has developed in Islamic succession law is that the son takes twice the share of the daughter because the son has more obligations, such as maintenance, which the daughter supposedly does not have. This interpretation has strengthened the patriarchal family structure (Bouraoui). When the wife, as in Tunisia, has the obligation to maintain the family, this gives her a status of equality (Seife) *vis-à-vis* the man not only in terms of rights, but also obligations. Succession in Muslim communities in South Africa will be discussed below in more detail.

Even if some South African Cape ulama prefer an interpretation of the maintenance obligation as one-sided and non-mutual, it still remains open to individual couples to enter into contractual agreements that divide the duty of maintenance between them, or exempts one of them from that duty under specified conditions.

Divorce – by delegated talaq or for specified reasons

An important provision in the Cape exemplary contract covers various conditions of divorce. As a prelude to divorce, an attempt to reconcile 'the unfortunate event of a breakdown in the marriage' is required. For three months the parties are to enter a reconciliation process. Who is to lead this reconciliation process is not specified; this is left to the circumstances and persons available at the time.

The reconciliation provision has certain implications for the husband who seeks to issue a *talaq*. Because he is under a contractual obligation to enter reconciliation for three months, his pronouncement of an irrevocable *talaq* before the three months are over would be ineffective. In other words, three *talaq*s issued in one sitting would not have the force of a final divorce. Only after the three months of reconciliation can the husband start the process of divorce by *talaq*. That process according to the Quran lasts over at least three periods of menstrual purity.[123]

The bride's right to divorce is both general and specific. First, she is given a general delegation of *talaq*, which she may use for any reason and at any time, just like her husband. Presumably her exercise of this power would be subject to the same restrictions of reconciliation. Specifically she is also given a right to divorce for certain reasons: in the event of her husband's polygamy, and in that of violation of any stipulations in the marriage contract.

Neither spouse is required to ask an extra-judicial Muslim body, e.g. the Muslim Judicial Council, to sanction the wife's or the husband's pronouncement of divorce.

Unlike the practice in Egypt (prior to 2000, when a new law was introduced), the exemplary Cape marriage contract does not tie the delegation to the wife of the power of *talaq* to certain conditions. The wife is not obliged to compensate the husband or confer on him any financial advantages. The absence of such a condition conforms to the spirit of the Quranic verse which warns husbands against using their divorce powers to irritate their wives.[124]

From the point of view of contractual law, each spouse is free, however, to link the exercise of *talaq*, whether delegated or not, to certain conditions. The wife, for example, could insist on a clause which makes the husband's exercise of *talaq* conditional on his granting her financial favours should the divorce put her at a financial disadvantage, and her chances of remarriage be seen as slim.

Khula *divorce*

The exemplary contract does not say anything about a *khula* divorce. In practice, however, the wife's right to *khula* is recognized in the Cape.[125] The purpose of it and the conditions under which it is to be exercised are debatable. It is well known that *khula* as such is not expressly mentioned in the Quran, only indirectly in the verse which allows an exception to the rule that the husband is not to demand the return of the dower upon divorce,[126] contrary to what is allowed under African laws and customs. *Khula* is thus interpreted by some of the Cape ulama as a right of the wife, but dependent on the financial disposition of the husband. If he would have issued a *talaq* – either at his own wish or at the wish of the wife – but in fact does not do so simply for the reason that he does not want to, or cannot pay, or cannot pay the deferred dower, then divorce by *khula* is to take place. This has been called an 'invention' (innovation) – or an equitable interpretation, to put it more positively – of the learned jurists to relieve a wife from a stingy or an impoverished husband. Once she forgives or waives the debt of the deferred dower, then the husband is to issue a *talaq*. Under this interpretation, the right to *khula* is not regarded as an absolute right of the wife, equal to that of the husband's *talaq*, and to be exercised whenever she wishes a divorce, regardless of whether her husband would have divorced her or not by *talaq* but for fear of the financial consequences. The *khula* is made a conditional right.

Certainly the various hadiths on *khula* indicate that this was subject to a variety of opinions, the interpretation of which depends on the basic principle from which one starts: if with the premise of Islamic law that spouses are to have equal bargaining power,[127] then *khula* would be considered the wife's equivalent of *talaq*. Just as a husband using *talaq* incurs certain financial losses, so does the wife when she chooses to use *khula*.

Post-divorce alimony

As in the case of *khula*, alimony payments by the husband, called *mutaa* (the consolatory gift), are not regulated in the exemplary contract. This is probably because the deferred dower proposed in the contract is equivalent to a large sum, namely a suitable house. Nonetheless in practice in the Cape, the *mutaa* is paid.[128] The usual amount is analogous to that owed in cases of divorce in non-consummated marriages: half of the average customary *mahr*, if no *mahr* was paid, or half of the *mahr* that was actually paid.

The practice sets even further conditions on the payment of the *mutaa*. Its payment is conditional, being paid when the husband has been at fault in the breakdown of the marriage. The burden of proof rests on the woman claiming the *mutaa*. The fault of the husband is easy to prove when he has left for another woman, but if this is not the case, then it is difficult for the wife to prove his fault. Because of this difficulty of proof, a particular kind of *mutaa* is granted in the Cape. It is a gift that is conferred on the wife in recognition of her indirect services to maintaining the family. Since a wife is exempt from having direct responsibility for the material maintenance of the family, the gift awarded is a consolatory compensation for having relieved the husband in part of his non-material family duties.

By way of comparison, the Quran does not, nor do the hadiths, specify that *mutaa* is to be conditional on who was responsible for the breakdown of the marriage. It can be inferred from these sources that it is an unconditional payment. This inference is reinforced when we perceive *mutaa* and *khula* as two sides of the same coin. *Mutaa* has been usually seen as a consolatory gift to women from the husbands who issue *talaq*. Women who exercise a right to divorce by *khula* also give consolatory gifts to their husbands by cancelling all debts which their husband might have owed them. Fault does not play a role. Thus if *mutaa* is decoupled from fault, as in the case of cancelling debts as part of *khula*, then the balance of power between the spouses is maintained.

Post-divorce claim by the wife on her contributions to the husband's wealth

The exemplary Cape marriage contract regulates the contributions made by each spouse (exclusive of the obligatory maintenance payments by the husband). Contribution means one spouse gives something (presumably funds) that helps the other spouse acquire, save or increase property or possessions. The value of any contribution is to be assessed in a fair way and not underestimated. Rules and practices in the Cape community observed by the imam vary according to the social class to which the woman belongs. In the merchant class, often a woman works for the family business. She is entitled upon divorce to a salary for the years she worked. Among the working class, a wife is entitled to keep her salary for herself. If she has been made redundant and does the household work at home, then the husband is to pay her what she had been earning. Also a working-class woman is to be paid for services rendered in the house if she has no servant. The latter opinion is based on the view of several old juridical opinions that a wife is entitled to a servant as part of her maintenance claims.

While a divorced wife is entitled to make these claims before the extra-judicial body of Muslim arbitrators, such as the Muslim Judicial Council in Cape Town, the iman has observed in practice that it is expected that she not stubbornly insist on these rights, but be prepared to enter negotiations and compromise as part of the divorce-settlement process.

It was unfortunate in the Ryland case that the court found no evidence of a practice in the Cape community allowing women to claim contributions to the marital assets and wealth of their husbands. Nor did the court have the benefit of a variety of Islamic law opinions on women's rights to claim a share in the marital assets. For example, Iranian law allows divorced women to claim their contributions to the wealth of the husband (Jones 1996, 324, n. 7). Even the expert witness of the husband in the Ryland case had concluded in his MA thesis that a claim to contributions to the marital wealth can be based not only on habitual practices (*adah (adat)*, *urf*), but also on the social needs of the community (Moosagie 52). It seems that the court had not questioned him on this point.

Extra-judicial interpretations in the Asian Muslim communities of Islamic marriage and divorce law

The Asian Muslim community, especially in Natal has produced highly qualified lawyers, trained in South African law as well as in Islamic law at Islamic centres in India (Deoband) or Pakistan (Darul Uloom). They are practitioners as well as scholars, and have published on Islamic law, drawing on orthodox texts and actual practices in South Africa. The practices reflect either cases brought before the *shurta*, or Muslim Judicial Council, and personal contracts and agreements drawn up by Muslim lawyers for their clients.

The views of some of these practitioners will be cited here in order to compare them with Cape Town. The main source of reference is a handbook published in Durban (Omar 1993).[129]

Madhab *(school of law) issues*

The first difference between the Western Cape and the Natal region lies in the *madhab* used as a point of reference. The Islamic experts in the Ryland case both agreed that the Shafii school of law applied because of the Malaysian and Indonesian origins of the Malay Muslim community. It was also agreed that other schools of law could be applied if found to be more compatible with the social circumstances in the Cape. In the Durban area the starting point is the Hanafi school of law, as found in India and Pakistan, but it is also agreed that a choice of *madhabs* is possible when required by modern social circumstances. Evidence has been brought forward to show how even the Hanafi jurists of old showed a preference for other schools of law, particularly when they felt that the Hanafi rules resulted in hardship for women seeking a dissolution of the marriage. This reflects the practice of Hanafi qadis in India sending wives to Shafii qadis in cases of absent husbands who were not paying maintenance (Qureshi 309).

Marriage contracts

As regards marriage contracts, I could not obtain any exemplary contract, unfortunately, for the Durban area. The handbook on Islamic law does not deal with this subject. In principle it would seem that the exemplary marriage contract for the Cape would be equally valid in the Durban area.

Concepts of divorce

The Durban handbook regards divorce basically as a unilateral right of the husband (*talaq*). This privilege is also safeguarded by its extra-judicial nature. The wife, on the other hand, has no right to divorce *per se*, only a right to have the marriage dissolved. This is not an extra-judicial dissolution at her behest, but requires a hearing before a judicial body. Her wish for divorce may be granted only if she proves certain circumstances.

It is curious that the handbook does not dwell much on restrictions on *talaq*. The word *talaq* as used in the Quran and in the hadiths refers to seemingly unlimited power wielded by the husband in pre-Islamic times to dissolve the marriage. Islam came to circumscribe this power by laying down certain conditions, e.g. it can be pronounced only when the wife is not having her menses, it has to be pronounced over three menstrual periods, and the husband must pay whatever he owes on the dower plus a consolatory gift. The later approval of an 'instant *talaq*' (*talaq al bidaa*) (Moosa, N. 119), which the Sunni allowed a husband to cut corners and pronounce it in one sitting, is not analysed. The *talaq* in one sitting was highly controversial among the medieval jurists. The Hanbali jurist Ibn

Taimiyya – one of the greatest minds, who had been taught hadith by a woman, Zainab bint Makki, in Damascus – railed in 718/1318 against the innovative *talaq* as detrimental to women, but the Shafii jurist al Subki defended it as a means of unburdening those men and women caught in compromising circumstances (Rapoport 2002, 218–37). Islam did not confer on the wife this ancient pre-Islamic power to pronounce *talaq*, but it did give her a right to walk out of the marriage by way of *khula*. She could return her dower, forgive any further debts her husband owed her, and leave (see chapter on Egypt above). Whether *talaq* should be used as a term for divorce in general is therefore doubtful. A more generic term would be *shiqaq*, meaning a breakdown of the marital relationship, or a breach of the limits of God.[130] Alternatively one could adopt the approach taken in a Bukhari hadith, which used two separate words for divorce, depending on which spouse wanted to leave the marriage. *Talaq* would be used if the husband wanted termination and *shiqaq* would be used if the wife wanted termination.[131]

Women's right to divorce

Rather than discussing the academic debates on restricting the exercise of *talaq* or the widening of the possibilities of *khula* (Qureshi), [132] the Durban handbook emphasizes what tends to happen in the daily lives of women. It serves to guide the communal decision-making bodies about the rights of women who come to ask for a dissolution of their marriage when the husband does not exercise *talaq*. It is to remind these bodies that the Hanafi law has liberalized itself. Of the four Sunni *madhab*s it had restricted the right of the wife to have a marriage dissolved so much that it was practically impossible for her to leave, similar to the old Mosaic tradition which ties women's hands. The handbook points out that the Hanafi jurists came to adopt the Maliki or Shafii positions.

The basic grounds for which a wife is said to be able to have her marriage dissolved are as follows:

when the husband is missing and has left nothing behind for maintenance;
when he is absent from home, but has breached the duty to maintain;
when he breaches his duty to maintain either due to inability or refusal;
when he breaches his duty to have sexual intercourse with his wife;

when he is castrated;
when he is impotent;
when he is insane;
when he has a disease dangerous to the wife;
when he is cruel to his wife (beating, assaulting).

The burden of proof lies on the wife. In most instances she has to wait a while and give the husband a chance to correct his ways, e.g. an insane husband has to have undergone treatment for one year before the wife may petition. Otherwise, the wife may get immediate dissolution in the case of a castrated or missing husband if she can show that she has no maintenance and would be tempted to have an extra-marital affair. This affects particularly younger wives of older polygamous men.

Lack of equal social and economic status between the spouses is not named as a ground for terminating or annulling the marriage, as once allowed among Hanafi jurists, especially who were accustomed to a more pluralistic and open society than the Medinans (Coulson 1991, 49, 94).

The exact extent to which *khula* is practised in the Durban area has still to be examined. Indications are, however, that if a wife followed the example of Rubayyi, daughter of Muawwidh,[133] who simply left her husband, paid back the dower then informed Umar about this. He required her to undergo only one period of *idda* – thus unilaterally divorcing herself by *khula*. She would still be required to undergo scrutiny by the Muslim dispute-settlement councils in the Durban area before she could remarry.

The assumption in the handbook is that women may not exercise extra-judicial divorce, so that even a woman seeking a *khula* divorce must go before an adjudicating body, while a husband exercising *talaq* need not. This opinion is not based on the principles of equality as evidenced in the Quran and the hadiths. If we interpret the Quranic verses regarding who is to handle disputes between spouses, along with the hadiths on women exercising *khula* by simply returning the dower and walking away in the spirit of equality, we see another divorce pattern emerging. Islam gave each marriage partner her/his own form of divorce. Both have in their own hands the means to an extra-judicial divorce. The husband has the *talaq*, the wife has the *khula*. Each form of divorce has financial consequences. If the husband exercises *talaq*, he is liable to pay the deferred dower and a *mutaa* consolatory gift. If the wife exercises *khula*, she is liable to returning the dower and waiving the debt of a deferred dower or other debts. If either party wants to avoid these financial burdens, then the court, representing the community, offers a last resort out of the deadlock. According to the Quran the community is to use arbitrators to try to get the parties to agree, either to stay married, or to reach an agreement about the conditions of the dissolution of the marriage. From a commonsense point of view, this arbitration process is particularly needed when neither spouse can or wants to bear the financial consequences of a marital breakdown.[134] The long-standing practice in Egypt of treating divorce as a long process of arbitration and negotiation between the quarrelling spouses to reach a financial settlement bears this argument out.

Thus the Islamic scheme of divorce has essentially three pillars. The adjudicated or arbitrated decision is only one of them. The other two pillars are *talaq* and *khula* as extra-judicial forms of divorce.

Certainly the Durban handbook is rooted in the social reality of the Muslim communities and is designed to protect women, who are regarded as being economically more vulnerable than men. A divorce by the communal adjudicating body offers a woman certain advantages over an extra-judicial *khula*, at least according to the Maliki school. If a woman were unhappy in her marriage for reasons caused by her husband, and thought *khula* was the only and most efficient way out of the marriage, she would be out of pocket, since she had to return the dower. If later she discovered that she actually could have gone to court to get a divorce because of her husband's wrongs, then she was entitled, under Maliki rules, to claim back the dower she had returned (Bellefonds II:434–5). The advantage can today, of course, be relative. If it costs the wife more time and money to prove her case before an adjudicating body than the value of the dower she would have to return, then the court would offer no particular advantage.

Problematic exercise of talaq

The exercise of *talaq* by the husband is often problematic in practice in the Durban area.[135] Husbands have been known to pronounce *talaq* and give their wives the impression that it was irrevocable and thus final. But as soon as the ex-wife finds another husband to marry, the first husband alleges that the *talaq* was in fact revocable. This is especially a problem when the husband has given a conditional *talaq*, e.g. when he says that the next time he beats his wife, she is divorced, and alleges that he intended only a revocable *talaq*. Such problems are solved on a case-by-case basis.

Maintenance during marriage

One interesting statement in the Durban handbook relating to divorce on grounds of lack of maintenance speaks of the wife's waiver of the husband's duty to maintain. It is said that she may receive a court divorce on grounds that her husband is absent and does not maintain her if she has not waived her rights to maintenance. This differs from the more restrictive view in the Cape standard marriage contract, where the right to maintenance cannot be waived. The difference of opinion reflects the differences among the jurists of past ages about wives' ability to maintain themselves in the event of absent husbands. The Shafiis tended not to permit divorce if the wife had enough to maintain herself during her husband's absence (Qureshi 309). Instead of divorcing her husband, she was to claim from him arrears owed to her as a debt. The Hanafis traditionally have never allowed a wife to divorce on grounds of lack of maintenance, irrespective of her inability to maintain herself. She was, however, permitted to waive the maintenance debt, but not in advance of its accruement, only after it had accrued (Meron 304).

Post-divorce alimony

The position taken in Durban is that a divorced woman does not get maintenance or alimony payments beyond the *idda*. The key to this approach is the view that maintenance has a definite meaning in Islamic law. It is *nafaqa*, and the duty of the husband to provide it is restricted to an existing marriage. This is similar to the rules of African customs and laws. Any other payments after divorce cannot be called maintenance. Such payments are made for the limited period of the *idda* or constitute a consolatory gift or benefit called *mutaa*. This conforms to the Hanafi arguments that the legal nature of maintenance is a gift or a debt arising out of a marriage contract. Once that contract ends, there is no legal basis for continuing the maintenance in the form of alimony payments. Thus there was no good reason for distinguishing between a marriage dissolved by death or divorce. If a widow had no claims on post-marriage maintenance, why should a divorcee have claims? (Meron 303).

The hadith cited in the Durban handbook in support of these arguments is the well-known report of the case of Fatima bint Qais. The version in the older Maliki collection of hadiths says that Fatima's husband was away on a trip, during which he divorced her and informed her of the *talaq* through his agent. The divorce was irrevocable and final. He sent no more barley for her maintenance. It is said that she was very angry, and complained to the Prophet. He told her that her husband was legally no longer liable for her maintenance, sending her to spend her *idda* outside her conjugal home. What precise remedy Fatima wanted was not made very clear. She could have been raising three possible claims: one for continued alimony/maintenance after divorce; one for maintenance during the *idda* required after the final divorce; and/or one for the right to stay in the house of her former husband during the *idda* under the same conditions of maintenance as before the divorce. From the Prophet's answer, it can be inferred that she was indeed making all three claims, all of which were denied. From a practical point of view, the Fatima decision prevents the ex-spouses from living in the same house: either the husband has to be absent, as in the case of Fatima, or the divorced husband has to leave the house. The latter case arose when Abd Allah b. Umar divorced his wife in the house of the Prophet's wife, Hafsah. He then avoided the house on the way to the mosque since he found it repugnant to be in the house where a divorcee lived.[136]

Later hadith reports indicate that there was great debate on what Fatima actually wanted, and on the rule to be derived from her case. In the Bukhari version, Aisha is reported to have been upset by what Fatima was telling other women. It seems that Fatima was saying that once divorced irrevocably, a woman is to leave her husband's house and not get any maintenance during her third and last *idda.*[137] Aisha advocated the opposite position, namely that a wife was to stay in the house of her husband and be maintained for the period of all three *idda*s. Only upon expiration of the last *idda* did she have to leave and lose all claims to further maintenance. In the collection of Dawud, Umar too expressed disapproval of what Fatima was saying. Aisha explained that Fatima actually wanted to leave her husband's house because she was alone there, since the Prophet told her that she would be safe at another man's house, which his Companions frequented. Because of these conditions, the Prophet allowed her to leave the house. Apparently Aisha was being kind to Fatima, for other reports said that she was a difficult and arrogant woman, quick to anger, and that no one wanted to keep her during the *idda.*[138] Umar too objected to Fatima's interpretation of what the Prophet said, but on sexist grounds. He felt that she could not be believed as she was a woman.[139] In support of Aisha's position, the Bukhari collection of *talaq* hadiths is prefaced by a citation from the Quranic verses on *talaq*. It is clearly said that the husbands were not to turn out their wives unless they were guilty of sexual imprudence, e.g. as when a divorced wife would bring in her lover or would meet there with another prospective husband. The divorced wives were to live in the same style as before (sura 65:6–7). For pregnant women this period could last until delivery; or if she were breastfeeding, until the child was weaned. For non-pregnant women, it was to last for three menstrual cycles.

The result was varying interpretations by the jurists. Certainly the problem raised is not easy to solve. Fatima's predicament is as difficult today as it was then. The chances for social quarrels were heightened when a divorced woman remained in the house in which her ex-husband brought his new wife. The husband, in order to avoid this problem, would be subject to double financial burdens, for he would have to finance an extra dwelling for the ex-wife during her *idda*. The Maliki and Shafii view was that an irrevocably divorced woman could live in the house of her ex-husband for the duration of the *idda*, but without maintenance. She was allowed to leave the house by day to earn her own living. The Hanafis preferred that she stay in the house in seclusion, and therefore argued that she was entitled to maintenance for however long the *idda* lasted. The Hanbalis followed literally the original report of Fatima bint Qais in the Malik Ibn Anas' *Muwatta*, and the report of Umar avoiding the house of his divorced wife. The Hanbalis solved the problem quite neatly. The nature of the possible claims was divided into various categories. Once irrevocably divorced, an ex-wife had no claims to housing or maintenance for herself, only during the *idda* following the two revocable *talaq*s. But if she were breastfeeding, then she could make claims for suckling wages. If she were pregnant, she had to maintain herself or be maintained by her family (she could not remarry until she had delivered). After the birth she could lay claim to maintenance for the child (Spectorsky 1993, 57). The logical consequence of this for a *khula* divorce, which was automatically irrevocable, was that a woman paid back to her husband not only her *mahr*, or marriage dower, but also had to maintain herself during the ensuing *idda*.

One issue in the debate emerges clearly: that post-alimony payments cannot be expected after the ending of the marriage contract. There is no further contractual basis – unless the parties themselves enter into a charitable contract or a contract of paying for work services.

In practice some Indian families try to negotiate, at the start of the marriage, financial security for their daughters in the event of divorce by insisting that the husband make a settlement of the fruits of revenue-producing properties he might have or acquire on the wife for her lifetime without forfeiture (Qureshi 301–3). This is part of what is known in India as the 'special allowance', over and beyond the minimal maintenance that a husband owes in clothing and food.

Post-divorce gift (mutaa)

The Durban leaders have kept abreast of legal developments in Indian Muslim laws. They disapproved of the judgment in the famous case of Shah Bano decided by the Indian Supreme Court in 1985.[140] The court had to interpret the provisions of a criminal procedure statute which penalized a husband of sufficient means who did not maintain his ex-wife, who had insufficient means to do so. The Indian case law up to that time had interpreted the term 'maintain' to refer to the payment of a deferred dower upon divorce, and to no other kind of payments. In the Shah Bano case the Supreme Court expanded the term 'maintain' to include *mutaa*. The Quran requires a husband to make a 'generous' *mutaa* according to his means. The court interpreted 'generosity' to mean a large enough gift to sustain the ex-wife, if she was incapable of maintaining herself, as was the case with the elderly Shah Bano, who was being divorced after more than 20 years of marriage.

The Supreme Court decision provoked an outcry. Parliament, under pressure from leaders of the Muslim community in India, enacted a new law, The Muslim Women (Protection of Rights on Divorce) Act, 1986. This requires the children and relatives of a hapless divorced woman to maintain her, not her husband. The Egyptian statute on lodging for the divorced wife if she is custodian of the children would not have helped Shah Bano, whose children were already grown. The Tunisian legislation would have been of help, as it allows a court to order reparations in the form of post-divorce payments to the spouse who is not at fault. In Shah Bano's case her husband was clearly at fault. Nor did the Indian law provide, as in Iranian legislation, for the right of the woman to claim from the husband the monetary value of contributions she had made during the marriage for the material benefit of her divorcing husband.

Leaders of the Durban Muslim community supported the solution of the Indian parliament. It was thought unfair to place the burden of maintenance for a divorced woman who cannot earn a living on an ex-husband rather than on her relatives. It is true that from the hadiths on *nafaqa* and *sadaqa* (see the chapter on Tunisia above) it is to be inferred that the pre-Islamic practice of some tribes was that married women were expected to maintain themselves or to look to their own blood relatives for support, especially when the husband had no surplus after supporting himself and his own needy blood relatives. Islam introduced the notion that a married man is also to treat his needy wife as a needy relative, as part of the family, as long as she is married to him. The preference in Durban for the supportive role of the blood family for a divorced woman reflects the cultural importance of the extended family for the Asian community in South Africa. It may also account for the ready acceptance of marriage among cousins of the same family.

The Islamic rules for maintenance of family and for succession embody the idea of the extended family. It is not only the spouse and children who have to be maintained, but also indigent blood relatives. It is not only the nuclear family members who inherit from one another – collaterals too have their portions. Many of the contemporary family-law statutes in Muslim countries have recognized the legality of claims of the extended family.[141] Again, this approach is similar to that of African customs and laws (Jones-Pauly 1998).

Early studies on extended Asian families in the Durban area have indicated the impact that the apartheid regime had on the extended family, and the latter's economic importance. The extended family and the joint family have long Indian traditional roots, but apartheid and urbanization have contributed to its demise. As a valued goal, however, the feelings in favour of the extended family were found to be strongest in the Muslim community in Durban (Schoombee); and the extended family was a positive factor in the economic success of Indians (including Muslims). This success rested on family firms, key to whose ongoing prosperity was the father-son relationship, although in some exceptional instances a daughter or widow rose to positions of control (Jithoo).

When the family was unable to support the divorced wife, it has been the opinion in Durban that the Islamic state – in the case of South Africa, presumably the Muslim community, then the state – has to support her. This conforms to a Maliki hadith according to which the state is ordered to pay when the divorced wife lives in a rented place and the husband cannot continue to pay the rent during her *idda*.[142]

Islamic succession/inheritance practices in South Africa

As mentioned, one of the most serious problems which the non-recognition of Muslim marriages imposes on Muslims relates to inheritance. It was only by way of wills or gifts that the Muslim community was able to escape the harshness of South African case law. In a commercial community like that in Durban, Muslim lawyers gained great experience in drawing up wills, bequests and gifts that would save the family inheritance from being disbursed to persons not interested in the family business or to the state (by escheat).

In Cape Town, wills and testaments tend to be drawn up by ulama. This is common mainly among wealthy Asians, living not only in Cape Town but also in Zimbabwe.[143] Other dispositions of property for distribution after death include *waqf* (religious family or public trusts) and gifts.

The gender distribution among persons wanting to devolve property is fairly evenly divided between women and men. Women tend to be well-off because of inheritance from their blood family. For an unknown reason it appears that there are more women testators in Natal and Transvaal.[144]

Devolving inheritance on children not of the marriage bed

Two problems in particular in the devolvement of property by will or testament arise from the peculiar circumstances of South African Muslim communities. One problem relates to children whose parents are not married at the time of conception. Another problem relates to the devolution of properties or valuables to married women relatives who have entered into a community of property agreement with their husbands under South African civil law.

It is not unusual in the Cape Town community for couples to get married because the woman is already pregnant. Under traditional Islamic rules, a child is recognized as a child of the marriage bed if born six months or more after the parents' marriage. Thus if the child is born less than six months after the marriage,[145] then its filiation with the father can be doubted, and the child would inherit only from the mother. To solve this problem, modern-day fathers have drawn up wills to give a share in their goods to these children. If the parents have not married at all, the fathers draw up deeds of *inter vivos* gifts to the children.

Devolving property on women relatives in community of property

Regarding the second problem of inheritance by women relatives who are married in community of property, an exemplary will as drawn up by an imam in Cape Town makes provision for devolving property on a female relative, with the stipulation that it becomes her exclusive property independent of any community of property agreements made between the recipient and her husband.

Inheritance conflicts between spouses and the extended family

There is a basic conflict between South African statutory inheritance law and Islamic succession laws when it comes to the surviving spouse sharing with the extended family of the deceased. South African law allows the surviving widow or widower to inherit the estate as the sole beneficiary, if the only other heir is a collateral relative of the deceased, while under Islamic laws, the widow would have to share the estate with the collateral relative (Omar 1988, 5). In the face of this conflict, the lawyers tend to advise the relatives to enter into redistribution agreements with the surviving spouse that follow Islamic law. Such agreements can be reached before or after the death of the relative concerned. If they concern landed property, then the agreements must conform to the legal formalities with which lawyers rather than imams are familiar.

Adopted children as non-heirs

Adopted children are another problem for estate planners. Under South African statutory law they may inherit, whereas under Islamic rules, an adopted child does not qualify as an heir *per se*. If the adopted child happens to be a relative, then s/he would inherit in the capacity of that relationship. The problem of adopted children is resolved in the Durban Muslim community by use of a bequest: the adopted child is bequeathed up to one-third of the estate. In the event of the adopted child predeceasing the parent, the bequest devolves on the grandchildren

Dilemmas with regard to succession/inheritance: gender and extended family

Apart from the particular problems noted above, there are elements of Islamic inheritance rules which pose general social dilemmas for members of the Muslim communities. Islamic inheritance rules are characterized essentially by two features: first, gender inequality because the son receives twice the share of the daughter, and the surviving husband twice as much as the surviving wife, with the exception of the grandmother and grandfather, who receive equal shares; and secondly, competition from collateral relatives, such as uncles, who are co-inheritors if the surviving children are daughters; otherwise, a son in general would exclude them. With respect to the latter, there is a clear division of opinion between the Sunni and Shii schools of thought, which affects the interests of women. The Sunnis find that if the deceased has left only daughters, then the collateral relatives may also inherit along with them. If any sons are left, they exclude the collaterals. The Shii find that daughters alone may exclude collaterals. It is well known that this difference of opinion is based on the political problems relating to the succession to the Prophet. The Shii favoured making Fatima, the sole surviving child and daughter of the Prophet, and her husband the heirs, excluding the uncles of the Prophet. The Sunni favoured the uncles (Coulson 1971, 126).

Exercising the Sunni or Shii option

An exemplary will in Cape Town thus provides for testators to exercise an option. The will specifies whether it is intended to be executed under the Sunni or Shii school of thought. The testament is also to specify whether it has been certified by a learned Islamic jurist as being in accord with Islamic rules or not.

Equalizing shares of daughters and sons by way of usufruct

Many parents do not like to make differences between the inheritance shares of their daughters and sons. Two methods most commonly used to achieve equality are the creation of a trust and gifts (*hiba*). A trust is usually created in a will for the minor children. Upon their reaching majority age under Islamic rules (*bulugh* or puberty, that is, 15 years of age), they are entitled to access the trust funds. As it is usually the revenues from a trust which are inherited, the entitlements of the sons and daughters are regarded as usufruct under Islamic rules and therefore to be distributed in equal portions. A similar practice has long existed in East Africa, called *shirika*, where the daughters and sons share equally in the revenues of the property as long as the latter remains undivided (Caplan 44). In the Indian Muslim community in Malawi the testator can confer the property as a whole on the children, specifying that they are to share the revenues equally and leave the capital intact.[146] In certain parts of Jordan, daughters inherited in fact equally but sons were known to buy out sisters (Wahin).

In contrast to these customs and practices, some legal practitioners in Durban who draw up testamentary trusts, whereby the corpus stays intact and only the revenue is distributed, have advised that the revenue has to be divided according to Islamic rules, that is, daughters receive half as much as sons (Omar 1988, 23).

Equalizing inheritance shares by way of gift and debt

When an *inter vivos* gift is made, it must be delivered to the child in order to be valid. The nature and amount of the gift is then listed in the will along with proof that the properties given away had been registered in the name of the testator, that is, it was his/her property to give away in the first place. When the estate opens for succession, the sons will take twice the amount of the daughters, but the daughters will already have been compensated by gifts. A gift *inter vivos* is also used to increase the share of the surviving wife, who would be entitled under Islamic rules to only one-eighth if there are children and one-fourth if no children. The gift usually consists of the marital home. She is given one-half of the house as a gift before the testator dies.

In the Durban area some Islamic experts caution parents against fostering resentment among the children. The parents are advised that when making gifts to their children, they should give in equal amounts. This does not solve the concern of the parents about the daughter inheriting less than the son. So it is advised that when a parent wishes to favour one child over another with a gift *inter vivos*, the reason specified should be for services rendered, for example, to the parents. This position accords also with that of Islamic law experts in some Muslim communities in southern Tanzania. A difference in opinion between Durban and Tanzanian Muslims lies in whether such a donation is obligatory or not. The Durban position is that it is not obligatory, rather it is the voluntary decision of the parent. The southern Tanzanian position is that it transforms into an obligation under certain circumstances. If the gift for services is made *inter vivos*, it is a voluntary gesture. If no *inter vivos* gift has been made, then after the death of a parent, a 'gift' from the estate is deemed obligatory, especially to the surviving child, usually a daughter, who has rendered services such as taking care of the parent in her/his old age. Such a gift takes on the nature of a debt which has to be settled before distribution of the estate to the heirs. This construct could be useful for South African courts with regard to circumstances that arose, for example, in Juleiga Daniels' case. She alleged that her husband had orally given her the house, but the court refused to give legal effect to this because it was oral and thus did not fulfil the South African formalities. The court could have tried to interpret that allegation as a practice in the community that allows a spouse to create an oral debt as an implied term of a Muslim marriage contract.

Equalizing inheritance shares on the basis of agreement and need

Methods of removing gender discrimination and equalizing the inheritance shares of daughters are not regarded as an evasion of traditional Islamic rules. These methods are motivated by social circumstances and by the notion that differences of opinion among the jurists about Islamic rules are a product of varying social circumstances. Nowadays in South Africa education is required for daughters and sons, and it is a must for earning a good living. Education too affects marriage prospects: an educated woman also fetches a more attractive and financially secure partner. When the children are minors at the time of a parent's death, an equal division of inheritance is needed to ensure their further education. Should the children already be grown up, then the educational needs of their children (grandchildren of the deceased) can be paid for by inheritance.

This issue of equalizing inheritance shares is not peculiar to South Africa. Many extended family councils among Muslims in southern Tanzania also decide to agree to an intestate division that is equal for daughters and sons especially when the children of the deceased are of school age (Jones-Pauly 1998). School fees do not discriminate between boys and girls, being the same for both. It is not clear whether this approach, which is based on the principle of need rather than the status and gender of an heir, has raised objections among orthodox ulama in western Tanzania, who have been trained abroad in Arab centres and not in African social circumstances. But should there be opposition, it could be satisfied with the response that Islamic rules honour family agreements. That is to say, the other heirs are permitted to enter into an oral agreement to give their inheritance portions to the children so that daughters and sons inherit equally. This would mean that testators could try, before their death, to get potential collateral heirs to enter into an agreement to devolve their shares on the children of the deceased.

Inheritance inequality and the South African Constitution – a comparative view

While there are many mechanisms at the disposal of Muslim families to equalize the shares between men and women, the issue is usually solved before death. Otherwise, the traditional intestate inheritance rules would prevail. At face value, these rules are incompatible with constitutional equality.

The incompatibility between Islamic succession law and the Constitution is not peculiar to the South African Muslim communities. African laws and customs governing succession have raised similar problems. A look at how the two systems compare will give some insight into how the Islamic law might be treated.

Mthembu/Letsela case – African laws and customs on inheritance

African laws and customs generally exclude women from intestate succession altogether and recognize male primogeniture. Islamic rules do not exclude women, but in general they reduce their shares compared to those of men. The African exclusion was given statutory approval in the 1920s.[147] This statute was challenged by a woman of the Zulu community in 1996. She had married a South Sotho man in 1992 under African rites. They lived in a house together with their daughter. He held the leasehold title to the house. Living with him in the house was not only his wife and their child but also his parents and a sister. He was murdered, dying intestate. The father of the deceased claimed the house as primary male heir under African laws and customs, since the deceased left no sons. The surviving spouse brought an action to have the African rule declared invalid because it was inconsistent with the Constitution and offended against public policy and natural justice.[148] Justice le Roux of the Transvaal Provincial Divisional Court rejected the application, finding that the African law and custom of primogeniture was not unconstitutional. The reasons were as follows: the Constitution guarantees the exercise of freedom to live one's life according to one's communal laws, and prohibits discrimination only if it is unfair and unreasonable. The court found that the African law and rule is fair and reasonable: the rule of primogeniture because it entails not only the right to inherit from the deceased, but also the duty to take care of the survivors of the deceased. In other words, the fathet-in-law had a duty to maintain the surviving spouse and her daughter. He could not evict them, since they had the right to continue to use the property. The court dismissed the application to declare the African law of succession unfair discrimination, and therefore unconstitutional. It mentioned, however, future remedies for the applicant widow. If the father-in-law was trying to say he had no duty to maintain the applicant and her daughter on the grounds that the marriage was not properly performed under African rites and therefore was null and void, thus rendering the child a child outside of the marriage bed, then the wife could petition for a declaration that the application of African law and custom would be inequitable and inappropriate under the circumstances. A potential denial of the validity of the marriage rested on the fact that the balance (2,000 rands) of the *lobola* (marriage dower) had not actually been paid before the husband had been murdered. The wife had only a copy of a receipt of the first instalment of the *lobola* (900 rands).

The case went to appeal.[149] To establish the African custom and law (Zulu and Sotho), Justice Mpati of the Supreme Court of Appeal of South Africa cited several well-established written authorities (Bekker, Bennett, Kerr), which confirmed the rule that women do not inherit under African laws and customs. Instead, the male head of the extended family inherits and is liable for maintaining the women and minor children left behind. The Supreme Court upheld the lower court's judgment, repeating the latter's argument that the African rule had an essential social purpose. The court also did not find the rule contrary to *boni mores*, as 'many Blacks, even to this day, would wish their estates to devolve in terms of Black law and custom [23]'. This allegation of what the community wants as opposed to what is actually practised was simply a confirmation of the written authorities on African laws and customs rather than empirically based.

This position is surprising. The court did not investigate any possible differences between Sotho and Zulu customs relating to gender (Webster 257, 259). It did not even call for evidence of whether its allegation had any sociological truth and whether practice was deviating from the rule formulated and frozen in the books on customary law. The court would have done well to consider the more sociological approach that the Botswana Court of Appeal took in 1992.[150] The latter court rejected the generalities made in the standard textbooks on African law and custom, and required evidence of the actual practices in the specific area where the disputing parties lived. It cited Nigerian case law in which it has been held that the continued existence of a custom that does not meet the demands of modern society cannot be taken for granted.[151] It also cited old South African case law, according to which custom is to be established by at least ten witnesses.[152]

In 1998 a report from the South African Law Commission[153] had already noted that the principle of primogeniture had long been assumed to be a 'keystone', but in fact the practice varied. Not the first-born, but rather the last-born son was inheriting the land. There was also evidence that the preference for males was changing, as bread-winning widows were taking over their husbands' lands. The commission was especially keen to find out whether the standard description of the custom was still true.

The decision of the South African courts against the Zulu widow became a burning issue in South Africa. A draft bill was introduced to change the custom, but was withdrawn. The Law Commission again discussed reforms of the order of succession to ensure inheritance by widows and children.[154] It was proposed that the existing Intestate Succession Act apply to everyone in South Africa regardless of custom, and that the maintenance liabilities imposed by customary rules on the male heir be abolished or curtailed.

The pro-custom judgment has now been replaced by the Constitutional Court's decision in the consolidated cases of Bhe and Shibi in October 2004.[155] In the first case, Ms Bhe and her partner had two minor children when he died in 2002. The parents and one child were living in a makeshift shelter, typical of Khayelitsha, a poor black township founded near Cape Town in the 1980s under apartheid, with a population of half a million. Ms Bhe was a domestic worker and her partner a carpenter. They had begun to build a home with state subsidies before he died. One daughter lived with them while the second resided temporarily with her paternal grandfather in the Eastern Cape, on the other side of the country. The relationship between the grandfather and Ms Bhe deteriorated. They both claimed inheritance of the deceased's real estate. The grandfather had plans to sell it in order to recoup funeral expenses, while Ms Bhe sought the land for herself and the children. The Khayelitsha magistrate awarded the land to the grandfather on the grounds of African law and custom (not specifying which of the African groups) which permit only male relatives to succeed. In the second case, of Shibi, the applicant's sole brother had died. His nearest male relatives, two cousins, laid claim to the estate worth 11,468 rands, under the African rule of male primogeniture. In both cases the lower courts, the Cape High Court and the Pretoria High Court, in turn all ruled against the male relatives, and the Constitutional Court confirmed these judgments. It seems that the lower courts may now be more in tune with the Constitutional Court's judicial activism than previously. The Constitutional Court found the customary rules violated the constitutional provisions of equality (section 9) and human dignity (section 10) of the female person. It reiterated that the rights to equality and human dignity along with the right to life are the source of all other rights. While the Constitution requires the courts to uphold cultural legal pluralism, all laws and rules must be in harmony with the Constitution. The obligations of South Africa under CEDAW (the UN Convention on the rights of women) were also cited as mandating the elimination of harmful social and cultural practices affecting the welfare and dignity of a person. African law and custom had not kept pace with changing circumstances; primogeniture inherently violated equality and dignity.

Only the dissenting opinion of Justice Ngcobo addressed the issues raised in the Mthembu case, where the Supreme Court of Appeal had taken the opposite view to the Constitutional Court, upholding African laws and customs that prevented women from inheriting while warning male heirs not to abuse their powers. Justice Ngcobo wanted to determine what the actual practice was and then to assess whether that practice was reasonable or fair. Discrimination, or derogation from the principle of equality or freedom, can only be justified by reasonableness. Derogation from dignity seems an impossibility. The dissenting opinion argued for distinguishing inheritance from succession in indigenous law: men are to succeed to the position of administering an estate but are obliged to take care of the women and minor children left behind. The senior men succeed to the status of head of the family with all its duties attached. They do not necessarily inherit the estate with the right to dispose of it as they like. This dissenting opinion did not address the issue of why the status cannot be conferred on men and women jointly. Nor did the opinion discuss the underlying principle of African inheritance rules, which are based more on the needs of close family members (relatives, children and spouses) of the deceased rather than on status within the family (Jones-Pauly 1998).

Both the Mthembu and Bhe/Shibi cases have important implications for the application of Islamic inheritance rules. In terms of establishing actual practices in any one Muslim community or region as they evolve according to the use of *ijtihad* (i.e. using one's judgment to find solutions appropriate to the circumstances rather than blindly following classical arguments from past ages), any litigation before South African courts would involve examining a multitude of sources: the standard textbooks, the Quran, the hadiths and the actual updated practices of differing economic and social classes in the community (or communities) from which the parties come. This is not an easy task. The following paragraphs will examine ways of approaching the discourse on Islamic inheritance rules.

Approaching Islamic succession/inheritance law in a new light

The basic outline of Islamic inheritance rules are to be found in the Quran. Within the cultural context in which the inheritance verses were revealed, they were to some extent revolutionary. In the pre-Islamic Bedouin culture and during the early years of Islam, inheritance was not a matter purely of blood relationship or status. Individuals who were not related could pledge to inherit from each other as part of a security pact (Ghazali, Taha).[156] The right to inherit among blood relatives depended on whether one belonged to the category of persons who could be held responsible for avenging the death of a relative,[157] as well as on customs that varied from place to place.[158] Islam introduced into this system fixed shares for specified blood relatives and those of a given marital status.[159] Islam left room for continuing existing customs by allowing bequests of up to one-third of the estate (Coulson 1971, 239–40)[160] and by allowing emancipated slaves and emancipating owners to inherit from one another.[161] Under the general principles of contract, the heirs may deviate from the prescriptions of the state or jurists by agreeing to a mutually negotiated division of their own making.

Shares for daughters – an innovation

Islamic law of inheritance was also revolutionary in respect of gender compared to the existing Mosaic law. Under the latter, daughters were at first totally excluded from inheritance; even when the deceased father left behind only daughters, the estate went to the uncle. This changed when the daughters of Zeflohad complained that this was an unjust custom. While the right to inherit was conferred on daughters, it was nonetheless limited. They could inherit only if there were no sons, as in the case of Zeflohad.[162] A similar story arose in an Islamic hadith, where it was again an Ansari woman who complained – living up to the reputation of Ansari women as being independent-minded and watchful of their rights. She came to the Prophet with her two daughters complaining that the paternal uncle had taken everything. She wanted the daughters to have the right to inherit because they needed property to marry.[163] A Quranic verse was revealed granting the daughters inheritance rights.[164] The Prophet then divided the estate so that the two daughters received the larger portion, namely two-thirds. The remainder was divided between their mother and their uncle. The verse – revealed as a result of a mother trying to get a change in what she regarded as an unjust rule – was revolutionary in one way: the inheritance of the daughters was not conditional on the absence of a son; sons and daughters could inherit together. One daughter alone was given half; two daughters were given two-thirds. The son was given the equivalent of two daughters, i.e. two-thirds.

Fixed Quranic shares gave security to daughters in competition with male relatives. The very fact that the shares were only fractions instead of the entire estate, as was possible under Mosaic rules, meant questions were bound to arise. One particularly troubling question was what was to happen to the remainder of the estate after all fixed shares were distributed and without exhausting the entire estate. So if one surviving daughter got half, where was the remaining half to go? Was her share a minimum, which could be augmented in the absence of other heirs or by a bequest from the deceased? This debate was reflected in the well-known story of Abi Waqqas.[165] He had only one daughter and asked the Prophet how much of his property he could give away as *sadaqa*. He seems to have assumed that as his daughter had only a Quranic share of one-half he could do as he liked with the other half (Powers 44). He was even so bold as to ask whether he could give away two-thirds, implying that his daughter's share would be one-third. The Prophet answered that he might give away up to a third, and this proportion was so large because it was not good to leave behind poor relatives. The answer left open the question of how the estate was to be divided. If the daughter had her fixed share of one-half, and her father gave one-third away, then there remained one-sixth. Because the Prophet said that a third is a large proportion, this could mean that the remaining one-sixth could go to the daughter, who would then have two-thirds of the estate.

Shares for sisters – an innovation

A similar story arose in relation to sisters. Jabir had seven sisters as his sole heirs, and he asked the Prophet how much he could bequeath to them – a third or a half? The Prophet found that this was not generous enough. The verse was revealed that two sisters receive a Quranic share of two-thirds.[166] This was analogous to the above story of the mother and her two daughters. It was revealed that two or more daughters get two-thirds of their father's estate. The treatment of sisters was equally revolutionary compared to the Mosaic rules of the time, which excluded sisters from inheritance.[167] Only uncles were allowed to inherit.

The politics of daughters' shares

In time, however, the question of inheritance by a daughter became fraught with political issues. The Prophet had several spouses as heirs, but only one daughter as his descendant heir. Ali, the husband of the Prophet's daughter, claimed a share in his wife's share when the Prophet died. It would have been half of the estate, possibly even two-thirds, if the Prophet had left a bequest of one-third as Waqqas had wanted to do. Aisha, the Prophet's widow, refused Ali's claim.[168] She pointed out that the Prophet had said there would be no inheritance of his estate because it consisted to a large extent of spoils of war and that he wanted what he personally owned to be used to maintain his wives and his servants.

The result was war and differences of opinion between Sunni and Shii jurists. According to the Shii, followers of the Prophet's son-in-law Ali, a sole daughter takes one-half of the estate, and if there is a half remaining, she takes that too (Coulson 1971, 124). Other Sunni hadiths counter this position, to the disadvantage of the daughter. The residuary amount is given to male relatives (agnates). One such report is that already cited above of the Ansari mother who sought shares for her two daughters. While the Quranic verse was revealed giving the two daughters a two-thirds share, the verse is silent on the shares of the uncles. This leaves it open for interpretation and/or for the insertion of the old customary laws. The hadith is said to supplement the Quranic verse by telling the end of the story: after the Revelation, the Prophet is said to have given the uncles the residuary. So the final distribution was as follows: the Quranic share of two-thirds to the two daughters; the Quranic share of one-eighth to the widow,[169] and the remainder (five-twenty-fourths) to the uncle.

Because of the political dispute over the successor to the Prophet, daughters and agnates were pitted against one another. A formula had to be developed for establishing the hierarchy of shares and who could exclude whom. First the debts had to be paid, then any bequests up to one-third. For the remainder of the estate the Quranic shares were first assigned, then whatever was left over was to go to the agnates. If there was nothing left over, then the agnates got nothing. A highly complex mathematical system of calculating shares based on these simple basic rules evolved. However, the Quranic authority for this system is very limited. The result is a huge edifice of rules resting on a narrow base. To illustrate this immense complexity, there is a saying among the learned that whoever knows the law of inheritance has half the world's knowledge. The rules were developed by learned jurists who had strong agnatic biases. The caliphs succeeding the Prophet were often at the mercy of learned jurists and of local customs when faced with inheritance disputes; often they had to rescind their decisions when challenged by local jurists. There are several reported examples, especially in respect of female relatives. Grandmothers and paternal aunts were not named in the Quran as Quranic heirs. Despite or because of this, they went to the caliphs to lay claim to shares. Caliphs Abu Bakr and Umar refused at first to recognize their claim, precisely because it was not mentioned in the Quran, but they relented when witnesses testified to the practice of the Prophet or to local practice. The key argument was that inheritance was a reciprocal matter. If custom allowed the grandchildren to inherit from these females, it was only equitable to allow the latter to inherit from the descendent line.[170]

Historical agnatic bias against women – Ibn Masud's solution

In one well-known case there was a dispute about how to share the estate when three females of varying degrees of relationship to the deceased were the only survivors. They were a daughter, a son's daughter and a sister. One solution was to give the daughter and sister the Quranic shares of one-half each, with the result that the estate was exhausted and the son's daughter went empty-handed. But another solution, reported to be that of the learned Ibn Masud, was different. He gave the daughter half, the son's daughter one-sixth and the remainder to the sister.[171] This was based on a legal fiction that the son's daughter could be treated as a daughter, thus meeting the Quranic share of two-thirds for two daughters. The daughter and the son's daughter did not share the two-thirds on an equal basis. The daughter received her Quranic share of one-half, while the remaining one-sixth went to the son's daughter. The solution shows an agnatic bias: according to the Quran, only the daughter is named as an heir, and she would thus have been entitled to one-half. The Quran says nothing about a grandchild inheriting; as for a sister, it says that she is an heir only if there are no descendants,[172] so technically she would not have inherited given the presence of a descendant, the daughter. One obvious solution would be that the daughter takes her one-half and also the rest of the estate. But this solution would have been too suggestive of the Shii political favouritism towards the daughter of the Prophet. Thus the solution was to interpret the Quranic one-half for a single daughter literally, as the maximum limit on her share. The remainder could not be given to her and would simply be assigned to other relatives.

Thus inheritance is one area of Islamic law where the customary rules and political stakes forced the classical version of inheritance laws to go in a certain direction, which was not necessarily inevitable. The Quranic text itself is not explicit about the direction inheritance law should have taken. The differences between the Sunni and Shii illustrate the point well. The Sunni confined the sole daughter(s) to a fixed share and did not allow them to exclude the male members of the wider extended family. The Shii made a sole daughter(s) the primary heir with the power to exclude male agnates Otherwise, in the presence of a son she is treated as a secondary residuary heir as under custom. The incorporation of practices of the day into Islamic rules of inheritance indicates the acceptance of changing practices, a principle which would include changing practices of today.

Overcoming the political past: **ijtihad** *for reinterpreting inheritance verses*

Without the political and customary law influences, the Islamic rules of inheritance could have been based on another set of principles – the Quranic principles of equality and charity. The Quran noted that if there has been partiality in the division of the estate, then this is to be corrected for the sake of peace.[173] This can be interpreted in many ways. It could mean that the verses dealing with fixed shares were to be interpreted so that there is as little partiality and as much equality as possible – all with the aim of preserving peace and equity.

When we apply the principles of minimum partiality and maximum equality to the division of the estate between sons and daughters, the double portion assigned to a son would not result in fact in great disparity between a daughter and a son. The partiality towards the son would not be great. To illustrate this point: a mother or father leaves two heirs: a son and a daughter. The Quranic share for a son is that of two daughters, that is, two-thirds, and for a daughter one-half. The result is that the estate is as it were overdrawn, and the shares have to be reduced accordingly (*awl*). The mathematics is as follows:

son 2/3 + daughter 1/2 = 4/6 + 3/6 = 7/6
awl: son = 4/7 daughter = 3/7

The result is that the son gets only 1/7 more than the daughter, which is not much. Their shares are more nearly equal than would be the case under the system calculated by the jurists.

The jurists, however, had preferred to make an exception to the daughter's one-half Quranic share in the presence of a son, again a male bias. They gave the son two-thirds, made the daughter a residual heir, and gave her only one-third, instead of her Quranic one-half. This solution was much closer to the Mosaic rule that the son (the eldest) received two portions of the estate. This was not the spirit in which the fixed shares for women were revealed for Islam. The clarity of the determinate share for the daughter as guaranteed in the Quranic verse 4:7[174] is thus compromised.

Classical Islamic jurists based the notion of a double portion for the son on a logical deduction from the principle of residuality, which in turn derived from the political power of the agnatic *asaba*, who sought to succeed the Prophet, and the principle of pacification: the *asaba* had to be pacified. In effect the jurists likened the daughters by analogy to the *asaba* agnates. We can ask whether these principles are valid for all political and social situations in the many pluralistic Muslim societies and sub-societies. Such an approach undermines the idea that the verses on inheritance in the Quran are among the clearest and therefore the most difficult to reinterpret, an idea that is to be doubted. Obviously the verses were not clear enough, so the principle of residuality had to be invented as an extra-Quranic notion.

Reducing the daughter to a residuary heir permits an outcome that goes against the Quranic rules of one-half for a daughter and two-thirds for two daughters (or more). For under the classical rules, if a parent left a son and two daughters, he would inherit two-thirds while the two daughters would share one-third, i.e. one-sixth each. If a parent left two sons and two daughters, the two sons would share in the two-thirds, each receiving one-third while the two daughters would still get only one-sixth each.

If we reduced the prominence of the principle of residuality and emphasized more the equalizing principle of the Quran, along with the notion of Quranic heirs with fixed shares, then we would have another distribution. Using the logic of fixed Quranic heirs, we could treat the two sons and the two daughters in the same way. The two sons would receive two-thirds (reduced by *awl* to one-half) and the two daughters two-thirds (reduced by *awl* to one-half). The result is equality.

A few more arithmetical examples will illustrate how daughters could achieve more equality in inheritance – not complete equality, but more than the present system allows.

A. 1 son		1 daughter
Classical:	2/3 (two portions)	1/3 (residual share)
New:	2/3 = 4/6 (two portions)	1/2 = 3/6 (Quranic share)
	4/6 + 3/6 = 7/6	
	awl: 4/7	3/7

Under the new approach the disparity is reduced: the son receives only 1/7 more than the daughter, instead of 1/3 more.

B. 1 son		2 daughters
Classical:	2/3 (two portions)	1/3 (residual share) each getting 1/6
New:	2/3 (two portions)	2/3 (Quranic share)
	2/3 + 2/3 = 4/3	
	awl: 2/4	2/4 each getting 1/4

Here the new approach results in the same inequality as the classical, with the son taking twice as much as each of the daughters.

C. 2 sons		1 daughter
Classical:	2/3 (two portions)	1/3 (residual share)
New:	2/3 (two portions)	1/2 (Quranic share)
	4/6 (2/3) + 3/6 (1/2) = 7/6	
	awl: 4/7	3/7

The sons together get only 1/7 more than the daughter, but each son gets 2/7 and the daughter with her 3/7 gets slightly more than each son (1/7 more).

If instead of having the two sons share the 2/3 and we gave 2/3 to each son = (4/6 = 8/6) and the daughter her Quranic 1/2 (3/6), the results would be slightly less for the daughter. The sons would take 2/3 + 2/3 (a total of 4/3 = 8/6), the daughter her 1/2 (3/6). We then need *awl* (8/6 +

3/6 = 11/6), which would allow 8/11 for the two sons, each getting 4/11, and the daughter 3/11. She would receive only 1/11 less than each son.

D. 2 sons		2 daughters
Classical:	2/3 (each 1/3)	1/3 (each 1/6) (residuary)
New:	2/3 (double portion)	2/3 (Quranic)
	4/6 + 4/6 = 8/6	
	awl: 4/8 (1/2)	4/8 (1/2)

In the classical solution the daughters get one half of the sons' portion. In the new Quranic solution, the sons and daughters share equally with 1/2.

If we were to assign each son 2/3, the total estate would be 4/3 + 2/3 = 6/3. The sons would take 4/6 (1/3 for each son), and the daughters would take 2/6 (1/3 for each daughter). This would result also in equality of shares.

Admittedly the classical inheritance system is an elegant arithmetical edifice. If we were to adopt (what I would call) the more authentically Quranic system, the portions of the daughters and sons would be calculated strictly on the basis that the daughter always gets her Quranic share of one-half and the son two portions. The results will vary from case to case and thus not always be consistent with the principle of equality, but at least equality will occur more often. In contrast, the classical system is consistent, but always results in a wide margin of inequality between daughters and sons.

Answering contemporary arguments against egalitarian inheritance

Modern vindicators for the gender bias of a classical inheritance interpretation have not delved into the politico-historical background. Some are justifying the gender difference in favour of 2:1 for the sons on the ground that the men have more financial obligations under classical interpretations than women (Chaudhry). They have to pay a marriage portion (*mahr*) and they have sole responsibility for maintaining the wife or wives. Of course the Quran allows a wife to forego the *mahr*, or the *mahr* is symbolic or quite small or consists of the husband working for the wife's family for a while. Hence the Quran does not of necessity mandate this connection between inheritance portions and dower (Shahrur). As for maintenance, it is not necessarily the sole obligation of the husband. The wife had to pay for extras and for her medical costs or for any trips taken for ritual purposes. The

South African Muslim communities as well as the courts should scrutinize in depth modern apologies for non-egalitarian inheritance shares.

Quranic premium on generosity towards the needy heirs

If the modern Muslim jurists insist on rejecting a new Quranic approach to inheritance and insist on retaining the classical inheritance interpretations premised on gender disparity, there is always another road to be taken towards equality. The basis of this approach is the Quranic principle of charity which could counterbalance the intransigence of classical jurists who laid great store by the status of the heir in terms of her/his blood line to the praepositus. This was partly because the blood-line became a vehicle for political power. Whoever could establish a blood-line to the Prophet could claim the community leadership. Charity, on the other hand, would have reflected more the spiritual meritocracy which Islam introduced as a revolutionary idea to counter clericalism or chieftaincy based on family relationship. Charity can be achieved either through liberalizing the rules of bequests or giving priority to the principle of neediness. Generally the classical view was that a bequest is limited to only one-third of an estate. This rule is based on a prophetic hadith, not the Quran. The classical jurists differed on whether the bequest could be made to favour a relative or could only be made to an outsider. While these arguments may have been based on the aim to keep social peace within a family, the emphasis today is less on peace than on fulfilling the educational needs of children, who are dependent much longer on the economic resources of their parents than in earlier times. On the basis of changing social circumstances, one can allow the freedom to bequeath up to one-third of an estate to the child who has the most need irrespective of gender. If both sons and daughters are equally needy, the bequest can be used to equalize the shares. If both are equally well-off then the bequest can be used for a needy relative or non-relative.

If bequest is still too limited a device to achieve justice to the equal needs of children, then the Quranic verse on the purpose for leaving property may come to our rescue. It was written that children, both female and male, are to share in the properties of their parents. This laid down a clear principle of inheritance based on descendancy without gender bias. The ensuing verse went on to say that if at the time of division of the estate there are relatives, orphans and poor, then they too are entitled to means from the property so that they can survive or earn a livelihood (*risq*). The attitude, presumably of the children who expected to be the sole heirs, is to be one of kindness and justice.[175] The verses specifying the specific fractional portions for parents and spouses then ensue. The classical logic used to interpret these verses is premised on the specific preceding the general, that is, after all the specific shares are dealt out, then what is left is for the general category of the needy. This logic is not infallible. If the spirit of the Quran is generosity and equality, then the general governs the specific. If after the distribution of the estate to the specific heirs with fixed shares, there is left for the needy less than what the specific heirs really need, then the needy should be given their share first. What is left over shall be divided among the less needy specific heirs.[176]

Debts towards daughters under a regime of egalitarian inheritance rules

The Quran also provides that the debtor has the first claim in the estate, then come legacies, and finally inheritance shares.[177] What a debt or obligation (*dain*) consists of is open to question. If it is found that a daughter has taken care of a parent more than her brother, then the debt or obligation that the heirs owe her should be reflected in the distribution of the estate so that she would inherit at least the same as a son or more.[178]

Ottoman Islamic law precedents – equal shares for daughters and sons

As pointed out above, the inheritance rules were in flux in the 1st century of Islam so that certain local customs were not upset. The rulers were petitioned to introduce shares and rules which were not explicitly provided for in the Quran. The Ottomans followed this precedent and introduced various changes in the inheritance law. For example, all lands which were deemed the ruler's land by virtue of conquest were at the disposal of the state. The state could grant, against a fee, usufruct to private persons for purposes of cultivation. These lands were called *miri* (derived from *emir*, the ruler) land. Upon the death of the possessor, the lands devolved on the children to the exclusion of the spouse in equal shares to daughters and sons (Ottoman Land Code) (Fisher; Jones 1995). The idea was to prevent fragmentation especially of agricultural lands. This meant that if someone left no sons and only daughters, then the daughters inherited all. The state did not have an interest in a distant uncle with no ties to the area inheriting land along with the daughters, as would have been the case under classical interpretations. A distant uncle, it was thought, would have little interest in taking care of the land and so would have become an absentee landlord from whom it would be difficult to collect taxes (Jones 1995).[179] The Land Code protected the land from absentee descendant heirs as well by providing that if an heir did not cultivate for three consecutive years, then the state could offer the land to anyone else against a fee (Art. 74). The Ottoman Land Code was amended in 1913 (Fisher 78) to extend the rule of equal inheritance to certain *mulk*, that is, private lands, and to give more rights to the surviving spouse, female or male. It also reinterpreted the classical glosses. The Quranically named heirs were hierarchized and female children allowed to exclude collateral male relatives (as permitted in Shiite interpretations favouring the Prophet's daughter). The children (grandchildren in case of prior decease) had priority and excluded all other relatives. If there were no children then the land passed to the spouse without gender bias. In the absence of children and a spouse, then collateral relatives were entitled to inherit.

Modern applications of Ottoman principles

The classical inheritance rules which resulted in fragmentation in the extreme were designed with a nomadic society with moveable properties such as animal herds in mind. It was not suited for landed properties. The Ottoman approach has been supplemented in other Muslim lands today where agricultural land is at a premium and must be economically viable, such as in Tunisia and Zanzibar (Jones 1975 and 1996a). The Ottoman rule of equal shares for daughters and sons is still applied in some Muslim societies as viable and fair (Wahin).[180]

Another issue of non-equality that can plague the South African legislation for inheritance among Muslims is the classical interpretation that no non-Muslim relative may inherit from Muslim relatives, but the reverse is allowed. The rule derives from the legal fiction that all land belongs to the Muslim ruler by virtue of conquest, so if a non-Muslim were to inherit, the implication was that the inherited piece of land could be deemed no longer to be under the control of the Muslim ruler. As this fiction has no roots in reality any more, maintaining this interpretation, which has no direct basis in the Quran, would perpetuate basic unfairness and violate principles of human dignity of non-Muslim relatives.[181]

On the Swahili coastal areas of East Africa, property used for the survival of the family was held in common for all heirs. A combination of rules was devised based on a property system which typologizes types of property according to their role in gaining income and sustaining livelihood. For example, disposal over trees is treated differently from disposal over the soil itself, or disposal over work tools or structures is governed too by rules different from those for the underlying soil. Hence land that was held in common by the family would remain undivided, while revenues from the land or crops planted on the land were divided among the children only, and without gender bias. The prescribed rule of half to the daughter was deemed applicable only in the extreme case of having to sell or partition the underlying common property as a last resort option for reasons of survival.

Consequences of Bhe/Shibi case for Islamic inheritance law in South Africa

In any event, under the ruling of the South African Constitutional Court in Bhe/Shibi, the classical interpretation that denies women equality in inheritance by daughters and sons would be in violation of the constitution. In the light of the practice of several South African Muslims to give equal shares to their children as well as the urgent need for *ijtihad* (that is, re-interpretation of the sources), the South African courts should not fear taking on the task of interpreting the inheritance verses in keeping with the spirit of equality. The state can contemplate enacting a law which applies to all citizens regardless of indigenous or religious interpretations, but with a proviso that in cases of conflicts or ambiguities, then the courts are to take into account the cultural mindset of the parties involved.[182] The courts as well as the legislature may refer to the efforts of Muslim women and jurists in Muslim majority countries who have drafted egalitarian family and succession codes.[183]

The Bhe/Shibi decision can be invoked to re-examine the issue of discrimination and inequality at the hands of religion and not just the state. The Constitutional Court highlighted the injustice of the apartheid state that had enacted laws that humiliated Blacks, especially Black women, and excluded them from enjoying equal rights under state law as well as under customary laws. It cannot be forgotten that the apartheid state justified its very existence and is ideology of discrimination on theological arguments. The state Constitution provided for a 'Christian state' and prominent theologians interpreted biblical passages to sustain a tyranny of inequality. The past makes clear the dangers of accepting religious interpretations which perpetuate a model of discrimination no matter how well intended for the 'protection' of the targeted group. The theologians who then joined the struggle against apartheid charged into the battlefield of exegesis and hermeneutics with the aim to achieve an egalitarian interpretation of scriptures. If the courts have occasion to deal with issues of Islamic law, then they should not forget to take a historical perspective on the dynamics of how any religious law can lose sight of and pervert its original spirit of egalitarianism.

Theological and power disputes within the Muslim communities

The South African courts were not confined to handling disputes relating to family and inheritance matters of Muslims. An important body of litigation dealt with control over mosques, control over the community and the recognition of 'sects'. In these cases the courts varied in the extent to which they delved into the terminology and substance of Islamic law.

Religious trusts

One early case concerned Sunni Muslims.[184] In 1903 two merchants drew up a deed for transferring land in Natal for the construction of a mosque. The deed transferred the property to five trustees of the Mahommedan Mosque of Estcourt. Whether the transfer and the trust constituted what is known under Islamic law as *waqf* was not specified clearly. In 1935 there arose a controversy about replacing three of the deceased trustees. A meeting of all worshippers was convened to decide on a constitution for the mosque and the conditions for creating a trust. Whether the trust was to satisfy Islamic law or Roman-Dutch law was not specified. The conveyance to the new trustees had to be registered with the Registrar of Deeds. The Registrar needed a court order recognizing the transfer and the appointment of new trustees. A protest from a member of the community resulted in court litigation. The court knew of no precedent case which affirmed the jurisdiction of a court to confirm appointment of trustees.

The court affirmed its own jurisdiction as the defendant did not argue the issue of who had the power of appointment. Only who was to be appointed was at issue. The court justified its jurisdiction by way of analogy to an earlier case where the court had ordered the sale of trust property and use of the proceeds to purchase another property for the trust. Likening the transfer of the trust properties to the sale, the court then established the criteria the trustees would have to meet in order to make a transfer in accordance with the authority of the community affected. For this purpose the court did not refer to Islamic law. It relied rather on general democratic criteria. These were: first, the majority of the beneficiaries in the community had expressed an opinion in favour of a certain position; secondly the changes were to their benefit and consistent with the purposes of the trust. The court established who the members of the mosque were. They were not only the residents of Estcourt Township, but also persons living in Weenen County. At an assembly of community members, a constitution for the mosque and trust were adopted. The court found that the criteria for transfer by the trustees were satisfied. The court ordered that the plaintiff transfer the trust property to the newly elected trustees.[185]

Over half a century later in 1999 the Supreme Court of Appeal heard another case (Hoosen) involving an Islamic trust.[186] In 1985 a trust deed had been made in favour of the Islamic Propagation Centre International. It was registered according to South African law with the Master of the Supreme Court. The deed provided for five trustees, later increased to seven. They were to hold office for life. The value of the trust was substantial as it included income-generating properties. The aims of the trust were to further Islam – to promote charitable activities and to propagate the Islamic faith among Muslims and non-Muslims. The powers of the trustees included not only managing the trust and its business interests, but also appointing personnel and agents. Any major decision had to be reached by a vote of two-thirds of the trustees. In the event that a fellow trustee vacated his position, the trustees were to elect another person to fill the vacancy. The trust appears to have been a *waqf*, as it was a trust of perpetual succession, never to be ended.

Two of the respondents in the case were an original trustee and his daughter-in-law. When he had became physically paralyzed after a stroke, he granted power of attorney in 1997 to his daughter-in-law to attend the trustees' meetings on his behalf. Some of the other trustees lodged a complaint in the Durban Division to have the power of attorney annulled. The disagreement was not surprising, since through the years factionalism had erupted among the trustees and eventually prejudiced the management of the trust.

The trial court upheld the power of attorney to the daughter-in-law. The other trustees went to appeal.

Again the court was to reach a decision that relied on the South African law of trusts, unrelated to the Islamic rules of a religious *waqf*. The court had to decide whether a trustee may give a power of attorney to a person not elected by the other trustees. The court looked at two criteria to determine its decision. One was the role of the trustees, and the other was the terms of the trust agreement. It found that according to an early precedent, the trustees are ultimately responsible for the implementation of decisions. The power of attorney to the daughter-in-law conferred discretion to act on behalf of the trustee, but it would not have been possible to hold her responsible personally for her decisions; the trustee himself would remain liable, yet he would be bound by her decisions. In regard to the terms of the trust agreement, the court found that the agreement had no provisions relating to delegation of power of attorney. At most it provided for the trustees to appoint agents and servants to perform services for the trust. It provided that all affairs were to be controlled by the trustees. Whether the term 'trustees' implied a person delegated with authority from an elected trustee could not be determined from the terms of the trust deed. The court then resorted to analogy. It analogized power of attorney to agency. The rules of agency as laid down in the case law permit delegation of power for important matters only where the personal attributes and skills of the principal are not of 'material importance' for the performance of the powers delegated.

On the basis of this analogy, the court had to establish the powers to be exercised by the daughter-in-law as quasi agent and whether the tasks at hand required personal attributes and skills that only her father-in-law could exercise for managing the trust's affairs with the other trustees. The court found that these personal attributes and skills consisted of the following: imbued with the spirit of Islam; personal confidence of potential donors in the trust; and the personal trust of the other trustees in one another. This highly personalized view of the skills that a trustee needed resulted in the court denying the right of the trustee to give a power of attorney. At the same time, the court observed that the delegating trustee was 'the guiding spirit behind the trust'[187]. Why the father-in-law as the key figure among the trustees should not have been able to designate the person whom he presumably felt was endowed with the same personality traits and skills as himself is not clear.

What is curious, among other things, is that the court did not concentrate on the clause in the trust deed that provided for a procedure to settle issues which were not provided for in the trust deed. The trustees were to make a decision and the decision was to be treated as though it were a clause in the trust deed. Why the court did not require the trustees to vote on the issue of delegating the powers of attorney is unclear.

In conclusion, the court found that the trustee's power of attorney to his daughter-in-law was not valid.

The costs of the litigation were ordered to be paid out of the trust funds, for the action arose out of a conflict over interpretation of the terms of the trust deed.

The emphasis of the court on the importance of the personal religious attributes of the trustees and the trust of potential donors raises a suspicion that the gender of the person appointed by the paralyzed trustee was the unsaid issue. There is nothing in the Islamic rules of religious trust which prohibits a woman from being a trust administrator (Jones 1975). A *waqf* trustee may, for example, in Andhra Pradesh, India, appoint a proxy (*naib*) when unable to fulfil her/his duties for good reasons, and the proxy is held personally responsible and must stand under the supervision of the trustee.[188] As for the question of potential donors, an Islamic religious trust is not essentially a matter of a financial investment. The funds dedicated for religious purposes are to reach the persons who should benefit from charity, but when the funds are depleted, the trust is terminated.

The primary concern of the Islamic law of *waqf* is not the administration of the trust *per se.* Foremost is the purpose of the *waqf* (Bulbulia). Does it serve God/Allah? The trust constitutes a dedication of material goods to God/Allah. God/Allah never sells property, nor transfers it. No one may profit by the sale of such assets. Persons of specific categories may benefit from the dedication, that is, they may make use of the revenue of the properties. Among the beneficiaries there must be the poor and needy, though the jurists disagreed over the point in time when a *waqf* should benefit this category of persons. Is it for the duration of the *waqf*, or only when the named beneficiaries no longer existed? (Anderson, J. 1959; Crecilius 1991). Hence the order of the court in the Hoosen case that the costs of the litigation were to be borne by the trust, is questionable, since it is not the trustee who is to benefit from the funds, but the needy.[189]

The fate of *waqf*s in Islamic societies has been varied (Anderson, J. 1959; Crecilius 1991). Tunisia (Jones 1975) abolished them just as Abu Hanifa had recommended because they tied up property (Coulson 1991, 87). Doing good for the poor and needy could be achieved through the institution of *zakat*, the charitable tax. India has tried to harness the wealth for good purposes. The kind of *waqf* that was at issue in the Hoosen v Deedat case seems to be of the sort which the Indian legislator has sought to promote. The purpose of India's Central Waqf Act, 1954 (Act 29 of 1954) aimed to transform the trusts' boards into 'creative organs for educational, social, economic and cultural renaissance' (Alim MK, 1). For this reason the law regulates in detail how a government-created board is to supervise all trustees appointed in a *waqf* deed to manage the *waqf* properties and promote its wealth-creating potential. This is to avoid a *waqf* becoming an economic burden because of its inalienability.

The case raises an issue similar to that in the matrimonial case of Ryland, which modernized the South African law on recognition of Muslim marriage contracts. At issue was which terms of an agreement can be deemed to be implied terms, that is, terms which were intended to apply Islamic rules. The trust deed in Hoosen was unclear on the point of delegation of power. To help resolve this problem, the court should have considered interpreting the South African jurisprudence on trusts in the light of the Islamic rules of religious trust and vice versa in order to reach a decision that would have been more comprehensive and reflective of the plurality of South African *mores*.

Religious sects

The South African courts were also seized of litigation on doctrinal questions as to who could form a mosque. In 1983 the issue of the right of Ahmadis to establish associations arose.[190] The Ahmadis have been declared in Pakistan to be a banned heretical sect.

The organization called AAIL constituted a voluntary association of Ahmadi Muslims with a written constitution. The Muslim Judicial Council was also a voluntary association of certain Muslim sheikhs, imams and theologians, who were also trustees of a Cape Town mosque (Long and Dorp Streets) as well as trustees of the Malay part of a cemetery at Athlone in the Cape.

The Muslim Judicial Council refused the AAIL to have their members buried in the Athlone cemetery or to worship in the Long and Dorp Streets mosque. When the AAIL began to collect money to construct a mosque, the council disseminated information to the Muslim communities that the Ahmadis were non-Muslims and apostates.

To counter the propaganda, the AAIL brought an action in court for a declaration that they are Muslims, entitled to burial and visitation in the mosque. It also sought an order to refrain the council from disseminating false defamatory malicious matter against the Ahmadis.

The Muslim Judicial Council pleaded that the AAIL had no *locus standi* to bring an action. It had not suffered a wrong as an association, rather its members had suffered. Secondly, the council pleaded that an association cannot be defamed, only a person.

The court dealt first with the issue of *locus standi*. It found that the AAIL is a voluntary religious association of a corporate character, that is, it has perpetual succession and its own property independent of its members as provided in its constitution. The constitution also conferred on the AAIL the power to sue and be sued.

The court then examined the case law on when a corporate association can sue. The basic principle is that a person, legal or natural, must have a direct interest in the suit. A direct interest was defined to mean that a judgment would prejudicially affect their interests in a given matter.

The court found that the AAIL as an association would not be prejudicially affected, and therefore had no direct interest in the matter and could not sue on the issues being alleged. The reasons given by the court were that the Council was refusing access to members of the AAIL not because of their membership in the AAIL but because the members were said to be non-Muslims. This kind of action was a matter of the liberty of individuals. They could have brought a suit in their own name, but not the AAIL on their behalf. The South African case law only exceptionally permitted an action brought by a person having an indirect interest in the litigation.

In respect to the defamation issue, it was true that the council had published material against the AAIL as such. The court reviewed those writings in the South African legal literature which favoured defamatory actions brought by a non-trading corporation, as well as writings which took positions to the contrary. The court took the easier way out by declaring that the defamation actions were directed against the Ahmadis as individuals and not because they were members of the AAIL.

The court concluded that the AAIL lacked *locus standi* to bring an action for the nature of the relief sought. In the end, the court avoided having to resolve doctrinal matters.

More than a decade later, after the apartheid era had ended, the South African courts were again confronted with an action in defamation against Ahmadis: this time, as specified in the AAIL judgment, in their individual capacity.[191] Not long after the AAIL judgment in 1983, Sheikh Jassiem had brought an action for damages against Sheikh Nazim Mohamed for an imputed statement that Jassiem 'is 'n sympathizer mit dei Ahmadis' (a sympathiser of the Ahmadis). Jassiem also brought proceedings against the Muslim Judicial Council, alleging that Nazim had acted on behalf of and with the authority and approval of the council. Sheikh Jassiem further sued the council for damages for allegedly inciting the trustees of the Loop Street mosque to dismiss him as imam of that mosque.

At the trial level the defamation claims were consolidated and decided in favour of Jassiem. His claim for damages for incitement to dismiss was rejected. Only the council went to appeal.

Several doctrinal issues were at stake. The court recounted in detail the history of the Ahmadis. The Ahmadiyya movement was founded in then British India in 1889 by one Mirza. He was known as a devout Muslim. In 1891 he claimed that he was himself the 'promised Messiah' and made claims to prophethood. Muslim religious leaders condemned him as an apostate on the ground that Muhammad was the final Prophet and no other prophets would follow. At the core of the various protests was the question of whether Mirza claimed to be a prophet, flying in the face of the orthodox teaching that no Prophet would come after Muhammad. In the course of time the movement grew despite orthodox opposition in Afghanistan, Egypt, Persia and Pakistan. The movement split into the Lahore Ahmadis and the Qadiani Ahmadis. The Qadianis believed, unlike the Lahores, that Mirza was indeed a Prophet. A *fatwa* from Al Azhar University in Egypt in 1962 declared that the Qadianis had deviated from Islam.

In South Africa in the 1980s there were only 200 Lahores and even less Qadianis among the 260,000 strong Sunni Muslim community in the Western Cape. The Muslim Judicial Council was an unelected body that claimed authority over the Muslims in Western Cape. It had on occasion declared certain individuals to be apostates and no longer members of the Muslim community. Both plaintiff and defendant were at some time members of the Council. Jassiem left, however, in the 1960s because of a difference of opinion on a ritual issue. He became imam at the Imam Yasien Mosque when his father, a former imam, appointed him to this post. For some years Jassiem allowed the Lahore Ahmadiyyas to pray in the mosque. Upon receiving the Al Azhar *fatwa* from Cairo, the council decided to issue its own *fatwa* condemning all followers of Mirza. When they requested Jassiem to join them in a campaign against the Qadianis and the Lahores, Jassiem refused to commit himself. He continued to allow Lahores to come to his mosque. The council then declared Jasseim to be an apostate. Jassiem defended his position by saying that the Lahores had recited the Kalimah Shahada and so were professing Muslims. For this reason he could not refuse them entry to the mosque.

The council issued in fact a *fatwa* in 1965 against Ahmadis and sympathizers. It called them apostates and prohibited any association between a Muslim and them. This meant, for example, that not even the services of an Ahmadiyya tailor could be hired. Jassiem was ostracized socially. Many no longer attended prayers at his mosque. In 1970 under pressure from the council Jassiem signed a document stating his repentance for encouraging Ahmadis. As a result many Lahores no longer came to his mosque. Jassiem continued to believe, however, that the Lahores were not apostates and were Muslims. He was condemned for continuing to sit on a local authority committee on which an Ahmadi was a member. In 1973 Jassiem married the sister of a man regarded in Cape circles as a Lahore or at least a Lahore sympathizer. Before a meeting with members of the council, Jassiem's brother-in-law denied that Jasseim himself was an Ahmadi.

The court recounted the religious qualifications of the contestants. Jassiem came from a family of imams on his mother's and father's side, going as far back as his great-grandfather. He had studied at Al Azhar in the 1920s and 1930s, but without graduating. Upon return to Cape Town he was a religious teacher. He had even taught Nazim, chairperson of the Muslim Judicial Council. He had studied in Mecca in the 1950s.

The court then listed the main issues at the defamation trial: whether calling a Muslim an Ahmadi or Ahmadi sympathizer is an insult and whether the person allegedly defamed was Muslim; what defines a Muslim; whether a Muslim ceases to be a Muslim or becomes an apostate if he refuses to condemn Lahore Ahmadis as apostates.

The trial court found that calling a Muslim an Ahmadi or Ahmadi sympathizer constituted defamation in the closely knit Cape Muslim community as evidenced by the social ostracism and loss of esteem which Jassiem had suffered. The appellate court agreed that in South Africa in a defamation action, it was not necessary to prove loss of social reputation in the society at large. It could occur in a particular segment of the society as long as the plaintiff establishes that s/he has such a relationship with that social segment and that the allegedly defamatory statement was calculated to harm that relationship. There was therefore in the eyes of the appellate court, no need that Jassiem prove he was a Muslim, only his relationship to the Muslim community. He did not have to prove the falseness of the statement that he was a non-Muslim and apostate. This in turn meant that the defence (namely, the council) did not have to prove the truth of their statement that he was not a Muslim. This was in keeping with a case in 1937 in which it was defamatory in Transvaal to accuse a European of advocating marriage between Africans and Europeans. Defamatory meant that such a person would incur hatred of her/his European citizens. It was not necessary to establish the truth or falsity of the defamatory statement, namely whether such marriages were right or wrong.[192]

The appellate court ruled in effect that South Africa has distinctive community groups. It can be adjudged that a member of a group has lost esteem. Caution, however, is to be exercised in such cases. Each case should be treated as a question of fact. The principle is that esteem can be lost only in the context of a particular group and not in the society at large. Thus the idea that a statement is defamatory only if esteem is lost in the general society was no longer appropriate for South African society.[193]

The trial court also accepted expert evidence from both the plaintiff and defendant on who is a Muslim and whether Lahore Ahmadis were apostates. The trial court noted that it had to reach a decision on which expert opinion was acceptable because Islam lacked a central body for settling dogmatic disputes, an *ecclesia*. The trial court decided in favour of the expert opinion submitted for Jassiem that the Lahore Ahmadis were not apostates.

The appellate court did not agree. It found that the question of who is a Muslim or who has become an apostate is a matter of ex-communication. Ex-communication involves matters of tenets of faith. It ruled that a court cannot reach a decision on the justifiability of whether a person is to be ex-communicated or not by way of 'conventional judicial standards'. The court implied that an exception can be made when the parties assert that a determination of the fairness of ex-communication is necessary for the defence of establishing the truth of a statement and for the public benefit. It would seem that Nazim of the Muslim Judicial Council did not wish to push this point because they had walked out of an earlier trial and left the court to make a judgment by default in favour of the Ahmadiyya association which had alleged defamatory action on the part of the council as it had denounced the advertisement of the Ahmadiyya association for fund-raising. At that time the council had argued that no secular court could decide in an ecclesiastical dispute.[194]

The appellate court took cognizance of the fact that Islamic law provides for a procedure for determining whether ex-communication is appropriate and that the Muslim Judicial Council had not followed this procedure before issuing a statement against Jassiem.[195] It also found that Nazim had not been authorized by the council to make defamatory statements against Jassiem.

Damages were awarded to Jassiem against Nazim for defamatory statements.

The judgment is important for various reasons. One is that it reveals the reluctance of the appellate courts to have issues of law so formulated that they will entangle the courts in decisions of religious dogma. Secondly, it shows a certain readiness of the courts to extend to the Muslim community the South African case law on controlling religious decision-making bodies when faced with a complaint of unfairness. In 1983 the question of fairness of hearings before religious bodies had to be settled in connection with the New Protestant Church in Africa.[196] The Presbytery Commission initiated investigations of rumours against a preacher in the church. It failed to inform him of the nature of the rumours. A report was made. The preacher had a chance to present his case at a Presbytery hearing. He lost his case and was suspended. He then lodged a complaint in a state court to have the Presbytery's decision reviewed and set aside. The court examined the constitution of the Presbytery and decided that the Presbytery had not acted according to its own constitutional procedure, in effect, the hearings were irregular. They also had not conformed to the requirements of natural justice in so far as the preacher had not been given a hearing at the start of the rumour and the appeal procedure amounted to a new hearing.

As noted above, the Muslim Judicial Council had refused in another court dispute involving their public statements against the Ahmadis, who were raising funds for a mosque, to have a state court intervene in questions of dogma. As a result, a default judgment was issued against the council.[197] The council was criticized for its 'boycott' of the state judicial process.[198] It seems to have changed its position when it remained in the proceedings involving defamation against Jassiem until the bitter end. The appellate court proved sensitive enough to frame the issues in such a way as to avoid having to decide questions of dogma.

Nonetheless the court seems to have left open the door to reserve to itself the power to decide on the procedural fairness of a decision that a body such as the council might eventually take after holding hearings to determine whether a member of their community should be ex-communicated as a sympathizer of the Ahmadis.[199]

This is important for future actions by Islamic dispute settlement bodies in South Africa. If a woman feels that the decision of such a body in a matrimonial dispute is unfair, she could choose either to take the case afresh to the courts or petition for a review of the extra-judicial decision. Such an approach would save a lot of debate on the question of whether there should be a Sharia Court in South Africa, on a par with courts for African law and custom. One knotty legal problem of a substantive nature could still arise. That is related to the proprietary consequences of a decision by a Muslim body ex-communicating a member of the community. Ex-communication in effect renders a person an apostate. This can have serious implications on the rights to maintenance and to inheritance. The general Islamic rule is that the apostate is barred from inheriting from Muslim relatives or the surviving spouse(s). There is a difference of opinion on whether the Muslim relatives or surviving spouse(s) of an apostate may inherit from the latter's estate. Jurists often opined, however, that in the case of an apostate woman, her estate could be inherited by her Muslim relatives or surviving spouse (Coulson 1971, 186). South African courts will probably find themselves faced with complex questions of the relationship between dogma and proprietary rights. These matters will offer them opportunities for fundamental re-examination of Islamic legal opinions, demanding a careful determination of the fundamental principles.

Islamic dispute settlement – extra-judicial conflict resolution in the Muslim communities

Issues of adjudicatory authority in Islam and other revealed religions

The Mohamed v Jassiem judgment is a vivid example of lively debates in the Islamic communities in South Africa. As the appellate court in that case observed, there was no one Islamic body that had the last word on a question of doctrine. This is not to be interpreted as a weakness in Islam. It is rather a sign of the freedom of thought that Allah/God's revelations in the Quran intended for all of the monotheistic religions in the world at the time. Judaism had a priesthood, whose members issued authoritative decisions, but no central authority. For that reason Mosaic law was famous for a high degree of freedom of thought that permitted differences of opinion. The Christians had in contrast introduced a highly hierarchical priesthood with a centralized authority and a suppression of freedom of doctrinal opinion. The concept of freedom of opinion took root in European Christian lands outside the realm of religious thought. Such freedom survived only through the vibrancy of the non-religious, or secular, Renaissance movement. The Muslims refused to introduce a priesthood or a central authority. The face of authority was not a human being or an office, but rather the Book, the Quran. Muslim jurists developed a concept of freedom of thought by publishing a variety of interpretations and founding several schools of law. The exercise of freedom of thought had as its object to maintain the balance between the integrity of the central authority of the Book/Quran and the possibility of differences of opinion among the believers. That led to the development of a legal science for determining in what areas the Quran enjoined unity of opinion if at all and in what areas it provided for variety of opinion. The challenge today is to find a way to arbitrate among a wide variety of opinion-holders and decision-makers.

Reliance on outside advisory opinions in South Africa

The question of judicial and interpretive authority in the Muslim communities has long been an unresolved issue in South Africa. The famous Transvaal *fatwa*, issued, as already mentioned, at the start of the 20th century, illustrates the problem graphically. A question was sent from the Transvaal to the then mufti of Egypt and great reformer, Muhammad Abduh, about eating meat slaughtered by Christians and inter-*madhab* worship in one and the same mosque. The mufti of Egypt considered that the circumstances in South Africa for a Muslim minority required positive answers to the questions (Green; Skovgaard-Petersen) – yes, they could eat meat slaughtered by Christians and worshippers of different schools of law could intermingle in the same prayers in the same mosque. The query would be similar to a question about inter-denominational worship among Christians.

Today the Muslim communities in South Africa continue to recognize the authority of Al Azhar, though the time needed for an answer from Egypt is said to take too long. The Indian community in South Africa also turns to the Darul Uloom in Deoband, India for *fatwa*s.[200] With the establishment of Islamic learning institutions in South Africa (e.g. the Islamic College in Cape Town) and the increase in the number of graduates in Islamic theology and law, this dependency may be called into doubt. The South Africans have reached a high standard of solid critical Islamic law scholarship, capable of analysing and criticizing the *fatwa*s issued from other Islamic centres from a methodological and substantive point of view.[201]

Muslim South African dispute-settlement bodies

Against this background, it is not surprising that there are several Muslim bodies in South Africa in addition to the Muslim Judicial Council (founded in 1945), such as the Cape Malay Association (founded 1923), Majlis as Shira al Islami, Islamic Council of South Africa (ICSA), Muslim Youth Movement (MYM), Muslim Students Association Call of Islam (aligned with the African National Congress), Cape Islamic Association, Muslim Assembly, Islamic Unity Convention, Deobandi Jamiat, Barelvi Jamiat, Majlis al-'ulama, Qibla (Moosa, E, Esack 6, 31, 33, 41, 83, 212; Mahida 44–53). Some of these groups sought to represent themselves to the major parliamentary party, the African National Congress, as the exclusive representative of Muslims. In August of 1994 in Durban a Muslim Personal Law Board was founded to unify various groups and opinions. Because of acrimonious debates among different schools of thought, the Board was disbanded only a year later. One rather remarkable event was that the exiled Tunisian Muslim fundamentalist Rashid al Ghannouchi (Hamdi 1998) was reported to have attended the opening meeting of the Board.

Under South African law the present status of the Islamic dispute settlement bodies is extra-judicial. They would offer what the South African Law Commission calls alternative dispute resolution mechanisms, alternative to the courts.

The extent of the powers of any one such dispute-settlement body in the Muslim communities is currently determined by the body itself and the disputants using it. In the light of the case law in South Africa, the courts would have an interest in reviewing the decisions of these extra-judicial bodies, but only if a party sues in the courts seeking review. The main interest of the courts is in the fairness of the procedure. They are particularly concerned that all parties are heard.

Cape views on conflict-resolution

How do the South African Muslim groups view extra-judicial conflict-resolution? The Western Cape view differs from that of Durban. One of the problems raised in the Eastern Cape is that of defining the limits of the powers of interpretation of the learned ulama, imams and trained jurists who constitute the *shurta* (councils in consultation with members of the community). There is no mufti or qadi in South Africa. Persons of such statue are *mujtahid*s, jurists who are regarded by the community as capable of interpreting the sources of the law, the Quran and the hadiths, in a manner befitting the circumstances, practices and customs in the Muslim communities in South Africa.[202] They are allowed to go beyond blind application of textbook Islamic law and apply their own logic and reasoning. The members of the *shurta* are regarded by some in the Cape as persons of limited knowledge and authority in Islamic law.

Two basic solutions have been offered to what is seen in the Cape as a problem of the absence of a qadi or mufti. One is the establishment of a Sharia Court or the appointment of Muslim law assessors to a state court, as in the case of Malawi, Botswana and Tanzania. The Cape community has still to consider adapting the Sinai Bedouin practice to the situation in South Africa. Among the Bedouin a qadi is not appointed by the state. Instead, disputing parties agree upon taking a case before a highly learned jurist and select the persons who will guarantee the execution of the decision of the learned jurist (Stewart).

Given the view that the authority of the members of the *shurta* in the Cape is restricted, the *shurta* tends to limit its functions to cases of marital disputes. It tries to reconcile the parties or counsel them about rights and duties. It generally does not believe it has authority to issue an order of divorce as a qadi or state-appointed judge would have. As a result, the power of divorce lies solely in the hands of the husband who alone exercises the power of *talaq*. The *shurta* would limit its role to determining whether his *talaq* were pronounced at a certain time in the menstrual cycle of the wife, or pronounced while he was sober or not, or pronounced in a rage. These findings would determine whether the *talaq* were valid or not. Otherwise, if the husband refuses to exercise *talaq*, when the wife wishes to be divorced, the *shurta* may not feel competent to issue a *tamlik*, which is a forced *talaq*. It would limit itself instead to finding a ground for declaring the marriage null. It also means that the *shurta* does not feel competent to confirm a wife's right to initiate divorce by *khula* (returning her dower as a sign of her divorcing her husband).

This restrictive view on the limits of authority of the *shurta* has far-reaching consequences for the Muslim marriage contract. The parties to a Muslim marriage have to rely mostly on the terms of divorce, which they write into their marriage or post-nuptial contract. In case of dispute over the meaning of the terms of the contract, the *shurta* would have the power of interpretation. As for a *khula* divorce initiated by the wife, whether a *shurta* would issue her a divorce would depend on whether it interprets *khula* to be a form of forced *talaq* or a right in itself or whether the terms of the divorce contract cover a *khula* divorce.

Durban views on conflict-resolution

In Durban, however, there seems to be hardly any concern about the lack of a qadi. On the question of who should have authority to reach decisions, there is a tendency among the learned jurists to have confidence in the *shurta*, or judicial council of the community, to take decisions, as long as a qadi is absent in South Africa (Omar 1993, 22).

Perspective of South African couples on extra-judicial bodies

Couples marrying under Muslim rites also have their views on extra-judicial decision-making bodies. One of three couples interviewed after the Ryland case about the contents of their marriage contracts made an interesting point about dispute-settlement among Muslims.[203] They felt that the extra-judicial rulings of some of the religious leaders in the communities (ulama) to whom couples took their disputes were unfair in some cases towards women. As a result, they sought to incorporate into the marriage contract protection against such rulings.

While such couples are motivated by the equality ethos of the South African Constitution, it should be noted that marriage contracts are a double-edged sword in Islamic law. This has been the experience in Egypt. In a contract the wife can not only attain protection of her rights, but equally can agree to give up many rights, e.g. the right to monogamy, or curtailing the amount of maintenance the husband owes, or agreeing to compensate him when he demands *talaq* in exchange for compensation (see chapter on Egypt above). The only safeguard lies eventually in the courts, and that is only if the courts decide that the terms of a marriage contract which are not compatible with the ethos of the Constitution relating to gender equality are not enforceable.

Eventually the surest safeguard for fair dispute settlement lies in the women themselves. The brunt of negotiation and representation of their interests will rest on them. They and their families have to be enabled to negotiate a bargain based on interpretations of Islamic law that have as their first premise an equal balance of power between spouses. A conscious-raising campaign among women about taking the initiative is required.

Law reform and conflict resolution

The South African Law Commission took up the issue of extra-judicial dispute settlement in 1997. It published a paper on Alternative Dispute Resolution (ADR) for comment.[204] Arbitration was excluded as a form of ADR since another working paper was being circulated for purposes of revising the Arbitration Act 42 of 1965. Arbitration is used mainly in industrial disputes. The purpose of the Alternative Dispute Resolution paper was to debate how the 'overburdened court system'[205] could be relieved by more formalized alternative dispute settlement mechanisms and how these mechanisms could provide more affordable access to justice. The term 'alternative' was redefined as 'appropriate', meaning: what process is 'best suited' to the particular nature of the dispute or conflict?[206] Finding appropriate alternatives is of particular concern in South Africa because of the history of apartheid. During apartheid the courts were perceived largely as bastions of injustice applying statutes which were unjust and therefore constituted pseudo law. As part of their resistance to apartheid in the urban areas, the people founded community courts. Non-governmental organizations have also initiated various forms of dispute resolution in the communities.[207]

The Law Commission envisioned two major forms of alternative dispute resolution: mediation, defined as leaving the final decision to the parties; private adjudication or private arbitration, defined as allowing the parties to choose the decision-makers. The difference between the alternative dispute settlement and the judicial settlement is that the success of the former depends on the willingness of the parties to accept the outcome, whereas a court settlement compels acceptance. A combination of approaches would also be possible, such as mediation in the course of matrimonial court litigation. Private contracts in South Africa may contain clauses for dispute resolution outside court by experts appropriate for the issue in dispute.[208] The Law Commission's paper did not broach the question of whether by analogy a clause in a Muslim marriage contract specifically regulating the procedure for resolution of disputes between the spouses would or ought to be recognized.

While the African approach and that of various social organizations to alternative dispute resolution are mentioned in the Law Commission's report, the Islamic approaches in family matters were not included much less the Mosaic or Christian. They were included only by way of implication in the discussion of the pros and cons of an alternative community court system.[209] Three basic requisites recommended for all community courts are gender and age representation among the court members, resistance to communal political pressures (in effect, a plea for objectivity and independence), and adherence to the constitutional Bill of Rights.

Islamic rules for extra-judicial conflict resolution

The Islamic communities continue to control the process of settling disputes according to their interpretations of Islamic laws. In classical Islamic law the matter is not simple, nor is integrating a gender perspective. When mediation or conciliation is sought between the spouses, this is regarded essentially as an extension of the negotiations of the marriage contract (Goolam). Where arbitration is used instead, this tends to take on more of the character of a court process, for the decision by a third independent party is in principle binding.

A major issue arises when the parties do not wish to accept the recommendations of mediators or conciliators. What rules will then govern? There are two Quranic verses concerning matrimonial dispute settlement. In one,[210] it was said that if a wife feels threatened by a disobedient or recalcitrant (*nushuzann*) husband, then the two may decide to reach an amicable settlement between themselves. This in effect confers on the wife the same power to negotiate as the husband for reaching mutual decisions on the consequences of divorce. The other verse[211] speaks of dissension (*shiqaq*) between the spouses. This means in a practical sense that they are incapable of talking with each other. In that situation two decision-makers are to be appointed, one from each spouse's family. The issue arose among the jurists as to who had the authority, though, to appoint the family decision-makers. Some were of the opinion that the ulama or the government or a court judge (qadi) or heads of family clans had the power of appointment. Others opined that the spouses themselves appointed the decision-makers, or at least dictated the conditions and extent of their powers (Goolam 145, 147). In this method of dispute settlement the wife was dependent on her relationship with her family. The extent to which they represented either her interests and theirs combined, or exclusively her interests alone, would depend on the gender sociology of the community or even the family. If the spouses did not determine the extent of the powers of the decision-makers, another contentious issue would arise. In the absence of agreement between the spouses on the extent of the powers of decision-makers or persons who are to resolve the conflict, might the law automatically confer on the decision-makers the power to grant a divorce? The jurists' opinions were divided. Some were of the view that the decision-makers might order divorce and determine the terms of property settlements, since the quarrelling spouses would not be in a position to reach a fair agreement. Others were of the opposite opinion, for the Quranic verse refers to reconciling the spouses, thus implying that the power of the decision-makers was limited to reconciliation only. This would mean that the decision to divorce would be left to the husband or the wife. The husband would have to decide whether it was in his financial interest to pronounce *talaq* (and pay the deferred dower and consolatory gift) or the wife would have to decide whether it was in her financial interest to walk out and offer a *khula* (repayment of the marriage dower or forgiving any debts the husband might owe her).

There was also controversy among the jurists regarding the binding character of the decision of the persons appointed to resolve the conflict: even when the spouses had agreed to confer on the mediators the power to decide for divorce, the spouses could change their mind. If the mediators agreed on divorcing the parties, but one of the spouses dissents, what would happen? Some jurists argued that the divorce pronounced by the mediators was valid, others argued that it was not valid. The issue turned on the legal nature of the power of the mediators: were they mere agents of the spouses, always subject to the will of the latter, or did they acquire an authority independent of the spouses? For other jurists, the decisive factor was who had appointed the decision-makers. If the court (qadi) had appointed them, then their decision was binding, as quasi-agents of the court. If the family had appointed them, then the decision was not binding. Some jurists emphasized the nature of the issue on which the mediators were deciding. If the nature of the dispute was one of divorce, divorce was normally a matter of a voluntary decision by the husband (*talaq*, combined with payment of the deferred dower plus the *mutaa* gift).[212] Thus to confer on the decision-makers the power to pronounce divorce would amount to a forced divorce, contrary in effect to the voluntary nature of divorce. Hence the mediators' decision to divorce was thought binding but subject to the husband's consent. This opinion ignored the right of the wife to exercise her claim to divorce on her terms (*khula*, combined with repayment of the dower and relinquishing the husband's debts towards her).

In summary, when regulations or laws for the Muslim communities are being debated in South Africa, the diversity of the Islamic legal approach should be taken into account. The fact that there is such a diversity of opinion facilitates the task. The principles most compatible with the constitutional principles of gender quality and fair hearing can be chosen.

Extra-judicial dispute settlement in non-Muslim religious communities

The question of an extra-judicial authority to reinterpret the religious law is not peculiar to the Muslim communities in South Africa. For example, in the Hebrew community, the power of the husband to block the religious remarriage of an ex-wife was a problem. The religious leaders refused to reconsider orthodox interpretations so as to force the husbands to issue a religious divorce. The solution had to be provided by the South African state legislator. A law was enacted to solve the problem.[213] Under the law the state courts may refuse to issue a civil divorce decree sought by either spouse until evidence has been brought of a religious divorce. While the law is neutrally formulated, the intention was to remedy cases in which the Hebrew husband sought divorce in court, walked away with a decree nisi, but refused to grant a *ghet*, a religious divorce thus preventing his ex-spouse from remarrying under her religious law. Now the husband in order to get a civil divorce must divorce his first wife religiously. The law does not solve the problem completely. If a wife has sought a civil divorce by a state court, but the ex-husband does not want the divorce, he could hold up the civil divorce proceedings by not granting a religious *ghet*.

The South African law is applicable only to religious divorces, not to African customary law divorces. That means that Muslim or Catholic divorces would be subject to the 1996 law. It is of benefit in practical terms to the Muslim woman. If her husband seeks to divorce her in a state court but does not pronounce the religious *talaq* or revokes an earlier *talaq* in order to prevent her from remarrying (which seems to be a common occurrence), then he is also barred from obtaining the civil divorce and remarrying. Otherwise, if the Muslim wife seeks the divorce in a state court, her ex-husband can refuse to issue a *talaq*, thus blocking her state civil divorce. The only possible escape lies in the authority granted under the statute to the court to 'make any other order that it finds just', which might include an injunctive order to a religious body to declare the marriage dissolved. In the Muslim community this again raises problems of whether the *shurta* believes it has the inherent authority to divorce or is limited to merely counselling the parties.

Considerations for statutory recognition of Muslim marriages

After dealing with one religious community, the South African Law Commission carried on an investigation for the Muslims. This involved the matter of whether Muslim marriages should be recognized by enacting a statute governing Islamic personal status.

Muslims relied on the judiciary, not statutes, for recognition of marriages celebrated under Islamic rites. At most the statutes appointed Muslim marriage officers, whose duty is to register the marriage with the state. The only advantage of this statute was statistical. It permitted the state to approximate how many Muslim marriages there are. Even this purpose was totally undermined since there was no incentive attached to registration. Registration was not even made a requirement for purposes of justiciability in the courts. The courts were at first divided on the question of whether to recognize Muslim marriages that had been voluntarily registered, and the dominant opinion eventually went against recognition of any Muslim marriage, whether registered or not. The ground was that Muslim marriages are de jure polygamous. One minority opinion, as cited above, found that a Muslim marriage could also be regarded as de jure monogamous, on the basis of evidence from the hadiths.[214] The only other marriage that was considered de jure polygamous was the marriage under African law and custom. Judicially the polygamous African marriage suffered the same fate as the Muslim marriage at the hands of the courts. The status of the African marriages changed only by way of statutory legislation. So it has been thought that the Muslim marriage should be treated like the African and thus be regulated by statute.

Already under the apartheid regime in 1978 Mr P. T. Poovalingam (then Asian representative in the House of Delegates)[215] introduced a private bill to recognize Islamic family and succession laws and customs. The bill was deferred on the promise that the South African Law Commission would first investigate the situation in the Muslim communities then make recommendations on what laws were needed.[216] The eventual aim of the investigation was to determine what principles of Islamic law conflicted with South African law. Ten years later in 1988, the commission drew up 61 questions to be answered in written form by various religious leaders.

The timing was bad. The year was 1988 when popular resistance to apartheid had reached a high. Political opinion in the Muslim community was divided over how far Muslims should resist participating in the apartheid regime or make use of token suffrage rights granted by the apartheid regime to the non-European population. Not surprisingly, the community was divided over whether to cooperate with the South African Law Commission. A group in Johannesburg had distributed a call for boycotting the questionnaire. They were members of the Muslim Youth Movement and the Call to Islam (Esack 242). Opposing them was a council of Muslim theologians in Port Elizabeth, the Mujlisul Ulama, who distributed letters calling for cooperation with the commission. The Ulama argued that the initiative taken by the commission would serve the interests of the Muslim community in South Africa.[217]

In post-apartheid South Africa, the Law Commission took up the issue again and was mandated to investigate the eventual recognition and application of Muslim personal law in South Africa per statute.[218] Two women out of eight members sat on the project committee.

The commission's report on Muslim marriages was organized along the lines of the law recognizing marriages under African traditional law (Recognition of Customary Marriages Act, 1998).[219] The report dealt essentially with recognition, registration by a marriage officer, marriage age, equal capacity of both spouses to acquire assets, regulation of community of property, divorce (possible only by court decree[220]), mediation by community leaders in divorce, conversion of the marriage into a de jure monogamous marriage under the civil law.

The issues posed by the Law Commission were several: conditions for recognition of de facto monogamous Muslim marriages; conditions for recognition of de facto polygamous Muslim marriages; the relation between a civil monogamous marriage and a subsequent or preceding Muslim marriage; recognition of divorce by *talaq*; effective dispute resolution mechanisms; regulation of proprietary rights, maintenance, succession, social welfare benefits; and constitutional aspects.

The commission started its discussion with the last issue, namely that of the constitutional parameters within which Muslim marriages would operate. This is a point that was hotly contested during the constitutional debates. The issue was whether the personal status laws of the various cultural communities in South Africa should be exempted from the Bill of Rights. The more orthodox African traditional leaders argued for exempting the African family and succession laws and customs and orthodox Muslim religious leaders repeated the same arguments for Islamic personal laws (Esack 244). On the African continent this debate is not new. The Kenyan Constitution has provisions of exemption, while the Tanzanian constitutional Bill of Rights subjects personal laws to constitutional review (Jones 1995, 1995a). The difference between these two approaches can be explained in part by zeitgeist. The Kenyan Constitution was written at a time when pan-Africanism and racial discrimination were the larger issues. The Tanzanian Bill of Rights was written at a time when the gender issues and human rights had come to the fore. The South African Constitution left the question open and did not take a specific position. The South African Law Commission merely concluded that it would be for the legislature to decide whether it wishes, or not, to recognize personal or religious laws. But in case of recognition, the legislature was to assure that the '[r]ecognition ... be consistent with ... the other provisions of the Constitution' (Art. 15 (3) (b)).

The South African Law Commission framed the constitutional aims against which recognition of Muslim personal law would have to be measured:

> maintaining a secular and unitary state;
> maximizing the individual's right of choice in religion;
> protecting women in regard to the economics of family life, especially after divorce;
> preventing unfair discrimination.

The commission also formulated the specific core constitutional principle against which recognition of Muslim marriages would be measured, namely:

> equality (Art. 9).

This was the commission's only conclusion. It felt that equality was a principle of Islamic law. In support of this proposition, it cited Quranic verses and one-line hadiths which would support equality. Verses and hadiths to the contrary were not cited nor the problems of interpretation discussed.[221]

The concrete proposals that the commission made in regard to the contents of a draft law on recognition of Muslim marriages were more of a technical nature and did not raise controversial issues. The guiding principles proposed were as follows:

> guarantee of the right to choose a marriage system compatible with one's religious beliefs or compatible with the civil secular law;

age of consent at 18 years of age;
informed consent from both parties;
designation of Muslim religious marriage officers with the duty to solemnize the marriage and register it;
a marriage formula for Islamic rites;
prohibition of incestuous marriages (including the Islamic rules of fosterage);
permitting a marriage contract, which expressly provides for the application of Islamic law;
providing for divorce in case of polygamy of the husband;
registration of de facto monogamous Muslim marriages before a Marriage Officer;
regulation of marriage with or without community of property or provision of other rules on matrimonial property regime.

After controversial discussions with members of various Muslim communities and women's groups, a draft was submitted in 2003 to the Minister for Justice and Constitutional Development.[222]

The South African Commission for Gender Equality has also created an alternative draft law for Muslim Marriages, but it was embargoed (Manjoo).[223]

Overall review of draft Muslim Marriages law

The most prominent features of the draft law are –
Minimum age of marriage would be 18 years.
Husbands could marry polygamously and issue unilateral *talaq*. The wife could divorce only before court and could offer a *khula* divorce.
The husband would pay a marriage portion (*mahr*).
There would be no community of property unless the parties agree otherwise.
Custody would be governed by the principle of child welfare.
Inheritance would be excluded from the law.

The draft explicitly provided for equality within a Muslim marriage – both husband and wife would be 'equal in human dignity' (Art. 3). Yet throughout the draft equal dignity does not translate into equal rights. The drafters had not used the opportunity to go the Tunisian way of a modern *ijtihad* (critical reinterpretation) of Islamic law. Some of the more problematical aspects are highlighted below. The draft obviously represents compromise. Serious *ijtihad* would be apparently left to the courts, not the legislature.

Age of marriage, marriage guardians, and definition of Muslim

Although 18 would be the legal age for marriage, a minor would be able to marry with the consent of both parents or a guardian in the absence of the mother. Hence the draft law deviated from the conservative interpretations that only the father's consent is needed. At the same time the Home Minister would be given the authority to permit the marriage of a minor or to delegate this power to a Muslim individual or group (s. 5 (6)). It was unclear whether the minister would need to intervene in addition to the parents' consent to an underage marriage or only in case of lack of parental consent. If the minister's consent were not obtained, the minister might still bless the marriage with post de facto consent. The only constraint was that the minister or delegate would have to show that the marriage would be in the interests of the parties.

The draft did not set a minimum age limit under which no parent or minister may agree to the marriage. Hence the draft law would not provide sufficient safeguards against marriages with underaged minors outside South Africa from countries where child marriages are practised or children betrothed at a very early age. What seems at stake here was the notion of what is the age of majority from a conservative perspective. The age of majority was deemed in medieval Islamic law, as in other legal systems at the time, to be the age of puberty, estimated on average to be 12–15 years of age. There is no Quranic verse on this. Age of majority, however, is an evolving legal concept that is based on realism and facts that change the social meaning of age (Ghazali).[224] Age represents a society's view on how long it takes a young person to reach a stage of having been trained to undertake a living independent of parents. If our contemporary society is now taking much longer than the medieval society to prepare our youngsters for life, then the marriage age is set higher.

The draft avoided the controversial issue of whether or not a woman needs a guardian to marry. The draft only stated that a husband and wife are equal in dignity (Art. 3). It did not specify equality at the actual marriage ceremony. A proxy would apparently allow someone to substitute for the person to be married, as long as that proxy satisfied the Muslim marriage officer that the person to be married had consented (Art. 5 (1) (b)). The term proxy was not defined in the draft. It would seem that the notion of proxy would be an indirect way of allowing a guardian to act as a proxy. This would raise the issue of whether the proxy is used consistently for the bride rather than the groom. If so, then one asks whether the draft foresaw the gender issue of whether an adult woman would not be treated as equal to an adult man in so far as she would give her consent through a proxy but he would not. At stake is whether both parties to the marriage need only to give consent without requiring in addition the consent of a guardian or *wali*. This is an old issue in Islamic law. The Hanafi and the Shafii have long disagreed about whether a woman even needs a *wali*, much less to marry without the consent of a guardian. At one time some jurists held that a full aged man too needed a *wali* (Spectorsky 1982, 463). Those jurists who decided against egalitarianism then opened the door to a Pandora's box of other subordinate issues. One such issue in earlier writings was whether a husband would have a legal remedy outside divorce if he discovered after the consummated marriage that his wife was mentally ill or had a sexual disease. Could he sue the *wali* for failure to disclose defects or refuse to pay the full dower? (Spectorsky 1982, 463). To avoid such disputes, the South African legislator and courts should make clear that proxy does not mean guardian and that a woman's consent like that of a man does not need to be supplemented by the guardian's consent. Furthermore the reason given why a proxy is needed, especially in the case of a bride, would have to be scrutinized in depth and with care.

The draft also avoided the contentious issue of whether a Muslim woman may marry a non-Muslim man. The classical interpretation of various Quranic verses has been discriminatory towards women. If a woman finds a Muslim marriage officer who is willing to marry her to a non-Muslim, the issue would arise as to whether the courts may recognize it as a marriage 'according to Islamic law'. The courts would have to choose between a classical interpretation of Islamic law or rely on an *ijtihad* reinterpretation of the Quranic verses in the spirit of the South African Constitution. The relevant Quranic verses are, in their language, egalitarian. Sura 2:221 states: 'Do not marry unbelieving women until they have faith (in one Allah/God), a slave woman is better than an unbelieving (free woman) ... For the woman, do not marry to an unbeliever until they have faith (in one Allah/God). A man slave who believes is better than a (free) unbeliever.' Subsequently sura 5:5 reminds men of their obligations when marrying non-Muslim women: ' ... Lawful to you are those women who have faith (in one Allah/God and women of the people of the book. Give them their dowers …'

The verses from sura 2 thus were revealed with the intent to treat men and women equally. Neither was to marry an unbeliever. Each is to marry a believer. The verses did not use the word Muslim, as found in sura 2:128 ('Oh Lord make us Muslim bowing to your will …'). Sura 5 in turn simply reminds men that just because they are marrying a believer of the pre-Islam monotheistic religions (Christianity or Judaism), does not mean that she is not due her dower when her own law may not require a dower or requires her to pay a dower. Yet because the verse addresses only men (and rightfully so because it addresses dower, a duty on men), this verse has been interpreted to mean that Muslim women may not have the same right to marry men of the Book (Christian or Jewish believers). The reason given was not Quranic, but stemmed rather from psychological and biological myths without empirical evidence. It was thought that women are too weak to resist demands to convert from Islam into another monotheistic religion. It is presumed that men have no weaknesses. Islamic history, however, had presumed the reverse. When Muslims conquered certain parts of the Persian Empire, Caliph Umar wrote to his governor of Al Madain that it had come to his attention that several Arab Muslim men including the governor himself, Hudhayfah, had married women of the area, who were of the Book (Kitabi: Christian or Jewish believers in one God), and he wanted the governor to divorce his wife. The governor in turn questioned Umar's approach. He wanted to know whether such marriages were permissible or forbidden. Umar had to respond that they were permissible (under Quranic injunctions), but Umar felt that the non-Arab women were quite captivating. Arab Muslim men would not be able to resist them and they would take them from their Arab Muslim wives back home. The governor then agreed to divorce. Other men who had also married believers of the Book did not follow suit necessarily. When they returned home to the Arabian peninsula, some divorced their Madain wives and others kept them.[225] Why should one not presume today that the Muslim men and women are equally too weak to resist the influence of a spouse who is an adherent of the Book and thus should be limited to marrying only Muslim partners? Without this presumption, one can give both men and women the chance to show the strength of their beliefs with an equal right to intermarry. This issue illustrates how outdated or inaccurate empirical or historical information can impede a logical egalitarian interpretation of the Quran.

The draft defined a Muslim marriage for purposes of recognition by the state as a marriage between a man and a woman (Art. 1 (xviii)). A Muslim is further defined as one who believes in the oneness of Allah and the Prophet as the Final Messenger of God (Art. 1 (xvii)). The first definition in itself violates the South African Constitutional Court decision which struck down the gender specific language of the Marriage Act and thus permitted same sex marriages.[226] No Muslim marriage officer would be obliged to bless a same sex marriage, but were there one, then such a marriage under the draft law would not be recognized. The definition of Muslim as someone who accepts the Prophet as the final messenger seemed designed to render the Ahmadi marriage a kind of marriage that cannot be statutorily recognized unless a special Ahmadi marriage law were enacted (see supra on religious sects and litigation).

Male polygamy

The draft paralleled the South African law-maker's prior decision to allow polygamy for African customary marriages. The draft did not adopt the Tunisian way of interpreting the Quranic verses to mean that no human man can possibly treat women equally as a condition for polygamy. The draft provided two constraints on exercising the gender-biased privilege. The man's unilateral decision would be curtailed to the extent that he must seek the permission of a court to become polygamous. The wife would be informed but not given veto power. The draft prescribed the one criterion according to which it could grant polygamy. It would have to decide whether the husband could treat more than one wife 'equally' (Art. 6 (8)). The term equally was not defined; it is simply provided that equal treatment would be determined according to the prescriptions of the Holy Quran. The terminology is noteworthy. The earlier draft had specified the meaning of equality using the conservative interpretations relating to material equality between wives (each had to be materially maintained at the same standard). The current draft resembled more closely the arguments set forth by Tunisian Islamic jurists, who argued that moral and emotional equality is intended, not just material comfort for each wife. The draft left it to the courts to determine what the Quran prescribes, rather than the hadiths or opinions of ancient jurists. This was the one time the draft referred to Quranic prescriptions. Otherwise, the draft used the catch-all phrase, 'according to Islamic law', without defining sources or the concept.

Given that polygamy in the South African Muslim communities is practically extinct, the draft provision seemed to be a nod towards conservatives who do not wish to harmonize this social factual reality with law. The law reformers do not seem to appreciate how they could convince conservatives of how elegantly the Quran presents choices and offers solutions in the face of varying social contexts. The Scriptures were revealed in a society which was polygamous in fact. How could it introduce changes in such a society so that it would see the error of its ways? The Quran acknowledges that men do marry more than one wife. It was a fact of life then. Yet the Quran very cleverly hems in this one-sided male privilege with many conditions. All depends on the different sociological conditions existing at any one point in time and space. The Quran foresees many possible contingencies. It acknowledges the communal practice of marrying more than one wife when there has been a war and women with children are vulnerable. But the Quran does not make this a duty. For if the state can defend the vulnerable victims of war, then men no longer need to come to the rescue. Polygamy is not for the pleasure of a man. But if a man is more motivated by pleasure than a desire to do public charity (for a man could also simply provide maintenance for widows and orphans without marrying them and benefiting sexually or winning prestige in the community), then the Quran provides an impossible standard – the man is to love all the wives (and that means all their ensuing children) equally. Because the verse was revealed at a time just after a major war, it is highly circumscribed and conditioned. If there were a war in which more women get killed than men, as occurs in wars with high collateral damage, then the verse has no meaning, or else is to be interpreted to allow women by implication to marry more than one man. Similar to the issue of verses seeming to allow slavery, the verse is highly discouraging of polygamy, and so for that reason alone should never be applied to permit South African Muslim men to marry more than one wife unless circumstances are extreme or the man can bring evidence of almost saint-like qualities. The wording of the draft law (the court 'must grant' approval if satisfied the man can maintain equality) would be questionable in so far as it assumed a man can fulfil the equality condition. For a more realistic approach, the wording should be changed at the very least to the court 'may grant'. The presumption would be against the husband.

Some proponents of polygamy will argue that restricting or banning polygamy reflects a cultural bias towards monogamy and thus imposes Christian cultural imperialism as practised under the long years of non-recognition of African and Muslim marriages in South African history, precisely because they were potentially polygamous. The response is that the issue of non-recognition is resolved once all persons of South Africa can have marriages recognized according to their cultural/religious or sexual preferences. What is at stake in the debate on polygamy is gender equality. If women were granted the same polygamous rights as men, then men would not be privileged. Privileging men with polygamy is simply reverting to power imbalances that characterized the apartheid era – simply disguised in the form of cultural gender bias rather than general cultural bias.

Under the draft the penalty for entering a polygamous marriage without court consent would be a fine of R20,000, not even imprisonment as in Tunisia.[227] Whether the marriage remained valid was unclear. It could be provided that the marriage be null and void but any children would be treated as though the parents were married (although legally this is irrelevant because no child is to be discriminated against on the basis of parental conduct).

Talaq *and* khula

Conservative Islamic interpretations permitted the husband to issue a *talaq* (unilateral divorce). Without any recourse to an adjudicator, in effect it was a private divorce. The draft retained in part this view as well as the traditional categories of revocable and irrevocable *talaq*. The *talaq*, however, was constrained by the requirement that it would not become effective unless registered before a marriage officer and two witnesses, then brought before a court for confirmation. The court would not examine the fairness or grounds of the *talaq*. The only aspect of the *talaq* the wife could contest was its procedural correctness, whether it was pronounced 'according to Islamic law'. At most the wife could contest the timing of the *talaq*, e.g. whether it was not pronounced in the proper part of her menstrual cycle as prescribed by the Quranic sura devoted to *talaq* (sura 96). It was further constrained by the provision that the husband and wife go before a mediation council before having the *talaq* confirmed by court (Art. 13). A problem lay in the fact that the mediation council could reach a settlement between the parties regulating the terms of the divorce or of reconciliation without any further scrutiny from the court. The court would have only to examine the settlement from the point of view of minor children. If no children were involved, then the court would have basically a rubber stamp function.

Leaving the issues of *talaq* up to what is 'according to Islamic law', has also far-reaching consequences for inheritance, for Islamic law constitutes no more than a myriad of private judicial opinions supplemented by comparative official jurisprudence from other Muslim state and community courts/forums around the world. This process of consultation would be similar to some extent to uncovering the positions of various common law jurisdictions around the world. The inheritance issue at stake arises from a dispute over whether a wife could be deemed a spousal heir when her husband had issued an irrevocable *talaq* before consummating the marriage but while he was terminally ill (Spectorsky 1982, 462, n. 8). The Ottoman Land Code of 1274/1858 reached a compromise without going into the details of the nature of the divorce, whether it were revocable or irrevocable, or whether the marriage was consummated or not. It took as the major criterion the time when the husband died. The code acknowledged the wife as a spousal heir if the husband were terminally ill when he issued the *talaq*, revocable or irrevocable, and died *before* the wife's waiting period of *idda* ended, regardless of whether it turned out during the waiting period that she were pregnant or not. However, if the husband died after the *idda* had ended the wife could inherit only if the divorce had been revocable (Fisher, Art. 6).

A similar problem did not exist for husbands as spousal heirs. They inherited automatically even when the wife had brought a suit in court to divorce and she died before the conclusion of the case. Her instigation of court proceedings did not have the weight of a revocable *talaq*. Widows would be subject to unequal treatment in inheritance because of the privilege of *talaq* and its many complicated consequences, unless the draft law made a wife's pronouncement of a *khula* divorce as having the weight of an irrevocable divorce and made it independent of the consent of the husband (as in the case of Pakistan) just as a *talaq* is independent of the consent of the wife. The Tunisian Code of Personal Status streamlines the situation, showing the advantages that egalitarianism offers for simplifying the law. It avoids these problems by requiring divorce only before a court of law on the ground of breakdown on the authority of the Quranic verse: 'If you fear a breach (*shiqaq*) between them (spouses), then appoint adjudicators (*ahkama*) from (his and her families) …' (4:34). The reference to adjudicators from both sides was taken to refer to the customary practice of the desert nomads who did not make a clear distinction between arbitration and adjudication (Lyon 182). All parties for any kind of dispute, family or non-family, entered into contractual agreements about who should be the judge or arbitrator and who should be responsible for enforcement and execution for any one dispute. In the modern context of the more centralized authority this has been replaced by the practice of settling disputes before courts with appointed judges (Stewart).

The draft South African law would require the wife to bring her action for divorce before a court of law – specifying the grounds for divorce. While this right would also be given to the husband, it is only theoretical (Art. 1 (x)); practically it would have no meaning as long as a husband could exercise *talaq* without going through the trouble of specifying why he wants a divorce.

The wife would be given a separate right of divorce, the *khula*. Like the husband who issued a *talaq*, the wife would have to register her *khula* before the marriage officer and two witnesses. But the likeness stopped there. The draft defined this form of divorce as an 'agreement' for transfer of property in exchange for termination of the marriage. The draft did not adopt the more progressive interpretation applied in Pakistan and Egypt that the wife needs no agreement from the husband to get a *khula* divorce. Because the draft treated this form of divorce as a mutual settlement, it required further a court confirmation of the divorce. Yet one could raise the question, why waste the time of the court when the parties agree? The draft did not realize that the *khula* is not an agreement, but equivalent to *talaq* in so far as under *talaq* the husband has the financial obligation to finish paying the deferred dower. In *khula* the wife has the financial obligation to forfeit the deferred dower or return the prompt dower. The draft did not, however, protect the wife against pressure which a husband could place on a wife when negotiating a *khula* divorce. Here the South African legislator or courts would do well to learn from the Egyptian experience and read the concerns of the classical jurist Ibn Taimiyya that one can hardly assume that a man would not pressure his wife when it comes to getting a financial advantage out of a divorce (Ibn Taimiyya 256–7, *talaq*).

*Marriage dower (***mahr***)*

The dower was defined as something of value or benefit that is an *ex lege* (pursuant to the law) consequence of marriage (Art. 1). It was not made clear whether it would be obligatory or simply the result of an agreement between husband and wife. The draft attempted to distinguish the *mahr* from a price for sex (Ali, K.). It provided that the *mahr* contract would be presumed to establish a family and to lay the foundations for affection and companionship (Art. 1 (vi)). The *mahr* has had a turbulent history because its price can be so high as to deter young men from marrying since they compete against older wealthier men. Some governments choose to regulate it for that reason (see chapter on Tunisia above) (Jones-Pauly 2008).[228] The origins of the *mahr* are complicated. The word used in the Quran is not *mahr* but rather *sadaqa*. The practice was that the *sadaqa* was a compensation to a woman for losing her business. Khadija, the first wife of the Prophet, a businesswoman in her own right, was a prime example of this dilemma. A woman who agreed to leave her family business or her own business wanted compensation for taking the risk of moving to the husband's place. Or if the wife stayed at her family's home or wherever she had a business, and the husband would visit her, then he would compensate her or her family for his stay (Purohit 135–6). While the *lobola* which is permitted and justiciable under African customary laws is the parallel of the Islamic *mahr*, and justified by its function of showing respect for the marriage and serving as a deterrent against easy divorce, both institutions have a gender bias. The *mahr* is the sole obligation of the husband, and *lobola* the sole obligation of the husband's family. The gender unfairness of both institutions has not been legally tested. The only practice that might serve as a counterweight to the non-egalitarian aspects of the marriage portion is the tradition that the Muslim woman brings into the marriage many household goods which she herself has made or bought or which her family has supplied. Their value can be a counterweight to the husband's contribution. Where this is not a practice or it has fallen into disuse, then the gender bias of the *mahr* should be more seriously taken into account and corrected. The Quran provides a corrective for the gender bias. It allows a woman to forego it from the start of the marriage negotiations, not just at the time of a *khula* divorce.[229]

Adjudication: sources of law and personal qualifications – only Muslim judges

The draft often referred to the general term 'according to Islamic law' without defining the term. It did not specify an Islamic rule, whether representing a conservative or progressive interpretation. Specifying the rules was left to a complicated consultative procedure. The first instance judge seized of the matter (who should be of the Muslim faith) is to be advised by two Muslim assessors named by the Minister for Justice and Constitutional Development. If the case goes on appeal to the Supreme Court of Appeal, where no Muslim judges sit, and even if they happened to sit, the appellate court would be required to submit its draft decision to the scrutiny of an accredited Islamic institution. The court would not be bound by their views but should consider them.

The draft did not take into account the safeguards of the Egyptian Family Courts Establishment law, which include requiring a woman social worker or psychologist to be an assessor for a Muslim judge.

There is a certain irony in the ample use of the term 'according to Islamic law' in the draft. The draft was the result of an extensive consultative process undertaken in the spirit of the new South African democracy. It would be ironic if the interpretation of Islamic law were left only to some experts of an Islamic institution or Muslim assessors or judges who choose to apply only one Islamic law opinion, for as exemplified throughout this book, Islamic rules are myriad and reflect many different premises, reasonings and empirical realities. Islamic law by nature lends itself to a consultative process. Parties have to be informed of all of the possible arguments and disagreements among jurists on how to resolve a problem in light of all Islamic legal sources and practices. Then it is the parties who eventually may have to decide what rules they find most relevant and just for the resolution of their issues.

The draft law limited the faith of the judge sitting at the first instance trial level to being Muslim. As defined in the draft, it would exclude an Ahmadi (Art. 15). Only in urgent matters would a non-Muslim judge be able to hear a dispute about a Muslim marriage.

The requirement that the judge be a Muslim[230] represented a compromise with those who believe that only a Muslim can apply Islamic law,[231] even though this would not reflect a unanimous interpretation. It seemed designed to encourage Muslim women and men to go to court rather than remaining within the confines of the Muslim communal dispute resolution mechanisms. Yet this requirement would be discriminatory against non-Muslims who have married Muslims according to Islamic law. The definition of Muslim marriage in the draft is not confined exclusively to two Muslims marrying each other. If a Muslim man, for example marries a woman of the Book, i.e. a Christian or Jewish woman, and if they are embroiled in a dispute, why should not fairness for the non-Muslim party call for the judges hearing the case to come from each of their communities? Such would certainly be in the spirit of the Quran which says that in case of a spousal dispute, then the parties are to be heard by family members from both spouses,[232] meaning that Jewish or Christian family members could sit down with Muslim family members even if the marriage took place in a Muslim ceremony.

On the other hand, requiring the judge to be a Muslim or of any specific faith may raise some serious problems of 'immorality of law' (Fuller). It would mean getting into the definition of who is a Muslim or not, who is a good Muslim or not. This would resurrect the spectre of personal definitions of who we are that was so perniciously used under the apartheid regime. Such definitions carry the seeds of their own contradictions, which compromise the integrity (morality) of the legal system in itself. At the very most, the legislature might consider making this provision in the draft optional ('may' be a Muslim).[233]

Including the institution of assessors in the draft law reflected the long history of the colonial pluralistic legal system. Assessors were in effect substitutes for legal experts used in conflict of law cases because the local customary or religious law was regarded essentially as 'foreign' to the state law which the conquering invaders imposed on the land. The particularistic terms which the draft law used imply that certain laws like Islamic or African customs and rules are not yet an integral part of the South African constitutional human rights legal system. Mainland Tanzania and Tunisia have broken through this historical juggernaut by not insisting that the presiding judge be a Muslim, since the personal status law for family matters applies to all persons regardless of religion, but judges are to take into account the cultural practices of litigants. These two countries have less communal and sectarian strife than their neighbours, who have opted for communitarian or sectarian laws, e.g. Egypt (with its Coptic minority and Kenya with a concentration of Muslims on the coast).

A more inclusive, and hence more South African, approach might be to require all law students to take university courses and bar exams in Islamic laws and African customary laws. Such would deepen the dialogue and provide for a fair scholarly exchange of views. The role of *ijtihad*, applying reason, reality, mercy, generosity and equality to interpreting religious sources, needs to be thoroughly understood in the South African system, much in the same way that the African legal principle of *ubuntu* has been brought to bear on South African jurisprudence. This certainly would be in the scholarly, if not political tradition, of the 19th-century Indian Subcontinent Muslim exegetist, Sir Syed Ahmed Khan, who wrote not only a new commentary on the Quran and hadiths from the perspective of a rationalist epistemology but also published a commentary on the Bible, to the chagrin of traditionalists (see chapter on Pakistan).

Conclusions

The South African courts have a checkered history regarding Muslim marriages, mainly because they regard such marriages as potentially polygamous even when de facto monogamous. The courts in the pre-apartheid era proved to be more or less tolerant. Subsequent courts in the apartheid era foreclosed any type of mutual respect and recognition.

The current constitutional era in South Africa has set a new parameter, namely equality. Apartheid presumed to rest too on equality, equal but separate, apart. Now it is equality without a but. The lower high courts have needed time to adjust to the Constitutional Court's clear message of equality. The last few decisions in which same sex marriages have been approved and African customary inheritance rules against women struck down, show that the lower courts are beginning to understand the new jurisprudence and are integrating a human rights culture in the society.

The South African personal status laws regarding African customs and rules, and the draft law for Muslim marriages reflect by contrast an evolutionary approach. The laws reflect diversity, even a clash of principles, especially in regard to gender discrimination. Eventual consistency in the legal principles as a common ground, however, is to be created at the apex of the judiciary, the Constitutional Court. In practical terms, it is left to the choice of the litigants, depending on their degree of social and legal awareness, to decide to live out diversity or to seek the realization of basic human rights principles.

Unlike any of the other societies portrayed in this book, the South African courts have an advantage when encountering diversity. Perforce when dealing with religious or customary laws the courts live up to the challenge of delving into the history of these laws and revealing their evolution, flexibility and ultimate rationality. Previously the South African courts were blocked, as South Africa's legal system for over forty years served only one group holding the political and economic power, a system that overlooked and ignored human justice. What the South African courts can do for Islamic law and other religious or customary laws is to unblock them as well. They are in a better position than most to pave the way towards tackling the last bastions which resist human rights justice. These are mainly the religious institutions which choose not to measure the very core of their structures and doctrines against the rigours of human rights justice, all in the name of religious freedom, a false freedom of conscience, similar to the false equality that apartheid propagated (separate but equal). The latest decisions of High Courts in South Africa, recognizing a de facto polygamous Muslim and a de facto monogamous Hindu marriage, respectively, have extended the statutory laws to cover inheritance by widows in polygamous marriages. These statutory laws providing for widows to share in the estate do not explicitly define marriage as monogamous and hence have been interpreted in a new spirit of equality. Again the courts have managed to fill the gaps without the legislature having to interfere. The issue remaining is whether polygamy as a privilege of men violates the principle of equality and might one day become a legitimate reason for discriminating against marriage patterns and cultural choices, such as polygamy, which do not grant both spouses equal privileges in their sexual choices.[234]

5

CONCLUSIONS

When Islam was first revealed as a monotheistic religion in the 7th century it reflected the customs of the day, responded to injustices at the time while recognizing the achievements of its two other sister monotheistic religions, Christianity and Judaism. Islam recognized and praised the prophets of the latter two religions. The reciprocal acknowledgement of Muhammad as Prophet has not taken place.

At the time Islam appeared, clericalism was the order of the day. Islam aimed to break the hold of the clerical class in the pre-existing religions. Islam introduced long before Protestantism the concept that the individual believer is responsible directly to Allah/God without clerical intermediaries, including understanding the scriptures, interpreting them and voluntarily following their injunctions. Inherent in this approach were the principles of freedom from hierarchism and equality before Allah/God and the law. The law was not there to compel; compulsion was instead by one's conscience. Islam also emphasized that each believer learn and be able to read. That is why the Quran means 'read' and why the Prophet was reported to have said, go all the way to China, a non-Muslim society, to learn. The message is clear and often repeated in the Quran: the believer is not to stay cocooned in narrow-mindedness, self-conceitedness, self-righteousness or hypocrisy, knowing better than others.

With regard to women in particular, it is well known that the Quran retained some of the Arab and Arabo-African customs while planting the seeds for revolutionizing some pre-existing religious laws. In this regard the Quranic verses reveal a brilliant subtlety: while a verse seems to recognize a custom or rule that was already familiar to the people, even though it might be unjust towards women, the verses give food for thought so that what is familiar can be taken in a direction towards more justice. The verses on polygamy and adultery offer good examples of this subtlety. The polygamy verses presume that men because they are accustomed to unlimited polygamy want to continue this privilege. The Quran raised the issue of just how many wives can a man take on? Should the number be unlimited as in African, Arab and Semitic cultures or limited as in Christian culture? Is it two or three or four wives or two plus three plus four, adding up to nine? The Quran then raises another issue that goes beyond the debate of numbers. It turns the debate to the issue of why a man takes on several wives, what duty he fulfils if at all and how this affects the women. The Quran in effect points out the polygamist has an important duty, which is, to make each wife feel she is being equally loved. For women, however, this is a nigh impossibility, for as the Quran says in another passage, you can never do (enough) justice to a woman (4:129). In effect, the Quran undermines the polygamist by conditioning the exercise of this ancient custom on a premise that is impossible to fulfil. The second example that illustrates Quranic subtlety relates to consensual sexual relations (not rape). The Revelations contain strong warnings against intercourse between unmarried persons. Nonetheless the verses contain the seeds of rationalizing the social attitudes towards sexuality and leading attitudes towards a new direction. The verses clearly recognize that adultery and pre-marital sex are regarded as an anathema in the other religions and harshly punished with death. Yet at the same time, the Quran warns against meting out drastic punishment with ease. It introduces new kinds of evidentiary standards which can serve as an antidote against reaching harsh judgments rashly and against the prevailing trial by ordeal. The Quran requires four witnesses to the sexual act. In effect two lovers had practically to invite people into their bedroom to be convicted, also a nigh impossibility. Without this level of evidence, only a confession would suffice, but initiated by the person herself or himself. The confession thus has to be voluntary. Confessions become then a matter of conscience; confession is for a particular kind of person, a person who cannot live with her or his conscience and who has a need to ask the community to punish them, similar to the story in the American novel *The Scarlet Letter* of the adulterous Puritan priest whose conscience killed him. Self-confession is reinforced by the Quranic injunctions forbidding spying on others to get them in trouble with the law (sura 49:12).

While, as shown, certain passages reveal a brilliant approach to dealing with certain injustices, there are certain customs of the day which the Quranic injunctions reinforced. Two examples of such are the verses governing adjudication and dower. Custom at the time allowed conflicting parties to choose their own judges or arbitrators as well as the persons who were going to guarantee that the judgment or decision would be enforced. The Quran acquiesced in this system by applying it in spousal disputes, in which each party chooses an adjudicator or arbitrator. Similarly this applies in cases of murder. Relatives of the murdered victim can negotiate for victim compensation or for capital punishment of the perpetrator. Whether compensation or capital punishment were chosen, both sides had to agree on who would guarantee the payment of compensation or the death of the culprit so that execution would not result in a blood-feud. Regarding the dower, there were several pre-Islamic Arab customs by which a man married. If the wife had her own business or was needed in her family's business and she did not wish to move to her husband's place of residence, the husband paid a sum that would compensate her or her family if he convinced her to move away. Or if she stayed on in the place of her business and the husband visited her, then he had to pay for his keep. Khadija, the first wife of Muhammad, presented an early example of such a business woman. She had hired Muhammad as her agent then proposed marriage to him. The Quran recognized these customary options by providing that the husband and his family present the dower, unlike the early Mosaic rule under which the wife and her family brought wealth into the marriage (which was later eclipsed by the custom of the husband providing the bridewealth). At the same time, the Quran says that the wife may waive the dower if she so chooses. She is given the power to negotiate, not just to consent to or refuse marriage with a given man. In line with custom, the verses confer on her the right to keep whatever she earns, just as her husband has the same right. There was no community of property: customarily the wife and the husband had their own sources of livelihood or businesses before marrying, and if the marriage ended in divorce, each would be able to continue to earn a living. This raised certain juridical issues about maintenance, which are not resolved explicitly in the verses: such as, if a wife had her own means, had children from a prior marriage and was also responsible for her aged parents, and her husband, too, had obligations to his parents and children from a prior marriage, to what extent did the spouses have mutual responsibility to provide each with material support in addition to their parents and children? In some instances it was argued that the husband would owe the wife only one dress for summer and one for winter, while she would be responsible for her medical needs and travel to religious shrines.

Whether one identifies in the Quranic verses old customs being recognized or reforms being suggested, there is one overarching principle. That is negotiability. Negotiating a contract to deviate from the old customs or suggested reforms was possible at any time. Freedom to negotiate was paramount. Thus non-compulsion formed the core of the Islamic system. At the same time the reality of the viciousness of humankind is ever present in the Quran. Those who are strong and have the upper hand in negotiating will want to take advantage of the weaker. To protect the weaker, the Quran issues dire warnings against taking advantage of the weaker in negotiations. Society is to make the weaker stronger (sura 4:75). Hypocrites are often warned that they shall end up in hell. Hence any negotiation or contract which violates these basic principles is not legitimate and would have to be renegotiated.

One area where the Revelations were revolutionary is that of divorce. Islam conferred on the husband and wife the right to divorce. This contrasted with the pre-Islamic laws. Mosaic law gave the husband absolute power over divorce, the wife having no right to leave him without his consent; the Roman Catholic canonical law prohibited divorce; and Arab custom permitted a man to hold a woman in suspense so that she never knew whether she were divorced or not. Only ancient Egyptian law had permitted divorce by either spouse. Islam sought a middle ground among these opposing cultural perceptions about divorce. While permitting divorce by either spouse, Islam imposed certain restrictions which did not make divorce an easy matter. For example, the entire Quranic chapter that is devoted to divorce by the husband explains that the husband is to utter three divorces (*talaq*s) over a period of three menstrual periods; he was dependent on his wife informing him whether she was in her period or not. If the wife were pregnant then he could not divorce her before the pregnancy ended. The wife too receives an equivalent power to divorce when she felt that the husband was disobedient or recalcitrant and not acting upright towards her. The restriction on her was financial – to return the dower if she had accepted one. So if she had not accepted a dower, then custom had it that whatever trousseau she had brought into the marriage or whatever contributions she had made to the wealth of her husband, she was to leave all with him, unless of course she negotiated otherwise.

In inheritance matters, we see a mixture of introducing radical reform and recognizing past customs. Need is the first principle of inheritance – which surviving relatives needed the most? It is not status or the degree of relationship with the deceased. Nor is need gender specific. Whoever needs the most, whether male or female, is given priority, as expounded in some Tanzanian judgments. If, however, relatives or dependents were not in need, then status came into play – that is, the children, the parents, the spouse were to receive specified shares. Children's shares were the largest, and daughters were discriminated against. The male child could receive twice as much as the female. Such would certainly have made the son beholden to maintain his unmarried sister (single, divorced, or widowed), as was mandated under pre-existing Mosaic, African and Hindu inheritance laws. The Quranic passages distinguish themselves from the pre-existing laws by giving the daughter a share in the estate of her parents that is larger than the share of distant male relatives albeit smaller than that of the son. This reflected a recognition of her right to economic independence. On the other hand, the Quran, as shown above in the case of the polygamous and adultery verses, offers a revolutionary alternative to the pre-existing inheritance patterns of the day. If one were to read the verses of inheritance literally, the only time a son could inherit consistently more than a daughter would be when there were only two surviving children, one son and one daughter. Otherwise, if there are more than two children, the daughters would receive more than the sons or only slightly less, depending on the ratio of female to male children. Furthermore, none of the inheritance provisions are set in stone. Family members were still allowed to negotiate a distribution that deviated from the fixed shares for whatever reasons as long as need was not an issue. In other words, flexibility is the hallmark of even the inheritance system.

If one were to summarize the revolutionary aspects of the Quran which affect women's rights, the following picture would emerge – She could marry herself with her own free will. She could not be inherited by her in-laws upon her husband's death. Before marrying she could agree to a dower of any value, whether high or low, or only symbolic. Or she could waive the dower entirely. She could negotiate whether she would stay at her place of business or go to her husband's place and be allowed to set up her own business or find her own source of income over which she alone could dispose. Her claim on her husband was principally for supporting their common children. If she brought children into the marriage they were her responsibility. If she did not want to stay in the marriage, she could divorce her husband and simply pay back the dower if she had accepted one from the start of the marriage. If her husband wanted to divorce her against her will, she could claim that her husband had not followed the proper detailed Quranic procedure that lasted over a period of time of at least three months. Once she was divorced, she could claim no long-term alimony but could claim a one-time gift for compensation for being thrown out of the marriage bed. It was expected that she continue to earn her living. If her husband died and she was not needy, she could claim little from his estate (between one-fourth to one-eighth), if needy then more; if her parents died, and was not needy, she could claim more than she could from her husband's estate (one-third). Her most serious competitor was her brother, but only if she were the sole surviving daughter and her brother the sole son. Otherwise, she had better chances to claim more from her parents' estate if there were more than two children surviving. If she were in more need than her brother, then she could claim more on that basis; and if she had helped her sick parents, she could claim a debt against the estate. Finally, in penal matters, if a woman had a jealous husband or overly zealous brother who sought to tarnish her moral or sexual reputation, she was protected by the rule of four witnesses and the rule against spying. With respect to a jealous husband, she had additional protection. She could demand that she take an oath to deny the accusation of an affair. Whether she lied or not was a matter between her and Allah/God, not between her and her husband, her family or the community.

Regarding a dress code, it was common at the time when Islam was introduced that people wore something distinctive so that others knew with whom they were connected, what their religious or family affiliation was. Muslim Arabs were known for placing a premium on simplicity of dress. They were not the richest in the early years of Islam. When the Prophet died, he left very little. He was known to wear only a simple woollen cloak. This also distinguished him as a Muslim. As the Arabs conquered the wealthier lands of the Persians and Byzantines, the historical reports show that the Persians in particular despised the Muslims coming from the Arabian peninsula for what the Persians considered shabby dress and shoes. Women who were enslaved were known to bare their breasts. Women in general were known to wear ornaments as a display of wealth. Islam's stress on egalitarianism made Muslims sensitive to issues of disparities in appearance. Both sexes were warned Quranically to stay modest in their clothing, and women in particular to stay modest in their ornaments and cover their bosoms, whether slave or free. The same principle applied to wedding feasts. They were not to be extravagant, for such would emphasize the disparity between those in need and those without need. Furthermore, the practice of five prayers a day at all hours of the day and night, including the early morning, had an impact on dress as well. The call to prayer obliged both Muslim women and men to be on the streets while it was still dark. This meant that non-Muslims should be able to recognize who was a Muslim, man or woman, so that they would not be molested or suspected of engaging in some dubious behaviour. The kind of outer cloak that the Prophet wore was recommended for all so that one could easily recognize a Muslim. There rose a controversy among Muslims about whether women in particular had to veil their faces for this reason. This was certainly an issue in the Christian community since the Bishop of Milan had issued in the 4th century a notice requiring all good Christian women to veil their faces. The Persians too were known to have women veiled. The discussion in the Muslim community, caught between varying dress codes of the day, led to confusing the Quranic verses enjoining Muslims to wear an outer cloak, which would distinguish them from non-Muslims, with the verses which speak of veils for covering women's bosoms and which discouraged women from elaborate display of their ornaments. The outer cloak then was transformed into total veiling, which became the means for identifying who is a Muslim woman; whether she was on her way to prayers or not became irrelevant. In some societies it is reported that the veil aids clandestinity and hypocrisy, that is, women, for fear of the unjust application of the laws of adultery, resort to using the full veil for clandestine meetings. This truly is a sign of how much the true spirit of the Quran is ignored, as pointed out by the Tunisian intellectuals Taalbi and Haddad. To overemphasize a dress code is missing the point of the Quranic verses that stress modesty of dress and spirit for both men and women, regardless of gender. Achieving the virtue of modesty without hypocrisy is far more difficult than merely focusing on dress codes.

Through the centuries the choices which the Quran made available to society were continuously narrowed. This phenomenon is not unique to Islamic law. It occurs in any legal system, religiously based or not. In Islamic law this process was the result of jurists defining the choices made available in the Quran according to their own social perceptions and prevailing pre-Islamic *mores*. Consequently Islamic law was taken into the direction of what was already familiar to the people, that is, what was already known and accepted in the pre-Islamic monotheistic and polytheistic communities.

The revolutionary chances the Quran offered for liberating women became circumvented by all sorts of legal fictions. The result was that a woman's independent dignity was compromised. She was deemed to be in need of the guardianship of a man, whether it was her father, her brother, her uncle or her husband. She retained only nominal control over her resources and her right to engage in any legal venture, including a marriage contract. Her free exercise of consent was hemmed in by jurists who added that in addition to her consent to marriage, she needed the consent of her male guardian (in most schools of thought except the Hanafi).

Consent by males became the dominant feature in Islamic law to the extent that when a wife wanted to initiate divorce and pay the husband compensation (*khula*), she had to obtain his consent, similar to the pre-exisiting Mosaic practice. Regarding the husband's right to divorce (*talaq*) her without her consent, the jurists expanded his right (except among Shii) by allowing him to shortcut the timetable laid out in the Quran. Instead of waiting over three menstrual periods he could simply repeat three times the word *talaq* in one sitting. This circumvented the minimum of three menstrual periods needed to divorce regardless of whether the wife were pregnant or not. The ease with which the husband could divorce then affected the rules of dower. The dower took on more prominence as a financial institution that could serve as a brake on easy divorce. This shifted the balance of power between the sexes. The dower became practically mandatory, the wife's right to waive was largely suppressed, and male relatives of the bride dominated the negotiations in order to obtain as high a dower as possible. The inflated dower was then divided into two parts – one prompt and one deferred. The deferred dower was of much higher value than the prompt dower. This difference was justified as an instrument to obstruct the *talaq* which had been made easy for husbands. It was to offset the jurists' relaxing the Quranic restrictions on the exercise of *talaq*. It was argued that a husband would think twice before divorcing because he would incur a financial burden. This in turn led to another shift. The wife's right to waive the dower, including the deferred dower, occupied the jurists. Some wanted high standards of evidence to prove that a wife had waived payment of the deferred dower and thus relieved the husband of the burden of thinking twice about divorcing her. Some jurists were content with less stringent standards of evidence. The inflated value of the deferred dower also affected the interpretations of the Quranic verses which refer to the husband giving the divorced wife a compensatory gift for having divorced her (*mutaa*). The expensive deferred dower rendered the *mutaa* superfluous and it was relegated to the category of voluntary piety, no longer obligatory. If the husband were pious he would pay, if not he need not pay. Because of easy divorce without compensation, the deferred dower became as well a source of income for women, who were encouraged after divorce to remarry and not be independent and earn their own income. This emerged as a result of the jurists developing a concept of marital obedience that resembled the Christian notion of obedience, which was a one-sided obedience – that of the wife towards her husband. This did not reflect on how the Quran used the word disobedience or recalcitrance (*nushuz*). The Quran uses the word for both man and woman without distinction. The word implied that if neither the husband nor the wife obeyed each other, or were recalcitrant or disrespectful towards each other, this was ground for considering divorce. The jurists' depreciation of the value of such Quranic verses on disobedience meant that the husband's consent for everything the wife did became imperative. She could no longer exercise her right to her own earnings because she had to obtain the consent of the husband to work or undertake business.

These various constraints did not abolish the woman's rights; they in effect constrained her from exercising them. This all culminated in the juridical notion of the husband as protector and guardian of his wife. The result was an expansion of the man's rights, including polygamy. The jurists emphasized more and more the numbers aspects (four or nine wives?) of the Quranic verse over the equity concerns. The ability of the husband to maintain and guarantee complete obedience from his wives became a criterion for exercising polygamy. The jurists further developed the power of the husband to chastise or punish a woman physically if she disobeyed. Rules were formulated to determine the extent of physical punishment allowable.

Over time the jurists relied not so much on doctrinal arguments based on Quranic exegeses and social realities as biological argumentation, similar to what was happening in the Christian and Judaic worlds as well. The fairer sex became the weaker sex, biologically no longer in need of material or economic independence but of total guidance by her husband and dependence on his material support for her. Bringing children into the marriage from a previous marriage was no longer acceptable, as it meant an extra burden on the new husband. The mother had to leave her small children behind as she was now dependent on her new husband for consent to engage in any economic activity she might want to undertake to support her children. The juridical containment of women evolved into a notion that women had to be sequestered to make sure that they did not try to regain their rights to exercise their Allah/God-given freedoms, especially for the elite urban women. If they left the confines of their homes they could not be seen and had to cover their faces, as though they carried the curtains and walls of their homes around with them.

The financial burdens placed on the man as a result of the more costly deferred dower, to be paid upon divorce and his obligation to pay maintenance during the marriage impacted on the inheritance rules. In inheritance the principle of need was ignored by the jurists who gave priority to the concept of status. Distant relatives like grandmothers and uncles, who had customarily received shares in an estate in pre-Islamic times, but were not mentioned in the Quran, recovered from the jurists their status as heirs. This meant that the children and the spouse relict had even more heirs competing with them. The burden of added competition fell on the daughter. Regardless of how many sons and daughters a parent left, the sons could exclude distant relatives and receive twice the portion of the daughters. If only one daughter or several daughters constituted the sole heir(s), most of the jurists (excepting the Shii), held that they did not receive the same powers as sons to exclude distant relatives; she had to share with distant relatives. The justification was said to be balance. The jurists had conferred on the son as a man far more financial burdens to meet than on the woman and therefore this entitled him to more inheritance. He had in effect more needs than she. In a round about way, the principle of need was reconstructed in a formalistic way that favoured the man. If the social reality, however, proved that the woman had more burdens, this was not usually taken into account in the juridical treatises.

Despite its egalitarian non-clerical message, Islam sustained the ancient institution of enslavement. The jurists developed over the centuries many rules governing relations among the enslaved themselves and between the enslaved and their enslavers. Differences between the freedoms and punishments for enslaved women versus free women were highlighted and legalized. For example, an adulterous or fornicating female slave was to be whipped, while a freed woman was to be stoned. The reasons for the difference lay in a bias of the jurists towards protecting the slave as property of the owner. Killing by stoning a slave for adultery or fornication would raise the issue of how much would the enslaver be compensated for the loss of a valuable asset. It also raised the moral question of to what extent could an owner be held responsible for the sexual behaviour of her or his property. The enslaver was further protected by the jurists under an exceptional rule. A free man who committed adultery with the female slave of his wife without the latter's permission would be whipped, not stoned. Regarding the marriage dower (*mahr*), the bridegroom who married an enslaved woman was obliged to pay the slave owner the dower; this in turn influenced jurists to make the dower obligatory for the free woman, ignoring the Quranic freedom of the woman to waive the dower. As for the right to work, a woman slave could work without the permission of her enslaved husband during the day, but had to be back home by night. The free Muslim woman, in contrast, had to obtain permission from her husband to work even during the day outside the home. Only a few prominent jurists pointed out the inequity of this discrimination against free women.

In conclusion, the direction in which the jurists took the law to curtail the freedoms of women was only in part a patriarchal perversion of the Quranic verses and hadiths. The juristic interpretations were equally a result of the politics of how to get Islam as a new religion accepted in a hostile environment, for the sources of Islamic law – the Quran and the hadiths – contained two kinds of seeds: one for emancipation and one for continuing familiar pre-Islamic mentalities. Deriving a rule from the two primary sources was a matter of choice between the emancipatory direction on the one hand and the tried and true on the other. Choice was and is inherent in the verses and hadiths. This was the source of their brilliance. Jurists, depending on their own social milieu, logic, and economic bias, chose often, but not always, the line of least resistance so that Islam could fit into the landscape of the familiar and not be totally rejected. This basic brilliance of the Quran to offer the choice to be progressive or conservative, emancipatory or patriarchal, has often been overlooked. The tendency of the more conservative interpreters is to deny this basic choice in order to achieve a monopoly of power over the politics of Islamic law.

A major debate on the direction of Islamic law arose during the last century of the Muslim empire, the Ottoman Empire, and continues today. The debate raises some existential questions for Muslims as to the nature of Islamic law. Islamic law was critiqued as inherently anti-woman and incapable of taking emancipatory directions. To understand the terms of this debate, one has to look at the political context. This was at a time when the Ottoman Empire was confronted with non-Islamic economic powers from Europe. The issues were framed in terms of a religio-political contest: Islam versus non-Islam and Oriental political and military power versus Western political and military power. One sector of the Ottoman economy and Islamic law which especially felt the impact of the debate was that of slavery, which was the economic basis of the Ottoman Empire and the southern United States. Islamic law itself as developed by the imperial jurists was struck a powerful blow when the British declared war on slavery around the world. The British began signing treaties with what they regarded as their executive counterparts in the Arab and Muslim lands: the sultan, the emir or the chief. The treaties aimed to bind the latter to abolish slavery. The British did not sign with the learned jurists or ulama who had formulated the rules on slavery and devised ways for their enforcement. The consequences of this anti-slavery movement were far-reaching. It was the rulers not the learned jurists who became responsible for making changes in Islamic law and treating it as state or ruler's law, thus raising a serious question about whether enforcement of law by the state were compatible with the Quranic prohibition against compulsion in religion (2:256). As a result, former enslavers (i.e. slave owners), sought to sue the ruler or state for loss of property. They were joined by administrators of trust lands tied up in religious *waqf* which had been formed to provide maintenance of slaves for life and the succeeding generations of their children. Some individual slaves themselves changed nationality and citizenship in order to fall under the jurisdiction of the British and escape that of a Muslim ruler thus heightening political animosity between the Oriental and the Western approaches.

The degree of sincerity and enthusiasm shown throughout the Ottoman Empire for abolishing a large part of Islamic law, namely the law of enslavement, varied within the Empire. One sees a clear difference between Tunisia and Egypt for example. The Bay of Tunis, though held at the point of gunboat diplomacy, consulted with the ulama and his ministers about which Islamic law principles could be used to justify emancipation of the enslaved. The result was a well-reasoned inspiring document of emancipation that appealed to the egalitarian strain in Islam, which had been neglected for so long and hidden in the shadow of the strains placed on Islamic law – to proliferate differentiations between the believer and the non-believer, the enslaved and the slaved, the Arab and the non-Arab, the son and the daughter, the man and the woman. In Egypt enthusiasm was not high. The difference may be because of the cultural differences. The Berber tradition in Tunisia was more egalitarian and ready to challenge authority. Egypt by contrast had a long history of enslavement stretching back to ancient pharaonic times, tied to the eternal rise and fall of the Nile river waters. Tunisia also had a longer history of political stability during the Ottoman era than Egypt. This can be traced to the tendency of the Tunisian rulers to concentrate on consolidating their own power within their borders and being satisfied to continuously improve their hard-won gains in designing an administrative infrastructure in the modernization process that integrated Islam and outside challenges. Egyptian rulers were more ambitious, seeking to challenge Constantinople's power and to expand beyond Egyptian borders. The ulama too in Tunisia tended to play a more conservative role, being dependent on appointments by the ruler, while the Egyptian ulama, although having a tradition of conservatism were known for championing the lower classes against the vicissitudes of power. In the Indian Subcontinent the economy was more dependent on a caste system rather than slavery *per se*. At issue for the learned Islamic law scholars was how to react to the mutiny against British rulers. The scholars split basically into two camps – one conservative, in favour of Muslim princes who had sought to rebel against the British but lost, and the more liberal, who championed critical independent thought among Islamic scholars and jurists. In South Africa slavery had benefited the upsurge in the Muslim population at first because Christians could not be indentured or enslaved while Muslims could be. Once the British abolished slavery regardless of religion, the recognition of Islam and Islamic law became the issue. As the state marginalized Islamic law and Muslims were fragmented along ethnic lines, the private exercise of Islamic law became paramount. This in turn allowed in practice much freedom and diversity in practice depending on cultural and empirical circumstances.

One of the earliest foremost legal thinkers for choosing to take up the challenge to search for other principles on which to base Islamic law, was the Tunisian intellectual and government minister Khayr ad Din. His influence spread as far as the Indian Subcontinent to Sir Syed Ahmed Khan, the spiritual and intellectual father of present day Pakistan. Khayr ad Din did not start with the premise of rejecting Islamic law, as the Turkish head of state Ataturk eventually did, but with the premise that just as the classical jurists had plucked out the seeds in the sources which acknowledged the habits of the day – discriminating between freed and enslaved and between the genders – the latter day intellectuals could pick and choose the other dormant seeds in the same sources that permitted economic, social and gender equality. With emancipation of the enslaved came inevitably thoughts about emancipating the woman.

Thus the first procedural reform in Islamic law in Tunisia consisted of the government becoming the law-maker, the source of *ijtihad*, over and above the legal scholars. This change persists to this day in all the four countries studied in this book. The ulama are consulted officially, but the final political will to reform lies with the government. Because the government, even when only nominally democratic, is beholden to the people, it has to vie with those who are popular scholars and mosque leaders in the debate on what kind of Islamic principles are to apply, those of liberation and egalitarianism or those of difference and discrimination. It is in this power struggle that the jurists again play a crucial role. Though appointed by the state, these modern jurists have the duty to be independent, as the Islamic classical jurists of old (Arabi), and to exercise the right to issue diverging opinions on a point of law without fear of being threatened with violence by government, or more importantly, fellow conservative Muslims. In all four countries in this book the higher judiciary has proven to be the one body which tends – with some setbacks in some instances – to sustain any reforms which the government and legislature have managed to introduce. Sustaining this independence and a critical intellectual understanding of the constitutional principles of equality is crucial for sustaining a trajectory of reinterpreting the choices embedded in the sources of Islamic law.

The Tunisian story in the first chapter of this book has revealed that women's rights had a long tradition there. The constraints imposed on women by the jurists were circumvented to some extent by use of the Islamic principle that anything is negotiable. As a result the marriage contract permitted a woman to continue to work without consent of her husband. The dower which her father negotiated often consisted of land for building a house so that if the daughter were divorced at the whim of her husband she at least had her own place to live so as not to burden her original family. Women also had the tradition of bringing into the marriage household goods the value of which matched the value of the dower. This gave wives confidence when the husband in a quarrel sought to remind the wife of how much he had sacrificed financially for her. In this fertile soil of practice only a few decades after the European colonialization of the country began, the Tunisian intellectual Taalbi boldly championed the principles of reform of Khayr ad Din and responded to the European charges that the very sources of Islam were inherently non-progressive. He pointed out the passages in the sources which are progressive but had been overshadowed by the non-progressive. His successor in the 1930s, Haddad, a theologian/jurist, continued on the same path. He confronted head-on the issue of women's emancipation. He critiqued the conservative ulama for being unjust towards women. His analysis of the texts showed that the classical conservative rules were not based on doctrine or logic, but rather on biological and sociological assumptions, which were out of touch with empirical reality. These assumptions and perspectives were fantasies reflecting social hypocrisy. He reinterpreted empirically and doctrinally the Quranic verses and hadiths on veiling, divorce, women's right to work and equality of women to men. Veiling for him was not doctrinal. It represented a symbol, a symbol to portray the notion that a woman could not compete with a man for work and that her sole biological function was to care for a man. Haddad's work was seminal for the future programme of the then existing independence party, which later gained power, Bourguiba's Destour Party. The orientation of the party was civilian, that is rooted in the civil society, not military. It had its origins in the socialist trade union movement. Its very roots anchored its pro-women's rights stance. The ulama had lost credibility because they were identified with the colonial power which was more interested in sustaining a more conservative Islam rather than reforming it. By the time Tunisia won Independence, a commission had drafted a code of family law which for the first time in Islamic modernity reflected an *ijtihad* (reinterpretation of the sources) that chose the liberal over the conservative trajectory of the Quran and hadiths.

The Tunisian *ijtihad* introduced the scheme of Islamic law which makes the woman an equal partner to the man and applies universally to all Tunisian citizens regardless of religion. It could draw on its long experience in harmonizing modernity and Islamic principles plus the general traditional practice of Tunisian women to engage in entrepreneurship, such as the weavers living in Qairawan, one of the oldest centres of Islamic learning in North Africa. Politically the government entered into a quid pro quo relationship with the people. It formulated a social pact with the population at large and the women in particular. If the state were to provide economic and social development by furthering education and providing health and employment then the women had to agree to curb the birth rate. A pragmatic mobile health system and an *ijtihad* interpretation that protected the women's right to control her reproductive life have proven successful. The ministry created for women's affairs became a valued partner in the government and was given much power to educate women about their rights and to offer arbitration services for family conflicts to be settled in such a way as to do justice to the woman. Both the husband and the wife must seek divorce on the same grounds in the courts; thus private divorce by the husband has been eliminated. Today it is the professional middle class women and rural employed women who sustain the *ijtihad* that has lasted over half a century. The courts have women judges and advocates, who also ensure liberal interpretations of the codified *ijtihad.* There is only one area of law where *ijtihad* did not penetrate deeply. That was in inheritance, which the classical jurists had transformed into a complex mathematical system. The law-maker has, however, offered other legal devices that can circumvent the orthodox inheritance law. For one, women are often appointed as administrators of an estate and so attain a position of authority to negotiate with other heirs in terms of needs. Or fathers and husbands supplement the daughter's or wife's share in an estate through a life insurance policy or a bequest. The judiciary has declared the life insurance to fall outside the general inheritance rules because of its contractual nature. Now couples may choose to enter into communal property agreements in which husband and wife are practically co-owners or partners controlling jointly the family assets. So when the husband dies, the wife becomes the sole remaining partner controlling the assets and need not compete with collateral or ascendant heirs.

In general in the Islamic world, the post-Second World War independence movements raised expectations of a more woman-friendly Islamic law through use of *ijtihad.* Of the four countries we studied in this book, Pakistan was the one country other than Tunisia which also exercised *ijtihad*, not as thoroughly as in Tunisia, which abolished polygamy as un-Islamic. Pakistan only curtailed the husband's privilege to exercise polygamy, based on emphasizing the Quranic verses on equal love for each wife over the passages dealing with the numbers and material equity. Egypt by contrast began its reform process in the 1920s and 1930s, refusing requests from Tunisian intellectuals to abolish polygamy. The latter had thought Egypt, as the first independent Arab state, should set an example. Egypt adopted instead a more gradual approach through procedural manoeuvres. It decided to ignore the rule that only one school of law applied throughout the Ottoman Empire, the Hanafi. It decided to take an eclectic approach and combine the rules from the different schools in order to maximize fairness. For example, a major issue for the government was the poverty of wives who were left behind without maintenance from husbands who went off to the military or emigrated. The Hanafi law had made it difficult for the wives to divorce and remarry. The new law adopted the Maliki school which provided more grounds for a wife to get a divorce such as on grounds of lack of maintenance. The reluctance of the subsequent revolutionary Egyptian government to introduce a thorough-going *ijtihad* can be attributed to several factors. One was the preoccupation of the government with the Arab-Israeli war in which Egypt took the lead. The other was the presence of ulama who were not discredited among the people and who opposed the militaristically based socialism of the post-Second World War revolutionary government of Nasir and advocated a more capitalistic policy. A final factor was that the socialist orientation of the leaders placed more weight on introducing a constitution that reflected a policy to carve out a separate but contained space for secular tendencies in a religious milieu.

In family law matters maintenance has long been a dominating issue in Egypt. Since in orthodox Islamic law maintenance and obedience were closely tied, the predominance of the maintenance issue led to imprinting upon the consciousness of women and men that the foremost duty of the woman was to obey. Hence even when the woman exercised her right to initiate divorce (*khula*), the jurists upheld the notion that the *khula* divorce was not valid without the consent of the husband. This gave him a chance to negotiate with his wife so that she gave up not only her dower but any financial assets she might have brought into the marriage and waived even maintenance for the children if she sought to keep them. The legislature then introduced a law which essentially tried to abolish these customary practices and returned to a more pro-gender equality version of the *khula* divorce in which the wife had only to return her dower, equivalent to the husband's duty to pay off the deferred dower if he initiated divorce. The legislature retained, however, one aspect of the customary practices by requiring the wife to relinquish in addition to the dower any debt claims including past maintenance that she might hold against the husband. Women in certain parts of Egypt have tended to apply the Quranic provision that they have the right even to waive the dower at the start of the marriage or any time during the marriage with the result that the husband can use the dower money to pay for migrating abroad to find a job. For these women, there is no more dower to return if they choose to divorce by *khula*. Otherwise, it is mainly the higher court rather than the law-maker which has exercised a more far-reaching *ijtihad*. In matters of post-divorce the higher court has awarded post-divorce maintenance under certain circumstances if needed to protect the minor children. Regarding *khula*, as the legislature had not dealt with the controversial issue of whether the husband needed to consent to a *khula* divorce, the higher court held, based on *ijtihad*, that no consent is needed. Already the fact that the husband may divorce without going to court and the wife must go to court even for a *khula* divorce entails discrimination. The court's decision to give the wife the freedom to divorce without being constrained by the husband was a step towards equalizing the situation. While the new law was pro-equality, some commercial lawyers, citing examples from their practice, opined that the law brought an added advantage to the government. Often wealthier men were placing their assets in the name of their wives in order to avoid high taxation. The law conferring on wives the right to divorce and thus run off with the assets would discourage such evasive practices.

The highest Egyptian court has also taken the more pro-woman trajectory found in some hadiths which disapprove of female circumcision, a common practice among women in Egypt. The higher court, unlike in Tunisia, still has to compete nonetheless with the opinions of the official mufti and the rector of the Al Azhar University, which produces both conservative and liberal Islamic legal scholars. What no doubt lends popular support to the highest court in controversial cases such as *khula* and circumcision is the fact that the mufti and the Al Azhar rector air differences of opinion in public. Hence the *ijtihad* of the court does not have to contend with a solid wall of opposition. This reflects the long Islamic juristic tradition of freely competing opinions. The social welfare orientation of the court from the era of socialist egalitarianism is also reflected in the court's tendency to try to harmonize constitutional values and Islamic law.

When Pakistan became the first state created for the Muslim minority in the Indian Subcontinent, so that they could be a territorially sovereign Muslim majority just after the Second World War, *ijtihad* was still the dominant approach to reclaiming the strain of pro-women rights in Islam. It was not, however, in the Pakistani context far-ranging since the pre-Independence Muslim intellectual tradition was divided between very liberal and very conservative and no one group had predominated over the other. Political instability also plagued the country as martial law became the rule rather than the exception.

In time Pakistan became affected by two events that sent shock waves among Muslims, of a magnitude resembling the era of the abolition of slavery and the elimination of the Islamic law of enslavement. One seismic shock came with the fall of the Shah in the nearby state of Iran and the rise of a clerical, non-egalitarian Islamic power base, determined to give credence to the pro-male trajectory of Islamic law and to reject *ijtihad* as a reformatory tool in gender relations. The second event was the Soviet invasion of Afghanistan and the support which Pakistan as an ally of the United States gave to the Afghani freedom fighters who rooted the ideology of their fight in the notion of a religious *jihad*, a religious fight against secular socialism. One month after the Iranian revolution, the Pakistani head of state, General Ul Haq, introduced through executive fiat the Islamic penal laws which had prevailed during the days of the Mughal Empire dating back to the 1500s and 1600s, similar to what was about to occur in Iran and later on in Afghanistan under the Taliban. Ul Haq's executive ordinance criminalized adultery and fornication between unmarried persons, including rape. It gave rise to a flood of court cases initiated by private charges brought to the police and prosecuted by the ruler/state. The ordinance represented a convergence of popularist biases against the sexual choices of women and an extension of the ruler/state power. While the Quranic provisions for needing four witnesses to the sexual act in order to protect both men and women from being spied upon and unnecessarily prosecuted were written into the law, the government expanded its powers beyond the Quran and hadiths thus circumventing the Quranic provisions. If there were insufficient Quranic evidence to convict – and there never could be with the requirement of four witnesses to the sexual act – the ruler/state gave itself nevertheless the power to prosecute on the basis of circumstantial evidence as in any other secular criminal case. If men accused of rape were convicted, the penalties were high – up to 25 years of imprisonment. On the other hand men were acquitted for lack of proof beyond a reasonable doubt. At the same time, if women failed to prove their rape charge they were in turn convicted for consensual adultery or fornication. Failure to prove was taken as circumstantial evidence of consent or as presumptial evidence of consent. The rule of proof of consent beyond a reasonable doubt was ignored. The judiciary played an uneven role in this misapplication of Islamic law. Many courts were complicit in this reversal of justice, many were not. A recent revision of the law has removed the state discretionary power and placed it back into the secular penal code inherited from the British, but it retains the basic Islamic provisions of the executive ordinance punishing adultery. Unproven rape charges may no longer be converted into charges of fornication or adultery against women.

The expansion of the discretion of the ruler/state to prosecute premarital sex led to an uncontemplated but logical result. It led to a surge of honour killing. A brother, a husband, a father, any male relative could kill their female relative or wife simply on the pretext of suspicion of *zina*. The irony was that a judicial sentencing to stoning was extremely rare and if it occurred, then the highest appellate court always found fault with the evidence or procedure and nullified the order of stoning. This was totally the opposite in Iran or Afghanistan. Ironically there was no need for stoning in Pakistan. Men took it upon themselves to execute the women extra-judicially. They based their honour killings on a hadith which used the Arabic word for honour in a word play which gave the reader a choice – to favour the more popularist and customary notion of male control over women or to follow the more pro-woman emancipatory approach which gave women control over their own honour and sexual lives, answerable only to God. The highest Pakistani court came to the rescue of women by issuing a judgment in the first year of this millennium which declared honour killing contrary to the Constitution. The highest Shariat court has also found honour killing contrary to its interpretation of the Quran and the hadiths that do justice to women.

In the past the highest Pakistani courts exercised jurisdiction independent of the executive and sought to moderate the blind adherence to orthodox Islamic injunctions by the executive. The courts were keen to confer on themselves the power of *ijtihad*. The judiciary even had the audacity to strike down the death penalty of stoning to death for adultery as unIslamic and hence unconstitutional. It reversed itself when the executive interfered in this independence and thus undermined the courts' credibility so that the binding nature of the judgments of the highest courts has suffered. Nonetheless many, not all, of the highest courts have sustained a steady course of *ijtihad* and moderateness. Only recently, as mentioned above, has the legislature supported the highest courts and the women's movement with a new law which punishes honour killings but still allows some room for the courts to consider the popularist pro-male interpretation of Islamic injunctions. This challenges the highest courts to undertake an even more meticulous *ijtihad*, that is, to ground *ijtihad* in a more philosophical basis which exposes the constitutional weaknesses of the lay popularist superficial knowledge of Islam and presses the government to commit itself to countering popularist Islamic law and accept the independence of the modern trained judiciary.

Here Pakistan could learn some lessons from the South African highest appellate courts. South Africa offers the best example of how Islamic law at first presented itself as a cultural phenomenon which suffered during the apartheid era of discrimination just as African customary laws did simply because they were of non-Christian or non-European origin and allowed polygamous marriages. Once the post-apartheid courts began to recognize a Muslim marriage as justiciable before the courts, some of the lower courts took this as a sign that the various customary and religious laws could legitimately diverge from, even contradict, the constitutional provisions of equality and human dignity for women. This represented a tendency to revert to the separate but equal doctrine of the apartheid era. The highest court has reversed this trend by holding all cultural and religious groups to the constitutional standards even if this means the nullification of a particularistic rule. The highest court has negated certain gender inequities in African customary inheritance laws. This has radical implications for the equally discriminatory Islamic law as understood by conservative religious bodies.

The South African Law Reform Commission has drafted a Muslim personal law based on democratic and open discussions with representatives from the entire spectrum of Muslim intellectuals. The draft clearly reflects more of a blind adherence to Islamic law as largely unchangeable than an *ijtihad* approach based on the Tunisian model. The government would have found support for *ijtihad* from certain groups of Muslims who practise pro-women Islamic law by way of contractual agreements, which are negotiated with the help of liberal imams. The chapter on South Africa shows how one can achieve a comprehensive gender-equality interpretation of Islamic law in family and inheritance matters. Until the government is prepared to have the draft law rethought, or even if the draft law were passed with its vague references to 'according to Islamic law' without defining the term Islamic law, it will remain for the highest court to harmonize the constitutional equality provisions with orthodox Islam. That might entail it learning how to exercise an *ijtihad* that releases the emancipatory strains in Islam. This may well mean that the courts would have to re-examine the concept of whether the state should refuse to enforce Islamic injunctions because they constitute a religious system based on voluntarism. In case the courts would refuse to entangle the state in applying Islamic injunctions, it would then become the duty of the legislature to learn how to incorporate at least the values of Islam and the values of African customary laws into a universalistic pro-gender equality law which is compatible with Islamic *ijtihad* but does not use state force to replace the religious conscience which can be judged only by Allah/God.

Thus despite differences in history and politics, all four countries presented in this book show that the key organ for sustaining the progressive strains in Islam against the pressure of the less egalitarian strains is an independent judiciary well trained in constitutionalism, international human rights and the notion of Islamic law as a process of choices, capable of being reconciled with contemporary social and ethical changes. The courts cannot, of course, be left alone to accomplish their tasks or totally rely on the legislative or executive branches. Popular civil rights movements lend backbone and courage to the courts, such as evidenced by the public outcries from women's movements in each country, supported by cross-border solidarity.

NOTES

Acknowledgements

1 Sura 49:13: Oh People, We have created you from a single pair, a man and a woman, and made you into nations and tribes so that you may know, not despise. In the sight of Allah the honoured are those who deal mercifully (with others). God is all knowing.

1
Tunisia – The Ideal Islamic Reform

1 Malik, *Muwatta: kitab nikah.*
2 Bukhari, *Sahih: kitab nikah; bab as shurut; kitab as shurut, bab shurut fi'l talaqi.*
3 This conclusion by analogy was not a logical necessity and so was rejected by Hanbali jurists. The Hanbalis opined that an initial contract may prohibit entry into a subsequent contract.
4 Malik, *Muwatta: kitab nikah.*
5 Dawud, *Sunan: kitab nikah, bab shuruti fil nikah.*
6 Interview, Samia Ben Khalifa, daughter of the Sheikh ul Islam, Sidi Ben Arous, Tunis, January 1998.
7 Interview, Prof. Nabiha Gueddana, Office National de la Famille et de la Population, Tunis, January 1998.
8 Bukhari, *Sahih: kitab nikah; bab wa ina imra'a khafat min ...*
9 Malik, *Muwatta: kitab nikah.*
10 Preamble of the *Ahd al-Aman* (Fundamental Pact) of 1274 A.H./1857 A.D.
11 He wrote about the Islamic congress in Jerusalem in 1931: 'Abd al Aziz at Ta'albi, *Khalfiyat al mutamar al islami bi'l Quds, 1931/1350*, edited by Ahmad Ibn Milad and Hammadi as Sahili, Beirut, Dar al garb al islami, 1988.
12 *L'esprit libéral du Coran*, appearing under the name of César Ben Attar (the lawyer of Ta'albi), Ta'albi and al Hadi al Sab'i (Sebai) (his translator), Paris, 1905; later

edited by Muhammad al Mukhtar as Sallami, translated by Hamadi as Sahili, Beirut, Dar al garb al islami, 1985.

13 Bukhari, *Sahih: bab hijab.*

14 I reached this position in the same way as, but independently of, the Egyptian Sheikh Muhammad al Ghazali (p. 62).

15 See Dawud, *Sunan: kitab libas, bab Sura Al Nur*, reporting on Um Salamah arguing that Maimuna need not be veiled much less lower her gaze in front of a blind man. The Prophet is reported to have anwered that it did not matter: what mattered was that she was looking at the blind man. The second report points out that only the Prophet's wives were addressed in the first report, since the Prophet had told another woman that she could spend her *idda* with the same blind man (Ibn Umm Maktum) without covering herself.

16 Muslim, Sahih, *kitab nikah*; *bab nadb min ra'y al mar'a.* I have reached this conclusion independently of the Egyptian Sheikh Muhammad Al Ghazali (b. 1917, d. 1996), who also used this hadith to criticize those jurists and imams who preach that a woman has to protect a man from arousing himself in front of women. For such an opinion from a Malaysian Sheikh that the veil protects men from themselves, see Samira Ahmed's film *Unveiling Islam*, broadcast in the UK on Channel 4 television, January 2004.

17 Bukhari, *Sahih: bab hijab.*

18 Dawud, *Sunan: kitab libas.*

19 Malik, *Muwatta: kitab salat.*

20 Malik, *Muwatta: kitab salat.*

21 Malik, *Muwatta: kitab salat.*

22 Malik, *Muwatta: kitab talaq, bab muhakkun.*

23 Malik, *Muwatta: kitab talaq.*

24 Malik, *Muwatta: kitab talaq.*

25 Bukhari, *Sahih: kitab nafaqat, bab mughib.*

26 Malik, *Muwatta: kitab talaq.* When Fatima bint Qais informed the Prophet that she had received a marriage proposal from a certain Abu Jahm, he told her that this man beat his wives and so discouraged her from marrying him.

27 Al-Haj Maulana Fazlul Karim, *Al Hadis*, Book I, New Delhi, Islamic Book Service, 1989, p. 212, citing Abu Dawud. Abu Dawud, *Sunan: kitab nikah*; *bab li zawjaka alaika haqq* ('rights of your wife over you').

28 Malik, *Muwatta: kitab 'uqul*; *bab 'uqul al ma'a.*

29 Dawud, *Sunan: kitab nikah*; *bab adrabuhunna* ('beat them').

30 Bukhari, *Sahih: kitab nikah*; *bab mauidhati al rajuli abntahu zaujiha.*

31 Malik, *Muwatta: kitab jami'*; *bab bil rifq bil mamluk*; Dawud, *Sunan: kitab adab; bab mamluk.*

32 Dawud, *Sunan: kitab adab; bab mamluk.*

33 Interview, Awni Aziz Dajani, Tunis, January 1998.

34 At Tabari, Tarikh, *History* (official history of Islam), Year 23, para. 2767.

35 Malik, *Muwatta: kitab nikah*; *bab jama'.*

36 Originally s. 1313 of the Buergerliches Geseztbuch of 1895 (*Die Beratung des Buergerliches Gesetzbuchs*, similar to the Reichsgesetz of 6 February 1875); became s. 8 of the Ehegesetz 1946.

37 Bukhari, *Sahih: kitab nikah; bab kufrani al aishiri wa huwa al zauju* ('to be ungrateful to the husband').
38 Muslim, *Sahih: kitab riqaq.*
39 Malik, *Muwatta: kitab talaq.*
40 A similar situation was observed by the author during field work among the Muslim community on the cashew plantations of southern Tanzania in the 1990s.
41 Bukhari, *Sahih: kitab nikah; bab man tafa nisa'ihi* (also Anas bin Malik).
42 Ibid., *kitab nikah; bab la yatazawwaj akbar 'arba in.*
43 At Tabari, Tarikh, *History*, Year 23, paras. 2755–56.
44 Bukhari, *Sahih: kitab nikah; bab gairati an nisa'i.*
45 Dawud, *Sunan: kitab nikah* (hasan).
46 Muslim, *Sahih: kitab birr; bab al ihsan ila al banat.*
47 Bukhari, *Sahih: kitab shurut; bab shurut fil nikah.*
48 Malik, *Muwatta: kitab talaq* (Yahya b. Sa'id on a question put to Sa'id al Musayyab).
49 According to frequent anecdotes, this continues today in wealthy strata of Arab societies where divorces are frequent, and some women use the full veil as a way of protecting their freedom to go everywhere and do whatever they wish, includeing having affairs without being easily detected.
50 Al-Haj Maulana Fazlul Karim, *Al Hadis*, Book I, New Delhi, Islamic Book Service, 1989, p. 201.
51 Dawud, *Sunan: kitab al taharah; bab ha'id.*
52 Malik, *Muwatta: kitab hajj.*
53 Bukhari, *Sahih: kitab nikah.*
54 Ibid., *kitab nikah; bab anzhri lilai al mar'ata kala at tazwiji*; Dawud, *Sunan: kitab nikah* (Jabir b. 'Abd Allah on how he chose a wife).
55 Muslim, *Sahih: kitab nikah.*
56 Bukhari, *Sahih: kitab tibb*, report by Rubai bint Muath bin Afra.
57 Ibid., *kitab al dabbah wal said; bab dabbah al ma ati.*
58 Written notes from Zahia Jouirou, Historian, University of Tunis, Manouba, from her field study of her home village Menzel el Harb in the Sahel, 1999.
59 Malik, *Muwatta: kitab nikah; bab walimah.* A contemporary example of efforts to control expenses is the Marriage Functions (Prohibition of Ostentatious Display and Wasteful Expenses) Ordinance II of 2000 and the Punjab Marriage Functions (Prohibition of Ostentatious Display and Wasteful Expenses) Act V of 2003, upheld as constitutional by the Supreme Court of Pakistan, Ch. Muhammad Siddique and ors. v Government of Pakistan and ors, Constitutional Petition No. 23 of 1999 and 21 of 2004, decided 5 November 2004.
60 Interview with Hamadi Sahli, retired Professor of History, Tunis, March 1999.
61 Muslim, *Sahih: kitab nikah; bab al wasiya bin nisa'i.*
62 Bukhari, *Sahih: kitab talaq.*
63 Malik, *Muwatta: kitab talaq; bab muhakkun.*
64 Bukhari, *Sahih: kitab talaq; bab talaq fil sukr.*
65 Malik, *Muwatta: kitab talaq; bab jami' at talaq.*
66 Deuteronomy 24:4.
67 Bukhari, *Sahih: kitab talaq; bab ahaqq bi raddahinna.*
68 Ibid., *kitab talaq; bab talaqa at thlaki; tallaqaha thlathan.*

69 Malik, *Muwatta: kitab talaq; bab khul'.*
70 Ibid.
71 Ibid., *kitab talaq; bab mut'a.*
72 Ibid., *kitab talaq; bab khiyar.*
73 Ibid., *kitab talaq; bab jami' at talaq.*
74 Ibid., *kitab talaq; bab rajul yamusu.*
75 Sura 2:226.
76 Malik, *Muwatta: kitab talaq; bab ila.*
77 Bukhari, *Sahih: kitab talaq; bab itha arrada binafyi al waladi; sadaqi.*
78 Sura 2:229, known as *khul'.*
79 Ali, *The Meaning of the Holy Qur'an*, Intro. to Sura 65 – *At Talaq.*
80 Malik, *Muwatta: kitab talaq; bab el batta.*
81 Sura 2:228.
82 Bukhari, *Sahih: kitab talaq; bab khul'.*
83 Malik, *Muwatta: kitab talaq; bab khayar.*
84 Bukhari, *Sahih: kitab nikah; bab wa ina imr'a khafat min ...*
85 Malik, *Muwatta: kitab talaq; bab khul'.*
86 Ibid., *kitab nikah; bab jami' al nikah.*
87 Ibid., *kitab talaq; bab talaq al marid.*
88 Ibid., *kitab talaq; bab talaq al ha'id.*
89 Deuteronomy 24:1.
90 Malik, *Muwatta: kitab talaq; bab tamlik.*
91 Ibid., *kitab talaq; bab 'azl* (on the freedom of men to decide whether or not to refrain from impregnating captive slave women, who had no say in the matter).
92 Dawud, *Sunan: kitab talaq.*
93 Interview, Kacem Bousnina, 2000.
94 Suras 65:6; 2:233.
95 See the decision of the Reichsgericht, 8 April 1929, Vol. 125, p. 54ff (*Entscheidungen des Reichsgerichts in Zivilsachen*), in which a wife spent her afternoons and evenings as a piano player in a cinema house for silent films in Berlin.
96 §1360a of the Civil Code. For a popular account of wives' dependence, see *Wieviel Haushalts und Taschengeld darf die Gattin denn beanspruchen?* ['How much housekeeping and pocket money may a wife claim?'], *Hofer Anzeige*, 18 June 1996, p. HV.
97 Malik, *Muwatta: kitab talaq; bab 'idda (mutawaffan fil bait)*; Bukhari, *Sahih: kitab dabbah; bab dabbah al imra'a.*
98 Bukhari, *Sahih: kitab nafaqat; bab amali al imra'a.*
99 Muslim, *Sahih: kitab zakat; bab nafaqa 'ala al aqrabin.*
100 Ibid., *kitab zakat; bab sadaqa min bait zaujhi*; Bukhari, *Sahih: kitab zakat; bab zakat min bait zaujhi*; disputed by Abu Dawud.
101 Bukhari, *Sahih: kitab nafaqa; bab lam yanfiqi al rajulu.*
102 Al-Haj Maulana Fazlul Karim, *Al Hadis, Mishkat ul Masabih*, Vol. II, New Delhi, Islamic Book Service, 1989, p. 197.
103 Muslim, *Sahih: kitab zakat; bab nafaqa bil nafs.*
104 Bukhari, *Sahih: kitab nafaqat; bab fadl ala al ahl, bab nafaqa ala al ahl wal iyali.*
105 Dawud, *Sunan: kitab zakat; bab sadaqa.*

106 Malik, *Muwatta: kitab nikah*; *bab 'idda fil bait.*
107 Ibid.
108 Bukhari, *Sahih: kitab zakat*; *bab sadaqa min bait zawajiha*; Dawud, *Sunan: kitab zakat*; *bab sadaqa*, *kitab al ijara*; *bab sadaqa.*
109 Bukhari, *Sahih: kitab nafaqa*; *bab lam yunfiqi al rajulu.*
110 Muslim, *Sahih: kitab zakat*; *bab nafaqa wa sadaq ala aqrabin wal zawaj.*
111 Ibid.; Bukhari, *Sahih: kitab zakat*; *bab sadaqa min bait zawajiha.*
112 Muslim, *Sahih: kitab zakat*; *bab nafaqa ala aqrabin wal zawaj*; Bukhari, *Sahih: kitab zakat*; *bab sadaqa ala zawaj wal aitam.*
113 Decree prescribing the emancipation of slaves, 23 January 1846.
114 Decree of 13 August 1956, *JOT* (*Journal Officiel de la Tunisie*), 28 December 1956.
115 Decree of 18 July 1957 and of 25 July 1957, *JORT* (*Journal Officiel de la République de la Tunisie*), 26 July 1957).
116 Decree of 19 March 1874 (*Jam'iya al 'ahbas*).
117 1 June 1959, *JORT*, No. 30 of 1 June 1959.
118 Code of Personal Status (CSP) Art. 9: 'Man and woman may conclude marriage themselves or by way of a wakil ...'
119 Art. 18 CSP: contracting several marriages [i.e. polygamy/polygyny] is prohibited.
120 Art. 30 CSP: divorce may take place only before a court. Art. 31(3): the court may pronounce divorce on the petition of the husband or the wife.
121 Interview, April 1999, Kacem Bousnina, former governor of Sfax. See Enda-Inter-arabe, p. 85, ftn. 2 on no female-led enterprises before the 1970s.
122 Art. 140 of the Code of Property Rights (*majallat al huquq al 'ainiyat*).
123 Report of Tunisia's Minister of Religious Affairs arguing that the style of hijab imported from the Gulf violates Tunisian cultural tradition. At www.prohijab.net quoting Khaleej Times, 30 December 2005.
124 Leyla Sahin v Turkey, Application 44774/98, Judgment, 29 June 2004, European Court of Human Rights, para. 108.
125 Carthage, 13 August 1992, in Tunisian External Communication Agency, Women of Tunisia, Civil and Legal Gains, Tunis, March 1993, p. 13.
126 Information on crèches from République Tunisienne, Rapport de La Tunisie sur l'Application de la Convention Internationale sur les Droits de l'Enfant, 1995, p. 67.
127 Malik, *Muwatta: kitab nikah*; *bab mahr wa hiba.*
128 At Tabari, Tafsir al Tabari, Sura An Nisa', Misr, Dar al Maarif, n.d.
129 Mohd. Ahmed Khan v Shah Bano Begum, All India Reports (A.I.R.) 1985, S.C. 945, at 951, 952.
130 Law No. 98–94 of 9 November 1998, *JORT*, 13 November 1998, p. 2225 and 27 November 1998, p. 2316.
131 Sura 4:32: '... to men is allotted their profits and gains; to women is allotted their profits and gains ...'
132 Interviews with the Sheikh of Tunduru, Tanzania and the High Court Muslim Judge, Dar es Salaam, Tanzania, 1997.
133 L'Office National de la Famille et de la Population, 1995, p. 326.
134 Source of information in this paragraph is Mohamed Ayad's contribution, L'Office National de la Famille et de la Population, 1995, pp. 299–318.

135 Dawud, *Sunan: kitab nikah*; *bab ha'id.*
136 Ibid.
137 Malik, Muwatta. *kitab 'uqul*; *bab 'uqual al mar'a.*
138 Dawud, *Sunan: kitab nikah*; *bab haqq.*
139 Malik, *Muwatta: kitab talaq*, *bab 'azl.*
140 Ibid., *kitab al 'uqul*; *bab 'uqul al janin*; Bukhari, *Sahih: kitab al diyat; bab janini* (Abu Huraira).
141 Infanticide Act, 1938, c. 36.
142 Bukhari, *Sahih: kitab muhaddin*; *bab ithm az zunat.* See also the pledge of women before the Prophet not to kill one's children (Bukhari, *Sahih: kitab ahkam*; *bab bai' an-nisa'.*
143 Interviews, Baccouche and Hachida.
144 Malik, *Muwatta: kitab rahn*; *bab manbudh.*
145 Bukhari, *Sahih: kitab shahadat*; *bab idha zakiy* (Abu Jamil).
146 Court of Appeal in Tunis, Case No. 20462, 14 Nov 1994.
147 Bukhari, *Sahih: kitab talaq*; *bab man ajaza talaq.*
148 Decree 95-407 of 6 March 1995 (*JORT*, 17 March 1995) amending Decree 90-519 of 22 March 1990.
149 Directive of the Ministry of Religious Affairs of 10 May 1993 (*JORT*, 21 May 1993).
150 Decree 93-1952 of 31 August 1993 (*JORT*, 1 October 1993).
151 Decree of 18 July 1957 (*JORT*, 26 July 1957).
152 Decree 93-1549 of 26 July 1993 (*JORT*, 3 August 1993).

2
Egypt – Conservative Incremental Reform

1 *Al Ahram Weekly* (Cairo), 18 February 2000, on the interests that the British government had in the precise titles adopted by the Egyptian dynasty.
2 Sura An Nisa, 4:127: 'They ask thy instructions concerning the women ... In the Book concerning the orphans of women to whom ye give not the portions prescribed, and yet whom ye desire to marry, as also concerning the children who are weak and oppressed; that ye stand firm for justice to orphans.'
3 Sura An Nisa, 4:75: 'And why should ye not fight in the cause of Allah and of those who, being weak, are ill-treated (and oppresed)? Men, women, and children, whose cry is. Our Lord! Rescue us from this town, whose people are oppressors ...'
4 Interview, Mervat Tilawi, former Minister for Social Affairs, member of the National Council of Women, Cairo, February 2000, on the need for a comprehensive state campaign on what Islam means.
5 *Kitab al ahkam as shari'iyya fi'l ahwal as shakhsiyya* ('ala madhab al Imam Abi Hanifa an Numan), 1875, (translated into French as 'Code du Statut personnel et des successions') and *Murshid al hayran.*
6 Law No. 25 of 1920, 12 July 1920.
7 Law No. 25 of 1929.
8 Law No. 100 of 1985.

9 *Journal Officel*, No. 8, 27 January 1921.

10 Bukhari, *Sahih: kitab ahkam; bab hal yaqdiy* (Aisha on Hind bint Utba bin Rabia asking to use her husband's property for his children). In the version in Muslim, *Sahih*, the wife asks for 'us', (herself and the children) (*kitab aqdiyy; bab hind*).

11 Art. 1, Law No. 25 of 1920.

12 Art. 3, Law No. 25 of 1920.

13 Art. 4, Law No. 25 of 1920.

14 Art. 5, Law 25 of 1920.

15 Art. 7, Law 25 of 1920.

16 Art. 9, Law 25 of 1920.

17 Art. 9, 2nd paragraph, Law 25 of 1920.

18 Art. 10, Law 25 of 1920.

19 Bukhari, *Sahih: kitab ahkam; bab shahdati (aahlu al jihaz)*, prohibiting a judge to take a case if he has personal knowledge of the situation at issue.

20 Ibid., *kitab ahkam; bab hal yaqdiy* (where the husband exercising *talaq* is likened to a judge). The Prophet was greatly angered over a report that a husband had issued his *talaq* in a fit of anger.

21 Decree-Law No. 25 of 1929 concerning certain questions of personal status, 24 February 1929.

22 Art. 16, Decree-Law 25 of 1929.

23 Treated as abrogated in the 1999 official edition of the personal status law for Muslims (*Ahwal as shakhsiyya li'l muslimun*), Cairo, Ministry for Trade, Resources and Minerals, 1999.

24 Art. 17, Decree-Law 25 of 1929.

25 Art. 12, Decree-Law 25 of 1929.

26 Art. 13, Decree-Law 25 of 1929.

27 Art. 6, Decree-Law 25 of 1929.

28 Art. 7, Decree-Law 25 of 1929.

29 Art. 8, Decree-Law 25 of 1929.

30 Art. 9, Decree-Law 25 of 1929.

31 Art. 10, Decree-Law 25 of 1929.

32 Art. 11, Decree-Law 25 of 1929.

33 Art. 1, Decree-Law 25 of 1929.

34 Art. 2, Decree-Law 25 of 1929.

35 Art. 5, Decree-Law 25 of 1929. An exception was made for a *talaq* pronounced before consummation.

36 Art. 5, Decree-Law 25 of 1929.

37 Regelung der Personenstandsangelegenheiten der Koptisch-Orthodoxen, Arts. 128–132, 145–146, §40 of Regulation of the Personal Status Matters of the Orthodox Coptics.

38 Art. 19, Decree-Law 25 of 1929.

39 Malik, *Muwatta: kitab nikah; bab sadaqah wa hiba; irkha as satur.*

40 Art. 99, Law 78 of 1931.

41 Ibid.

42 Art. 347, Law 78 of 1931.

43 Art. 345–6, Law 78 of 1931, which is still in existence in the 1999 edition of the personal status laws (*Ahwal as shakhsiyya li'l muslimun*).
44 Law No. 44 of 10 June 1979, modifying personal status provisions.
45 Art. 1, introducing Art. 6a, Presidential Decree of 1979.
46 Art. 1, introducing Art. 5a, Presidential Decree of 1979.
47 Art. 1, introducing Art. 23a, Presidential Decree of 1979.
48 Sura 4:128.
49 Sura 4:34.
50 Art. 2, Presidential Decree of 1979.
51 Ibid.
52 Sura 2:241.
53 Art. 3, Presidential Decree of 1979.
54 Art. 1, introducing Art. 18bis, Presidential Decree of 1979.
55 Led by activist Advocate Mona Zulficar of Shalakany Law Office, Cairo. Her fame spread to southern Africa too: 'Egyptian women want out of the old order', *Mmegi/The Reporter*, Vol. 11, No. 31, 5–11 August 1994, p. 24.
56 The 'house laws' regulate family matters in individual aristocratic 'houses' (families) in Germany and have been tolerated and upheld by the courts. On a house law that required heirs to marry only Protestants of 'noble birth' see a judgment of the Bavarian Supreme Regional Court (Nr. 527 BayObLG, FamRZ 1997, p. 705, and accompanying commentary by Joachim Goebel, *Eheschließungsfreiheit und erbrechtliche Protestativbedingungen*, p. 656).
57 Art. 2 of Law 100 of 1985.
58 Sura 16:10ff, 50, 59, 72, 76, 90.
59 Art. 16 of Law 25 of 1929.
60 Art. 165, *Codes Egyptiens et Lois Usuelles en vigueur en Egypte,* 51ème edition, Cairo, 1939, n.p.
61 Interview, Dr Hania Mohamed Sholkamy, Cairo, February 2000. See also Fahmi, p. 80.
62 Art. 1 of Law 100 of 1985, adding Art. 11a to Decree-Law 25 of 1929.
63 Art. 2 of Law 100 of 1985 amending Art. 1 of Law 25 of 1920.
64 Sura 4:32.
65 Bukhari, *Sahih: kitab adhan; bab istithan, khuruj ila al masjid; kitab nikah; bab istithan.* Also in Malik, *Muwatta: kitab salat.*
66 Bukhari, *Sahih: kitab nikah; bab khuruj an nisa'i.*
67 Ibid., *kitab istithan; bab hijab.*
68 Muslim, *Sahih: kitab nikah; bab imtina.*
69 Ibid., *kitab nikah, bab itizal.*
70 Sura 4:34, 4:128.
71 Sura. 4:34–35.
72 Personal Status Rules of the Coptic Orthodox Church, §42.
73 Personal Status Rules of the Coptic Orthodox Church, §46.
74 See National Council for Human Rights, Arab Republic of Egypt, *Annual Report of The National Council for Human Rights, 2004/2005*, observing that women constituted only 3.6 per cent of members of parliament and 9 per cent of all senior posts (Cairo, p. 282).

75 Art. 2 of Law 100 of 1985, amending Art. 1 of Law 25 of 1920.
76 Ibid.
77 Sura 2:256.
78 Rules of Personal Status of the Coptic Orthodox Church, §33 (7).
79 Ibid., §128.
80 Art. 1 of Law 100 of 1985, adding Art. 18 bis2 to Decree-Law 25 of 1929.
81 Decree-Law 25 of 1929, Art. 16.
82 Nuruddin v Kaimuddin and others, *PLD* 1997 Karachi 386.
83 Sura 4:3.
84 Atiya, p. 63.
85 See also Bukhari, *Sahih: kitab nikah; bab yaqillu ar rijalu wa yakathuru an nisa'u.*
86 Ibid., *kitab nikah; bab shurut; kitab as shurut; bab shurut fi-t talaq.*
87 Sura 4:128, Bukhari, *Sahih: kitab nikah, bab ina amra'itu khrafat.* See also Malik, *Muwatta: kitab nikah*, relating the story of the wife of Rafi bin Khadij, the daughter of Muhammed bin Maslama Ansari.
88 Bukhari, *Sahih: kitab nikah, bab ya qallu ar rijalu wa yakthuru an nisa'u ...*
89 For a clear explanation of the conditions for exercising *ijtihad* and the absence of claims by the imams of the schools of law to absolute finality, see Abdul Waheed v Asma Jehangir, *PLD* 1997 Lahore 301, at 342. A decision of the Egyptian Constitutional Court agrees – stating that *ijtihad* is allowed in controversial issues where the Sharia is flexible (*Al Jarida ar rasmiyya* (*Official Gazette*), No. 3, 18 January 1995, p. 58, at p. 67). It notes further that the opinions of the legal scholars are not holy, i.e. not infallible.
90 Bukhari, *Sahih: kitab nikah, bab wa ini umr'atu khafat.*
91 Art. 1 adding Art. 11a to Law 100 of 1929.
92 Sura 2:228.
93 Sura 65:1. Bukhari, *Sahih: kitab talaq; bab man tallaq; bab qauli Allah taaliy.* Also in Malik, *Muwatta: kitab talaq; bab talaq al ha'id.* For even more hadiths on the prohibition against *talaq* during the menses, see Muslim, *Sahih: kitab talaq; bab tahrim talaq al ha'id.*
94 Bukhari, *Sahih: kitab talaq; bab idha tullakati el ha'idu.*
95 Malik, *Muwatta: kitab talaq; bab talaq al ha'id* (Ibn Shihab).
96 Sura 65:4.
97 Malik, *Muwatta: kitab talaq; bab talaq al ha'id.*
98 Ibid., *kitab talaq; bab talaq al marid.*
99 Sura 33:28.
100 Bukhari, *Sahih: kitab talaq; bab man khrayyara nisa'hu.*
101 Malik, *Muwatta: kitab talaq; bab ma yabaina min at tamlik* (Malik and Nafi).
102 Sura 2:241.
103 Personal Status Rules of the Coptic Orthodox Church, §40.
104 Courtesy of conversations with administrative personnel at the Ministry of Justice, Cairo.
105 *Al Jarida ar rasmiyya*, No. 3, 18 January 1996.
106 Ibid., p. 79.
107 Ibid., p. 76.
108 Bukhari, *Sahih: kitab talaq; bab al mutallaqati idhi khrushiyi.*

109 Malik, *Muwatta: kitab talaq; bab 'idda al mar'a fil baitihi idhi talaq fihi.*
110 Sura 65:1.
111 See also Malik, *Muwatta: kitab talaq; bab nafaqa.*
112 Constitutional Court Judgment, *Jarida ar rasmiyya*, No. 3 of 18 January 1996, p. 68.
113 Malik, *Muwatta: kitab talaq; bab jami' at talaq.*
114 Sura 65:1.
115 Sura 4:34–35, 128–130.
116 Sura 4:34.
117 *Al Jarida ar rasmiyya*, No. 3, 29 January 2000, to take effect on 1 March 2000.
118 Allam, Abeer, 'Women forge destinies of their own', Cairo, *Middle East Times* (Cairo), 10–16 February 2000, p. 10.
119 Interview, Dr Fathi Naguib, Deputy Minister of Justice and member of the newly established National Women's Council, Cairo, February 2000.
120 Art. 3 of the preamble.
121 Imam Mahmoud Shaltut, Great Shaykh of al Azhar, *Mas'alat at taqrib bayna al madhahib al islamiyya* (Centre for the Rapprochement of Islamic Sects), Cairo: Dar al taqrib [sic], 1383 A.H.
122 Part I, Art. 15 (1).
123 Ibid., Art. 3.
124 Ibid.
125 Ibid., Art. 4.
126 Art. 71.
127 Part 3, Art. 17.
128 Allam, Abeer, 'Urfi delivers the goods at half the price', *Middle East Times* (Cairo), 17–23 February 2000, p. 10.
129 Art. 17.
130 Part 3, Art. 19.
131 Art. 18 (second paragraph).
132 The Maldives have a similar problem. The Ministry of Justice is under pressure to appoint a woman to the bench for the first time, but the potential candidate wishes not to be appointed to the family court system because she fears being stereotyped (C. Jones-Pauly, Mission Report, The Maldives, United Nations Population Fund (UNFPA), December 2005).
133 Tadros, Mariz, 'By the skin of her teeth', *Al Ahram Weekly* (Cairo), 17–23 February 2000, p. 15.
134 Art. 21.
135 Ibid.
136 Fakhr ad Din Muhammad ibn Umar Razi (b. 543/1149, d. 1210), *At Tafsir al kabir,* Misr: al Matba'ah al baniya al misriyah, Vol. 11, 1983, p. 66, explaining the meaning of Sura An Nisa 4:128 ('If a wife fears disobedience on her husband's part, there is no blame on them if they arrange an amicable settlement between themselves. And such settlement is best, even though men's souls are swayed by greed. And if you do good and practice self-restraint, Allah is well acquainted with all that you do.')
137 Sura 65:6.

138 See below on the Constitutional Court case upholding the constitutionality of the *khula* statute.
139 Art. 20 (paragraph 5).
140 Interview, Zanzibar, September 1997.
141 Sura 2:229.
142 Bukhari, *Sahih: kitab talaq; bab ash shiqaq.*
143 Malik, *Muwatta: kitab talaq; bab khul'.*
144 Bukhari, *Sahih: kitab talaq; bab khul'.*
145 Dawud, *Sunan: kitab talaq; bab khul'.*
146 Ibid.
147 Art. 18a.1 of amended Decree-Law 25 of 1929.
148 Malik, *Muwatta: kitab talaq; bab nafaqa.* Dawud, *Sunan: kitab talaq; bab nafaqa.*
149 Art. 277, draft Egyptian Code of Personal Status.
150 Balqis Fatima v Najm-ul-Ikra, Qureshi, *PLD* 1959 Lahore 566, followed in Amanullah vs. Husna, *PLD* 1997 Karachi 306.
151 Bukhari, *Sahih: kitab talaq; bab khul'.*
152 Sarwar Jan v Abdur Rhaman, 2004 CLC (Civil Law Cases) 17.
153 Ibid., p. 23.
154 Interview, a Cairo commercial lawyer who has handled several conveyances of wealthy husbands to wives, February 2000.
155 Tadros, Mariz, 'By the skin of her teeth', *Al Ahram Weekly* (Cairo), 17–23 February 2000, p. 15.
156 *Jarida ar rasmiyya*, No. 52 (Supplement), 26 December 2002, Higher Constitutional Court, 15 December 2002/11 Shawal 1423 A.H., Alaa Abul Maati Abul Fetouh vs The Prime Minister, The Speaker of the People's Assembly and Mrs Alya Saeed Muhammad.
157 Sura 2:229: 'And if the spouses fear you cannot keep the limits of God, then there is no blame on any one for her obtaining her freedom.'
158 *Al Ahram Weekly* (Cairo), 17–23 February 2000, p. 3.
159 The National NGO Commission for Population and Development, FGM Task Force Position Paper by Marie Assaad and Aziza Hussein, Cairo, October 1997.
160 Courtesy of the FGM Task Force, Cairo.
161 FGM Task Force Position Paper, *International Women's Rights Action Watch*, Vol. 11, No.2, December 1997, University of Minnesota.
162 *Ruz al-Yusuf*, Issue of 17 October 1994.
163 Ibid.
164 Muslim, *Sahih: kitab 'ilm*; Bukhari, *Sahih: kitab ikhtilaf fil sunna wa 'ahadith.*
165 Cited in great gratitude to the late Honourable Mohammed Annabi, appellate judge of Tunis, a scholar and my mentor, who referred often to the writings of Ibn Hazm.
166 Interview, Dr Hania Mohamed Sholkamy, health anthropologist, London, 1999.
167 Abu-Sahlieh, Sami A. Aldeeb, 'To Mutilate in the Name of Jehovah or Allah: legitimization of male and female circumcision', St Sulpice (Switzerland), 1994, at www.fgmnetwork.org/, p. 5 (accessed 30 May 2010).
168 See awareness campaign of Fatma Khafagy, 'Honour Killing in Egypt', Association of Legal Aid for Women, Cairo, 2005.

169 Sura 16:123; Genesis 17:10–14.

170 Muslim, *Sahih: kitab tahara*; *bab khisal al fitra*; Bukhari, *Sahih: kitab libas*; *bab taqlim al azfar.*

171 Bukhari, *Sahih: kitab istithan*; *bab al khitan bada al kibari.*

172 Suras 24:30 and 24:31.

173 Interview, former Minister of Social Affairs and member of the Supreme Council of Women, Cairo, February 2007.

174 Interview, Cairo, February 2000.

175 Observations at the Dar al Ifta, Cairo, February 2000.

176 Citing *Adab al mufti wa al mustafti* by Ibn as Salah (d. 1245), who wrote that the office of mufti was not tied to being male or free, in other words a slave as well as a woman could become a mufti and issue *fatwa*s to qadis, ftn 17, citing *Fatawa wa masail Ibn as Salah*, ed. Abd al Mu'ti Amin Qal'aji, Beirut: Dar al Ma'rifah, 2 vols., 1986/1406, I, p. 42.

3
Pakistan – Orthodox Modernity

1 The author was brought up in Bhopal on the legends of the Begums. The Begum Sikandar received from the British government in appreciation of her services during the rebellion jurisdiction over the district (*pergunnan*) of Bairsea (Sanad granting Pergunnah Bairsea to the State of Bhopal, 1860, signed by Canning, 27 December 1860, in Aitchison, Charles Umpherston, compiler, *A Collection of Treaties, Engagements and Sanads Relating to India and Neighbouring Countries*, Vol. IV ('Central India Agency'), Calcutta: Government of India, Central Publication Branch, 1933, p. 117. See also reference from Maulana Abul Kalam Azad, asserting that Maulana Munawaruddin was detained during the Mutiny by Begum Sikander Jehan at www.globalwebpost.com/farooqm/study, accessed 30 May 2010.

2 His son Faiz Tyabji authored the standard work *Principles of Muhammedan Law*, 1st edn., in 1913. Its various subsequent editions were consulted regularly in East African courts. After Partition the book was retitled as *Muslim Law: The Personal Law of Muslims in India and Pakistan*, Bombay, 4th ed., 1968.

3 Sura 2:221: 'Do not marry unbelieving women until they have faith (in one Allah/God), a slave woman is better than an unbelieving (free woman) … For the woman, do not marry to an unbeliever until they have faith (in one Allah/God). A man slave who believes is better than a (free) unbeliever.' Sura 5:5: '… Lawful to you are those women who have faith (in one Allah/God) and women of the people of the book. Give them their dowers …'

The verses from sura 2 treat men and women equally. Neither is to marry an unbeliever. Each is to marry a believer. For the term 'believer', the verse does not use the word Muslim, as sura 2:128 does ('Oh Lord make us Muslim bowing to your will …'). Sura 5 in turn reminds men that just because they are marrying a believer or a non-Muslim of the pre-Islam monotheistic religions (Christianity or Judaism), this does not mean that she is not due her dower when her own law may not require a dower but rather require her to bring in a dowry. Yet because the verse is addressed only to men (and rightfully so because it addresses dower, a duty on men), it has been interpreted to mean that Muslim women may not have the same right to marry men of the Book. The reason given is not Quranic, but rather based on psychological and biological myths without empirical evidence. It is thought that women are too weak to resist demands to convert from Islam to another monotheistic religion, and presumed that men have no weaknesses.

4 Comparable to the position taken by the modern Muslim and Egyptian-European Tariq Ramadan. See his 'Rethinking the use of Muslim law', *Boston Globe*, 31 March 2005, where he proposes a moratorium on the application of classical interpretations of the penal (*hudud*) law until the ulama can reach a consensus on this issue.

5 Parry, Clive, *Consolidated Treaty Series*, Dobbs Ferry, N.Y.: Oceana Publications, 1979–1986, XLV British Foreign State Papers (B.S.P.), p. 726.

6 Ibid., 110 *CTS*, p. 267.

7 Ibid., 110 *CTS*, p. 269.

8 Ibid., 114 *CTS*, p. 497.

9 Ibid., 113 *CTS*, p. 467, XI Aitchison, p. 108.

10 Ibid., 146 *CTS*, p. 209.

11 For various reasons, including the action taken by the British to cut the Afghan King's tax revenue on imported British goods.

12 Constitution (Twenty-sixth Amendment) Act, 1971. It stated that the privy purse privilege of the princes was against the egalitarian social order. It also overrode the Indian Supreme Court's decision that the presidential order to abrogate the privilege was unconstitutional.

13 For example, in Mohd. Ahmed Khan v Shah Bano Begum, A.I.R. 1985, S.C. 951 and Danial Latifi v Union of India (2001) 7 SCC 740, interpreting Islamic sources to challenge the classical interpretation that a divorced woman was not entitled to any post-divorce maintenance even if she had been married many years and would be left destitute by the divorce. The Court harmonized Islamic law sources with the statutory law, the Criminal Procedure Code (Amendment) Act of 2001, which applies to all women, whether Muslim or not.

14 In 2004 a conference was organized to bring together members of the All India Muslim Personal Law Board and Muslim women activists in India. See Sikand, Yoginder, 'Muslim women and gender Justice', 15 October 2004, at www.countercurrents.org, accessed 20 May 2010.

15 Muslim Family Laws Ordinance of 1961 and Punjab/Sindh/N.W.F.P./ Baluchistan and Muslim Personal Law (Shariat) Application Act, 1962. The latter law invalidates the customary rules which prevented women from inheriting certain types of landed property.

16 Marriage Functions (Prohibition of Ostentatious Display and Wasteful Expenses) Ordinance II of 2000 and Punjab Marriage Functions (Prohibition of Ostentatious Display and Wasteful Expenses) Act V of 2003, in Ch. Muhammad Siddique and ors v Government of Pakistan and ors, Constitutional Petition No. 23 of 1999 and 21 of 2004, decided 5 November 2004.

17 The pluralism of Islamic law opinions was later recognized but in a restricted matter. An explanation note for Art. 227 of the 1973 Constitution explained: 'In the application of this clause to the personal law of any Muslim sect, the expression "Quran and Sunnah" shall mean the Quran and Sunnah as interpreted by that sect.'

18 Compare early Islamic history, in which the Abbasids (758–1258 A.D., based in Raqqah and Baghdad, deriving their name from the blood uncle of the Prophet) deposed the Umayyads (661–750 A.D., based in Damascus, who were in-laws of the Prophet through the Prophet's wife Aisha), arguing that their revolt was in the name of the Quran and the *sunna*. Followers were required to take an oath to the *kitab wal sunna*. Some rebels even added to the oath *wa al Rida* (also a member of the Prophet's family), thus personalizing the issue. The backbone of the revolt were the Khurasan, assimilated descendants of Arab soldiers who had settled in the conquered Persian empire, who were dissatisfied with being taxed similarly to non-Muslim locals, and who joined the Bani Hashemites (members of the Prophet's family) against the Umayyads. The Abbasids used the colour black then adopted green which the Alids used. The latter favoured Fatima and Ali, who had fled the Arabian peninsula to the Arab soldier frontier town of Kufa in Iraq. The Umayyads eventually settled in Andalusia in 756, where a liberal medieval Moorish culture flourished, and in 929 declared a 'western caliphate' to rival the 'eastern caliphate' (analogous to the western and eastern Catholic Church). On the Islamic Inquisition in this period see Makdisi, p. 18.

19 Revival of the Constitution of 1973 Order, 1985, Presidential Order (P.O.) No. 14 of 1985, 2 March 1985.

20 Criminal Law (Second Amendment) Ordinance, 1990 (Qisas and Diya Ordinance).

21 Abolishment of Whipping Act, 1996. Whipping had been introduced by the British in the Indian Subcontinent in Act IV of 1909, and supplemented by the Pakistani ruler Ayub Khan in 1963 in the Whipping (West Pakistan Amendment) Ordinance, 1963 (XLII of 1963) and the Whipping (West Pakistan Amendment) Ordinance, 1969 (VI of 1969).

22 Criminal Law amendments starting in July 1994, Ordinance XLI of 1991 amending Penal Code XLV of 1860, again in February 1995 and December 1996. Based on sura 2:178: 'Believers, the law of equality is prescribed to you in cases of murder: The free for the free, the slave for the slave, the woman for the woman, but if any remission is made by a relative of the slain, then grant any reasonable demand and compensate him with handsome gratitude. This is a concession and a mercy from your Lord. After this, whoever exceeds the limits shall be (subject to) grave penalty.' Sura 2:179: 'In the law of equality (*qisas*) life is saved to you and to those who understand that you may restrain yourselves.' Sura 5:45: 'We ordained therein for them: life for life, eye for eye, nose for nose, ear for ear, tooth for tooth, and wounds equal for equal. But if any one remits the retaliation by way of charity it is an act of atonement and if any one fail to judge by the light of Allah they are unenlightened.'

23 Chief Executive Order No. 24 of 2002, *Gazette of Pakistan*, Extraordinary, August 2002.

24 The Indian Supreme Court had once ruled in favour of executive orders which amend the Constitution (Golak Nath, AIR 1967 SC 1643), but overruled itself in Kunwar Shri Vir Rajendar v The Union of India, AIR 1970 SC 1946 and Keshavananda Bharati v the State of Kerala, AIR 1973 SC 1461.

25 Criminal Law (Amendment) Act 2004, *PLD* 2005 Statutes 77, 11 January 2005 Gazette, Pakistan – Extraordinary Part II, amending the Penal Code of 1860.

26 *Zina* means adultery, sex between unmarried persons or pre-marital sex (latter are cases of fornication).

27 Preamble to the 1973 Constitution: 'Wherein the Muslims shall be enabled to order their lives in the individual and collective spheres in accordance with the teachings and requirements of Islam as set out in the Holy Quran and Sunnah …'

28 B. Z. Kaikus and others v President of Pakistan and others, *PLD* 1980 Supreme Court (SC) 160.

29 Sura 2:256: 'Let there be no compulsion in religion. The Truth stands out clear from error, whoever rejects evil and believes in Allah has grasped the most trusty handhold that never breaks.' See C. Jones-Pauly, 'Tensions between Islamic Law and Human Rights from the Perspective of Comparative Law', at www.human rights.ch, accessed 20 May 2010.

30 B. Z. Kaikus and others v President of Pakistan and others, *PLD* 1980 Supreme Court (SC) 160, at 179.

31 Constitution (Third Amendment) Order, 1980 (P.O. No. 14 of 1980), section 2, (with effect from September 17, 1980).

32 B. Z. Kaikus and others v President of Pakistan and others, *PLD* 1980 Supreme Court (SC) 160, at 181.

33 Presidential Order No. 14 of 1985, effective 2 March 1985.

34 See Makdisi on how ignoring religio-philosophical principles in the process of equating *shar'*, i.e. Revelation, the source of principles, with Islamic law preserves traditionalism in Islamic law.

35 Art. 203C (1).

36 Ibid., (3A).

37 (2A) An appeal shall lie to the Supreme Court from any judgment, final order or sentence of the Federal Shariat Court: (a) if the Federal Shariat Court has on appeal reversed an order of acquittal of an accused person and sentenced him to death or imprisonment for life or imprisonment for a term exceeding fourteen years; or, on revision, has enhanced a sentence as aforesaid; or (b) if the Federal Shariat Court has imposed any punishment on any person for contempt of the Court. [Constitution (Second Amendment) Order, 1982 (P.O. No. 5 of 1982) section 6 (with effect from 22 March 1982)].

38 Federal Shariat Court, Annual Report 2003, Secretariat of the Law and Justice Commission of Pakistan. Islamabad, 2004, at www.ljcp.govpk, p. 7, accessed 30 January 2004.

39 Muhammad Safeer v Mst Zaria Bibi and The State, SD 2004 Fed. Sh. Crt 142, declaring a High Court order null and void in a case of *qazf* (*qadhf*) (accusation by the husband that the wife is adulterous).

40 Section 217 of the Penal Code (Strafgesetzbuch 'Kindestoetung'). This is to be distinguished from section 218 which punishes abortion after the 21st week of pregnancy.

41 As explained in criminal law lectures (Prof. Loos) at the University of Goettingen, 1988.

42 See also *Leipzig Kommentar*, Berlin: de Gruyter, 10th ed 1989, p. 217:1. The Law has been on the books since 1891 (after the German defeat of France). One of the superior court judges made a study of the application of this law in one of the provinces, concluding that of 130 murder cases in Lower Saxony, four involved infanticide. He found that a mother killed because she feared the economic burden of the child. The judge characterized the inner driving force that leads to such an act as reckless egoism: he found the act was well planned and not a result of emotional irrationality or the result of an unbalanced mind (Joachim Siol, Oberlandesgericht Oldenburg, Sitzungsbericht zum 53. Deutschen Juristentag, Berlin, 1980, Munich: C.H. Beck, 1980, p. M125).

43 Infanticide Act, 1939, 162 Geo. 6, c. 36.

44 Thomas Aquinas's *Summa Theologica* (mid-13th century) agrees that adultery is a mortal sin, after the most grievous sin of murder (2nd Part of the Second Part, *Treatise on Prudence and Justice*, Ques. 73, 'Of Backbiting, Reply to Objection 2 Whether backbiting is the gravest of all sins').

45 Fazal Din v Taj Din, *PLD* 1983 Fed. Sh. Crt. (FSC) 33, where the brother-in-law was acquitted at the first-instance trial of charges of the rape and murder of his sister-in-law, then convicted upon appeal and sentenced to imprisonment and whipping for rape and to hanging for murder. This is not a new problem. In the days of slavery jurists concerned themselves with illicit relations between a husband and the slave of his wife or vice versa or between a slave-woman's husband and her mistress.

46 Muhammad Ashraf v The State, *PLD* 1987 Fed. Sh. Crt. (FSC) 33, where the defendant pleaded that the cause of his raping the victim was a family dispute over a water course. In Ajaib v The State, *PLD* 1994 (27) Supreme Court Monthly Review 1497, political party faction was cited as a cause.

47 Iqbal Shah v The State, *PLD* 1981 Fed. Sh. Crt. (FSC) 284, where two cases arose out of a vendetta. X was accused of rape. He had a close friend with a daughter. The brother of the father of the woman prosecuting X for rape then abducted the daughter of the friend of the accused X. The brother was in turn brought to trial for damaging the eye of the woman he had abducted when she resisted.

48 Mukhtar Ahmad v The State, *Pakistan Criminal Law Journal* 2005 Fed. Sh. Crt, (FSC) 1065.

49 Mst Bashiran and anor v The State, *PLD* 1988 Supreme Court (Shariat Appellate Division) 186. The higher court overturned the trial court's conviction for *zina* subject to *taazir* on the ground that the ex-wife manifested no *mens rea* to break the law. She believed the *talaq* document was genuine and not as it in fact turned out to be falsified.

50 Mr Justice Dr Javad Iqbal, Judge, Supreme Court of Pakistan, Crimes Against Women in Pakistan, *PLD* 1988, 195.

51 Citing statistics from the first eight years of the Ordinance showing more men than women imprisoned. See report on release from jails of over 1,000 women, I.A. Rehman, 'Fault lines in law-making', *Dawn*, 13 July 2006.

52 Muhammad Sharif v The State, *PLD* 1985 Supreme Court (SC) 319; Muhammad Asghar v The State, 2004 *Pakistan Criminal Law Journal* 2004, 201.

53 Muhammad Naeem v The State, 2005 *The Supreme Court Monthly Review* (*SCMR*) 284 (Vol. 38, No. 2), at 289. See also Riaz v Station House Officer, *PLD* 1998 Lahore 35 (Justice Ranjha).

54 Iqbal, Nasir, 'FSC sets guidelines for trial courts: misuse of Zina Ordinance', report dated 31 Jan 2006, Dawn Internet Edition, 1 February 2006/2 Muharram 1427 at www.dawn.com/2006/02/01/nat1.htm, accessed 1 March 2006.

55 Ghulam Sarwar v The State, *PLD* 1984 Supreme Court (SC) 218.

56 Nawaz Masih v The State, *PLD* 1981 Fed. Sh. Crt. (FSC) 272.

57 Rozenberg, Joshua, 'Rape and the sobering argument of consent', *Daily Telegraph*, (London), News, 13 April 2006.

58 See for example infra Umer Farin and 2 ors v The State, *PLD* 1983 Fed. Sh. Crt. (FSC) 1. Another decision acquitted the abductor once it was established that the abductee was a willing partner, but discussed general practice to the contrary (Ghulam Shabbir v The State, *PLD* 2004 Supreme Court (SC) Shariat Division 32).

59 Annual Report, Federal Shariat Court, 2003, p. 35. The figures are not broken down into the types of cases being appealed.

60 Classical interpretations refer to a four-fold confession, not just one.

61 I am aware of only one case in which stoning was even ordered.

62 For example, Bukhari, *Sahih: kitab al muharabin min 'ahl al kafir wal rida; bab 'akham 'ahl al dhimmi*, relating how the Prophet asked a man and a woman from the Jewish community who had told him of their adultery, what the penalty was in the Torah. The Prophet ordered them to be stoned (according to their own law, the Torah, not the Quran).

63 The Maldives have debated reforms to be made in their judicial guidelines, which limited the penalty imposed on unmarried pregnant women to whipping, but only if the woman confessed or if there were two (not four) witnesses to the act of intercourse.

64 It was argued that rape is not *zina* but rather *hiraba* or *jirah*, which are forms of assault, and not gender-specific (Quraishi). Another word (Sonbol) used is *ightisab* (coercion). For a discussion see Norman, Julie, Rape Law in Islamic Societies: theory, application and the potential for reform, Center for the Study of Islam and Democracy (CSID), Sixth Annual Conference, Washington, D.C. 22–23 Apr 2005, at www.islam-democracy.org/documents/pdf/6th_Annual_Conference-Julie Norman.pdf, accessed 30 May 2010.

65 The hadith in Dawud's *Sunan* is not helpful in regard to whether rape had different witnessing requirements than the usual two witnesses, but did name a penalty. It related that a man lusting after a woman attacked her. She resisted by shouting and he ran off. He was arrested by men in the community and brought before the Prophet on the basis of a description by the woman. At the hearing another man stood up and confessed that he had been the assaulter. This satisfied the Prophet

that the woman had not consented and she was absolved. But the Prophet imposed stoning to death on the man (*kitab hudud*, as reported by Alaqmah b. Wail and Asbat bin Nasr). In another instance (not necessarily involving rape), the man was also stoned but not the woman – she was released simply on the basis of her statement. The man was stoned because he confessed (*kitab hudud,* from Sahl b. Saad). Sahl gives another version in which the man who confessed named his partner. She denied the charge, and the man was simply lashed, while she was acquitted. But Ibn Abbas added another version: the man was unmarried, and the woman he named denied she had consented; he had no other proof of her consent. He was lashed for false accusation, 80 lashes instead of 100 for *zina.*

66 Bukhari, *Sahih: kitab ikrah; bab istikaraha.* No punishment was specified for the rapist, but the woman was absolved of any liability. It was also stated that if a woman were forced into prostitution, then Allah would forgive her (according to sura 24:33 about enslaved women being forced into prostitution).

67 On payments for defloration of a woman, without indication of whether it involved rape or not see Sharh Al Zurqani *'ala Muwatta al Imam Malik*, ed. Muhammed ibn Abd al Baqi, Misr: Matba'at Mustafa Muhammad, 1936, 4 Vols., *kitab aqdiya*; *bab istikaraha*, Vol. 3, p. 196.

68 In Malik, *Muwatta,* Nafia reported that Umar ordered no whipping for an enslaved woman when she had been raped (coerced into intercourse). Instead he decreed the slave who had raped her and was in charge of the household should (only be) lashed (*kitab hudud*).

69 The Pakistani courts often cite Abdul Qadir Shaheed, outlining the conflicting reasonings among the jurists about imposing the death penalty as *taazir* (Shaheed, Vol. 3, pp. 88–89).

70 Sura 5:33: 'The punishment of those who wage war against Allah and His Messenger, and strife with might for spreading evil, (slander and disorder) in the land is combating them by killing them, crucifixion, or mutilation of hands or feet or exile from the land. That is their disgrace in this world and a heavy punishment awaits them in the hereafter.' Sura 5:34: 'Except those who repent before they fall into your power, in that case know Allah is forgiving and merciful.'

71 Sura 2: 178–9: 'Oh to those who believe, the law of equality is prescribed in murder (killing) … but if any remission is made by the (relative) of the slain (victim) then grant any reasonable demand and compensate with handsome gratitude. This is a concession and mercy from your Lord … In the law of equality there is saving of life to you …'

Sura 4:45: 'We ordained "life for life, eye for eye, nose for nose, ear for ear …" But if anyone remits the retaliation by way of charity it is an act of atonement … and if any fail to judge by Allah's light (in the Revelation), then they are no better than wrongdoers.'

72 Sura 2:256: 'Let there be no compulsion in religion. The Truth stands out clear from error, whoever rejects evil and believes in Allah has grasped the most trusty handhold that never breaks.'

73 Hazoor Bakhsh v Federation of Pakistan, *PLD* 1981 Fed. Sh. Crt. (FSC) 145.

74 Ibid., at 177.

75 Dawud, *Sunan: kitab hudud; bab rajm.* Bukhari, *Sahih: kitab hudud; bab rajm.*

76 Hazoor Bakhsh v Federation of Pakistan, *PLD* 1981 Fed. Sh. Crt (FSC) 145, at 172, 235. See Noeldeke.

77 Art. 203 D (1) of the Constitution: (1) The Court may, either of its own motion or, on the petition of a citizen of Pakistan or the Federal Government or a Provincial Government, examine and decide the question whether or not any law or provision of law is repugnant to the injunctions of Islam, as laid down in the Holy Quran and Sunnah of the Holy Prophet, hereinafter referred to as the Injunctions of Islam.

78 Hazoor Bakhsh v Federation of Pakistan, *PLD* 1981 Fed. Sh. Crt. (FSC) 145, at 178.

79 Ibid., 178–189, 189.

80 Ibid., 196.

81 Ibid., 210.

82 Hazoor Bakhsh v Federation of Pakistan, *PLD* 1981 Fed. Sh. Crt. (FSC) 145, at 198.

83 Ibid., 200.

84 See Burhan al Din al Marghian, Hidaya, trans. by Hamilton, Charles as *The Hedaya or guide: a commentary on the Mussulman law, translated by order of the Governor-General and Council of Bengal*, London: T. Bensley, 1791, relating differences of opinion among the jurists on whether the master (or mistress – this is not made clear) may impose the *hadd* or only a qadi, and on whether the *hadd* could be imposed only on a Muslim or on a non-Muslim also.

85 Hazoor Bakhsh v Federation of Pakistan, *PLD* 1981 Fed. Sh. Crt. (FSC) 145, at 198. See Muhammad bin Abd Allah al Khatib at Tabrizi, *Mishkat al Masabih*, ed., Muhammad ad Din Albani, 2nd ed., Beirut: al Maktab al Islami, vol. II, 2nd edn., p. 1061; Hadith no. 3570, in Kamali, Mohammad Hasan, *Principles of Islamic Jurisprudence*, Cambridge: Islamic Texts Society, rev. edn., 1991, p. 222.

86 Muhammad Ibn Idris as Shafii, Ar *Risala*, Part II, *bab 'ahadith, mansukh.*

87 Sura 4:25: '... Wed them from the permission of their owners, and give them their dowers, according to what is reasonable. They should be chaste, not lustful, nor taking paramours. When they are taken into wedlock, if they fall into shame (*fahsha*) their punishment is half that for free women. This permission is for you who fear sin; but is better for you to practise self-restraint, and Allah is oft forgiving, most merciful.'

88 Malik, *Muwatta,* on Abu Bakr Siddiq who sentenced a man who had confessed to impregnating a slave girl without being married to her to whipping and banishment to Fidak, near Medina: *bab hudud*, reported from Safiyya.

89 Dawud, *Sunan: kitab hudud*, *bab* report from Habib b. Salim on Abd al Rahman b. Hunain, as Al Nuaman bin Bashir.

90 Sura 24:3: 'Let no man guilty of adultery (*zina*) or fornication marry any but a woman similarly guilty, or an Unbeliever; nor let any but such a man or an Unbeliever marry such a woman. To the believers such a thing is forbidden.' [Christian and Mosaic laws also imposed a similar interdiction.]

91 Muhammad Ibn Idris as Shafii, Ar *Risala*, Part II, *bab: ihtisan.*

92 At Tabari, Tarikh, *History*, Year 23, paras. 2741–42.

93 At Tabari, Tarikh, *History*, Year 17, paras. 2529–33. The story is worth summarizing in order to show the extreme caution taken to convict anyone of adultery. The governor of Basra, Al Mughirah b. Shuabah, later emissary to the Persian ruler Bundar, was married. When people began to hear about the affair he was conducting, they closely observed him – they in fact spied upon the house of the woman concerned, a widow named Umm Jamil, al Raqta, daughter of the Amir b. Saasaah tribe. It was not uncommon for a mature widow to offer her services to governors. One day, the people observing her house pulled aside the curtain and saw the two in flagrante delicto. When this was reported, Umar appointed Abu Bakrah as governor in Al Mughirah's place. On the arrival of his rival, Al Mughirah offered him one of his beautiful maids. Abu Bakrah's house adjoined that of Al Mughirah, and one day when the wind blew open a door, there were Umm Jamil and Al Mughirah, though the men present saw only her buttocks – they stared at her as she got up. Al Mughirah then wanted to leave for prayers, but Abu Bakrah forbade him and sent him back to Medina to appear before Umar for a hearing. Abu Bakrah gave his evidence along with the other men. Abu Bakrah said he saw Al Mughirah heaving like a stick but could see him only from behind. Another said he identified the lady as Umm Jamil by standing on his tiptoes and stretching his neck. One said he did not see Al Mughirah heaving like a stick but he did see him breathing very heavily, but he might have confused the woman with someone else. Al Mughirah presented his defence: he had never slept with anyone except his wife, and Umm Jamil must have looked like his wife to the other men present. How could his accusers identify what he did in any case, for he stood with his back to them and in front of the woman, so who could tell who she was and what was going on? Besides no one had the right to spy on him in his home. He was making love to his wife. In the end, there were no four witnesses who had witnessed the actual intercourse and identified the parties. The accusations were unproved and therefore false – so Umar acquitted Al Mughirah and flogged three of the witnesses. Al Mughirah became rather arrogant and told Umar to get rid of these nobodies, but Umar sharply silenced him and told him in effect he had come close to being stoned.

94 Hazoor Bakhsh v Federation of Pakistan, *PLD* 1981 Fed. Sh. Crt (FSC) 145.

95 Ibid., 168, 197, 198.

96 Art. 203E (9) of the Constitution: The Court shall have power to review any decision given or order made by it. (Amended by Constitution (Amendment) Order, 1981 (P.O. No. 5 of 1981) section 3 (with effect from 13 April 1981).

97 Federation of Pakistan v Hazoor Bakhsh, *PLD* 1983 Fed. Sh. Crt. (FSC) 255.

98 Ibid., 313.

99 Ibid., 312. See also the 1981 judgment, at 177 (Hazoor Bakhsh v Federation of Pakistan, *PLD* 1981 Fed. Sh. Crt. (FSC) 145). See Encyclopedia of Islam on Kharijites.

100 As found in the Explanation to Art. 227 (1) of the Constitution: (1) All existing laws shall be brought in conformity with the Injunctions of Islam as laid down in the Holy Quran and Sunnah, in this Part referred to as the Injunctions of Islam, and no law shall be enacted which is repugnant to such Injunctions. Explanation: In the application of this clause to the personal law of any Muslim sect, the

expression 'Quran and Sunnah' shall mean the Quran and Sunnah as interpreted by that sect.

101 Federation of Pakistan v Hazoor Bakhsh, *PLD* 1983 Fed. Sh. Crt. (FSC) 255, at 294.

102 2A. The principles and provisions set out in the Objectives Resolution reproduced in the Annex are hereby made a substantive part of the Constitution and shall have effect accordingly. (P.O. No.14 of 1985, Art. 2 and Sch. item 2 (with effect from 2 March 1985)).

Annex – Objectives Resolution – Whereas sovereignty over the entire universe belongs to Allah Almighty alone and the authority which He has delegated to the State of Pakistan, through its people for being exercised within the limits prescribed by Him is a sacred trust;

This Constituent Assembly representing the people of Pakistan resolves to frame a Constitution for the sovereign independent State of Pakistan;

Wherein the State shall exercise its powers and authority through the chosen representatives of the people; Wherein the principles of democracy, freedom, equality, tolerance and social justice as enunciated by Islam shall be fully observed; Wherein the Muslims shall be enabled to order their lives in the individual and collective spheres in accordance with the teachings and requirements of Islam as set out in the Holy Quran and the Sunnah; Wherein adequate provision shall be made for the minorities to profess and practise their religions and develop their cultures; [It has been asserted that the original Resolution read: 'Wherein adequate provision shall be made for the minorities to *freely* profess and practise their religions and develop their cultures.' – See Cowasjee, Ardeshir, 'The sole statements', *Dawn*, No. 4, 9 July 2000.] Wherein the territories now included in or in accession with Pakistan and such other territories as may hereafter be included in or accede to Pakistan shall form a Federation wherein the units will be autonomous with such boundaries and limitations on their powers and authority as may be prescribed; Wherein shall be guaranteed fundamental rights including equality of status, of opportunity and before law, social, economic and political justice, and freedom of thought, expression, belief, faith, worship and association, subject to law and public morality; Wherein adequate provisions shall be made to safeguard the legitimate interests of minorities and backward and depressed classes; Wherein the independence of the Judiciary shall be fully secured; Wherein the integrity of the territories of the Federation, its independence and all its rights including its sovereign rights on land, sea and air shall be safeguarded;

So that the people of Pakistan may prosper and attain their rightful and honoured place amongst the nations of the World and make their full contribution towards international peace and progress and happiness of humanity.

103 Citing Ibn al Muqaffaa advisor to the Abbasid caliph Al Mansur, who took a dim view of freedom of opinion, each juristic group being in his opinion 'infatuated with its own … and slight[ing] the doctrines of others'.

104 Act VII of 1996, Abolition of the Punishment of Whipping Act, 1996, Section 3: Except in cases where the punishment of whipping is provided for as Hadd …

105 Section 2, Definition … 'hadd' means the punishment of crimes laid down in the Holy Quran and Sunnah.

106 Iqbal Shah v State, *PLD* 1981 Fed. Sh. Crt. (FSC) 284.
107 Ordinance VIII of 1979, *Gazette of Pakistan*, Extraordinary, Part I, 9 February 1979.
108 Mst Nek Bakhat v The State, Muhammad Rafiz v The State, Ali Hussain and others v The State, *PLD* 1986 Fed. Sh. Crt. (FSC) 174.
109 Ibid., 179.
110 Sura 24:6: 'And for those who launch a charge against their spouses, and have no evidence of their own, their solitary evidence can be received if they bear witnesses four times with oath by Allah that they are solemnly telling the truth.' 24:7: 'And the fifth oath should be they solemnly invoke the curse of Allah on themselves if they are telling a lie.' 24:8: 'But it would avert the punishment of the wife if she bears witness four times with an oath by Allah that the other is telling a lie.' 24:9: 'And the fifth oath should be that she solemnly invokes the wrath of Allah on herself if the accuser is telling the truth.' 24:10: 'If it were not for Allah's grace and mercy on you, and that Allah is oft-returning, full of wisdom (you fare badly).'
111 Sura 24:4: 'And those who launch a charge against chaste women, and produce not four witnesses, flog them with 80 stripes and reject their evidence ever after. For such men are wicked transgressors.' 24:5: 'Unless they repent thereafter and amend their conduct. For Allah is oft forgiving and merciful.'

While the verse is designed to protect the reputation of women, not men, supposedly if a woman accused another woman, the former would be subject to the same penalty. It is well known that the verse was revealed when the youngest wife of the Prophet, Aisha, was accused of a sexual affair when she fell behind in the desert and was alone with a young man. The verse does not distinguish between married and unmarried women and so applies to both.
112 At Tabari, Tarikh, *History*, Year 23, para. 2775.
113 Ibid., Year 17, paras 2532–3.
114 Bukhari, *Sahih: kitab hudud*; *bab al taarid*, report by Abu Huraira about an Arab Bedouin who came to the Prophet complaining that his wife had given birth to a child with a black skin, so it could not possibly be his, implying his wife had committed adultery. The Prophet asked him what colour his own camels were. He replied, red, but admitted some of their offspring were grey because some ancestors had been grey. So the Prophet reminded him that he must have had black ancestry too. The matter was settled. In another *sunna* of Bukhari, *Sahih: kitab hudud, bab al ikhtirafi bil zanna* – a report from Abu Huraira and Zaid bin Khalid – a man told the Prophet he had paid sheep and given a slave to ransom for his son's adulterous relationship with a woman. The Prophet said that the woman should be asked and only if she confessed should she be stoned.
115 Bukhari, *Sahih: kitab hudud* – a report by Ibn Abbas about Maiz bin Malik: Maiz confessed to the Prophet, who then asked whether he was sure – had he not perhaps kissed the lady, or winked [or 'squeezed', according to Dawud, Sunan] or looked at her? When he answered 'yes' to the question of whether he had had sexual intercourse with her, then the Prophet ordered stoning.
116 Sura 49:12: 'Believers! Avoid suspicion as much: for suspicion in some cases is a sin: And spy not on each other behind their backs. Would any of you like to eat

the flesh of his dead brother? Nay, you would abhor it. Fear Allah: For Allah is Oft-Returning, Most Merciful.'

117 At Tabari, Tarikh, *History*, Year 23, para. 2743.

118 Muhammad Sarwar and anor v The State, *PLD* 1988 Fed. Sh. Crt. (FSC) 42. Similarly in Bashiran and anor v Muhammad Hussain and anor, *PLD* 1988 Supreme Court (SC) 186.

119 Sessions Courts' first instance jurisdiction over *hudud* cases fell under Art. 20 (1 proviso) of the Offence of Zina Ordinance. The Federal Shariat Court (FSC) would serve as an appellate body in competition with the High Court which supervises the Sessions Courts. Their competition is becoming an arena of dispute among the courts. See Federal Shariat Court, Annual Report 2003, Islamabad: Secretariat of the Law and Justice Commission of Pakistan, 2004, at www.ljcp.govpk, p. 7 – ACCE, questioning whether the provincial High Courts may hear appeals from sessions courts in *hudud* offences, as the appellate jurisdiction of the FSC is not very clear. See Judiciary website of the government of Pakistan stating that the Shariat Court had 'exclusive' appellate jurisdiction in *hudud* cases (at www.infopak.govpk).

120 This was not the first case in which the Federal Shariat Court had saved a woman from the mandatory stoning penalty. In Mst Jehan Mina v The State, *PLD* 1983 Fed. Sh. Crt. (FSC) 183 (Justices Qazilbash and Haq) the Federal Shariat Court reduced a death sentence for an unmarried pregnant woman to three years' imprisonment because of her tender age.

121 Shamim Akbar and anor v The State, *PLD* 1985 Fed. Sh. Crt. (FSC) 307.

122 Justice Fakhruddin H. Shaikh in Muhammad Yusuf and anor v The State, *PLD* 1988 Fed. Sh. Crt. (FSC) 22, at 24, 25.

123 Shaukat Ali v The State, Sindh Baluchistan Law Reporter (SBLR) 2004 Fed. Sh. Crt. 53.

124 Muhammad Imran v The State, *Pakistan Criminal Law Journal* 2005 Fed. Sh. Crt. (FSC) 1596.

125 *PLD* 1983 Fed. Sh. Crt. (FSC) 1.

126 In another, later case the Federal Shariat Court held that confessions before the police were not acceptable. Confessions to *zina* must be made before the court (Zubeda Begum and anor v The State, *PLD* 1986 Fed. Sh. Crt (FSC) 268).

127 Why 15 when the Ordinance prescribed 30 is not clear. Similarly in Abdur Rashid v The State, *PLD* 1986 Fed. Sh. Crt. (FSC) 290, at 295, where the sentence of 15 stripes was raised to 30.

128 Dawud, *Sunan: kitab hudud*, as reported by al Harari.

129 Bukhari, Sahin, *kitab hudud*, as reported by Qasim bin Muhammad about Ibn Abbas; Dawud, *Sunan: kitab hudud*, as reported by Hilal bin Umaiya.

130 Bukhari, *Sahih: kitab hudud, man zhhara al fahish*, as reported by Sahl bin Saad about Az Zubair.

131 Mst Bakhan v The State, *PLD* 1986 Fed. Sh. Crt. (FSC) 274.

132 Ibid., 278.

133 Ibid., 281.

134 It would be worthwhile revisiting Ibn Taimiyya (Hanbali, d. 1328/728) on the intimidation of women. With regard to divorce, he observed that one cannot

simply accept at face value a wife's renunciation or forfeiture of the marriage dower (*mahr*), for he surmised that a woman is likely to agree to the opposite of what was in her marriage contract either out of fear or as the price for obtaining a divorce free of harassment (Ibn Taimiyya, Book 5 (*talaq: halat al mushabahat*), pp. 256–7).

135 Shabbir Ahmad v The State, *PLD* 1983 Fed. Sh. Crt. (FSC) 110 (Justice Siddiq).

136 Muslim, *Sahih: kitab hudud*; *bab itiraf*.

137 It does not seem to depend on whether or not such a man is a Muslim or Pakistani, as evident from the story of Nathaniel Hawthorne's *Scarlet Letter*, a novel about the American Christian Puritan priest who allowed his lover, a married woman, to suffer humiliation as he watched in silence her being scathed and tried. In the end his sin bore so heavily on his conscience that, in grief, he took his own life.

138 Dawud, *Sunan: kitab hudud*, as reported by Al Lajlaj.

139 Safia Bibi v The State, *PLD* 1985 Fed. Sh. Crt. (FSC) 120.

140 Ibid., 125. See also Rani v The State, *PLD* 1996 Karachi 316.

141 Safia Bibi v The State, *PLD* 1985 Fed. Sh. Crt. (FSC) 120, at 123.

142 i.e., the woman has a right to deny consent.

143 Malik tended to think the alleged rapist should marry the woman, but wait at least until the end of her *idda*. If she were not pregnant, then marriage was safe. If she were pregnant then the man should wait until the woman's credibility was established (*Muwatta: kitab hudud*).

144 Safia Bibi v The State 1985 *PLD* Fed. Sh. Crt. (FSC) 120, at 127.

145 *PLD* 1985 Supreme Court (Shariat Appellate Bench) 319.

146 Bukhari, *Sahih: kitab hudud*; *bab ightirafi bil zanna*, as reported by Ibn Abbas (not in Dawud or Malik).

147 Dawud, *Sunan: kitab hudud*, as reported by Al Lajlaj.

148 Ibid., as reported by Buraida.

149 Deuteronomy 22:23–7 (Old Testament) also provides explicitly for this protection, which released a woman who was coerced into sex from a sin deserving of death. Only her rapist was to be stoned.

150 Similar to Deuteronomy 22:28–9 and Exodus 22:16–17, which provided that a man who had intercourse with an unmarried chaste woman and was found out, had to marry her without any right of divorce ever, but if the guardian refused marriage, then the man had to pay the guardian the marriage dower.

151 Presidential Decree No. 5 of 1970, amended by the Revolutionary Council Decree No. 2 of 1976, repealed by and re-enacted in Act No. 4 of 1985, repealed in part in January 2005 (Act No. 4).

152 Sura 46:15: 'We have enjoined on human beings kindness to their parents. In pain did their mother bear them, and in pain did she give them birth … At length when they reach the age of full strength and attain 40 years, they say, Oh my lord, grant me that I may be grateful for Your favour You bestowed upon me, and upon both my parents …'

153 *PLD* 2005 Lahore 589.

154 Bundesverfassungshof, Urteil, 12 Jan 2005, XII ZR 60/03, and XII ZR 227/03, not allowing secret DNA tests by the father. Here there is a certain discrimination involved, as unmarried men who sire children are not under this restriction.

155 See above, Sura 49:12: 'Believers! Avoid suspicion as much: for suspicion in some cases is a sin: And spy not on each other behind their backs. Would any of you like to eat the flesh of his dead brother? Nay, you would abhor it. Fear Allah: For Allah is Oft-Returning, Most Merciful.' See At Tabari, Tarikh, *History*, Year 23, para. 2743.

156 Mst Nek Bakhat v The State, Muhammad Rafiz v The State, Ali Hussain and others v The State, *PLD* 1986 Fed. Sh. Crt. (FSC) 174.

157 Mst. Bakhan v The State, *PLD* 1986 Fed. Sh. Crt. (FSC) 274 and Safia Bibi v The State, *PLD* 1985 Fed. Sh. Crt. 120.

158 See application of that provision supra in a 2005 case of *zina*: Muhammad Imran v The State of Pakistan, Criminal Law Journal 2005 Fed. Sh. Crt. (FSC) 1596.

159 Ghulam Sarwar v The State, *PLD* 1984 Supreme Court (SC) 218.

160 Ibid., 221.

161 As also in Muhammad Azam v Muhammad Iqbal, *PLD* 1984 Supreme Court (SC) 114.

162 As in the case of a married woman with five children – no marks of violence, semen swabs from her vagina were not compared with those of her attacker, and her complaint was lodged two months after the attack. The lower sessions court changed the charge from rape to consensual *zina*, but the Federal Shariat Court acquitted on the basis of no proof beyond reasonable doubt because of contradictory testimony (Mukhtar Ali v The State, *Pakistan Criminal Law Journal* 2005 Fed. Sh. Crt. (FSC) 1065).

163 Jamila Bibi v Muhammad Yaseen, *PLD* 1983 Fed. Sh. Crt. (FSC) 523.

164 Shabbir alias Kakku and other v The State, Sindh and Baluchistan Law Reports (SBLR) 2004 Fed. Sh. Crt. (FSC) 35.

165 Muhammad Sharif v The State, *PLD* 1985 Supreme Court (SC) 319.

166 Ghulam Shabbir v The State, *PLD* 2004 Supreme Court (SC) Shariat Division 32.

167 Muhammad Asghar v The State, 2004 *Pakistan Criminal Law Journal* 201.

168 See above Ghulam Sarwar v The State, *PLD* 1984 Supreme Court (SC) 218. Followed in Ghulam Shabbir v The State, *PLD* 2004 Supreme Court (SC) Shariat Division 32.

169 Parvez v The State, *PLD* 1985 Fed. Sh. Crt. 134.

170 Dawud, *Sunan: kitab hudud*; *bab 'afw*, as reported by Abd Allah b. Amr

171 Wahid Iqbal v The State, 2003 *Pakistan Criminal Law Journal* 1928.

172 Malik, *Muwatta: kitab rahm* (pledges for judgments), a Sunnah of Umar; Bukhari, *Sahih: kitab talaq*, ordering the husband to be imprisoned if he does not utter divorce when the *idda* has expired.

173 There has also been a case report on deadly sexual violence committed against minor boys (Muhammad Afzal alias Kaka v The State, Sindh and Baluchistan Law Reports (SBLR) 2004 Fed. Sh. Crt. (FSC) 20).

174 Malik, *Muwatta: kitab hudud*; *bab rajm*. Abu Walqid Laithi reported that when Umar was in Syria he sent Laithi to follow up on a matter which a husband had brought before Umar. The husband claimed he saw his wife with another man. Laithi was

sent to ask the wife, prompting her not to confess, for there were insufficient witnesses. She did confess on her own accord, however, and Umar ordered stoning. This must have been before the revealing of the Quranic verse on taking the *liaan* procedure, for the subsequent Sunnah of the Holy Prophet showed that the wife was summoned for the oath. See also Bukhari, *Sahih: kitab hudud*, as reported by Ibn Abbas about Maiz bin Malik, who confessed openly and was obviously distraught. The public was divided – some said he should be pardoned and others not.

175 An issue which arose recently in a case of a man who murdered his wife. The mother of the deceased demanded compensation (*diya*). As the man was poor, the Supreme Court granted him release on bail so that he could arrange for payments in instalments of the *diya* (Arshad Mehmood v The State, 2005 Supreme Court *Monthly Review* 1524).

176 Malik, *Muwatta: kitab rahn* (pledges for judgments), as reported by Abu Huraira on Saad ibn Ubaida questioning the Prophet, repeated in *kitab hudud; bab rajm.*

177 Malik, *Muwatta: kitab rahm* (mortgages, pledges).

178 Bukhari, *Sahih: kitab hudud*, as reported by Al Mughirah *ma'a imra'tihi rajullan fa qatalahu.*

179 Dawud, *Sunan: kitab hudud*; *bab rajm* (stoning).

180 Dawud, *Sunan: kitab talaq*; *bab li'an.*

181 Bukhari, *Sahih: kitab talaq*; *bab li'an.*

182 Ali Muhammad v The State, *Pakistan Criminal Law Journal* 1993 Lahore 557 (Justice Ausaf Ali Khan).

183 Ibid., 563.

184 Thomas Aquinas, *Summa Theologica*, Supplement Question 60, Of Wife Murder (mid-13th century). There must have been women who murdered husbands, but this was apparently not deemed a subject worthy of study.

185 Supra Mst Jehan Mina v The State, *PLD* 1983 Fed. Sh. Crt. (FSC) 183.

186 Ghulam Yassen and 2 ors v The State, *PLD* 1994 Lahore 392 (Justice Khul-ur-Rehman Ramday).

187 Ibid., 396.

188 See above Muhammad Sarwar and anor v The State, *PLD* 1988 Fed. Sh. Crt. (FSC) 42.

189 See note 115 above: Bukhari, *Sahih: kitab hudud*, as reported by Ibn Abbas about Maiz bin Malik.

190 Muhammad Ibrahim v Abdul Razzaq, *Pakistan Criminal Law Journal* 1997 Quetta 263 (Justices Amir-ul-Mulk Mengal and Javed Iqbal).

191 Nasiruddin and others v The State, *PLD* 2002 Quetta 42 (Justice Aman ul Allah Khan).

192 Muhammad Akram Khan v The State, *PLD* 2001 Supreme Court (SC) 1 (Justices SH. Riaz, Ahmed, Rana Bhagwandas and Mian Muhammad Ajmal).

193 The Federal Shariat Court in a 2004 judgment had rejected a petition which alleged that the restrictions imposed on the use of arms such as requiring their registration, were unIslamic. See Abdul Majid v Government of Pakistan, *PLD* 2004 Fed. Sh. Crt. (FSC) 1, relating to the Pakistan Arms Ordinance 20 of 1965 and Arms Rules 1924.

194 Art. 9, Constitution of 1973 of Pakistan as amended: 'No person shall be deprived of life or liberty save in accordance with law.'

195 Art. 8 (1), Constitution of 1973 of Pakistan, as amended: 'Any law, or any custom or usage having the force of law, in so far as it is inconsistent with the rights conferred by this Chapter [Fundamental Rights], shall, to the extent of such inconsistency, be void.'

196 Ghulam Yassen and 2 ors v The State, *PLD* 1994 Lahore 392.

197 Catholic Haiti had a Penal Code (Arts. 284–88) which prescribed imprisoning the wife and her lover, but the husband had the exclusive right to enter a criminal charge – no one else could. The husband was fined if he brought a concubine into the marriage home. If he killed the wife and/or her lover when caught in the act, the murder was excusable (Art. 269). Under international pressure to introduce laws against trafficking in persons, the Council of Ministers decriminalized adultery in 2005, even though it believed adultery is against the natural order of obligations.

198 Sura 4:34 is usually translated to mean 'Men are in charge (*qawwamun*) of women …' A pro-woman interpretation would be 'Men are upright towards women …'

199 Hazoor Bakhsh v Federation of Pakistan, *PLD* 1981 Fed. Sh. Crt. (FSC) 145.

200 In 2004, 17,521 petitions were filed in the Supreme Court, which rendered 9,938 decisions (Supreme Court of Pakistan, *Annual Report 2004*, at www.spc.com.pk).

201 National Commission for Women Ordinance No. XXVI of 2000, *Gazette of Pakistan*, Extraordinary, Part I, 17 July 2000.

202 Gillani, Waqar, 'Pakistan: Women's Commission Recommends Qisas Law Be Amended' – report on workshop held 25–27 March 2004 in Islamabad, *The Daily Times* (Pakistan), 2 Apr 2004, at www.wluml.org (News).

203 Criminal Law (Amendment) Act 2004, assented to on 11 Jan 2005, *Gazette of Pakistan*, Extraordinary Part II, amending various sections of the Penal Code, Act XLVI of 1860. The Amendment of section 311 of the Penal Code states: 'Provided that if the offence has been committed in the name or on the pretext of honour, the imprisonment shall not be less than 10 years.' The maximum sentence imposable for honour crimes is 25 years' imprisonment.

204 See note 202 above.

205 See Jahangir, Asma, 'Pakistan: The Women's Commission and the Hudood Ordinances', *Daily Times*, (Islamabad), 12 September 2003, available also at the Asian Human Rights Commission.

206 e.g. in the 2003 case of Ms Shazia and Hassan Solangi, in which police collusion with a clan council in carrying out a decision by a *jirga* (local trial council) to have the couple executed because they had eloped against the wishes of the clan (Suo Moto case No. 4 of 2003, *PLD* 2004 Supreme Court (SC) 556). This illustrates tribal resistance to Islamization of the laws.

207 In a murder and rape case involving a girl aged between eight and nine the Panchayat tried to unfairly 'fix' the responsibility for the crime (see Muhammad Idrees and anor v The State, *PLD* 2004 Supreme Court (SC) Shariat Appellate Division 342).

208 See note 135 above.

209 Syed Naseem Shah and ors v The State, *PLD* 2005 Supreme Court (SC) Shariat Appellate Division 181.
210 See note 191 above.
211 Muhammad Akram Khan v The State, *PLD* 2001 Supreme Court (SC) 1.
212 See note 184 above, Thomas Aquinas on wife-murdering.

4
South Africa – Constitutional Challenges for Islamic Law

1 I have deliberately avoided using the singular word 'community' in a theological sense in order to emphasize the diversity within and between groups.
2 Dadoo, Suraya, 'South Africa: many Muslims, one Islam', *IslamOnline*, at www.islamonline.net/English/artculture/2003/06/article08.shtml, 30 June 2003.
3 I wish to thank then Priv. Doz. Dr Roland Loimeier, University of Bayreuth (Germany) for sharing information on the Hanafis in the Cape.
4 August v Rens, 5 May 1836, Menzies Rept., Vol. I, 203.
5 Soetje Magmoet v Registrar of Deeds, Supreme Court, Cape of Good Hope, Juta Reports, 1888, Vol. V, 179.
6 Ngqobela v Sihele (1893), Supreme Court Cases, Vol. 10, 1892–93, 346.
7 Malgas v Gakavu, Eastern District Reports, 1891–92, Vol. 6, 225.
8 Bronn v Frits Bronn's Executor and Others, 3 Searle 313 (1860), at 321.
9 Mashia Ebrahim v Mahomed Essop, Transvaal Law Reports, Supreme Court, 1905, 59.
10 Estate Oeslodien v Estate Mustapha and others, Supreme Court Reports of the Cape of Good Hope, Vol. 25 (1908), 853.
11 Nalana v Rex (1907) T.S. 407.
12 Bronn v Frits Bronn's Executors, 3 Searle, 313 (1860), at 328.
13 Kaba v Ntela, Transvaal Supreme Court Reports, 1910, 964, at 967.
14 Reference to Marroko v The State, Hertzog, 110, 10 C.L.J. 245.
15 Rex v Mboko (1910), Transvaal Supreme Court Reports, 1910, 445, at 448.
16 Ibid., 449.
17 Mokwena v Laub, South African Law Reports (Transvaal Division and Witwatersrand Local Division), 1943, 63.
18 The statutory law at the time provided that the material interests of a partner to a non-recognized marriage – or rather 'union' as it came to be known – could be recognized and enforced. See Act 38 of 1927, allowing a marriage under civil law (de jure monogamous) even though both partners were already living in an African customary union because the latter was regarded as non-existent.
19 Nkambula v Linda, South African Law Reports, 1951 (I) 377.
20 There was a similar argument in Ngqolbela v Sihele, 10 S.C. (1893) 346, cited in Kaba v Ntela, Transvaal Supreme Court Reports, 1910, 964, at 970.
21 Kariem v Latief, Supreme Court (Cape of Good Hope Provincial Division), 1910, 154.
22 Ex Parte Abrahams, The South African Law Reports (1937) Eastern Districts Local Division, Supreme Court of South Africa, 107.

23 Law No. 25, 1891.

24 Act No. 13, 1857, For Removing all Doubts regarding the Validity of the Marriages of Certain Military Settlers, June 29, 1857 (*Statutes of the Cape of Good Hope, 1652–1886*, Vol. II, edited Foster, Joseph et al., Cape Town: W.A. Richards, 1887).

25 Bronn v Frits Bronn's Executor and Others, 3 Searle 313 (1860), 321.

26 Native Code, Natal, No. 19 of 1891.

27 Seedat's Executors v The Master (Natal), South African Law Reports (Appellate Division), 1917, 302.

28 On a claim for the dower (*lobola*) see Nomgogwana Nomadudwana vs. Makosi Totsholo, Case No. 20, Selected Decisions of the Native Appeal Court (Cape and O.F.S.), 1938, Vol. 10, 43.

29 Docrat v Bhayat (1932), The South African Law Reports (1932) Transvaal Provincial Division, 125.

30 Executors Estate Fatha Mahmomed v Moose and Others, The South African Law Reports 1946, Natal Provincial Division, 516, at 519.

31 Sura 4:19: 'O ye who believe! Ye are forbidden to inherit women against their will …'

32 Estate Mehta v Acting Master, High Court, 1958 (4) South African Law Reports 252.

33 Seedat's Executors v The Master (Natal), South African Law Reports (Appellate Division), 1917, 302.

34 Suid-Afrikaanse Nasionale Trust en Assuransie Maatskappy Bpk. v Fondo, 1960 (2) South African Law Reports, Supreme Court, 467.

35 Nkabinde v S.A. Motor & General Insurance Co. Ltd., 1961 (1) South African Law Reports (Durban and Coast Local Division) 302.

36 Baker v Bolton (1808) 1 Camp. 493.

37 See note 34 above, Suid-Afrikaanse Nasionale, at 467, arguments of counsel for the insurance company, at 468. Also in Zulu and Another v Minister of Justice and Another, 1956 (2) South African Law Reports (Natal Provincial Division) 128, at 130.

38 Kader v Kader, South African Law Reports (Rhodesia Appellate Division), 1972 (3) SA 203.

39 Osman v Osman, 1983 (2) South African Law Reports 706.

40 See note 10 above Oeslodien Estate.

41 Ismail v Ismail, 1983 (1) South African Law Reports (Appellate Division), 1006, at 1008–1009 (counsel arguments).

42 Cited in Ibid., 1025.

43 Ibid., 1024.

44 Ibid., 1025, citing Indians Relief Act 22 of 1914 (General Law Amendment Act 57 of 1975).

45 Ibid., 1020.

46 See note 19 above Nkambula.

47 Ngake v Mahahle en 'n Ander, 1984 (2) South African Law Reports 217.

48 Cumming v Cumming, 1984 (4) South African Law Reports (Transvaal Provincial Division) 585.

49 Muslim, *Sahih: kitab hiba; bab tahrim ar ruju fil sadaqa.*

50 Citing Brey v SIR, 1978 (4) SA 399 (CPD).

51 Act 200 of 1993 (Interim Constitution) adopted on 27 April 1994; Constitution of 1996 (Act 108 of 1996). The Constitution came into force on 4 February 1997.

52 Freedom of religion, belief and opinion 15. (3) a. This section does not prevent legislation recognising i. marriages concluded under any tradition, or a system of religious, personal or family law; or ii. systems of personal and family law under any tradition, or adhered to by persons professing a particular religion. b. Recognition in terms of paragraph (a) must be consistent with this section and the other provisions of the Constitution.

53 Equality 9. (3) The state may not unfairly discriminate directly or indirectly against anyone on one or more grounds, including race, gender, sex, pregnancy, marital status, ethnic or social origin, colour, sexual orientation, age, disability, religion, conscience, belief, culture, language and birth. (4) No person may unfairly discriminate directly or indirectly against anyone on one or more grounds in terms of subsection (3). National legislation must be enacted to prevent or prohibit unfair discrimination.

54 Language and culture 30. Everyone has the right to use the language and to participate in the cultural life of their choice, but no one exercising these rights may do so in a manner inconsistent with any provision of the Bill of Rights.

55 Cultural, religious and linguistic communities 31. (1) Persons belonging to a cultural, religious or linguistic community may not be denied the right, with other members of that community: a. to enjoy their culture, practise their religion and use their language; and b. to form, join and maintain cultural, religious and linguistic associations and other organs of civil society. (2) The rights in subsection (1) may not be exercised in a manner inconsistent with any provision of the Bill of Rights.

56 At http://www.sacs.org.za 4 July 1996, SAPA Local.

57 Office of the President, Speech before Parliament, 6 February 1998, at http://www.sacs.org.za.

58 Statement of the Department of Constitutional Development, 22 September 1998, at http.//www.sacs.org.za.

59 Office of the Deputy President, Speech before the Commission for the Promotion and Protection of the Rights of Cultural, Religious and Linguistic Communities, 4 August 1998, at http://www.sacs.org.za.

60 Whitehead, Alfred, *The Aims of Education: a Plea for Reform*, Address to the Mathematical Association, London 1916, reprinted in Blanshard, Brand, ed., *Education in the Age of Science*, New York: Basic Books 1959.

61 Moegamat Faud Ryland v Theorayah Edros, 1997 (2) South African Law Reports (Supreme Court, Cape of Good Hope Provincial Division) 690.

62 Capacity Building Workshop on the Lessons from Ryland v Edros (see note 61 above), 23 April 1997, Breakwater Lodge, Cape Town, Democracy in Action Article, 'Ryland v Edros: a new South African story', Cape Town, Legal Resources Centre, Gender Law Programme.

63 Judgment, *Jarida ar rasmiyya* No. 3 of 18 January 1996, p. 76.

64 Interview, Justice Farlam, Cape Town, July 1997; see for example, Ahmadiyya AAIL (SA) v Muslim Judicial Council, 1983 (4) SA 855 and Ahmadis v MJC, 1984 (4) SA 855.

65 See note 61 above, at 701 (g) – 704.

66 Interpretation of Bill of Rights 39. (1) When interpreting the Bill of Rights, a court, tribunal or forum a. must promote the values that underlie an open and democratic society based on human dignity, equality and freedom; b. must consider international law; and c. may consider foreign law. (2) When interpreting any legislation, and when developing the common law or customary law, every court, tribunal or forum must promote the spirit, purport and objects of the Bill of Rights. (3) The Bill of Rights does not deny the existence of any other rights or freedoms that are recognised or conferred by common law, customary law or legislation, to the extent that they are consistent with the Bill.

67 See note 19 above Nkambula.

68 See note 61 above Ryland, at 709 (d).

69 Ibid., at 709 (f).

70 Prescription Act 68 of 1969, sect. 13 (1) (c).

71 See note 61 above, at 711 (h), where *idda* was defined as three months after termination of the marriage by the third *talaq*, when in fact, the Quran enjoins the following in sura 2:229: 'A *talaq* (divorce) is only permissible twice: after that, the parties should either hold together on equitable terms, or separate with kindness …'

This verse is the basis of the jurists' view that the husband may pronounce two revocable *talaqs*, but the third is final and irrevocable.

72 Sura 65:1 – 'Oh Prophet! When ye do divorce women, divorce them in their prescribed periods and count (accurately) their prescribed periods … And fear Allah your Lord: And turn them not out of their houses, nor shall they (themselves) leave, except in case they are guilty of some open lewdness, those are the limits set by Allah: and any who transgresses the limits of Allah, does verily wrong his (own) soul: Thou knowest not if perchance Allah will bring about thereafter some new situation.'

73 Sura 4:35: 'If ye fear a breach between them, appoint arbiters, one from his family and the other from hers. If they wish for peace Allah will cause their reconciliation. So Allah hath full knowledge and is acquainted with all things.'

74 Sura 2:241: 'For divorced women, gratification (*mut'a*) on a reasonable scale. This is incumbent on those who fear God.'

75 Defendant's Additional Expert Summary, 11 September 1995, submitted by A. Andrews, Defendant's Attorney, Legal Resources Centre, Cape Town.

76 See note 61 above Ryland, at 715 (j).

77 Plaintiff's Expert Summary in Terms of Rule 36 (9) (B), 4 September 1995, submitted by Farouk Mowzer & Associates, Mitchell's Plain.

78 Ibrahim cited in Ryland v Edros at 718 (e) (see note 61 above).

79 Ibid., 717 (e).

80 Interview, Dr Ebrahim E.I. Moosa, expert for the defendant, Ryland v Edros, Cape Town, July 1997 (see note 61 above).

81 Sura 4:32: 'And in nowise covet the things in which Allah has bestowed his gifts more freely on some of you than on others: to men is allotted what they earn in

profits and to women what they earn in profits: but ask Allah of his bounty for Allah hath full knowledge of all things.'

82 Sura 65:6: 'Let the women live in the same style as ye live, according to your means: Annoy them not, so as to restrict them. And if they carry (life in their womb) spend on them until they deliver their burden: and if they suckle your (offspring) give them your recompense: and take mutual counsel together according to what is just and reasonable …'

83 'Divorce – Epoux iraniens', *Journal du droit international* (*JDI*), Vol. I (1999), pp. 136–44, with a critical note by Ali Bencheneb.

84 Freedom of religion, belief and opinion 15. (3) a. This section does not prevent legislation recognising i. marriages concluded under any tradition, or a system of religious, personal or family law; or ii. systems of personal and family law under any tradition, or adhered to by persons professing a particular religion. Recognition in terms of paragraph (a) must be consistent with this section and the other provisions of the Constitution.

85 Interview, Justice Farlam, Cape Town, July 1997.

86 See note 61 above Ryland, at 709 (d).

87 Art. 18–22 of the Tunisian Code of Personal Status.

88 Hafiza Ismail Amod (born Peer) v Multilateral Motor Vehicle Accidents Fund (High Court Durban and Coast Local Division), 1997 (2) Butterworths Constitutional Law Reports (BCLR) 1716 (D).

89 Ibid., 1722.

90 Mokwena v Laub (Transvaal Division and Witwatersrand Local Division), 1943 South African Law Reports 63, at 67; Zulu and Another v Minister of Justice and Another (Natal Province Division) 1956 (2) South African Law Reports 128, at 130.

91 See note 34 above Suid-Afrikaanse Nasionale, at 467.

92 *South African Law Commission*, Project 103, Capping of Claims on Multilateral Motor Vehicle Accidents Fund, 4 September 1995. The RAF board which oversees the Multilateral Motor Vehicle Accidents Fund was chastised for not following the recommendations of the *South African Law Commission* to update its processing of claims from dependents in relationships not solemnized under the Christian-oriented Marriage Act (Chap. 37, Oversight of the RAF, para. 37.40ff, at www.transport.gov.za/library/docs/raf/s15-37.pdf).

93 Estate Mehta, 1958 (4) South African Law Reports 253.

94 See note 38 above Kader.

95 Amod v Multilateral Motor Vehicle Accidents Fund, CCT 4/98, decided 27 August 1998, http://www.law.wits.ac.za/judgements/1998.

96 Hafiza Ismail Amod (born Peer), Commission for Gender Equality, amicus curiae, and Multilateral Motor Vehicle Accidents Fund, Supreme Court of Appeal of South Africa, Case No. 444/98, judgment 29 September 1999, http://www.law.wits.ac.za.judgements, 1999 (4) SA 1319.

97 Interpretation of Bill of Rights s. 39. (2) When interpreting any legislation, and when developing the common law or customary law, every court, tribunal or forum must promote the spirit, purport and objects of the Bill of Rights.

98 Zimnat Insurance Co Ltd v Chawanda, 1991 (2) SA 825 (ZS), in Amod, at 1325 (f).

99 See note 34 above Suid-Afrikaanse Nasionale, 467.

100 Monamodi v Sentraboer Co-operative Ltd (Witwatersrand Local Division) 1984 (4) 845.

101 Interview with M.S. Omar, Durban, July 1997.

102 Sura 4:92: 'Never should a Believer kill a Believer. (If it so happens) by mistake, (compensation is due): If one so kills a Believer, it is ordained that he should free a Believing slave and pay compensation to the deceased's family, unless they remit it freely. If the deceased belonged to a people at war with you and he was a Believer, the freeing of a believing slave is enough. If he belonged to a people with whom you have a treaty of mutual alliance, compensation should be paid to his family, and a Believing slave be freed. For those who find this beyond their means (is prescribed) a fast for two months running: by way of repentance to Allah, for Allah hath all knowledge and all wisdom.'

103 Malik, *Muwatta: kitab talaq; bab 'idda.*

104 Act No. 120, 1998, *Government Gazette*, 2 December 1998.

105 Juleiga Daniels v Robin Grieve Campbell and ors, Case CCT 40/03, Judgment by Sachs, J., 11 March 2004.

106 Intestate Succession Act 81 of 1987, s. 1 (4).

107 Maintenance of Surviving Spouses, Act 27 of 1990, s. 1.

108 *South African Law Commission*, Discussion Paper 101, Project 59, closing date for comments 31 January 2002, Clause 8.

109 Bukhari, *Sahih: kitab al fara 'id, kauli an nabiyi.* See discussion on inheritance below.

110 *Al Qalam*, The cyber Pen, at http://mandla.co.za/al-qalam/Default.htm.

111 Ismail, Zakiyya, Couples draw up own marriage contracts, *Al Qalam*, January 1997, at http://mandla.co.za/al-qalam/jan97/couples.htm.

112 Dr Mohammed Allie Moosagie, Bachelor of Theology (Miftah Al Ulum, Jalalabad, India); Masters degree and PhD in Islamic Law, University of Cape Town, Department of Religion; Head of the Department of Islamic Law at the Islamic College of Southern Africa; Head of the Academy of Islamic Research, Masjid al-Quds Islamic Centre; Senior Member of the Fatwa Committee of the Muslim Judicial Council; Member of the United Ulama Council of South Africa, Adjudicator in matrimonial disputes at the Masjid al-Quds Islamic Centre (qualifications as designated in the Plaintiff's Expert Summary in terms of Rule 36 (9) (B), 4 September 1995, Case No. 16993/92, Ryland and Edros (see note 61 above), courtesy of Justices Farlam and Traverso of the Supreme Court of South Africa, Cape of Good Hope Provincial Division).

113 Courtesy of Dr Moosagie, December 1998.

114 Interviews, Dr Moosagie Cape Town, July 1997 and December 1998.

115 Sura 24:6–10: 'And for those who launch a charge against their spouses, and have no evidence but their own, their solitary evidence (can be received) if they bear witness four times ... and the fifth (oath) ... they solemnly invoke the curse of Allah on themselves if they tell a lie ...'

116 Sura 4:3: '... But if you fear you shall not be able to deal justly (with them), then only one.' When read in conjunction with sura 4:129, this is impossible: 'You are never able to be fair and just as between women, even if it is your ardent desire ...'

117 Sura 4:32: '... to men is allotted what they earn, and to women what they earn ...'

118 Sura 4:4: 'And give the women their dower (*sadaqa*) as a gift, but if they renounce willingly as something that pleases them (and with) pleasure remit any part of it to you, take it and enjoy it with right good cheer.'

119 See Abdullah Yusuf Ali, *The Meaning of the Holy Quran*, Brentwood, MD: Amana Corporation, 1412/1992, ftn. 544 to, sura 4:33. Sura 4:34 goes on to say that 'Men stand by women in time of need by the means of strength God has given them and by means of sustenance out of their own wealth …'

120 Sura 3:195: 'And the Lord hath accepted of them: "Never will I suffer to be lost the work of any of you, be he male or female, you are members of one of another. Those who have left their homes and were driven out therefrom, and suffered harm in my cause and fought and were slain … verily I will admit them into gardens …" '

121 Sura 9:71: 'The Believers, men and women, reciprocate towards one another (and are not exalted above the other) …'

122 Sura 16:97: 'Whoever does works for the good (including making peace and serving the welfare), man or woman … we shall bestow on each their reward according to the best of their actions.'

123 Sura 65:1 *et seq.*

124 Sura 2:231: 'When you divorce women ... do not take them back to injure them or to take undue advantage; if any one does that, he wrongs his own soul.'

125 Interview, Dr Moosagie, Cape Town, July 1997.

126 Sura 2:229: 'It is not lawful for you to take back your gifts (from your wives), except when both parties fear that they would be unable (to keep) the limits ordained by Allah. If you do indeed fear that they would be unable to keep the limits of Allah, there is not blame on either one of them if she give something for her freedom. These are the limits ordained by Allah. So do not transgress them. If any do transgress the limits ordained by Allah, such persons wrong (themselves as well as others).'

The root word *khala'a* has many meanings: to cast off, to arrogate to oneself, to repudiate.

127 Suras 4:34 and 9:21 (standing by each other, reciprocal protectors of each other); 4:34 and 4:128 (disobedience of wife and husband towards each other); 2:228 (similar rights).

128 Interview, Dr Moosagie (see note 112 above), July 1997, Cape Town.

129 Mahomed Shoaib Omar: the author is a highly respected Durban lawyer. He qualified in commerce and law at the University of Natal, has a certificate in Islamic Law from the Darul Uloom in Karachi, Pakistan and is an Attorney of the Supreme Court of South Africa. He draws on Maulana Ashraf Ali Thanvi's *Al Hilahal Najizah* and on the *Kitab ul Faskh Wath Tafriq* by the Muslim Personal Law Board of India (Bihar and Orissa).

130 Suras 4:35 and 2:229.

131 Bukhari, *Sahih: kitab talaq*; *bab shiqaq*.

132 Balqis Fatima v Najm-ul-Ikra, Qureshi, *PLD* 1959 Lahore 566, followed in Amanullah v Husna, *PLD* 1997 Karachi 306.

133 Bukhari, *Sahih: kitab talaq; bab khul'.*

134 Sura 4:35.

135 Interview, M.S. Omar, Durban, July 1997.

136 Malik, *Muwatta: kitab talaq; bab 'idda al imra'a fil bait.*

137 Bukhari, *Sahih: kitab talaq; bab Fatimah bint Qais.*

138 Dawud, *Sunan: kitab talaq; bab Fatimah bint Qais.*

139 Ibid.

140 Mhd. Ahmed Khan v Shah Bano Begum, AIR 1985 Supreme Court 945. The Indian Supreme Court adopted the principles of Shah Bano in Danial Latifi & Anr v Union of India, JT (Judiciary Today) 2001 SC 218; (2001) 7 SC 740.

141 Code of Personal Status of Tunisia, Art. 43ff (support for ascendants in proportion to ability), Book 9 (Inheritance); Code of Personal Status, Egypt, Art. 395 ff (support for ascendants and needy relatives in proportion to their inheritance shares), Part II (Inheritance); Iranian Civil Code, Art. 1196 ff (support for ascendants and descendants).

142 Malik, *Muwatta: kitab talaq; bab 'idda al imra'a fil bait.*

143 Interview, Dr Moosagie, Cape Town, July 1997.

144 Interview, Dr Moosagie, Cape Town, December 1998.

145 e.g., Art. 71 of the Tunisian Code of Personal Status.

146 In re Osman Hussein, 1923–60 The African Law Reports Malawi 276 (1954). The High Court recognized the legality of this practice as an inheritance custom among Indian merchant families.

147 Black Administration Act 38 of 1927, § 23.

148 Mthembu v Letsela and Another, 1997 (2) SA 936 (Transvaal Provincial Division); Justice Mynhardt in 1998 (2) SA 875 (T).

149 Mildred Hleziphi Mthembu and Henry K. Letsela, The Supreme Court of Appeal of South Africa, Case 71/98, Judgment 30 May 2000 (reported in 2000 (3) SA 219).

150 Kweneng Land Board v Kabelo Listers Matlho, Pheto Motlhabane, Court of Appeal of Botswana, Civ Appeal No. 10/91, July 1992.

151 John Apoesho & Another v Awodija & Another, 1964 Nigerian Monthly Law Reports (NMLR) 8 (Supreme Court).

152 Van Breda & Others v Jacobs & Others, 1921 SALR 330 (Appellate Division).

153 *South African Law Commission*, Harmonisation of the Common Law and Indigenous Law (Draft Issue Paper on Succession), No. 12, Project 108, May 1998, p. 4ff.

154 *South African Law Commission*, Discussion Paper 93, Project 90, closing date 22 September 2000.

155 Bhe and Others v Magistrate, Khayelitsha and Others, Shibi v Sithole and Others; SA Human Rights Commission and Another v President of the RSA and Another, Case CCT 49/03, CCT 169/03, CCT 50/03, Constitutional Court, 2005 (1) BCLR 1 (CC), 15 Oct 2004.

156 Sura 4:33 regarding the right of inheritance on the basis of Muslim affinity – '(To benefit) everyone we have appointed shares and heirs to property left by parents and relatives, to those also to whom your right hand was pledged, give their due

portion. For truly Allah is witness to all things.' This was supposedly abrogated by sura 8:75 on giving priority to blood relatives: 'And those who accept faith subsequently and adopt exile, and the fight of the faith … they are of you. But kindred by blood have prior rights against each other in the book of Allah. Verily Allah is well acquainted with all things.' For hadiths that support the thesis of abrogation see Dawud, *Sunan: kitab al fara'id – Sura al Anfal* (8:75).

157 Dawud, *Sunan: kitab al fara'id, dhawu al arham* (on the controversial issue of whether the maternal relatives could inherit).

158 Sura 2:180: 'It is foreordained when death approaches any of you if leaving any goods make a bequest to parents and next of kin according to that (custom) which is well-known as just. This is due from the God-fearing.' See in Malik, *Muwatta: kitab fara'id*, a series of reports on the grandmothers who sought to claim shares on the basis of precedent, even though they were not named in the Quran. The Ansaris favoured recognizing grandmothers as heirs, while Caliph Umar was at first against it.

159 Sura 8:75 versus sura An Nisa 4:33.

160 Bequests are permitted in principle in the Quran (see sura 2:180, partly abrogated, and sura 5:106), but in hadiths Sunni jurists specifically limited bequests to only non-relatives. Shii opined that the duty to make a bequest to an heir was abrogated, but not the right to make such a bequest.

161 Malik, *Muwatta: kitab mirath al wila*; Bukhari, *Sahih: kitab fara'id, ma yarithu an nis'u min al wala'I*; Dawud, *Sunan: kitab fara'id.*

162 Numbers 27:8 where Zeflohad's daughters complained against the old customary rule, which they found unjust.

163 Dawud, *Sunan: kitab fara'id.* Dawud was of the opinion that they were the daughters of Sad b. al Rabi.

164 Sura 4:11: 'Allah commends to you regarding your children to the male share (of your good fortune) that of two females. If only women, two or more, then disperse two-thirds of what you leave behind. If only one, then she gets one-half.'

165 Malik, *Muwatta: kitab rahn, Abi Waqqas*; Bukhari, *Sahih: kitab fara'id, mirath al banati.*

166 Dawud, Sunan *kitab fara'id*; sura 4:176.

167 Numbers 27:10.

168 Bukhari, *Sahih: kitab fara'id, kauli an nabiyi.*

169 Sura 4:12.

170 Malik, *Muwatta: kitab fara'id*; Dawud, *Sunan: kitab fara'id.*

171 Bukhari, *Sahih: kitab fara'i*d *mirath al jaddi …*; Dawud, *Sunan: kitab fara'id*; Coulson, 1971, 54ff.

172 Sura 4:12: '… If the man or woman whose inheritance is in question has left neither ascendants or descendants, but has left a brother or a sister, each one of the two gets a sixth, but if more than two they share in a third …' Sura 4:176: '… About those who leave no descendants or ascendants as heirs, if it is a man that dies, leaving a sister, but no child, she shall have half the inheritance. If a woman, who left no child, her brother takes her inheritance. If there are two sisters, they shall have two-thirds of the inheritance. If there are brothers and sisters, they share, the male having twice of the female … Allah hath knowledge of all things.'

It is inferred that sura 4:12 refers to uterine brothers and sisters because the first part of the verse speaks of wives as heirs while sura 4:176 refers to brothers and sisters from the paternal side. This inference is not conclusive or inevitable, since the second part of sura 4:12 is explicitly gender-neutral ('If the man or woman … has left …').

173 Sura 2:182: 'If anyone fears partiality or wrongdoing on the part of the testator and makes peace between (the parties) they have done no wrong. Allah is oft forgiving, most merciful.'

174 Sura 4:7: 'From what is left by parents and those nearest related, there is a share for men and a share for women, whether the property is small or large – a determinate share.'

175 Sura 4:7–8.

176 Land Act 1/2002 of The Maldives reflects this spirit of preventing greed and excessive accumulation of wealth in a small community. Heirs already holding a specified square footage of real estate may not inherit (including bequests) as much as the other heirs who are landless (ss. 15, 17, 25).

177 Sura 4:12: 'In what your wives leave your share is half if they leave no child, but if they leave a child you get a fourth, after payment of legacies and debts/obligations. In what you leave their share is a fourth but if you leave a child they get an eight after payment of legacies and debts/obligations.'

178 Conclusions reached by a Muslim assessor for the Primary Court, Tunduru, Tanzania (Interviews, 1998).

179 The Ottoman Code was far more progressive than the German law governing agricultural estates in northern German at the time. Only well after the Second World War did the German Constitutional Court strike down the law (the *Hoeferordnung*) which prohibited women from inheriting agricultural estates.

180 Regulations for the Maldivian Land Act 1/2002, amended 3 May 2004, limiting bequests to descendants and ascendants. Only spouses and children inherit *miri* (government held) land.

181 Tanzania has already solved the issue by enacting a succession law which prohibits any religious bar to inheritance among relatives. The Ottoman Sultan's land decree of 1293/1871 set a precedent by providing that Muslims and non-Muslims were in general on an equal footing with regard to the acquisition and transfer of land and entitled to equal treatment.

182 As in the case of the Tanzanian Law of Marriage Act of 1971, which provides a uniform matrimonial law for all but allows the courts to take into account the customs/religion of the parties (Art. 107).

183 e.g. Cherif Chamari, Alia, Coordinator, Collectif 95 Maghreb-Egalite, One Hundred Steps, One Hundred Provisions: for an egalitarian codification of family and personal status laws in the Maghreb, London, Women Living Under Muslim Laws, November 2003; Bethesda, MD, Women's Learning Partnership, pp. 169–203, n.d.

184 Trustee Mahomedan Mosque, Estcourt v Mahommed Sayed, 1937 South African Law Reports (Natal Provincial Division, Supreme Court of South Africa) 241.

185 Ibid.

186 Naushad Hoosen and Others v Yasmin Deedat and Others, Supreme Court of Appeal of South Africa, 16 July 1999, [1999] 4 All SA 139; [1999] ZASCA 49; http://www.uovs.ac.za/law/appeals.

187 Ibid., paragraph 32.

188 §19 of Andhra Pradesh Wakf Rules, 1974.

189 The Wakf Act of 1954 in India prohibits the use of trust funds for covering litigation costs relating to the removal of a trustee from office or to disciplinary action (§41A).

190 AAIL (SA) [Ahmadiyya Anjuman Ishaati-Islam Lahore (South Africa)] and Another v Muslim Judicial Council (Cape) and Others, 1983 (4) South African Law Reports (Cape Provincial Division) 855.

191 Mohamed and Another v Jassiem, 1996 (1) South African Law Reports (Appellate Division) 673.

192 Ibid., at 705–706, citing Brill v Madeley, 1937 TPD 106.

193 Ibid., at 709.

194 Ibid., at 684–5 and 686–7.

195 Ibid., at 713 (D-G) and 714 (I).

196 Grundling v Van Rensburg No. 1984 (4) SA (Witswatersrand) 680.

197 See note 191 above, at 685–6.

198 See note 191 above, at 686–7.

199 See note 191 above, at 714–15.

200 Dr Mohammed Allie Moosagie, Plaintiff's Expert Summary in terms of Rule 36 (9) (B), 4 September 1995, Case No. 16993/92, Ryland and Edros (see note 61 above) (courtesy of Justices Farlam and Traverso of the Supreme Court of South Africa, Cape of Good Hope Provincial Division), p. 80.

201 Moosagie, Mohammed Allie, Unpublished MA Dissertation, University of Cape Town, Department of Religious Studies (*circa* 1994), Chapter IV (a critique of the methodology in two fatwas from Al Azhar and Darul Ulum and an analysis of Quranic hermeneutics).

202 Ibid., pp. 47 and 52, citing the Egyptian Hanafi jurist Ibn Abidin (d. 1256/1836).

203 *Al Qalam*, January 1997, at http://mandla.co.za/.

204 *South African Law Commission* (*SALC*), Issue Paper 8, Project 94, Alternative Dispute Resolution, 15 July 1997, ISBN 0621273198.

205 *SALC*, Issue Paper 8, Project 94, Alternative Dispute Resolution, Chap. 1, para. 1.3.

206 *SALC*, Issue Paper 8, Project 94, Chap. 2, paras. 2.1–2.3.

207 e.g., the Community Dispute Resolution Trust, *SALC*, Issue Paper 8, Project 94, Chap. 2, para. 2.16.

208 *SALC*, Issue Paper 8, Project 94, Chap. 3, para. 3.11, citing Chelsea West (Pty) Ltd v Roodebloem Investments (Pty) Ltd, 1994 (1) South African Law Reports 837 C.

209 *SALC*, Issue Paper 8, Project 94, Chap. 3, para. 3.45ff.

210 Sura 4:128.

211 Sura 4:35.

212 Sura 2:241.

213 Divorce Amendment Act 95 of 1996. Based on recommendations from the *South African Law Commission*, Project 76, Jewish Divorces Report, October 1994. See opposition to a similar proposed law in England, Lords Hansard, 30 June 2000, Divorce (Religious Marriages) Bill (H.L.), Hansard, House of Lords, Volume No. 614, Part No. 115, at http://www.publications.parliament.uk/pa/ld199900/ldhansrd/vo000630/index/00630-x.htm (last visited 10 May 2010). Opposition was based on the argument that the orthodox Mosaic law was capable of being interpreted in favour of the wife so that a judicial decision in effect could solve the problem (assuming that there was the political will in the community). Eventually Parliament passed the bill which became the Divorce (Religious Marriages) Act 2002, Chapter 27, 24 July 2002.

214 Estate Oeslodien v Estate Mustapha and Others, Supreme Court Reports of the Cape of Good Hope, Vol. 25, 1908, 853, at 861.

215 *South African Law Commission*, Project 59, 1988, Annex Questionnaire, p. iii.

216 *South African Law Commission*, Islamic Marriages and Related Matters, Project 59, 1988.

217 Mujlisul Ulama of South Africa, Port Elizabeth, 5 January 1988, untitled.

218 *South African Law Commission*, Project 59, Islamic Marriages and Related Matters, Issue Paper 15, May 2000, ISBN 0621300896.

219 Act No. 120, 1998, Government Gazette, 2 December 1998.

220 Art. 8, Recognition of Customary Marriages Act, 1998.

221 *SALC*, Project 59, Issue Paper 15, p. 10: 'And women shall have rights similar to the rights against men, according to what is equitable … (Sura 2:228); To men is allocated what they earn and to women what they earn (Sura 4:32). The best of you are those who are best to their families and I am the best to my family (hadith). Fear Allah with respect to the treatment of your women (hadith).'

222 SALRC, Project 59, Islamic Marriages and Related Matters Report, July 2003, containing the amended draft Muslim Marriages Act and the original draft of 2001 (SALRC Discussion Paper 101).

223 Personal communication from its drafter, Rashida Manjoo, 6 April 2006.

224 Al Azhari trained Muhammad Ghazali (d. 1996), Egyptian jurist and popular publicist who strongly criticized his fellow exegetic and hadith scholars who were losing touch with reality in not measuring their interpretations against the problems of the real world, e.g. how was it possible to support arguments against a woman becoming head of a country when the real world proved in fact that women made just as good presidents as men and did not take the country down to ruin.

225 At Tabari, Tarikh, *History*, Year 14 of Islam, paras. 2374–5.

226 Minister of Home Affairs and Another v Fourie and anor, Case CCT 60/04, Lesbian and Gay Equality Project and Eighteen Others v Minister of Home Affairs, Case CCT 60/04, South African Constitutional Court, 1 December 2005, [2005] ZACC 19; 2006 (3) BCLR 355 (CC). The Government was appealing against judgments that favoured equal rights.

227 Arts. 21 and 22 of the Code of Personal Status of Tunisia.

228 In the Tunisian Code of Personal Status (Arts. 3, 12), the *mahr* may have only a symbolic value, e.g. one dinar (commentary of 1957 edition of Code). The

Maldivian Family Act (4/2000) (Art. 10) allows the woman to demand that the *mahr* consist of work by the husband, e.g. for her family for a limited time.

229 Sura 4:4: 'And give the women (on marriage) their *sadaqa* (dower) as a free gift, but if they, of their own good pleasure, remit any part of it to you, take it and enjoy it with good cheer.' Sura 2:237: 'If you divorce them before touching them, but after you had set the dower for them, the compensation shall be half the dower, unless they voluntarily forfeit their rights, or the party responsible for causing the divorce chooses to forfeit the dower. To forfeit is closer to righteousness. You shall maintain the amicable relations among you. God is Seer of everything you do.'

230 The Pakistani Muslim Family Laws Ordinance of 1961 foresees that the chairperson of a local council which has jurisdiction over issues of polygamy and *talaq* may be a non-Muslim: Art. 2(b) Definitions – ... where the chairman of the Union Council is a non-Muslim, or he himself wishes to make an application to the Arbitration Council, or is, owing to illness or any other reason, unable to discharge the functions of Chairman, the Council shall elect one of its Muslim members as Chairman for the purposes of this Ordinance.

231 The Pakistani criminal law applies Islamic law to non-Muslims but allows them to have a non-Muslim judge to apply the provisions. The Offence of Zina (Enforcement of Hudood) Ordinance VII of 1979 punishes non-Muslims, men or women, when found guilty of *zina*, but does not subject them to the death penalty. Art. 21 provides that 'if the accused is a non-Muslim, the Presiding Officer (of the court) *may* [emphasis added] be a non-Muslim'.

232 Sura 4:34.

233 See note 231 above.

234 In the matter between Fatima Gabie Hassam and Master of the High Court and others, High Court Cape of Good Hope Provincial Division, Case 5704/2004, Judgment by Van Reenen, J, 18 July 2008; In the matter between Shaloshinie Govender and the Master of the High Court Durban and others, High Court of South Africa Durban and Coast Local Division, Case 6715/2008, Judgment by M.F. Moosa, AJ, 6 November 2008. Confirmed by the Constitutional Court in Case CCT 83/08 [2009] ZACC 19, 15 July 2009, Nkabinde, J.

BIBLIOGRAPHY

Abdal-Rehim, Abdal-Rehim Abdal-Rahman, 'The family and gender laws in Egypt during the Ottoman period'. In Sonbol, Amira El Azhary (ed.) *Women, the Family, and Divorce Laws in Islamic History*. Syracuse, NY: Syracuse University Press, 1996, pp. 96–111.

Abdelnasser, Walid M., 'Islamic organizations in Egypt and the Iranian revolution of 1979: the experience of the first few years'. *Arab Studies Quarterly*, Vol. 19, No. 2 (1997), pp. 25–39.

Abu Zahrah, Muhammad, *Ibn Hazm: Hayatun wa-'asruh*. Cairo: Dar al fikr al 'arabi, 1954.

Agha, Saleh Said, 'Abu Muslim's conquest of Khurasan: preliminaries and strategy in a confusing passage of the Akhbar al Dawlah Al Abbasiyyah'. *Journal of the American Oriental Society*, Vol. 120, No. 3 (2000), pp. 333–47.

Ahmad, Aziz, 'Sayyid Ahmad, Jamal al-Din al-Afghani and Muslim India'. *Studia Islamica*, Vol. 13 (1960), pp. 55–78.

Ahmed, Leila, *Women and Gender in Islam: Historical Roots of a Modern Debate*. New Haven, CT: Yale University Press, 1992.

Akhavi, Shahrough, 'The dialectic in contemporary Egyptian social thought: the scripturalist and modernist discourses of Sayyid Qutb and Hassan Hanafi'. *International Journal of Middle East Studies*, Vol. 29 (1997), pp. 377–401.

El Alami, Dawoud Sudqi, *The Marriage Contract in Islamic Law in the Shari'ah and Personal Status Laws of Egypt and Morocco*. London: Graham & Trotman, 1992.

El Alami, Dawoud and Hinchcliffe, Doreen, *Islamic Marriage and Divorce Laws of the Arab World*. London: Kluwer Law International, 1996.

Ali, Kecia, *Money, Sex, and Power: the Contractual Nature of Marriage in Islamic Jurisprudence of the Formative Period.* Unpublished PhD thesis, Duke University, 2002. Ann Arbor, MI: University Microfilms International.

Ali, Mohammed Khursheed, *The Waqf Laws.* Hyderabad: Asia Law House, 4th edn. 1995.

Ali, Shaheen Sardar, 'Testing the limits for family law reform in Pakistan: a critical analysis of the Muslim Family Laws Ordinance 1961'. *International Survey of Family Law.* Cambridge: Cambridge University Press, 2002, pp. 317–35.

Amin, Qasim, *Tahrir al-mar'a wa-l-tamaddun al-Islami.* Cairo: Dar al-Shuruq, 1988, trans. Petersen, Samiha Sidhom, as *The Liberation of Women and The New Woman. Qasim Amin: Two Documents in the History of Egyptian Feminism.* Cairo: American University in Cairo Press, 2000.

Anderson, J.N.D., 'Law as a social force in Islamic culture and history'. *Bulletin of the School of Oriental and African Studies*, Vol. 20, No. 1/3 (1957), pp. 13–40.

—— 'Waqfs in East Africa'. *Journal of African Law*, Vol. 38, No. 3 (1959), pp. 152–64.

Anderson, Lisa, *The State and Social Transformation in Tunisia and Libya, 1830–1980.* Princeton, NJ: Princeton University Press, 1986.

Aouij, Emna Chtioui, *Les Droits de la Femme.* Tunis: SNIPE *La Presse*, pp. 32–3, repr. 1999.

Arabi, Oussama, *Early Muslim Legal Philosophy: Identity and Difference in Islamic Jurisprudence.* Los Angeles, CA: G.E. von Grunbaum Center for Near Eastern Studies, 1999.

Atiya, Nayra, *Khul-Khaal: Five Egyptian Women Tell Their Stories.* Cairo: American University in Cairo Press, 1984.

Azer, Adel, 'Law as an instrument for social change: an illustration from population policy'. In Nelson, Cynthia and Koch, Klaus Friedrich (eds.) *Law and Social Change in Contemporary Egypt.* Cairo Papers in Social Science, Vol. 2, Monograph 4. Cairo: American University in Cairo Press, 2nd edn. 1983, pp. 60–97.

Baker, John Hamilton and Milsom, Stroud Francis Charles, *Sources of English Legal History: Private Law to 1750.* London: Butterworths, 1986.

Bakhtiar, Laleh, *Encyclopedia of Islamic Law: A Compendium of the View of the Major Schools.* Chicago, IL: ABC International Group, 1996.

Baklouti, N., 'Éléments de signification dans le mariage traditionnel (région de Gabès). *Cahiers des arts et traditions populaires*, No. 10 (1990), pp. 87–103.

Bekker, Jan C., *Seymour's Customary Law in Southern Africa.* Cape Town: Juta, 5th edn. 1989.

de Bellefonds, Y. Linant, *Traité de droit musulman comparé.* Vol. I, *Théorie générale de l'acte juridique*; Vol. II, *Mariage, la dissolution du mariage*; Vol. III, *Filiation, incapacités, libéralités entre vifs.* Paris: Mouton, 1965.

Ben Achour, Yadh, *Politique, religion et droit dans le monde arabe.* 2 vols. Tunis: Cérès Productions, 1992.

Bencherifa, Muhammad (ed.), *Muhammad Ibn Iyad, Madahib al-hukkam fi nawazil al-ahkam.* Beirut: Dar al garb al-islami, kitab aliskan, 1990, p. 225.

Bennett, Thomas, *A Sourcebook of African Customary Law for Southern Africa.* Cape Town: Juta, 1991.

Bergmann, Alexander and Ferid, Murad, *Internationales Ehe- und Kindschaftsrecht.* Frankfurt a.M.: Verlag für Standesamtswesen, 1993.

Berkey, Jonathan P., 'The Mamluks as Muslims: the military elite and the construction of Islam in medieval Egypt'. In Phillip, Thomas and Haarmann, Ulrich (eds.) *The Mamluks in Egyptian Politics and Society.* Cambridge: Cambridge University Press, 1998, pp. 163–73.

Binous, Jamila, Harzallah, F., Hamzaoui, S., Ben Romdhane, H., Mahfoudh-Fraoui, D. and Tahar-Baklouti, L.V., *Tunisiennes en avenir: comment les femmes vivent.* Tunis: Cérès, Fondation Friedrich Naumann, 1992.

Botiveau, Bernard, 'Les récentes modifications du code égyptien du statut personnel: genèse d'un débat sur le droit de la famille'. *Bulletin du CÉDEJ*, No. 17 (1985), pp. 343–71.

—— *Loi islamique et droit dans les sociétés arabes: mutations des systèmes juridiques du Moyen-Orient.* Paris: Karthala, and Aix-en-Provence: Iremam, 1993.

Bouraoui, Soukaïna, 'Ordre masculin et fait féminin'. In Camau, Michel and Abdelkefi, Jellal (eds.) *Tunisie au présent: une modernité au-dessus de tout soupçon?* Paris: Éditions du CNRS, 1987.

Brown, Nathan J., *The Rule of Law in the Arab World: Courts in Egypt and the Gulf.* Cambridge: Cambridge University Press, 1997.

Brunschvig, Robert, *Études d'Islamologie*, Vol. II. Paris: G.P. Maisonneuve et Larose, 1976.

Bulbulia, M.A.E., 'Application of the concept of *wakf* in South Africa'. *Rebus* (1981), pp. 155–7.

Cachalia, Firoz, 'Citizenship, Muslim family law and a future South African constitution: a preliminary enquiry'. *Tydskrif vir Hedendaagse Romeins-Hollandse Reg*, Vol. 56 (1993), p. 392.

Caplan, Ann Patricia, *Choice and Constraints in a Swahili Community: Property, Hierarchy and Cognatic Descent on the East African Coast.* London: Oxford University Press and the International African Institute, 1975.

Chadbourne, Julie Dror, 'Never wear your shoes after midnight: legal trends under the Pakistan Zina Ordinance'. *Wisconsin International Law Journal*, Vol. 18 (Summer 1999), pp. 179–280.

Charfi, Mohamed, 'La dot à travers le passé et le présent en Tunisie'. *Revue tunisienne de droit*, 1977, pp. 258–60.

Chaudhry, Zainab, 'Comment: the myth of misogyny: a reanalysis of women's inheritance in Islamic law'. *Albany Law Review*, Vol. 61 (1997), pp. 511–55.

Cheriet, Boutheina, 'Gender, development and policy formation'. In Nelson, Cynthia and Altorki, Soraya (eds.) *Cairo Papers in Social Science*, Vol. 20, Monograph 3, Arab Regional Women's Studies Workshop, Autumn. Cairo: American University in Cairo Press, 1997, pp. 94–8.

Chejne, Anwar G., *Ibn Hazm.* Chicago, IL: Kazi, 1982.

Cherif, Mohamed-Hédi, *Pouvoir et société dans la Tunisie de Husayn Bin 'Ali (1705–1740).* Tunis: Publications de l'Université de Tunis, 1984.

Cherif, Mohamed El-Hédi, 'Réformes et Islam chez Bourguiba'. In Ferchiou, Sophie (ed.) *L'Islam pluriel au Maghreb.* Extract from *L'Annuaire de l'Afrique du Nord, 1994.* Paris: Éditions du CNRS, 1996, pp. 59–67.

van der Chijs, Jacobus Anne (compiler), 'Nederlandsch-Indisch Plakaat-Boek 1602–1811, Statuen von Indien'. *Landsdrukkerij, 1885–1900*, Vol. 60, pp. 416–31.

Cohn, Marcus, *Wörterbuch des jüdischen Rechts.* Basel: Karger, 1980.

Cook, Michael, *Early Muslim Dogma: A Source-critical Study.* Cambridge: Cambridge University Press, 1981.

Cooper, John, Madelung, Wilfred F. and Jones, Alan, *The Commentary on the Qur'an by Abu Ja'far Muhammad b. Jarir Al-Tabari*, Vol. I. Oxford: Oxford University Press, 1989.

da Costa, Yusuf, 'Assimilatory processes amongst the Cape Muslims in South Africa during the 19th century'. *South African Journal of Sociology*, Vol. 23, No. 1 (1992), pp. 5–11.

Coulson, Noel, 'The state and the individual in Islamic law'. *International and Comparative Law Quarterly*, Vol. 6, No. 1 (1957), pp. 49–60.

—— *Succession in the Islamic Family.* Cambridge: Cambridge University Press, 1971.

—— *A History of Islamic Law*. Edinburgh: Edinburgh University Press, 1964, reproduced 1991.

Craig, Michael, 'Perinatal risk factors for neonaticide and infant homicide: can we identify those at risk?' *Journal of the Royal Society of Medicine*, Vol. 97, No. 2 (2004), pp. 57–61.

Crecelius, Daniel, 'The *Waqf* of Muhammad Bey Abu Al-Dhahab in historical perspective'. *International Journal of Middle East Studies*, Vol. 23 (1991a), pp. 57–81.

—— and Bakr, Abd al-Wahhab (trans.), *Al-Damurdashi's Chronicle of Egypt 1688–1755: Al-durra al-musana fi akhbar al-kinana*. Leiden: Brill, 1991.

CRÉDIF, *Tunisian Women in Figures*. Tunis: CRÉDIF, 1996a.

—— *Femmes et hommes dans le milieu rural en Tunisie: données statistique*. Tunis: CRÉDIF, 1996b.

——/UNESCO, *Droits de la femme et de la petite fille en Tunisie*. Tunis: CRÉDIF, 1994.

Davids, Achmat, 'My religion is superior to the law: the survival of Islam at the Cape of Good Hope'. *Kronos*, Vol. 12 (1987), pp. 57–71.

Delanoue, Gilbert, 'Les intellectuels et l'état en Égypte aux XIXe et XXe siècles'. In Delanoue and Al-Bishri, Tariq (eds.) *Les Intellectuels et le Pouvoir: Syrie, Égypte, Tunisie, Algérie*. Cairo: CÉDEJ, 1986.

Dien, M. Izzi, *The Theory and the Practice of Market Law in Medieval Islam: A Study of Kitab Nisab al-Ihtisab of 'Umar b. Muhammad al-Sunami (fl. 7th–8th/13th–14th Century)*. Cambridge: E.J.W. Gibb Trust, 1997.

Doi, Abdur Rahman I., *Woman in Shari'ah*. London: Ta-Ha, 1989.

Early, Evelyn A., *Baladi Women of Cairo*. Boulder, CO, and London: Rienner, 1993.

Eccel, A. Chris, *Egypt, Islam and Social Change: Al Azhar in Conflict and Accommodation*. Berlin: Schwarz, 1984.

Enda Inter-arabe, *The Thousand and One Paths to Empowerment: Coping Strategies of Poor Urban Women in Tunisia*. Tunis: n.p., n.d. (ca. 1999).

Engineer, Asghar Ali, *The Rights of Women in Islam*. London: Hurst, 1992.

Esack, Farid, *Qur'an, Liberation and Pluralism: An Islamic Perspective of Interreligious Solidarity against Oppression*. Oxford: One World, 1997.

Fadel, Mohammed, 'Two women, one man: knowledge, power and gender in medieval Sunni legal thought'. *International Journal of Middle East Studies*, Vol. 20, No. 2 (1997), pp. 185–204.

Fahmi, Hoda, *Divorcer en Égypte: étude de l'application des lois du statut personnel*. Cairo: CÉDEJ, 1987.

Fahmy, Khaled, 'Police and the people in nineteenth-century Egypt'. *Die Welt des Islams*, Vol. 39, No. 3 (1999), pp. 340–77.

Ferchiou, Sophie, *Les femmes dans l'agriculture tunisienne*. Aix-en-Provence: Edisud, 1985.

— 'Le role des femmes dans la transmission du patrimoine familial selon la législation islamique en Tunisie'. In Gadant, Monique and Kasriel, Michèle (eds.) *Femmes du Maghreb au présent: la dot, le travaille, l'identité*. Paris: Éditions du CNRS, 1990, pp. 37–51.

Fisher, Stanley, *Ottoman Land Laws: Law Extending Right of Inheritance to the State in Mevquve Land, 1284/1867, New Land Code of 1331/1913*. Oxford: Oxford University Press, 1919.

Frazer, James George, *The Golden Bough. A Study in Comparative Religion*. 12 vols. London: Macmillan, 1890, trans. von Bauer, Helen Elizabeth Franziska, as *Der Goldene Zweig: Das Geheimnis von Glauben und Sitten der Völker*. Leipzig: Hirschefeld, 1928.

Fuller, Lon, *The Morality of Law*. New Haven, CT: Yale University Press, 1964.

Gargouri-Sethom, S. 'Le mariage à Chenini, Nahal, M'dou: aspect économique'. *Cahiers des arts et traditions populaires*, Tunis, No. 10 (1990), pp. 71–85.

Gätje, Helmut, *Koran und Koranexegese*. Zürich and Stuttgart: Artemis, 1971.

Al Ghazali, Muhammad, *Sunna al nabawiya bayna ahl al-fiqh wa ahl al hadith*. n.p.: Al-Shuruq, 1989.

de Goeje, M.J., *Mémoire sur les Carmates du Bahrein et les Fatimides*. Leiden: Brill, 1886.

Goitein, S.D., *A Mediterranean Society: The Jewish Communities of the Arab World as Portrayed in the Documents of the Cairo Geniza*. Vol. III, *The Family*. Berkeley, CA: University of California Press, 1978.

Goolam, Nazeem M.I., 'Conflict resolution in Islamic societies'. In Jones-Pauly, Christina and Elbern, Stefanie (eds.) *Access to Justice in Africa: The Role of Court Administrators and Law Adjudicators in the African and Islamic Contexts*. The Hague: Kluwer Law International, 2000, pp. 137–60.

Green, Arnold H., *The Tunisian Ulama 1873–1915: Social Structure and Response to Ideological Currents*. Leiden: Brill, 1978.

Haddad, Tahar, *Our Women in the Shari'a and Human Society* (*Imra'ana fil shari'a wal mujtama*). Tunis: Dar at tunisiya lil nashr, 1985.

Hamdani, Sumaiya, 'The dialectic of power: Sunni/Shi'i debates in tenth-century North Africa'. *Studia Islamica*, Vol. 90 (2000), pp. 5–22.

Hamdi, Mohamed Elhachmi, *An Analysis of the History and Discourse of the Tunisian Islamic Movement al-Nahda: A Case Study of the Politicisation of Islam*. Unpublished PhD thesis, University of London, 1996.

— *The Politicisation of Islam: A Case Study of Tunisia*. Boulder, CO: Westview, 1998.

Hannoum, Abdelmajid, 'Historiography, mythology and memory in modern North Africa: the story of the Kahina'. *Studia Islamica*, Vol. 86 (1997), pp. 85–130.

Harb, Muhammad Talat, *Fasl al kitab fi al marah wa al hijab*. Egypt: Matbaat al Taraqqi, 1901.

— *Tarbiyat al marah wa al hijab*. Egypt: Matbaat al Manar, 1914.

Hassan, Fayza, 'Women's destiny, men's voices'. *Al Ahram Weekly*, No. 46, 3–9 February 2000.

Hatem, Mervat F., 'Economic and political liberation in Egypt and the demise of state feminism'. *International Journal of Middle East Studies*, Vol. 24 (1992), pp. 231–51.

Hattenhauer, Hans (ed.), *Allgemeines Landrecht für die Preussischen Staaten von 1794*, Articles 204ff. Neuwied: Luchterhand, 2nd edn. 1994.

Hejaiej, Monia, *Behind Closed Doors: Women's Oral Narratives in Tunis*. London: Quartet, 1996.

Hijab, Nadia, *Womanpower: The Arab Debate on Women at Work*. Cambridge: Cambridge University Press, 1988.

Hill, Enid, *Mahkama! Studies in the Egyptian Legal System: Courts and Crimes, Law and Society*. London: Ithaca, 1979.

— *Al Sanhuri and Islamic Law*. Cairo Papers in Social Science, Vol. 10, Monograph 1. Cairo: American University in Cairo Press, 1987.

Hodgson, Marshall G.S., *The Venture of Islam: Conscience and History in a World Civilization*. Vol. I, *The Classical Age of Islam*. Chicago, IL: University of Chicago Press, 1974.

Holdsworth, William Serale, *A History of English Law*, Vol. III. London: Methuen, 1923.

Hoodfar, Homa, *Between Marriage and Market: Intimate Politics and Survival in Cairo*. Berkeley, CA: University of California Press, 1997.

Hopwood, Derek, *Habib Bourguiba of Tunisia: The Tragedy of Longevity*. New York: St. Martin's, 1992

Huntington, Samuel P., *Political Order in Changing Societies*. New Haven, CT, and London: Yale University Press, 1968.

Hussels, Martin,'Renaissance oder endgültiger Tod des §217 StGB'. *Neue Zeitschrift für Strafrecht*, 1994), pp. 526–8.

Ibn Iyad, Muhammad. In Benscherifa, H. (ed.) *Madhahib al hukkam fi nwazil al ahkam.* Beirut: Dar al-garb al-islami (kitab al iskan), 1989.

Ibn Taimiyya, *Fatawin an-nisa'.* Beirut: Dar al qalam, 1987.

Ibrahim, Ahmad, 'Ancillary orders on divorce in the Shari'ah courts of Malaysia'. *Islamic and Comparative Law Quarterly*, Vol. 7 (1987), p. 185.

Institut National du Patrimoine, *La femme tunisienne à travers les ages.* Exposition au Palais de La Abdalliya, La Marsa, Tunis, November, 1997.

Issa, Hossam, 'L'état de droit en Égypte: mythe idéologique et réalités politiques'. *Annuaire de l'Afrique du Nord*, Vol. 34 (1995). Paris: Éditions du CNRS, 1997.

Jackson, Sherman, *Islamic Law and the State: the Constitutional Jurisprudence of Shihab al-Din al-Qarafi.* Leiden: Brill, 1996.

Jeppie, Shamil, 'Commemorations and identities: the 1994 tercentenary of Islam in South Africa'. In Sonn, Tamara (ed.) *Islam and the Question of Minorities.* Atlanta, GA: Scholars Press, 1996, pp. 73–91.

Jithoo, Sabita, 'Indian family businesses in Durban, South Africa'. *Journal of Comparative Family Studies*, Vol. 22, No. 3 (1985), pp. 365–76.

Johanson, Baber, 'The valorization of the human body in Muslim Sunni law'. In Stewart, Devin J., Johansen, Baber and Singer, Amy (eds.) *Law and Society in Islam.* Princeton, NJ: Markus Wiener, 1996, pp. 71–112.

Jones, Christina, *Law and Development: The Law of Bequests in the Context of Reform of Property Law in Tunisia.* Unpublished PhD thesis, University of London, 1975. Ann Arbor, MI: University Microfilms International.

—— 'Concepts of equality in cases of discrimination against women: examples from Africa'. In Ludwar-Ene, G. and Reh, M. (eds.) *Gender and Identity.* Hamburg: LIT, 1995a, pp. 169–286.

—— 'Menschenrechte und Landfrauen in Tansania: ein Vergleich mit der deutschen Höfeordnung'. *Frauen in der einen Welt*, Vol. 1 (1995), pp. 86–99.

—— 'Plus ça change, plus ça reste le même: the New Land Reform Zanzibar Project'. *Journal of African Law*, Vol. 40, No. 1 (1996a), pp. 19–42.

—— 'Anwendung des islamischen Rechts in der Bundesrepublik Deutschland'. *Deutsche Richterzeitung*, 1996, pp. 322–8.

Jones-Pauly, Christina, 'The law and morality of support in the extended family in Germany and Tanzania: changing perceptions of family forms'. In Eekelaar, J. and Nhlapo, R.T. (eds) *The Changing Family.* Oxford: Hart, 1998, pp. 265–86.

—— 'Indian roots of equity: was the import of English law in African colonies illegal?' *Droit et Cultures*, Vol. 32, No. 2 (1999), pp. 243–58.

—— 'Use of the Quran in key Pakistani cases on *zina* (adultery and rape) and *qadf* (false accusation of immorality)'. *Arabica: Journal of Arabic and Islamic Studies/Revue d'études arabes et islamiques*, Vol. 47, Nos. 3–4 (2000), pp. 539–53.

—— 'Marriage contracts of Muslims in the diaspora: problems in the recognition of *Mahr* contracts in German law.' In Quraishi, A. and Vogel, F. (eds.) *The Marriage Contract: Case Studies in Islamic Family Law*. Cambridge, MA: Harvard University Press, 2008, pp. 299–330.

Jongmans, D.G., 'Mzia et horma: relations entre service, estime sociale et prospérité dans une société en transformation'. *Cahiers des arts et traditions populaires*, Tunis, No. 3 (1969), pp. 101–33.

Jonker, Carla, 'Exploration anthropologique pour une étude du ménage familial en Kroumirie'. *Cahiers des arts et traditions populaires*, Tunis, No. 4 (1971), pp. 55–84.

Jouirou, Zahia, 'Le Vécu religieux des femmes dans un village tunisien'. Tunis: Faculté des Lettres Manouba, University of Tunis, n.d. (manuscript).

Kader, Soha Abdel, *Egyptian Women in a Changing Society 1899–1987*. Boulder, CO, and London: Rienner, 1987.

Karam, Azza M., *Women, Islamisms and the State: Contemporary Feminism in Egypt*. New York: St. Martin's, and London: Macmillan, 1998.

Karaman, Hayrettin, 'Sectarian preference in the Ottoman jurisprudence'. In Çiçek, Kamal (ed.) *The Great Ottoman-Turkish Civilization*, Vol. 3. Ankara: Yeni Turkiye, 2000.

Kazem, Safynaz (ed.), *The Mirror of Mai, Bahithat Al-Badia and Aisha Al-Taymouriya, Al-Anissa Mai (Mai Ziyada)*. Cairo: Al-Hilal, 1999.

Kechichian, Joseph A., 'The role of the ulama in the politics of an Islamic state: the case of Saudi Arabia'. *International Journal of Middle East Studies*, Vol. 18 (1986), pp. 53–71.

Kennedy, Charles H., 'The implementation of the hudood ordinances in Pakistan'. *Islamic Studies*, Vol. 26, No. 1 (1987), pp. 307–19.

—— Repugnancy in Islam: who decides? Islam and legal reform in Pakistan'. *International and Comparative Law Quarterly*, Vol. 41 (1992), pp. 769–87.

Kerr, Alastair James, *The Customary Law of Immovable Property and of Succession*. Grahamstown: Rhodes University, 2nd edn. 1976.

Khadduri, Majid (trans.), *Shafi'i, Risala.* Cambridge: Islamic Texts Society, 1987.

Khamis, Safia M., *Application of the Protection of Spinsters Act in Zanzibar.* Unpublished MA dissertation, University of Zimbabwe, ca. 1992.

Khayr ad Din, *Essai sur les réformes nécessaires aux états musulmans*, annotated Magali Morsay. Aix-en-Provence: Édisud, 1987.

Kilani, Taoufik, 'Quelques aspects de l'interruption voluntaire de grossesse: stratégie de l'O.N.F.P.' *ONFP Magazine* (Tunis), No. 3 (July 1996), p. 15.

Klein, Ira, 'Materialism, mutiny and modernization in British India'. *Modern Asian Studies*, Vol. 34, No. 3 (2000), pp. 545–80.

Krawietz, Birgit, *Die Hurma: Schariarechtlicher Schutz vor Eingriffen in die körperliche Unversehrheit nach arabischen Fatwas des 20. Jahrhunderts.* Berlin: Duncker & Humblot, 1991.

Labidi, Lilia, 'Islam and women's rights in Tunisia'. Paper presented at Österreichische Orient-Gesellschaft, *Islam in a Pluralistic World*, 15 November 2005.

—— and Hachma, Çabra, *Sexualité et tradition.* Tunis: Dar Annnawras, 1989.

Lakhdar-Ghoul, Latif, 'Dar-Ajoued: approche préliminaire d'une prison domestique'. *Institut des Belles Lettres Arabes*, Vol. 56, No. 171 (1993), pp. 49–64.

Lambert-Hurley, Siobhan, 'Princes, paramountcy and the politics of Muslim identity: the Begum of Bhopal on the Indian national stage, 1901–1926'. *Journal of South Asian Studies* (Australia), Vol. 26, No. 2 (2003), pp. 165–91.

Lapidus, Ira, 'The separation of state and religion in the development of early Islamic society'. *International Journal of Middle East Studies*, Vol. 6, No. 4 (1975), pp. 363–85.

Largueche, Dalenda, 'Confined, battered, and repudiated women in Tunis since the eighteenth century'. In Sonbol, Amira El Azhary (ed.) *Women, the Family, and Divorce Laws in Islamic History.* Syracuse, NY: Syracuse University Press, pp. 259–76.

Lee, Suzy, 'Note: saving Amina Lawal: human rights symbolism and the dangers of colonialism'. *Harvard Law Review*, Vol. 117 (May 2004), pp. 2,365–86.

Lev, Yaacov, *State and Society in Fatimid Egypt.* Leiden: Brill, 1991.

Lewis, Bernard, *Cultures in Conflict: Christians, Muslims, and Jews in the Age of Discovery.* New York and Oxford: Oxford University Press, 1995.

Lohlker, Rüdiger, *Shari'a und Moderne: Diskussionen über Schwangerschaftsabbruch, Versicherung und Zinsen*. Stuttgart: Deutsche Morgenländische Gesellschaft, 1996.

Lüddeckens, Erich, *Ägyptische Eheverträge*. Wiesbaden: Harrassowitz, 1960.

Lyon, Stephen, *Power and Patronage in Pakistan*. Unpublished PhD thesis, University of Kent, 2002.

Mahfouz, Naguib, *Palace of Desire*. Cairo: American University in Cairo Press, 1997.

—— *Miramar*. Cairo: American University in Cairo Press, 1998.

Mahida, Ebrahim Mahomed, *Islam in South Africa: A Bibliography*. Durban: Centre for Research in Islamic Studies, University of Durban-Westville, 1993.

Makdisi, George, 'The juridical theology of Shafi'i: origins and significance of *Usul al Fiqh*'. *Studia Islamica*, Vol. 59 (1984), pp. 5–47.

Manjoo, Rashida, 'The recognition of Muslim personal laws in South Africa: implications for women's human rights'. Working Paper, Human Rights Program, Harvard Law School, July 2007.

Marsot, Afaf Lutfi al-Sayyid, *Women and Men in Late Eighteenth-Century Egypt*. Austin, TX: University of Texas Press, 1995.

Medimegh, Aziza Darghouth, *Droits et vécu de la femme en Tunisie*. Lyon: L'Hermès-Edilis, 1992.

Mehdi, Rubya, *The Islamization of the Law in Pakistan*. Richmond: Curzon, 1994.

Meron, Ya'akov, *L'obligation alimentaire entre époux en Droit Musulman*. Paris: Hanefite, Librairie générale de droit et de jurisprudence, 1971.

M'Halla, Moncef, 'Tradition et modernité chez T. Haddad à travers Notre Femme dans la loi et la société'. *Cahiers des arts et traditions populaires*, Tunis, No. 7 (1980), pp. 125–39.

Ministry of Public Health, National Family and Population Board (ONFP), *Major Phases of the Program and Decennial Characteristics*. Tunis: ONFP, 1966–96.

El Mokhtar, Mohamed, *La littérature juridique et l'évolution du Malikisme en Mauritanie*. Tunis: Publications de l'Université de Tunis, Imprimerie officielle de la République Tunisienne, 1981.

Moors, Annelies, *Women, Property and Islam: Palestinian Experiences 1920–1990*. Cambridge: Cambridge University Press, 1995.

Moosa, Ebrahim, 'The fate of Muslim personal law'. At http://www.uct.ac.za/depts/religion/mpl.htm, accessed 7 May 2010.

Moosa, Najma, *Unveiling the Mind: A Herstory of the Historical Evolution of the Legal Position of Women in Islam*. Cape Town: Community Law Centre, 2004.

Moosagie, Mohammed Allie, *Islamic Law and Social Change: A Legal Perspective*. Unpublished MA dissertation, University of Cape Town, 1989.

Morrisson, Christian and Talbi, Bechir, *Long-Term Growth in Tunisia*. Paris: OECD Development Centre, 1996.

Muir, Sir William, *Life of Mahomet*. London: Smith, Elder, abr. edn. 1877.

Nada, Atef Hanna, *Impact of Temporary International Migration on Rural Egypt*. Cairo Papers in Social Science, Research Series No. 3, Vol. 4, Monograph 3. Cairo: American University in Cairo Press, 1991.

Najjar, Fauzi M., 'Egypt's laws of personal status'. *Arab Studies Quarterly*, Vol. 10, No. 3 (1998), pp. 319–44.

Nassar, Heba, 'Socio-economic factors affecting education and employment of women'. In Biegel, Reiner and Zghal, Riadh (eds.) *Éducation et formation professionelle des femmes dans le monde arabe et en Europe*. Euro-Arab Dialogue Programme. Tunis: Konrad Adenauer Stiftung, 1997, pp. 181–212.

National Council of Resistance of Iran, Foreign Affairs Committee, *Women, Islam & Equality*. Auvers-sur-Oise, France, 1995.

National Union of Tunisian Women, *Women of Tunisia: Their Struggle and Their Gains*. Tunis: Tunisian External Communication Agency, 1993.

Nawid, Senzil, 'The state, the clergy, and British imperial policy in Afghanistan during the late 19th and early 20th centuries'. *International Journal of Middle East Studies*, Vol. 29, No. 4 (1997), pp. 581–605.

Neusner, Jacob, *A History of the Mishnaic Law of Women*, Part IV and V. Leiden: Brill, 1980.

Noeldeke T. and Schwally, F., *Geschichte des Qurans*, Part I. Leipzig: Dieterich'sche, 1909, pp. 248–52.

Al Nowaihi, Mohamed, 'Changing the law on personal status within a liberal interpretation of the Shari'a'. In Nelson, C. and Koch, K.F. (eds.) *Law and Social Change in Contemporary Egypt*. Cairo Papers in Social Science, Vol. 2, Monograph 4. Cairo: American University in Cairo Press, 2nd edn. 1983, pp. 98–116.

Office National du Planning Familial et de la Population, *Législation et politique tunisiennes en matière de population: analyse et perception*. Tunis: Office National du Planning Familial et de la Population, 1974.

—— *Family Planning in Tunisia: Foundations, Results, Prospects*, Tunis: Office National de la Famille et de la Population, 1995.

Omar, Mahomed Shoaib, 'Islamic personal and South African law – some problems highlighted'. *De Rebus* (October 1982), pp. 485–503.

— *The Islamic Law of Succession and Its Application in South Africa.* Durban: Butterworths, 1988.

— *Selected Essays in Islamic Law. Incorporating Contemporary Issues.* Durban: n.p., 1993.

Pensa, Henri, *L'Avenir de la Tunisie.* Paris: Librairie africaine et coloniale, 1903.

Powers, David S., 'The will of Sa'd b. Abi Waqqas: a reassessment'. *Studia Islamica*, Vol. 58 (1983), pp. 33–53.

Purohit, Nishit, *The Principles of Mohammedan Law.* Pune: C.T.J., 1985.

Al Qairawani, Abdullah bin Abi Zaid, *Risala al Qairawani.* n.p.: Halabi, 1949.

Quadri, Anwar Ahmad, *A Sunni Shafi'i Law Code.* New Delhi: Islamic Book Service, 1992.

Quraishi, Asifa, 'An Islamic critique of the rape laws of Pakistan from a woman-sensitive perspective.' *Michigan Journal of International Law*, Vol. 18 (1997), pp. 287–320.

Qureshi, M.A., *Muslim Law of Marriage, Divorce and Maintenance.* New Delhi: Deep & Deep, 1995.

Raban, Uri, '*Al Walad li-l-Firash*' on the Islamic campaign against *zina*'. *Studia Islamica*, Vol. 78 (1993), pp. 5–26.

Ragaï, Doria (Shafik), *La femme et le droit religieux de l'Égypte contemporaine.* Paris: Librairie Orientaliste Paul Geuthner, 1940.

Rahimuddin, Muhammad, *Notes, Muwatta' Imam Malik.* Lahore: Sh. Muhammad Ashraf, 1991.

Rapoport, Yossef, 'Matrimonial gifts in early Islamic Egypt.' *Islamic Law and Society*, Vol. 7, No. 1 (2000), pp. 1–36.

— *Marriage and Divorce in the Muslim Middle East, 1250–1517.* Unpublished PhD thesis, Princeton University, 2002. Ann Arbor, MI: University Microfilms International.

Rautenbach, Christa, *Muslim Personal Law and the Meaning of 'Law' in the South African and Indian Constitutions.* At www.puk.ac.za/lawper/1999-2/rauten.html, 7 May 2010.

Razi, Fakhr al Din Muhammad ibn Umar, *Al Tafsir al kabir.* Egypt: Al Matba'ah al bahiyah al misriyah, 1983.

Redding, Jeffrey, 'Constitutional Islam: theory and Pakistan'. *Virginia Journal of International Law*, Vol. 44, No. 3 (2004), pp. 759–827.

Rejeb, R. Ben, 'Grossesse hors mariage et maternité provisoire: à propos du vécu psychologique de vingt mères célibataires'. *Institut des Belles Lettres Arabes*, Vol. 56, No. 171 (1993), pp. 65–72.

Rejeb, Souad et al, 'La mère au travail et son enfant: simple sondage sociologique'. *Institut des Belles Lettres Arabes*, Vol. 54, No. 167 (1991), pp. 85–93.

Rispler-Chaim, Vardit, *Islamic Medical Ethics in the Twentieth Century*. Leiden: Brill, 1993.

Rosberg, James H., *The Emergence of an Independent Judiciary in Contemporary Egypt*. Unpublished PhD thesis, Massachusetts Institute of Technology, 1995. Ann Arbor, MI: University Microfilms International.

Rosen, Lawrence, *The Anthropology of Justice: Law as Culture in Islamic Society*. New York and Cambridge: Cambridge University Press, 1989.

Rosenthal, Franz (ed.), *The History of al-Tabari*. Albany, NY: State University of New York Press, 1989.

Rugh, Andrea B., *Religious Community and Social Control in a Lower-Class Area of Cairo*. Unpublished PhD thesis, American University, Washington, DC, 1978. Ann Arbor, MI: University Microfilms International.

Sabbagh, Abdulkarim, *Frauen im Islam: zum Problem sozialer Modernisierung, am Beispiel besonders Ägyptens*, Würzburg: Sabbagh, 1986.

Al Sabbagh, Muhammad Lutfi, with Dawood, Al-Amin and al-Awwa, Muhammad Salim, *The Right Path to Health: Health Education through Religion: Islamic Ruling on Male and Female Circumcision*. Alexandria: World Health Organization, 1996.

Saeed, Javaid, *Islam and Modernization: A Comparative Analysis of Pakistan, Egypt, and Turkey*. Westport, CT: Praeger, 1994.

Salem, Lilia B., 'Hypothèses à propos des hiérarchies sociales qui charactérisent la société tunisienne'. *Les Cahiers de Tunisie*, Vol. 32, Nos. 129–30 (1984), p. 24.

Sarsar, Mohamed Chafik, 'Essai sur le constitutionalisme et la constitutionalisation dans l'espace Arabo-Musulman au XIXe siècle'. *Actualités Juridiques Tunisiennes*, No. 6 (1992), pp. 53–62.

Scholl, Claus, *Das Eheverbot der Wartezeit unter besonderer Berücksichtigung rechtsvergleichender, rechtspolitischer und internationalprivatrechtlicher Aspekte*. Unpublished Dr Jur dissertation, University of Bonn, 1971.

Scholl, Claus, 'Die statistische Relevanz relativer Eheverbote: ein Beitrag zur Rechtstatsachenforschung'. *Zeitschrift für Standesamtwesen*, 1973, p. 153.

Schoombee, G.F. and Mantzaris, E.A., 'Attitudes of South African Indians towards extended and nuclear family groups in South Africa'. *Journal of the University of Durban-Westville*, New Series, Vol. 1, pp. 75–89.

Schwab, Dieter, *Geschichtliches Recht und moderne Zeiten: ausgewählte rechtshistorische Aufsätze*. Heidelberg: Müller, 1995.

Seife, Susan, *Effects of Outside Employment on Lower-Class Iranian Women and Their Children*. Unpublished PhD thesis, Syracuse University, 1985. Ann Arbor, MI: University Microfilms International.

Sethom, Samira, 'Étude de quatres contrats de mariage Sfaxiens du XIXe siècle'. *Cahiers des arts et traditions populaires*, Tunis, No. 1 (1968), pp. 19–36.

Shah, Nik Noriani Nik Badli, 'Sisters in Islam: state legislation in Malaysia.' Paper presented at the Harvard Law School Conference on the Islamic Marriage Contract, January 29–31, 1999.

Shaham, Ron, *Family and the Courts in Modern Egypt: A Study Based on Decisions by the Shari'a Courts 1900–1955*. Leiden: Brill, 1997.

Shaheed, Abdul Qadir Apudah, *Criminal Law of Islam*, Vol. 3. Karachi: International Islamic, 1987.

Shahrur, Mohammed, *Nahwa usul jadida lil fiqh al islamiya. Fiqh al mara' al wasiya – al irth – al qiwama – al ta'dduya – al libas*. Damascus: al Ahali lil Tib'ah wa al Nashr wa al Tawzi', 2000.

Shaltut, Imam Mahmoud, Great Shaykh of al Azhar, *Mas'alat at taqrib bayna al madhahib al islamiyya*. Cairo: Dar al taqrib, 1383 A.H.

As Sharif, Mohammed Al Habib, *Majallat al 'ahlwal as shakhsiyya*. Tunis: Dar al mizan, 1997.

Shatzmiller, Maya, 'Women and property rights in al-Andalus and the Maghrib: social patterns'. *Islamic Law and Society*, Vol. 23 (1995), pp. 219–57.

Shepard, William E., *Sayyid Qutb and Islamic Activism: A Translation and Critical Analysis of Social Justice in Islam*. Leiden: Brill, 1996.

Sholkamy, Hania Mohamed, *Children's Health and Well-Being: An Ethnography of an Upper Egyptian Village*. Unpublished PhD thesis, London School of Economics, 1998.

Shoshan, Boaz, *Popular Culture in Medieval Cairo*. Cambridge: Cambridge University Press, 1993.

Siegel, Reva B., '"The rule of love": wife-beating as prerogative and privacy'. *Yale Law Journal*, Vol. 105, No. 3 (1996), pp. 2,118–207.

Sisters in Islam, *Are Women and Men Equal Before Allah?* Selangor: SIS Forum, 1991.

Skovgaard-Petersen, Jakob, *Defining Islam for the Egyptian State: Muftis and Fatwas of the Dar al-Ifta.* Leiden: Brill, 1997.

Smith, Charles D., *Islam and the Search for Social Order in Modern Egypt: a Biography of Muhammad Husayn Haykal.* Albany, NY: State University of New York Press, 1983.

Société tunisienne d'étude du XVIIIe siècle, *L'Abolition de l'esclavage en Tunisie: à travers les archives 1841–1846.* Tunis: Alif, 1990.

Sonbol, Amira El Azhary, 'Law and gender violence in Ottoman and modern Egypt'. In Sonbol (ed.), *Women, the Family, and Divorce Laws in Islamic History.* Syracuse, NY: Syracuse University Press, 1996, pp. 277–89.

—— 'Rape and law in Modern Ottoman Egypt'. In Ilkkaracan, Pinar (ed.), *Women and Sexuality in Muslim Societies.* Istanbul: Women for Women's Human Rights, 2000, pp. 309–26.

Spectorsky, Susan, 'Ahmad ibn Hanbal's Fiqh'. *Journal of the American Oriental Society*, Vol. 102, No. 3 (1982), pp. 461–5.

—— *Chapters on Marriage and Divorce: Responses of Ibn Hanbal and Ibn Rahwayh.* Austin, TX: University of Texas Press, 1993.

Spellberg, Denise A., *Politics, Gender, and the Islamic Past: The Legacy of 'A'isha bint Abi Bakr.* New York: Columbia University Press, 1994.

Spenlen, Jeannette, *Sexualethik und Familienplanung im muslimischen und christlichen Ägypten.* Frankfurt a.M./New York: Lang, 1994.

Sraïeb, Noureddine, *Le Collège Sadiki de Tunis 1875–1956: Enseignement et Nationalisme.* Tunis: Alif, Éditions de la Méditérranée, n.d.

—— 'Des droits de l'homme et de l'état de droit dans la pensée politique tunisienne du XIXe siècle'. *Annuaire de l'Afrique du Nord,* Vol. 34 (1995). Paris: Éditions du CNRS, 1995, pp. 93–9.

Stern, Gertrude, *Marriage in Early Islam.* London: Royal Asiatic Society, 1939.

Stewart, Frank Henderson, *Texts in Sinai Bedouin Law.* Wiesbaden: Harrasowitz, 1988.

Stowasser, Barbara F., *Women in the Qur'an: Traditions and Interpretation.* New York: Oxford University Press, 1996.

Stratz, Hans-Wolfgang, in Staudinger, Kommentar BGB, s. 8 Ehegesetz, Rdn. 3 and 9, 12. Auflage. Berlin: Sellier and de Gruyter, 1990.

Sugier, Clémence, 'Les bijoux de la mariée à Moknine'. *Cahiers des arts et traditions populaires*, Tunis, No. 1 (1968), 141–56.

Sultan, Jahan Begam H.H. Nawab, *Muslim Married Couple.* New Delhi: Award, 1916 (repr. 1980).

Ta'albi, Abdelaziz, César Ben Attar, Csar and Al Hadi Al Saba'i, *L'esprit libéral du Coran*. Paris: n.p., 1905.

At Tabari, Abi Ja'far Muhammad ibn Jarir, Tarikh at Tabari, *Tarikh al rusul wa al muluk*, from Muhammad Abu al Fadl Ibrahim. Egypt: Dar al Ma'arif, 11 vols. 1960–77.

Taha, Mahmud Muhammad, *Risala al thaniyah min al-Islam: the Second Message of Islam*, trans. An-Na'im, Abdullahi Ahmed. Syracuse, NY: Syracuse University Press, 1987.

Taamallah, Khemais, 'Évolution de la famille tunisienne à travers quelques indications sociales'. In *Collectif: Structures familiales et rôles sociaux*. Actes du Colloque de l'Institut Supérieur de l'Éducation et de la Formation Continue, Tunis, 3–4 February 1994. Tunis: CERES, 1994, pp. 89–97.

Tayob, Abdelkader, 'Tabari on the Companions of the Prophet: moral and political contours in Islamic historical writing'. *Journal of the American Oriental Society*, Vol. 119, No. 2 (1999), pp. 203–10.

Toledano, Henry, *Judicial Practice and Family Law in Morocco: The Chapter on Marriage from Sijilmasi's Al 'Amal al mutlaq*. Boulder, CO: Social Science Monographs, 1981.

Tucker, Judith E., *Women in Nineteenth-century Egypt*. Cambridge: Cambridge University Press, 1985.

Van Wyk, Helgard de Jager, Personal Disposable Income in South Africa by Income Group and Population Group, 1960–2005. Report No. 279. Pretoria: Bureau of Market Research, UNISA, 2000.

Visagie, G.G., Regspleging en Reg aan die Kaap van 1652 tot 1806. Cape Town: Juta, 1969.

Vivien, Kassandra, *Siwa Oasis*. Cairo: IPL, n.d.

Vogel, Frank E., 'Islamic governance in the Gulf: a framework for analysis, comparison, and prediction'. In Sick, Gary G. and Potter, Lawrence G. (eds.) *The Persian Gulf at the Millennium: Essays in Politics, Economy, Security, and Religion*. New York: St. Martin's, 1997, pp. 249–95.

Vogel, Frank E. and Hayes, Samuel L. III, *Islamic Law and Finance: Religion, Risk, and Return*. The Hague: Kluwer Law International, 1998.

Wahin, Lars, 'Inheritance law in the Jordanian hill country'. *British Journal of Middle Eastern Studies*, Vol. 21, No. 1 (1994), pp. 57–84.

Walther, Wiebke, 'Die Frau im Islam heute'. In Endel, Werner and Steinbach, Udo (eds.) *Der Islam in der Gegenwart*. Munich: Beck, 4th edn. 1996.

Waltz, Susan E., 'Another view of feminine networks: Tunisian women and the development of political efficacy'. *International Journal of Middle East Studies*, Vol. 22 (1990), pp. 21–36.

Weber, Max, 'Die protestantische Ethik und der "Geist" des Kapitalismus'. *Archiv für Sozialwissenschaft und Sozialpolitik*, Vol. 20, pp. 1–54, Vol. 21, pp. 1–110 (1905).

Webster, David, 'Abafazi Bathonga Bafihlakala: ethnicity and gender in a KwaZulu border community'. In McAllister, Patrick A. and Spiegel, Andrew D. (eds.) *Tradition and Transition in Southern Africa*. Johannesburg: Witwatersrand University Press, 1991, pp. 243–71.

Welchman, Lynn and Hossain, Sara (eds.), *Honour: Crimes, Paradigms and Violence against Women*. London: ZED Books, 2005.

Wheeler, Brannon M., *Applying the Canon in Islam: the Authorization and Maintenance of Interpretive Reasoning in Hanafi Scholarship*. Albany, NY: State University of New York Press, 1996.

Wickering, Deborah, *Experience and Expression: Life among Bedouin Women in South Sinai*. Cairo Papers in Social Science, Vol. 14, Monograph 2. Cairo: American University in Cairo, 1991.

Yamani, Maha A.Z., *Polygamous Life and Law in Contemporary Saudi Arabia*. Reading: Ithaca, 2008.

Yearbook of Islam and the Middle East, Vol. I. The Hague: Kluwer, 1994.

—— Vol. II. The Hague: Kluwer, 1995.

Yousaf, Chaudhary Ejaz, 'Promulgation of an appropriate Islamic criminal justice system in a multi-religious Islamic country: problems and challenges'. *Pakistan Law Digest Journal*, 2004, pp. 1–10.

Zaidi, Z.H. (ed.), *Qaim I Azam: M.A. Jinnah Papers Project*. Islamabad: National Archives of Pakistan, 2004.

Zouari, Ali, 'Sanaa et maalma dans la région de Sfax'. *Cahiers des arts et traditions populaires*, Tunis, No. 2 (1968), pp. 29–32.

Zulficar, Mona, 'The Islamic marriage contract in Egypt'. In Quraishi A. and Vogel, F. (eds.) *The Islamic Marriage Contract: Case Studies in Islamic Family Law*. Cambridge, MA: Harvard University Press, 2008, pp. 231–74

INDEX